BEST PRACTICES
IN SCHOOL PSYCHOLOGY

STUDENT-LEVEL SERVICES

BEST PRACTICES
IN SCHOOL PSYCHOLOGY

STUDENT-LEVEL SERVICES

NASP

EDITED BY

PATTI L. HARRISON & ALEX THOMAS

Published by the National Association of School Psychologists

Copies may be ordered from:
NASP Publications
4340 East West Highway, Suite 402
Bethesda, MD 20814
301-657-0270
301-657-3127, fax
866-331-NASP, Toll Free
e-mail: *publications@naspweb.org*
www.nasponline.org/publications

Best Practices in School Psychology: Student-Level Services
ISBN: 978 0932955-54-8 (print)

Best Practices in School Psychology (4-book series)
ISBN: 978-0-932955-52-4 (print), ISBN: 978-0-932955-51-7 (electronic)

Printed in the United States of America

19 10 9 8 7 6 5

Table of Contents

Introduction 1

Interventions and Instructional Support to Develop Academic Skills

1   Best Practices in Instructional Strategies for Reading in General Education 9
        Rebecca S. Martinez

2   Best Practices in Increasing Academic Engaged Time. 19
        Maribeth Gettinger and Katherine Miller

3   Best Practices in Fostering Student Engagement 37
        Amy L. Reschly, James J. Appleton, and Angie Pohl

4   Best Practices in Setting Progress Monitoring Goals for Academic Skill Improvement. 51
        Edward S. Shapiro and Kirra B. Guard

5   Best Practices in Promoting Study Skills 67
        Robin Codding, Virginia Harvey, and John Hite

6   Best Practices in Homework Management 83
        Lea A. Theodore, Melissa A. Bray, and Thomas J. Kehle

7   Best Practices on Interventions for Students With Reading Problems 97
        Laurice M. Joseph

8   Best Practices in Oral Reading Fluency Interventions. 115
        Edward J. Daly III, Maureen A. O'Connor, and Nicholas D. Young

9   Best Practices in Delivering Intensive Academic Interventions With a Skill-by-Treatment
        Interaction. 129
        Matthew K. Burns, Amanda M. VanDerHeyden, and Anne F. Zaslofsky

10 Preventing Academic Failure and Promoting Alternatives to Retention 143
        Mary Ann Rafoth and Susan W. Parker

11 Best Practices in Services for Gifted Students 157
        Rosina M. Gallagher, Linda C. Caterino, and Tiombe Bisa-Kendrick

12 Best Practices in Planning for Effective Transition From School to Work for Students With
        Disabilities. 173
        Fred Jay Krieg, Sandra S. Stroebel, and Holly Bond Farrell

13 Best Practices in Facilitating Transition to College for Students With Learning Disabilities 185
        Raymond Witte

Interventions and Mental Health Services to Develop Social and Life Skills

14 **Best Practices in Applying Positive Psychology in Schools** 199
Terry M. Molony, Maureen Hildbold, and Nakeia D. Smith

15 **Best Practices in Social Skills Training** 213
Jennifer R. Frey, Stephen N. Elliott, and Cindy Faith Miller

16 **Best Practices in Fostering Student Resilience** 225
Amity L. Noltemeyer

17 **Best Practices in Assessing and Promoting Social Support** 239
Michelle K. Demaray and Christine K. Malecki

18 **Best Practices in Classroom Discipline** 251
George G. Bear and Maureen A. Manning

19 **Best Practices in Assessing and Improving Executive Skills** 269
Peg Dawson

20 **Best Practices in Solution-Focused, Student-Driven Interviews** 287
John J. Murphy

21 **Best Practices in Group Counseling** 305
Julie C. Herbstrith and Renée M. Tobin

22 **Best Practices in Delivering Culturally Responsive, Tiered-Level Supports for Youth With Behavioral Challenges** 321
Robyn S. Hess, Vanja Pejic, and Katherine Sanchez Castejon

23 **Best Practices in Classroom Interventions for Attention Problems** 335
George J. DuPaul, Gary Stoner, and Mary Jean O'Reilly

24 **Best Practices in School-Based Interventions for Anxiety and Depression** 349
Thomas J. Huberty

25 **Best Practices in Interventions for Anxiety-Based School Refusal** 365
Shannon M. Suldo and Julia Ogg

26 **Best Practices in Promoting Appropriate Use of Restraint and Seclusion in Schools** 381
Brian M. Yankouski and Thomas Massarelli

27 **Best Practices in Making Manifestation Determinations** 399
Robert J. Kubick Jr. and Katherine Bobak Lavik

28 **Best Practices in Service Learning for School-to-Work Transition and Inclusion for Students With Disabilities** 415
Felicia L. Wilczenski, Paula Sotnik, and Laura E. Vanderberg

Index 427

Best Practices in School Psychology: Series List 443

Introduction

BEST PRACTICES IN SCHOOL PSYCHOLOGY: OVERVIEW OF THE SERIES

Best Practices in School Psychology is the sixth iteration of an intraprofessional collaborative effort to provide a single source for contemporary knowledge about many valued topics within school psychology. It has been more than 30 years since the first edition of *Best Practices in School Psychology* was published. In those 30 years and six editions, there have been substantial changes in the quantity of chapters, range of topics, and intended outcomes of school psychology services. However, the purpose of all editions of *Best Practices in School Psychology*, including the current edition, has remained constant over the years: to provide the current, relevant, and valued information necessary for competent delivery of school psychological services. Thus, chapters across editions have focused on *practices* by school psychology practitioners. Although chapters are not intended to be detailed reviews of research, research documentation is included in the chapters to provide an evidence-based foundation for recommended best practices.

This edition of *Best Practices in School Psychology* is designed to be a comprehensive resource, allowing readers to refer to chapters in the process of gaining information about specific, important professional practice topics and updating readers about contemporary techniques and methods. The primary target audience is school psychology practitioners who provide services in school settings, as was the case for previous editions. Similarly, the chapters may provide useful resources for other school-based professionals, as well as those who provide services to children in other settings. *Best Practices* also may serve as a helpful supplement for graduate courses when used in conjunction with primary course textbooks. As a compilation of best practices on major topics, *Best Practices in School Psychology* will assist school psychology practitioners, graduate students, interns, faculty, and others by providing readings on many specific areas of interest.

The content in this edition of *Best Practices in School Psychology* is expanded from earlier editions to include a broader range of topics, with considerable attention to multitiered, problem-solving, and evidence-based approaches for the delivery of effective school psychology services. The school psychology services outlined in this edition focus on improving student outcomes through data-based and collaborative activities in schools. Chapters emphasize prevention and intervention efforts for both student-level and systems-level services that recognize the importance of culture and individual differences across students, families, schools, and communities.

This edition of *Best Practices* was developed over 5 years, with multiple focus groups consisting of practitioner school psychologists, as well as graduate students and faculty, assisting the editors with organization and new topics for chapters to represent current and future needs. In addition, chapter authors and reviewers identified additional chapter topics.

The result is that this edition is organized a bit differently than previous editions. This edition is a four book series, with each book corresponding to one of the four interrelated components of the broad framework of the 2010 National Association of School Psychologists (NASP) *Model for Comprehensive and Integrated School Psychological Services* (i.e., the NASP Practice Model; see http://www.nasponline.org/standards/2010standards/2_PracticeModel.pdf): (a) *practices that permeate all aspects of service delivery*, including data-based and collaborative decision making; (b) *student-level services*, including instructional and academic supports and social and mental health services; (c) *systems-level services*, including school-wide learning practices, preventive and response services, and family–school collaboration; and (d) *foundations* of school psychological services, including diversity, research and program evaluation, and legal/ethical/professional practices.

About half of the chapters in this edition are updates of chapters included in earlier editions, and the other half focus on new and topical issues of importance in contemporary school psychology. Although it is impossible to include chapters for *all* areas of relevance to school psychology, it is hoped that the resulting 150 chapters provide a good representation of major services and issues in the field.

Organizational Framework of the Series

Each of the four books in the series has two or three separate sections corresponding to the specific domains of school psychology established in the 2010 NASP Practice Model. The titles of the four books and of the sections within each are outlined below:

1. *Best Practices in School Psychology: Data-Based and Collaborative Decision Making*

   Introduction and Framework
   Data-Based Decision Making and Accountability
   Consultation and Collaboration

2. *Best Practices in School Psychology: Student-Level Services*

   Interventions and Instructional Support to Develop Academic Skills
   Interventions and Mental Health Services to Develop Social and Life Skills

3. *Best Practices in School Psychology: Systems-Level Services*

   School-Wide Practices to Promote Learning
   Preventive and Responsive Services
   Family–School Collaboration Services

4. *Best Practices in School Psychology: Foundations*

   Diversity in Development and Learning
   Research and Program Evaluation
   Legal, Ethical, and Professional Practice

Chapter Structure

Typically, chapters include the following components, which provide readers with a predictable chapter structure:

Overview. Includes a definition and history of the topic and may provide situations for which a practicing school psychologist may wish to consult the chapter. This section orients the reader to the major issues, characteristics, and needs related to a chapter topic. It is introductory and establishes the context for the information presented.

Basic Considerations. Provides background information, research, training, experience, equipment, and other basics that school psychologists should know to effectively deal with the topic.

Best Practices. The heart and most extensive part of a chapter. Authors were asked to provide best practices and to include options and perspectives so that school psychologists can mesh their professional orientation with other successful possibilities.

Summary. A synopsis of the topic, which includes a brief review and discussion of the best practices.

References. Publications and resources that support the chapter authors' information. Authors were asked to not make exhaustive lists, because chapters are intended to focus on evidence-based practices and not simply present a compilation of research.

Unlike previous editions of *Best Practices*, the current edition does not include Annotated Bibliographies at the end of each chapter. Instead, readers have online access to each chapter's Annotated Bibliography on the NASP website (http://www.nasponline.org/publications). Annotated Bibliographies include articles, books, Web-based information, and other resources suggested by authors of each chapter for follow-up reading to gain a more detailed view of best practices for the topic discussed in a chapter.

It is our hope that this edition of *Best Practices in School Psychology* will support current and future school psychologists in their ongoing quest for improved procedures and practices and the acquisition of professional skills needed to enhance students' success in their schools, homes, and communities.

INTRODUCTION TO THE BOOK: BEST PRACTICES IN SCHOOL PSYCHOLOGY: STUDENT-LEVEL SERVICES

This book includes two sections of chapters about school psychology practices related to student-level services, including instructional and academic supports and social and mental health services.

Interventions and Instructional Support to Develop Academic Skills

Chapters in this section focus on the Interventions and Instructional Support to Develop Academic Skills domain of the 2010 NASP *Model for Comprehensive and Integrated School Psychological Services*. The domain represents practices for student-level services (see http://www.nasponline.org/standards/2010standards/2_PracticeModel.pdf, p. 5):

School psychologists have knowledge of biological, cultural, and social influences on academic skills; human learning, cognitive, and developmental processes; and evidence-based curricula and instructional strategies. School psychologists, in collaboration with others, demonstrate skills to use assessment and data collection methods and to implement and evaluate services that support cognitive and academic skills. Examples of direct and indirect services that support the development of cognitive and academic skills include the following:

- School psychologists use assessment data to develop and implement evidence-based instructional strategies that are intended to improve student performance.
- School psychologists promote the principles of student-centered learning to help students develop their individual abilities to be self-regulated learners, including the ability to set individual learning goals, design a learning process to achieve those goals, and assess outcomes to determine whether the goals were achieved.
- School psychologists work with other school personnel to ensure the attainment of state and local academic benchmarks by all students.
- School psychologists apply current empirically based research on learning and cognition to the development of effective instructional strategies to promote student learning at the individual, group, and systems level.
- School psychologists work with other school personnel to develop, implement, and evaluate effective interventions for increasing the amount of time students are engaged in learning.
- School psychologists incorporate all available assessment information in developing instructional strategies to meet the individual learning needs of children.
- School psychologists share information about research in curriculum and instruction with educators, parents, and the community to promote improvement in instruction, student achievement, and healthy lifestyles.
- School psychologists facilitate design and delivery of curriculum and instructional strategies that promote children's academic achievement, including, for example, literacy instruction, teacher-directed instruction, peer tutoring, interventions for self-regulation and planning/organization, etc.

- School psychologists use information and assistive technology resources to enhance students' cognitive and academic skills.
- School psychologists address intervention acceptability and fidelity during development, implementation, and evaluation of instructional interventions.

Interventions and Mental Health Services to Develop Social and Life Skills

Chapters in this section focus on the Interventions and Mental Health Services to Develop Social and Life Skills domain of the 2010 NASP *Model for Comprehensive and Integrated School Psychological Services*. The domain represents practices for student-level services (see http://www.nasponline.org/standards/2010standards/2_PracticeModel.pdf, pp. 5–6):

School psychologists have knowledge of biological, cultural, developmental, and social influences on behavior and mental health; behavioral and emotional impacts on learning and life skills; and evidence-based strategies to promote social–emotional functioning and mental health. School psychologists, in collaboration with others, demonstrate skills to use assessment and data-collection methods and to implement and evaluate services that support socialization, learning, and mental health. Examples of professional practices associated with development of social, emotional, behavioral, and life skills include the following:

- School psychologists integrate behavioral supports and mental health services with academic and learning goals for children.
- School psychologists facilitate design and delivery of curricula to help students develop effective behaviors, such as self-regulation and self-monitoring, planning/organization, empathy, and healthy decision-making.
- School psychologists use systematic decision-making to consider the antecedents, consequences, functions and potential causes of behavioral difficulties that may impede learning or socialization.
- School psychologists address intervention acceptability and fidelity during development, implementation, and evaluation of behavioral and mental health interventions.
- School psychologists provide a continuum of developmentally appropriate mental health services, including individual and group counseling, behavioral coaching, classroom and school-wide social–emotional learning programs, positive behavioral support, and parent education and support; this may include attention to issues such as life skills and personal safety for students with lower levels of functioning.
- School psychologists develop and implement behavior change programs at individual, group, classroom, and school-wide levels that demonstrate the use of appropriate ecological and behavioral approaches (e.g., positive reinforcement, social skills training, and positive psychology) to student discipline and classroom management.
- School psychologists evaluate implementation and outcomes of behavioral and mental health interventions for individuals and groups.

ACKNOWLEDGMENTS

It is fascinating to compare the assembling and publication of this sixth edition of *Best Practices in School Psychology* with the circumstances surrounding the first edition. The comparison highlights the growth and diversity of the profession, the organizational vitality and commitment of NASP, and the increasing influence and importance of school psychologists during the intervening 30+ years.

In 1982, when work began on the first edition, NASP had 7,500 members (2014 membership exceeds 25,000), and training, field placement, practice, and credentialing standards for school psychology were at a much earlier stage of development. For the first edition of *Best Practices*, the acknowledgments section thanked six individuals who assisted in reviewing the 39 chapters and in typesetting—yes, literally setting type of the text. Selection of font style and size, space between lines, paper stock, cover art, selection of the printer, obtaining copyright, design of shipping cartons, method of shipping, cost, and the like were made by the coeditors, and communications with authors and reviewers were primarily by U.S. mail along with occasional phone calls. Three thousand copies of the first edition of *Best Practices* were printed and then trucked to, stored at, and eventually distributed from a school psychologist's garage in Connecticut. The introductory price to members, including shipping, was $22. Times change.

For this sixth edition of *Best Practices*, there are hundreds of people to thank and acknowledge. First, the approximately 300 authors of our 150 chapters spread across four books deserve our gratitude. We appreciate the dedication, enthusiasm, and efforts of this highly talented group.

In addition to our editorial review, an earnest effort was made to have each chapter peer-reviewed by at least three school psychologists (two current practitioners and a university- or other non-school-based school psychologist). We must heartily thank the reviewers who read first drafts, provided important feedback to authors, and shared their suggestions for improvement of the chapters. Once these reviews were received, the reviewed chapters were forwarded to the author along with copies of comprehensive reviewer notations and editor comments. It was a time-consuming process for the reviewers, and our authors' final manuscripts substantially benefited from these extensive reviewer efforts. Reviewers who contributed to this edition, and who receive our appreciation, are:

Melinda Adkins	Ronald S. Palomares	Candis Hogan
Elsa Arroyos	Anna M. Peña	Susan Jarmuz-Smith
Barry Barbarasch	Madi Phillips	Rita Lynne Jones
Brian J. Bartels	Pamela M. Radford	Regina K. Kimbrel
John Biltz	Alecia Rahn-Blakeslee	Misty Lay
Alan Brue	Tracy Schatzberg	Mary Levinsohn-Klyap
Elliot J. Davis	Nicole Skaar	Monica McKevitt
Bill Donelson	Marlene Sotelo-Dynega	Katherine Mezher
Amy N. Esler	Vicki Stumme	Sara Moses
René Fetchkan	Jackie Ternus	Mary Alice Myers
Beth Glew	Lori Unruh	Ed O'Connor
Bryn Harris	Ellie L. Young	Leslie Z. Paige
Denise Hildebrand	Ashley Arnold	Shamim S. Patwa
Daniel Hyson	Michelle S. Athanasiou	Debbie Phares
Jessica (Dempsey) Johnston	Susan Bartels	E. Jeanne Pound
Cathy Kennedy-Paine	Jill Berger	Stephanie Rahill
Laurie McGarry Klose	Brandee Boothe	Nancy Peña Razo
Brian Leung	Kelly R. Swanson Dalrymple	Margaret Sedor
Jane Lineman-Coffman	Emma Dickinson	Carole A. Sorrenti
Courtney L. McLaughlin	Katie Eklund	Patricia Steinert-Otto
Dawn Miller	Pam Fenning	James M. Stumme
Karin Mussman	Marika Ginsburg-Block	Lynne Ostroff Thies
Karen O'Brien	Julie Hanson	Nate von der Embse
Rivka I. Olley	Jasolyn Henderson	

This sixth edition of *Best Practices* is the first edition that does not include Jeff Grimes as coeditor. Jeff worked with Alex Thomas as coeditor of all previous editions and made many contributions to the framework and content of *Best Practices* editions over the years. Further, Jeff has been a long-time leader in school psychology, and our field has benefitted greatly from his commitment, wisdom, and vision. We thank Jeff for all he has done for *Best Practices* and school psychology.

The efforts of Mike Schwartz have proved invaluable to the completion of this edition. Mike Schwartz has been the copyeditor for every chapter in this and in the last two editions of *Best Practices*. He read and reread each of the chapters and contributed substantive comments and perspectives in addition to making sure that references were properly cited, tenses agreed, tables aligned, verbs and nouns were compatible, and ideas remained focused. We thank him for his talent and good humor.

The look and feel of this edition, and the consistency and ease of reference, is due to the metadiligent efforts of Linda Morgan, NASP Director of Production. She actively participated in the myriad details associated with this work and took the lead in the design and presentation. Additionally, she fact checked and triple fact checked every reference and citation. NASP is fortunate to have her talents, and this edition of *Best Practices* is richer due to her involvement.

There are other people at the NASP national office who quietly and competently worked to enhance this edition of *Best Practices*. We thank Brieann Kinsey, Manager of Editorial Production, for her time fact checking, proofreading, and ensuring that what was printed was accurate and consistent with the overall "feel" of the publication. We also thank Denise Ferrenz, Director of Publications, for dealing with the multitude of planning, publication, and marketing considerations associated with a project of this magnitude.

Alex Thomas
Patti Harrison

EDITOR NOTE

Authors were invited to write chapters for this edition of *Best Practices* because of their expertise and experience in a specific topic. In a number of cases, these authors have written other publications or developed resources on the same topic and reference these materials in their *Best Practices* chapters. Therefore, authors were instructed to include a disclosure statement at the end of their *Best Practices* chapters, in line with the 2010 NASP *Principles for Professional Ethics*, Standard III.V.6 (see http://www.nasponline.org/standards/2010standards/1_%20Ethical%20Principles.pdf), which requires school psychologists to disclose financial interests in resources or services they discuss in presentations or writings.

Disclosure. Alex Thomas and Patti Harrison have financial interests in publications they coauthored or coedited and that are referenced by authors of several chapters in this edition of *Best Practices in School Psychology*. These include, for Alex Thomas, previous editions of *Best Practices in School Psychology* and, for Patti Harrison, *Contemporary Intellectual Assessment: Theories, Tests, and Issues; Adaptive Behavior Assessment System;* and *ABAS-II: Clinical Use and Interpretation.*

Section 1
Interventions and Instructional Support to Develop Academic Skills

1

Best Practices in Instructional Strategies for Reading in General Education

Rebecca S. Martinez
Indiana University

OVERVIEW

A candid look at student achievement in the 21st century points to an educational system that continues battling to ensure that all children experience academic success. School psychologists who have been in education for any period of time certainly have witnessed countless programs, curricula, and initiatives ebb and flow. Most ubiquitous and notable among these efforts are those aimed at undertaking the literacy crisis in the United States. According to the Nation's Report Card, which summarizes the academic achievement of a nationally representative sample of elementary and secondary students, approximately 25% of all students read below a basic level. These percentages are greater for poor (37%), Black (42%), and Latino (37%) students (National Center for Education Statistics, 2011). Nevertheless, the ability to read critically and write well is the foundation for lifelong success both in and out of school. Phyllis C. Hunter, a nationally renowned reading consultant who specializes in helping teachers recognize and correctly implement scientifically based reading programs (Reading Rockets; http://bcove.me/wqnsdtkv), describes reading as the new civil right. Hunter is unwavering in the conviction that a school's first and most important mission is to teach children to read and read well.

Of all the potential solutions that exist to address this country's education problems, none is more tangible than efforts aimed at improving teachers' capacity to deliver excellent instruction, especially in reading. We know that improvements in instruction invariably lead to improvements in learning outcomes (Barber & Mourshed, 2007). Fortunately, a vast literature on effective instructional pedagogy, particularly in the area of reading, has identified both general and specific instructional strategies (and interventions) most likely to promote academic achievement for all students. Leaders in the top performing school systems understand that "the quality of the outcomes of any school system is essentially the sum of the quality of the instruction that its teachers deliver" (Barber & Mourshed, 2007, p. 26). We know what works. Indeed, much of the variation in children's reading achievement rests squarely on a teacher's instructional effectiveness in the classroom (Strickland, Snow, Griffin, Burns, & McNamara, 2002).

In the area of reading, using effective instructional strategies can in effect bring most struggling readers to average reading levels (e.g., Foorman, Francis, Fletcher, Schatschneider, & Mehta, 1998). Even for students who are English language learners (ELL), quality of instruction is more important than language of instruction (Cheung & Slavin, 2012) for improving educational outcomes. An excellent teacher is a curriculum and instruction virtuoso. She has the remarkable ability to use daily student data to inform what materials she will select and the methods she will employ to instruct each and every pupil in her charge. It is indisputable: "It all comes down to the teacher" (Strickland et al., 2002, p. 4) and the instructional strategies available in his or her teaching arsenal.

This chapter describes instructional principles and strategies, both broad and specific, that have been identified in various literatures (e.g., education, special education, educational psychology, and school psychology) as being the most effective at helping all children learn to read and read better. The chapter addresses the National Association of School Psychologists (NASP)

Model for Comprehensive and Integrated School Psychological Services (NASP 2010a) domain of Interventions and Instructional Support to Develop Academic Skills and is intended to address the area of reading instruction and intervention. It is anticipated that the information presented in this chapter will allow school psychologists to recognize when excellent instructional practices in reading are occurring and when these practices need improvement so school psychologists can work collaboratively with teachers in continuing to improve teachers' instructional practices and thus student academic outcomes.

The three core components of excellent classroom pedagogy comprise effective strategies in (a) instruction, (b) classroom management, and (c) classroom curriculum design (Marzano, 2007). In this chapter, the focus is on the first component, the use of effective instructional strategies and principles as applied to improving students' reading. While there is no shortage of literature on effective instructional strategies, the goal of this chapter is to present with broad brushstrokes some of the most salient features of effective instructional practices and principles, emphasizing those that promote reading mastery at the elementary and secondary levels.

BASIC CONSIDERATIONS

If it all comes down to the teacher with regard to classroom instruction and intervention, where does this leave the school psychologist? Among their many professional roles, school psychologists are charged with promoting effective learning environments that prevent academic problems as well as working with teachers and other educators to cultivate these supportive learning environments (NASP, 2010b). Although instruction and curriculum are regarded as domains of the classroom teacher, if school psychologists are going to advocate effectively for students within the educational system, then they must have knowledge about pedagogy, including awareness of evidence-based curricula (the what) and effective instructional methods (the how) and what these look like when implemented (or not implemented) in the classroom.

It is essential that school psychologists become proficient at recognizing the features of excellent classroom instruction and work skillfully and collaboratively with teachers when that instruction falls short. This work can be a delicate undertaking, but no professional is better prepared to carry on this pursuit than the school psychologist. A school psychologist's training in consultation and collaboration (and, in some

cases, pedagogy) allows the school psychologist to work closely with educators to advocate on behalf of students by making sure appropriate interventions and instructional supports are in place.

By and large, school psychologists can champion for students by capitalizing on their unique positions within a school system as both outsiders and insiders. As outsiders, school psychologists are in a unique role to objectively appraise the educational culture in which they work. Because they are not teachers, school psychologists are outsiders to the classroom, and therefore can be impartial when evaluating classroom ecologies and teaching effectiveness and unbiased when observing and assessing individual students. These assessment tasks are especially important when evaluating students who have been referred for special education consideration.

Alternatively, as insiders to the school system in which they work, school psychologists generally are highly regarded by staff for their skills and knowledge about best practices in education and psychology. Consequently, school psychologists have credibility with teachers and administrators and are frequently sought out for their expertise, wide skill set, and ethical acumen. School psychologists thus are in the best position to confer closely with teachers, administrators, and other related services personnel in support of excellent instructional practices that provide every student an opportunity to succeed academically. Examples of this type of work include developing and offering tailored professional development sessions, facilitating discussion around a book study, creating intervention briefs that summarize the literature and interpret it for teachers' practical use, investigating and reporting on the evidence base of certain programs or curricula, and consulting individually with teachers about areas in which they would like more support or professional development.

What Good Reading Instruction Looks Like

Most students—roughly 50–60%—learn to read regardless of the method of instruction employed by their teachers (Olson, 2004). However, for struggling readers, explicit, systematic, and intense instruction in the five essential components of early reading (i.e., phonemic awareness, phonics, fluency, vocabulary, and comprehension) is the key to help them break the reading code in English. If struggling students are identified early through a systematic multitiered system of service delivery and taught using instruction that is based on science, most have an excellent chance being remediated to satisfactory reading levels (Moats, n.d.).

Early Reading

The 2004 Individuals with Disabilities Education Act and the 2001 No Child Left Behind Act define the essential components of early reading as explicit and systematic instruction in (a) phonemic awareness; (b) phonics; (c) vocabulary development; (d) reading fluency, including oral reading skills; and (e) reading comprehension strategies. Explicit instruction means that material is taught overtly such that the teacher models what students need to do to demonstrate mastery of each new skill, while systematic instruction refers to the sequencing of complex tasks into more manageable chunks so students are not overwhelmed with difficult new material (Vaughn, Wanzek, Murray, & Roberts, 2012). Further, it is the general education teacher who is responsible for providing this instruction to all students (Fuchs & Fuchs, 2005) and implementing it with fidelity for at least 90 minutes daily (McCook, 2006). In consultation sessions and during problem-solving meetings, school psychologists can promote the importance of the general education teacher in providing reading instruction to all students, including struggling students, and discourage the idea that only specialists, such as special education teachers, should provide intense reading instruction.

Despite widely acknowledged best practices (backed by science and the law) in teaching reading to young children, there historically have been two distinct philosophies about how to teach young children to read, and school psychologists ought to be familiar with both: (a) whole language and (b) scientifically based approaches. Whole language is an approach to reading instruction that emphasizes a natural process of learning to read by fostering children's interaction with meaningful, authentic literature. The whole language philosophy is intuitively appealing, and, indeed, more than half of all students learn to read when instructed this way (Olson, 2004). However, the remaining students for whom reading does not come easily cannot and will not break the code and become independent readers if taught only by a whole language approach. According to Moats (n.d.):

> For more than three decades, advocates of "whole language" instruction have argued—to the delight of many teachers and public school administrators—that learning to read is a "natural" process

for children. Create reading centers in classrooms; put good, fun books in children's hands and allow them to explore; then encourage them to "read," even if they can't make heads or tails of the words on the page. Eventually, they'll get it. So say the believers. (p. 6)

It is important for all educators to understand that students who do not learn to read automatically must be taught to read explicitly and systematically using a scientifically based approach. Understanding of the scientifically based approach to teaching reading began in the 1990s, when the National Reading Panel was convened to review research and summarize the essential features of effective, scientifically based reading instruction. These areas are commonly known as the Big Ideas in beginning reading: phonemic awareness, phonics, fluency, vocabulary, and comprehension (National Institute of Child Health and Human Development, 2000). Good readers must master each of these elements and each must be incorporated in effective early reading instruction, especially for non-readers, poor readers, and ELLs.

School psychologists can be of great assistance in promoting the scientifically based reading instruction agenda first and foremost by ensuring schools can recognize when whole language programs claim to be based on science (Moats, n.d.) and instead help schools select reading curricula firmly grounded in what works. One way school psychologists can accomplish this goal is by serving on the textbook adoption committee and advocating for adoption of curricula that emphasize the Big Ideas in beginning reading.

Secondary Reading

There are many struggling readers at the secondary level and teaching them to read, while ensuring they gain content area knowledge, is no easy task. The key concept to remember regarding effective reading instruction for struggling readers at the secondary level is that every teacher is a teacher of reading (Shanahan & Shanahan, 2008). Secondary teachers simply cannot take for granted that reading instruction in elementary school makes reading instruction at the secondary level dispensable (Shanahan & Shanahan, 2008). This sentiment may be frustrating to secondary teachers who see themselves as content instructors rather than reading teachers (Shanahan & Shanahan, 2008). Further, unlike elementary teachers who may have had at least some coursework in how to teach children to read, secondary teachers frequently have no preservice training in teaching reading.

Although many efforts aimed at remediating early reading failure focus on intensifying instruction in decoding and phonics, it is not as simple an approach with secondary students. Slavin, Chamberlain, and Daniels (2007) noted that at the secondary level:

> It matters a great deal how reading is taught. [Secondary] reading is different from elementary reading. The students are far more sophisticated in their interest and social skills, and those who are struggling in reading have little patience for methods or materials designed for younger children. Students are likely to have uneven reading skills and gaps, so teaching everyone the same content is both inefficient and demotivating. (p. 1)

To improve literacy-related instruction in the content areas (e.g., science and social studies) at the secondary level, Torgesen et al. (2007) offered five recommendations: (a) provide explicit instruction and supportive practice in the use of effective comprehension strategies throughout the school day; (b) increase the amount and quality of open, sustained discussion of reading content; (c) set and maintain high standards for text, conversation, questions, and vocabulary; (d) increase students' motivation and engagement with reading; and (e) teach essential content knowledge so that all students master critical concepts. School psychologists can work closely with teachers to select and implement appropriate interventions that bolster secondary students' basic reading skill (e.g., fluency) and improve their comprehension and understanding of the content.

BEST PRACTICES IN INSTRUCTIONAL STRATEGIES FOR READING IN GENERAL EDUCATION

In this section four core principles underlying instructional effectiveness are presented. These instructional principles are not specific or unique to reading and thus can be applied to improving outcomes in other academic areas (e.g., writing and mathematics), although examples related to improving reading are highlighted. These core instructional tenets are (a) conducting frequent formative assessments and using data to inform instructional decisions within a multitiered model of service delivery, (b) altering instructional dosage as necessary, (c) differentiating instruction to

meet the needs of all students, and (d) having ample knowledge about specific evidence-based strategies and interventions that promote student achievement. Teachers may not readily use or implement all four of these principles all of the time in their classrooms, and no school psychologist should use these as a checklist to classify teacher instructional efficacy. Nonetheless, school psychologists must be willing and prepared to work collaboratively with teachers who are amenable to learning about and adopting one or more of these principles in their daily work. The four principles of instructional excellence are described next.

Formative Assessment Within a Multitiered Model

One of the most effective characteristics of excellent instruction involves formative assessment within a multitiered model of service delivery and using assessment results to modify instruction accordingly. Excellent teachers understand the importance of formative assessment and incorporate it throughout their teaching. Indeed, frequent formative assessment is associated with substantial learning gains, and the more ambitious the goals a teacher sets for students the greater the student gain (Jenkins & Terjeson, 2011). Still, formative assessment alone is not sufficient to trigger the kind of radical change necessary to ensure all students are learning. If classroom (and school-wide) assessment activities are not directly and actively linked to prevention and intervention efforts or aligned to curriculum and instruction, then these assessment activities are essentially worthless (Ikeda, Neesen, & Witt, 2008). Consequently, effective teachers do not hesitate to obtain and use data, including formative assessment data, to remediate skills deficits in struggling students (Barnett, Daly, Jones, & Lentz, 2004) and enrich activities for high achieving students. This process is the essence of using data to inform instructional decisions.

School psychologists can be especially instrumental in assisting teachers in understanding the purpose of assessment and how to use assessment information to modify instruction. In the best case scenario, there is virtually no lag between discovering that a student is struggling in a particular skill (e.g., letter identification, phonemic awareness, reading fluency, math calculation) and the swift application of research-based instructional practices and interventions aimed directly at helping students master a skill before moving on to a more complex or difficult skill. Testing, assessment, and evaluation are sometimes regarded negatively in education settings, but school psychologists can help eliminate faulty beliefs about assessment and instead present assessment as a way to empower teachers' work by demonstrating how assessment data provide the information teachers need to tailor their instruction to ensure positive academic gain for all students.

Effective teachers also find resourceful ways to involve students in the formative assessment process, including (but not limited to) having students graph their own progress and set attainable but challenging goals. Students who chart/measure their own progress and are active participants in the intervention process are more invested in their own growth and therefore may be more motivated to achieve. Chapius (2009) offers seven specific approaches to help teachers involve students in monitoring their own progress: (a) provide a clear and understandable vision of the learning goal, (b) use examples of strong and weak work, (c) offer students individualized and frequent descriptive feedback, (d) teach students to self-assess and set goals, (e) design lessons to focus on one aspect of quality at a time, (f) teach students how to revise their work, and (g) engage students in self-reflection and let them document and share their learning progress. School psychologists who have the opportunity to provide direct academic interventions to struggling students can model these approaches for teachers. School psychologists can also create a series of worksheets with specific instructions for some of these approaches and share these templates with teachers for use with their own students.

With regard to which formative assessment tool to use to measure and monitor academic growth (or decline), curriculum-based measurement (CBM) has an exceptionally strong research base (see, e.g., Ardoin, Christ, Morena, Cormier, & Klingbeil, 2013). CBMs are standardized, time efficient, relatively inexpensive, and quick to administer and score. There are numerous name brands of CBM, including AIMSweb (http://www.aimsweb.com), Dynamic Indicators of Basic Early Literacy Skills (http://dibels.uoregon.edu), System to Enhance Educational Performance (http://www.isteep.com/login.aspx), and EdCheckUp (http://www.edcheckup.com). In the early elementary grades tasks may include letter naming fluency, letter sound fluency, phoneme segmentation fluency, and nonsense word fluency. In the later grades tasks may include oral reading fluency and reading comprehension (i.e., Maze tasks). CBM is an exemplary screening and progress-monitoring tool because CBM parallels both the five targets of effective early reading instruction (i.e.,

phonemic awareness, phonics, fluency, vocabulary, and comprehension) and the areas in which a child can be found to have a specific learning disability in reading.

Considering assessment and intervention together is essential in helping the committee responsible for determining special education eligibility determine if a child meets eligibility requirements for a specific learning disability. If a child has been provided with research-based interventions administered with fidelity over sufficient time and the child continues to be in poor standing relative to his or her peers and fails to make sufficient progress, then a strong case can be made that the child meets the criteria for a specific learning disability (providing exclusionary factors and other related information have been considered; Case, Speece, & Molloy, 2003).

Unfortunately, in a majority of preservice education classes around the country, future teachers are not taught how to assess children's reading difficulties or how to ameliorate these difficulties using science-based reading instruction (Walsh, Glaser, & Dunne-Wilcox, 2006). Consequently, and assuming that school psychologists have sufficient training to provide effective professional development to teachers in the area of reading instruction, school psychologists can be ambassadors for CBM and evidence-based instructional practices by providing teachers professional development in these areas and offering ongoing, embedded coaching as teachers learn how to implement these effective practices in their daily instruction.

Instructional Dosage

Effective teachers use formative assessment data to guide their instructional decisions, including the decision to intensify their teaching for struggling students and enrich their instruction for advanced students. The process of intensifying instruction based on need can be described as instructional dosage. Too frequently educators believe that they cannot provide effective, intense instruction or interventions to struggling students because they do not have a particular curriculum or they have not learned about the newest and latest program, when in fact all they need to do is understand how to intensify (i.e., alter the instructional dosage) existing sound instructional practices.

Perhaps the best paradigm to illustrate instructional dosage is by Faggella-Luby and Deshler (2008), who described a framework that encompasses four dimensions of instructional dosing or intensification: (a) group size, (b) instructional period (session length), (c) frequency (number of sessions per week), and (d) and duration (total number of sessions). Simply stated, by helping teachers adjust these four dimensions in their teaching, school psychologists can help teachers address the needs of struggling students without the need of an outside program or curriculum. Each of these dimensions is described in detail below.

Flexible grouping is a core component of effective instruction, and excellent teachers teach to both large and small groups of students. In terms of instructional dosage, reducing the teacher-to-student ratio alone increases the intensity of the instruction and allows for more individualized attention (i.e., differentiation). The smaller group size also increases individual student's opportunities to respond and receive corrective feedback. Both opportunity to respond and corrective feedback are critical components of excellent instruction.

With regard to deciding how small an instructional group needs to be so that instruction may be maximally effective, researchers have demonstrated that academic gains are similar for students participating in one-on-one instruction as for those receiving instruction in groups of three (Vaughn et al., 2003). That is, teachers will generally get more bang for their buck if they instruct small groups of three than if they spend most of their time providing one-on-one instruction to struggling students.

Struggling students also need longer and more frequent instructional periods. Session length, frequency, and duration are modifiable dimensions that can be applied to increase intensity. One of the key elements of the federally funded Reading First program includes an uninterrupted 90-minute period of core reading instruction. For most students, a scientifically based core reading program delivered for 90 minutes a day is sufficient for them to grasp basic reading skills. Students who struggle in reading, however, may benefit from increasing the 90 minute block by 30–90 additional minutes of effective instruction. School psychologists can encourage teachers to use the instructional time to reteach concepts that students have not learned, incorporate specific interventions to address weak or fragile skills, or incorporate aspects of the core curriculum intended for struggling readers.

The heavy instructional time commitment dedicated to reading often poses a dilemma for teachers whose daily schedules are already overflowing with activities. This is also where school psychologists can be especially supportive. School psychologists can help teachers, administrators, and parents understand the dire need to make sure children learn to read, even at the expense of other instructional content or elective courses. School psychologists understand that even though such a position may be unpopular and will likely be met with resistance, they will persevere in advocating for students by pursuing staff and parent buy-in for prioritizing reading instruction. School psychologists can help staff make small changes, such as assisting administrators in designing the master schedule to spotlight reading for struggling students over other, less urgent school activities and consulting with teachers on their class schedules to allow for more reading instruction.

Differentiated Instruction

Closely related to the concept of instructional dosage is the notion of differentiated instruction, or differentiation, which is a teaching paradigm wherein teachers explicitly take into account their students' diverse strengths and needs when planning how they will deliver their instruction and what classroom routines they will implement. Because of today's diverse student body, teachers must modify their instruction and curriculum if they aim to make sure each and every student has the opportunity to learn. Excellent education is not a one-size-fits-all practice. Excellent teaching is difficult and teachers must masterfully manage a continuous teach–assess–differentiate cycle from the moment they start the school day until the bell rings at the end of the day. Consider this powerful statement:

> If you teach the same curriculum, to all students, at the same time, at the same rate, using the same materials, with the same instructional methods, with the same expectations for performance and grade on a curve you have fertile ground for growing special education. (Germann, 2003, cited in Tilly, 2003)

Tomlinson and Imbeau (2010) presented eight core tenets of differentiated instruction: (a) teacher focuses on the essentials; (b) the teacher modifies content, process and products; (c) assessment and instruction are inseparable; (d) the teacher attends to student differences; (e) the teacher balances group and individual norms; (f) all students participate in respectful work; (g) the teacher and students work together flexibly; and (h) the teacher and students collaborate in learning. These principles of differentiation are described next.

Differentiated instruction that focuses on essential skills is geared toward all children learning the big ideas about a concept or a skill. The teacher decides what core objectives all children need to master, and then adjusts the complexity and expectations of what students must know and be able to do based on knowledge of where each student is individually. In this way, the teacher ensures that struggling students grasp the big ideas while advanced students can move on to more complex features of the big idea without having to do the same activities they have already mastered. Oftentimes new tasks are presented in an "I do, We do, You do" format, where the teacher models the task (I do), the student and the teacher practice the task together (We do), and then students repeat the task independently (You do) (Kosanovich, 2012) using activities at different levels of complexity.

In a differentiated classroom, there is a clear sense that the teacher respects individual and group differences. Teachers who differentiate are aware—and accept—different readiness levels, abilities, interests, school experiences, and cultural and linguistic influences and plan their instruction accordingly. They do this by considering these differences when planning instruction and ensuring that all students participate in equally engaging daily classwork. Teachers who differentiate are masterful at fostering a sense of respect where all students are given opportunities to engage with each other and learn the material at their pace, in tasks that are equally important and interesting (Tomlinson & Imbeau, 2010). For example, ELL or special education students are actively engaged in an instructionally meaningful small group activity, perhaps with a teaching assistant, when the teacher is delivering whole group instruction.

The teacher who differentiates is also flexible and amenable to modifying a lesson as the need arises. The teacher continuously works in partnership with students, collaboratively working toward the goal of learning. School psychologists can assist teachers in their differentiation efforts by informing teachers about students with whom they may have not had much experience. For example, if a teacher has limited or no experience working with ELL students, then school psychologists can help allay the teacher's concerns about effectively serving language minority students by discussing ways to offer meaningful and scaffolded instruction.

Knowledge of Evidence-Based Strategies and Interventions

Excellent instruction, especially in reading, includes the application of evidence-based intervention strategies

matched to students' unique needs (i.e., instructional match; Burns, 2007). Excellent teachers have a broad range of evidence-based reading strategies and interventions at their disposal. These teachers have a vast knowledge of interventions and are aware of resources for finding these interventions. When excellent teachers come across a new intervention or program and they are not sure about its evidence base, they do research to make informed decisions, an area in which school psychologists can be especially helpful.

No Child Left Behind requires schools to use scientifically validated practices and interventions. To this end, in 2002 the Institute of Education Sciences founded the What Works Clearing House (http://ies.ed. gov/ncee/wwc), a website that reviews the research on educational practices and programs and provides practice guides and intervention reports so teachers can make appropriate decisions. Similarly, in school psychology, the Task Force on Evidence-Based Interventions in School Psychology (http://www. indiana.edu/~ebi) came together and created coding manuals to help school psychologists identify effective interventions and assist scholars in the field in designing and promoting high quality research in school psychology.

Teachers who have gaps in their preservice training may benefit greatly from school psychologists who provide them with resources to become aware of and access these interventions. Practical ways a school psychologist can make these resources available to teachers might include making a master list of the best websites for interventions, providing teachers with evidence briefs and instructions or directions for implementing certain interventions, and role-playing with teachers how these interventions can be implemented with fidelity in the classroom.

Most high quality, research-based instructional strategies share two important features: they are easy to set up and implement, and they do not require any special training. One practical resource for evidence-based interventions is the Evidence-Based Intervention (EBI) network (http://ebi.missouri.edu). The EBI network includes intervention briefs, which are summaries of the research for each intervention, as well as videos modeling the interventions. Examples of the evidence-based interventions featured on the network include cross-age peer tutoring; guided reading; story detective; cover, copy and compare; repeated readings; incremental rehearsal; partner reading; mystery motivator; and response cards. School psychologists can use this website to help teachers understand what a research-based intervention is and how to incorporate it in their reading instruction to ensure all students make acceptable academic gains.

SUMMARY

Reading instruction is perhaps a school's single most important task. However, approximately one quarter of all students have not mastered basic reading skills by fourth grade. Fortunately, reading failure is a remediable problem. Decades of reading research have demonstrated that evidence-based instructional strategies, implemented by effective teachers, can help to resolve this country's reading crisis. School psychologists play a central role in helping school staff understand and adopt such practices, policies, and programs. Four broad principles of effective instruction were described in this chapter: (a) formative assessment within a multitiered model, (b) instructional dosage, (c) differentiated instruction, and (d) knowledge of evidence-based strategies and interventions. Promoting scientifically based practices in the schools—especially regarding reading instructional practices—is one sure way school psychologists can champion for all students.

REFERENCES

Ardoin, S. P., Christ, T. J., Morena, L. S., Cormier, D. C., & Klingbeil, D. A. (2013). A systematic review and summarization of the recommendations and research surrounding curriculum-based measurement of oral reading fluency (CBM-R) decision rules. *Journal of School Psychology, 51*, 1–18.

Barber, M., & Mourshed, M. (2007). *How the world's best performing school systems come out on top*. Retrieved from http://mckinseyonsociety.com/how-the-worlds-best-performing-schools-come-out-on-top/

Barnett, D. W., Daly, E. J., Jones, K. M., & Lentz, F. E. (2004). Response to intervention: Empirically based special service decisions from single-case designs of increasing and decreasing intensity. *The Journal of Special Education, 38*, 66–79.

Burns, M. K. (2007). Reading at the instructional level with children identified as learning disabled: Potential implications for response to intervention. *School Psychology Quarterly, 22*, 297–313.

Case, L. P., Speece, D. L., & Molloy, D. E. (2003). The validity of a response-to-instruction paradigm to identify reading disabilities: A longitudinal analysis of individual differences and contextual factors. *School Psychology Review, 32*, 557–582.

Chapius, J. (2009). *Seven strategies of assessment for learning*. New York, NY: Pearson.

Cheung, A. C. K., & Slavin, R. E. (2012). Effective reading programs for Spanish-dominant English language learners (ELLs) in the elementary grades: A synthesis of research. *Review of Educational Research, 82*, 351–395.

Faggella-Luby, M. N., & Deshler, D. D. (2008). Reading comprehension in adolescents with LD: What we know; what we need to learn. *Learning Disabilities Research & Practice, 23*, 70–78.

Foorman, B. R., Francis, D. J., Fletcher, J. M., Schatschneider, C., & Mehta, P. (1998). The role of instruction in learning to read: Preventing reading failure in at-risk children. *Journal of Educational Psychology, 90*, 37–55.

Fuchs, D., & Fuchs, L. (2005, May). *Operationalizing response to intervention (RTI) as a method of LD identification*. Retrieved from http://tennessee.gov/education/speced/doc/sefuopertifaq.pdf

Ikeda, M. J., Neessen, E., & Witt, J. C. (2008). Best practices in universal screening. In A. Thomas & J. Grimes (Eds.), *Best practices in school psychology V* (pp. 103–114). Bethesda, MD: National Association of School Psychologists.

Jenkins, J. R., & Terjeson, K. J. (2011). Monitoring reading growth: Goal setting, measurement frequency, and methods of evaluation. *Learning Disabilities Research & Practice, 26*, 28–35.

Kosanovich, M. (2012). *Using instructional routines to differentiate instruction: A guide for teachers*. Portsmouth, NH: RMC Research Corporation, Center on Instruction.

Marzano, R. J. (2007). *The art and science of teaching*. Alexandria, VA: ASCD.

McCook, J. E. (2006). *The RTI guide: Developing and implementing a model in your schools*. Horsham, PA: LRP Publications.

Moats, L. C. (n.d.). *Whole-language high-jinks: How to tell when "scientifically-based reading instruction" isn't*. Washington, DC: Thomas B. Fordham Institute. Retrieved from http://www.edexcellence.net/publications/wholelanguage.html

National Association of School Psychologists. (2010a). *Model for comprehensive and integrated school psychological services*. Bethesda, MD: Author. Retrieved from http://www.nasponline.org/standards/2010standards/2_PracticeModel.pdf

National Association of School Psychologists. (2010b). *Principles for professional ethics*. Bethesda, MD: Author. Retrieved from http://www.nasponline.org/standards/2010standards/1_%20Ethical%20Principles.pdf

National Center for Education Statistics. (2011). *The Nation's report card: Reading 2011* (NCES 2012–457). Washington. DC: Author.

National Institute of Child Health and Human Development. (2000). *Report of the National Reading Panel. Teaching children to read: An evidence-based assessment of the scientific research literature on reading and its implications for reading instruction* (NIH Publication No. 00-4769). Washington, DC: Author.

Olson, R. K. (2004). SSR, environment, and genes. *Scientific Studies of Reading, 8*, 111–124.

Shanahan, T., & Shanahan, C. (2008). Teaching disciplinary literacy to adolescents: Rethinking content-area literacy. *Harvard Educational Review, 78*, 40–59.

Slavin, R. E., Chamberlain, A., & Daniels, C. (2007). Preventing reading failure. *Educational Leadership, 65*, 22–27.

Strickland, D., Snow, C., Griffin, P., Burns, M. S., & McNamara, P. (2002). *Preparing our teachers: Opportunities for better reading instruction*. Washington, DC: National Academies Press.

Tilly, W. D., III. (2003, December). *Heartland Area Education Agency's evolution from four to three tiers: Our journey—Our results*. Paper presented at the National Research Center on Learning Disabilities Responsiveness-to-Intervention Symposium, Kansas City, MO

Tomlinson, C. A., & Imbeau, M. B. (2010). *Leading and managing a differentiated classroom*. Alexandria, VA: ASCD.

Torgesen, J. K., Houston, D. D., Rissman, L. M., Decker, S. M., Roberts, G., Vaughn, S., Wexler, …Lesaux, N. (2007). *Academic literacy instruction for adolescents: A guidance document from the Center on Instruction.* Portsmouth, NH· RMC Research Corporation, Center on Instruction.

Vaughn, S., Linan-Thompson, S., Kouzekanani, K., Bryant, D., Dickson, S., & Blozis, S. (2003). Reading instruction grouping for students with reading difficulties. *Remedial and Special Education, 24,* 301–315.

Vaughn, S., Wanzek, J., Murray, C. S., & Roberts, G. (2012). *Intensive interventions for students struggling in reading and mathematics: A practice guide.* Portsmouth, NH: RMC Research Corporation, Center on Instruction.

Walsh, K., Glaser, D., & Dunne-Wilcox, D. (2006). *What education schools aren't teaching about reading and what elementary teachers aren't learning.* Washington, DC: National Council for Teacher Quality.

2 Best Practices in Increasing Academic Engaged Time

Maribeth Gettinger
Katherine Miller
University of Wisconsin–Madison

OVERVIEW

How students spend their time in classrooms is a topic of considerable importance for teachers, school psychologists, and administrators. The amount of time students are actively engaged in learning is a strong predictor of academic achievement. A best-evidence synthesis of research on teaching and learning confirmed that, in addition to motivation and high-quality instruction, the time that students are on task during appropriate learning activities accounts for significant variation in achievement outcomes (Fullan, Hill, & Crevola, 2006). Simply put, the more time students are actively engaged in learning, the higher their achievement will be.

Given the importance of time as a determinant of learning, the purpose of this chapter is to describe best practices for school psychologists to help teachers evaluate, extend, and enhance academic engaged time. The chapter is predicated on the contention that academic engaged time plays a key role in contributing to student achievement. As such, best practices for increasing academic engaged time are well situated within the National Association of School Psychologists (NASP) *Model for Comprehensive and Integrated School Psychological Services* (NASP, 2010) practice domain encompassing Interventions and Instructional Support to Develop Academic Skills. In fact, academic engaged time has been accorded special significance by school psychologists because components of engaged time are manipulable facets of classrooms that teachers, through problem solving and consultative support from school psychologists, are often able to control.

Despite the importance of academic engaged time, descriptive studies reveal that (a) as little as half of each school day is typically devoted to academic instruction, (b) students are engaged in learning activities only 28–56% of the time they spend in school during a given year, and (c) the level of students' on-task behavior may be as low as 45% in some classrooms (Fisher, 2009). In response to concerns about low academic engagement among students, the National Education Commission on Time and Learning was established in 1991 to conduct a comprehensive examination of time use in America's schools. In 1994, the National Education Commission on Time and Learning released its report, *Prisoners of Time*, which concluded, "it would be unreasonable to believe that … the quality … of American schools could be improved without substantial changes in the amount and use of time allowed for teachers and students to do their work" (National Education Commission on Time and Learning, 1994, p. 15). With increasing accountability for student outcomes, schools must find ways to ensure that all students have adequate learning time to achieve a minimum level of proficiency. The need to focus on instructional time is so urgent that the National Education Commission on Time and Learning updated and reissued its report in 2005 to underscore the importance of maximizing academic engaged time (National Education Commission on Time and Learning, 2005). A key role for school psychologists is to engage teachers in problem solving to restructure their use of classroom time and instruction to ensure that all learners accrue sufficient amounts of engaged learning time.

The concept of academic engaged time is particularly significant as schools move toward implementation of multitiered instructional support systems. Because increases in student engagement covary with gains on curriculum-based measures and standardized tests, academic engaged time may be used to gauge students' response to instructional practices or to assess the overall quality of Tier 1 instruction. Moreover, within multi-leveled models, tiers of instruction are differentiated on the basis of several dimensions, including the intensity of instruction. For many learners, academic engaged time is a proxy for instructional intensity. That is, the more engaged learning time, the more explicit and effective instruction is for students.

Carroll's Model of School Learning

Current interest in academic engaged time can be traced to several theories that implicate time in the learning process, beginning with Carroll's (1963) original model of school learning. The major premise of Carroll's model is that learning is a function of two time variables: the amount of time students spend in learning relative to the amount of time they actually need for learning. According to Carroll, students master instructional objectives to the extent that students are allowed and are willing to invest the time required to learn the content. Carroll's model can be expressed as a simple mathematical equation: degree of learning $= f$ (time spent/time needed). Based on this equation, the degree to which a learner succeeds in learning a task is dependent on the amount of time the learner spends in relation to the amount of time he or she needs. That is, the closer individuals come to achieving equilibrium between the amount of time they require for learning and the amount of time they actually engage in learning, the higher their level of mastery.

By placing time as a pivotal variable in school learning, Carroll's model initiated a major shift in educational thought and research on the teaching–learning process and spawned decades of research focusing on learning time and school achievement (Gettinger & Walter, 2012). The current conceptualization of academic engaged time is linked to the emergence of research during the 1970s, which defined teaching effectiveness in terms of specific classroom behaviors. The primary goal of teaching-effectiveness research was to determine the relationship between observable classroom processes and student performance, with the intent of identifying teaching practices and behaviors associated with school learning and, in particular, student engagement (Gettinger & Walter, 2012). The search for relations between class-room processes (e.g., teaching behaviors) and outcomes (e.g., student achievement) came to be known as *process–outcome research*. It was the most common paradigm for

identifying variables that contribute to academic engaged time.

Beginning Teacher Evaluation Study

The earliest and most extensive process–outcome research program to document the relationship between time and learning was the Beginning Teacher Evaluation Study conducted during the 1980s (Fisher & Berliner, 1985). The Beginning Teacher Evaluation Study was a landmark study on teaching effectiveness that generated results with far-reaching educational implications dealing with time, instructional processes, and classroom environments. In particular, through systematic observations of classrooms over a 6-year period, Beginning Teacher Evaluation Study researchers developed an operational definition of what they termed *academic learning time*. Specifically, academic learning time is the time students are engaged in academic tasks of appropriate difficulty on which they achieve at least 80% accuracy. The Beginning Teacher Evaluation Study researchers found that student achievement was most highly associated with academic learning time (Fisher & Berliner, 1985).

Research spanning more than three decades has continued to support the original Beginning Teacher Evaluation Study findings documenting a strong positive relationship between academic learning time and student achievement across multiple skill domains and developmental levels (Black, 2002). In recent years, academic learning time has been replaced with the broader concept of academic engaged time to reflect the inclusion of learner-centered variables such as initiative, self-motivation, and self-regulatory strategies. Whereas students' cognitive, affective, and behavioral engagement contributes to academic success, the most reliable approaches to assessing engaged time rely on observable criteria. Thus, the focus of this chapter is on time-based indices of observed academic engagement.

BASIC CONSIDERATIONS

School psychologists play an important role as instructional consultants to help teachers maximize academic engaged time for all learners, thus potentially minimizing the number of students who require Tier 2 or Tier 3 interventions. A student's level of academic engaged time signals how well he or she is responding to Tier 1 instruction and can serve as the basis for making decisions about the need for supplemental instruction. Best practices for consulting with teachers to increase academic engaged time are based on two fundamental considerations for school psychologists: (a) an understanding of the components of academic engaged time and (b) knowledge of approaches for assessment of classroom time usage.

Components of Academic Engaged Time

Having a clear understanding of the components of learning time is necessary for applying the construct of academic engaged time to classroom practices. School learning time, from which the concept of academic engaged time is derived, is best understood as a superordinate concept that encompasses subordinate, more refined concepts of time. Theoretical conceptualizations of academic engaged time identify multiple components along a continuum as illustrated in Figure 2.1. Learning time components can be ordered on a vertical continuum, moving from time that is

Figure 2.1. Continuum of Components and Determinants of Academic Engaged Time

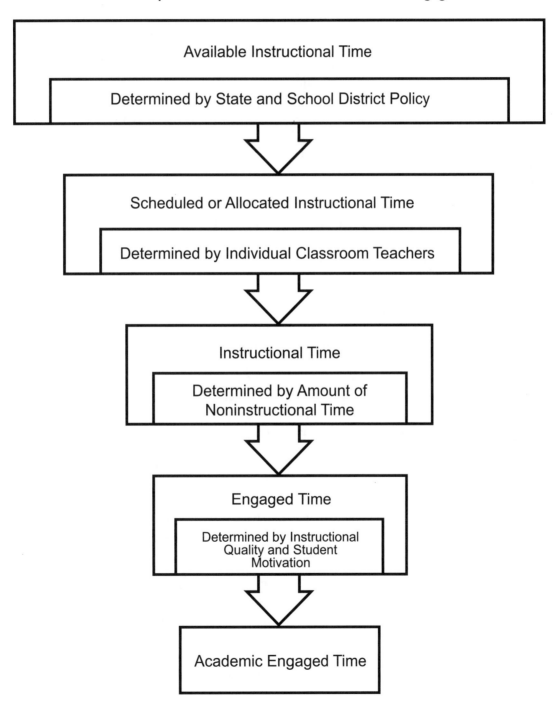

broadly described, easily measured, and typically mandated (shown at the top of the figure), to time that is narrowly focused, challenging to measure, and often difficult to modify (shown at the bottom of the figure).

Available Time

The first component of academic engaged time is available time. This represents the total number of minutes, hours, or days that potentially can be devoted to instruction. Available time is typically established by school district policies and state-mandated time requirements.

Scheduled Time

The second component, scheduled or allocated time, is a more precise subset of available time. It is the amount of time determined by classroom teachers for instruction in each content domain, such as science or math. Scheduled time represents the upper limit of in-class opportunities for students to be engaged in learning.

The process by which scheduled time is converted to productive learning time depends on classroom instruction and management practices as well as on student characteristics. Despite variation across classrooms in the amount of time scheduled for instruction, Marks (2000) found that most variability in academic engaged time is attributable to differences in individual student characteristics and not classrooms. This may be due to several reasons. First, as implicated in Carroll's (1963) model, some students simply require more time for learning than do others. The lowest achieving students may need three to six times as much time to learn the same content as the highest achieving students. Thus, individual differences in the amount of time needed for learning (within a constant amount of scheduled time) contribute to variable achievement more so than do differences in scheduled time.

A second reason why variability in academic engaged time is linked to learner characteristics is that students in the same classroom often self-allocate variable time for independent study, in particular studying outside of school. For example, one student may self-allocate 20 minutes every day to study spelling words, whereas another may spend only 5 minutes each day. Over a 5-day period, this results in considerable variability in study time across students, ranging from 25 to 100 minutes. Thus, the amount of self-determined or self-scheduled learning time will vary across individual learners, even in the same classroom with constant allocated time.

Instructional Time

As shown in Figure 2.1, scheduled time can be further broken down into instructional time (third component of academic engaged time) versus noninstructional time. Instructional time is the amount of scheduled time specifically devoted to learning and instruction. Noninstructional time, by contrast, is the portion of scheduled time that is spent in nonclassroom activities (e.g., recess) or noninstructional events (e.g., making transitions between activities). Whereas a 60-minute period may be scheduled for instruction, some portion of that time is often lost to noninstructional activities having little to do with learning. A vast portion of instruction, for example, is eroded by factors such as time spent in maintaining discipline or dealing with interruptions, such that less than 50% of a school day is typically spent in academic instruction.

Multiple classroom events may reduce the amount of scheduled time that is converted to actual instructional time. The two most common sources of lost instructional time are *transition time* and *wait time* (Kubitschek, Hallinan, Arnett, & Galipeau, 2005). Transition time is noninstructional time that occurs before (e.g., teacher gives back homework at the start of an instructional activity) and after (e.g., children put away materials after a science lesson) instructional periods. Whereas the amount of transition time is typically the same for all students in one classroom, the second source of lost instructional time, wait time, varies across individual students. Wait time is the amount of time an individual student must wait to receive instructional help (e.g., waiting for the teacher's attention after the student raised a hand).

Observational research confirms that an increasing amount of instructional time continues to be "stolen" from classrooms to accommodate noninstructional activities. For example, if 60 minutes are scheduled for a history lesson, and the teacher devotes the first 10 minutes to collecting essays and answering questions about upcoming assignments and the last 5 minutes having students prepare for gym class, then the amount of instructional time is only 45 minutes, or 75% of the scheduled time.

Engaged Time

Moving down the continuum in Figure 2.1 is engaged time, or the proportion of instructional time during which students are cognitively and behaviorally on task or actively engaged in learning, as evidenced by paying attention, completing assigned work, interacting appropriately with peers, taking notes, listening, solving problems, or participating in relevant discussion. Engaged time includes both passive attending and active responding. Students rarely spend the total amount of instructional time provided by teachers actively engaged in appropriate activities. Students may be bored, confused, involved in other activities, distracted, or out of the classroom. Even in well-managed classrooms with effective instruction and multiple opportunities to learn, disparities exist among students in their individual levels of engaged time. In fact, classroom observations reveal considerable variability in average engagement rates among students in elementary classrooms, ranging from as low as 45% up to 90% (Wharton-McDonald, Pressley, & Hampston, 1998).

Academic Engaged Time

Finally, academic engaged time is a certain percentage of engaged time that represents the amount of time during which learning actually occurs for students. Academic engaged time is the most carefully delineated concept of learning time in the literature. It is the portion of time during which students are actively engaged in relevant academic instruction that leads directly to measurable learning.

An index of academic engaged time is derived by subtracting from the total instructional time not only the amount of time spent on classroom management tasks but also time spent on instructional activities that do not translate into successful learning. In other words, the qualities of both relevance and success are critical for discerning academic engaged time. Neither succeeding at irrelevant tasks nor failing at worthwhile tasks contributes to effective learning. Students gain the most from their learning time when they experience a balance of high and medium success, with most activities targeted at a high success level (80–85%). Thus, accurately measuring and ensuring success is critical for increasing students' academic engaged time. Evidence of success may include answering questions correctly, completing work accurately, or demonstrating understanding through other performance indicators. Systematic and repeated monitoring of academic progress using curriculum-based probes provides specific information about students' success on well-defined learning tasks.

Conclusion

A high level of academic engaged time occurs when (a) students are covering content that holds their interest and is viewed as being important and relevant, (b) students are paying attention or are on task for most of the class period, and (c) students are experiencing a high level of success or accuracy with most of the assignments they complete. Whereas each element of learning time depicted in Figure 2.1 demonstrates some relationship with achievement, academic engaged time has been shown to have the strongest link with school learning and achievement (Gettinger & Walter, 2012). For example, research demonstrates that students in schools with more allocated minutes per day have outcomes only slightly better compared to students with less allocated or available time. The link between time and achievement, however, increases when students are given more instructional time, and it is even greater when students' academic engaged time increases. Although the distinctions among the time components in Figure 2.1 may seem obvious, they are important because they make apparent why any strategy to maximize learning time must focus on providing the "right" kind of time, rather than just adding more time to the school day.

Analysis of Time Use

A second basic consideration for school psychologists is familiarity with strategies to evaluate classroom time usage. Implementing a problem-solving process to develop best practices for increasing academic engaged time begins with a comprehensive time-use analysis using the framework presented in Figure 2.1. This analysis determines how effectively time is used in classrooms and the extent to which time may be lost within each component of academic engaged time. To leverage available school time so as to maximize academic engaged time (and, in turn, enhance achievement outcomes), educators must understand what is happening in their schools and classrooms. When teachers are guided by school psychologists in gathering time-use data themselves, they are more likely to apply what they have learned to their own classroom practices.

Group Analysis

An analysis of learning time may be accomplished by school psychologists working with a group of teachers. With a group approach, the school psychologist facilitates discussion among teachers (e.g., all first-grade teachers in a school). Collaboratively, teachers work through the framework in Figure 2.1, using their knowledge of school operations and estimates of how they allocate class time: First, prior to group meetings, teachers are asked to maintain personal logs of their time usage during a typical 1- or 2-week period. Second, as a group, teachers use their time-use logs to record the number of available hours or minutes available in a school day and the amount of scheduled time for different academic subjects in the top portions of Figure 2.1. Third, teachers examine common ways across all classrooms whereby scheduled time is typically lost (e.g., recess, transitions, early dismissals, disruptions). Once lost time is subtracted from scheduled time, the amount that remains represents usable instructional time. This is recorded in the third level of Figure 2.1. Fourth, teachers estimate and compare engagement rates in their individual classrooms across different instructional formats (e.g., teacher-led discussion, independent seatwork), academic domains (e.g., science, reading), and learning tasks (e.g., writing essays, doing computation problems). These amounts are recorded as engaged or on-task time in Figure 2.1. Fifth, teachers construct a profile of success among students in their classrooms (e.g., high, average, or low) to estimate the proportion of students for whom academic engaged time may be further reduced because the work is too difficult or poorly aligned with student skills.

This type of collaborative group analysis of time use provides a forum for identifying sources of lost time as well as problem solving and brainstorming ways to maximize learning time for all students. Within a multitiered model, group analysis of instructional time contributes to the enhancement of Tier 1 core instruction.

Individual Classroom Analysis

An alternate procedure entails a more focused analysis of time use within an individual classroom. Individual analysis is more appropriate than group analysis for developing supplemental interventions for struggling students who accrue less engaged learning time compared to other students receiving Tier 1 instruction. Similar to the group approach, an individual analysis relies on the framework in Figure 2.1. Assessment may involve both data gathering by a teacher and observations by a school psychologist to analyze time usage in the classroom and academic engaged time for individual students. First, the teacher constructs a written schedule of classroom activities or content areas and computes approximate percentages (or actual number of minutes) of both scheduled and instructional time for each activity, as well as sources and amounts of noninstructional time. Second, activities, or content areas, are ranked from highest to lowest, based on the percentage of scheduled time devoted to instruction in that area. Third, teachers rate students in terms of their

overall achievement and engagement in each area. This process allows teachers to see whether there is a relationship between achievement and instructional time and, in turn, whether scheduled time and instructional time accommodate the learning-time needs of students.

Appendix A illustrates a time-use analysis format completed by a fourth-grade teacher. In this teacher's class, several students were not making adequate progress toward literacy benchmarks, especially in writing. The teacher's analysis revealed that less than half of the available time (75 minutes) for the morning literacy block was being converted to engaged learning time. This analysis served to focus the teacher's efforts on identifying ways to recover lost time and incorporate more opportunities for writing throughout the day.

A benefit of self-analysis procedures is that teachers, either in groups or individually, reflect on the extent to which their classrooms are characterized by high versus low levels of academic engaged time and, in turn, think about what may be facilitating or impeding the accumulation of sufficient engaged learning time. To encourage reflective practice, teachers may also respond to specific probes from a school psychologist about classroom time usage. Appendix B provides an example of an instructional time checklist that facilitates teachers' analysis of their classroom time usage and prompts them to focus on items checked *no* or *somewhat*.

Conclusion

An understanding of the components of academic engaged time and corresponding analysis of classroom time usage are basic considerations underlying the implementation of best practices to increase academic engaged time. As professionals who are familiar with effective teaching and classroom management practices, school psychologists are well qualified to facilitate teachers' analysis of their use of classroom time and to provide direct training to assist teachers in implementing best practices to increase academic engaged time.

BEST PRACTICES FOR INCREASING ACADEMIC ENGAGED TIME

Beginning with the Beginning Teacher Evaluation Study, research has consistently shown that the more time students are engaged in learning activities, the higher their achievement. Whereas schools and teachers may allocate an appropriate amount of time for learning, descriptive studies reveal that students are not always engaged during that allocated time. In some classrooms, for example, students spend less than 50% of allocated instructional time directly engaged in learning academic content. Thus, increasing student engagement is more important than merely adding minutes to the day. Providing more instructional time will not have a significant effect on student learning unless the additional time is devoted to instruction, with students being engaged in appropriate learning activities. School psychologists can assist teachers in making better use of existing time and finding ways to increase the proportion of time during which students are engaged in appropriate instructional activities.

Best practices for increasing academic engaged time are often synonymous with strategies to provide Tier 1 academic and behavior support. Focusing on classroom management, for example, may seem an unusual approach to extending learning time. In many schools, however, frequent and recurring disruptive behavior leads to correspondingly big losses in learning time. Thus, preventing the occurrence of disruptions through effective positive behavior support has the effect of maximizing academic engaged time for all students.

Three major factors have been shown to contribute to academic engaged time: (a) classroom management (managerial strategies that maximize engaged time), (b) instructional design (teaching and instruction designed to keep students engaged in learning), and (c) student self-regulation (self-regulatory methods to maintain behavior and cognitive engagement). Two factors (classroom management and appropriateness of instruction) rest primarily with teachers, and the third (self-management) rests more with students. The purpose of the following sections is to describe best practice strategies to increase academic engaged time derived from research aimed at enhancing each group of factors summarized in Table 2.1.

By using assessment information (e.g., classroom time-use logs, observational data), school psychologists can provide individual consultation or direct training to assist teachers in increasing academic engaged time using the strategies listed in Table 2.1. Because the intent of these strategies is to maximize learning time for all students, they are conceptualized primarily as Tier 1 strategies. Nonetheless, many best practices described in the following sections also increase engaged time for small groups or individual students with attention difficulties, organization problems, and overall low engagement. Tier 2 and 3 strategies are designed to extend best practices for increasing academic engaged time, provide more opportunities or time for learning, and, when necessary, adjust the difficulty level of material to ensure high levels of success and engagement.

The following sections describe best practices that are intended to serve as guidelines for school psychologists in their role as classroom consultants. Not every procedure may be effective or efficient for all classrooms and teachers. Because of individual teaching styles and classroom arrangements, school psychologists must work within a problem-solving approach to analyze time use, target areas in which learning time can be increased, identify students whose academic engaged time is below average, and develop strategies that are tailored to teachers' personal styles and learners' individual needs. A critical role for school psychologists is to facilitate teachers' utilization and, when necessary, modification of the following procedures in their classrooms.

Table 2.1. Practices for Maximizing Academic Engaged Time

Managerial Strategies	Instructional Strategies	Student-Regulated Strategies

• Design classroom space to facilitate monitoring and management of student behavior
• Develop and enforce consistent rules, expectations, and classroom routines
• Reduce transition time
• Minimize class size and learning group sizes
• Establish authoritative management style and positive teacher–student relationships
	• Promote active student participation in learning:
	  • Questioning techniques
	  • Active responding
	• Provide sufficient scaffolding and structure:
	  • Strong academic focus
	  • Frequent feedback
	  • Explicit task directions
	• Provide adequate teacher attention
	• Adjust design of instruction to:
	  • Differentiated instruction
	  • Motivation to learn
	  • Diverse teaching methods
	  • Instructional pace
		• Teach students to employ metacognitive and study strategies
		• Incorporate self-monitoring procedures into the classroom
		• Support students' self-management skills
		• Have students set their own goals for learning
		• Use homework effectively to enhance student learning

Managerial Strategies

From the first day of school, even in early childhood classrooms, educators must consider how various classroom management strategies and environmental factors affect students' engagement and, ultimately, students' achievement. Researchers continue to study what teachers do in the classroom to promote academic engagement and minimize the amount of learning time that is lost due to interruptions. One major finding across all studies is that the manner in which teachers organize and manage their classrooms affects the level of engagement among students. Brophy (1986), one of the earliest researchers to consider the importance of classroom environments, found that poor classroom management can erode instructional time and decrease opportunities for students to learn. According to Brophy, student engagement rates depend on a teacher's ability to organize the classroom to facilitate efficient transitions between activities and to minimize time spent getting organized or dealing with misconduct. Small interruptions to the daily activities of a classroom continuously add up and can result in significant loss of learning time. Effective educators make every effort to minimize these interruptions. Several managerial strategies have been shown to promote academic engaged time, including (a) designing classroom space to facilitate close monitoring of student behavior, (b) establishing consistent rules and expectations and efficient classroom routines, (c) implementing procedures to reduce transition time, (d) minimizing class size and learning group sizes, and (e) adopting an authoritative management style and creating positive teacher–student relationships (see Table 2.1).

Classroom Arrangement

Academic engaged time is maximized when teachers systematically monitor and reinforce the behavior of their students during learning activities. There are multiple ways to arrange classroom environments to facilitate close monitoring, and these modifications are often feasible for teachers to implement because they are minimally intrusive and require few resources. Environmental changes that have the greatest impact on increasing academic engaged time include (a) planning seating arrangements that allow the teacher to view student behavior from anywhere in the classroom; (b) decreasing the amount of time spent at the teacher's desk by frequently circulating the room and going to students when they have questions rather than requiring students to come to the teacher; (c) utilizing student volunteers for handling classroom materials (rather than having the teacher do so) and adding organizational aides such as shelves, hooks, and labels to facilitate this; (d) creating clear pathways in areas of high congestion; and (e) providing secluded study carrels in proximity to the teacher for students who may require extra help.

Related to continuous monitoring of classrooms are managerial procedures to limit disruptive and off-task behavior, especially during instructional activities. Disruptive behaviors pose the greatest threat to academic engaged time because these behaviors interfere not only with the student's own learning, but also the learning of other students. To minimize inappropriate behavior and the resulting loss of instructional time, teachers must be consistent in responding to disruptions and handling misbehavior immediately and efficiently. At the same time, school psychologists can assist teachers in planning and implementing systematic reinforcement contingencies to strengthen and support student engagement. There is strong evidence, for example, regarding the effectiveness of token economy interventions and group contingencies for increasing students' engagement (Harmin & Toth, 2006).

Expectations and Routines

A second group of managerial strategies to increase academic engaged time includes having clearly defined and taught rules, high expectations for engagement during learning activities, and consistent classroom routines. Teachers who explicitly communicate their behavioral expectations to students, beginning the first day of school, establish an environment in which task engagement is maximized and interruptions to learning time are minimized. Rules and expectations are most effective when they are clearly posted to support students' awareness and knowledge of them.

Teachers who are successful in maximizing academic engaged time expect their students to meet behavioral and academic expectations, and these teachers provide consistent, immediate, and effective consequences for doing so. According to Adkins-Coleman (2010), "Successful teachers … demand effort from the moment students enter the classroom, and they require students to remain engaged for the entire class period" (p. 50). Teachers can preserve engaged learning time through implementing consistent routines for noninstructional activities as well. Doing so, for example, may include handling noninstructional obligations (e.g., taking attendance) *after* students have begun working on assignments, or completing all noninstructional activities during a predetermined time of day set aside specifically for such activities. Soliciting assistance from the administration to minimize external interruptions (e.g., intercom announcements, unscheduled visitations) is another effective way to protect instructional time and increase engaged learning time.

Transitions

Another set of managerial strategies that maximize academic engaged time involve efficient transition procedures. Transitions, such as going to the bathroom, sharpening pencils, or entering and exiting the classroom, can decrease academic engaged time. A key factor in successfully reducing transition time is to ensure that students understand and follow transition routines. For example, teachers can develop specific entrance and exit routines for students who leave the classroom for related services. Moreover, transition routines should be explicitly taught and practiced until students are able to carry these routines out quickly and appropriately. Teachers with well-managed classrooms often invest considerable time teaching these routines early in the school year and reviewing these routines throughout the year as necessary (Bohn, Roehrig, & Pressley, 2004).

Another strategy to minimize time spent in whole-group transitions is the use of verbal or nonverbal cues. Although the specific type of transition cue varies across classrooms (e.g., flickering lights, using key signal words or phrases), what is most critical is that all students be able to recognize and interpret the cue. In one third-grade classroom, for example, a teacher and her students used concepts from a science unit to cue classroom transitions. When it was time for independent seatwork, the teacher told her students it was "time to go deep-sea fishing." "Time to surface" was the cue to transition to the rug for whole-class discussion.

As an additional strategy, teachers can establish a time limit for each transition and use positive reinforcement for students who complete the transition within the time limit. For example, to reduce the amount of time needed to move from small science groups to whole-class math instruction, a sixth-grade teacher recorded the amount of time students needed to get ready for the math lesson. Over a period of several weeks, students were challenged to reduce this amount of time until a targeted goal for transition time was achieved.

A key role in this process for school psychologists is to record the actual number of instructional minutes used for academic purposes versus transitional or disciplinary activities. Once teachers are aware of when and how much instructional time is typically lost due to disruptive behaviors or transitions, school psychologists can (a) assist teachers in implementing management strategies during targeted times and (b) continue to record classroom time use to evaluate the effectiveness of strategies in minimizing time loss.

Small Learning Groups

Another aspect of classroom management and organization that affects academic engaged time is the size of the class or learning group. Blatchford, Russell, Bassett, Brown, and Martin (2007) documented that students in small classes (15 students or fewer) are significantly more engaged in learning and exhibit more learning-related behaviors, such as being on task and completing work assignments, than do students in large classes. Because manipulating class size may not be an option in all schools, teachers can achieve similar benefits of small class size by minimizing the number of students in learning groups. Small learning groups, especially groups that are teacher directed, have been shown to promote a high level of student engagement. With small classes or small learning groups, less time is spent redirecting misbehavior, and in turn, both the quality and amount of interaction between teachers and students increase. Both outcomes are conducive to increasing academic engagement among students.

Authoritative Teaching Style

Across all developmental levels, there is evidence that a management approach that is authoritative in nature and emphasizes positive student–teacher relationships contributes to higher overall learning time among students. Teachers who adopt an authoritative approach to classroom management set high standards for academic learning and expect all students to achieve them. Ross, Bondy, Gallingane, and Hambacher (2008) characterize this method as a *warm demander* approach. These researchers found that in warm-demander classrooms, teachers push students to succeed because they genuinely want them to be successful and believe that all students are capable of doing so. Students in these classrooms experience little wasted time and exhibit high levels of academic engaged time.

Beyond an authoritative management approach, the quality of students' relationships with teachers also has a significant impact on engagement and learning. Elementary students who report feeling appreciated by their teachers are more likely to demonstrate higher engagement in learning compared to students who feel unimportant or ignored by teachers (Furrer & Skinner,

2003). Similarly, in classrooms where teachers facilitate positive social interactions between students, there are higher overall rates of academic engagement. Accordingly, school psychologists can provide professional development opportunities for teachers that focus on the importance of teacher–student relationships and assist teachers in identifying strategies that promote positive interactions with students.

Conclusion

How well teachers manage their classroom contributes to maximizing academic engaged time. By helping teachers to implement best practice managerial strategies, school psychologists contribute to minimizing student disruptions, maintaining student engagement, ensuring smooth transitions, and organizing classroom routines, all of which have the effect of preserving allotted time for instruction and learning. Through consultation, modeling, or professional development activities, school psychologists can be instrumental in helping teachers acquire and implement effective classroom management practices to increase academic engaged time.

Instructional Strategies

Effective instructional practices constitute the second category of best-practice strategies aimed at maximizing engaged learning time (see Table 2.1). Findings from several studies have yielded a substantial body of knowledge about instructional variables that are linked to an increase in academic engaged time. Instructional variables include both (a) teaching behaviors that directly involve students in the learning process and provide sufficient structure and attention and (b) instructional design features that match task requirements with student ability, motivation, interests, and learning-time needs.

Promote Active Participation in Learning
In recent years, a teaching approach that supports students' active participation in learning has been shown to increase academic engaged time (Young, 2010). Ensuring a minimum level of participation among all students in every lesson is crucial for maximizing engaged time. School psychologists need to know, however, that teachers often find this aspect of teaching difficult to implement. Through direct training and in-class coaching or modeling, school psychologists can assist teachers in developing a teaching style that ensures all students make active learning responses (e.g., writing, answering questions, reading out loud) rather than passive responses (e.g., listening).

Questioning techniques. One well-researched
mechanism to ensure that all students remain engaged in whole-group teaching is the use of effective questioning techniques (Good & Brophy, 2003). According to Good and Brophy, questions that promote engagement are clear, purposeful, brief, and formulated to extend students' thinking. Low-achieving students typically accrue lower amounts of academic engaged time, in part because they have fewer opportunities to respond to questions. An effective questioning strategy that increases engagement among all students follows three sequential steps (Chuska, 1995). The teacher poses a question to the entire class. Then, the teacher gives students wait time to think about the question and formulate a response. After a sufficient amount of time (5–10 seconds), the teacher calls on an individual student to respond. Using this method requires all students to be responsible for constructing an answer to the question because the teacher may call on any student.

Active responding. Beyond effective questioning
techniques, there are additional strategies to promote active engagement. Existing assignments and teacher-guided activities can be easily modified to incorporate a higher degree of active student participation and responding. For example, math problems can be solved in cooperative learning groups instead of as independent seatwork assignments. Similarly, students can be directed to discuss topics directly with one another during large-group discussion rather than have the teacher ask and respond to questions. Again, modeling by school psychologists is instrumental in the implementation of these strategies.

Provide Sufficient Scaffolding and Structure
Students accrue more academic engaged time in classrooms where teachers are responsive, give frequent feedback, and provide sufficient structure and support for learning (Young, 2010). Teaching practices aimed at providing the necessary structure for student learning include (a) adopting a strong academic focus, (b) providing frequent performance feedback, and (c) being explicit with task directions. School psychologists can provide instructional consultation, inservice training, or in-class coaching to assist teachers in effectively utilizing these three techniques.

Strong academic focus. To maximize academic
engaged time, it is critical, first, to incorporate a strong academic focus. Academic focus is reflected in the total amount of time devoted to academic versus nonacademic

activities and in the type of instructional interaction that prevails in the classroom. Instruction with a strong academic focus is linked with explicit learning goals, and students are held accountable for reaching those goals.

Frequent performance feedback. Providing appropriate feedback is the second key element of supportive, structured teaching. Although strategies may vary, providing feedback that is frequent and individualized and that provides specific suggestions for rethinking or redoing work is an effective means of enhancing academic engaged time. One way for teachers to maximize effective feedback is to have individual conferences with students. Conferences allow teachers to provide correction, suggestions, and praise for hard work, and ensure that students understand the specific strengths and limitations of their work. This type of feedback enhances students' perceptions of their own competence and perceived personal control during academic tasks (Jang, Reeve, & Deci, 2010).

Explicit task directions. A significant amount of academic engaged time is lost when students fail to understand task requirements, thus underscoring the importance of ensuring that expectations for learning are made explicit. This may be achieved by having students paraphrase directions and asking the students to plan in advance how to address problems that might occur while they are working. In addition, directions should be provided in a visual format and placed where students can access the directions independently as needed. For some tasks, outlines or study guides help students organize and focus their attention on lessons. Additional strategies include keeping directions simple, giving directions once and only when students are attending, directing students to begin work after all instructions are given, and then moving throughout the room to monitor students and provide assistance as needed. Research demonstrates that clear directions help students to understand learning requirements and increases the amount of time students spend in completing assigned tasks (Marzano, Pickering, & Pollack, 2001).

Promote Teacher Attention

In addition, and somewhat axiomatically, students are more academically engaged when they are receiving attention from the teacher, whether individually or in a group. Students are more academically engaged in classrooms where there is greater supervision, monitoring, and interaction with teachers. Specifically, teachers who spend a substantial portion of time involved in interactive instructional activities (e.g., demonstrating, explaining), rather than in noninteractive tasks (e.g., grading papers), are effective in keeping students engaged in academic tasks. Small-group activities also promote higher levels of engagement than do either individual work or whole-class work because these activities afford more opportunities for attention from the teacher and more active roles for students, both of which lead to increased academic engagement (Rimm-Kaufman, La Paro, Downer, & Pianta, 2005).

Improve Instructional Design

In addition to specific teaching behaviors, several instructional design features have been shown to increase academic engaged time. Small modifications to the way lessons are presented can make significant differences in the level of engagement among students.

Differentiated instruction. First, engaged time is enhanced when learning activities are geared to students' ability. To be academically engaged, students must be both challenged and able to experience a high rate of success. Simply assigning more time to a topic will not automatically increase students' academic engaged time. As noted by Carroll (1963), the relationship between time and learning is linked to the amount of time students require for learning. There are individual differences in how much exposure, practice, or instruction is actually needed for learning. Therefore, instruction that is designed to be differentiated based on such individual student needs (time needed, developmental appropriateness, pace, and flow of delivery) will maximize academic engaged time.

Student motivation. A second aspect of instructional design that increases academic engaged time is the extent to which teachers and school psychologists foster students' motivation for learning. Students will be engaged versus disengaged in learning in large part as a function of motivation. Specifically, students initiate and maintain involvement in learning activities when they believe that sustained engagement will lead to desired outcomes. One factor that influences motivation and, in turn, engagement is the relevance of learning content to the students' personal lives. Essentially, students who do not understand why it is important to complete a given task are less likely to do so. When individuals view goals as being salient to their future success, they are more motivated to achieve those goals (Rock & Thead, 2009). Even uninteresting material that is presented with a meaningful rationale or introduced with an intriguing real-world issue can help draw students into the subject matter and engage them in learning.

Diverse teaching methods. Using multiple and diverse teaching methods is another aspect of instructional design to increase academic engaged time. Students often become disengaged if the same format (e.g., teacher lecture) is repeatedly used. Because students learn differently, not all students may be able to benefit from a strict lecture format. Therefore, blending lecture formats with other teaching approaches (e.g., questioning, discussions) will promote active learning and engagement for a greater proportion of students.

Instructional pace. Adjusting the pace of a lesson is another feature of instructional design that promotes academic engaged time. A quick, smooth, and efficient instructional pace increases the amount of content covered as well as the amount of active learning time available during a class period or school day. Breaking lessons into small steps, changing the topic or procedure when the teacher notices a decline in student engagement, and maintaining high expectations for student involvement are all examples of effective strategies for delivering fast-paced instruction (Harmin & Toth, 2006).

Conclusion

Instruction in which the teacher assumes a central role in the teaching process, while also taking steps to maintain active student participation in learning, contributes to increases in learning time. Teachers who create a strong academic focus, emphasize academic goals, provide many opportunities for active responding, display high levels of interaction with students, and give frequent feedback are likely to have classrooms with high levels of academic engaged time. School psychologists can provide professional development opportunities for educators to become more aware of the importance of incorporating these strategies into their classroom teaching. Many of these strategies represent small modifications that require minimal time or energy on the part of educators, but can still have a significant impact on students' levels of engagement.

Student Self-Regulated Strategies

Unlike managerial and instructional strategies that focus on classroom environment factors to promote engagement, student self-regulated strategies focus on "within-learner" or cognitive and metacognitive variables to maximize academic engaged time. Consistent with Carroll's (1963) model, the amount of time students spend engaged in learning is, to some extent, self-determined. Even when teachers consistently implement best practices for increasing learning time, students may spend less time than they need to (or less time than what is provided) due to low motivation, limited self-efficacy, or lack of self-monitoring skills. Moreover, even when students appear to be behaviorally engaged, their academic learning time may be limited if they use ineffective learning strategies or allocate their attention to irrelevant or inappropriate task dimensions. Self-regulation strategies enable students to effectively and efficiently use their instructional time in order to maximize academic engaged time. In other words, these methods serve to involve students directly in increasing their own academic engagement. Best practice self-regulated approaches include teaching students to employ (a) task-appropriate cognitive and study strategies, (b) self-monitoring procedures, and (c) self-management skills (see Table 2.1). Although appropriate for all grade levels, these strategies are effective primarily with middle and high school students. In addition, school psychologists most often function as interventionists, providing supplemental instruction in self-regulated strategies to small groups of students.

Study Strategies

The first student-regulated practice is to promote students' acquisition and implementation of study strategies for using time efficiently, as well as cognitive strategies for achieving higher success on learning tasks. Explicitly teaching students how to use study strategies (through a three-step sequence of modeling, guided practice with feedback, and application) can increase academic engaged time because students learn to approach learning tasks in a structured, organized, and efficient manner, thus minimizing wasted time.

Cognitive learning strategies also support active engagement during independent work periods because students are better equipped to understand material on their own without relying on teachers for how-to guidance or support. For example, teaching students to use question-generation or prediction strategies during individual reading periods enhances their learning and retention of material because such strategies have been shown to keep students cognitively engaged and forces them to interact with the text while they read (Guthrie, Wigfield, & You, 2012). Similarly, when students are taught to use a systematic error-correction procedure for writing and spelling tasks, their engagement and overall success during the allocated study time significantly increase (Harris, Graham, Mason, & Sadler, 2002).

Self-Monitoring

A second student-regulated method for increasing academic engaged time is self-monitoring. A key to students' school success lies in the ability to monitor their own comprehension and performance during learning tasks. When students fail to recognize road-blocks to their own learning or are not aware of the time demands of assigned tasks, they neither plan nor adjust their study time accordingly. There is evidence that many students fail to monitor their own learning, even when instruction has been delivered so as to maximize academic engaged time. Without adequate training and practice using self-monitoring strategies, even highly motivated students may fail to regulate their own learning time. Furthermore, self-monitoring alone can be a highly effective intervention to increase students' on-task behavior, thus contributing to higher rates of academic-engaged learning time (Levendoski & Cartledge, 2000).

Research has identified specific ways in which students can be taught to monitor their learning time and, in turn, maximize their engagement. Self-correcting techniques, for example, teach students to monitor their own accuracy in responding and progress toward goals. The use of flash cards, answer tapes, or self-checking stations are effective instructional tools for increasing self-checking behaviors among students. Another method to build self-monitoring skills involves having students keep a personal log of the duration of their study time, frequency of engaged behaviors (answering questions, writing responses), and overall work completion (Rock, 2005).

Implicit in all self-monitoring procedures is the need for students to self-observe and self-evaluate. Evidence-based resources and methods are available for school psychologists to help teachers individualize self-observing and self-recording procedures to match students' needs and preferences, especially young children or students with disabilities. Kern, Dunlap, Childs, and Clarke (1994), for example, increased engagement by having students record on sheets taped at the corner of their desks (or inside their notebooks) whether they were or were not on task at signaled intervals. As another example, Daly and Ranalli (2003) developed a self-monitoring tool called "countoons,"

which are cartoon illustrations of students' appropriate and inappropriate behaviors paired with a contingency for meeting an established criterion of appropriate behavior. The drawings also contain space for children to record the frequency of their own behavior. This tool is particularly appealing for young learners or students who struggle with reading. While many of these strategies can easily be implemented at the core-instruction level, school psychologists can foster further development during more intensive interventions with students.

Self-Management

Self-management skills enable students to guide their own learning behaviors, experience a high degree of autonomy in the classroom, and maximize their engaged time. To manage the range of ability levels among diverse learners and enable each child to accrue maximum learning time, a systematic self-management approach aimed at developing independent learning skills is often necessary. Even young children can learn to guide themselves through daily classroom routines and activities with minimal assistance from a teacher (hence, less wait time) and minimal loss of engaged learning time.

Several strategies have been shown to be effective for teaching students to become independent learners. For example, students can be taught a systematic, step-by-step approach to task completion. This often consists of providing students with a series of self-questions designed to help them prepare for and adequately complete new tasks. Guiding questions can be used to cue or prompt students to gather necessary materials, review directions, approximate the amount of time for the assignment, and determine whether they have the skills necessary to complete the assignment. These guiding questions may be posted in the classroom or provided to students on individualized job cards (e.g., "What materials do I need?" "How much time do I have to complete this assignment?"). Such a strategy has been used effectively with individual students or with an entire classroom (Rock, 2005).

Student Goal Setting

A student-regulated approach aimed at increasing academic engaged time involves having students set their own goals for learning and engagement. Goal-setting strategies provide opportunities for students to establish and evaluate their performance relative to daily personal learning goals. Through setting goals for learning, students become empowered and demonstrate high levels of task engagement as they work to achieve their goals. Harmin and Toth (2006), for example, described a goal-setting procedure wherein at the beginning of the day the teacher invites students to identify one goal for themselves and to record it in an individualized log book. At the end of the day, students reflect on how successful they were at reaching their goals and share this with this class. Harmin and Toth found that establishing daily goals maintained students' engagement in learning activities throughout the day.

Use of Homework

Student-regulated strategies, particularly self-monitoring and goal setting, are effective for increasing the degree to which students complete homework assignments. Some experts conceptualize the effective use of homework as a way to maximize academic engaged time by extending learning time beyond the typical school day (Cooper, Robinson, & Patall, 2006). Both assigning homework and having a supervised study period at school can significantly boost students' engaged learning time. Homework is most beneficial when it is relevant to learning objectives, matched to students' ability levels, assigned in regular amounts, well explained, and used as a source of corrective feedback.

In terms of designing and using homework to extend academic engaged time, homework appears to be most effective when it is planned for a specific purpose and when that purpose is clearly explained to students. For example, telling students to "read the next chapter" fails to provide sufficient guidance for many students. Academic engagement in homework assignments is low when students do not fully understand how to approach the task. Providing study guides, graphic organizers, or discussion questions to accompany the chapter, however, allows students to understand the learning goals and to exercise autonomy over their engaged learning time.

Other strategies that allow teachers to use homework as a mechanism for extending learning time beyond the classroom include providing frequent feedback on homework accuracy, charting homework completion over time, establishing home routines and a system for allowing students to access homework help as needed, teaching effective homework time-management skills, and incorporating a menu of homework assignments (Cooper et al., 2006). School psychologists can also facilitate training opportunities for parents to learn many of these same strategies to help their children engage in a more productive use of homework time.

Conclusion

In addition to classroom instruction and management practices, student-regulated strategies constitute important best practices for increasing academic engaged time. School psychologists may increase engaged time among individual students by providing small-group instruction related to study skills and learning strategies, self-monitoring techniques, and self-management skills. When used appropriately, homework can also extend learning time beyond allocated or scheduled instructional time and can serve to encourage students to apply self-regulated strategies in other settings.

SUMMARY

The potential for learning time to be an important element of school reform depends largely on whether the time is used effectively and on its use as a resource for students most in need of greater academic engaged time, such as low-income students and others who have little opportunity for learning outside of school. Increasing academic engaged time for all students can improve learning and effectively close the achievement gap between low-achieving students and their higher achieving peers. The best practices for increasing academic engaged time described in this chapter have been shown to enhance the rigor and relevance of learning tasks and to improve the overall quality of teaching. Thus, understanding the components of academic engaged time and having knowledge of well-documented procedures for increasing academic engaged time are useful for school psychologists, in performing their roles as instructional consultants, and for teachers, in optimizing Tier 1 or core classroom instruction for all learners.

The link between learning time and academic success is well documented in educational research. It is clear, however, that the nexus between more instructional time and higher learning depends upon the degree to which available time is devoted to high-quality instruction and the extent to which students experience success in learning. Any addition to allocated time will improve achievement only to the extent that time is actually used for instruction and, in turn, converted to academic engaged time. Simply assigning more study time to a topic will not automatically increase the student's learning. When best-practice instructional, managerial, and student-regulated strategies are implemented, then more instructional time will pay off in greater learning because academic engaged time is increased.

In one form or another, learning time plays an important role in understanding, predicting, and controlling instructional processes across a range of activities. For researchers and practitioners, not only is academic engaged time an instructional time variable, it is actually a metric or quantifiable index of the quality of instruction. That is, when students accrue greater academic learning time, it signals that high-quality instruction is likely occurring in the classroom. Researchers must continue to address what can be done to enhance or increase academic engaged time for all learners, and school psychologists must continue to help teachers translate these findings into effective classroom practices. Supporting teachers to make good use of existing time, whereby students experience high success on meaningful tasks, is more likely to increase academic engaged time (and, in turn, student achievement) than simply allocating more instructional time. Overall, academic engaged time will be maximized, and improved academic outcomes will likely result, when (a) instructional time is used effectively, (b) classrooms are well managed to keep students motivated and engaged in learning, and (c) students are taught to be independent, self-guided learners.

REFERENCES

Adkins-Coleman, T. A. (2010). "I'm not afraid to come into your world": Case studies of teachers facilitating engagement in urban high school English classrooms. *Journal of Negro Education, 79,* 41–53.

Black, S. (2002). Time for learning. *American School Board Journal, 189*(9), 58–62.

Blatchford, P., Russell, A., Bassett, P., Brown, P., & Martin, C. (2007). The effect of class size on the teaching of pupils aged 7–11 years. *School Effectiveness and School Improvement, 18,* 147–172. doi:10.1080/09243450601058675

Bohn, C. M., Roehrig, A. D., & Pressley, M. (2004). The first days of school in the classrooms of two more effective and four less effective primary-grade teachers. *The Elementary School Journal, 104,* 269–287.

Brophy, J. (1986). Teacher influences on student achievement. *American Psychologist, 41,* 1069–1077. doi:10.1037/0003-066X.41.10.1069

Carroll, J. B. (1963). A model of school learning. *Teachers College Record, 64,* 723–733.

Chuska, K. (1995). *Improving classroom questions: A teacher's guide to increasing student motivation, participation, and higher level thinking.* Bloomington, IN: Phi Delta Kappa Educational Foundation.

Cooper, H., Robinson, J. C., & Patall, A. (2006). Does homework improve academic achievement? A synthesis of research, 1987–2003. *Review of Educational Research, 76,* 1–62.

Daly, P. M., & Ranalli, P. (2003). Using countoons to teach self-monitoring skills. *Teaching Exceptional Children, 35*(5), 30–35.

Fisher, C. W., & Berliner, D. C. (1985). *Perspectives on instructional time.* New York, NY: Longman.

Fisher, D. (2009). The use of instructional time in the typical high school classroom. *The Educational Forum, 73,* 168–173. doi:10.1080/00131720902739650

Fullan, M., Hill, P., & Crevola, C. (2006). *Breakthrough.* Thousand Oaks, CA: Corwin Press.

Furrer, C., & Skinner, E. (2003). Sense of relatedness as a factor in children's academic engagement and performance. *Journal of Educational Psychology, 95,* 148–162. doi:10.1037/0022-0663.95.1.148

Gettinger, M., & Walter, M. J. (2012). Classroom strategies to enhance academic engagement. In S. L. Christenson, A. L. Reschly, & C. Wylie (Eds.), *Handbook of research on student engagement* (pp. 653–674). New York, NY: Springer.

Good, T. L., & Brophy, J. E. (2003). *Looking in classrooms* (9th ed.). Boston, MA: Allyn & Bacon.

Guthrie, J. T., Wigfield, A., & You, W. (2012). Instructional contexts for engagement and achievement in reading. In S. L. Christenson, A. L. Reschly, & C. Wylie (Eds.), *Handbook of research on student engagement* (pp. 601–634). New York, NY: Springer.

Harmin, M., & Toth, M. (2006). *Inspiring active learning: A complete handbook for today's teachers.* Alexandria, VA: Association of Supervision and Curriculum Development.

Harris, K. R., Graham, S., Mason, L. H., & Sadler, B. (2002). Developing self-regulated writers. *Theory Into Practice, 41,* 110–115.

Jang, H., Reeve, J., & Deci, E. L. (2010). Engaging students in learning activities: It is not autonomy support or structure but autonomy support and structure. *Journal of Educational Psychology, 102,* 588–600. doi:10.1037/a0019682

Kern, L., Dunlap, G., Childs, K., & Clarke, S. (1994). Use of a classwide self-management program to improve the behavior of students with emotional and behavioral disorders. *Education & Treatment of Children, 17,* 445–458.

Kubitschek, W. N., Hallinan, M. T., Arnett, S. M., & Galipeau, K. S. (2005). High school schedule changes and the effect of lost instructional time on achievement. *High School Journal, 89,* 63–71.

Levendoski, L. S., & Cartledge, G. (2000). Self-monitoring for elementary school children with emotional disturbances: Classroom application for increased academic responding. *Behavioral Disorders, 25,* 211–224.

Marks, H. M. (2000). Student engagement in instructional activity: Patterns in the elementary, middle, and high school years. *American Educational Research Journal, 37,* 153–184. doi:10.3102/00028312037001153

Marzano, R. J., Pickering, D. J., & Pollack, J. E. (2001). *Classroom instruction that works: Research-based strategies for increasing student achievement.* Alexandria, VA: Association for Supervision and Curriculum Development.

National Association of School Psychologists. (2010). *Model for comprehensive and integrative school psychological services.* Bethesda, MD: Author. Retrieved from http://www.nasponline.org/standards/2010standards/2_PracticeModel.pdf

National Education Commission on Time and Learning. (1994). *Prisoners of time: Report of the National Education Commission on Time and Learning.* Washington, DC: U.S. Government Printing Office.

National Education Commission on Time and Learning. (2005). *Prisoners of time: Report of the National Education Commission on Time and Learning* (rev. ed.). Washington, DC: U.S. Government Printing Office.

Rimm-Kaufman, S. E., La Paro, K. M., Downer, J. T., & Pianta, R. C. (2005). The contribution of classroom setting and quality of instruction to children's behavior in kindergarten classrooms. *The Elementary School Journal, 105,* 377–394. doi:10.1086/429948

Rock, M. L. (2005). Use of strategic self-monitoring to enhance academic engagement, productivity, and accuracy of students with and without disabilities. *Journal of Positive Behavior Interventions, 7*, 262–268, doi:10.1177/10983007050070010201

Rock, M. L., & Thead, B. K. (2009). Promote student success during independent seatwork. *Intervention in School and Clinic, 44*, 179–184.

Ross, D. D., Bondy, E., Gallingane, C., & Hambacher, E. (2008). Promoting academic engagement through insistence: Being a warm demander. *Childhood Education, 84*, 142–146. doi:10.1177/1053451208326055

Wharton-McDonald, R., Pressley, M., & Hampston, J. M. (1998). Literacy instruction in nine first-grade classrooms: Teacher characteristics and student achievement. *The Elementary School Journal, 99*, 101–128.

Young, M. R. (2010). The art and science of fostering engaged learning. *Academy of Educational Leadership Journal, 14*(1), 1–18.

APPENDIX A. INSTRUCTIONAL TIME ANALYSIS COMPLETED BY A FOURTH-GRADE TEACHER

	Literacy Block	Science Block	Math Block
Available time	75 minutes, 8:30–9:45	60 minutes, 9:45–10:45	75 minutes, 10:45–12:00
List all possible sources of reductions in available time	Waiting for tardy students; taking attendance; announcements; retrieving writing journals; reading books	Transition to and from the science lab; retrieving science journals and pencils	Retrieving math notebooks; transition to and from the checking center for math problems
Lost minutes	20 minutes	8 minutes	10 minutes
Instructional time	55 minutes	52 minutes	65 minutes
Average engagement rate (paying attention and doing work)	60%	95%	85%
List all possible sources of reductions in instructional time	Wait time for the teacher to help individual students with writing or reading results in lost time for students who need extra help	Very little lost instruction time because all students are engaged in hands-on activities	Overcrowding at checking stations; some students do not know how to do problems and lose learning time by doing nothing
Engaged time	32 minutes	49 minutes	55 minutes
Desired goal	55 minutes	45 minutes	55 minutes
Need for change?	Yes	No	No

APPENDIX B. INSTRUCTIONAL TIME CHECKLIST

	Yes	No	Somewhat	Changes to Implement
Does my daily schedule minimize noninstructional, organizational time and maximize instructional time?				
Does the available or scheduled time for specific activities and content areas reflect my students' instructional needs?				
Do I start and stop planned activities and instruction within 3 minutes of the scheduled start and stop times?				
Have I structured my teaching activities to maximize the number of opportunities for all students to be actively engaged in learning?				
Are all my students working on materials appropriate to their skill levels?				
Have I minimized the amount of time required to make transitions?				
Are students in my class, on average, engaged in learning activities at least 75% of the time?				
Am I able to minimize interruptions and disruptions in class?				
Do students who require more-than-average time for learning receive sufficient time?				
Do I have strategies in place to minimize students' wait time and/or to keep students engaged in learning while waiting for me to respond to their questions?				

3

Best Practices in Fostering Student Engagement

Amy L. Reschly
University of Georgia
James J. Appleton
Gwinnett County Public Schools
Angie Pohl
University of Minnesota

OVERVIEW

School psychologists have long been aware of the importance of academic engaged time for understanding students' learning difficulties and as a target of intervention efforts. In recent years, however, engagement has expanded to include other aspects of students' behavior, cognition, and emotion at school and within learning. Student engagement has emerged as a metaconstruct, bringing together many separate lines of research (e.g., belonging, motivation, extracurricular participation; Fredricks, Blumenfeld, & Paris, 2004). Furthermore, interest in student engagement is interdisciplinary and international (Christenson, Reschly, & Wylie, 2012). Student engagement is also a construct that resonates with educators, many of whom clearly see the importance of engagement to student achievement (Finn & Zimmer, 2012).

The purpose of this chapter is to provide school psychologists with an overview of student engagement and to summarize evidence-based and promising intervention strategies. Specifically, school psychologists will learn about (a) the subtypes of student engagement, (b) best practice recommendations for promoting each subtype of engagement and for comprehensively fostering student engagement, and (c) considerations for implementing school-wide practices to promote student engagement. This chapter is aligned with the National Association of School Psychologists (NASP) *Model for Comprehensive and Integrated School Psychological Services* (NASP, 2010) domain of Interventions and Instructional Support to Develop Academic Skills.

BASIC CONSIDERATIONS

Engagement is a broad, fairly new construct. The advancement of the construct through theory and research and the application of engagement to practice are still evolving. This section is organized into summary statements followed by brief explanations to highlight important facets of the engagement construct.

Facets of Student Engagement

Engagement is multidimensional: Although scholars have yet to arrive at a consensus regarding the types and definition of engagement, there is general agreement that engagement involves aspects of emotion, cognition, and behavior. Christenson, Reschly, and Wylie (2012) offered the following overarching definition:

> Student engagement refers to the student's active participation in academic and co-curricular or school-related activities and commitment to educational goals and learning. Engaged students find learning meaningful and are invested in their learning and future. It is a multidimensional construct that consists of behavioral (including academic), cognitive, and affective subtypes. Student engagement drives learning; requires energy and effort; is affected by multiple contextual influences; and can be achieved for all learners. (pp. 816–817)

We conceptualize student engagement as having four dimensions or subtypes: academic, behavioral, cognitive, and affective. The model of engagement presented in this chapter grew out of our intervention work through Check & Connect (Christenson, Stout, & Pohl, 2012), a comprehensive student engagement intervention model. We believed it was important to separate behavioral engagement from academic engagement as it became clear that some students were engaged behaviorally but were not yet academically engaged with school, information that would lead to different intervention strategies.

We also have speculated that there may be a hierarchy among these forms of engagement, wherein changes to affective and cognitive engagement precede changes to behavioral and academic engagement (e.g., students feel that they belong, teachers care about them, students begin to see the relevance of their schoolwork for their future goals, leading to observable changes in indicators of behavioral and academic engagement). The subsequent review of best practices for promoting student engagement is organized around this four subtype model of student engagement. Indicators of each of the four subtypes of engagement may be found in Figure 3.1.

Student engagement underlies school dropout theory and effective intervention: Scholars agree that dropout is best conceptualized as a long-term process of disengagement from school. Both theory and research support this conceptualization. According to Finn (1989), student engagement and eventual school completion are composed of a cycle of participation–success–identification, which then promotes students' ongoing participation. For most students this cycle continues over several years and leads to school completion. Some students, however, do not begin school with the attitudes and behaviors necessary for successful participation. As the requirements of schooling change, students are more likely to demonstrate impaired or reduced participation, experience less successful outcomes, and have lowered identification or belonging, eventually culminating in dropout.

A number of studies provide support for this theory. For example, it is possible to predict dropout and completion from early elementary school based on such variables as attendance, school behavior, and attachment to school (e.g., Alexander, Entwisle, & Horsey, 1997). Participation in class and extracurricular activities are linked to more positive outcomes for students (e.g., Feldman & Matjasko, 2005; Finn & Rock, 1997). Studies of school dropouts provide support for the importance of the social aspects of schooling, often noting that students did not feel as if they belonged at school, teachers disliked them, or their friends had dropped out (Bridgeland, DiIulio, & Morison, 2006).

The most promising interventions to promote school completion address student engagement comprehen-

Figure 3.1. Four Subtypes of Student Engagement

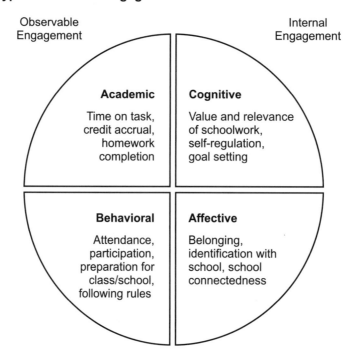

sively; that is, they address not just the academic and behavioral deficits students at risk for dropping out often exhibit but the social and interpersonal aspects of schooling as well. Check & Connect (Christenson, Stout, & Pohl, 2012) serves as an example of an evidence-based intervention model for promoting student engagement comprehensively. Check & Connect is a structured mentoring intervention designed to engage students who are showing early warning signs of disengagement from school and learning, The core elements of Check & Connect—relationships, problem solving and capacity building, and persistence—are elements that school psychologists can readily incorporate into their practice in order to promote students' engagement in school and with learning (Christenson, Stout, & Pohl, 2012).

Student engagement is the cornerstone of high school reform: In 2004, the National Research Council and the Institute of Medicine (2004) published a volume that argued student engagement should serve as the basis of high school reform initiatives. Effective schools engender student feelings of "I can" (perceptions of competence and control), "I want to" (personal values and goals), and "I belong" (social connectedness to peers and teachers). It is clear from this conceptualization that academic and social–emotional aspects of students' school experiences are essential to school-wide improvement efforts. These recommendations are closely aligned with the NASP Practice Model (NASP, 2010), suggesting the important role that school psychologists can play in putting these recommendations into practice through their work with other school personnel to support academic, behavioral, and social competence; facilitate effective instruction; and promote safe, positive school climates. In doing so, school psychologists can foster student engagement for all students.

Engagement is alterable and associated with important outcomes: Research has consistently found associations between engagement and achievement, high school completion, lower risk health and sexual behaviors, and social–emotional well-being (Christenson, Reschly, & Wylie, 2012). In addition, engagement is amenable to intervention efforts. Therefore, the proliferation of interest in engagement is not surprising. Engagement is also thought to be the link between contexts—homes, schools, peers—and student outcomes.

It has been suggested that engagement mitigates the effects of academic and demographic risk on student outcomes. In other words, student engagement promotes resilience (Finn & Zimmer, 2012). Finn and Rock (1997) illustrated this phenomenon when they divided a group of students who were demographically at high risk

for poor outcomes (i.e., low-income ethnic minority students) into three groups based on their academic performance: those who were higher achieving and likely to graduate, those who were likely to graduate but lower achieving, and those who dropped out. After controlling for things such as family structure, the groups differed as expected in terms of teacher- and student-reported engagement.

BEST PRACTICES FOR PROMOTING STUDENT ENGAGEMENT

This chapter is organized around guidelines for school psychologists to promote four subtypes of engagement in schools: academic, behavioral, cognitive, and affective (see Figure 3.1). An understanding of the subtypes of engagement is important for determining intervention targets. Engagement is a construct that is relevant for all youth, includes important contexts for assessment and intervention (homes, schools, peers), and addresses students' academic and behavioral needs as well as their social and emotional well-being.

Engagement interventions are conceptualized across multitiered universal and individualized levels (targeted and intensive) of intervention. It should be noted that engagement subtypes and interventions are interrelated. For example, an intervention to address self-regulation (cognitive) may also affect time on task or homework completion (academic). In addition, the literature on engagement is still primarily correlational in nature. More research is needed on the effects of engagement interventions. There is also a need for longitudinal research. It is likely there are developmental changes in the engagement construct with age and level of schooling (Christenson, Reschly, & Wylie, 2012). In each engagement section that follows, brief descriptions of each subtype of engagement, summaries of research, and intervention recommendations are presented.

Academic Engagement

Academic engagement refers to engagement in instruction, academic work, and tasks. It is composed of indicators such as academic engaged time, homework completion, and credits earned (high school). These indicators are typically readily available to educators.

Recommendations for Practice
Making the most of available time: School psychologists may consult with teachers and teams to enhance academic engaged time for students. This consultation is impor-

tant because although research has clearly indicated that the amount of time students spend engaged in learning is highly predictive of academic achievement, it has also demonstrated that large portions of the school day are not devoted to instruction and that many classrooms have low levels of academic engaged time even within the allotted instructional time (Gettinger & Walter, 2012). As a member of the school team often operating outside of the classroom, school psychologists can observe classroom instruction, practices, and procedures and offer objective, specific recommendations to teachers on how to modify their practices to ensure academic engagement. School psychologists can help teachers to design interventions that target instructional variables (e.g., creating variety, matching to instructional level, ensuring understanding, using group versus individual instruction, and providing feedback to students) as well as allotment and use of time (e.g., smooth transitions, classroom routines). A summary of practice recommendations to enhance academic engaged time on which school psychologists can draw may be found in Table 3.1a–d.

Monitor homework completion: School psychologists can consult with teachers and families, as well as work with individual students, to promote students' homework completion, which research has shown is reliably associated with student achievement (Cooper, 1989). A number of variables related to homework completion have been identified and may serve as appropriate targets for individual and classroom-level interventions, including exogenous factors (students' ability, motivation, study habits; subject matter; grade level), assignment characteristics (deadlines, purpose, amount), initial classroom factors (facilitators such as links to curriculum, provision of materials), classroom follow-up (feedback, testing of related content, use in class discussion), and home–community factors (other demands on student time; home environment, such as noise or materials; parent, sibling, and others' involvement; Cooper, 1989). General guidelines for monitoring and promoting homework completion that are aligned with these intervention targets can be found in Table 3.1a–d.

Monitor failures and credits: School psychologists and/or other school personnel should regularly examine elementary and secondary students' course grades. In high school, credits should be examined at the end of each semester and timely interventions implemented to help students who are off track recapture credits. These interventions, which may be implemented by school psychologists, could involve provision of additional help while students retake courses during the traditional school year, online credit recovery options, and summer school options.

In high schools, a certain number of credits, typically set by each state, are required to earn a high school diploma. Course grades and sometimes high-stakes assessments, depending on state requirements, are used to determine whether credits are earned. Although elementary and middle school students do not typically earn credits toward high school graduation, the corollary is course failures. Course failure in math or English in the sixth grade, alone or in combination with other risk indicators, is highly predictive of failure to graduate from high school (Balfanz, Herzog, & Mac Iver, 2007). The strong relationships between middle and high school course success and graduation are utilized within many current early warning systems, alerting practitioners and administrators in advance of problems at the end of high school.

Formal Intervention

One formal intervention school psychologists may want to examine is the Homework, Organization, and Planning Skills intervention. A randomized trial of middle school students with attention deficit hyperactivity disorder found significant effects of the program over wait-list control students in terms of parent-rated organized action, planning, and homework completion (Langberg, Epstein, & Becker, 2012).

Behavioral Engagement

Behavioral engagement may be defined through observable appropriate behaviors in class, unstructured times during the school day, and extracurricular activities. Indicators of behavior engagement include attendance (absences, tardies, skipping), behavior (suspensions, office referrals, detentions), and participation in the classroom and extracurricular activities. Behavioral engagement has been associated with various outcomes of interest, including achievement, high school dropout and completion, and general physical and emotional well-being (e.g., substance use, sexual behavior). Furthermore, indicators of behavioral disengagement are among the most common concerns expressed by educators and parents.

Recommendations for Practice

Implement timely attendance and behavior interventions: It is critical that school psychologists and/or other school personnel intervene when attendance and behavior data begin to indicate student disengagement. Early intervention is important because attendance, behavior, and

Table 3.1a. Strategies to Promote Academic Engagement

Tier	Strategy Description

Universal	• Enhance classroom managerial strategies (Gettinger & Walter, 2012)
	  ▪ Establish efficient and consistent classroom routines
	  ▪ Decrease class and group sizes
	  ▪ Minimize classroom disruptions/effectively manage off task behavior
	  ▪ Reduce transition time
	• Utilize student-mediated strategies (Gettinger & Walter, 2012)
	  ▪ Teach metacognitive, self-monitoring, and study strategies to students
	  ▪ Have students set their own goals for learning
	  ▪ Ensure effective use of homework to enhance learning
	• Apply principles of effective instruction
	  ▪ Provide direct instruction
	  ▪ Create scaffolding for learning
	  ▪ Provide guided practice
	  ▪ Provide frequent feedback
	  ▪ Use mastery learning principles to guide instructional planning and delivery
	  ▪ Maximize instructional relevance (e.g., clearly state purpose, graph progress toward goals)
	  ▪ Ensure appropriate instructional match
	  ▪ Provide clear directions
	  ▪ Use multiple teaching methods
	• Facilitate home–school support for learning
	  ▪ Provide home support for learning strategies related to content area
	  ▪ Enhance bidirectional communication with families
	  ▪ Encourage parents to volunteer in the classroom
	• Utilize a variety of interesting texts and resources
	• Support student autonomy by providing choices within courses and assignments
	• Ensure appropriateness of homework assignments (Cooper, 1989)
	  ▪ Set clear purpose and time requirements
	  ▪ Coordinate assignments across classes/teachers so students are not overwhelmed
	  ▪ Do not use to test or give as punishment
	  ▪ Have teachers collect, check for completeness, and give intermittent instructional feedback
	  ▪ Use parents as support, not for instruction
	  ▪ Follow general time guidelines: 10-minute rule per grade (e.g., Grade 1: 10 minutes per night; Grade 4: 40 minutes per night)
	• Ensure that there are both academic pressure (high expectations, well-structured learning environment) and support for learning (caring environment; Lee & Smith, 1999)
	• Attend to the effect of the organization/structure of the school on learning (e.g., smaller learning communities, academies)
	• Reinforce students frequently based on effort and amount of work completed
	• Increase time on task and substantive interaction through cooperative learning, whole class, or group instruction and peer-assisted learning strategies
	• Enhance teacher–student relationships and/or teacher–student support

Individualized	• Utilize after-school programs (tutoring, homework help)
	• Intensify partnering and communication efforts with families (e.g., home–school notes, assignment notebooks, enrichment activities)
	  ▪ Ensure adequacy of educational resources in the home
	  ▪ Help parents to understand and set expectations
	• Implement individual self-monitoring interventions
	• Foster positive teacher–student relationship for marginalized students

preparation (e.g., being prepared for and participating in assignments, coming on time, not disrupting class), even in the early grades, are associated with student achievement across grade levels, race, and gender (Finn, 1989). In addition, these early attendance, behavior, and participation patterns are important for establishing later patterns of engagement and disengagement (e.g., Alexander et al., 1997). Frequent absences interfere with learning and also inhibit the development and maintenance of relationships with teachers and peers, which are important to students' affective engagement. In a similar vein, misbehavior interferes with the learning

Table 3.1b. Strategies to Promote Behavioral Engagement

Tier	Strategy Description
Universal	• Examine discipline policies ▪ Strive to eliminate out-of-school suspension ▪ Ensure that policies are considered fair, nonpunitive, and understood by students ▪ End reliance on negative consequences as a means of managing student behavior • Encourage social interactions and planning for the future through smaller learning communities that target vocational interests (e.g., academies) • Connect with families (Epstein & Sheldon, 2002) ▪ Link families to an accessible school contact ▪ Enhance communication with families, particularly those who are not native English speakers ▪ Provide educational workshops • Offer social skills training and bullying prevention in curriculum for all students • Provide after-school and summer programs • Facilitate participation in extracurricular activities; increase range and number of activities, including different levels of competition • Use coordinated, collaborative home–school interventions to address attendance • Involve students in hands-on-learning that is directly related to future career paths or interests • Create an orderly, routine environment that promotes consistency • Offer professional development for classroom management strategies • Gather student input about classroom rules, school climate, and evaluation of coursework/assignments; use feedback to make appropriate changes • Ensure that school climate, school culture are respectful to all students
Individualized	• Provide additional, supplemental supports for students not responding to positive behavioral support systems implemented school-wide • Devise an individualized approach to addressing attendance or participation issues at school; strive to understand student perspective and unique family circumstances • Assign a truancy officer to work with families and students with attendance problems (Epstein & Sheldon, 2002) • Implement programs that work to build specific skills such as problem solving, anger management, or interpersonal communication • Provide an adult mentor who works with students and families long-term to foster engagement in school and deliver the message that school is important (e.g., Check & Connect) • Develop specific behavior plans or contracts to address individual needs • Provide intensive wraparound services • Provide alternative programs for students who have not completed school • Encourage parents to monitor and supervise student behavior • Implement student advisory programs that monitor academic and social development of secondary students (middle or high) • Implement school-to-work programs that foster success in school and relevant educational opportunities

and climate of other students and is a source of stress for educators.

When designing interventions targeting student attendance and behavior, school psychologists should consider the three primary domains associated with attendance and disciplinary difficulties: the school environment (e.g., school climate, teacher–student relationships, harshness of school rules, student perceptions of school), home environment (e.g., family conflict, mobility, socioeconomic status), and student characteristics (e.g., academic performance, social skills; Goldstein, Little, & Akin-Little, 2003). Interventions,

whether universal or individualized, which are targeted across domains rather than to one domain, are more likely to be effective. Thus, school psychologists should work with students, families, and other school personnel to design interventions that target each domain in an effort to improve behavior and attendance. Table 3.1a–d provides specific strategies for promoting attendance and positive behavior.

Encourage and facilitate extracurricular participation: School psychologists can identify students' strengths and interests and then work to connect students to extracurricular activities that are tied to those strengths and interests.

Table 3.1c. Strategies to Promote Cognitive Engagement

Tier	Strategy Description

Universal	• Teach, model, and promote the use of self-regulated learning strategies such as planning, goal setting, self-monitoring of progress, strategy selection, and self-evaluation (Zimmerman, 2002).
	• Facilitate the goal setting process (Greene et al., 2004)
	  ▪ Help students set long-term, future-oriented goals and short-term goals that include the action steps to be taken in order to reach future goals and task-specific goals
	  ▪ Discuss the relevance of academic tasks and skills to students' future goals
	• Promote a mastery goal orientation
	  ▪ Keep the focus on understanding, skill development, and personal improvement
	• Encourage educators and administrators to foster a mastery-oriented goal structure in the classroom and school; remind them of the TARGET acronym (Epstein, 1989)
	• Provide students with choices when completing assignments
	• Provide students with authentic, challenging assignments that relate to life outside of school and to their interests
	• Model learning strategies when teaching specific concepts; provide student models when possible (Schunk & Mullen, 2012)
	• Provide feedback that emphasizes self-control and the link between effort/practice and improvement
	• Provide professional development training to teachers (e.g., goal setting and self-regulation combined with informed feedback that focuses on improvement and enhancing intrinsic motivation)
	• Encourage parents to deliver messages related to motivational support for learning (high expectations, talk to their child about school and schoolwork, valuing of education)

Individualized	• Enhance student's personal belief in self through repeated contacts, goal setting, problem solving, and relationship building (e.g., Check & Connect) • Aid the student in defining goals for the future; discuss the connection between education and those goals for the future • Explicitly teach cognitive and metacognitive strategies such as managing time, chunking assignments, studying for tests, using mnemonic devices, taking notes, making outlines, and comprehending textbooks • Implement self-monitoring interventions (e.g., graph progress toward goals) • Discuss the link between the student's effort and the outcome/behavior/success achieved to increase the student's perceived self-control, self-efficacy, and self-determination (Schunk & Mullen, 2012) • Provide specific, positive feedback emphasizing student effort and the strategies used to master a skill or complete a task (Schunk & Mullen, 2012) • Design tasks that are specifically related to the student's interests and future goals • Help the student set challenging but reachable goals so that the student can experience success and draw on that success for motivation

Participation in these activities enhances outcomes for youth in several ways, such as promoting connections to school and positive social networks, providing opportunities to interact with competent adults, and developing individual interests and strengths (Gilman, Meyers, & Perez, 2004). Outcomes associated with participation in extracurricular activities include higher academic achievement, reduced rates of high school dropout and substance use, less sexual activity (for girls), better psychological adjustment (e.g., higher self-esteem, less social isolation), and reduced delinquent behavior (Feldman & Matjasko, 2005).

School psychologists may be concerned with students at either end of the participation continuum: those who do not participate in any activities and those who are overscheduled. Results indicate that overscheduling of adolescents' activities is not as widespread as some media reports suggested (Fredricks, 2012). In general, adolescents' well-being increases with number of hours and time in extracurricular activities. However, those who are at the highest levels of participation do show decreased academic well-being. In addition, school psychologists may also want to pay attention to students who try out for but are not selected for certain teams and activities. Some research suggests negative effects for those not selected.

Enhance out-of-school time: School psychologists and other personnel may seek opportunities to enhance students' out-of-school time (including before and after school, weekends, and summers). These opportunities may take place at school or other community organizations. School psychologists and other personnel may

Table 3.1d. Strategies to Promote Affective Engagement

Tier	Strategy Description
Universal	• Implement advisory programs with advisers monitoring engagement data • Systematically build relationships/connections for all students; have educators identify students who may not have a connection with a staff member (i.e., list all student names at grade levels and determine who knows the student) and match staff members and alienated students for future regular mentor-like contact • Address size through implementation of smaller learning communities • Enhance peer connections through peer-assisted learning strategies • Implement a mentoring program (use of college-age students) • Increase participation in extracurricular activities • Combine social support for students (from teachers, peers, parents, and community) with high levels of academic press (i.e., teacher belief that they are challenging students and student perception that they are being challenged; Lee & Smith, 1999) • Promote a positive school climate • Intervene early, persistently, and across the contexts of school peers, school adults, and the home and community to change student developmental trajectories • When evaluating results, be sure to check for delayed outcomes associated with early interventions
Individualized	• Build personal relationships with marginalized students; enhance relationships with one caring adult • Personalize education (e.g., alter assignments to match personal interests and goals; Oyserman et al., 2002) • Assist students with personal problems • Provide extra support for students in a timely fashion • To improve generalizability, intervene across peer, family, and community contexts when possible

connect students to existing programs or seek to implement new programs to ensure there are out-of-school options available to all students.

When attempting to connect students to out-of-school programs, school psychologists and others should consider (a) the student's perceptions of the social status of the proposed activity, (b) intrinsic interest, (c) the quality of the social networks, and (d) the nonparental adult involved with the proposed activity (Gilman et al., 2004). For example, facilitating a student's participation in an activity or with people the student dislikes may not have the desired outcomes. Thus, in addition to logistical concerns, such as transportation and fees, educators should support student autonomy and choice whenever possible.

When examining existing programs, school psychologists should consider that these programs vary greatly in terms of quality, structure, rigor, and intensity. Programs high in rigor (demanding, challenging, relevant activities) are most likely to help participants obtain positive achievement gains (Shernoff, 2010). School psychologists may vet programs to ensure that students are connected to those high in rigor.

When considering when to implement new out-of-school programs and which programs to implement at their site, school psychologists should understand that research has demonstrated that both summer and after-school programs resulted in positive academic benefits for high-risk students. Thus, school psychologists should focus their attention on practical issues when determining timing and intervention programs, such as staffing, cost, and duration. Age and program structure are also important considerations. In reading, both elementary and secondary students benefit from summer and after-school programs. In mathematics, however, achievement benefits are limited to secondary level. In addition, one-to-one tutoring in reading for at-risk students appears to be very promising (Lauer et al., 2006).

Formal Interventions

The following formal interventions are evidence-based interventions and intervention models that either directly or indirectly promote behavioral engagement that school psychologists may consider implementing in their schools.

Good Behavior Game: The Good Behavior Game is a universal (Tier 1) classroom management intervention in which children are rewarded for engaging in appropriate behavior during class time. The Good Behavior Game has been widely implemented and researched by several scholars, across cohorts, and with different age groups and has been found to show immediate effects on classroom behavior (on task, disruption), and distal effects years later on important indicators such as special education placement, high school graduation, and college attendance (e.g., Bradshaw, Zmuda, Kellam, & Ialongo, 2009).

Positive behavioral interventions and supports: Positive behavioral interventions and supports (PBIS) is a framework for implementing evidence-based interventions to enhance social and academic outcomes for all students. PBIS has four key elements: (a) use of data for decision making, (b) measureable outcomes, (c) evidence-based practices, and (d) systems that support implementation of evidence-based practices (http://www.pbis.org). PBIS at Tier 1 is focused on teaching appropriate behavior to students and creating an environment in which all adults use common language and practices and are consistent in their application of reinforcement. A number of studies provide evidence of the effectiveness of PBIS on improving problem behavior, including bullying and peer victimization, and improving academic achievement (see Sugai & Simonsen, 2012, for a summary). PBIS also has implications for students' affective engagement through the promotion of a positive school climate among students and between staff and students.

Behavior Education Program: The Behavior Education Program is a Tier 2 intervention intended to be implemented within a continuum of positive behavior support in schools. The Behavior Education Program is composed of a daily check-in/check-out system in which students are provided immediate feedback on their behavior, progress relative to goals is graphed, and both immediate and long-term reinforcement is given to students based on their performance. The Behavior Education Program provides a way for students to receive positive adult attention at school and seeks to increase home–school collaboration through daily progress reports (Crone, Hawken, & Horner, 2010).

Check & Connect: As described earlier, Check & Connect is a comprehensive intervention designed to enhance student engagement for marginalized, disengaged students in grades K–12. Rigorous research of Check & Connect has demonstrated findings such as increased rates of persistence, attendance, credit accrual, and school completion as well as reduced rates of truancy, suspensions, and course failures (Christenson, Stout, & Pohl, 2012). Although evidence for Check & Connect demonstrates increases in academic and behavioral engagement, the personalized interventions implemented by the mentors target all four subtypes of engagement. Mentors promote engagement through such strategies as connecting students to tutoring programs, developing behavior contracts, facilitating

problem solving and goal setting, and promoting participation in extracurricular activities in the school and community. Recognizing the importance of multiple contextual influences on student engagement, including the home, school, and community, Check & Connect mentors also work to create positive relationships in and among all three environments in order to provide consistent support for student engagement in learning (Christenson, Stout, & Pohl, 2012).

Cognitive Engagement

Cognitive engagement can be defined broadly as students' investment in their learning, effort directed toward learning, and use of self-regulated learning strategies to understand material, accomplish tasks, and master skills (Fredricks et al., 2004). Indicators of cognitive engagement include use of self-regulated learning strategies such as setting goals, managing time, using study skills, putting forth effort, maintaining self-efficacy and motivation, and persisting in the face of challenges; interest in learning; perceived relevance of school to personal aspirations; valuing of learning; and control of schoolwork. Researchers have demonstrated that these indicators of cognitive engagement are interrelated and are associated with positive academic outcomes for students (e.g., Greene, Miller, Crowson, Duke, & Akey, 2004).

Recommendations for Practice

Teach and promote self-regulated learning strategies: School psychologists can explicitly teach students the strategies needed to be self-regulated learners. They can teach students the three phases of self-regulated learning: the forethought phase (before the task), the performance phase (during the task), and the self-reflection phase (after the task; Zimmerman, 2002). School psychologists may work with students on academic tasks they have been assigned and promote self-regulated learning by asking students questions before, during, and after the task to facilitate the kind of thinking they should be doing as they approach a task independently. For example, in the forethought phase, the school psychologist can ask questions related to students' confidence in their ability to complete the task, valuing of the task, interest in the task, purpose for completing the task, goals for the particular task, and strategies they will use to complete the task. In the performance phase, they can encourage students to apply the strategies they have selected and facilitate self-monitoring of whether or not those strategies are working. In the self-reflection phase they can ask students about what went well in the task, what did not go well, to what students attribute their success or failure, and what they will do differently in the future. See the formal interventions below for specific interventions to teach self-regulated learning strategies.

School psychologists can also consult with teachers and help them to understand the importance of self-regulated learning for cognitive engagement and the connection it has to academic achievement (e.g., Zimmerman, 2002). They can share strategies for how teachers can incorporate self-regulated learning strategy instruction into their classrooms.

Enhance self-efficacy: Self-efficacy refers to a student's perceived capabilities for learning or performing a task. School psychologists can promote student self-efficacy by implementing the following research-based practices or sharing them with educators (Schunk & Mullen, 2012).

- Encourage students to set challenging but reachable mastery learning goals and monitor their progress toward achieving those goals. This is particularly important for those students who are disengaged from learning because they have experienced repeated failures in the past. If they can experience even small successes, their self-efficacy is likely to increase, which will lead to increased cognitive engagement as well.
- Allow students to observe and work with students similar to themselves who can model how to learn target skills.
- Provide students with specific feedback that praises effort and the use of specific strategies in learning a skill or completing a task. By doing so, the school psychologist is helping students to attribute their successes and failures to their effort and choice of strategies rather than their ability. This promotes students' perception that they have agency in learning and are capable of changing their level of effort or their choice of strategies in order to successfully complete a task or learn a skill.

Self-efficacy beliefs are associated with student engagement in learning, use of self-regulated learning strategies, putting forth effort, persistence in the face of challenges, and academic achievement (Schunk & Mullen, 2012). In enhancing self-efficacy, school psychologists are also promoting cognitive engagement and academic achievement.

Promote a mastery goal orientation: Promoting a mastery orientation means helping students to approach academic tasks as opportunities to learn new knowledge or skills rather than as opportunities to prove how smart they are or how they compare to others. School psychologists can promote a mastery goal orientation when working with students by focusing on what the students will learn from a task or intervention rather than on the students' performance relative to peers. School psychologists can also help students to see failures as learning opportunities and give students the chance to try again on tasks or improve their performance based on the feedback they have been given.

In order to foster a mastery goal orientation in classrooms, school psychologists can consult with teachers and emphasize that classroom goal structures, or what students perceive to be emphasized in the classroom, are associated with students' cognitive engagement (Ames & Archer, 1988). A helpful acronym that school psychologists can share with teachers to help them structure their classrooms to promote a mastery goal orientation is TARGET (Epstein, 1989), which reminds teachers to ensure that *tasks* are meaningful and relevant, the *authority* is shared between the teacher and students, all students are *recognized* for progress and effort, *grouping* is heterogeneous and flexible, *evaluation* is criterion-referenced, and *time* is flexible in the class, allowing for self-pacing when needed.

Ensure activities are meaningful, relevant, and interesting: To foster student engagement in academic tasks, school psychologists can consult with teachers to design and implement authentic, real-world tasks to teach curricular standards. Authentic work, or work that students perceive as meaningful, valuable, significant, worthy of effort, and connected to the real world, fosters cognitive engagement (Newmann, Wehlage, & Lamborn, 1992). Because interest in an academic task also has an impact on students' engagement with that task, school psychologists can work with students to identify a student's interests and then consult with teachers on how to incorporate the student's interests into academic tasks when possible.

Facilitate future-oriented thinking: School psychologists can help students to set long-term goals for their education, career, and life after high school, and then set short-term goals to help the students meet those future goals. When students are presented with academic tasks, school psychologists can work with students to help students see the relevance of the task to their short-term and long-term goals. Students who perceive their schoolwork as instrumental to achieving their future goals are more likely to value the work and engage cognitively in order to move closer to reaching their proximal goals and ultimately their future goals, such as graduating from college or securing a particular job (e.g., Greene et al., 2004).

Formal Interventions

Few evidence-based interventions to promote cognitive engagement currently exist. Those that do generally target self-regulated learning and cognitive strategy use in the core subjects of reading, writing, science, and mathematics. School psychologists may implement these interventions themselves or make educators aware of these evidence-based interventions.

Self-regulated strategy development: Self-regulated strategy development is a writing strategies instructional approach in which the instructor explains, models, and prompts students' use of self-regulated strategies in completing an academic task. Results from numerous studies with elementary and secondary students with and without disabilities demonstrated that the self-regulated strategy development approach is effective in helping students improve their quality of, knowledge of, approach to, and self-efficacy in writing (Harris, Graham, Mason, & Friedlander, 2007).

Concept-Oriented Reading Instruction: Concept-Oriented Reading Instruction is an instructional framework that promotes reading engagement through strategy instruction, modeling of strategies, opportunities for practice, and motivational support. Results from several studies showed that students receiving Concept-Oriented Reading Instruction demonstrated superior motivation, strategy use, and reading comprehension compared to students receiving traditional reading instruction (Guthrie et al., 2004).

Self-Regulation Empowerment Program: The Self-Regulation Empowerment Program is a more recent intervention developed to help secondary students become more strategic, motivated, and regulated during more complex and comprehensive academic activities. The Self-Regulation Empowerment Program is closely aligned with the three phases of self-regulated learning (see above) and focuses on training students in task analysis, goal setting and strategic planning, self-recording, self-evaluation, strategic attributions, and adaptive inferences. Initial research findings suggest that the intervention leads to increased behavior self-management, self-efficacy, and academic achievement (Cleary, Platten, & Nelson, 2008).

Affective Engagement

Affective engagement refers to students' emotional experiences when they are in the learning context and/or explicitly involved with learning. Affective engagement is often represented through terms such as identification, school connectedness, and belonging. Researchers are able to directly link other subtypes of engagement to academic achievement outcomes; affective engagement tends to directly influence constructs affecting achievement (including the other subtypes of engagement) rather than achievement itself (Finn & Zimmer, 2012). Additionally, affective engagement is positively related to other valued outcomes, such as motivation, persistence with rigorous academic work, and expectations for success (Goodenow, 1993).

Recommendations for Practice

Promote belonging and bonding with school: School psychologists may work with teachers and administrators to appreciate the importance of positive adult–student connections throughout the school day and year. In addition, school psychologists may ensure that instructional periods also include the availability of additional support to enable students to be successful academically. School psychologists may also work to implement and evaluate school programs that facilitate frequent positive contact between staff and students and to use students' engagement data to link those showing signs of increased risk to more intensive support, such as advisement or mentoring programs. The availability of universal and more intensive programs is needed to provide additional support and facilitate bonding and belonging at school. School belonging has been related to persistence with rigorous coursework, academic self-efficacy, stronger self-concept, and task goal orientations (Goodenow, 1993).

Support student beliefs on the value of school: School psychologists and others can support student recognition of the value of school by assisting students and their families in recognizing the link between current behavior (successes and failures) and proximal and distal outcomes, such as desired careers. One avenue for developing student recognition of the value of school is through graduation and career planning. Assisting at-risk youth to connect perceptions of future success with current school involvement has been linked to increased bonding to school, concern with school performance, relevant plans for reaching "possible selves," attendance, realistic possible selves, and less trouble at school (Oyserman, Terry, & Bybee, 2002).

Pair social support with academic press: An important concept for school psychologists and educators is working to create a community of support that is focused both on promoting students' affective engagement and communicating high expectations. Both are necessary to realize gains in student achievement (Lee & Smith, 1999). School psychologists and other interventionists can improve the reach of their affective engagement interventions if their efforts to enhance social support for students are provided with continued high expectations for academic achievement.

Formal Interventions

There are few formal interventions designed to solely address affective engagement. Rather, affective engagement is often addressed through more comprehensive interventions that may target various behaviors, types of engagement, or indicators of risk. Check & Connect, described previously, is one example. Another example is ALAS (Achievement for Latinos Through Academic Success), which is a multifaceted intervention with positive results for students staying in and progressing in school. ALAS provides a counselor/mentor who monitors engagement indicators such as attendance, behavior, and academic performance, while developing social and task-related skills within students, assisting families with school involvement, connecting families to community services, and positioning students for improved school bonding (Larson & Rumberger, 1995).

Implementation Considerations

In this section, general implementation considerations for promoting student engagement school-wide are described. It is important that school psychologists work with others to coordinate often fragmented efforts present in many school systems and evaluate the effects of engagement practices and interventions relative to goals.

Systematically monitor student population and follow up with students at risk: Two of the most important considerations for system implementation of engagement efforts are systematic monitoring of student population on key variables (e.g., attendance and behavior difficulties, homework completion, participation, reported cognitive and affective engagement) and the establishment of a process for follow-up with those showing signs of increased risk. School psychologists can lead efforts to monitor indicators predictive of important outcomes, such as graduation, as well as student perceptions of these indicators. The training of school psychologists in assessment, consultation, research methodology, and intervention uniquely position them to be among the leaders of such an effort.

Maintain and use data on student perceptions: Routinely collecting, analyzing, and reporting on student percep-

tions can provide school psychologists and other educators with an understanding of typical changes during the academic year and across grade levels, as well as significant deviations from these patterns. This information is useful for identifying students who are in need of additional support and to inform and evaluate school-wide interventions. Students' self-attributions for academic success are related to greater involvement and attentiveness at school, homework completion, and level of effort. Research underscores the importance of students' perceptions of their cognitive and affective engagement—indicators such as relationships, belonging, and relevance of schoolwork for future goals—to their school performance and behavior (Appleton, Christenson, Kim, & Reschly, 2006).

Increase support during transitional periods: Research suggests that transitions are a time of vulnerability for many students in their K–12 careers. For instance, perceived support from friends was linked to a greater sense of school membership following the ninth-grade transition (Isakson & Jarvis, 1999), and student struggles with passing courses and attending in ninth grade were particularly predictive of failing to graduate from high school (Allensworth & Easton, 2007; Balfanz et al., 2007). Ninth-grade students' perceptions of support in the relationships between students and teachers were linked to better than expected grades and lower failure and absence rates. As school psychologists lead efforts to systematically monitor the student population for signs of disengagement, they may use this information to plan for additional support for all students, small groups at increased risk for disengagement during and following a transition, and individuals.

Early Warning Systems

One emerging application of engagement research is in the form of early warning systems. Early warning systems typically use existing academic and behavioral engagement data, often in the form of attendance, disciplinary, and course success data (e.g., Allensworth & Easton, 2007; Balfanz et al., 2007). One of the primary applications of this work is to determine the number of students at high risk for dropout. An important concept to convey to educators and families is the dynamic nature of student risk and the frequency with which these data may be updated within these systems. School psychologists may be responsible for compiling and analyzing data such as these for the purposes of systems consultation and/or for use by school-based decision-making teams. School psychologists may also work with individual teachers, families, and students to link these assessment data to the implementation of interventions to address student risk and disengagement.

SUMMARY

Despite some differences in conceptualization and measurement, it is agreed that engagement is an alterable, multidimensional construct that is associated with important outcomes such as academic performance and involvement in delinquent behavior. Our perspective is rooted in the process of disengagement students undergo prior to dropping out of school and the potential that indicators of engagement provide for early intervention. Academic, behavioral, cognitive, and affective engagement underscore student outcomes. The most effective engagement-based interventions attend to the contextual influences of communities, families, and peers in addition to the school's effectiveness at meeting student needs for competence, autonomy, and relatedness. School psychologists and other educators have important influences on student engagement beginning with classroom teachers' frequent student interactions and including the universal and intensive intervention efforts school psychologists may lead. Advisement and other mentoring programs, early warning systems, and self-regulation-enhancing interventions represent some intervention approaches that make use of a student engagement paradigm. Early actions to influence engagement have the potential to provide increased return across students' educational tenure.

AUTHOR NOTE

Disclosure. Amy L. Reschly has a financial interest in books she edited or coedited referenced in this chapter.

REFERENCES

Alexander, K. L., Entwisle, D. R., & Horsey, C. S. (1997). From first grade forward: Early foundations of high school dropouts. *Sociology of Education, 70*, 87–107.

Allensworth, E. M., & Easton, J. (2007). *What matters for staying on-track and graduating in Chicago public high schools*. Chicago, IL: Consortium on Chicago School Research.

Ames, C., & Archer, J. (1988). Achievement goals in the classroom: Students' learning strategies and motivation processes. *Journal of Educational Psychology, 3*, 260–267.

Appleton, J. J., Christenson, S. L., Kim, D., & Reschly, A. L. (2006). Measuring cognitive and psychological engagement: Validation of the Student Engagement Instrument. *Journal of School Psychology, 44*, 427–445.

Balfanz, R., Herzog, L., & Mac Iver, D. J. (2007). Preventing student disengagement and keeping students on the graduation path in urban middle-grades schools: Early identification and effective interventions. *Educational Psychologist, 42*, 223–235.

Bradshaw, C. P., Zmuda, J. H., Kellam, S. G., & Ialongo, N. S. (2009). Longitudinal impact of two universal preventive interventions in first grade on educational outcomes in high school. *Journal of Psychology, 101*, 926–937.

Bridgeland, J. M., DiIulio, J. J., & Morison, K. B. (2006). *The silent epidemic: Perspectives of high school dropouts*. Washington, DC: Civic Enterprises.

Christenson, S. L., Reschly, A. L., & Wylie, C. (Eds.). (2012). *Handbook of research on student engagement*. New York, NY: Springer.

Christenson, S. L., Stout, K. E., & Pohl, A. (2012). *Check & Connect: A comprehensive student engagement intervention: Implementing with fidelity*. Minneapolis, MN: University of Minnesota, Institute on Community Integration.

Cleary, T. J., Platten, P., & Nelson, A. C. (2008). Effectiveness of self-regulation empowerment program with urban high school students. *Journal of Advanced Academics, 20*, 70–107.

Cooper, H. (1989). Synthesis of research on homework. *Educational Leadership, 47*, 85–91.

Crone, D., Hawken, L., & Horner, R. (2010). *Responding to problem behavior in schools: The Behavior Education Program* (2nd ed.). New York, NY: Guilford Press.

Epstein, J. L. (1989). Family structures and student motivation: A developmental perspective. In C. Ames & R. J. Sternberg (Eds.), *Teaching thinking skill: Theory and practice* (Vol. 3, pp. 259–295). San Diego, CA: Academic Press.

Epstein, J. L., & Sheldon, S. B. (2002). Present and accounted for: Improving student attendance through family and community involvement. *Journal of Educational Research, 95*, 308–318.

Feldman, A. F., & Matjasko, J. L. (2005). The role of school-based extracurricular activities in adolescent development: A comprehensive review and future directions. *Review of Educational Research, 75*, 159–210.

Finn, J. D. (1989). Withdrawing from school. *Review of Educational Research, 59*, 117–142.

Finn, J. D., & Rock, D. A. (1997). Academic success among students at risk for school failure. *Journal of Applied Psychology, 82*, 221–234.

Finn, J. D., & Zimmer, K. (2012). Student engagement: What is it? Why does it matter? In S. L. Christenson, A. L. Reschly, & C. Wylie (Eds.), *Handbook of research on student engagement* (pp. 97–131). New York, NY: Springer.

Fredricks, J. A. (2012). Extracurricular participation and academic outcomes: Testing the over-scheduling hypothesis. *Journal of Youth Adolescence, 41*, 295–306.

Fredricks, J. A., Blumenfeld, P. C., & Paris, A. H. (2004). School engagement: Potential of the concept, state of the evidence. *Review of Educational Research, 74*, 59–109.

Gettinger, M., & Walter, M. J. (2012). Classroom strategies to enhance academic engaged time. In S. L. Christenson, A. L. Reschly, & C. Wylie (Eds.), *Handbook of research on student engagement* (pp. 653–673). New York, NY: Springer.

Gilman, R., Meyers, J., & Perez, L. (2004). Structured extracurricular activities among adolescents: Findings and implications for school psychologists. *Psychology in the Schools, 4*, 31–41.

Goldstein, J. S., Little, S. G., & Akin-Little, K. A. (2003). Absenteeism: A review of the literature and school psychology's role. *California School Psychologist, 8*, 127–139.

Goodenow, C. (1993). Classroom belonging among early adolescent students: Relationship to motivation and achievement. *Journal of Early Adolescence, 13*, 21–43.

Greene, B. A., Miller, R. B., Crowson, H. M., Duke, B. L., & Akey, K. L. (2004). Predicting high school students' cognitive engagement and achievement: Contributions of classroom perceptions and motivation. *Contemporary Educational Psychology, 29*, 464–482.

Guthrie, J. T., Wigfield, A., Barbosa, P., Perencevich, K. C., Taboada, A., Davis, M. H., … Tonks, S. (2004). Increasing reading comprehension and engagement through Concept-Oriented Reading Instruction. *Journal of Educational Psychology, 96*, 403–423.

Harris, K. R., Graham, S., Mason, L. H., & Friedlander, B. (2007). *Powerful writing strategies for all students*. Baltimore, MD: Brookes.

Isakson, K., & Jarvis, P. (1999). The adjustment of adolescents during the transition into high school: A short term longitudinal study. *Journal of Youth and Adolescence, 28*, 1–26.

Langberg, L. M., Epstein, J. N., & Becker, S. P. (2012). Evaluation of the Homework, Organization, and Planning Skills (HOPS) intervention for middle school students with attention deficit hyperactivity disorder as implemented by school mental health providers. *School Psychology Review, 41*, 342–364.

Larson, K. A., & Rumberger, R. W. (1995). ALAS: Achievement for Latinos Through Academic Success. In H. Thornton (Ed.), *Staying in school. A technical report of three dropout prevention projects for junior high school students with learning and emotional disabilities* (pp. A-1–A-71). Minneapolis, MN: University of Minnesota, Institute on Community Integration.

Lauer, P. A., Akiba, M., Wilkerson, S. B., Apthorp, H. S., Snow, D., & Martin-Glenn, M. L. (2006). Out-of-school-time programs: A meta-analysis of effects for at-risk students. *Review of Educational Research, 76*, 275–313.

Lee, V. E., & Smith, J. B. (1999). Social support and achievement for young adolescents in Chicago: The role of school academic press. *American Educational Research Journal, 36*, 907–945.

National Association of School Psychologists. (2010). *Model for comprehensive and integrated school psychological services*. Bethesda, MD: Author. Retrieved from http://www.nasponline.org/standards/2010standards/2_PracticeModel.pdf

National Research Council & the Institute of Medicine. (2004). *Engaging schools: Fostering high school students' motivation to learn.* Washington, DC: National Academies Press.

Newmann, F., Wehlage, G. G., & Lamborn, S. D. (1992). The significance and sources of student engagement. In F. Newmann (Ed.), *Student engagement and achievement in American secondary schools* (pp. 11–39). New York, NY: Teacher College Press.

Oyserman, D., Terry, K., & Bybee, D. (2002). A possible selves intervention to enhance school involvement. *Journal of Adolescence, 25*, 313–326.

Schunk, D. H., & Mullen, C. A. (2012). Self-efficacy as an engaged learner. In S. L. Christenson, A. L. Reschly, & C. Wylie (Eds.), *Handbook of research on student engagement* (pp. 219–235). New York, NY: Springer.

Shernoff, D. J. (2010). Engagement in after-school programs as a predictor of social competence and academic performance. *American Journal of Community Psychology, 45*, 325–337.

Sugai, G., & Simonsen, B. (2012). *Positive behavioral interventions and supports: History, defining features, and misconceptions*. Retrieved from http://www.pbis.org/school/pbis_revisited.aspx

Zimmerman, B. J. (2002). Becoming a self-regulated learner: An overview. *Theory Into Practice, 41*, 64–70.

4

Best Practices in Setting Progress Monitoring Goals for Academic Skill Improvement

Edward S. Shapiro
Kirra B. Guard
Lehigh University (PA)

OVERVIEW

Progress monitoring has become a critically important tool for improving the academic outcomes of all students, including students with disabilities. Consistent with the requirements of laws such as No Child Left Behind and the 2004 Individuals with Disabilities Education Improvement Act, progress monitoring provides direct links between assessment and the instructional process. A large and substantial research literature has emerged showing how progress monitoring can be used across academic areas, including reading, mathematics, composition, spelling, and other academic content areas, to improve student outcomes (e.g., Jenkins & Terjeson, 2011). Among its many uses, progress monitoring can be used to create instructional groups (e.g., Menzies, Mahdavi, & Lewis, 2008), identify specific skill deficits (e.g., Flynn, Hosp, Hosp, & Robbins, 2011), screen students for potential early school failure (e.g., Clemens, Shapiro, & Thoemmes, 2011), assist in eligibility decision making (e.g., Shinn, 2007), and evaluate academic progress for students with intellectual disabilities (e.g., Allor, Mathes, Roberts, Cheatham, & Champlin, 2010). Progress monitoring has value when used across all students; that is, those at risk for academic problems, those already identified as in need of special education, and those in general education.

Within the field of school psychology, the National Association of School Psychologists (NASP) *Model for Comprehensive and Integrated School Psychological Services* (NASP, 2010) defines the roadmap for training and practice. Progress monitoring plays a prominent role in the domain of Interventions and Instructional Support to Develop Academic Skills. Progress monitoring also relates to data-based decision making and accountability. In particular, as data-based problem solvers, school psychologists use data derived through progress monitoring in assisting the instructional decision-making process to maximize student outcomes. Additionally, progress monitoring can play an important role at the universal, targeted, and intensive levels of the delivery system for school psychological services. The NASP Practice Model (NASP, 2010) reinforces that knowledge and skills in progress monitoring continue to be essential to the practice of school psychology.

System-wide approaches for promoting academic success, such as response to intervention (RTI), depend on data-based decision making in order to determine if students are benefiting from the instruction they are receiving. Progress monitoring is considered one of the core components of RTI. For students who are identified as needing additional supports, progress monitoring provides educators with periodic data on student response to targeted interventions. School psychologists can help educators then use this information to determine if these students require some modification to the supports they are receiving (Fuchs & Vaughn, 2012; Gersten et al., 2009).

Progress monitoring has multiple components: establishing and measuring academic goals; providing a vehicle for understanding how students are progressing toward established goals; creating opportunities for class-, school-, and district-wide screening to identify students potentially at risk for academic failure; and offering data that can provide accountability evidence to parents, teachers, and educators about the impact of school-wide curricula and intervention programs. When progress monitoring is done on a frequent basis, it offers students a chance to see how they are moving toward goals and offers a clearer understanding of the impact of the instruction they are receiving (e.g., Lannie & Martens, 2008; Sutherland & Snyder, 2007).

One of the best resources for identifying empirically supported measures for progress monitoring is the set of tool charts for screening and progress monitoring available through the National Center on Response to Intervention (NCRTI; http://www.rti4success.org). The tool charts provide a user-friendly overview of progress-monitoring tools developed by commercial publishers that were evaluated for their technical adequacy and impact on student achievement. Specifically, the NCRTI website offers analysis of measures that have been examined by technical experts and provides consumers with available options for conducting progress monitoring. The tool charts synthesize available research support on a variety of progress monitoring measures in order to assist practitioners in identifying appropriate measures for their schools.

As much as progress monitoring is important to the problem-solving process, concerns have been raised as to the sensitivity of curriculum-based measurement progress monitoring in reading to short-term student growth. In particular, measures demonstrate problems with establishing reliable and valid trends when evaluating student progress or intervention effectiveness over fewer than 20 weeks (Christ, Zopluoglu, Monaghen, & Van Norman, 2013). Indeed, Christ et al. (2013) indicate a need for significant caution when using progress monitoring in making decisions about student progress in reading. Shapiro (2013), in commenting on the Christ et al. (2013) study, noted that the findings suggest a need for extending interventions for periods longer than the typically recommended 6 or 8 weeks. The concerns raised by Christ et al. (2013) are likely to alter the future best practice recommendations typical to current use of progress monitoring measures.

In this chapter, the current best practices in goal-setting processes for use in progress monitoring will be examined. The practices described are those most commonly found in schools today, with acknowledgement that these practices may need to be altered in the future based on the research conducted by Christ et al. (2013). However, until further research can provide evidence of the most effective improvements to progress monitoring applications, the methods described in this chapter represent current school-based practice.

BASIC CONSIDERATIONS

Conceptually, progress monitoring can be divided into two primary methods of assessment: general outcomes measurement and specific subskill mastery measurement (Fuchs & Deno, 1991). General outcomes measures represent standardized, repeated metrics that serve as indices of student progress across curriculum objectives. Among general outcomes measurement models, curriculum-based measurement has been shown to have strong research-supported effects on student performance. Teachers who use curriculum-based measures plan more effective instruction and achieve greater student outcomes than those who do not use curriculum-based measures (e.g., Stecker, Fuchs, & Fuchs, 2005).

Types and Applications of Progress Monitoring

Indeed, when teachers use curriculum-based measurement feedback to inform instructional modifications, outcomes are even higher than when the monitoring process alone is used (e.g., Ball & Gettinger, 2009). Additionally, when curriculum-based measurement data for individual students is aggregated across classrooms, grades, schools, or districts, educators can reliably examine patterns of growth across the academic year. This is an essential step in ensuring students are provided with high-quality instruction and intervention (Ardoin & Christ, 2008). There is no doubt that curriculum-based measurement has become an accepted methodology for conducting the general outcomes measurement form of progress monitoring (e.g., Ball & Christ, 2012).

Case reports and professional descriptions of specific subskill mastery models have been published, but the empirical support for specific subskill mastery models is less sophisticated and less well developed than for general outcomes measurement models. For example, Howell and Nolett (1999) describe a procedure known as curriculum-based evaluation, which is a specific subskill mastery model of progress monitoring. In their model, specific skills of students are evaluated with intervention strategies targeted on the skills found to be deficient. Reassessment of the skills continues across time as the student shows acquisition of the targeted skills. Reports of models using these principles have been described by Burns and his colleagues (e.g., Burns, 2002, 2004; Burns & Helman, 2009; Burns & Kimosh, 2005).

Studies using a specific subskill mastery approach suggest it is a meaningful tool for monitoring student progress. For instance, VanDerHeyden and Burns (2009) utilized single-skill mathematics probes once each week to monitor students' response to specific instruction to develop those individual skills. Results indicated that students who failed to demonstrate criterion performance on single skill probes after intervention continued to struggle to master subsequent math skills at the same rate and with the same proficiency as students who did reach the criterion score. This approach has also demonstrated promise as a progress monitoring measure in reading and with students who are English language learners (Burns & Helman, 2009).

Alternative approaches to curriculum-based measurement and specific subskill mastery measurement have been proposed for progress monitoring. In particular, technological advances have provided for the development of computer adaptive testing, where students answer items using a computer software program. Each item administered to the student during a computer adaptive test is presented based on the student's performance on the previous item. Scores obtained on a computer adaptive test are placed on a single scale that reflects a developmental process across grades from kindergarten to Grade 12. As such, the measure can reflect small changes over time and allow educators to set goals for expected end-of-year performance. In addition, because the measure is based on student ability and is closely linked to curriculum standards, outcomes of computer adaptive testing provide specific information about a student's skill abilities and deficits at each administration. Computer adaptive testing has been shown to be cost-effective compared to other progress monitoring measures (McBride, Ysseldyke, Milone, & Stickney, 2010). These features and emerging evidence make computer adaptive testing a promising new tool for progress monitoring (Ball & Christ, 2012; Shapiro, 2012; Shapiro & Gebhardt, 2012).

Goal Setting as a Core Element of Progress Monitoring

Although the use of progress monitoring is viewed as a critical component of the RTI process, progress monitoring must be used within the context of a problem-solving model to be an effective tool. A key part of a problem-solving process is the setting of goals for expected outcomes that provide the framework within which potential solutions to problems are evaluated.

The first step in goal setting is to select the target for outcomes. Targets identify the expected level of performance to be achieved, assuming success of the implemented intervention strategy. When targets are met or exceeded, professionals can be assured that the intervention has met its established objectives. In cases where the individual has greatly exceeded the target, adjustments of the goal can be made along the way to the outcome. Likewise, when the progress of individuals compared to targets suggests that the intervention is not likely to be successful in reaching the goal, changes in the intervention can be made prior to the point in time when the goals should be accomplished. Clearly, setting goals that are realistic yet challenging is crucial to making the ongoing decisions within a problem-solving model.

Goal setting can be done at both group and individual levels of analysis. At the group level, teams may set goals for the performance of entire grades or schools, looking at data aggregated across individuals to determine if goals have been met following the implementation of selected strategies to address the problem area. For example, in an RTI model, it is expected that the implementation of a high-quality, scientific, research-based instructional program implemented with integrity at Tier 1 should result in successful outcomes for at least 80% of all students (NCRTI, 2012). When universal screening data find substantially fewer students successfully meeting competencies, the implication is that changes are needed in the delivery of the core program, or within Tier 1. These changes are necessary to improve outcomes for all children before we can determine the degree to which supplemental instructional programs at Tier 2 (strategic) and Tier 3 (intensive) are affecting outcomes. As such, problem-solving teams may put goals in place that reflect a focus on improving the collective outcomes of student performance within the core program.

At the individual level, when students are identified through an RTI process as needing more strategic or intensive instruction, it is critical that goals be established at the individual student level. This allows school psychologists to assist educators in measuring student progress toward expected outcomes against appropriate expectations. By setting goals and monitoring a student's progress against those goals, the impact of instruction can be assessed in an ongoing manner, and adjustments in instruction and goals can be made as the instruction is proceeding. Progress monitoring at the level of individual students plays a major role in deciding when a student needs to be moved to a different level of instructional need (from strategic to intensive, from strategic to benchmark). Progress monitoring data also provide input as part of a comprehensive educational evaluation used when school psychologists examine the determination of eligibility for special education services. When services are provided within the context of students already receiving special education services, progress monitoring continues to play a key role in determining the impact of specially designed instruction.

A key element of effective goal setting, whether used at group or individual levels, is the establishment of benchmarks specifying the minimal expected perform-ance across students. Benchmarks indicate the level of student performance that, if achieved, predicts with a high degree of probability that the student will be successful on future assessments of that academic area. Benchmarks are determined empirically by examining the relationship between scores on predictor measures and longitudinal outcomes for students. One of the most well-established benchmarking processes was provided by Good (Good, Simmons, Kame'enui, Kaminski, & Wallin, 2002), who identified scores on the Dynamic Indicators of Basic Early Literacy Skills (DIBELS), which predicted later reading achievement. Specifically, DIBELS benchmarks were set so that approximately 80% of students who achieved them were successful in reading performance at the subsequent grade-level

material. Those considered in the some-risk category had a 50% likelihood of positive outcomes, and those placed in the at-risk category had only a 20% chance of achieving success (Good et al., 2002). Benchmark scores and cut points for risk have been revised for the newest version of DIBELS, DIBELS Next (Good & Kaminski, 2011; Powell-Smith, Good, Latimer, Dewey, & Kaminski, 2011).

For example, Figure 4.1 shows the performance across a group of second-grade students on a measure of oral reading fluency obtained using DIBELS Next at the fall, winter, and spring screenings. As evidenced from the figure, 56% of students were found to be meeting the benchmark goal of 52 words read correctly or more in 1 minute at the fall. When the team of second-grade teachers and the school psychologist examined these data, they recognized the need to enhance and focus aspects of the core second-grade reading program in order to improve the development of skills across all students in their classes. Specifically, a review of additional classroom and district assessments, as well as an analysis of the curriculum, revealed a need to strengthen phonics and vocabulary instruction. These activities were provided within the existing second-grade English language arts instructional block.

As reflected in the data collected at the middle and end of the year on these same students, the collective efforts across teachers were successful, with 71% of students now reaching the benchmark for oral reading fluency (87+ words correct per minute). Additionally, the number of students requiring intensive instructional

Figure 4.1. Outcomes of DIBELS Next Oral Reading Fluency at Fall, Winter, and Spring Benchmarks for Grade 2 Students

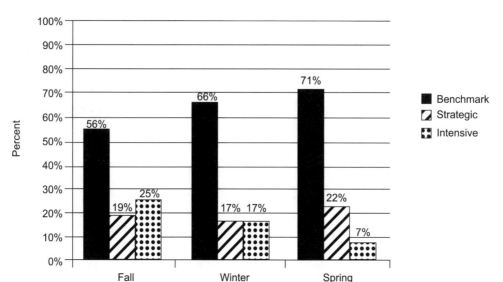

support fell from 25% (fall) to 7% (spring), offering further evidence for the positive impact of the supplemental interventions.

The purpose of this chapter is to provide a methodology and framework for how to select goals for progress monitoring. Effective goal setting requires that school psychologists assist other educators in using decision rules to determine goals that are reasonable yet challenging for students at the individual level or for groups of students. Guidelines for goal setting using decision rules for different goal-setting situations are offered. In their leadership role, school psychologists can provide guidance and direction for using effective, empirically supported decision making. The decision rules suggested here were derived predominately from the experience of the first author's work in the implementation of models of RTI that have been in place for more than 7 years.

BEST PRACTICES IN SETTING PROGRESS MONITORING GOALS

There are two basic conceptual frameworks within which goal setting is done, and these two approaches work together to identify reasonable but challenging expectations for students. In a normative approach, the team uses a comparison group for goal setting. A key to using a normative framework for goal setting is the degree to which the normative group is representative of the specific group or student for whom the goal will be set. Unless the normative group used for comparison shares common characteristics with the targeted group, goals based on the normative group will be problematic. In particular, teams can use either local or national normative groups for the basis of comparison. As can be seen below, the use of local normative groups can pose difficulties in interpretation of outcomes, especially if the local normative context deviates substantially from what is being used as the basis for determining that a student is meeting district- or state-defined levels of proficiency.

For example, Shapiro (2011) provided data from curriculum-based measurement normative data sets collected across three school districts, each representing different levels of socioeconomic status (SES). Although SES should not be used as the sole predictor of academic achievement, there is a substantial literature base suggesting that poverty level can often be used as one of the best predictors of overall academic outcomes (e.g., Ransdell, 2012; Whipple, Evans, Barry, & Maxwell, 2010). For example, Shapiro (2011) found

that a student reading 79 words correctly per minute in spring in the low SES district would be approaching the 75th percentile of the distribution, while this same student reading at the same level in the high SES district would be reading at the 25th percentile. The impact of a team using a local normative comparison for purposes of setting goals could result in substantial underreporting or overreporting of successful outcomes unless the normative group against which the student is being compared is clearly identified. In addition, should students move from district to district, parents, teachers, and students themselves can be greatly surprised by how their performance compares to that of their peers.

An alternative to local normative data as the basis for comparison is to use national normative comparison groups. Data sets that provide norms across large numbers of districts, racially and ethnically diverse students from a range of socioeconomic backgrounds, and geographic regions of the country are publicly available. Hasbrouck and Tindal (2006) have reported aggregated data in reading for more than 20 states and for more than 16,000 students per grade (http://www. readnaturally.com/pdf/oralreadingfluency.pdf). AIMSweb (http://www.aimsweb.com) has provided normative data for measures of reading, math computation, math concepts and applications, writing, spelling, early literacy, and other areas reported across their extensive database. In addition, AIMSweb provides statewide data collection through their subscription service, as well as a district-wide database. Similarly, computer adaptive tests provide national normative databases derived from the large number of computer adaptive test users.

Using national normative samples allows comparisons to be made with the performance levels expected of typical performing students from across the country and equates more closely with data sets that are used in well-developed, published, norm-referenced tests. Employing a combination of local and national norms provides the user of these data with opportunities to evaluate how student performance compares with a national sample of same-grade peers as well as against the local peers within the particular school. Such cross-group comparisons become especially important given the weight placed on the predictability of the curriculum-based measures to potential outcomes on high-stakes achievement tests.

Related to normative models of goal setting is the use of criterion- or competency-based models to establish goals. In this model, targets for student performance are determined based on the attainment of scores that predict successful academic outcomes with high probability. These scores are identified as benchmarks for performance. In particular, student performance on measures of high-stakes, state-developed tests of achievement has become the index against which student outcomes are judged. These tests are used to assess competency based on state-defined curriculum standards. Scores are then assigned to categories on the basis of performance. Although the exact titles may differ somewhat from state to state, students' performance is identified as either advanced, proficient, basic, or below basic.

As they help teams engage in the goal-setting process, school psychologists are often influenced by both normative and competency-based approaches to goal setting. School psychologists need to make sure that educators are pragmatic and use a combination of methods for goal setting. Identification and selection of goals can be based on the expected outcomes for students compared to normative national populations, normative local populations, and competency standards established by the state assessment. Additionally, the development of national Common Core State Standards provides another set of criterion comparisons (see http://www.corestandards.org for more information on the Common Core State Standards Initiative). Considerations also can include benchmarks predictive of success on the high-stakes tests and the expected growth rates for students both locally and against a national normative peer group.

Decision Rules for Selecting Goals at the Group Level

When school psychologists work with a team to look at data aggregated across students within grades, and the team wants to set a goal for the group of students, the team needs to consider several factors. First, if a large number of students are identified as not at benchmark, then the collective objective of the team is to move that group of students toward attaining the benchmark at the next point of universal screening. Such outcomes were illustrated in Figure 4.1.

Second, for students below the benchmark, the team needs to use the expected rate of progress for students performing at benchmark at that grade level as the amount of change they will set as the goal. The rate of improvement, or slope, is a key indicator that sets the criterion against which the group of students under discussion will be compared. Closing the gap for those students whose starting point is below benchmark would be a critical goal for the team to consider. For example,

if students who attain benchmark at the fall and remain at that level at winter and spring improve at a rate of 1.0 words correct per minute per week, then the target rate of improvement for students below that benchmark level would need to be at a rate greater than 1.0 in order for students to catch up to the benchmark level. Interested readers may want to consult the Rate of Improvement website developed by practicing school psychologists for excellent tools and resources related to rate of improvement (http://rateofimprovement.com/roi/).

The process of setting reasonable goals for a group between benchmarking periods is based on logical analysis that is designed to try to close the gap between students identified as at risk for academic failure and their typically achieving peers. The steps involved in this process are described below.

Step 1. Determine the average rate of improvement for typical students at the specific grade level: The average rate of improvement can be obtained in one of two ways. If normative data for the skill area are available, such as those from AIMSweb or from national data sets such as those from Hasbrouck and Tindal (2006), the rate of improvement for students at the percentiles of the distribution that typically define the benchmark levels would be used. In most state assessments, the 40th to 50th percentiles mark the point defined as benchmark or proficient, so using the same point of the distribution is logical for setting the expected rate of growth for students in that grade. In the absence of normative data, we could calculate the rate of improvement for students beginning and ending the year at benchmark using data from measures such as the DIBELS Next. For example, according to the DIBELS Next benchmarks, a second-grade student who begins the year at benchmark in oral reading fluency scoring 52 words correct per minute and ends the year at 87 words correct per minute would achieve a gain of 35 words in 36 weeks of school, or a rate of improvement of 0.97 words correct per minute per week.

Step 2. Multiply the average rate of improvement by a value between 1.5 and 2.0: Given that students below benchmark levels must catch up to their peers, the rate of improvement that must be attained for these students needs to be higher than that expected of typically performing students. As a general guideline for setting challenging goals, Fuchs, Fuchs, Hamlett, Walz, and Germann (1993) and Hosp and Hosp (2003) suggest multiplying the rate of a typically performing student by a value in the range of 1.5 to 2.0. The value obtained would be identified as the range of expected rate of improvement.

Step 3. Determine the number of weeks between benchmark periods (i.e., number of weeks until the next benchmark assessment): Multiply the number of weeks by the expected rate of improvement. This will yield the expected gain for that time frame.

Step 4. Subtract the expected gain from the next benchmark goal: Using benchmark level for the next assessment period, the resulting number would identify the amount of gain that would be likely for students moving at the expected rate of improvement set by the team.

Step 5. Determine the number of students in the some-risk category who are at or above the result of Step 4: Using a set of data listing all students, the team finds the score obtained in Step 4 and identifies the number of students who fall at or above that score. This will provide an indication of the number of students who are likely to move to benchmark levels assuming the expected rate of improvement set by the team and the addition of specific, targeted intervention strategies beyond the core program.

Step 6. Add the number of students found in Step 5 to the number currently scoring in the benchmark (no-risk) group level and divide by the total number of students across all groups: The assumption is that all students currently at benchmark will remain at this level. Adding those students whose progress moves at the expected rate of improvement will increase the benchmark group by this number. Dividing by the total number will yield the anticipated percentage of students meeting the benchmark score. As a result, this percentage can be set as the new goal for the next benchmark assessment period.

This process is best illustrated by example. Looking at Figure 4.2, students who scored at 52 or more words

correct per minute met the beginning-of-the-year benchmark. As can be seen, students who scored between 37 and 51 words correct per minute were classified in the strategic (some-risk) category. As the team looked at these data to select the goal that they wanted to set for the group to achieve by the winter benchmark assessment, the team decided to focus on those students with the most potential to improve their skills and move from some risk to benchmark levels of performance. The team began by finding the expected rate of improvement for second-grade children on the DIBELS Next oral reading fluency measure. Using the benchmarks established by the DIBELS Next, second-grade students should achieve a total of 87 words correct per minute after 36 weeks of school, for an expected rate of improvement of 0.97 words correct per minute per week. Following the steps above, multiplying the rate of improvement by 1.5 and the result by 18 weeks from the start to middle of the school year and subtracting from the winter benchmark of 72 words correct per minute, resulted in a value of 46 words correct per minute.

Examining Figure 4.2, all those students scoring at 46 words correct per minute or better on the measure would be those most likely to improve to the low-risk category by the winter benchmark, assuming that those currently at low risk would remain at low risk. In looking at the data, the team added 4 students who scored at 46 or better (some risk) plus 31 students (low risk) and divided by the total number of students (59), and set the goal for the group at 63% of students meeting benchmark at the next assessment period (winter). The outcomes shown in Figure 4.1, where 66% of students attained benchmark levels of performance by the winter

Figure 4.2. Distribution of Grade 2 Students on DIBELS Next Oral Reading Fluency at Fall

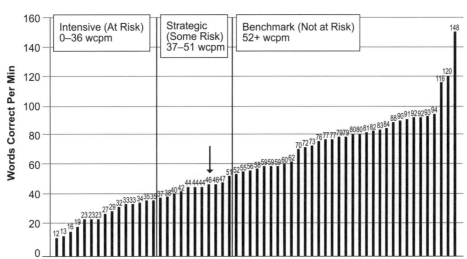

assessment, indicate that the group goal for winter was indeed achieved.

Decision Rules for Selecting Goals at the Individual Student Level

Selecting appropriate goals for individual students begins with identifying the correct level at which a student should be monitored. A student who is functioning below enrolled grade level will demonstrate little progress over time if monitored at levels that significantly exceed his or her instructional level. For students who are performing below enrolled grade level, it makes sense to set targets that show gains within their instructional level. At the same time, students' performance will ultimately be judged against their enrolled grade level on high-stakes measures of achievement, regardless of their functional instructional level. For this reason, comparison of student attainment to both instructional and enrolled grade level is an important part of the decision-making process. Student performance should thus be measured at the student's highest instructional level, with efforts to move that student toward grade level viewed as paramount in the instructional process.

The decision-making process is described in a series of steps that provide clear, practical applications of the goal-setting process.

Step 1. Goal setting when the student is below enrolled grade level: The process of establishing targets and setting goals for students begins with determining the correct level at which a student should be monitored. This is the level at which instruction is most likely to be successful given a student's skill development. Instructional level in reading is determined through a process called survey level assessment. Essentially, a student's performance is examined at a series of grade levels beginning with the student's enrolled grade level until the highest level at which the student's performance falls at least at the 25th percentile is found. Using a set of reading passages that are predetermined to be at specified grade levels, students are administered three randomly selected, 1-minute passages from the pool of passages available for the grade level. Procedures derived from curriculum-based measurement (Shinn & Shinn, 2002) are used to administer and score the passages, using words read correct per minute as the primary metric for determining instructional level. Median scores across the three passages at each grade level represent the score assigned to the student's performance. Using goal charts such as those shown in Figure 4.3, student performance at each grade level can be plotted. The bars of the goal chart shown in Figure 4.3 represent the 25th–75th percentile range on normative data collected across large numbers of typical performing students at each grade level. Specifically, the normative data are derived from

Figure 4.3. Survey-Level Assessment of Milo, a Grade 3 Student Assessed at Grades 3, 2, and 1 Levels

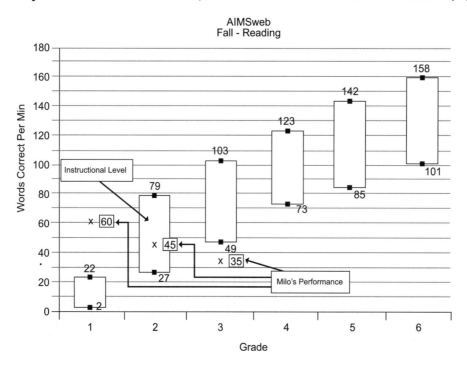

AIMSweb. The normative data shown in Figure 4.3 are similar to data produced by the aggregation of normative data sets as reported by Hasbrouck and Tindal (2006). The process is best illustrated by example. As shown in Figure 4.3, Milo was a third grader who was administered a survey-level assessment in the fall and scored a median performance of 35 words correct per minute on third-grade material, 45 words correct per minute on second-grade material, and 60 words correct per minute on first-grade material. The highest grade at which Milo's performance reached the 25th percentile would be second-grade level, which is deemed the instructional level and the level at which he would be monitored.

Step 2. Set goal for the progress monitoring period: Once the instructional level is determined, the next step is to establish progress monitoring goals for the student. The goal provides targets for expected rates of improvement against which the student's actual level of progress can be measured. As discussed previously, two types of targets can be selected: those based on normative performance of typically performing students or those based on standards that represent benchmarks used as key scores that predict a student's likelihood of successful performance at subsequent levels. Although normative goal-setting methods can be selected for all students, it is more sensible to use normative goal-setting methods when a student's instructional level is found to be below his or her enrolled grade level and to use benchmarks as goal levels when the student is monitored at his or her enrolled grade level.

Typically, students performing at least one or more grade levels below their enrolled grade will need to have their performance accelerated beyond the rate typical for their grade in order to catch up and eventually achieve at their enrolled grade level. Achieving at grade level and meeting benchmarks, especially when using measures of oral reading fluency, are the strongest predictors of success on high-stakes tests (e.g., Goffreda & DiPerna, 2010; Shapiro, Keller, Lutz, Santoro, & Hintze, 2006). Therefore, achieving benchmarks is important. However, students who are starting well below their enrolled grade level will need to have interim goals that move them toward benchmarks in incremental steps rather than setting unrealistic and often unattainable goals that would place the student at frustrational levels of performance.

Normative levels for students' rates of improvement have been established and are available from several sources. One of the most widely used sources is Fuchs et al. (1993), who determined rates of improvement (i.e., slope) for reading, math computation, math concepts, and spelling among typical performing students in two school districts across two consecutive years. Based on their data, expected gains in reading, math computation, and spelling were established, and these rates of improvement have been widely used in setting goals for students. As seen in Figure 4.4, the rates vary across grades, and realistic or ambitious goals can be set. In addition to the data obtained by Fuchs et al. (1993), we may also use the normative data collected and reported by AIMSweb or Hasbrouck and Tindal (2006). Each of these databases offers empirically derived slopes for large numbers of students, obtained by examining the typical changes from beginning to middle to end of the year within and across grades. The slopes for students performing at various percentile ranks within the grades can also be determined, which allows goal setting to be individualized on the basis of the targeted student's percentile rank. Those using computer adaptive testing are also provided with similar rates of expected gains for typically performing students. The values for expected rate of improvement are given in the metric used by the particular product, such as scaled scores (e.g., STAR Reading Assessment, Renaissance Learning, http://www.renlearn.com/default.aspx) or RIT scores (http://www.nwea.org/products-services/computer-based-adaptive-assessments/map).

Using the same example of Milo, the team identifies the expected rate of improvement for a student at the third-grade level based on the Fuchs et al. (1993) data. Based on this information, the team members identify a goal of 1.0 words correct per minute per week as the expected rate of improvement. This would be equivalent to a student at the 50th percentile (mean performance only was reported by the Fuchs et al. data set), who is a typical third grader. However, because Milo is a third grader functioning at the second-grade level, the team might decide to set a more ambitious goal intended to accelerate Milo's progress and move him closer to being successful with third-grade material. As such, an expected rate of growth of 1.5 words correct per minute per week would be selected, the level identified by Fuchs et al. (1993) as an ambitious level of growth (see Figure 4.4).

Using the AIMSweb database, the team would find that the average third grader is found to make progress at approximately 1.1 words correct per minute per week. This is the approximate rate of growth found among typically performing third-grade students at the 25th and 50th percentile ranks. Given that Milo's

Figure 4.4. Goals for Rate of Improvement in Reading and Math Computation Performance

Reading (words correct per min)

Grade	Reasonable	Ambitious
1	2.0	3.0
2	1.5	2.0
3	1.0	1.5
4	0.85	1.1
5	0.50	0.85
6	0.30	0.65

Math Computation (digits correct per min)

Grade	Reasonable	Ambitious
1	0.30	0.50
2	0.30	0.50
3	0.30	0.50
4	0.70	1.15
5	0.75	1.20
6	0.45	1.00

Note. From "Formative Evaluation of Academic Progress: How Much Growth Can We Expect?" by L. S. Fuchs, D. Fuchs, C. L. Hamlett, L. Walz, & G. Germann, 1993, *School Psychology Review*, 22, 27–48. Copyright 1993 by the National Association of School Psychologists. Adapted with permission.

performance in third-grade material was below the 25th percentile, and a typical student at the 50th percentile of third grade would move at approximately 1.0 words per minute per week, we would select the 1.0 rate of growth as the selected, ambitious target for monitoring at the second-grade level.

Regardless which target is selected, the rate of growth is multiplied by the number of weeks across which progress monitoring will be conducted to establish the aimline for the student. Assuming we decide to select the 1.0 words correct per minute per week and that Milo will be monitored for the next 18 weeks until the midyear benchmark, we would expect an increase of 18 words (1.0 × 18 weeks = 18.0 words) over the baseline rate of 45 words correct per week at the midyear benchmark.

An alternative way to select the appropriate target rate for Milo is to try to move him to at least the 50th percentile of the distribution for the midyear benchmark. Looking at Figure 4.5, the 50th percentile would be a score of approximately 75 words correct per minute at midyear. To reach that level, Milo would have to increase a total of 30 words across 18 weeks, or a weekly increase of 1.67 words correct per minute per week. The team would need to decide if such a rate was too challenging for Milo. In Milo's case, the team decided to use a 1.67 words correct per minute per week goal.

Figure 4.6 displays the progress-monitoring graph for Milo for 10 weeks (from the 6th through the 16th week of school). Initial baseline performance on second-grade material of 45 words correct per minute is shown along with the target of 75 words correct per minute for 16 weeks postintervention. The line connecting these two data points represents a growth rate of 1.67 words correct per minute per week. Milo's weekly progress-monitoring data are recorded until the end of the 16 weeks, just prior to the midyear benchmark data collection point. The actual rate of improvement attained by Milo was 2.85 words correct per minute per week, indicating that he had performed at a rate greater than the expected level.

Step 3. Determine if the student is ready to move to a higher level of monitoring: When students have an instructional level below their enrolled grade level, a key objective is to accelerate their progress during the course of the year so that they may be moved to an instructional level closer to grade level. One of the key reasons for getting students as close to grade level as possible is that the demands of high-stakes tests require students to be assessed at their enrolled grade level, regardless of their instructional level. Thus, the closer a student is to functioning at grade level, the higher the probability of successfully demonstrating proficiency on the high-stakes test. In addition, the key question that must ultimately be answered is whether the student is making adequate progress compared to peers at his or her enrolled grade level.

The impact of the instructional intervention in place for Milo resulted in performance that reached between 75 and 83 words correct per minute (across the last three data points) by the midyear point (see Figure 4.6). Examining Figure 4.5, we can see that Milo's performance is now approaching the 50th percentile of second-grade level material. When a student demonstrates growth that reaches or approaches at least the 50th percentile of his or her instructional level, the team determines if the student has acquired the skills that would allow his or her instructional level to be raised. To do so, the team repeats a survey level assessment at the enrolled grade level, in Milo's case the third-grade level, where three randomly selected third-grade

Figure 4.5. Milo's Expected Rate of Improvement From Fall to Winter at the Grade 2 Level

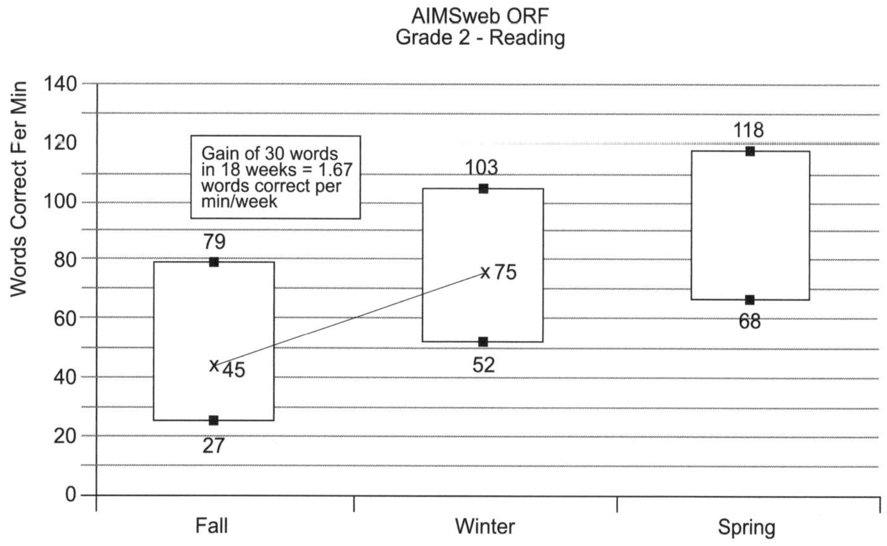

AIMSweb ORF
Grade 2 - Reading

Note. ORF = oral reading fluency.

passages are administered. If the student's performance is at least at the 25th percentile of that grade level, then the student's instructional level is raised, progress monitoring now begins at the higher level, and the goal is reset for the next instructional period. If the student's performance has not reached at least the 25th percentile of the next grade level, then instruction and monitoring continue at the same instructional level (in Milo's case, the second-grade level). If performance maintains or accelerates at the current rate, then the student should be examined again at the next data decision point (usually at least 4–6 more data points) to determine if he or she is ready to move to the higher instructional level.

In Milo's case, when a survey-level assessment was conducted at midyear using passages at the third-grade level, he achieved a median score of 70 words correct per minute, which was just above the 25th percentile (see Figure 4.7). Thus, his instructional level was raised, and a very reasonable goal of 1.1 words correct per minute per week was set as the expected rate of improvement, with a target gain of 20 words over the remaining 18 weeks of the school year. Progress monitoring continues with Milo at the third-grade level for the remainder of the year.

Additional Considerations About Monitoring at Grade Level

When a student is functioning and being monitored below enrolled grade level, whether the student's improvement at the instructional level generalizes to the higher enrolled grade level is of critical importance. Thus, some teams may elect to monitor the student's performance at the enrolled grade level as well as the student's instructional level. It is important to keep in mind that gains over time at levels higher than the instructional level are unlikely to be strong until the student is ready to be instructed at that higher level. For this reason, school psychologists may want to advise teams to periodically assess student performance at levels above instructional level, but frequent assessment at the enrolled grade level is not likely to yield data useful for making instructional recommendations.

Goal Setting When the Student Is at Enrolled Grade Level

When it is determined that progress monitoring will be at the student's enrolled grade level, the process for setting goals is similar to when performance is below enrolled grade level. However, the team uses attainment of benchmark targets as goals, rather than the normative expected rates of growth for grade levels. At the same time, as mentioned previously, it is important to consider the reasonableness of goals derived using normative rates of improvement as the basis for comparison.

Step 1. Determine the correct level at which the student should be monitored: The survey-level assessment described above is conducted and if the student is found to be reading at least at the 25th percentile for his or her enrolled grade, the level for monitoring should be the same as the student's enrolled grade level.

Figure 4.6. Progress Monitoring Graph for Milo

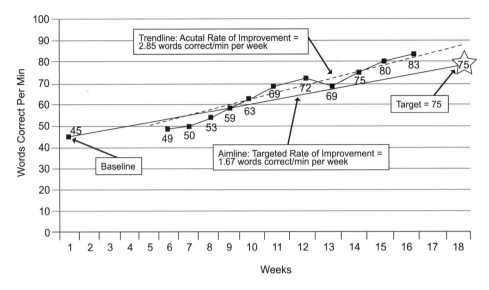

Step 2. Set the goal for progress monitoring period: If a student is performing at grade level, then targets for performance should be set at the lowest level defining the benchmark for the next assessment period. For example, according to the DIBELS Next benchmarks, students at the end of third grade should achieve a minimum score of 100 words correct per minute on oral reading fluency measures to meet the expected benchmark. The goal for a student who scored at 60 words correct per minute at the beginning of the year would be set as 100 words correct per minute to be achieved by the end of the school year. The goal rate of improvement for this student would be set as 40 words correct per minute across 36 weeks (one school year), or 1.11 words correct per minute per week.

To examine the degree to which this level of expected gain would be reasonable, the team could calculate the expected rate of improvement of a typical student in third grade who achieved the benchmark at midyear and maintained his or her performance to the end of the

Figure 4.7. Goal Chart Showing Milo's Expected Rate of Improvement From Middle to End of the Year Against Benchmarks for Grade 3 in Reading

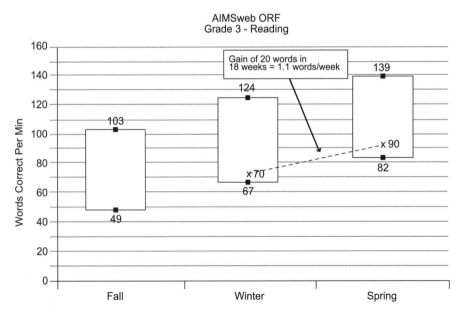

Note. ORF = oral reading fluency.

year. Using the DIBELS Next benchmarks, a typical student would have a goal of improving from a score of 70 words correct per minute in the beginning of the year to 100 words correct per minute at the end of the year, or 0.83 words correct per minute per week.

When comparing the rate of growth set for the targeted student, who was identified as at some risk, with the expected rate of improvement for students achieving at benchmark levels it is evident that the level of accelerated growth set for the target student was reasonable. In other words, we recognize that we need to accelerate rates of growth for students who are at risk beyond the rates expected of typical performers since these students need to catch up to their peers. Of course, we do not want to set rates that are unreasonable and that are unlikely to be achieved despite excellent instruction. As such, moving the target student at a rate of 0.28 words correct per minute per week above the expected rate would likely be viewed as a level that could be accomplished.

Determining whether the target rate of improvement selected for a student is reasonable is partially a subjective decision. Typically, students whose performance is far below the benchmark may need more time with the additional strategic or intensive intervention to make up the gap in their learning rate. Thus, a student found to be at 40 words correct per minute would need to gain 60 words correct per minute or 1.67 words correct per minute to reach the benchmark of 100 by the end of the school year. Considering that a typical student under typical instruction moves at the rate of 0.83 words correct per minute per week, setting a goal for this student that is almost double the rate of typical performers may be viewed as unrealistic and unnecessarily frustrating. School psychologists can directly assist teams by helping teams to understand that the use of normative data (i.e., understanding the rates expected of typical performing students) combined with the knowledge of benchmarks (i.e., the criterion level of performance predictive of success at the next higher level or skill) can be used together to establish reasonable and challenging goal levels for all students as well as groups of students.

Goal Setting for Other Academic Areas

Although the examples provided here are in the area of reading, it is important to note that procedures for applying goal setting to other academic areas are essentially identical. School psychologists play an important role in the problem-solving process by helping school teams to appropriately utilize goal setting across academic subjects, such as reading, mathematics, writing, and spelling. When looking to set goals for progress monitoring in areas other than reading, school psychologists and their fellow team members should identify the level at which the progress of the student or group should be monitored on the measure being utilized, identify appropriate goals using relevant measures, and monitor student progress toward those goals, as outlined here.

As an example, if a student was identified as slightly below benchmark on a measure of math computation, such as the AIMSweb M-COMP measure, the team should identify an appropriate goal using the steps outlined here to increase the student's total points on this measure. Therefore, the difference in the goal-setting process is in the metric being used (total points versus words read correct per minute for a measure of oral reading fluency), and is otherwise identical regardless of the academic area being progress monitored.

SUMMARY

Overall, goal setting plays a critical role in the progress monitoring process and ties together a complex series of decisions that include knowledge of normative levels and benchmarks, and a recognition that students who function below grade level may need more time to achieve grade-level success (see Figure 4.8). When goal setting is combined with the delivery of scientific, research-based interventions, effective use of progress monitoring, and decision rules that are part of a logical model, empirically based outcomes can be determined for students whose performance was initially at risk for academic failure. Goal setting and progress monitoring have been identified as a potential methodology through which decisions could be made to exit students from special education or other remedial services. Additionally, goal setting and progress monitoring are valuable approaches for evaluating instruction and intervention across a group of students (Ball & Christ, 2012). School psychologists play a critical role in assisting teams to fully understand how progress monitoring data play a critical role in data-based decision-making processes.

Despite the strengths of progress monitoring, significant concerns about curriculum-based measurement in reading have been raised (Ardoin, Christ, Morena, Cormier, & Klingbeil, 2013; Christ et al., 2013). In particular, concerns have been raised regarding the technical adequacy of progress monitoring measures, as well as the use of progress monitoring for decision

Figure 4.8. Flow Chart for Goal Setting Using Progress Monitoring

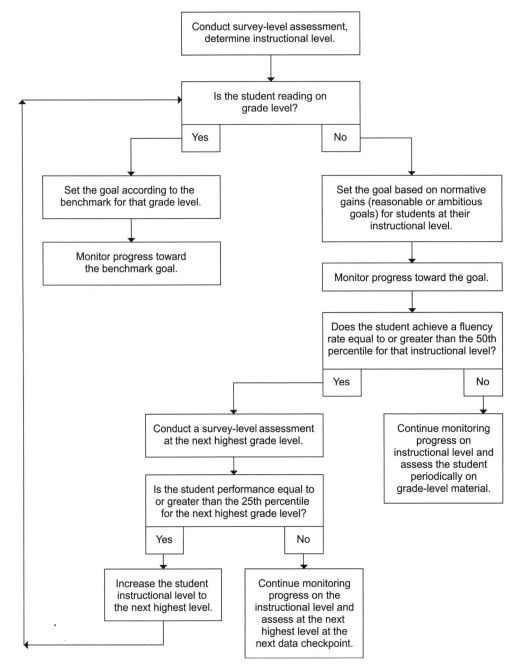

Note. From "Best Practices in Setting Progress-Monitoring Goals for Academic Skill Improvement" (p. 155), by E. S. Shapiro. In A. Thomas and J. Grimes, *Best Practices in School Psychology V*, 2008, Bethesda, MD: National Association of School Psychologists. Copyright 2008 by National Association of School Psychologists. Adapted with permission.

making. These concerns indicate that substantially more research is needed to ensure that progress monitoring has the technical strength for the nature of instructional decisions. At the same time, the use of team-based decision making using progress monitoring data can certainly contribute to the process of improving potential outcomes for students who are not achieving at the levels expected for their grade or age. Ongoing efforts to further elaborate and refine the decision-making process will provide a superb framework for enhancing the problem-solving model being used within an RTI process.

AUTHOR NOTE

Disclosure. Edward S. Shapiro has a financial interest in STAR Assessment and a financial interest in books he authored or coauthored that are referenced in this chapter.

REFERENCES

Allor, J. H., Mathes, P. G., Roberts, J. K., Cheatham, J. P., & Champlin, T. M. (2010). Comprehensive reading instruction for students with intellectual disabilities: Finding from the first three years of a longitudinal study. *Psychology in the Schools, 47,* 445–466. doi:10.1002/pits.20482

Ardoin, S. P., & Christ, T. J. (2009). Curriculum-based measurement of oral reading: Standard errors associated with progress-monitoring outcomes from DIBELS, AIMSweb, and an experimental passage set. *School Psychology Review, 38,* 266–283.

Ardoin, S. P., Christ, T. J., Morena, L. S., Cormier, D. C., & Klingbeil, D. (2013). A systematic review and summarization of the recommendations and research surrounding CBM-R decision rules. *Journal of School Psychology, 51,* 1–18. doi:10.1016/j.jsp.2012.09.004

Ball, C. R., & Christ, T. J. (2012). Supporting valid decision making: Uses and misuses of assessment data within the context of RTI. *Psychology in the Schools, 49,* 231–244. doi:10.1002/pits.21592

Ball, C. R., & Gettinger, M. (2009). Monitoring children's growth in early literacy skills: Effects of feedback on performance and classroom environments. *Education & Treatment of Children, 32,* 189–212. doi:10.1353/etc.0.0055

Burns, M. K. (2002). Comprehensive system of assessment to intervention using curriculum-based assessments. *Intervention in School and Clinic, 38,* 8–13. doi:10.1177/10534512020380010201

Burns, M. K. (2004). Empirical analysis of drill ratio research: Refining the instructional level for drill tasks. *Remedial and Special Education, 25,* 167–173.

Burns, M. K., & Helman, L. A. (2009). Relationship between language skills and acquisition rate of sight words among English language learners. *Literacy Research and Instruction, 48,* 221–232. doi:10.1080/19388070802291547

Burns, M. K., & Kimosh, A. (2005). Implementation guidelines: Using incremental rehearsal to teach sign words to adult students with moderate mental retardation. *Journal of Evidence-Based Practices for Schools, 6,* 148–150.

Christ, T. J., Zopluoglu, C., Monaghen, B. D., & Van Norman, E. R. (2013). Curriculum-based measurement of oral reading: Multi-study evaluation of schedule, duration, and dataset quality on progress monitoring outcomes. *Journal of School Psychology, 51,* 19–57. doi:10.1016/j.jsp.2012.11.001

Clemens, H. H., Shapiro, E. S., & Thoemmes, F. (2011). Improving the efficacy of first grade reading screening: An investigation of word identification fluency with other early literacy indicators. *School Psychology Quarterly, 26,* 231–244.

Flynn, L. J., Hosp, J. L., Hosp, M. K., & Robbins, K. P. (2011). Word recognition error analysis: Comparing isolated word list and oral passage reading. *Assessment for Effective Intervention, 36,* 167–178. doi:10.1177/1534508411398649

Fuchs, L. S., & Deno, S. L. (1991). Paradigmatic distinctions between instructionally relevant measurement models. *Exceptional Children, 57,* 488–500.

Fuchs, L. S., Fuchs, D., Hamlett, C. L., Walz, L., & Germann, G. (1993). Formative evaluation of academic progress: How much growth can we expect? *School Psychology Review, 22,* 27–48.

Fuchs, L. S., & Vaughn, S. (2012). Responsiveness-to-intervention: A decade later. *Journal of Learning Disabilities, 45,* 195–203. doi:10.1177/0022219412442150

Gersten, R., Compton, D., Connor, C. M., Dimino, J., Santoro, L., Linan-Thompson, S., & Tilly, W. D., III. (2009). *Assisting students struggling with reading: Response to intervention (RTI) and multi-tier intervention for reading in the primary grades.* (NCEE 2009-4045). Washington, DC: U.S. Department of Education. Retrieved from http://ies.ed.gov/ncee/wwc/publications/practiceguides/

Goffreda, C. T., & DiPerna, J. C. (2010). An empirical review of psychometric evidence for the Dynamic Indicators of Basic Early Literacy Skills. *School Psychology Review, 39,* 463–483.

Good, R. H., & Kaminski, R. A. (2011). *DIBELS Next assessment manual.* Eugene, OR: Dynamic Measurement Group.

Good, R. H., Simmons, D. S., Kame'enui, E. J., Kaminski, R. A., & Wallin, J. (2002). *Summary of decision rules for intensive, strategic, and benchmark instructional recommendations in kindergarten through third grade* (Technical Report No. 11). Eugene, OR: University of Oregon.

Hasbrouck, J., & Tindal, G. A. (2006). *Oral reading fluency norms: A valuable assessment tool for reading teachers. The Reading Teacher, 59,* 636–644. doi: 10.1598/RT.59.7.3.

Hosp, M. K., & Hosp, J. L. (2003). Curriculum-based measurement for reading, spelling, and math: How to do it and why. *Preventing School Failure, 48,* 10–17.

Howell, K. W., & Nolett, V. (1999). *Curriculum-based evaluation: Teaching and decision making* (2nd ed.). Belmont, CA: Wadsworth.

Jenkins, J., & Terjeson, K. J. (2011). Monitoring reading growth: Goal setting, measurement frequency, and methods of evaluation. *Learning Disabilities Research & Practice, 26,* 28–35. doi:10.1111/j.1540-5826.2010.00322.x

Lannie, A. L., & Martens, B. K. (2008). Targeting performance dimensions in sequence according to the instructional hierarchy: Effects on children's math work within a self-monitoring program. *Journal of Behavioral Education, 17,* 356–375.

McBride, J. R., Ysseldyke, J., Milone, M., & Stickney, E. (2010). Technical adequacy and cost benefit of four measures of early literacy. *Canadian Journal of School Psychology, 25,* 189–204. doi:10.1177/0829573510363796

Menzies, H. M., Mahdavi, J. N., & Lewis, J. L. (2008). Early intervention in reading: From research to practice. *Remedial and Special Education, 29,* 67–77.

National Association of School Psychologists. (2010). *Model for comprehensive and integrated school psychological services.* Bethesda, MD: Author. Retrieved from http://www.nasponline.org/standards/2010standards/2_PracticeModel.pdf

National Center on Response to Intervention. (2012). *RTI implementer series: Module 3: Multi-Level Prevention System: Training manual.* Washington, DC: U.S. Department of Education.

Powell-Smith, K. A., Good, R. H., Latimer, R. J., Dewey, E. N., & Kaminski, R. A. (2011). *DIBELS Next benchmark goals study* (Technical Report No. 11). Eugene, OR: Dynamic Measurement Group.

Ransdell, S. (2012). There's still no free lunch: Poverty as a composite of SES predicts school-level reading comprehension. *American Behavioral Scientist, 56*, 908–925. doi:10.1177/0002764211408878

Shapiro, E. S. (2011). *Academic skills problems: Direct assessment and intervention* (4th ed.). New York, NY: Guilford Press.

Shapiro, E. S. (2012). *New thinking in response to intervention: A comparison of computer-adaptive tests and curriculum-based measurement within RTI.* Wisconsin Rapids, WI: Renaissance Learning.

Shapiro, E. S. (2013). Progress monitoring with CBM-R and decision making: Problems found and looking for solutions (Commentary). *Journal of School Psychology, 51*, 59–66, 10.1016/j.jsp.2012.11.003

Shapiro, E. S., & Gebhardt, S. N. (2012). Comparing computer-adaptive and curriculum-based measurement methods of assessment. *School Psychology Review, 41*, 295–305.

Shapiro, E. S., Keller, M. A., Lutz, J. G., Santoro, L. E., & Hintze, J. M. (2006). Curriculum-based measures and performance on state assessment and standardized tests: Reading and math performance in Pennsylvania. *Journal of Psychoeducational Assessment, 24*, 19–35. doi:10.1177/0734282905285237

Shinn, M. M., & Shinn, M. R. (2002). *AIMSweb training workbook: Administration and scoring of reading curriculum-based measurement (R-CBM) for use in general outcome measurement.* Eden Praire, MN: Edformation.

Shinn, M. R. (2007). Identifying students at risk, monitoring performance, and determining eligibility within response to intervention: Research on educational need and benefit from academic intervention. *School Psychology Review, 36*, 601–617.

Stecker, P. M., Fuchs, L. S., & Fuchs, D. (2005). Using curriculum-based measurement to improve student achievement: Review of the research. *Psychology in the Schools, 42*, 795–819.

Sutherland, K. S., & Snyder, A. (2007). Effects of reciprocal peer tutoring and self-graphing on reading fluency and classroom behavior of middle school students with emotional or behavioral disorders. *Journal of Emotional and Behavioral Disorders, 15*, 103–118.

VanDerHeyden, A. M., & Burns, M. K. (2009). Performance indicators in math: Implications for brief experimental analysis of academic performance. *Journal of Behavioral Education, 18*, 71–91. doi:10.1007/s10864-009-9081-x

Whipple, S. S., Evans, G. W., Barry, R. L., & Maxwell, L. E. (2010). An ecological perspective on cumulative school and neighborhood risk factors related to achievement. *Journal of Applied Developmental Psychology, 31*, 422–427. doi:10.1016/j.appdev.2010.07.002

5

Best Practices in Promoting Study Skills

Robin Codding
Virginia Harvey
John Hite
University of Massachusetts Boston

OVERVIEW

According to the National Association of School Psychologists (NASP) *Model for Comprehensive and Integrated School Psychological Services* (NASP, 2010), the domain of Interventions and Instructional Support to Develop Academic Skills is one of two central aspects of direct and indirect service delivery that school psychologists provide. Academic competence is a multifaceted construct composed of (a) basic (e.g., reading, mathematics) and complex (e.g., critical thinking) skills as well as (b) enablers (e.g., interpersonal skills, motivation, engagement, study skills; DiPerna, 2006). Academic enablers are defined as student behaviors and attitudes that permit active participation in learning. Research has established the important connection between academic skills and enablers such that students at risk for school failure display fewer academic enablers than students with average or above-average achievement (Cleary, 2009). Therefore, if students possess the adequate academic skills but continue to struggle in school, academic enablers should be evaluated by school psychologists and subsequently addressed through interventions applied within a multitiered system of service delivery.

Preliminary evidence has suggested that the best predictor of student achievement after accounting for current achievement is student motivation followed by engagement for younger elementary-age children or study skills for later elementary, middle, and high school students (DiPerna, 2006). Research has also suggested that good study skills provide a protective effect against student participation in violence, whereas poor study skills constitute a risk factor, particularly during the middle school years (Henry, Tolan, Gorman-Smith, & Schoeny, 2012). Study skills are broadly conceptualized as a component of self-regulated learning and represent the application of strategies and tactics to learning while simultaneously managing time and resources efficiently (Richardson, Robnolt, & Rhodes, 2010). Therefore, study skills include the specific strategies that permit students to acquire, organize, remember, and use information as well as self-evaluation of the efficacy of those strategies.

School psychologists report study skills among the top four referral problems encountered in both elementary and secondary schools with greater frequency occurring during the middle and high school years (Cleary, 2009). However, few school psychologists are familiar with commercially available tools that directly address study skills or study skill strategies (Cleary, Gubi, & Prescott, 2010). The purpose of this chapter is to describe the importance of and place for study skill assessment and intervention by school psychologists within a multitiered system of service delivery. Core study strategies and their application will be described.

BASIC CONSIDERATIONS

Improving study skills can make substantial differences in students' achievement. Students with effective study habits plan and control their learning, think and inquire about the subjects they are learning, and reflect and self-evaluate their learning. They employ motivational, emotional, and behavioral self-regulation strategies; apply effective cognitive skills such as organizational and memory tools; and use metacognition strategies such as planning and monitoring (McCormick, Dimmitt, & Sullivan, 2013). Studying is an intentional skill, mastery over which requires motivation, effort, training, and practice (Gettinger & Seibert, 2002) along with self-regulation, which governs student planning, monitoring, and evaluation of the study strategies used (Richardson et al., 2010).

Study skills have been described as an essential element of student commitment to and engagement with school. Study skills, along with socioeconomic status, parental involvement with school, academic goals, and student–teacher interactions, were found to explain a considerable portion of academic performance, with higher values of each associated with better outcomes (Moreira, Dias, Vaz, & Vaz, 2013).

These data suggest that both home and school environments can facilitate school engagement and use of study practices. It is known that the presence of resources for studying, along with parental encouragement and expectations, are predictive of a child's academic goal setting (Moreira et al., 2013). Teacher leadership, support, understanding, and mastery learning orientation (i.e., promoting autonomy and interest) have also been associated with establishing a positive environment for student achievement. Effective study strategy development begins with social modeling (i.e., parents, teachers, peers) and gradually shifts to self-management (Schunk & Usher, 2011).

At the student level, research suggests a bidirectional relationship between academic goals and study skills. It may be that (a) use of effective study strategies results in good outcomes and consequently leads to higher student motivation and the experience of greater control over the school experience or (b) having learning goals facilitates the motivation to develop effective study strategies (Moreira et al., 2013). Those students who engage in goal setting, self-monitoring, and self-reflection achieve greater academic success (Schunk & Usher, 2011). Conversely, those students who do not exhibit these behaviors display poor organization and time management skills, inconsistent work completion and accuracy, school avoidance, and overall poorer academic outcomes (Cleary, 2009).

School success also requires that students possess appropriate attitudes and beliefs about learning (Richardson et al., 2010) including self-efficacy, task interest or value, and outcome expectations (Zimmerman, 2011). Self-efficacy refers to students' perceived learning skills or performance capabilities, and it is postulated to have an impact on persistence,

effort, and choice (Schunk & Usher, 2011). Task interest or value suggests that when a student understands the utility of the study activity he or she will be more likely to engage in the task, even if self-efficacy is low. Outcome expectations refer to student anticipation of the consequences to his or her actions. For example, students might be more likely to engage in effective study practices if they believe it will result in high test scores.

Although expectations for autonomous study skills increase as students progress through school, instruction in study skills and self-regulatory strategies are effective in addressing academic issues in the areas of reading, writing, and math regardless of age, grade, educational placement, and intervention length (Perry, Albeg, & Tung, 2012). Often instruction in study skills is neglected because it is assumed that students have mastered these skills at an earlier grade level, can learn these skills on their own, and are able to generalize strategies across academic disciplines independently.

Unfortunately, these assumptions are often unfounded. Research has consistently illustrated a gap between knowledge and use of effective study strategies. Although both successful and unsuccessful students rate good study skill strategies as more effective than poor strategies, only successful students report systematically using effective study strategies and *not* using ineffective strategies (Meneghetti, De Beni, & Cornoldi, 2007). These data support the necessity of teaching students to use effective strategies consistently and to evaluate the utility of study strategies through self-reflection (Zimmerman, 2011).

Effective study strategies are often elaborate and complex, which subsequently results in deeper information processing (Richardson et al., 2010). For example, strategies such as self-testing, checking comprehension while reading, and rereading misunderstood text as well as rephrasing text into one's own words appear to differentiate students with good study skills from those with poor skills (Meneghetti et al., 2007). Those with poor study skills are more likely to skip misunderstood text, repeat information literally, and study with background TV or music. Students with effective study habits also use various techniques and change their strategies as appropriate. All students need to know a variety of learning methods, as well as methods to monitor their own learning success, so that they can determine whether the employed strategies are working or need modification (Richardson et al., 2010). Furthermore, appropriate strategies vary according to students' learning styles, personal habits, the subject area, and teachers' approaches. Even excellent students are unlikely to use every type of study skill (Meneghetti et al., 2007).

Fortunately, study skills are quite teachable. Instruction in study skills can be provided at every system level. School psychologists can help determine which learning principles are being neglected and then help students and teachers learn and adopt a variety of strategies to address areas of deficiency. Study skills can and should be taught universally to the entire student population as a preventive measure (Gettinger & Seibert, 2002). Study skills can also be taught as secondary or tertiary interventions to students when they do not employ the age-appropriate study and self-regulation strategies necessary to be academically successful.

Targeted interventions to improve deficient study skills can take place in small groups, and such efforts can successfully prevent the need for further assessment and restrictive placement. Students who are in need of intensive specialized education programs also benefit from study skills instruction. School psychologists can be involved in improving study skills (a) indirectly, when they serve as consultants to general or special education teachers, or (b) directly, when they work with students individually or in small groups to address areas of need (Harvey & Chickie-Wolfe, 2007).

BEST PRACTICES IN PROMOTING STUDY SKILLS

Best practice in promoting study skills includes school psychologists collaborating with general educators to teach study skills in conjunction with the established curriculum, as study skills taught in isolation are unlikely to be maintained or transferred from one setting to another. Because most studying and homework completion occurs at home, effective practice by school psychologists requires skillful collaboration with parents. Furthermore, since studying requires self-regulation, it is particularly important to include the student as a team member. Thus, effective work in this area requires that school psychologists, teachers, parents, and students work closely to determine appropriate procedures, designate responsibilities, monitor intervention success, and foster generalization.

The most important consideration for school psychologists working to improve study skills is to help students incorporate fundamental principles of effective learning into their studying regimen. Efficient learning requires (a) focusing on important information, (b) tying new information to previously learned material, (c) spacing and repeating trials, (d) incorporating corrective feedback, (e) monitoring learning, and (f) taking steps to modify learning strategies as needed. There are multiple study strategies available for incorporating each of these principles. For example, focusing on important information might be accomplished by outlining, mapping constructs, writing test questions, or previewing. Incorporating corrective feedback can be accomplished by reviewing corrected papers, interactive video learning, or using the writing process.

Study Skill Strategies

Study skills require that students engage in complex reading and thinking activities, which are facilitated through several essential elements: (a) organization of the study activity; (b) acquisition of knowledge from text, lectures, and teachers; (c) comprehension and engagement in effective test-taking strategies; (d) use of self-management strategies; and (e) assessment of motivation and affect (Richardson et al., 2010).

First, organization of study activities can be supported in both home and school in a variety of ways. Second, acquisition of knowledge requires that students have skills to employ the following behaviors: comprehend directions, take notes, preview texts, as well as understanding reading material and monitoring comprehension. Third, a variety of strategies can support adequate test preparation and test taking. Fourth, students need to use a variety of self-regulation or self-management strategies to plan for, monitor, and evaluate their studying behavior. Fifth, motivation and affect associated with studying behaviors should also be attended to given the impact of both on subsequent engagement in studying.

Organization
Organizing study sessions or assignment completion requires planning and forethought. School psychologists can help students organize materials within school and facilitate implementation of home–school collaborative interventions and consultation to ensure the necessary home support is provided.

Within the school, assignment books, calendars, folder systems, and desk organization can all support the opportunity for effective studying. Assignment books or sheets and calendars should be required of all students who are expected to complete work independently. If a student has considerable difficulty writing down assignments, even with monitoring by the teacher, then a peer can be seated next to the student to make sure assignments are recorded. Increasingly, schools are posting assignments on Internet websites, which can be helpful. However, the posts do not negate the need for students to plan their own studying. Students need specific guidance in learning how to break long-term assignments into small components and integrate the components into their assignment books. The use of a calendar becomes critical for older students who have multiple long-term assignments and multiple teachers.

Some students use folders for each subject or for homework. Others use loose-leaf notebooks organized by subject. Loose-leaf notebooks are efficient because handouts and notes from the textbook can be added in chronological order, but to be effective these notebooks must be organized. For example, students must place papers and assignments in the notebook or folder at the end of each class so the papers or assignments do not become misplaced throughout the day.

School psychologists can suggest that times be designated for school-wide or class-wide cleaning and organization of both desks and notebooks. Students with severe organizational problems will need an adult or a peer to help sort their papers. Unscheduled and scheduled checks, with rewards for good organization, are helpful. For students who become disorganized between classroom organization sessions, an individualized cleaning routine should be established, with neatness criteria, time line, and reinforcements specified.

At home, space for studying and parental support are important. To be successful students need to have resources and other materials at home as well as bring those required supplies from school. Home–school collaboration is imperative and school psychologists are essential for facilitating communication such that teachers confer with parents about problems with studying and parents are available to help with studying and organization. Parents should let teachers know when excessive time is being spent on studying so assignments can be modified. Study strategies must be appropriately monitored, and parents and teachers must collaborate to deliberately foster students' self-regulatory behaviors (Zimmerman, 2011).

School psychologists can ensure that systems such as use of checklists posted in lockers or verbal prompts from adults are established to remind students to check that all necessary study materials have been collected before dismissal. School psychologists can assess whether home support is provided for studying, communicate to parents that students of all ages need familial encour-

agement regarding academic goals and success, and establish a home–school intervention plan to facilitate needed home organization. Simple behavior management systems (e.g., school–home notes and behavior contracts) can be established to encourage bringing materials home. Early on, children need help from their parents in prioritizing activities, establishing consistent routines, and organizing materials for return to school. Generally, students need less supervision as they get older, and by junior high they often make and keep their own study schedule. Some adolescents, particularly students with learning disabilities, will continue to need considerable parental involvement.

School psychologists might assist parents and their children with establishing a routine study hour. This can be challenging in busy households, as it must take into account already scheduled extracurricular activities, chores, favorite TV shows, computer games, and recreational use of the Internet. Ideally, the family agrees upon a study hour during which the TV and other distractions are removed, and the entire family studies, reads, or completes paperwork. In determining the study time, the child's ability to concentrate at different times of the day should be considered. Some children can focus better in the early morning, others after supper, and others right after school. Many elementary school children are too tired after dinner to be able to concentrate efficiently, as demonstrated by their being easily frustrated and slow to complete tasks. Establishing a study location is also important, ideally an environment devoid of distractions. Some students find working in their own room difficult because they are tempted by distractions or they are lonely. These students may study better at the kitchen table while other students may work best at the public library.

When studying at home is not possible or parents are unable to provide sufficient support, the school psychologist can help develop alternative locations and supports. For example, many schools and community organizations such as Boys and Girls Clubs have after-school programs for elementary school students that include supervised study periods. Most high schools have advisories and supportive study halls during the school day as well as offer after-school help.

Comprehending Directions

Adults tend to assume that students understand verbal directions, yet students frequently do not understand what is said to them. Comprehension of directions can be checked by having students tell adults, in their own words, what needs to be done. It is helpful for younger students to write (or circle, if the directions are written) each action word, number each action, and cross off each number after completion (Kuepper, 1990). If students can understand directions, yet still do not follow them, they may not be attending to the directions or they may be choosing to disregard them. The former can be remedied by having the student read the directions subvocally before starting an assignment. Choosing to disregard directions needs to be further explored in a student interview to determine the function of noncompliance. If this appears to be an area of weakness despite universal instruction along with other signs of a potential language processing problem, then a speech and language evaluation can illuminate areas of concern and identify a potential language processing disability.

Note Taking

Students who use note taking while listening to lectures have deeper encoding, recall more information from class, and increase understanding of lesson content (Boyle & Rivera, 2012). Therefore, school psychologists should support and assess students' abilities in effective note taking, and provide supervised practice as appropriate. Notes should be orderly, labeled, and legible; written in the student's own words; and contain all key words and some supporting details. With success, the amount of material contained in the outlines can be faded to promote independence.

Guided notes and strategic note taking are two techniques that have been particularly effective (medium to large effect sizes) for improving tests and quizzes as well as increasing the quantity, accuracy, and details of recorded notes for students with all forms of disabilities (Boyle & Rivera, 2012). Guided notes are preprepared outlines of lectures with missing material; that is, typically one to eight words are missing from a given section. As the lecture proceeds, students fill in the missing portions of the outline, the format of which often reflects a traditional outline with Roman numerals and uppercase letters.

Strategic note taking provides cognitive prompts and cues to students during lectures such as (a) record three to six main points, (b) record new vocabulary words, and (c) briefly summarize lecture points linking ideas together. Note-taking paper can be developed to include these prompts or students can be taught the CUES (cluster main ideas together, use teacher cues to record key lecture points, enter vocabulary words into notes, summarize) strategy to facilitate the appropriate steps. Before the lecture students are encouraged to summar-ize previous knowledge of the topic, and after the lecture students write five key points and corresponding details (Boyle & Rivera, 2012).

Students, including those with learning disabilities, learn and study more efficiently when using laptop computers for note taking (Richardson et al., 2010). It is beneficial for students to add details to class notes as soon as possible after each lecture. This practice provides another learning trial, facilitates the ability to remember and correct details, and improves achievement. Students can also mark a review tally each time they review their notes, which encourages spacing their reviewing over time and thereby increasing academic achievement. School psychologists in collaboration with teachers can also support this practice class-wide by randomly selecting outlines to check for accuracy.

Previewing

Previewing takes very little time but is one of the most important techniques for understanding reading material, particularly at the secondary level when the majority of instruction is centered on textbooks (Garber-Miller, 2007). Nonfiction is preread by reviewing nontext cues (title, author, publication date, headings and subheadings, pictures, graphs, charts); reading the introduction, preface, and conclusion; and skimming the body. Fiction is preread by reading the front cover, back cover, and introduction, and skimming the first chapter to determine setting, character, and plot.

A number of creative techniques can be used to encourage active engagement with the structural and content analysis of texts and other classroom materials, each of which might be best matched with universal classroom practices but could be adapted for Tiers 2 and 3. For example, classrooms could be divided in half with one group acting as the textbook salesperson and the other as the potential purchasing teachers. Small groups could be used to assign students to (a) review specific chapters, identifying new content and what might have been previously learned; (b) provide brief overview and visual representation of each unit to be covered; and (c) identify key textbook features. Game formats such as generating scavenger hunts or awarding points to teams for locating and describing textbook features might also be considered (Garber-Miller, 2007).

Reading Comprehension

Teaching students reading comprehension strategies is an effective intervention for facilitating deep text elaboration, particularly when self-regulatory strategies are employed. Critical elements that cut across all successful techniques are that students are taught to (a) attend more carefully and (b) think more systematically as they read (Richardson et al., 2010).

Several methods assess a student's ability to comprehend assigned readings. First, it is useful to have the student orally review the textbook, explaining the pictures, graphs, and general material. Second, the school psychologists should ask the student to read aloud a passage and answer questions regarding the text, making note of both word-calling and question-answering accuracy. The student should be able to read with 90% word-calling accuracy and maintain at least 75% accuracy in answering comprehension questions. If the material is difficult enough that the student cannot read with that level of accuracy, then additional instructional support is needed. Third, devise a cloze test. This is done by photocopying approximately 300 running words from the text. The first sentence is left complete, blanking out every fifth word until there are 50 blanks, and leaving a complete sentence at the end. The student then reads the passage, guessing the missing words, and should be able to guess at least 60% of those missing words. In the maze technique, the student is provided with several words from which to choose the correct answer for each blank (Williams, Ari, & Santamaria, 2011).

A number of self-regulatory strategies enhance reading comprehension, including questioning while reading; activating background knowledge to enhance comprehension; taking notes; highlighting, outlining, illustrating, and identifying the spatial or semantic organization of text; predicting outcomes; identifying main ideas and supporting statements; analyzing text structure; questioning; rapid reviewing; imaging; and thinking of examples.

Comprehension is also enhanced when students check for "clicks" (understanding) and "clunks" (nonunderstanding) at the end of each page. When nonunderstanding occurs, students should take remedial steps such as slowing down, rereading, looking up material, reading about the same topic in an easier source, asking for help, or making a visual map.

An effective comprehension strategy requires that students survey (look over the material before beginning to read to obtain a general framework, paying particular attention to the title, chapter headings and subheadings, charts and pictures, the introductory paragraphs, and the conclusion), question (before beginning to read students write down questions that reflect curiosity

about the topic or that convert headings and subheadings into questions), read (read through the material in the normal way and add unknown words to a list), and write (write answers to the previously generated questions and summarize the material in writing).

Summarizing text in the students' own words significantly increases the comprehension of written material (Westby, Lawrence, & Hall-Kenyon, 2010). Effective summarizing requires identifying and rewording both the main ideas and supporting information for each paragraph.

Reading comprehension can also be increased by generating graphic organizers; that is, developing a visual image that summarizes material. Some examples are time lines for history material, genograms or sociograms that depict relationships among characters in a novel, and a map in which the student places the main topic in the middle of a blank sheet of paper, branches subheadings from the main topic, and supporting details branch from the subheadings.

Finally, students can use computers in various ways to increase their reading comprehension (Kitsantas & Dabbagh, 2010). They can employ computer-assisted instruction materials developed by textbook authors and publishers or word-processing programs with functions for outlining and summarizing material. Students might also employ a word-processing program to take notes from reading material and manipulate the information to create hierarchical structures, inserting additional information from other sources such as class notes, deleting nonessential information, and reorganizing the material (Richardson et al., 2010). Students might use integrated software that facilitates moving from one source (file or program) to another and thereby view information from multiple perspectives. For example, some computer-based mapping programs are able to convert outlines into graphics and vice versa, enabling students to synthesize concepts and information.

Test Preparation and Test Taking

Test preparation strategies such as use of study guides or graphic organizers and mnemonics produce large effect sizes (Scruggs, Mastropieri, Berkeley, & Graetz, 2010). Teacher-provided study guides are most effective when incomplete so students can be actively engaged by adding their own elaborating information. Teachers can provide incomplete notes, have students complete them, and then check completed notes for accuracy. Another effective approach is to instruct students how to develop their own study guides. For example, students can be taught to employ graphic organizers that group the information they need to learn into meaningful units and can serve as a powerful study aid, contributing to students both acquiring and embedding content into memory (Dexter, Park, & Hughes, 2011).

One type of graphic organizer, Semantic Mapping and Semantic Feature Analysis, enables students to illustrate relationships between concepts and related ideas and thereby helps them connect information. This method has been shown to have powerful effects on immediate learning. Syntactic/Semantic Feature Analysis, a graphic organizer that focuses on comparing characteristics of main ideas, has been shown to be effective in helping students maintaining knowledge (Dexter et al., 2011). Semantic Mapping and Analysis can be used across content areas and can also be adapted to target specific instructional goals for individual students to effectively enhance understanding and retrieval of knowledge (see examples at http://www.prepit.org/reading/semanticWebsMaps.html).

Memory-enhancing strategies include calling up vivid emotions and humor, rehearsing and repeating, sandwiching new information within known information, and sorting information into categories. In addition, making hierarchies and organizational charts; using associative strategies such as a story, cues, acrostics, or peg words; using visual imagery; summarizing in own words; relating new to previously learned information; using graphic organizers; or reviewing notes can be helpful (Harvey & Chickie-Wolfe, 2007).

Studying with corrected tests and assignments as well as predicting possible test questions are well-established effective strategies (Meneghetti et al., 2007). Students should review tests and assignments that the teacher has corrected and returned until they (a) understand the provided feedback; (b) consider the results in the context of all learning; and (c) determine what worked well, what did not work well, and what should be changed. School psychologists can also teach and/or encourage students to develop and answer multiple choice, short answer, and essay questions while studying.

An essential element of studying pertains to the number of study sessions and the proximity of study sessions to actual test taking. Research has demonstrated that spaced practice results in more efficient learning than massed practice (cramming). Although many students find it difficult not to procrastinate, studying for a test should be spread over several days and divided into multiple small units (Son, 2004).

Test-taking techniques are also essential for student success, such as coming to the exam with everything needed; carefully listening to directions and asking for clarification; reviewing written directions carefully, including any sample items; jotting down memorized information as soon as possible; skimming through the entire test to determine the test's scope; setting up and keeping a schedule; reading each question carefully (on essays, responding precisely to words such as *discuss, describe, illustrate, explain, evaluate*; on multiple choice, being wary of words such as *always, never, everyone*); outlining the important points to be covered before responding to an essay question; attempting to answer every question; spending the most time on questions that carry the most points; keeping track of time; checking for the correct number on answer sheets; answering known questions first; immediately eliminating incorrect multiple choice answers; rereading essay questions and answers to check for completeness; writing neatly; and rechecking work before submitting it. School psychologists can refer students to resources, such as Test Taking Tips found at http://www.testtakingtips.com.

Self-Management

Self-management is an integrated aspect of using effective study strategies and consists of a number of elements including goal setting, self-monitoring, self-instruction, and self-reflection. Often a behavior management system to increase self-regulation is necessary to facilitate study skill use. Goal setting refers to student- or teacher-directed targets that help structure student effort, provide information on progress, and motivate students to persist until goals are achieved (Schunk & Usher, 2011). Students can be instructed to articulate learning goals according to their current level of knowledge and be taught to adjust those goals. Timing a student completing a worksheet or reading assignment can produce helpful planning guidelines from which goals and checkpoints can be determined. Goal setting is often one aspect of a treatment package but can also be instituted class-wide.

Self-monitoring is a commonly used intervention strategy for students at risk for and with disabilities (e.g., Perry et al., 2012) and requires students to observe and record their own behavior. In order to effectively engage in this procedure, the student must be able to discriminate whether the target behavior occurred or did not occur. Self-monitoring strategies are encouraged to assist students with attending to tasks, prevent impulsive responding, and temper frustration and can take the form of cue cards, prompt sheets, or self-recording cards. Students could record their attention to the task (e.g., "I copied the problem correctly"; "I worked slowly and followed the steps"), their productivity (number of problems completed), and/or their accuracy (number of correct problems completed).

Self-instruction or self-questioning is when students use self-statements to direct behavior and is often incorporated into checklists or heuristics that in turn serve as prompts, cues, and/or reminders. In mathematics, checklists are often used to generate sequential steps required to solve problems such as multiplying fractions in an orderly method (Montague, 2007). Heuristics work similarly; for example, Say, Ask, Check, reminds students to read the problem, ask themselves questions about the process of reading a problem, and check their work for each step. Students can develop study strategy portfolios (Harvey & Chickie-Wolfe, 2007), where they outline and commit to a study plan (noting where, when, and with which strategies they will study) and examine their study strategies by asking themselves questions such as: How do I know when I have studied enough? How do I keep myself motivated? How many hours do I plan to study and do I follow my plan? How prepared do I feel? What grade did I expect to get, and how does that compare with the grade I received? What strategies were most and least successful? Given all this information, how might I change my study plan in the future?

Zimmerman (2011) describes self-reflection as constituting self-evaluation and self-reactions. Self-evaluation refers to a process within which a student compares his or her performance to an established criterion set by a tutor, coach, mentor, teacher, or the student and is often provided reinforcement contingent on meeting the criterion. Self-reactions include self-satisfaction and adaptive inferences. Adaptive inferences are conclusions that a strategy employed for learning or studying should be altered in future applications.

Motivation and Affect

Some students will need to be led through successful experiences to help them understand that the effort expended relates to the outcome experienced and that success in school is not simply an effect of innate ability or luck (Zimmerman, 2011). Students need to understand the purpose of learning material, including why the teacher assigned the material, how the assignment relates to the students' learning goals, and how the information will be useful in the students' lives. Students often need help bridging information they are learning in math, science, and social studies to their lives. School psychologists can facilitate these discussions with students to bridge this gap through small groups or individual supports.

Research indicates that students often do not know how to apply study strategies to particular classes, feel use of study strategies would take too much time, and have difficulty integrating new strategies into routine study habits. Thus, study skills should be related to particular courses and monitored, associated with positive and responsive teacher–student relationships, and incorporated into students' goals (Richardson et al., 2010).

Study preferences can help develop consistent schedules. Some students prefer to address less-preferred work first while others prefer to complete easier work first. Students can be taught to use strategies such as setting a small goal and/or taking a break to reduce frustration with nonpreferred tasks. In addition, whatever students dislike about the way they handle studying can be subjected to a brainstorming session, and one of the solutions brainstormed can be chosen, tried, and evaluated. For example, a student may procrastinate and decide to try self-rewarding after completing an assignment. Students often need help understanding that emotions such as boredom, frustration, and anxiety while studying are normal and can be appropriately addressed.

While a moderate amount of anxiety benefits academic performance, excessive anxiety can result in poor performance (Gregor, 2005). Test anxiety affects one third to one half of intermediate-level students and is often identified by students during individual interviews, in written self-analyses, or on self-report scales. Sometimes excessive anxiety is made evident because a student performs poorly on actual tests after having performed significantly better on practice tests and other assignments. Both direct and indirect interventions can effectively reduce anxiety and improve test performance. Direct interventions include relaxation or slow breathing exercises, cognitive–behavioral therapy, exercise, meditation, yoga, or medication. Indirect interventions include instruction in study skills (Harvey & Chickie-Wolfe, 2007).

Assessment of Study Skill Needs

Comprehensive evaluation of study skills is needed, particularly at the secondary and tertiary levels of service delivery in order to appropriately match treatments to students' needs. Self-report measures that specify study skill strategy use or self-regulation along with informal interviews with teachers, parents, and students, and direct classroom observations is recommended (Cleary, 2009). Researchers have also suggested that none of these methods are sufficient to capture students' self-regulatory skills and recommend also using think-aloud protocols (i.e., assessment of students' verbalization of thoughts during task completion) and structured diaries (i.e., assessment of motivation, interest, and self-efficacy using a series of questions pertaining to student study sessions; Zimmerman, 2011).

Recommendations for school psychologists evaluating study skill problems are (a) observe student's behavior and academic performance, and compare the results with classmates' performance; (b) observe the classroom climate and compare it with the checklist presented in Table 5.1; (c) conduct a student interview selectively using the questions presented in Table 5.2; (d) observe a student completing an academic work session in a one-to-one setting, during which the student describes his or her work methods, describes how he or she studies, and shows textbooks, notebooks, and assignment books; (e) analyze classroom-completed and homework samples; (f) conduct parent and teacher interviews, using selected questions; and (g) employ formal inventories of learning/self-regulations strategies (Table 5.3).

With respect to test-taking strategies, school psychologists might also consider the related issue of test-taking accommodations. Many students who qualify for special education or 504 plans are provided with accommodations designed to support success during test taking. Unless carefully selected, research has repeatedly indicated mixed results on the benefits of accommodations (e.g., extended time) during test taking (Cormier, Altman, Shyyan, & Thurlow, 2010). The Dynamic Assessment of Test Accommodations is a data-based approach to accommodation selection (see Table 5.3). Its use can reduce the risk of well-intentioned accommodations failing to support successful test taking.

Application to Multitiered Systems

A positive learning environment provides students with challenging yet manageable assignments; clear directions, expectations, and standards; frequent verbal support and constructive written feedback; and regular, publicly acknowledged success. The teacher promotes students helping, sharing, cooperating, and collaboratively solving problems, and establishes an atmosphere of acceptance where respect and kindness toward both peers and adults is modeled and required. Each student's short- and long-term learning goals are collaboratively developed with the teacher, and teachers provide explicit instruction in and support for self-regulatory strategies leading to academic success

(Zimmerman, 2011). Within a multitiered system of service delivery, school psychologists can facilitate overall academic competence by observing for these universal classroom features and subsequently providing consultation and feedback to teachers.

When promoting study skills universally, it is often necessary to initially provide guided instruction and modeling augmented by teacher-based monitoring. As successful learning is demonstrated, direct instruction and teacher-based monitoring can be faded and replaced by student-based monitoring. Given the limited time allocated for classroom instruction, it may also be the case that school psychologists can advocate for universal promotion of study skills during homerooms or advisory periods. School psychologists can facilitate study skill instruction by direct instruction; consultation with teachers, paraprofessionals, or school volunteers; or through inservice training.

Zimmerman (2011) describes the following four phases as essential for permitting acquisition, application, and transfer of student study skills. First, effective study strategies should be modeled by (a) subdividing the strategy into steps, (b) providing an explicit explanation of the strategy and rationale for using the strategy, and (c) modeling use of the strategy. Second, multiple and varied opportunities to practice strategy use are generated with students' achieving increasing responsibility over strategy use. Third, students use the strategy independently through daily opportunities provided within the classroom. Students are prompted to consider the appropriate study strategy to employ with different classroom assignments. Fourth, students systematically apply study strategies independently. In order to achieve such independence, a range of study skill strategies must be instructed and students must be taught that application of strategies can be task and person dependent. Ultimately, students must learn how to organize their own study environments.

Universal Prevention Case Example

Administrators at Northeast High School expressed concern to the school psychologist, Ben Logan, that a large number of referrals for learning disability evaluation were occurring across ninth-grade English language arts classrooms. They indicated that these teachers had voiced frustration about students' writing assignments and test scores. Mr. Logan approached the teachers collaboratively, and a plan for consultation was developed. It soon became apparent after classroom observations that many students struggled with generat-

Table 5.1. Checklist for Qualities That Foster Study Skills

During observations and interviews, the school psychologist should focus on the following characteristics and develop a plan for implementation through collaborative consultation with teachers, parents, and students.

Organization
- Modeling and providing instruction in time management and organizational strategies
- Leading discussions take place, encouraging students in planning and prioritizing
- Encouraging students to write assignments in an assignment book
- For large projects, students submit weekly progress reports or smaller parts as completed

Comprehending directions
- Providing direct instruction specific to memory-enhancing strategies
- Providing assignments, both orally and in writing, that are clear

Note taking
- Students are taught effective note-taking skills and required to add details and review

Previewing and reading comprehension
- Students are taught methods to increase concentration and comprehension as they read
- Check-ins used to ensure students' ability to understand texts
- Alternative readings are used to ensure comprehension of materials when appropriate
- Self-instruction cues, heuristics, and checklists are generated for student use as a reference when problem solving
- Teachers and students should be encouraged to use cooperative learning or study groups

Test preparation and test taking
- Interview process is used to assess student homework and studying skills
- Students are taught to self-assess their own study strategies
- Cross-disciplinary collaboration is fostered
- Material to be covered on tests is clear
- Study guides are provided by teachers, or students are provided direct instruction in how to develop effective study guides
- Students know test question formats and are given example test questions
- Grading criteria and rubrics are shared with students
- Students collaborate in developing assessment measures or help develop test questions
- Tests are administered in a low-anxiety atmosphere
- Students are encouraged to use tests as opportunities to demonstrate knowledge
- Teams use data-based decision-making methods to determine effective test taking accommodations for eligible students

Self-management, motivation, and affect
- Lectures are concise, effectively structured, and followed by opportunities for students to use the newly acquired information
- Students are provided direct instruction on how to evaluate their own learning
- Students are provided opportunity to develop unique talents and to select learning topics
- Collaborative learning process takes place between students and teacher
- Students are taught to monitor and evaluate their own behavior
- Students are encouraged and reinforced to plan their studying using previously successful strategies
- Students are taught and provided opportunity to utilize personal learning guides by keeping a binder in which they keep historic and current forms, notes, and lists of successful strategies (Harvey & Chickie-Wolfe, 2007)

Assessment of study skills needs
- Family members are partners in their child's education and are encouraged to hold high, yet reasonable, expectations
- Regular communication between home and school is maintained
- Solution-oriented, conjoint consultation is fostered to address problem situations
- Classroom has minimal distractions and is quiet for independent work
- Students are given challenging yet manageable tasks
- Students are given some control over assignments and projects
- Teachers get to know students as individuals
- Academic and behavioral directions, expectations, and standards are clear
- Teachers frequently provide verbal support and write positive comments on papers
- Feelings of academic competence are encouraged by regular success and are publicly acknowledged
- Each student's short- and long-term learning goals are collaboratively developed
- Work is corrected promptly and includes specific and constructive qualitative feedback
- Effort and accuracy are emphasized when students complete tasks
- Classroom climate encourages students' helping, sharing, cooperating, and collaborating in problem solving
- Atmosphere of acceptance is established where respect and kindness toward both peers and adults is modeled and required

Table 5.2. Menu of Student Interview Questions

Organizational skills and note taking
- Where do you write down your assignments? May I see it? How do you break long-term assignments into smaller parts? Do you schedule those parts in your assignment book? Can I see notes that you have taken in a class? Do you ever go back and add details to your notes later?
- What do your parents expect from you in terms of studying? What happens when you do not meet your parents' expectations? Do other adults encourage you and support your doing well in school and who are they?
- How do the people in your family help you study or do homework? Or, how do they not help you?
- When you need help with studying, who do you ask for help? Do you have study buddies?
- Do you have a regular, quiet time to study at home? Is it enough time? What does the rest of the family do while you study? Do you set a schedule? Do you keep it? How do you stay on track?

Reading comprehension
- How do you approach a reading assignment in history or science?
- How do you approach reading a story or novel?
- What do you do to improve your understanding of your reading?
- What do you do when it is too hard?

Test preparation and test taking
- How do you prepare for a test or to give a performance? Do you spread out sessions or cram?
- What methods do you use to memorize?
- What strategies do you use when taking tests?
- What do you do afterward?

Self-management skills
- When you look at your previous grades, do you see patterns and trends? Which of your studying methods work well? Which ones don't? What do you think you should change?
- How do you monitor your own behavior? Do you reward yourself for good work and give yourself a consequence for unacceptable performance?
- Do you develop and use a study plan?
- For the next week, keep track of exactly how you study. What patterns do you see?
- What are your long-term goals? What are some jobs you would like to have as an adult?
- What are your goals for this year? What would you like to accomplish?
- What are things you spend time on now that will help you achieve your important goals? What are things you spend time on now that work against your goals? Who will help you achieve each of your goals? Who will make it difficult to achieve each important long- and short-term goal?

Motivation and affect
- What do you do especially well? What are some things you like to do for fun when you aren't in school? What are some things you like to do for fun when you are in school? What are some things you like to do for fun with your parents, with your brothers and sisters, with your friends?
- What do you do least well? What things are hardest for you to do?
- Are there any subjects that make you feel frustrated, bored, angry, or nervous? What do you do when this happens?
- What do you do when you don't feel like studying but the deadline is soon? How do you get over wanting to put studying off?
- Have you ever found that you were so excited about learning that you forgot to do something such as watch a favorite TV show? Explain that situation.
- What do you imagine that the very best student in the world does after school or when completing homework or while studying? How does that compare to what you do? What's holding you back from being the best student in the world? Which of the best student's habits and behaviors could you adopt?

Assessment of study skill needs
- Do your classmates and friends help you study and do well in school?
- How do your teachers help you learn? How could that be improved? Which of your assignments are too hard? Too easy? Which are just right?
- What do you think are your teachers' goals for you? What happens when you don't meet those goals?
- How do your teachers help you prepare for weekly or unit tests? How do your teachers help you prepare for the state tests? What could your teachers do differently to help more?
- Do you feel as though you are encouraged to develop your unique talents and learn about what you are interested in at home or at school? Can you give me some examples? How could that be improved?

Table 5.3. List of Self-Regulation and Learning Inventories

Title (Test Author)	Description	Ordering Information
Academic Competence Evaluation Scales (DiPerna & Elliott, 2000)	Three versions (teacher, K–12; student, grades 6–12; college); software available; 10–15 min. administration; links assessment to intervention	Pearson: http://www.pearsonassessments.com
Academic Intervention Monitoring System (Elliott, DiPerna, & Shapiro, 2001)	Tool for RTI Tier 1 and 2 intervention planning; uses teacher, student, and parent forms to identify evidence-based interventions and develop plans for monitoring outcome goals to address academic concerns; grades K–12	Pearson: http://www.pearsonassessments.com
Dynamic Assessment of Test Accommodations (Fuchs, Fuchs, Eaton, & Hamlet, 2003)	Three versions (grades 2–3, 4–5, 6–7); individual or group administration; administration of brief tests with and without accommodations to determine effectiveness of specific accommodation selection to national sample.	Pearson: http://http://www.pearsonassessments.com
Learning and Study Strategies Inventory (2nd ed.; Weinstein & Palmer, 2002)	Self-report (grades 9–12); 76 items; Web version; 30 min. administration; has psychometric limitations requiring consideration.	H&H Publishing: http://www.hhpublishing.com
School Motivation and Learning Strategies Inventory (Stroud & Reynolds, 2006)	Self-report (ages 8–18); two forms (child, teen); software available; 20–30 min. administration	Western Psychological Services: http://portal.wpspublish.com

ing and organizing notes from both class lectures and textbooks. Mr. Logan observed that many of the students, in addition to those being referred for evaluation, would benefit from direct classroom instruction on note taking to become self-regulated learners. Through consultation, Mr. Logan and the teachers developed lesson plans to teach students how to use strategic note taking, heuristics, and self-checking. Teachers agreed to randomly check notes for accuracy and offer rewards, initially, to encourage continued use. It became clear after several weeks that a majority of students were increasing the quantity and accuracy of notes and that data collected during observation showed overall increase in on-task behaviors during lectures and class discussions.

Tiered Supports for Study Skills

Social modeling that includes peers in addition to teachers and parents is a critical aspect of promoting study skill generalization and adaption into student routines (Schunk & Usher, 2011). Cooperative learning groups where students work in pairs or small teams within the school has been recognized as a highly effective instructional practice (Scruggs et al., 2010) and peer mentoring has increased the value of study skills as well as improved knowledge of and practice with study skills (Richardson et al., 2010). Therefore, it might be useful to organize study groups within classes or grades for students who are exhibiting challenges with study skills. Study groups need to be coconstructed, meaning that members of the group have shared perceptions and goals, complete assignments correctly, and also understand that both concepts and process can improve outcomes for all students.

A four-step process might be employed to improve use of effective study strategies: (a) modeling, (b) coaching, (c) behavioral rehearsal, and (d) reinforcement (DiPerna, 2006). Modeling from relevant adults and peers that includes explicit instruction in the strategy steps and the reason for those steps appears to be essential. Coaching requires the school psychologist to use verbal instruction to teach a skill and begins with detailed description of the strategy along with presentation of examples and nonexamples. Situations for when to use the study strategies are identified, barriers preventing the use of such strategies are outlined, and solutions to address the potential barriers are generated. Behavioral rehearsal involves covert rehearsal, where students employ mental imagery; verbal rehearsal, during which students recite the steps for performing the study strategy; and overt rehearsal, where students engage in supervised role-plays practicing strategy use. Finally, frequent performance feedback is offered throughout the process and reinforcement for making progress toward goals or using the study strategies is provided.

Student understanding of the impact of effort can also be fostered by having them track studying habit and outcomes using the student study plan (Appendix).

Individualized Intervention Case Example

Dr. Mina Habash, the school psychologist at Shaw Elementary School, has been approached by special education staff to assist in developing a Tier 3 intervention to address study skills weakness for students receiving individualized academic instruction as they transition to sixth grade. Through the consultation process, Dr. Habash recognizes that the students do not know how to delineate important information taught in class despite efforts by teachers to provide notes. Unfortunately, the students go home unable to effectively review taught information while studying. Dr. Habash works with the teachers as well as families during support nights after school to discuss the importance of students being actively engaged in the process of studying to promote motivation. She reviews and collaboratively designs research-based interventions including graphic organizers using semantic mapping. During classroom and family consultation, Dr. Habash provides an overview of ways in which well-developed graphic organizers can elicit student participation by helping illustrate relationships between concepts. In class, Tier 3 supports are then developed to teach students how to ask for clarification about main ideas and use teacher-generated organizers to make comparisons between previously understood knowledge while studying at school and home.

Multicultural Considerations

Research suggests that collaborative learning and self-regulation approaches employed within the classroom consider students' cultural values and strengths. For example, Latino students are often raised in collectivistic cultures and subsequently may value helping, sharing, and the success of the group (Rothstein-Fisch & Trumball, 2008). Such students might be particularly responsive to collaborative learning approaches. Student autonomy is important for self-regulation of study skills, and parental involvement can facilitate this autonomy. However, not every culture values self-regulation to the same degree. For example, Tang and Neber (2008) demonstrated that use of self-regulated learning strategies and self-efficacy was greater for students in the United States than for students in China. It was postulated that emphasis on the teacher, rather than the student, as the provider of knowledge in Chinese culture might be partially responsible for the finding. Therefore, a school psychologist working with Chinese American students to increase self-regulation may encounter a conflict with the students' parents regarding the value of such behaviors.

School psychologists might keep in mind that home support can be challenging for parents who were educated in a different country, who are unfamiliar with the U.S. educational system, who have a lack of knowledge about expectations for participation in school-related activities, who perceive institutional racism, or for whom a language barrier exists (Polo, Zychinski, & Roundfield, 2012). Immigrant children face unique challenges in U.S. educational settings in terms of acculturation, discrimination, and second language acquisition, and these can be addressed by school psychologists using approaches that explicitly address psychosocial and academic self-regulation (Fuertes, Alfonso, & Shultz, 2007).

Effectiveness of School Psychologists' Practices

School psychologists can determine the effectiveness of implemented interventions regarding study skills using single-case study methodology (Perry et al., 2012). Any well-defined problem behavior or academic outcome can be used as a monitoring tool. However, it is best to avoid teacher-assigned grades (as they are subjective) or time spent on homework. Instead, it is best to measure quality indicators, such as attention to task, productivity (number of tasks completed), or accuracy (number of correct tasks completed).

In conducting a single-case study, at least three to five data points are required during the baseline period prior to any implemented intervention, and data should be collected at least weekly throughout the intervention. After successful strategies have been identified, the team develops and implements strategies to promote generalization and maintenance. It is likely that goal setting and progress monitoring of study skills will need to occur in other settings, or in at other academic disciplines, for successful generalization to occur.

SUMMARY

Study skills significantly affect students' school functioning and can be taught at all ages and levels of ability. Teachers often do not provide instruction in study skills because they assume that students already have mastered them. Frequently, interventions to improve organization or study skills can be implemented with the aid of the school psychologist in prevention programs as well as in Tier 2 or 3 interventions. The most productive approaches to the assessment and intervention of study skills uses an ecological assessment involving classroom observations, analyses of work samples, consultation with teachers and parents, student interviews, and observation of the student at work to precisely identify areas of weakness and to design effective remediation. Effective remediation requires that the student, school psychologist, teachers, and parents work closely together to determine and monitor appropriate interventions.

AUTHOR NOTE

Disclosure. Virginia Harvey has a financial interest in books she authored or coauthored referenced in this chapter.

REFERENCES

Boyle, J. R., & Rivera, T. Z. (2012). Note-taking techniques or students with disabilities: A systematic review of the research. *Learning Disability Quarterly*, *35*, 131–143. doi:10.1177/0731948711435794

Cleary, T. J. (2009). School-based motivation and self-regulation assessments: An examination of school psychologists' beliefs and practices. *Journal of Applied School Psychology*, *25*, 71–94. doi:10.1080/15377900802484190

Cleary, T. J., Gubi, A., & Prescott, M. V. (2010). Motivation and self-regulation assessments: Professional practices and needs of school psychologists. *Psychology in the Schools*, *47*, 985–1002. doi:10.1002/pits.20519

Cormier, D. C., Altman, J. R., Shyyan, V., & Thurlow, M. L. (2010). *A summary of the research on the effects of test accommodations: 2007–2008* (Technical Report 56). Minneapolis, MN: University of Minnesota, National Center on Educational Outcomes.

Dexter, D. D., Park, Y. J., & Hughes, C. A. (2011). A meta-analytic review of graphic organizers and science instruction for adolescents with learning disabilities: Implications for the intermediate and secondary science classroom. *Learning Disabilities Research & Practice*, *26*, 204–213. doi:10.1111/j.1540-5826.2011.00341.x

DiPerna, J. (2006). Academic enablers and student achievement: Implications for assessment and intervention services in the schools. *Psychology in the Schools*, *43*, 7–17. doi:10.1002/pits.20125

DiPerna, J., & Elliott, S. N. (2000). *Academic competence evaluation scales (ACES)*. San Antonio, TX: Pearson.

Elliott, S. N., DiPerna, J. C., & Shapiro, E. (2001). *Academic intervention monitoring system (AIMS)*. San Antonio, TX: Pearson.

Fuchs, L., Fuchs, D., Eaton, S., & Hamlett, C. (2003). *Dynamic assessment of test accommodations*. San Antonio, TX: Pearson.

Fuertes, J. N., Alfonso, V. C., & Shultz, J. T. (2007). Counseling culturally and linguistically diverse children and youth: A self-regulatory approach. In G. B. Esquivel, E. C. Lopez, & S. G. Nahari (Eds.), *Handbook of multicultural school psychology: An Interdisciplinary perspective* (pp. 409–427). Mahwah, NJ: Erlbaum.

Garber-Miller, K. (2007). Playful textbook previews: Letting go of familiar mustache monologues. *Journal of Adolescent & Adult Literacy*, *50*, 294–299, doi:10.1598/JAAL.50.4.4

Gettinger, M., & Seibert, J. K. (2002). Contributions of study skills to academic competence. *School Psychology Review*, *31*, 350–365.

Gregor, A. (2005). Examination anxiety: Live with it, control it, or make it work for you? *School Psychology International*, *26*, 617–635, doi:10.1177/0143034305060802

Harvey, V. S., & Chickie-Wolfe, L. A. (2007). *Fostering independent learning: Practical strategies to promote student success*. New York, NY: Guilford Press.

Henry, D. B., Tolan, P. H., Gorman-Smith, D., & Schoeny, M. E. (2012). Risk and direct protective factors for youth violence: Results from the centers for disease control and prevention's multisite violence prevention project. *American Journal of Preventative Medicine*, *43*, S67–S75. doi:10.1016/j.amepre.2012.04.025

Kitsantas, A., & Dabbagh, N. (2010). *Learning to learn with integrative learning technologies (ILT): A practical guide for academic success*. Charlotte, NC: Information Age.

Kuepper, J. E. (1990). Best practices in teaching study skills. In A. Thomas & J. Grimes (Eds.), *Best practices in school psychology II* (pp. 711–721). Washington, DC: National Association of School Psychologists.

McCormick, C. B., Dimmitt, C., & Sullivan, F. R. (2013). Metacognition, learning, and instruction. In W. M. Reynolds, G. E. Miller, & Weiner, I. B. (Eds.), *Handbook of psychology, Vol. 7: Educational psychology* (2nd ed., pp. 69–97). Hoboken, NJ: Wiley.

Meneghetti, C., De Beni, R., & Cornoldi, C. (2007). Strategic knowledge and consistency in students with good and poor study skills. *European Journal of Cognitive Psychology*, *19*, 628–649. doi:10.1080/09541440701325990

Montague, M. (2007). Self-regulation and mathematics instruction. *Learning Disabilities Research & Practice*, *22*, 75–83. doi:10.1111/j.1540-5826.2007.00232.x

Moreira, P. S., Dias, P., Vaz, F., & Vaz, J. (2013). Predictors of academic performance and school engagement integrating persistence, motivation and study skills perspectives using person-centered and variable-centered approaches. *Learning and Individual Differences*, *24*, 117–152. doi:10.1016/j.lindif.2012.10.016

Perry, V. A., Albeg, L., & Tung, C. (2012). Meta-analysis of single-case design research on self-regulatory interventions for academic performance. *Journal of Behavioral Education*, *21*, 217–229.

Polo, A. J., Zychinski, K. E., & Roundfield, K. E. (2012). The Parental Schoolwork Support Measure–Youth: Development and psychometric evaluation. *Cultural Diversity and Ethnic Minority Psychology*, *18*, 297–306. doi:10.1037/a0028729

Richardson, J. S., Robnolt, V. J., & Rhodes, J. A. (2010). A history of study skills: Not hot, but not forgotten. *Reading Improvement, 47,* 111–123.

Rothstein-Fisch, C., & Trumball, E. (2008). *Managing diverse classrooms: How to build on students' cultural strengths.* Alexandria, VA: Association for Supervision and Curriculum Development.

Schunk, D. H., & Usher, E. L. (2011). Assessing self-efficacy for self-regulated learning. In B. J. Zimmerman & D. H. Schunk (Eds.), *Handbook of self-regulation of learning and performance* (pp. 282–297). New York, NY: Routledge.

Scruggs, T. E., Mastropieri, M. A., Berkeley, S., & Graetz, J. E. (2010). Do special education interventions improve learning of secondary content? A meta-analysis. *Remedial and Special Education, 31,* 437–449. doi:10.1177/0741932508327465

Son, L. K. (2004). Spacing one's study: Evidence for a meta-cognitive control strategy. *Journal of Experimental Psychology: Learning, Memory, and Cognition, 30,* 601–604. doi:10.1037/0278-7393.30.3.601

Stroud, K. C., & Reynolds, C. R. (2006). *School motivation and learning strategies inventory.* North Tonawanda, NY: Multi-Health Systems.

Tang, M., & Neber, H. (2008). Motivation and self-regulated science learning in high achieving students: Differences relate to nation, gender, and grade level. *High Ability Studies, 19,* 103–116.

Weinstein, C. E., & Palmer, D. R. (2002). *Learning and study strategies inventory* (2nd ed.). Clearwater, FL: H&H Publishing.

Westby, C. C., Lawrence, B., & Hall-Kenyon, K. (2010). Summarizing expository texts. *Topics in Language Disorders, 30,* 275–287. doi:10.1097/TLD.0b013e3181ff5a88

Williams, R. S., Ari, O., & Santamaria, C. N. (2011). Measuring college students' reading comprehension ability using cloze tests. *Journal of Research in Reading, 34,* 215–231. doi:10.1111/j.1467-9817.2009.01422.x

Zimmerman, B. J. (2011). Motivational sources and outcomes of self-regulated learning and performance. In B. J. Zimmerman & D. H. Schunk (Eds.), *Handbook of self-regulation of learning and performance* (pp. 282–297). New York, NY: Routledge.

APPENDIX. STUDENT STUDY PLAN

Name _____ Subject _____ Date _____

Planning: Methods I plan to use:

- Focus on important information
- Space and repeat my learning
- Use more than one approach
- Include corrected work
- Increase comprehension
- Keep motivated
- Number of hours I plan to study

Appraisal: Post-studying evaluation

- Comparison of plan and actual studying
- Did I study with anyone? How did that work?
- Did I have any problems or distractions?
- How did I know when I studied enough?
- Grade expected
- Grade received
- What worked? What didn't work? What should I change?

Best Practices in Homework Management

Lea A. Theodore
College of William and Mary (VA)
Melissa A. Bray
Thomas J. Kehle
University of Connecticut

OVERVIEW

Homework, defined as work to be completed by students during nonschool hours, has long been controversial among educators and school psychologists. Specifically, the dispute involves the extent to which homework is perceived as an effective contributor to academic achievement or personal attributes that positively influence student behaviors, both educationally and personally (Cooper, Robinson, & Patall, 2006). Despite these issues, homework historically has been associated with academic achievement and is a valuable supplemental pedagogical tool (Cancio, West, & Young, 2004; Reinhardt, Theodore, Bray, & Kehle, 2009).

As an essential component to the learning process, homework fosters academic and nonacademic benefits for students of all grades and ability levels (Reinhardt et al., 2009). The academic benefits include facilitating the retention and understanding of class material through practice, affording students opportunities to apply newly learned skills, and providing students with opportunities to demonstrate mastery of material (Epstein & Van Voorhis, 2001). Nonacademic benefits include increased development and enhancement of good study habits, time management skills, and self-discipline (Cooper & Valentine, 2001), as well as increased parental involvement in and collaboration with students' teachers and schools. In contrast to these benefits, failure to complete homework is associated with an increase in special education referrals and a decline in overall academic performance among students with learning disabilities (Lynch, Theodore, Bray, & Kehle, 2009). Given the long-term implications for scholastic performance, teachers use homework to reinforce classroom learning.

The importance of homework in fostering the learning process among students of all grade and ability levels is clear. As classrooms become more inclusive in composition, educators are increasingly challenged to ensure that all students achieve suitable academic progress and mastery. To this end, teachers often consult with school psychologists, who are uniquely qualified to assist by working directly with teachers, as well as by indirectly suggesting strategies to facilitate the homework assignment, organization, and completion process. Because of this important facilitative role, school psychologists must be knowledgeable about evidence-based interventions for improving homework compliance and performance.

The intent of this chapter is to provide school psychologists with useful strategies to assist parents and teachers in maximizing the benefits of homework while reducing the angst associated with the practice. Aligned with the National Association of School Psychologists (NASP) practice domain of Interventions and Instructional Support to Develop Academic Skills, from the NASP *Model for Comprehensive and Integrated School Psychological Services* (NASP, 2010), this chapter promotes a school-based problem-solving approach that promotes collaboration among school psychologists, teachers, and families, with the goal of enhancing all students' academic competence using a multitiered service delivery model. A cooperative team approach uniting schools and families with the knowledge of preventive and educative homework strategies is essential to fostering academic development among all students. In addition to the academic benefits, homework also influences students' attitudes, knowledge, and skills associated with effective learning (Rowell & Hong, 2002).

Consequently, homework best practices facilitate the consultation process and provide teachers and families with educational guidance regarding homework organization and management, regardless of students' ability levels. During the course of consultation, school psychologists may recommend preventive and remedial homework interventions that both enhance a student's academic skills and promote nonacademic benefits, such as improved time management skills, self-discipline, and organizational strategies (Rowell & Hong, 2002). In summary, this chapter promotes a greater understanding of the history of the homework debate, purposes of homework, its benefits and negative effects, expectations of appropriate amounts of homework, developmental differences with respect to homework assignments, special education, and best practices in homework management.

BASIC CONSIDERATIONS

Educational initiatives promulgated during the past decade, among them the reauthorized Individuals with Disabilities Education Act and No Child Left Behind, have brought accountability to the forefront of public education. These federal laws hold school systems responsible for fostering and documenting continuous academic improvement among all students, with and without disabilities. In this climate of accountability, where student performance is paramount, homework is a powerful instructional tool that enhances academic achievement by providing students with additional opportunities for learning beyond the school hours. Homework supplements in-school academic instruction by providing opportunities to practice newly acquired skills and concepts covered in class (Bang, 2011). As such, homework is a frequently employed teaching strategy because it can be highly influential in and beneficial to the learning process (Rowell & Hong, 2002).

History of Homework

Although homework has been used to supplement in-class learning for more than a century, the value of homework has been debated since the mid-1800s. During the 19th century, students could voluntarily leave school at 14 years of age. This meant that students who willingly remained to complete high school

expected homework to be part of the academic curriculum that was a requisite part of completing their education (Maltese, Tai, & Fan, 2012). At the turn of the century, and for approximately 50 years after, the educational community found little research to support the supposition that homework influenced student learning, and as such, homework was viewed as intrusive and unnecessary. In 1957, this antihomework sentiment changed with the launch of the Sputnik satellite by the Soviet Union. The Cold War underscored concern regarding the rigor of the American educational system and the preparedness of students to compete with contemporaries in the future (Eren & Henderson, 2011). The United States then focused on developing higher standards in education, with homework serving as an instrumental tool that would improve overall scholastic achievement by accelerating academic mastery. Notably, research on homework conducted during this time indicated that greater amounts of homework resulted in higher achievement (Maltese et al., 2012).

During the 1960s and 1970s, the Vietnam War shifted the spotlight away from education and homework and focused instead on truancy and behavior (Maltese et al., 2012) and personal and social freedoms (Keith, Diamond-Hallum, & Fine, 2004). In the 1980s, the publication of *A Nation at Risk: The Imperative for Educational Reform* (National Commission on Excellence in Education, 1983) and *What Works* (U.S. Department of Education, 1986), called attention to the waning academic excellence of America's students. Homework was again viewed as a necessary vehicle by which to increase educational standards, ensure global competition, and ultimately improve the economic status of the United States.

As the century turned again to a new millennium, an antihomework movement was begun by parents who believed that homework caused undue stress on their child (Cooper et al., 2006; Keith et al., 2004), despite support for homework as an integral method to improve academic achievement (Maltese et al., 2012). The cyclical nature of the merit of homework continues, with President Obama's administration pushing to strengthen the rigor of our nation's schools as well as emphasizing his priority of improving achievement in science, technology, engineering, and math education (Maltese et al., 2012) during a time of global economic crisis. Thus, it appears that when the United States is facing difficult economic times and an uncertain political future, there is a resurgence of interest in developing rigorous academic standards in the nation's schools, which translates into increases in homework.

Purpose of Homework

To comprehend the value and wide-ranging influence of homework on academic and nonacademic behaviors, it is important to first appreciate the purpose of homework for both instructional and noninstructional outcomes (Power, Karutsis, & Habboushe, 2001). Instructionally, homework serves four primary purposes: practice, preparation, extension, and integration.

Practice homework is used to reinforce instructional steps, practices, and methods covered in class. This type of homework is designed to reinforce learning and facilitate mastery of newly learned skills through rote practice. Preparation-oriented homework serves as an advance organizer to prepare students for material that teachers will present in upcoming lessons. When the teacher covers these concepts in class, students will have been prepared for the material and will therefore obtain the maximum benefit from introduction. Extension homework involves extending newly acquired skills to different situations and contexts. For example, students might apply new mathematical skills to the process of learning how to balance a checkbook. Integration homework helps students combine learned skills and concepts to create a more comprehensive final outcome, such as a multistep science project or an in-depth book report (Cooper et al., 2006).

In addition to its academic benefits, homework also has noninstructional implications, including enhancing personal attributes (e.g., learning time management, assuming responsibility, and achieving self-confidence), enhancing communication between parents and their children, satisfying school administrations' mandates regarding required time spent on homework (i.e., daily and weekly homework), and apprising parents of what their children are learning in school (Epstein & Van Voorhis, 2001). Clearly, homework serves a multitude of purposes that enhance both instructional and noninstructional outcomes (see Table 6.1).

Appropriate Amounts of Homework

There is an optimal amount of homework that results in maximally effective learning. The key to determining the appropriate amount of homework is to match the amount assigned to students with the academic subject and the students' grade level. Based on recommendations from the National Education Association and the National Parent Teacher Association, school psychologists can apply this rule of thumb for recommending a developmentally appropriate amount of homework for elementary-grade students: approximately a 10-minute increase in homework per grade level, beginning with 10 minutes of homework for first-grade students. Second graders, then, might be expected to complete 20 minutes of homework each night, third graders 30 minutes, fourth graders 40 minutes, and so on. In middle and high school, the 10-minute rule gives way to other factors. High school seniors, because of multiple subjects and college-bound expectations, might be expected to have 2 or more hours of homework each night (Cooper & Valentine, 2001; National Education Association, n.d.). Moreover, because assignments vary in complexity and duration (e.g., semester-long projects), homework times for students in high school may differ day to day depending on subject difficulty, time required to master new material, and the complexity of multiple assignments made by multiple teachers (Brock, Lapp, Flood, Fisher, & Tao, 2007; see Table 6.1).

Developmental Differences and Different Practices

As with all things developmental, there are differences in how students of various ages and developmental levels learn (e.g., practice, preparation, extension, and integration), so homework must be tailored to fit the needs of students, depending on their level of functioning. A student's developmental level influences the relationship between homework and academic achievement, with a stronger positive relationship existing between homework and achievement for students in middle and high school as compared to students at the elementary level (Bempechat, Li, Neier, Gillis, & Holloway, 2011). When consulting school psychologists explain why homework does not yield strong academic effects for students in elementary school, they should point out that academic researchers have found that younger children have not yet developed the effective study habits necessary to benefit from solitary homework completion. Additionally, young students have greater difficulty than older students ignoring environmental distractions, and they have overall shorter attention spans (Patall, Cooper, & Robinson, 2008). Although practice homework during the elementary grades may have modest effects on academic achievement, it gives students the opportunity to overlearn basic facts and, importantly, provides noninstructional advantages, such as developing positive personal attributes. These nonacademic gains include helping students develop good study habits; master basic facts and processes; establish self-discipline, time management, and independent learning

Table 6.1. Basic Considerations of Homework

Purpose of homework
- Practice homework reinforces learning
- Preparation homework introduces students to material that will be presented in future lessons
- Extension homework extends newly learned skills to different situations
- Integration homework combines learned skills and concepts to create a more comprehensive final product

Appropriate amounts of homework
- Elementary grades: The heuristic is a 10-minute increase per grade level:
  - Grade 1: 10 minutes of homework
  - Grade 2: 20 minutes of homework
  - Grade 3: 30 minutes of homework
  - Grade 4: 40 minutes of homework
- Middle and high school: Assignments vary in complexity so homework times will vary depending on
  - Level of difficulty
  - Time required to master material
  - Duration of multiple assignments and complexity

Developmental differences and different practices
- Homework must be tailored to fit the needs of students, depending on their developmental level
- At the elementary level
  - Homework does not yield strong academic effects
  - Homework does provide nonacademic benefits (i.e., developing good study habits), which relate to long-term student achievement
- There is a stronger positive relationship existing between homework and achievement for students in middle and high school

Special education and homework
- Students with attention and learning problems have significant homework problems because they
  - Have difficulty concentrating
  - Have problems completing homework
  - Make careless errors
  - Have difficulty beginning homework
  - Need several prompts and reminders to complete homework
- Students in special education who have difficulty with homework are at risk for
  - Poor academic achievement
  - Lower grades
  - Increased risk for dropping out of school
  - Attaining lower levels of employment
- The learning process is influenced by the amount of time that students spend engaged on a task
- Homework increases students' academic engaged time by supplementing learning at home

skills; and develop positive attitudes toward school and the learning process (Zimmerman & Kitsantas, 2005). Consulting school psychologists should point out that homework also provides increased opportunities for parental involvement and collaboration with their child's school, both of which are positively correlated with student achievement.

Given that the goal of homework in the early grades is to master basic facts and procedures, establish learning routines, and foster personal responsibility, school psychologists should emphasize that the amount of homework assigned during the elementary-level grades should not be a primary concern. Rather, these nonacademic benefits are important in and of themselves because they relate to long-term student achievement

by promoting lifelong learning benefits (Theodore, DioGuardi, Hughes, Carlo, & Eccles, 2009). Nonacademic benefits extend beyond the educational arena because students complete these tasks with minimal supervision and without the time constraints imposed during the school day. Homework requires students to marshal their capacity to focus and concentrate on the task at hand, to be mindful of how to proceed when completing the task, and to employ independent critical thinking skills on their own. Particularly at the elementary grade level, homework augments students' personal development by promoting a sense of responsibility and perseverance, which fosters structure and, perhaps more significantly, highlights the importance of learning (see Table 6.1).

Positive Effects of Homework

Proponents believe that there are many positive effects of homework, including the learning and retention of classroom material both immediately and in the long term. Homework also promotes appropriate study habits, the development of positive personal characteristics, and the involvement of parents in their child's learning. Significantly, the direct effects of homework on achievement and learning are the most common reasons homework is assigned (Patall et al., 2008). By having students complete additional assignments during noninstructional hours, students devote more time to learning material presented in class by practicing skills (i.e., practice homework), reviewing work, studying for exams, and, of course, cultivating nonacademic benefits. Homework runs along the continuum from basic skill practice in the early grades to the development of critical thinking skills in the upper grades (i.e., extension homework). In this manner, students retain information in the short term, and through the act of practice and critical thinking, information is transferred to long-term memory, ultimately becoming well-learned, crystallized knowledge. Homework also encourages the establishment of effective study habits in the elementary grades and cultivates self-discipline, which in turn promotes long-term understanding of academic material. In addition, homework encourages a curiosity about learning that may take place anywhere outside of the classroom, thereby improving attitudes toward school (Epstein & Van Voorhis, 2001) and lifelong learning.

Perhaps equally as important as the academic benefits of homework are the nonacademic benefits that homework may promote. The process of completing homework fosters discipline, organization, and independent learning in a manner that not only enhances academic performance but also nurtures responsible character traits that generalize to nonacademic contexts (e.g., sports, music, work). Importantly, the combination of academic and nonacademic benefits promote personal skills and attributes that promote long-term academic achievement (Epstein & Van Voorhis, 2001; Theodore et al., 2009).

Notably, homework practices also increase students' academic self-efficacy, that is, students' beliefs about their ability to learn. This enhanced personal belief is related to the amount of time students spend engaged on homework assignments, as well as the amount of energy they apply when completing those tasks (Zimmerman & Kitsantas, 2005). Highly efficacious students are active learners who set goals, employ deliberate plans of action to meet their goals, and maintain motivation and persistence until they realize their objective. It should be no surprise that students with high levels of self-efficacy are high achievers. Significantly, students' motivational beliefs mediate the relationship between homework practices and students' academic achievement. Self-efficacy is associated with self-regulation of learning as students direct their thoughts and behaviors toward achieving a goal (Bembenutty, 2011). Thus, self-regulation of learning behaviors requires that students identify appropriate strategies for learning and demonstrate initiative and discipline to realize their goals. Homework practices, then, promote self-regulation of student learning by enhancing students' academic self-efficacy.

Finally, homework allows parents active participation in their child's learning process by enhancing their understanding and appreciation of what their child is learning in the classroom. There are several benefits derived from parents being involved in their child's homework. By expressing interest in their child's homework, parents convey to their child the social value and significance of schoolwork and learning. Parents who invest in their child's homework communicate their own positive attitude about homework and education, which generalizes to the development of positive behaviors in school (Epstein & Van Voorhis, 2001). Parents can actively support their child's learning process by establishing a homework routine that includes setting a designated homework time; providing a quiet, nondistracting area in the home; ensuring that the materials necessary to carry out work are provided; supervising homework completion; and answering questions their child may pose. These constructive parental behaviors influence long-term academic achievement by promoting goal setting, goal attainment, and learning how to manage time in order to realize objectives (Patall et al., 2008). Moreover, parental involvement enhances communication between parents and children as well as between parents and teachers. In this manner, homework serves as a natural extension of the home–school collaboration. In sum, school psychologists should encourage parental involvement in homework because it results in higher rates of student achievement by facilitating communication with a child's teacher and by providing structure and support at home, which leads to positive learning behaviors and an acceptance of the value of learning (Van Voorhis, 2011; see Table 6.2).

Table 6.2. Positive and Negative Effects of Homework

Positive effects of homework

Academic
- Promotes appropriate study habits
- Increases learning and understanding of academic material
- Cultivates self-discipline
- Encourages curiosity about learning
- Improves attitudes toward school

Nonacademic
- Fosters discipline
- Improves organization
- Promotes independent learning
- Encourages responsible character traits
- Increases academic self-efficacy
- Enhances self-regulation of learning

Parental Involvement
- Helps parents become active participants in their child's learning
- Conveys the value and significance of school and the learning process
- Promotes positive attitudes about homework, which generalize to positive school behaviors
- Enhances communication between school and home

Negative effects of homework
- May result in boredom and fatigue if overexposed to academic material
- May become satiated with the acquisition of knowledge, which may result in burnout
- Leaves less time for recreational activities that promote academic and social–emotional skills
- Permits parental intrusion
  - May place a great deal of pressure on children to complete homework
  - May create confusion by using instructional techniques that differ from the child's teacher
  - May promote cheating
  - May foster dependence on others to complete assignments
- Highlights social inequities

Negative Effects of Homework

Despite the positive effects of homework on the learning process and outcomes, opponents have raised concerns about the negative effects of homework on students. First, there is concern that homework may lead to boredom and fatigue if students spend too much out-of-school time on, and are overexposed to, academic material. That is, if students are consistently barraged with academic material and activities, they may become satiated with the acquisition of knowledge, which may result in early academic burnout. Second, as students spend more time engaged in academic work, they have less time to play or be involved in recreational activities that promote physical, social, and emotional development. Third, parental involvement in the homework process, while generally beneficial, may cause unique problems at home. For instance, parents may pressure their child too much with respect to how, when, and where to complete homework, and they may create confusion in the learning process by using instructional techniques that differ from their child's teacher's. Significantly, involvement by others, particularly if the assistance goes beyond answering simple questions, may promote cheating as well as encourage dependence on others to complete assignments. Finally, homework may highlight extant social inequities: children from well-to-do homes may have access to more resources (e.g., computers, Internet); greater parental education, assistance, and support; and dedicated quiet areas where students can complete their work, all benefits that facilitate the acquisition, retention, and understanding of academic material that children from disadvantaged homes may not have as readily available (Cooper et al., 2006; see Table 6.2).

Special Education and Homework

The extent to which homework problems adversely affect the overall academic functioning of students with learning problems cannot be underestimated. It is well documented that students with attention and learning problems have significant homework difficulties that negatively affect academic performance, result in conflict between parents and their children, place children at greater risk for developing anxiety and depressive disorders, and may damage the collaborative relationship between parents and teachers (Lynch et al., 2009; Power, Werba, Watkins, Angelucci, & Eiraldi, 2006; Sheridan, 2009). Academically, students with attention and learning problems struggle with homework, in part because they have difficulty concentrating, which may result in incorrectly recording assigned work, having problems completing assignments, and making careless errors because of a propensity to rush through assignments (Bryan, Burstein, & Bryan, 2001). Further, students with attention and learning difficulties tend to have difficulty managing their emotions and behavior, which negatively influences productivity, including delaying beginning homework and needing nagging reminders to complete assignments (Lynch et al., 2009). This dynamic often contributes to further decline in academic achievement, lower grades, increased risk for dropping out of school, and lower levels of employment as a result of diminished education (Sheridan, 2009).

Given the negative implications stemming from homework noncompliance in students with attention and learning problems, it is particularly important that school psychologists encourage teachers to provide these students with additional opportunities for practice and to promote academic achievement in the classroom, with brief, direct follow-up homework to foster transference of learning from one setting to another. In this manner, homework assignments serve not only to reinforce prior learning but also to strengthen the nonacademic benefits that homework provides. In particular, research has suggested that the learning process, for both general and special education students, is influenced by the amount of time that a student spends engaged on a task. Thus, homework increases students' academic engagement by supplementing classroom learning in core academic areas (Dettmers, Trautwein, Ludtke, Kunter, & Baumert, 2010). As such, continued educational practice at home for students with and without disabilities is essential to fostering success in school. However, preparing parents for the task of supporting their exceptional child at home may be a currently underserved but essential role for school psychologists as educational consultants (see Table 6.2).

BEST PRACTICES IN HOMEWORK MANAGEMENT

A primary goal of school psychologists is that of facilitating and enhancing the academic functioning of all students. When students fail to complete homework assignments, their academic performance and attitude toward learning may be negatively affected. School psychologists play a vital role in working with administrators, educators, families, and students to promote effective homework practices, thereby improving scholastic achievement. However, since homework is primarily within the purview of classroom teachers, school psychologists typically serve as consultants and problem solvers to improve homework performance in both the home and school settings.

The NASP Practice Model (NASP, 2010) advocates for the delivery of school psychological services in a multitiered model. This model is composed of universal, targeted, and intensive interventions that employ evidence-based strategies designed to help children progress educationally. For students who are experiencing academic difficulties, this multitiered response-to-intervention (RTI) model may be especially useful for homework management. Given the current climate of inclusion for students with academic problems, it is essential that school psychologists have knowledge of the various strategies designed to assist students in the learning process to better help them succeed academically. Table 6.3 provides a list of the multitiered services that school psychologists may recommend to administrators, teachers, and parents to facilitate and improve effective homework practices. To this end, a three-tiered RTI approach to homework management follows.

Tier 1

At the school-wide level, school psychologists work with schools to provide universal prevention strategies to ensure effective homework practices. In collaboration with administrators and educators, school psychologists may promote the following approaches within their schools:

- Provide clear homework policies to parents and students that include expectations for homework completion and consequences for late and missed assignments.
- Institute a homework hotline where students may call to ask specific questions regarding a particular assignment (Dawson, 2008).

Table 6.3. Three-Tiered Model of Best Practices for Homework Management

Tier 1: Universal prevention

Schools:
- Provide clear homework policies to parents and students
- Implement a homework hotline
- Develop a website devoted to addressing questions, posting resources, displaying class assignments

Teachers:
- Establish a routine of when homework will be a assigned and when it will be collected
- Clearly state the homework assignment
  - Announce the purpose of the assignment
  - Write the assignment on the board
  - Provide explicit instructions regarding how to complete the assignment
  - Provide examples
  - Remind students of assignment due dates
  - Inform students how the work will be graded
- Make homework meaningful to students by tying assignment to class instruction
- Be mindful of developmentally appropriate amounts of homework (the 10-minute rule)
- Provide feedback in a timely manner
- Implement the flipped classroom

Parents:
- Establish homework routines at home
  - Identify a quiet area away from distractions where homework may be completed
  - Designate a specific time that homework is to be completed
  - Ensure that your child has the materials needed to complete the homework
- Communicate with your child's teacher
- Talk to your child about the assignments
- Monitor your child while he or she completes the work

Tier 2: Targeted interventions

Schools:
- Organize an after-school homework club

Teachers:
- In collaboration with school psychologists:
  - Teach students organizational strategies
  - Help students develop good study habits
  - Teach students appropriate study skills
  - Tailor assignment to the skill level of the student
  - Identify whether academic tutoring is warranted
- Provide homework accommodations
- Use incentive systems
- Implement a class-wide contingency for homework management

Parents:
- Continue communication with teachers
  - School–home logs
  - Daily report cards

Tier 3: Intensive interventions

School psychologists in collaboration with teachers may
- Conduct a functional behavior assessment to determine why a student is not completing homework
- Develop individually tailored behavior management plans

Note. From "Best Practices in Managing Homework," by Peg Dawson, 2008, in A. Thomas and J. Grimes (Eds.), *Best Practices in School Psychology V* (pp. 1073–1084), Bethesda, MD: National Association of School Psychologists. Copyright 2008 by the National Association of School Psychologists. Adapted with permission.

- Develop learning community management systems, such as Edline or Moodle, which are websites that provide support for individual classes. Teachers may post homework assignments, upcoming tests, class expectations, and grades, as well as provide resources for students. Sites such as Edline primarily assist parents in viewing whether their child completed the homework assignments.

- Establish a classroom routine at the beginning of the school year that informs students and parents of the manner in which homework will be assigned and how it will be collected (Cooper & Valentine, 2001).

- Ensure that homework assignments are clearly stated so that students know exactly what they are required to do when completing the assignment at home. To facilitate understanding of what students need to do, classroom teachers should (a) announce the purpose of the assignment, (b) write the assignment on the board or send an assignment sheet home, (c) provide explicit instructions regarding how to complete the assignment as well as provide examples, (d) remind students periodically of the date the assignment is due, and (e) inform students of how the assignment will be graded (Dawson, 2008).

- Assign homework that is an extension of what was taught in class. Otherwise, the learning opportunity will be wasted if students are not able to complete the work because it is too difficult. Along these lines, it is important to make certain that the skill level of the student matches the instructional level of the assignment. Therefore, homework should be well planned and closely linked to classroom instruction (Bembenutty, 2011).

- Teachers should be mindful of the developmentally appropriate amount of homework. As mentioned previously, teachers should follow the 10-minute rule whereby 10 minutes of homework is allotted for each grade level (Cooper & Valentine, 2001).

- School psychologists should conduct classroom guidance sessions on tips for organizing and completing homework independently.

- Teachers should provide timely and appropriate feedback that corrects homework errors, thereby improving learning and understanding of class material. When work is corrected and returned in a timely manner, that is, within 24 hours of turning in the assignment, students better see where mistakes were made so that they may learn from their correction. Assignments with instructive comments significantly enhance learning.

Flipped Classrooms

Teachers may consider incorporating a relatively new method of blended learning into their repertoire, known as flipped classrooms (Fulton, 2012; Strayer, 2012). This type of instruction involves having teachers make videos of their lectures that are posted to teacher or school websites for students to upload and watch at home. If students do not have Internet access at home, then the teacher can provide the student with a DVD or jump drive of the lecture. The classroom is considered flipped because the lecture is considered to be homework while class time is spent actively engaged in practical application of the lecture to bolster students' understanding of the lesson. The idea is that students learn material during their own time and come to class ready to participate in class discussions and activities designed to promote active learning. Thus, students work on assignments and projects in school, so that the teacher has the opportunity to provide individual assistance to students who are experiencing difficulty. A significant advantage to the flipped classroom is that it engages students in the learning process so that students become active learners because teachers can focus on higher order thinking and can work directly with students rather than lecture them. Significantly, since students watch the videos at home, they can learn at their own pace. Students who master a concept can move on to the next, while students who find the material challenging can watch the video as many times as they need to until they understand the material. Moreover, if students are not able to attend school (i.e., sick), they can catch up by watching the videos at home. Flipping classrooms may be done for all grades, from kindergarten through high school.

What Parents Can Do

In this first tier, parents may also play an important role in the homework monitoring process. Significantly, establishing homework routines during the elementary school years send a clear message to children that schoolwork and learning are important. Further, it cultivates a sense of stability and routine that may be employed as part of their child's behavioral repertoire as the child goes through school (Dawson, 2010). Related to the development of a homework routine is the manner in which homework is actually carried out. School psychologists may assist parents with facilitating the homework process by using the following guidelines:

- Identify a designated quiet area in the home where their child can work most effectively.

- Ensure that their child has the materials necessary to complete the assignments (e.g., pencils, crayons, scissors, calculator).
- Identify a specific time when homework is expected to be completed (e.g., after school, after dinner). When their child arrives home from school, it is a good idea for parents to speak with their child about specific needs for completing that night's homework. In addition, it would be beneficial to discuss how their child plans to fulfill the assignments (Cooper & Valentine, 2001). To assist in this process, it is recommended that children use a homework planner where assignments are systematically listed so that parents are made aware of exactly what work was assigned. Maintaining a homework planner also facilitates and encourages communication with teachers (Dawson, 2008). Moreover, having both teachers and parents sign off on homework guarantees supervision by both parties.

At home, school psychologists may encourage parents to monitor their child while their child completes the homework. Monitoring includes answering questions, looking over completed work, and helping their child study for exams (Keith & Keith, 2006). Parental involvement in homework completion should be kept to a minimum. Parents are cautioned to "provide the minimum help necessary for the child to be successful" (Dawson, 2008, p. 1079). The reason for minimal assistance is that children need to develop a sense of independence and accomplishment, and to foster these behaviors children need to independently navigate and complete as much of their homework as possible. If parents find that their child is unable to successfully complete homework assignments, then it is advisable for parents to consult with their child's teacher to better address their specific concerns.

Tier 2

Students in this tier have not made adequate progress with respect to academic achievement and are in need of more focused, targeted interventions. As mentioned previously, homework noncompliance adversely affects educational performance. Therefore, strategies designed to facilitate homework in this stage in the RTI process are warranted. School psychologists, in collaboration with administrators, teachers, and parents, may assist students in various ways.

Organizational Skill Development

School psychologists may assist students in this tier by teaching organizational strategies, helping them develop good study habits, and teaching them effective study skills, using such approaches as the Survey, Question, Read, Recite, Review method (Dawson, 2008). This method is a reading strategy that has been shown to be effective in the comprehension of reading material. This method is a reading strategy that has been shown to be effective in the comprehension of reading material. In the first step, the survey, students skim the reading passage and identify headings, subheadings, pictures, graphs, and other elements in order to get a better sense of the content of the reading material. Students then formulate (and write down) questions based on their survey of the reading, or read questions asked by the teacher or posed at the end of the chapter. The purpose of the questions is to allow students to focus on the reading. The next step is for students to read the book or chapter and find answers to their questions. They then recite their answers from memory (to themselves or a partner). Finally, students review the main points of the reading again to ensure mastery of the material.

Tutoring

It is important to assess whether additional academic support, such as tutoring, is warranted. The school psychologist and classroom teacher may work collaboratively to develop assignments that are tailored to the skill level of the student. For instance, a student's reading and math skills may be assessed using curriculum-based or diagnostic norm-referenced methods, and in collaboration with the teacher, specific assignments may be developed to address academic areas in need of remediation. Weekly informal assessment of the student's academic progress should be conducted until the student reaches mastery levels. The student's academic progress may be further facilitated at home with parents' continued structure and encouragement of homework completion (Keith & Keith, 2006).

After-School Interventions

School psychologists might work with counselors and teachers to coordinate an after-school homework opportunity for students who need the assistance. For example, it would be beneficial for school psychologists to organize an after-school homework club whereby students may complete assigned work either with a trained peer tutor or under the supervision of teachers or administrators who may support them (Keith & Keith, 2006). In collaboration with classroom teachers and counselors, school psychologists may also recommend strategies such as self-monitoring, where students learn to monitor and evaluate their own homework completion; the incorporation of real-world homework assignments where students are encouraged to generalize the skills they learned in the classroom to their everyday lives; graphing of students' homework completion (Bryan & Sullivan-Burstein, 1998); and inclusion of student interests into assignments to give meaning to their learning.

Effective Parent–Teacher Communication

Students' homework should be monitored more carefully in this second tier to ensure compliance. For interventions to have the greatest success, collaboration between parents and teachers is necessary. Learning, for children, occurs across settings, particularly home and school. By providing consistency across children's primary contexts, parents and teachers can work together to promote student success. School psychologists should encourage teachers to reach out to parents whose children are experiencing homework problems, as parents are an integral component in effectively dealing with challenging homework problems. Active parental involvement is an essential part of improving performance in critical learning environments and overall learning and development (Sheridan, 2009). Thus, school psychologists should incorporate parents into the intervention to maximize the home–school partnership to promote positive student outcomes. As such, school–home logs or daily report cards may facilitate communication about the student's progress between settings. In addition to written communication, weekly or monthly phone calls as well as parent conferences to discuss homework progress would enhance the home–school partnership and, ultimately, homework performance. In this manner, children are aware that their parents and teachers are invested in their learning and success.

Accommodations

School psychologists may work with classroom teachers to provide homework accommodations such as

- Breaking assignments into smaller and more manageable tasks.
- Modifying the amount and kinds of assignments.
- Providing the student with a peer tutor to help with homework.
- Providing the student with examples of work that the student may refer to when completing assignments at home.

- Assisting the student in completing some of the homework problems before leaving school so that the student understands how to complete the task.
- Providing time during the school day to begin homework assignments, particularly difficult or challenging material, so that the student may receive assistance and have a better understanding of what he or she needs to do to complete the work; teachers may wish to pair students or have the class work in small groups.
- Not penalizing students for handwriting or spelling errors.
- Providing and allowing students to complete work for extra credit.
- Assigning lesser amounts of homework, with easier items initially, and gradually increasing the amount and difficulty as the student becomes more proficient.
- Modifying grading.

Incentives

Students in Tier 2 may also benefit from incentive systems that involve use of positive reinforcement, such as extra time at recess or computer time for homework completion (Dawson, 2010). Another positive behavioral support is what is referred to as a mystery motivator, which because of its novelty may serve as a powerful incentive for change. Mystery motivators are unknown but powerful reinforcers that a student receives contingent upon meeting a specified criterion (Madaus, Kehle, Madaus, & Bray, 2003). This behavioral intervention involves several steps:

- Mystery motivators must be both practical and easy to obtain, as well as acceptable to parents and teachers.
- In collaboration with the classroom teacher, the frequency with which the student will be rewarded with a mystery motivator for completing homework should be determined. Initially, students should be rewarded at least 3–4 days each week in order to establish the behavior, but the frequency of reinforcement should be reduced in order to fade the rewards over time.
- A mystery chart with each day of the week may be developed with "mystery motivator" written using invisible ink for the days of the week that the student will be rewarded. Thus, in order for students to earn an unknown but appealing reward, they must complete their homework to have the opportunity to determine whether they will receive a reward. Alternatively, teachers may write down a reward on

an index card and place the index card in a manila envelope with a question mark on the front. This serves as a visual cue for students to complete their homework to earn an unknown reward (Kehle, Bray, Theodore, Jenson, & Clark, 2000).

Group Contingencies

School psychologists may assist teachers with employing a group-oriented contingency, or class-wide intervention, to enhance homework performance in their classrooms. Group-oriented contingencies, which may be categorized as independent, interdependent, or dependent, target the same behaviors, criteria, and reinforcement for each student in the class (Theodore et al., 2009).

- *Independent group contingencies:* These are established when the standards for reinforcement are the same for the entire class, but rewards are based on each student's individual performance.
- *Interdependent group contingencies:* These are in effect when the same reward is delivered to the entire class based on the class meeting a specified criterion. There are several variations to this type of contingency. For instance, teachers may use class averages, high and low student performances, the performance of the entire class, and division of the class into teams (Theodore, Bray, Kehle, & DioGuardi, 2003).
- *Dependent group contingencies:* These reinforce the entire class based on the performance of one or a couple of selected students.

Group contingencies are particularly attractive to teachers because they are efficient with respect to teacher time and resources, are easy to employ because the teacher is managing only one contingency program, and are motivating for students (Lynch et al., 2009). Research has shown that all three contingencies are effective in improving homework performance (Lynch et al., 2009; Reinhardt et al., 2009; Theodore et al., 2009). Therefore, the choice of which contingency to use depends on teacher preferences as well as the characteristics of the particular class.

Tier 3

Services in Tier 3 typically consist of specifically designed interventions for students for whom strategies in Tiers 1 and 2 were unsuccessful. At this juncture, the student's academic functioning has been negatively affected. Students who do not complete their homework or who complete their homework but do not turn in their assignments may require more intensive support from classroom teachers and parents. There are many reasons why homework noncompliance exists, and the teacher and school psychologist are responsible for working collaboratively to determine these reasons.

Individually tailored strategies should be designed to meet the specific needs of the student by addressing the conditions that may be causing and maintaining homework noncompliance. Prior to developing an effective behavior management plan, it is important to first understand the function of a behavior. School psychologists, in collaboration with the students' teachers, may work together to develop a functional behavior assessment for this purpose. The goal of the functional behavior assessment is to identify the reason that the student is not completing homework or is failing to turn in assignments. As part of the functional behavior assessment process, it is beneficial to collect information about the student by reviewing the student's academic records (i.e., grades, attendance, and medical and social history); interviewing parents and teachers, as well as the students themselves; and observing the targeted students in various demand-center contexts (Steege & Watson, 2009). At this point it is essential to determine the function of the homework noncompliance so that an effective intervention may be designed to help the student be successful. Designing homework interventions is a natural extension of the consultative process whereby school psychologists seek to understand the needs of the student, the teacher, and the parents (Theodore et al., 2009).

Once the function of the homework noncompliance has been determined, behavior management strategies, such as behavior plans, homework charts, and token economy systems, which combine positive reinforcement for homework completion with punishment to decrease missed or incomplete homework, may be employed to improve the homework compliance of students in Tier 3. When designing homework interventions, it is important to involve the student in the planning of the intervention as well as in the creation of possible rewards. When developing interventions, students should understand how the intervention will work, when it will be employed, what the cost will be (e.g., how many tokens/points will be lost each time a homework assignment is not turned in), the reinforcers that are available, the points/tokens needed to earn rewards, and when points/tokens may be redeemed for rewards. Particularly noteworthy is that rewards need to be altered on a regular basis so that the rewards do not lose their reinforcing power (Pfiffner, Barkley, & DuPaul, 2006). Effective rewards differ from student to student, so various rewards will be reinforcing for different students. School psychologists may be involved in brainstorming school-based rewards that the teacher can use for students with homework issues. However, most important, it is the continued communication and progress monitoring between parents and teachers that are integral to student success (see Table 6.3).

SUMMARY

Despite the widely questioned value of homework, it continues to be a common practice in our nation's schools because researchers and practitioners alike attest to the benefits. In an era of increased accountability for documenting student learning, homework serves as a frequently employed teaching strategy that is influential to the learning process. Research has documented that students who engage in the homework process have higher grades than students who do not complete their homework (Cooper et al., 2006). Further, a well-established positive correlation exists between homework and achievement, and this correlation has been shown to be moderated by grade level. That is, homework provides greater academic benefits to children in middle and high-school as compared to elementary-age students (Zimmerman & Kitsantas, 2005).

Although homework at the lower grade levels minimally influences academic achievement, it has important implications for shaping students' values and beliefs regarding learning, as well as promoting personal responsibility and independence (e.g., the development of good study habits, self-discipline, and time-management skills), which generalize to nonacademic contexts. In essence, practice homework for younger students establishes routines and instills proper study skills that cultivate a sense of self-discipline that in turn promotes long-term understanding of academic material. Homework also serves to encourage an inquisitiveness of learning that may take place anywhere outside of the classroom and that ultimately improves students' attitudes toward school (Epstein & Van Voorhis, 2001).

Given the significant implications of homework, it is incumbent upon school psychologists and classroom teachers to work collaboratively within a multitiered system to support children with homework problems. This may be accomplished by providing teachers, parents, and students with effective strategies, interventions, and classroom accommodations that enhance the academic functioning of all children and adolescents.

REFERENCES

Bang, H. J. (2011). Promising homework practices: Teachers' perspectives on making homework work for newcomer immigrant students. *The High School Journal, 95*(2), 3–31. doi:10.1353/hsj.2012.0001

Bembenutty, H. (2011). Meaningful and maladaptive homework practices: The role of self-efficacy and self-regulation. *Journal of Advanced Academics, 22*, 448–473. doi:10.1177/1932202X1102200304

Bempechat, J., Li, J., Neier, S. M., Gillis, C. A., & Holloway, S. D. (2011). The homework experience: Perceptions of low-income youth. *Journal of Advanced Academics, 22*, 250–278. doi:10.1177/1932202X1102200204

Brock, C. H., Lapp, D., Flood, J., Fisher, D., & Tao, K. (2007). Does homework matter? An investigation of teacher perceptions about homework practices for children from nondominant backgrounds. *Urban Education, 42*, 349–372.

Bryan, T., Burstein, K., & Bryan, J. (2001). Students with learning disabilities: Homework problems and promising practices. *Educational Psychologist, 36*, 167–180. doi:10.1207/S15326985EP3603_3

Bryan, T., & Sullivan-Burstein, K. (1998). Teacher-selected strategies for improving homework completion. *Remedial and Special Education, 19*, 263–276. doi:10.1177/074193259801900502

Cancio, E. J., West, R. P., & Young, R. K. (2004). Improving mathematics homework completion and accuracy of students with EBD through self-management and parent participation. *Journal of Emotional and Behavioral Disorders, 12*, 9–22. doi:10.1177/10634266040120010201

Cooper, H., Robinson, J., & Patall, E. (2006). Does homework improve academic achievement? A synthesis of research, 1987–2003. *Review of Educational Research, 76*, 1–62. doi:10.3102/00346543076001001

Cooper, H., & Valentine, J. C. (2001). Using research to answer practical questions about homework. *Educational Psychologist, 36*, 143–153. doi:10.1207/S15326985EP3603_1

Dawson, P. (2008). Best practices in managing homework. In A. Thomas & J. Grimes (Eds.), *Best practices in school psychology V* (pp. 1073–1084). Bethesda, MD: National Association of School Psychologists.

Dawson, P. (2010). Homework: A guide for parents. In A. Canter, L. Z. Paige, & S. Shaw (Eds.), *Helping children at home and school III: Handouts from ·your school psychologist* (pp. S2H11-1–S2H11-4). Bethesda, MD: National Association of School Psychologists.

Dettmers, S., Trautwein, U., Ludtke, O., Kunter, M., & Baumert, J. (2010). Homework works if quality is high: Using multilevel modeling to predict the development of achievement in mathematics. *Journal of Educational Psychology, 102*, 467–482. doi:10.1037/a0018453

Epstein, J. L., & Van Voorhis, F. L. (2001). More than minutes: Teachers' roles in designing homework. *Educational Psychologist, 36*, 181–194. doi:10.1207/S15326985EP3603_4

Eren, O., & Henderson, D. J. (2011). Are we wasting our children's time by giving them more homework? *Economics of Education Review, 30*, 950–961.

Fulton, K. (2012). Upside down and inside out: Flip your classroom to improve student learning. *Learning & Leading With Technology, 39*, 12–17.

Kehle, T. L., Bray, M. A., Theodore, L. A., Jenson, W. R., & Clark, E. (2000). A multicomponent intervention designed to reduce disruptive classroom behavior. *Psychology in the Schools, 37,* 475–481. doi:10.1002/1520-6807 (200009)37 : 5<475 ::AID-PITS7>3.0. CO;2-P

Keith, T. Z., Diamond-Hallam, C., & Fine, J. G. (2004). Longitudinal effects of in-school and out-of-school homework on high school grades. *School Psychology Quarterly, 19,* 187–211. doi:10.1521/scpq. 19.3.187.40278

Keith, T. Z., & Keith, P. B. (2006). Homework. In G. G. Bear & K. M. Minke (Eds.), *Children's needs III: Development, prevention, and intervention* (pp. 615–629). Bethesda, MD: National Association of School Psychologists.

Lynch, A., Theodore, L. A., Bray, M. A., & Kehle, T. J. (2009). A comparison of group-oriented contingencies and randomized reinforcers to improve homework completion and accuracy for students with disabilities. *School Psychology Review, 38,* 307–324.

Madaus, M. R., Kehle, T. J., Madaus, J., & Bray, M. A. (2003). Mystery motivator as an intervention to promote homework completion and accuracy. *School Psychology International, 24,* 369–377. doi:10.1177/01430343030244001

Maltese, A. V., Tai, R. H., & Fan, X. (2012). When is homework worth the time? Evaluating the association between homework and achievement in high school science and math. *The High School Journal, 96*(1), 52–71. doi:10.1353/hsj.2012.0015

National Association of School Psychologists. (2010). *Model for comprehensive and integrated school psychological services.* Bethesda, MD: Author. Retrieved from http://www.nasponline.org/standards/ 2010standards/2_PracticeModel.pdf

National Commission on Excellence in Education. (1983). *A nation at risk: The imperative for educational reform.* Washington, DC: U.S. Government Printing Office.

National Education Association. (n.d.). *Research spotlight on homework.* Washington, DC: Author. Retrieved from http://www.nea.org/ tools/16938.htm

Patall, E. A., Cooper, H., & Robinson, J. C. (2008). Parent involvement in homework: A research synthesis. *Review of Educational Research, 78,* 1039–1101. doi:10.3102/0034654308325185

Pfiffner, L. J., Barkley, R. A., & DuPaul, G. J. (2006). Treatment of ADHD in school settings. In R. A. Barkley (Ed.), *Attention deficit hyperactivity disorder: A handbook for diagnosis and treatment* (3rd ed., pp. 547–589). New York, NY: Guilford Press.

Power, T. J., Karutsis, J. L., & Habboushe, D. F. (2001). *Homework success for children with ADHD: A family-school intervention program.* New York, NY: Guilford Press.

Power, T. J., Werba, B. E., Watkins, M. W., Angelucci, J. G., & Eiraldi, R. B. (2006). Patterns of parent-reported homework problems among ADHD-referred and nonreferred children. *School Psychology Quarterly, 21,* 13–33. doi:10.1521/scpq.2006.21.1.13

Reinhardt, D., Theodore, L. A., Bray, M. A., & Kehle, T. J. (2009). Improving homework accuracy: Interdependent group contingencies and randomized components. *Psychology in the Schools, 46,* 471–488. doi:10.1002/pits.20391

Rowell, L., & Hong, E. (2002). The role of school counselors in homework intervention. *Professional School Counseling, 5,* 285–291.

Sheridan, S. M. (2009). Homework interventions for children with attention and learning problems: Where is the "home" in "homework?" *School Psychology Review, 38,* 334–337.

Steege, M. W., & Watson, T. S. (2009). *Conducting school-based functional behavioral assessments: A practitioner's guide* (2nd ed.). New York, NY: Guilford Press.

Strayer, J. F. (2012). How learning in an inverted classroom influences cooperation, innovation and task orientation. *Learning Environments Research, 5,* 173–191. doi:10.1007/s10984-012-9108-4

Theodore, L. A., Bray, M. A., Kehle, T. J., & DioGuardi, R. J. (2003). Contemporary review of group-oriented contingencies for disruptive behavior. *Journal of Applied School Psychology, 20,* 79–101. doi:10.1300/J370v20n01_06

Theodore, L. A., DioGuardi, R. J., Hughes, T. L., Carlo, M., & Eccles, D. (2009). A class-wide intervention for improving homework performance. *Journal of Educational and Psychological Consultation, 19,* 275–299. doi:10.1080/10474410902888657

U.S. Department of Education. (1986). *What works.* Washington, DC: Author.

Van Voorhis, F. L. (2011). Costs and benefits of family involvement in homework. *Journal of Advanced Academics, 22,* 220–249. doi:10. 1177/1932202X1102200203

Zimmerman, B. J., & Kitsantas, A. (2005). Homework practices and academic achievement: The mediating role of self-efficacy and perceived responsibility beliefs. *Contemporary Educational Psychology, 30,* 397–417. doi:10.1016/j.cedpsych.2005.05.003

7

Best Practices on Interventions for Students With Reading Problems

Laurice M. Joseph
Ohio State University

OVERVIEW

Approximately 33% of fourth graders and 24% of eighth graders read below grade level (National Assessment of Educational Progress, 2011). These statistics are troubling given the fact that reading is a critical skill that is not only necessary for achieving success across various content areas in K–12 and postsecondary education settings but also in employment settings. Today, more than ever, with advancements in technology, the majority of employment settings demand sufficient literacy skills. Individuals who are illiterate are not able to compete in today's global job market, and many will end up living in poverty. Moreover, social interactions may diminish for individuals who are not able to communicate or comprehend communications received via technology.

Given these statistics, it is no wonder that students with reading problems constitute the majority of referrals for school psychological services (Bramlett, Murphy, Johnson, Wallingsford, & Hall, 2002). According to the National Association of School Psychologists (NASP) *Model for Comprehensive and Integrated School Psychological Services* (NASP, 2010), it is critical that school psychologists achieve competence in using a problem-solving model to select and facilitate the use of interventions and instructional support that are aimed at helping students develop reading skills.

The purpose of this chapter is first to describe the critical reading skills that school psychologists should be aware of so that they have a better understanding of the skills that students need to obtain to become proficient readers. Next, a discussion about teaching critical reading skills within a multitiered service delivery model

is provided. This is followed by a discussion on phases of learning reading skills and implementing evidence-based instructional components using data-based problem-solving methods. Last, a description of various evidence-supported supplemental reading techniques is provided for school psychologists who consult with educators and parents about selecting and implementing effective reading interventions.

BASIC CONSIDERATIONS

There are reading skills that are considered to be critical for individuals to achieve during their K–12 school years so that they can function adequately in society upon graduation.

Critical Skills of Reading

The critical reading skills, sometimes referred to as the big ideas of reading, are phonemic awareness, alphabetic principle, fluency, vocabulary, and comprehension. Key legislation such as the 2004 No Child Left Behind Act has stipulated that these critical skills be addressed in school curricula across the nation. Moreover, students who are referred to school psychologists will likely demonstrate difficulties with one or more of these skills. What follows is a detailed discussion about each skill.

Phoneme Awareness

A phoneme is considered an individual sound, which is the smallest unit of sound in a word. Phonemic awareness is a specific skill that involves attending to and manipulating individual sounds (phonemes) of spoken words. There are approximately 41 phonemes in the English language. Daly, Chafouleas, and Skinner (2005) present a hierarchy of phonemic awareness skills:

- *Alliteration*: Refers to identifying and saying the first sound in a word, such as saying /c/ for the word *cab* and identifying words that have the same first sound, such as in the words *cap*, *cup*, and *can*.
- *Blending:* Involves stringing together the individual sounds of a word to make a whole word such as the sounds /c-u-p/ to form the word *cup*.
- *Segmenting:* Involves breaking a spoken word (e.g., *cup*) apart by saying each individual sound in that word (e.g., /c-u-p/). Children can also practice breaking the word apart by simultaneously clapping to each individual sound while saying them.
- *Manipulation:* Involves deleting, substituting, and reversing individual sounds in words to make new words. When the word *can* is articulated, children are asked to say the new word when the /c/ sound "walks away." When /f/ sound "comes over" to stand in the /c/ place, children are asked to say the new word, *fan*. Children may also reverse the sounds in the word *tap* to form another word *pat*. Children can also add sounds to a word such as adding /s/ to the word *pit* to form the word *spit*.

As children move from one hierarchical phase to another, they are likely to refine the skills that they learned in preceding phases (Anthony, Lonigan, Driscoll, Phillips, & Burgess, 2003).

Although the development of all phonemic awareness skills influences reading outcomes for children (Smith, Scott, Roberts, & Locke, 2008), educators should note that, among the phonemic awareness skills, phoneme segmentation was the best predictor of first graders' word reading performance (Nation & Hulme, 1997). Specifically, children should be able to segment initial and final sounds by the middle of their kindergarten year; segment and blend consonant–vowel, vowel–consonant, and consonant–vowel–consonant by the end of their kindergarten year; and segment and blend words with consonant blends by the beginning of their first grade year (Schuele & Boudreau, 2008).

Phonemic awareness is distinct from phonological awareness even though the terms are often mistakenly used interchangeably. Actually, phonemic awareness falls under the larger umbrella term phonological awareness. One way to distinguish phonemic awareness from phonological awareness is to classify phonological awareness as large segmentation skills and phonemic awareness as small segmentation skills (Carroll, Snowling, Hulme, & Stevenson, 2003). Large segmentation skills involve segmenting syllables and onsets and rimes. Onsets refers to the consonant sound that precedes the vowel such as /c/ in the word *can*. Rime refers to the portion of the syllable that comes after the initial consonant or consonants of a word. For the word *can*, the rime is /an/. Most children progress from segmenting syllables to segmenting onsets and rimes, and then to segmenting individual sounds of words (Thatcher, 2010). Phonemic awareness eases students' way into gaining an understanding of the alphabetic principle.

Alphabetic Principle

The alphabetic principle refers to understanding that there is an association between letters and sounds. Children begin to realize that written words are a representation of spoken words and objects in their environment when they begin to make letter–sound associations (De Graaff, Bosman, Hasselman, & Verhoeven, 2009). This is particularly the case for children who have acquired phonemic awareness as they form an awareness of the regular ways letters represent sounds, which makes it possible to identify words in context even if they can only be partially sounded out (Torgesen & Mathes, 2000).

Children who can make letter–sound associations are likely to develop reading fluency (Perfetti & Bolger, 2004). Explicit instruction on letter–sound associations can begin in kindergarten. It improved early reading skills of kindergartners at risk for not developing those skills (Coyne, Kame'enui, Simmons, & Harn, 2004). Moreover, kindergartners who received letter–sound association instruction outperformed their peers who received whole word instruction on reading words that were unfamiliar to them (Cardoso-Martins, 2001).

By the time children enter first grade, they move from simple to more advanced ways of making letter–sound associations. Many of the basic printed words that first graders encounter in stories are words with consonant–vowel–consonant patterns, and they require children to sequentially decode the words by making one-to-one letter–sound correspondences. For instance, children look at the letters /c-u-p/ and say each sound of the word (decode) and then blend the sounds together to produce the word *cup*. At more advanced levels, children hierarchically decode words by using letters in words to cue the sounds of other letters such as using the letter *e* at the end of the word *cake* to cue themselves to make a long vowel sound for the letter *a* (McCormick, 2003).

Appropriate types and sufficient amounts of instruction on the alphabetic principle are critical to children's overall reading achievement (Al Otaiba et al., 2008). Instruction on the alphabetic principle is usually done through a phonics approach. Having stated that, it should be noted here that the terms *alphabetic principle* and *phonics* are not synonymous. Phonics is a type of method for teaching children to make letter–sound associations.

Reading decoding skills are a good predictor of oral reading fluency (Cummings, Dewey, Latimer, & Good, 2011). Teaching students reading decoding skills helps children read words in stories or passages with a reduced number of hesitations and errors (Lo, Cooke, & Starling, 2011). In a review of studies, findings revealed that even students with reading problems in secondary grades benefited from explicit phonics instruction (Joseph & Schisler, 2009).

Fluency

Reading words in context such as in stories and in passages helps children apply their decoding and recognition skills (Carnine, Silbert, Kame'enui, & Tarver, 2004). Children often read words at slow rates when they have not learned to apply decoding skills efficiently (Allor & Chard, 2011). These students have not made the shift from intentional decoding to automatic word recognition (Kuhn, 2005), and this transition occurs through reading words repeatedly (Torgesen et al., 2001). Moreover, not being able to read words effortlessly hinders an ability to gain meaning from text (Ehri, 2005).

Children are likely to cross over the bridge from recognizing words accurately to comprehending text if they develop fluency (Kim, Wagner, & Lopez, 2012). Fluency refers to reading words in passages accurately, at a conversational pace, and in a proper expressive manner (National Reading Panel, 2000). Reading with expression (prosody) means exhibiting variations in pitch, loudness, and duration; pausing between sentences; stressing syllables; and using intonation that is reflective of the statements in the text (Couper-Kuhlen, 1986; Hudson, Lane, & Pullen, 2005). Reading with expression can be a sign that meaning was derived from text (Rasinski, 2012). On the contrary, children who read with little or no expression are not likely to comprehend the full meaning of the text (Benjamin & Schwanenflugel, 2010). For instance, less-skilled second- and third-grade readers were observed to make longer pauses both within and between sentences compared to their peers who were skilled readers (Schwanenflugel, Hamilton, Kuhn, & Stahl, 2004).

Carnine et al. (2004) suggested that oral reading passage fluency exercises should be incorporated into daily reading lessons in the elementary grades until children read approximately 135 words per minute with 97% accuracy on fourth-grade texts. Children will likely advance to higher level comprehension skills when their fluency levels are adequate (Kuhn et al., 2006). Moreover, feelings of frustration from working slowly and needing more time to accomplish assignments are minimized for fluent readers (Carnine et al., 2004). Reading fluently becomes especially critical in intermediate and secondary grades when students are expected to read more texts written in various genres (e.g., expository, persuasive).

Vocabulary

Children who were identified as having poor reading skills progressed through their school years with lower vocabulary than children with good reading skills (Cain & Oakhill, 2011). Vocabulary refers to knowing the meaning of words, and it is predictive of children's listening and reading comprehension performance with positive correlations ranging from .6 to .8 (Pearson, Hiebert, & Kamil, 2007). Vocabulary is also related to phonological decoding skills. For instance, young children who know the meanings of many words find it easier to make distinctions among words that differ on the basis of one phoneme, such as the words *fat* versus *fit* (Reese, Suggate, Long, & Schaughency, 2010).

With regard to vocabulary, size matters as it is related to reading comprehension performance (Stahl & Nagy, 2006). Children's receptive vocabulary is four times larger than their expressive vocabulary (Jalongo & Sobolak, 2011). Preschool-age children experience the highest rate of vocabulary growth (Farkas & Beron, 2004). Many children have accumulated about 42 million words by the time they reach the age of 4 (Hart & Risley, 2003), and actually speak about 10,000 words when they enter school (Childers & Tomasello, 2002). According to Byrnes and Wasik (2009), this figure breaks down to learning 5 to 6 new words per day, 38 new words per week, 2,000 new words a year, and 10,000 words by age 6.

These figures are not necessarily representative of children from low-income families who have limited oral language experiences (Hart & Risely, 2003), as these children are not accumulating vocabulary at a rate that is comparable to their advantaged peers. For instance, second-grade children who have limited oral language experiences knew 4,000–8,000 fewer word meanings than their peers with rich oral language experiences

(Biemiller, 2004). Higher achieving students acquired four times as many words as lower achieving students when they completed high school (Hirsch, 2003).

Children can increase their vocabulary by engaging in reading and writing activities. For children who struggle with understanding the meanings of words, vocabulary should be taught in a direct and systematic manner (Biemiller, 2004). Explicit forms of vocabulary instruction (i.e., deliberately explaining word meanings and providing key examples) had stronger effects for helping children increase their vocabulary over implicit forms of instruction (Marulis & Neuman, 2010). Teachers should spend most of vocabulary instruction time on explicitly teaching the meaning of words that are widely used in various texts and in mature conversations. These words convey ideas or feelings rather than objects. According to Beck, McKeown, and Kucan (2005), these types of words can be classified as Tier 2 words. Examples of Tier 2 words are *anxious*, *conflict*, and *aggressive*. Tier 1 words are already in most children's oral language repertoires. Examples are *cup*, *carpet*, and *room*. These words require little instruction time because they can be pictured and labeled and are already a part of most children's oral language repertoires (Morgan & Meier, 2008). Tier 3 words are words that are not widely used in conversations or found in most texts. These words are specific to content areas such as science, math, or social studies. Examples are *ions*, *chlorophyll*, and *molecule* (Beck et al., 2005).

Reading Comprehension

Reading comprehension refers to "the process of simultaneously extracting meaning through interaction and involvement with written language" (Shanahan et al., 2010, p. 5). Although instruction on comprehending text certainly begins in the elementary grades, it becomes the primary focus of reading instruction in the intermediate and secondary grades. Reading comprehension involves activating prior knowledge; understanding text structure; previewing, questioning, predicting, and knowing word meanings; identifying the main idea; making inferences; relating sentences and paragraphs to each other; and summarizing (Randi, Grigorenko, & Sternberg, 2005). Activating prior knowledge refers to ascertaining what is already known about the theme or topic of a story or passage. Understanding text structure refers to knowing key features that are included in narrative and expository texts. For instance, most narrative text contains information about the characters, setting, events, plot, conflict, and resolution. Expository texts may include,

for instance, compare and contrast, cause and effect, and problem and solution statements. Previewing involves examining key elements of a story or passage before reading the story or passage. For instance, students may obtain ideas about the topic and key concepts of the story or passage by examining the title, headings, vocabulary words (particularly those printed in boldface type), beginning and ending sentences, and graphics. After students preview the text, they are in a better position to begin generating questions about what they hope to learn from reading the text (Alber-Morgan & Joseph, 2013). As students begin to read the text, they can make predictions about the outcome of events in a story or passage. Making inferences refers to speculating about characters (e.g., a character's feelings) or actions (e.g., cause of the action) that are not clearly stated in the text. Students with learning disabilities have difficulties with these comprehension skills and do not have a repertoire of strategies that they can apply to gain meaning from text and monitor their understanding of text (Jitendra & Gajria, 2011).

Table 7.1 presents a summary of the critical skills with regard to their characteristics and research findings.

BEST PRACTICES IN INTERVENTIONS FOR STUDENTS WITH READING PROBLEMS

School psychologists can assist teachers in helping students learn critical reading skills in classrooms that contain a systematic multitiered service delivery approach to teaching reading.

Helping Students Learn Critical Reading Skills in a Multitiered Service Delivery Approach

Most multitiered delivery approaches of teaching reading consist of three tiers of assessment and intervention (Brown-Chidsey & Steege, 2010). Tier 1 involves providing large-group reading instruction and monitoring students' progress at the beginning, middle, and end of the school year. School psychologists can assist teachers in using the progress monitoring data to identify students who are not responding favorably to a Tier 1 level of reading instruction and who need Tier 2 reading interventions. Tier 2 involves providing supplemental small-group reading interventions to a group of students who did not respond well to the Tier 1 level of instruction. Assessment occurs more often in this tier, which is anywhere from twice a week to once a month. School psychologists can assist teachers in examining the

Table 7.1. Summary of Critical Reading Skills: Major Characteristics and Research Findings

Critical Skills	Characteristics	Research Findings
Phoneme awareness	Attending to and manipulating individual sounds of spoken words through activities such as isolating, blending, segmenting, deleting, substituting, and reversing sounds in words.	Phonemic awareness, particularly phoneme segmentation, is a good predictor of word reading skills (Nation & Hulme, 1997; Smith, Scott, Roberts, & Locke, 2008).
Alphabetic principle	Understanding and producing associations between letters and sounds by making one-to-one correspondences between letters and sounds and by using letters to cue the sounds of other letters in a word.	Kindergartners who were taught letter–sound correspondences outperformed their peers who received whole word instruction on reading words that were unfamiliar to them (Cardoso-Martins, 2001).
	A type of method for teaching children to make letter–sound correspondences is phonics.	Children who can make letter–sound correspondences are likely to develop reading fluency (Cummings, Dewey, Latimer, & Good, 2011; Perfetti & Bolger, 2004) and make fewer hesitations and errors while reading passages (Lo, Cooke, & Starling, 2011).
Fluency	Reading words in a passage accurately, at a conversational pace, and in a proper expressive manner (i.e., varying pitch, using intonation that reflects statements in text, stressing syllables, and pausing between sentences).	Oral reading passage fluency exercises should be incorporated into daily reading lessons in the elementary grades until children are able to read 135 words per minute with 97% accuracy on fourth-grade texts (Carnine, Silbert, Kame'enui, & Tarver, 2004).
		Children who are fluent readers are more likely to comprehend text at deeper levels (Kuhn et al., 2006).
		Children who read with little or no expression are not likely to comprehend the full meaning of text (Benjamin & Schwanenflugel, 2010).
Vocabulary	Knowing the meaning of words.	Vocabulary predicts children's listening and reading comprehension performance (Pearson, Hiebert, & Kamil, 2007).
	Vocabulary instruction time for school-age children should primarily be devoted to teaching the meaning of words that convey ideas or feelings, as these types of words are widely used in a variety of texts.	Children who know the meanings of words find it easier to make distinctions among words that differ on the basis of one phoneme (Reese, Suggate, Long, & Schaughency 2010).
		Explicit forms of vocabulary instruction had stronger effects over implicit forms, helping learners who struggle with acquiring meaning of words.
Comprehension	Gaining meaning from text through activating prior knowledge, understanding text structure, knowing word meanings, identifying main ideas, making inferences, and relating sentences and paragraphs to each other.	Students who experience difficulties comprehending text do not have a repertoire of strategies to aid them in monitoring their understanding of text (Jitendra & Gajria, 2011).
		Gaining meaning from text can be achieved through the use of strategies such as previewing, questioning, and predicting (Randi, Grigorenko, & Sternberg, 2005).

progress monitoring data collected in this tier to determine if the interventions are effective or if more intensive interventions are needed (i.e., Tier 3). Tier 3 involves providing supplemental one-to-one reading intervention to students who did not respond well to Tier 2 intervention. Assessment is very frequent and occurs anywhere from a daily to a weekly basis.

As students move from Tier 1 to Tier 2 and Tier 3 levels of instruction, school psychologists can collaboratively work with teachers to design interventions that involve an increase in the intensity and length of instruction. This often means that students receiving Tiers 2 and 3 interventions are given more demonstrations of how to perform a skill, more opportunities to practice with corrective feedback, more learning trials, including timed trials to perform skills fluently, and more opportunities to generalize content or skills. Researchers have shown that children who received small-group lessons in addition to whole-class reading instruction greatly improved on their reading skills and achieved greater gains than children who did not receive the supplemental small-group lessons (e.g., Fien et al., 2011; Pullen, Tuckwiller, Konold, Maynard, & Coyne, 2010).

Before describing specific evidence-based reading methods and techniques, it is important to mention that school psychologists have an ethical obligation to recommend the use of evidence-based instructional components and techniques across all tier levels of instruction rather than methods that have not been supported through research. Although there is no guarantee that any given evidence-based instructional component and technique will be effective for a particular student, there is a greater chance of obtaining positive outcomes if evidence-based methods are used with that student rather than unsupported methods (Brown-Chidsey & Steege, 2010). Thus, implementing evidence-based instructional components and techniques not only is effective but is an efficient way of helping students, as time is not wasted on implementing methods that are not likely to result in desirable outcomes (Konrad, Helf, & Joseph, 2011).

To enhance the efficiency of implementing evidence-based instruction methods across the tiers, school psychologists, educators, and other related service personnel should collaboratively use data-based problem-solving methods of practice to help students achieve desired reading skill outcomes. Data-based problem-solving models of practice permit school psychologists to use data to identify students' reading skill needs, target appropriate interventions, develop procedures for how interventions will be implemented, implement interventions with procedural integrity, monitor students' progress or their responsiveness to the intervention, and evaluate students' performance. If desired outcomes were not achieved, school psychologists can work with other professionals to determine which instructional components were effective and which were ineffective and make the necessary modifications until desired student outcomes are achieved.

There are evidence-based instructional components that should be incorporated across all tiers, across all reading skills, and within any reading program or technique according to a student's phase of learning. These instructional components consist of demonstration, guided practice, independent practice with corrective feedback, and programming for generalization of skills. Learning new reading skills usually progresses from acquisition to fluency to generalization phases (Daly et al., 2005). Acquisition refers to the phase at which students are beginning to learn how to perform a new skill. Fluency refers to demonstrating how to perform the skill without hesitation and with automaticity. Generalization refers to how well students are able to apply the skill in other contexts. School psychologists, teachers, and other related service personnel determine at which phase of learning students are currently functioning through data-based problem-solving methods such as those previously described.

Knowing which phase of intervention students are in need of helps educators implement the necessary instructional components that are designed to meet specific learning needs. Table 7.2 presents the instructional components that best address each phase of learning. For instance, demonstration, guided practice, and independent practice with corrective feedback are methods for helping students acquire skills. Timed independent practice trials and programming for generalization are ways students can become fluent with skills because they are receiving several opportunities to practice skills in multiple and varied contexts. Programming for generalization helps students learn to apply skills in contexts that differ from the one that the skill was initially taught.

These instructional components are designed to promote errorless learning (i.e., minimize time students spend practicing errors) and are implemented in a seamless manner that result in a "my turn, together, and your turn" process (Bursuck & Damer, 2011). It may not be necessary to implement all of these components. For instance, some students may have demonstrated acquisition of a skill; however, they are not fluent at performing that skill. Through data-based problem-solving methods, school psychologists can assist teachers in determining which components to implement according to the individual needs of their students (i.e., differentiating instruction).

Tier 1: General Reading Instruction Strategies for All Students

What follows provides a detailed description of instructional components and how they can be implemented to address acquisition, fluency, and generalization phases of developing reading skills.

Table 7.2. Evidence-Based Instructional Components Associated With Learning Phases

Instructional Components	Acquisition	Fluency	Generalization
Demonstration	Showing students how to perform a skill		
Guided practice	Taking turns performing the skill with the students		
Independent practice with corrective feedback	Giving students opportunities to perform the skill on their own with corrective feedback		
Timed independent practice trials		Having students complete short-duration (e.g., 1 minute) timed skill practice trials	
Programming for generalization		Providing additional opportunities for students to practice performing a skill in multiple contexts	Creating conditions for students to perform skill in multiple contexts

Reading Acquisition Phase

School psychologists can collaborate with teachers to design ways to demonstrate and create guided and independent reading practice activities for students who are at the acquisition phase of learning how to perform reading skills.

Demonstration (my turn). When students are at an acquisition phase of learning, teacher demonstration of how to perform a skill is often needed. This is best accomplished when teachers make explicit the process of performing the skill (Skinner, Logan, Robinson, & Robinson, 1997). Teachers can do this by verbalizing their behavior as the teachers are demonstrating the skill. For example, demonstrating the decoding of the word *sat* might involve the teacher's saying, "I see that the first letter in the word is *s*, and the *s* makes the /s/ sound. I see that the second letter is *a*, and it makes the /a/ sound because it is a short vowel sound. Then, I see the letter *t*, and it makes the /t/ sound. If I blend all the sounds together, they make the word *sat*."

Guided practice (together). During the acquisition phase of learning, guided practice immediately follows demonstration. This involves giving the student an opportunity to complete the task with teacher prompts and corrective feedback (Carnine et al., 2004). In the previous example, the teacher might give the following prompt: "Now I am going to point to the first letter of the word *sat* and I want you to tell me the sound the *s* makes," and so forth. If the student responds correctly, then the teacher says, "Good, the letter *s* makes the /s/ sound." If the student responds

incorrectly, then the teacher says, "Watch me, this is the letter *s* and it makes the /s/ sound. Now, try it again." The prompt is gradually faded as students demonstrate mastery of the skill. For example, the teacher might just point to the first letter of the word *sat* without providing verbal directions and wait for the student to make a response. Then, the student is provided with words he or she has already learned to decode so that the student can discriminate between decoding the newly targeted word (i.e., *s-a-t*) with words previously learned. Guided practice can be completed with a whole classroom of students using active student responding methods such as choral responding. Choral responding consists of all the students verbally responding in unison to teacher questions or prompts (Alber-Morgan, 2010).

Independent practice with corrective feedback (your turn). After a student has achieved completing a task successfully with teacher guidance, the student is asked to complete the task independently with minimal teacher direction. Using the same example, the teacher might say, "Now decode the word *sat* on your own." Corrective feedback is then given.

Reading Fluency Phase

In many classrooms, minimal time is devoted to helping children achieve fluency with skills. To prevent low-performing readers from falling even further behind their peers, a portion of classroom time needs to be devoted to having children practice skills and achieve fluency so they can begin to catch up with their peers (McCurdy, Daly, Gortmaker, Bonfiglio, & Perampieri,

2007). School psychologists can work with teachers to create daily short-duration timed reading skill probes to help students become fluent at performing the skills independently.

Once students are provided with demonstrations and guided and independent practice opportunities on reading a set of words, the teacher may ask the students to read as many words in the set as quickly as they can in 1 minute to build fluency. At the completion of the timed trial, the number of correct responses along with the number of errors is recorded. The timed trials are repeatable, and students are encouraged to record their performance on a graph or chart so they can monitor changes in their performance over time.

Reading Generalization Phase

Additional ways to build fluency is to provide students with opportunities to perform the reading skill in multiple contexts. School psychologists can work collaboratively with educators, staff, and parents to create opportunities for students to practice reading skills in a variety of contexts.

Ways of programming for generalization are providing natural contingencies of reinforcement, teaching enough examples, and programming common stimuli (Cooper, Heron, & Heward, 2007). Aiming for natural contingencies of reinforcement may involve, for instance, assessing students' preferences, choosing reading materials that are interesting and meaningful to the students, and providing students with choices of instructional arrangements (working in small groups or one-to-one). Teaching enough examples consists of providing examples that represent various contexts and response modes for which the skills are likely to be performed. For instance, students can be provided with various types of text genres (e.g., expository, narrative, opinion) where they may encounter the same words. Students can also be instructed to use various response topographies to complete tasks, such as saying the words and writing them. Finally, teachers can program common stimuli by making settings as similar

as possible to the teaching setting where the student first learned a particular skill. For instance, students can be given portable cue cards containing strategies for decoding words that can be used in various classrooms and at home.

Tiers 2 and 3: Supplemental Evidence-Based Reading Intervention Techniques

Teachers will most likely consult with school psychologists about students who need instruction that supplements the instruction (i.e., Tier 1 whole-class instruction) they are already receiving in the classroom. There are various supplemental evidence-based reading intervention techniques that are designed to help students obtain fundamental reading skills. These techniques can be used with students who need Tier 2 (small-group) or Tier 3 (one-to-one) level of instruction in the classroom. These procedures may also be implemented using cross-age or same-age peer tutors if the tutors receive sufficient training on the intervention procedures. The following techniques are not exhaustive of all possible evidence-based techniques. The techniques presented here incorporate many of the effective instructional components that were previously mentioned. Additionally, the techniques require minimal teacher preparation, are low cost, are easy to implement, and promote active student responding.

Table 7.3 presents a summarized list of these supplemental evidence-based instructional techniques that school psychologists and teachers may collaboratively select and implement across critical reading skills. As can be seen from the table, several of the techniques can be used to teach a variety of reading skills. Using the same technique to teach more than one skill can be particularly efficient with regard to preparation time, student training time, and cost of materials.

Sound and Letter Boxes

Sound boxes, commonly referred to as Elkonin boxes (Elkonin, 1973), are a technique that school psychologists may suggest for students who need help with

Table 7.3. Examples of Supplemental Evidence-Based Instructional Techniques That Can Be Implemented Across Critical Reading Skills

Critical Skills	Examples of Evidence-Based Instruction Techniques
Phoneme awareness	Sound boxes, time delay, recorded words
Alphabetic principle	Letter boxes, time delay, recorded words, incremental rehearsal
Fluency	Repeated readings with phrase drill error correction, listening passage preview
Vocabulary	Time delay, recorded words, incremental rehearsal
Comprehension	Paragraph shrinking; story mapping; Ask, Read With Alertness, Tell + Peer Discussion; RAP-Q; FIST; Click or Clunk

learning phoneme segmentation skills. This technique has also been described as a "say it–move it" activity (Blachman, Ball, Black, & Tangle, 2000). A rectangle is drawn on a dry-erase board, piece of paper, or cardboard. The rectangle is divided with drawn vertical lines to create a series of connected boxes according to the number of sounds heard in a given word. Tokens or other small objects that can easily slide into the boxes are placed below the connected boxes. The teacher orally presents a word, and the student is instructed to slide the token into the respective box as each sound in the word is slowly articulated. Initially the teacher models the procedure for the student. For example, the teacher says the word *h-a-t* by articulating each sound slowly and simultaneously placing a token in the first box when the sound /h/ is pronounced, placing a token in the second box when the sound /a/ is pronounced, and placing a token in the third and final box when the sound /t/ is pronounced. Then, the teacher and student complete the task together by articulating the sounds of a word slowly and placing the tokens in the student's respective boxes. After the teacher and student complete the task together, the teacher prompts the student to complete aspects of the task on his or her own. Last, the student completes the task independently with corrective feedback. During this phase, the student may be instructed to repetitively move his or her finger just below the connected boxes and blend the sounds together until the student is articulating every sound in the word quickly and effortlessly. Blank square-shaped tiles can be used rather than drawn connected boxes. This technique has been shown to be effective for helping preschool and kindergarten children develop phonemic awareness skills (e.g., Ball & Blachman, 1991; Keesey, Konrad, & Joseph, 2013; Maslanka & Joseph, 2002).

School psychologists may suggest the use of letter boxes as a variation of sound boxes for students who need help with making letter–sound correspondences. The same procedures are used except that tokens are replaced with letters (e.g., plastic letters, magnetic letters, or letter tiles). Eventually, students can be taught to write the letters in the boxes as they articulate each sound. The connected boxes are gradually faded by first removing the solid lines that divide the boxes and replacing them with dotted lines. Students are asked to articulate sounds of the word while sliding letters in the fading connected boxes. Next, the dotted lines are removed, leaving a large rectangle. Eventually, the rectangle is removed and students make the letter–sound correspondences without the supportive structure. This procedure has been used within the comprehensive Reading Recovery program when children need assistance making letter–sound sequences while they are attempting to decode words (Clay, 1993). Letter boxes are effective for helping primary-grade children with and without disabilities to decode words (Joseph, 2000, 2002).

Time-Delay Procedures

School psychologists may recommend the use of time-delay procedures for students who need help with basic reading skills, such as making letter–sound correspondences, recognizing words as a whole, and defining words. Initially described by Touchette (1971), time-delay procedures, in general, involve a teacher demonstrating a correct response immediately followed by asking the student to make that same response. This is referred to as a zero-second delay response. Then, the student is asked to respond on his or her own without the response being modeled. Typically, the student is given about 3 seconds to make a correct response, and if the student does not make a correct response within that time frame, then the teacher demonstrates how to make the correct response. This permits students to attempt a correct response before the teacher demonstrates it.

Time-delay procedures have been found to have a positive impact on reading skills for students with disabilities (e.g., Hughes & Frederick, 2006) and for English language learners (e.g., Bliss, Skinner, & Adams, 2006). Moreover, teachers find these procedures feasible to implement in the classroom with respect to preparation and instructional time (Hughes, Fredrick, & Keel, 2002). With time-delay procedures, students are likely to receive a lot of positive reinforcement because there is a high probability that students will make accurate responses and a low probability that they will make errors (Stevens & Schuster, 1988). Thus, students' learning rates increase with the use of these procedures (McCurdy & Condari, 1990).

What follows presents an example of implementing the steps of a time-delay procedure for teaching students to read words accurately.

Step 1: Initially, the teacher identifies and records on flashcards or on a computer screen the words that the student cannot read accurately during oral passage reading. These can be words selected from narrative or expository texts.

Step 2: The teacher decides how many instructional trials will be presented and determines how many words will be presented to the student within that predetermined number of instructional trials. The teacher will likely set the number of instructional trials based on observations of the student's acquisition level and behaviors during reading instruction. For instance, four new sight words could be presented for a total of 20 trials, resulting in 5 trials per word.

Step 3: The teacher presents a word printed on a flashcard and says the word (model) and then prompts the student to read the word by asking, "What word is this?" The student is expected to give a correct response immediately following the teacher's prompt. If the student does not make a correct response, then the teacher immediately models the correct response again and asks the student to repeat the correct response. This is called a zero-second delay trial. The teacher determines the amount of zero-second delay trials that are needed for the student based on the number of accurate responses that the student makes.

Step 4: The teacher then determines the delay time to be used in subsequent sessions, and this delay time will be the same (constant) for all remaining instructional sessions. For instance, the teacher may set a 3-second time delay, meaning that the student is given 3 seconds to make a correct response after a word is presented. If the student does not make a correct response within 3 seconds, then the teacher gives a prompt (i.e., models the correct response for the student) as was described in Step 2. If the student is unsure about the correct response, then the student is encouraged not to make a response and wait for the prompt. This reduces the number of instances that students make errors.

Step 5: The teacher sets the criteria for mastery. For instance, the criteria for mastery of each word may be that the student reads that word correctly on three consecutive learning trials.

Step 6: The 3-second time-delay procedure is repeated until the student has met the criteria for mastering reading the words.

Step 7: The teacher then asks the student to read passages that contain the words that the student has mastered to determine if the student is able to read the words effortlessly in connected text.

In this example, the delay in time is constant, as it remained at 3 seconds throughout most of the procedure. Time-delay procedures may also be progressive in nature. Progressive time-delay procedures may be implemented as a way to systematically fade the use of the prompt (i.e., teacher demonstrates correct response), especially as students demonstrate mastery of words (e.g., Casey, 2008). For instance, when students' rate of correct responding increases without the presentation of the prompt within the 3-second time delay, the teacher can systematically increase a 3-second time delay to a 4-second time delay before presenting the prompt. The delay time may continue to systematically progress from 5 seconds to 10 seconds and so on until the use of the prompt is completely faded. Thus, the delays in time get progressively longer as students consistently read words correctly.

Recorded Words

A variation of the time-delay procedure that has helped students increase their word recognition skills is the recorded words procedure (Bliss et al., 2006). School psychologists may suggest that this procedure be used during times when the teacher is not available to provide instruction to a student. The recorded words procedure has helped students increase their rate of reading words (Skinner & Johnson, 1995). This procedure involves the teacher recording a list of words that are presented a few seconds (e.g., 5 seconds) apart from each other. The following procedure is used for implementing recorded words.

Step 1: The teacher identifies about 15 words that the student was unable to read effortlessly while reading narrative or expository texts. The teacher places these words on a worksheet. The student is presented with a folder that contains the worksheet with the list of words on it.

Step 2: The student is instructed to sit at a table or at a desk that is partitioned off from the rest of the seats in the classroom (i.e., learning station). The student is instructed to put headphones on and play the recording of the list of words that corresponds to the words on the worksheet.

Step 3: The teacher provides the following instructions: "Now, try your best to read the words with the recording and not before or after the recorded word is presented. Pick up where you can if you fall behind." The student then reads the words aloud simultaneously with the recording of the words (i.e., zero-second time-delay trials).

Step 4: The student replays the recording. However, this time the student is instructed to attempt to read each word from the list within a short period of time (e.g., 5 seconds) before it is played (i.e., read slightly ahead of the recorded word) and evaluate his or her response and repeat the word after it is played if the word was read incorrectly.

Step 5: The teacher then asks the student to read passages that contain the words the student has mastered to determine if the student is able to read the words effortlessly in connected text.

This procedure provides students with opportunities to self-manage their reading behavior by monitoring and evaluating their responses. For instance, students may self-record whether they read each word correctly or not by placing a mark next to each word listed on their worksheet. After they complete the entire worksheet, they can review it to determine how many words they were able to read correctly and how many words they still need to practice reading. Because this procedure gives students opportunities to independently practice their reading skills at learning centers/stations in the classroom, the teacher is able to provide direct instruction and assistance on a rotation basis to other students in the room. It should be noted that the length of presentation time for each recorded word is important, as students have been found to make more accurate responses if each word is presented for 5 seconds rather than for just 1 second (Skinner & Johnson, 1995).

Interspersal Procedures

Interspersal procedures involve presenting a ratio of mastered to not-mastered content to help students gain momentum learning content that they have yet to master, while experiencing success (i.e., making correct responses) with content they have already mastered (Burns et al., 2009). School psychologists may recommend this technique for students who become easily frustrated or who perceive that much effort is required in reading words that they are not yet fluent with. Students may choose to engage and persist with the task for longer periods of time when words they have not mastered are presented with words they have mastered (e.g., Hulac & Benson, 2011). Interspersing not-mastered words with mastered words may consist of presenting three mastered words followed by the presentation of three not-mastered words, or it could involve interspersing one not-mastered word after every fourth mastered word (Cooke & Guzaukas, 1993).

Another way to intersperse words is presenting one not-mastered word with nine mastered words (Burns, 2004). This is referred to as the incremental rehearsal procedure. School psychologist may suggest the use of this interspersal drill and practice method for students who have particular difficulties with retaining and generalizing content and skills. Research has shown that incremental rehearsal has been found to have positive effects on helping students retain words (MacQuarrie, Tucker, Burns, & Hartman, 2002), increase fluency, improve comprehension (Burns, Dean, & Foley, 2004), and generalize skills to another

context (Joseph, Eveleigh, Konrad, Neef, & Volpe, 2012). The following procedure is used for the incremental rehearsal method.

Step 1: The teacher identifies 10 words that the student cannot read fluently in narrative or expository texts (i.e., not-mastered word) and identifies 9 words that the student can read fluently (i.e., mastered word). Then the teacher places all the words on flashcards, worksheets, or a computer screen.

Step 2: The teacher presents the first not-mastered word and models it for the student and then asks the student to repeat the first not-mastered word.

Step 3: The teacher then presents the first mastered word and asks the student to read it followed by the presentation of the first not-mastered word.

Step 4: The remaining sequence of words is presented: first mastered word, second mastered word, first not-mastered word, first mastered word, second mastered word, third mastered word, first not-mastered word, and so forth until the first not-mastered word is incrementally rehearsed among nine mastered words.

Step 5: The ninth mastered word is then removed and the first not-mastered word becomes the first mastered word (i.e., folded into the deck) and another not-mastered word is presented, and the procedure is repeated.

Step 6: The teacher then asks the student to read passages that contain the words that were mastered to determine if the student is able to read the words effortlessly in connected text.

Research has shown that students with significant reading and cognitive delays especially benefited from the amount of practice with words that is embedded in the incremental rehearsal procedure (Burns & Boice, 2009). Including mastered words with not-mastered words helps students gain momentum to read words effortlessly (Burns et al., 2009). However, as students' rate of reading words increases, the number of mastered words in the deck should be reduced and replaced with a more challenging ratio of not-mastered to mastered words. Otherwise, continuing to include many mastered words in the deck may actually slow down students' learning rates (Nist & Joseph, 2008), as the time spent on reading mastered words could be replaced with time students spend on reading words that they have yet to master (Skinner, 2008).

Repeated Readings

School psychologists may suggest that students engage in repeated reading exercises if the students are struggling with reading passages fluently. Repeated readings involve having students orally reread passages until an adequate level of fluency is achieved (Samuels, 1979). There has been substantial research over the last couple of decades verifying the effectiveness of repeated readings on students' oral reading fluency and comprehension performance (Therrien, 2004). In addition to providing students with opportunities to practice skills, repeated readings have also been coupled with other effective instructional components.

Students who continue to struggle with reading passages fluently may initially need to have the passages read to them. School psychologists can work with teachers to identify those students who need to listen to a teacher or older peer reading to them, or a recording of a passage or story before they actually read it themselves. This is often called listening while reading or listening passage preview (Daly & Martens, 1994). This gives the student an opportunity to observe how passages are read accurately, effortlessly, and with proper expression. Research has shown that students' oral reading fluency improved after students listened to a story being read to them (Begeny & Silber, 2006). In fact, students who were asked to follow along while listening to passages that were read to them increased their fluency over those who read passages independently without assistance (Daly & Martens, 1994). The following procedure is used for implementing repeated readings with demonstration.

Step 1: The teacher introduces the passage or story and asks the students to follow along and place their fingers on each word as each word is being read aloud.

Step 2: The teacher reads the story orally and checks to see if the students are following along with their fingers and, if not, the teacher redirects them.

Step 3: After the story is read aloud, the students are asked to read the story orally as a group or individually to the teacher. The teacher provides corrective feedback when errors are made.

Step 4: If several errors are made, then the teacher may model reading the story aloud to the students again followed by having the students repeat the reading of the story.

Research has shown that repeated readings are also most effective when error correction is provided (e.g., Alber-Morgan, Kamp, Anderson, & Martin 2007). An effective error correction procedure that school psychologists may recommend is called the phrase drill error correction procedure. This procedure is used to promote generalization of reading words correctly in connected text (Begeny, Daly, & Valleley, 2006). The student orally reads passages, and the teacher records the words that were incorrect. The teacher demonstrates reading the incorrect words correctly and then asks the student to practice reading the phrases that contained the incorrect words (Begeny et al., 2006). This procedure has been effective for helping students reduce the number of errors made and increase the rate of reading words correctly during repeated readings (Begeny et al., 2006; J. S. Nelson, Alber, & Gordy, 2004). The following procedure is used for implementing timed repeated readings with phrase drill error correction.

Step 1: The teacher presents a passage that is written at the student's instructional level. The teacher asks the student to read the passage aloud for 3 minutes. As the student begins reading, the teacher starts timing.

Step 2: The teacher records the errors the student made while reading the passage.

Step 3: When 3 minutes have elapsed, the teacher says, "Stop," and calculates the number of words read correctly per minute of oral reading time by dividing the number of words read correctly by 180 seconds and multiplying that figure by 60 seconds.

Step 4: For each word that was incorrect, the teacher models reading the word accurately and has the student reread each word and then reads the phrase in which each incorrect word occurred at least three times. If more than one word is incorrect in the same phrase, the teacher models the correct reading of all the words, and the student repeats the words and then rereads the entire phrase three times.

Step 5: After the student rereads all phrases that contained incorrect words, the student is asked to repeat the reading of the passage, and the number of words read correctly is recorded.

Step 6: The student is asked to repeat reading of the passage with phrase drill error correction until the student reads the passage accurately at an appropriate rate.

Summarizing Text Using Paragraph Shrinking

Greater reading outcomes may be evident if fluency interventions (e.g., repeated readings) are coupled with comprehension strategy instruction (Wexler, Vaughn, Edmonds, & Reutebuch, 2008). School psychologists can suggest using paragraph shrinking as a strategy to help students summarize passages that they have read (McMaster, Fuchs, & Fuchs, 2006). As a student comes to the end of each paragraph, the student stops reading and states the main idea and two details. Then the student uses not more than 10 words to write a summary of that paragraph. At the end of the passage, the student writes a summary of the entire reading selection using the 10-word summary sentences from each paragraph.

Another paraphrasing technique that school psychologists may recommend for students who are struggling with identifying the main idea and summarizing key elements of a passage or story is called the RAP strategy (read, ask, put; Schumaker, Denton, & Deshler, 1984). The student reads a paragraph, asks himself or herself the main idea and two details, and then puts the main idea and details in his or her own words. A variation of this strategy is RAP-Q. The Q stands for questions. Specifically, the students write questions on index cards (based on what they paraphrased), write the answer on the back of the card, and use the index cards for studying (Hagaman & Reid, 2008).

Graphic Organizers

School psychologists can recommend that students with comprehension difficulties use graphic organizers before, during, and after they read to derive meaning from text (Alber-Morgan, 2010). One type of graphic organizer that has been effective in improving comprehension is story mapping (Awe-Hwa, Vaughn, Wanzek, & Wei, 2004). It involves recording details about key elements of a story such as the characters, setting, plot, conflict, and resolution. Typically, students record details about these elements on blank spaces next to the labeled elements on a developed chart or a diagram. Another type of graphic organizer is a semantic map, which consists of diagramming concepts that are related to one another.

Question Generation

Generating questions before, during, and after reading is another effective strategy that school psychologists can recommend for students who experience difficulty with comprehending text. For instance, Ask, Read with Alertness, Tell + Peer Discussion was a strategy effectively used with urban youth (McCallum et al., 2011). This strategy involves students reading the title of a passage and asking themselves two questions about the topic before reading the passage. Students then read the passage and place a checkmark next to each paragraph if they understood it and place a minus sign next to each paragraph that they did not understand. Students were encouraged to slow their reading and focus on meaning for those paragraphs that did not make sense to them. Students then record answers to the two questions. After students finish writing the answers, they tell a peer their questions and answers.

Another self-questioning strategy, FIST, was used effectively with students with learning disabilities (Manset-Williams, Dunn, & Hinshaw, 2008). FI stands

for generating a question after reading the first sentence of a paragraph. ST stands for surveying the paragraph for the answer and answering the question in one sentence. The FI and ST are embedded cues within the passage, and when students come to these cues, they are asked to stop and complete the respective tasks.

There are some students who have difficulty generating their own questions. For these students, school psychologists may recommend that the students be provided with questions (e.g., Who is the main character?) that are listed on a worksheet, and the students can record their answers to those questions at predetermined stopping points marked in the text (Crabtree, Alber-Morgan, & Konrad, 2010). For instance, as students are reading a passage in the text, they may come upon a sticky note signaling them to stop and answer one or more questions that are printed on a worksheet. Students are permitted to revise their answers as they read and come to the next stopping point in the text. When this procedure was implemented with high school students, features were faded as the students became proficient with using them (Crabtree et al., 2010). For instance, the embedded stopping points were removed from the text, and each question on the worksheet was shortened as these students learned to stop, self-question, and comprehend text without those prompts.

Self-Monitoring

Students' reading performance is boosted when they are taught to self-monitor their reading behaviors (Joseph & Eveleigh, 2011). Self-monitoring involves observing one's own behavior and recording that behavior. School psychologists can assist in the development of self-recording devices such as charts, graphs, and electronic tools. For example, a school psychologist can help students self-record their performance by placing checkmarks next to task completion steps on cue cards.

Students can be taught to self-monitor their reading accuracy, productivity, and strategy use. Self-monitoring reading accuracy, for instance, can be completed with the use of the Click or Clunk technique (Wright, 2001). During silent or oral reading, students are given counters and a dry-erase board containing "Click" and "Clunk" columns. After students have read each sentence in a passage, they can ask themselves, "Did I understand that?" If the answer is yes, then the students say "click" and place a counter in the "Click" column, and if the answer is no, then the students say "clunk" and place a counter in the "Clunk" column. If the students say "clunk," then they reread the sentence to see if that helps them gain a better understanding of it. If rereading does not help them gain a better understanding, they can seek assistance. At the completion of this task, students count the number of instances that they said "click" and "clunk."

Mason (2004) taught students to self-monitor reading productivity during written retells. Students recorded on a chart the number of words or sentences/main ideas they used to retell a passage. J. M. Nelson and Mansett-Williamson (2006) taught middle school students with reading disabilities to self-monitor their strategy use by placing a checkmark next to the following strategies that were listed on a worksheet: (a) setting goals, (b) activating prior knowledge, (c) predicting content to be read in the text, (d) identifying the main idea, and (e) retelling key parts of the text. Afterward, instructors helped students make the connection between using the strategies and improving their reading performance. Several students may need these self-monitoring procedures explicitly taught to them before they can apply these procedures on their own. The previously described evidence-based instructional components (demonstration, guided practice, independent practice, and programming for generalization) can be implemented to help students learn to self-monitor their reading behaviors (Alber-Morgan & Joseph, 2013).

SUMMARY

Students with reading problems constitute the majority of academic referrals for school psychological services. Therefore, it is imperative that school psychologists have an understanding of the key reading skills that are necessary for students to become proficient readers. It is also important that school psychologists be knowledgeable about evidence-based reading instructional components and techniques so that they are able to assist teachers and parents in selecting and implementing methods that are likely to lead to desired outcomes for students. This is particularly crucial given the constraints on time for reading instruction during a typical school day. Moreover, school psychologists need to identify at which phase of learning students are functioning so they can assist in determining which instructional components and techniques are most appropriate and time efficient to implement.

REFERENCES

Alber-Morgan, S. (2010). *Using RTI to teach literacy to diverse learners K–8: Strategies for the inclusive classroom.* Thousand Oaks, CA: Corwin Press.

Alber-Morgan, S., & Joseph, L. M. (2013). Using self-questioning, summarizing, and self-monitoring to increase reading comprehension in inclusive middle and high school classrooms. In R. T. Boon & V. Spencer (Eds.), *Reading comprehension strategies to promote adolescent literacy in the content-areas for the inclusive classroom* (pp. 125–140). Baltimore, MD: Brookes.

Alber-Morgan, S. R., Kamp, E. M., Anderson, L. L., & Martin, C. M. (2007). Effects of repeated, error correction, and performance feedback on the fluency and comprehension of middle school students with behavior problems. *Journal of Special Education, 41,* 17–30.

Allor, J. H., & Chard, D. J. (2011). A comprehensive approach to improving reading fluency for students with disabilities. *Focus on Exceptional Children, 43,* 1–12.

Al Otaiba, S., Connor, C., Lane, H., Kosanovich, M. L., Schatschneider, C., Dyrlund, A. K., … Wright, T. L. (2008). Reading First kindergarten classroom instruction and students' growth in phonological awareness and letter-naming-decoding fluency. *Journal of School Psychology, 46,* 281–314. doi:10.1016/j.jsp.2007.06.002

Anthony, J. L., Lonigan, C. J., Driscoll, K., Phillips, B. M., & Burgess, S. R. (2003). Phonological sensitivity: A quasi-parallel progression of word structure units and cognitive operations. *Reading Research Quarterly, 38,* 470–487.

Awe-Hwa, K., Vaughn, S., Wanzek, J., & Wei, S. (2004). Graphic organizers and their effects on the reading comprehension of students with LD: A synthesis of research. *Journal of Learning Disabilities, 37,* 105–118.

Ball, E., & Blachman, B. (1991). Does phonemic awareness training in kindergarten make a difference in early word recognition and developmental spelling? *Reading Research Quarterly, 26,* 49–66.

Beck, I. L., McKeown, M. G., & Kucan, L. (2005). Choosing words to teach. In E. H. Hiebert & M. C. Kamil (Eds.), *Teaching and learning vocabulary: Bringing research to practice* (pp. 211–226). Mahwah, NJ: Erlbaum.

Begeny, J. C., Daly, E. J., III, & Valleley, R. J. (2006). Improving oral reading fluency through response opportunities: A comparison of phrase drill error correction with repeated reading, *Journal of Behavioral Education, 15,* 229–235.

Begeny, J. C., & Silber, J. M. (2006). An examination of group-base treatment packages for increasing elementary-aged students' reading fluency. *Psychology in the Schools, 43,* 183–195.

Benjamin, R., & Schwanenflugel, P. J. (2010). Text complexity and oral reading prosody in young readers. *Reading Research Quarterly, 45,* 388–404.

Biemiller, A. (2004). Teaching vocabulary in the primary grades: Vocabulary instruction needed. In J. F. Baumann & E. J. Kame'enui (Eds.), *Vocabulary instruction: Research to practice* (pp. 28–40). New York, NY: Guilford Press.

Blachman, B. A., Ball, E. W., Black, R., & Tangel, D. M. (2000). *Road to the code: A phonological awareness program for young children.* Baltimore, MD: Brookes.

Bliss, S. L., Skinner, C. H., & Adams, R., (2006). Enhancing English language learning fifth-grade students' sight-word reading with a time-delay taped word intervention. *School Psychology Review, 35,* 663–670.

Bramlett, R. K., Murphy, J. J., Johnson, J., Wallingsford, L., & Hall, J. D. (2002). Contemporary practices in school psychology: A national survey of roles and referral problems. *Psychology in the Schools, 39,* 327–335.

Brown-Chidsey, R., & Steege, M. W. (2010). *Response to intervention: Principles and strategies for effective practice.* New York, NY: Guilford Press.

Burns, M. K. (2004). Empirical analysis of drill ratio research: Refining the instructional level for drill tasks. *Remedial and Special Education, 25,* 167–173.

Burns, M. K., Ardoin, S. P., Parker, D. C., Hodgon, J., Kingbell, D. A., & Scholin, S. E. (2009). Interspersal technique and behavioral momentum for reading word lists. *School Psychology Review, 38,* 428–434.

Burns, M. K., & Boice, C. H. (2009). Comparison of the relationship between words retained and intelligence for three instructional strategies among students with below-average IQ. *School Psychology Review, 38,* 284–292.

Burns, M. K., Dean, V. J., & Foley, S. (2004). Preteaching unknown key words with incremental rehearsal to improve reading fluency and comprehension with children identified as reading disabled. *Journal of School Psychology, 42,* 303–314. doi:10.1016/j.jsp.2004.04.003

Bursuck, W. D., & Damer, M. (2011). *Teaching reading to students who are at risk or have disabilities.* Upper Saddle River, NJ: Pearson.

Byrnes, J. P., & Wasik, B. A. (2009). *Language and literacy development: What educators need to know.* New York, NY: Guilford Press.

Cain, K., & Oakhill, J. (2011). Matthew effects in young readers: Reading comprehension and reading experience aid vocabulary development. *Journal of Learning Disabilities, 44,* 431–443.

Cardoso-Martins, C. (2001). The reading abilities of beginning readers of Brazilian Portuguese: Implications for a theory of reading acquisition. *Scientific Studies of Reading, 5,* 289–317.

Carnine, D. W., Silbert, J., Kame'enui, E. J., & Tarver, S. G. (Eds.). (2004). *Direct instruction reading.* Upper Saddle River, NJ: Pearson.

Carroll, J. M., Snowling, M. J., Hulme, C., & Stevenson, J. (2003). The development of phonological awareness in preschool children. *Developmental Psychology, 38,* 913–923.

Casey, S. D. (2008). A comparison of within- and across-session progressive time-delay procedures for teaching sight words to individuals with cognitive delays. *Behavior Analyst Today, 9,* 162–171.

Childers, J. B., & Tomasello, M. (2002). Two-year-olds learn novel nouns, verbs, and conventional actions from massed or distributed exposures. *Developmental Psychology, 38,* 967–978.

Clay, M. (1993). *Reading recovery: A guidebook for teachers in training.* Portsmouth, NH: Heinemann.

Cooke, N., & Guzaukas, R. (1993). Effects of using a ratio of new items to review items during drill and practice: Three experiments. *Education and Treatment of Children, 16,* 213–234.

Cooper, J. O., Heron, T. E., & Heward, W. L. (2007). *Applied behavior analysis* (2nd ed.). Upper Saddle River, NJ: Merrill/Prentice Hall.

Couper-Kuhlen, E. (1986). *An introduction to English prosody.* London, England: Hodder Arnold.

Coyne, M. D., Kame'enui, E. J., Simmons, D. C., & Harn, B. A. (2004). Beginning reading intervention as inoculation or insulin: First-grade reading performance of strong responders to kindergarten intervention. *Journal of Learning Disabilities, 37,* 90–104.

Crabtree, T., Alber-Morgan, S. R., & Konrad, M. (2010). The effects of structured self-questioning on the reading comprehension of high school seniors with learning disabilities. *Education and Treatment of Children, 33,* 187–203.

Cummings, K. D., Dewey, E. N., Latimer, R. J., & Good, R. H. (2011). Pathways to word reading and decoding: The roles of automaticity and accuracy. *School Psychology Review, 40,* 284–295.

Daly, E. J., III, Chafouleas, S., & Skinner, C. H. (2005). *Interventions for reading problems: Designing and evaluating effective strategies.* New York, NY: Guilford Press.

Daly, E. J., III, & Martens, B. K. (1994). A comparison of three interventions for increasing oral reading performance: Application of the instructional hierarchy. *Journal of Applied Behavior Analysis, 27,* 459–469.

De Graaff, S., Bosman, A. M. T., Hasselman, F., & Verhoeven, L. (2009). Benefits of systematic phonics instruction. *Scientific Studies of Reading, 13,* 318–333. doi:10.1080/10888430903001308

Ehri, L. C. (2005). Learning to read words: Theory, findings, and issues. *Scientific Studies of Reading, 9,* 167–188.

Elkonin, D. B. (1973). USSR. In J. Downing (Ed.), *Comparative reading* (pp. 551–579). New York, NY: Macmillan.

Farkas, G., & Beron, K. (2004). The detailed age trajectory of oral vocabulary knowledge: Differences by class and race. *Social Science Research, 33,* 464–497.

Fien, H., Santoro, L., Baker, S. K., Park, Y., Chard, D. J., Williams, S., & Haria, P. (2011). Enhancing teacher read alouds with small group vocabulary instruction for students with low vocabulary in first-grade classrooms. *School Psychology Review, 40,* 307–318.

Hagaman, J. L., & Reid, R. (2008). The effects of the paraphrasing strategy on reading comprehension of middle school students at risk for failure in reading. *Remedial and Special Education, 29,* 222–234.

Hart, B., & Risley, T. (2003). The early catastrophe: The 30 million word gap. *American Educator, 27*(1), 4–9.

Hirsch, E. D. (2003). Reading comprehension requires knowledge of words and the world: Scientific insights into the fourth-grade slump and the nation's stagnant comprehension scores. *American Educator, 27*(1), 4–9.

Hudson, R. F., Lane, H. B., & Pullen, P. C. (2005). Reading fluency assessment and instruction: What, why, and how? *The Reading Teacher, 58,* 702–714.

Hughes, T. A., & Fredrick, L. D. (2006). Teaching vocabulary with students with learning disabilities using class-wide peer-tutoring and constant time delay. *Journal of Behavioral Education, 15,* 1–23.

Hughes, T. A., Fredrick, L. D., & Keel, M. (2002). Learning to effectively implement constant time-delay procedures to teach spelling. *Learning Disabilities Quarterly, 25,* 209–222.

Hulac, D. H., & Benson, N. (2011). Getting students to work smarter and harder: Decreasing off-task behavior through interspersal techniques. *School Psychology Forum: Research in Practice, 5*(1), 29–36.

Jalongo, M. R., & Sobolak, M. J. (2011). Supporting young children's vocabulary growth: The challenges, the benefits, and evidence-based strategies. *Early Childhood Education Journal, 38,* 421–429. doi: 10.1007/s10643-010-0433-x

Jitendra, A. K., & Gajria, M. (2011). Reading comprehension instruction for students with learning disabilities. *Focus on Exceptional Children, 43,* 1–16.

Joseph, L. M. (2000). Developing first-grade children's phonemic awareness, word identification, and spelling skills: A comparison of two contemporary phonic approaches. *Reading Research and Instruction, 39,* 160–169.

Joseph, L. M. (2002). Facilitating word recognition and spelling using word boxes and word sort phonic procedures. *School Psychology Review, 31*, 122–129.

Joseph, L. M., & Eveleigh, E. (2011). A review of the effects of self-monitoring on the reading performance of students with disabilities. *Journal of Special Education, 45*, 43–53. doi:10.1177/0022466909349145

Joseph, L. M., Eveleigh, E., Konrad, M., Neef, N., & Volpe, R. (2012). Comparison of the efficiency of two flashcard drill methods on children's reading performance. *Journal of Applied School Psychology, 28*, 317–337.

Joseph, L. M., & Schisler, R. (2009). Should adolescents go back to basics? A review of teaching word reading skills to middle and high school students. *Remedial and Special Education, 30*, 131–147.

Keesey, S., Konrad, M., & Joseph, L. M. (2013). Word boxes improve phonemic awareness, letter-sound correspondences, and spelling skills of kindergartners at risk of reading failure. Manuscript submitted for publication.

Kim, Y. S., Wagner, R. K., & Lopez, D. (2012). Developmental relations between reading fluency and reading comprehension: A longitudinal study from grade 1 to grade 2. *Journal of Experimental Child Psychology, 113*, 93–111.

Konrad, M., Helf, S., & Joseph, L. M. (2011). Evidence-based instruction is not enough: Strategies for increasing instructional efficiency. *Intervention in School and Clinic, 47*, 67–74. doi:10.1177/1053451211414192

Kuhn, M. R. (2005). A comparative study of small group fluency instruction. *Reading Psychology, 26*, 127–146.

Kuhn, M. R., Schwanenflugel, P. J., Morris, R. D., Morrow, L. M., Woo, D. G., … Stahl, S. A. (2006). Teaching children to become fluent and automatic readers. *Journal of Literacy Research, 38*, 357–386. doi:10.1207/s15548430jlr3804_1

Lo, Y., Cooke, N. L., & Starling, A. (2011). Using a repeated reading program to improve generalization of oral reading fluency. *Education and Treatment of Children, 2*, 115–140.

MacQuarrie, L. L., Tucker, J. A., Burns, M. K., & Hartman, B. (2002). Comparison of retention rates using traditional drill sandwich and incremental rehearsal flashcard methods. *School Psychology Review, 31*, 584–595.

Manset-Williamson, G., Dunn, M., & Hinshaw, R. (2008). The impact of self-questioning strategy use on the text-reader assisted comprehension of students with reading disabilities. *International Journal of Special Education, 23*, 123–135.

Marulis, L. M., & Neuman, S. B. (2010). The effects of vocabulary intervention on young children's word learning: A meta-analysis. *Review of Educational Research, 80*, 300–335. doi:10.3102/0034654310377087

Maslanka, P., & Joseph, L. M. (2002). A comparison of two phonological awareness techniques between samples of preschool children. *Reading Psychology: An International Quarterly, 23*, 271–288.

Mason, L. H. (2004). Explicit self-regulated strategy development versus reciprocal questioning: Effects on expository reading comprehension among struggling readers. *Journal of Educational Psychology, 96*, 283–296.

McCallum, R. S., Krohn, K. R., Skinner, C. H., Hilton-Prillhart, A., Hopkins, M., Waller, S., & Polite, F. (2011). Improving reading comprehension of at-risk high school students: The ART of reading program. *Psychology in the Schools, 48*, 78–86. doi:10.1002/pits.20541

McCormick, S. (Ed.). (2003). *Instructing students who have literacy problems*. Upper Saddle River, NJ: Pearson.

McCurdy, B. L., & Cundari, L. (1990). Enhancing instructional efficiency: An examination of time delay and the opportunity to observe. *Education and Treatment of Children, 13*, 226–238.

McCurdy, M., Daly, E. J., III, Gortmaker, V., Bonfiglio, C., & Perampieri, M. (2007). Use of brief instructional trials to identify small group reading strategies: A two experiment study. *Journal of Behavioral Education, 16*, 7–26. doi:10.1007/s10864-006-9021-y

McMaster, K. L., Fuchs, D., & Fuchs, L. S. (2006). Research on peer-assisted learning strategies: The promise and limitations of peer-mediated instruction. *Reading and Writing Quarterly, 22*, 5–25.

Morgan, P. L., & Meier, C. R. (2008). Dialogic reading's potential to improve children's emergent literacy skills and behavior. *Preventing School Failure, 52*, 11–16.

Nation, K., & Hulme, C. (1997). Phonemic segmentation, not onset-rime segmentation, predicts early reading and spelling skills. *Reading Research Quarterly, 32*, 154–167.

National Assessment of Educational Progress. (2011). *The nation's report card: Reading 2011*. Washington, DC: National Center for Education Statistics.

National Association of School Psychologists. (2010). *Model for comprehensive and integrated school psychological services*. Bethesda, MD: Author. Retrieved from http://www.nasponline.org/standards/2010standards/2_PracticeModel.pdf

National Reading Panel. (2000). *Teaching children to read: An evidence-based assessment of the scientific research literature on reading and its implications for reading instruction*. Washington, DC: National Institute of Child Health and Human Development.

Nelson, J. M., & Manset-Williamson, G. (2006). The impact of explicit, self-regulatory reading comprehension strategy instruction on the reading-specific self-efficacy, attributions, and effect of students with reading disabilities. *Learning Disability Quarterly, 29*, 213–230.

Nelson, J. S., Alber, S. R., & Gordy, A. (2004). Effects of systematic error correction and repeated readings on the reading accuracy and proficiency of second graders with disabilities. *Education and Treatment of Children, 27*, 203–214.

Nist, L., & Joseph, L. M. (2008). Effectiveness and efficiency of variations of flashcard drills on word recognition, maintenance, and generalization. *School Psychology Review, 37*, 294–308.

Pearson, P., Hiebert, E., & Kamil, M. (2007). Vocabulary assessment: What we know and what we need to learn. *Reading Research Quarterly, 42*, 282–296.

Perfetti, C. A., & Bolger, D. J. (2004). The brain might read that way. *Scientific Studies of Reading, 8*, 293–304.

Pullen, P. C., Tuckwiller, E. D., Konold, T. R., Maynard, K. L., & Coyne, M. D. (2010). A tiered intervention model for early vocabulary instruction: The effects of tired instruction for young children at risk for reading disability. *Learning Disability Research & Practice, 25*, 100–123. doi:10.1111/j.1540-5826.2010.00309.x

Randi, J., Grigorenko, E. L., & Sternberg, R. J. (2005). Revisiting definitions of reading comprehension: Just what is reading comprehension anyway? In S. E. Israel, C. C. Block, K. L. Bauserman, & K. Kinnucan-Welsch (Eds.), *Metacognition in literacy learning: Theory, assessment, instruction, and professional development* (pp. 19–40). Mahwah, NJ: Erlbaum.

Rasinski, T. V. (2012). Why reading fluency should be hot. *Reading Teacher, 65*, 516–522.

Reese, E., Suggate, S., Long, J., & Schaughency, E. (2010). Children's oral narrative and reading skills in the first 3 years of reading instruction. *Reading and Writing, 23*, 627–644.

Samuels, S. J. (1979). The method of repeated readings. *The Reading Teacher, 32*, 403–408.

Schuele, M. C., & Boudreau, D. (2008). Phonological awareness intervention: Beyond the basics. *Language, Speech, and Hearing Services in Schools, 39*, 3–20.

Schumaker, J. B., Denton, P. H., & Deshler, D. D. (1984). *The paraphrasing strategy.* Lawrence, KS: University of Kansas.

Schwanenflugel, P. J., Hamilton, A. M., Kuhn, M. R., & Stahl, S. A. (2004). Becoming a fluent reader: Reading skill and prosodic features in the oral reading of young readers. *Journal of Educational Psychology, 96*, 119–129.

Shanahan, T., Callison, K., Carrière, C., Duke, N. K., Pearson, P. D., Schatschneider, C., & Torgesen, J. (2010). *Improving reading comprehension in kindergarten through third grade: A practice guide* (NCEE 2010-4038). Washington, DC: U.S. Department of Education, National Center for Education Evaluation.

Skinner, C. H. (2008). Theoretical and applied implications of precisely measuring learning rates. *School Psychology Review, 37*, 309–314.

Skinner, C. H., & Johnson, C. W. (1995). The influence of rate of presentation during taped-words intervention on reading performance. *Journal of Emotional and Behavioral Disorders, 3*, 214–224.

Skinner, C. H., Logan, P., Robinson, D. H., & Robinson, S. L. (1997). Myths and realities of modeling as a reading intervention: Beyond acquisition. *School Psychology Review, 26*, 37–447.

Smith, S. L., Scott, K. A., Roberts, J., & Locke, J. (2008). Disabled readers' performance on tasks of phonological processing, rapid naming, and letter knowledge before and after kindergarten. *Learning Disabilities Research & Practice, 23*, 113–124. doi:10.1111/j.1540-5826.2008.00269.x

Stahl, S. A., & Nagy, W. E. (2006). *Teaching word meanings.* Mahwah, NJ: Erlbaum.

Stevens, K. B., & Schuster, J. W. (1988). Time delay: Systematic instruction for academic tasks. *Remedial and Special Education, 9*, 6–21.

Thatcher, K. L. (2010). The development of phonological awareness with specific language-impaired and typical children. *Psychology in the Schools, 47*, 467–480.

Therrien, W. J. (2004). Fluency and comprehension gains as a result of repeated reading. *Remedial and Special Education, 25*, 252–261.

Torgesen, J. K., Alexander, A. W., Wagner, R. K., Rashotte, C. A., Voeller, K. K. S., & Conway, T. (2001). Intensive remedial instruction for children with severe reading disabilities: Immediate and long-term outcomes from two instructional approaches. *Journal of Learning Disabilities, 34*, 33–58.

Torgesen, J. K., & Mathes, P. (2000). *A basic guide to understanding, assessing, and teaching phonological awareness.* Austin, TX: PRO-ED.

Touchette, P. E. (1971). Transfer of stimulus control: Measuring the moment of transfer. *Journal of Experimental Analysis of Behavior, 15*, 347–354.

Wexler, J., Vaughn, S., Edmonds, M., & Reutebuch, C. K. (2008). A synthesis of fluency interventions for secondary struggling readers. *Reading and Writing: An Interdisciplinary Journal, 21*, 317–347. doi:10.1007/s11145-007-9085-7

Wright, J. (2001). *The savvy teacher's guide: Reading interventions that work.* Retrieved from http://www.interventioncentral.org

8

Best Practices in Oral Reading Fluency Interventions

Edward J. Daly III
Maureen A. O'Connor
Nicholas D. Young
University of Nebraska–Lincoln

OVERVIEW

The purpose of this chapter is to describe interventions for oral reading fluency problems. School psychologist practitioners will learn evidence-based strategies for improving oral reading fluency. Protocols and descriptions of conditions for use described later in the chapter will help school psychologists to know how and when to apply them.

We must begin by grasping the role oral reading fluency plays in the many skills that need to be coordinated to read for meaning. To the independent observer, an accomplished reader says the words on the page accurately, fluidly, and with proper expression (i.e., inflection, tone, and rhythm) and then answers questions (implicit or explicit) about the text in a manner that assures the observer that the reader comprehended the text. The answers do not necessarily match the text word for word (nor do they need to), but the answers definitely relate aspects of the content either by review of what is in the text or by extension (i.e., articulating implications for other conditions or situations based on what can be derived from the text). This is the full scope of reading behaviors that are accessible to the observer.

The observer who has a stake in helping the aspiring reader to become an accomplished reader—most often a teacher, tutor, or parent/guardian—is often judging the proficiency of the reader. Expectations, of course, are adjusted according to some developmental standard: We do not expect a proficient second-grade reader to read Tolstoy's *War and Peace* in the same way he or she reads *Frog and Toad*. But, when the reader's behavior falls short of the interested observer's expectations, the observer should suspect a problem that needs to be resolved. This is often when the child is referred to the school psychologist. To investigate the problem, this otherwise fluid stream of reading behavior must be parsed into component parts in a way that facilitates intervention. Of course, comprehension is the ultimate goal of reading. So, the relevance, accuracy, and completeness of the reader's answers to questions (verbal or otherwise) about the text after it has been put aside are very important to the observer's judgment of the budding reader's proficiency.

The other noticeable feature of reading is the fluency (or lack thereof) of the behavior. At a minimum, oral reading fluency encompasses accuracy and rate of word reading; that is, reading words correctly and quickly. Although oral reading fluency may not be the end goal of reading, it is the most salient aspect of reading.

However, oral reading fluency as a construct is more complex than it would appear. First, there is the issue of what it is. For example, there is debate about whether definitions of oral reading fluency should also incorporate *prosody*—the expression used during reading—or even comprehension (Hudson, Pullen, Lane, & Torgesen, 2009; Kuhn & Stahl, 2003; Samuels, 2006). Oral reading fluency is also complex in terms of both the skill repertoire that it represents and how it contributes to comprehension. For instance, what is demonstrably visible—accurate and fluent word reading—is the culmination of a number of finely tuned prerequisite skills that must be coordinated to produce a fluid stream of uninterrupted reading behavior. Furthermore, many have questioned over the years whether this highly salient dimension of reading actually contributes to comprehension. This latter question is particularly important, because if it does not contribute to the ultimate aim of reading instruction, then teachers probably should not bother with it and nor should educators spend time developing interventions for students whose oral reading fluency is deficient. People who question the importance of oral reading fluency are really asking whether it is worth the time to focus on it during reading instruction.

We do not plan to settle the debate about whether prosody or even comprehension should be included in definitions of oral reading fluency. Our plan is to take a pragmatic approach to defining the boundaries of oral reading fluency. The single best measure of oral reading fluency is number of correctly read words per minute as operationalized by curriculum-based measurement (CBM; Deno, 1989). This operational definition is limited to accurate and fluent text reading. Its simplicity, solid psychometric characteristics (described below), and popularity recommend it highly. To date, no other attempt to operationalize or measure the construct of oral reading fluency has had the level of success achieved with the CBM measure. One of its most important characteristics is its sensitivity to instructional effects over time, which may be the reason why it is given such prominence in response to intervention (RTI). Oral reading fluency operationalized in this way, however, traveled a long and difficult road to gain respectability among educators.

In a historical analysis, Fuchs, Fuchs, Hosp, and Jenkins (2001) discovered a substantial drop in fluency tests in the 1970s in the United States and an emphasis on isolated word reading (as opposed to fluent text reading) in the reading intervention literature that persisted well into the 1990s. These observations resonate with personal experience for some of us. For those who conducted workshops and consultation in the late 1980s and early 1990s, the biggest challenge was to get educators to see any value at all in measuring oral reading fluency. Presenters were peppered with questions like, "Why don't you measure comprehension?" and "What about word callers?" These were legitimate questions in their own right, but the questioners never seemed quite satisfied with the responses given. Many believed that it was more important to work on comprehension directly and not be preoccupied with improving students' word or text reading fluency.

Changing Views on the Importance of Oral Reading Fluency

Several significant historical events caused a major shift in educators' view of oral reading fluency. Marilyn

Adam's (1990) classic book, *Beginning to Read*, which synthesized research on reading instruction, made a cogent and strong argument in favor of the importance of oral reading fluency. Next, the prominent National Research Council report (Snow, Burns, & Griffin, 1998) arrived at the same conclusion. The National Reading Panel (2000) then included oral reading fluency as one of the five critical literacy components, along with phonemic awareness, the alphabetic principle, vocabulary, and comprehension. Oral reading fluency is a valid instructional target, and that fact is now widely recognized among educators and curriculum publishers, thanks largely to influential integrative summaries of literacy research.

Cognitive researchers explain the construct of oral reading fluency in terms of *automaticity* of cognitive processes that allow for greater mental efficiency when it is achieved (Hudson et al., 2009). Presumably, automaticity allows for greater mental capacity and a lessening of response effort to make way for comprehension. However, oral reading fluency is also explainable within a behavior analytic framework in terms of the three-term contingency (antecedent–response–consequence) and in particular the stimulus control that is exerted by the text (Daly & Kupzyk, 2012). Both theoretical orientations acknowledge that improving oral reading fluency can contribute to comprehension. Interestingly, Hudson et al. (2009) point to possible bidirectional influences between oral reading fluency and comprehension, meaning that increases in comprehension may also improve oral reading fluency.

Oral Reading Fluency as a Legitimate Target for Instruction

Consistently high correlations ($\geq$.60) between oral reading fluency and comprehension measures have been found in psychometric studies (Jenkins, Fuchs, van den Broek, Espin, & Deno, 2003; Shinn, Good, Knutson, Tilly, & Collins, 1992). Furthermore, oral reading fluency is superior to existing comprehension measures as a measure of overall reading competence for early elementary grades (Good & Jefferson, 1998; Shinn, 1989; Shinn et al., 1992). Although this finding is not intuitively obvious since it might be thought that comprehension measures would be superior to the oral reading fluency measure, it is perhaps not all that surprising in light of the fact that measuring comprehension reliably and validly is extremely difficult to do. By contrast, CBM oral reading fluency is a simple and highly reliable measure of a critical reading skill that contributes meaningfully to comprehension (Shinn et al., 1992). Without at least some basic proficiency with oral reading fluency, independent comprehension is not even possible. CBM oral reading fluency has also been shown to be highly predictive of performance on high-stakes, statewide proficiency tests (Hintze & Silberglitt, 2005; McGlinchey & Hixson, 2004). Both positive and negative predictive power for meeting state cutoff scores was strong in all these studies.

Clearly, oral reading fluency is an essential target for literacy instruction. Unfortunately, in spite of its new-found popularity, fluency instruction is often neglected in many classrooms (National Reading Panel, 2000). This neglect can have deleterious effects of students' literacy growth. Lane et al. (2009) found that first- and second-grade students whose teachers knew (a) why reading fluency was important, (b) which skills were most important to becoming fluent readers, and (c) effective instructional methods improved their reading fluency more during the school year than students of teachers who did not know these things. For first graders, fluency growth was greatest for word reading fluency (the major emphasis in this grade), and for second graders, fluency growth was greatest for oral reading fluency of text (the major emphasis in this grade).

Therefore, given the high base rate for poor literacy skills among students nationally (according to the National Center for Educational Statistics, 33% of fourth-grade students were below basic levels of proficiency in 2011; see http://nces.ed.gov/) and the very real possibility that oral reading fluency is underappreciated and its role misunderstood by many educators, school psychologists are often called upon to provide consultation and collaboration for interventions and instructional support to develop academic skills (see National Association of School Psychologists [NASP] *Model for Comprehensive and Integrated School Psychological Services* [NASP, 2010]). CBM-oral reading fluency is currently the most common measure used in RTI due to its good psychometric properties, simplicity, and sensitivity to change. As such, it is a vitally important tool for the NASP Practice Model domain of Data-Based Decision Making and Accountability. School psychologists have been ahead of the curve in terms of appreciating the importance of oral reading fluency, and seem to be the professionals in the trenches who have been pushing schools toward a greater appreciation of its vital role in reading acquisition.

We now turn to basic considerations of background information and skills needed before oral reading fluency interventions can be recommended and administered.

BASIC CONSIDERATIONS

CBM oral reading fluency is measured by first having a student read randomly selected, equal difficulty-level passages for 1 minute each, and then scoring the number of correctly read words and errors per minute. Its reliability, validity, and efficiency were alluded to briefly in the previous section. CBM oral reading fluency's sensitivity to instructional effects makes it particularly appropriate for evaluating oral reading fluency interventions. Normative comparisons can be made to determine whether there is a discrepancy between the current level of performance and the expected level of performance before and after intervention in a sort of preassessment and postassessment design. Preassessment and postassessment will allow school psychologists to evaluate the degree to which the student is catching up to peers. Commercially available CBM oral reading fluency materials on websites like DIBELS (https://dibels.uoregon.edu/) and AIMSweb (http://www.aimsweb.com/) contain norms that can be used for this type of decision making.

Repeatedly measuring correctly read words per minute over time (e.g., once or twice a week) and plotting the results as a line graph can paint a dynamic picture of the student's progress in response to instruction. Use of a high-quality case study design facilitates decisions about instruction or intervention effectiveness for a particular student or even for a group of students. In practice, the most commonly used design is the AB design in which a baseline is first established (the A phase) and an intervention is subsequently introduced (the B phase). Stability and intervention effects are judged using visual analysis (Kazdin, 2011). Although not a true experimental design, Kazdin (2011) points out that the quality of inferences can be relatively high for individual students when (a) repeated measures of objective data (i.e., CBM oral reading fluency in this case) over time establish stability of performance during baseline, and (b) instruction produces an immediate and marked effect during the intervention phase.

An example of an AB design can be seen in Figure 8.1 for a case reported by Hofstadter and Daly (2011). Hofstadter and Daly evaluated the effects of a peer-mediated intervention and found large improvements in the target child's oral reading fluency. The example in Figure 8.1 clearly demonstrates both characteristics in the data: stability within each phase and a clear intervention

Figure 8.1. Oral Reading Fluency Results for a Peer-Tutoring Intervention

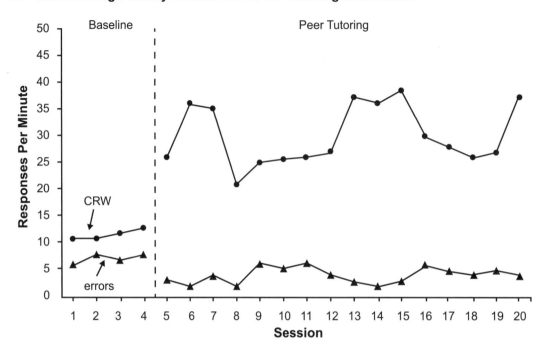

Note. CRW = correctly read words. From "Improving Oral Reading Fluency Using a Peer-Mediated Reading Intervention," by K. L. Hofstadter & E. J. Daly III, 2011, *Journal of Applied Behavior Analysis, 44,* 641–646. Copyright 2011 by the authors. Reprinted with permission.

effect (a visible change in behavior in the desired direction relative to baseline). A lack of stability in baseline (e.g., a lot of variability or a trend toward improvement) will compromise the ability to examine whether the intervention was effective. Therefore, it is advisable to measure baseline until performance stabilizes.

Unfortunately, the ideal of an immediate and marked effect during the intervention phase is not often achieved with oral reading fluency interventions. Realistically, improvements with a skilled behavior like oral reading fluency will take time. Therefore, a radical change in performance between baseline and intervention is not very likely. Nonetheless, a conclusion can be arrived at with a stable baseline, an increasing trend during the intervention phase, and a minimum of data overlap between phases (especially toward the end of the intervention phase).

Prerequisite Skills and the Emergence of Oral Reading Fluency

As noted earlier, oral reading fluency is one of the five critical literacy components that should be directly targeted for instruction (National Reading Panel, 2000). While oral reading fluency is believed to contribute to comprehension and phonemic awareness and phonics—

two of the other five literacy components that develop before oral reading fluency—appear to contribute significantly to oral reading fluency development. Phonemic awareness refers to the ability to segment words into constituent phonemes (individual sounds that make up the smallest unit of speech) and blend them in novel (i.e., previously untaught) ways to form new words. For example, the word *bat* has three phonemes that emerging readers should learn how to isolate as three separate sounds (/b/, /a/, /t/) when given the whole word. The emerging reader, however, also must learn how to arrange phonemes in novel ways and blend them successfully to form new words or combinations of phoneme sequences (e.g., the individual sounds /b/, /a/, /t/ can be blended in a new sequence to form *tab*). This ability to isolate and manipulate individual sounds is critical to later reading success (Adams, 1990; Ball & Blachman, 1991). But, it must be applied to written letters (and their combinations) for the reader to progress in his or her skills. Thus, students must learn letter recognition (Adams, 1990), how to read and spell letter combinations, and how those letter combinations form words. Mastery of letter combinations and how they form words is the domain of phonics instruction (National Reading Panel, 2000). Good phonics instruction teaches students to decode combinations of letters to read novel words.

Eldredge (2005) demonstrated that phonics skills contribute to accurate and fluent word recognition, which in turn contributes to word and text reading fluency. A longitudinal study by Speece and Ritchey (2005) examining oral reading fluency growth in a longitudinal sample of at-risk first-grade students sheds further light on how oral reading fluency develops in the early grades. They found that fluency differences between good readers and poor readers already begin to appear in first grade, just as students are beginning to learn to decode. Comparisons to a not-at-risk sample revealed that the at-risk first-grade students read less than half as many words correctly per minute and the number was growing at half the rate (measured as correctly read words per minute increase per week) of their peers. Yet, they also found that oral reading fluency growth in first grade and not oral reading fluency level accounted for a significant amount of oral reading fluency variance in the middle and at the end of second grade. Furthermore, letter–sound fluency and oral reading fluency in the middle of first grade were significant predictors of oral reading fluency at the end of first grade. In second grade, word reading accuracy and oral reading fluency earlier in the year were significant predictors of oral reading fluency level at the end of the year. Thus, as word reading is built on a bedrock of phonemic awareness and application of letter–sound correspondences to word reading, oral reading fluency should begin to develop by the middle of first grade. Growth (more so than initial level) predicts later oral reading fluency skill, suggesting that it is responsive to instruction.

Teaching word reading through phonics is appropriate for many words. But, there are also a number of words that do not have predictable phonetic properties (e.g., *the*, *said*, *come*) that must be learned as whole words. Although this class of words is relatively small given the regularities of the English language, it is therefore important to also teach sight-word recognition (Pikulski & Chard, 2005). Thus, a deficit in one or more prerequisite skills may contribute to an oral reading fluency problem, and instruction may need to be tailored to improve these prerequisite skills.

Selection of Texts for Oral Reading Fluency Instruction and Intervention

The texts used for oral reading fluency instruction influence instructional outcomes and therefore should be chosen carefully. The most important features of texts for oral reading fluency instruction are the types of words used in the text and the difficulty level of the text. Hiebert (2005) and Hiebert and Fisher (2005) demonstrated that the various types of texts often used for reading instruction differ significantly in terms of the number of high-frequency words (i.e., words that appear frequently in the English language), number of unique (i.e., appearing only once) or rare words, number of word repetitions within the text, and graphophonetic patterns (i.e., common phonetic patterns in a word, even in words that appear infrequently in the English language, e.g., *mat*). All of these factors have been shown to affect the degree to which students benefit from instruction. For example, Hiebert found that a content passage group (reading texts containing science and social studies texts) outperformed a literature passage group and that these two groups both outperformed a literature-based, control passage group (reading texts containing more rare, multisyllabic, or unique words) in terms of improving second-grade students' reading rate. The content and literature passage groups also performed better than the control passage group on a comprehension measure. The order of outcomes (content passage group > literature passage group > control passage group) conformed to the number of word repetitions, high-frequency words, and words with consistent graphophonetic patterns in the reading materials for each condition.

Hiebert and Fisher (2005) pointed out that texts containing rare and unique multisyllabic words may have a negative effect on poor readers' performance and/or may cause teachers to have to slow down instruction. They concluded that many reading programs' reading texts contain too many rare words to be profitable for students. The implication is that word reading instruction should be carried out in texts containing commonly appearing words in the English language while minimizing rare words and unique appearances of words. Therefore, some texts are better than others for teaching reading, and a critical difference is the nature of the words in the texts.

Difficulty level of the texts is another factor that influences oral reading fluency outcomes. Daly, Martens, Kilmer, and Massie (1996) manipulated difficulty level (instructional match versus instructional mismatch) while delivering instruction to four students with disabilities who had significant oral reading fluency deficits. Daly, Martens, et al. (1996) found that all four participants displayed greater generalized improvements in the instructional match condition than in the instructional mismatch condition, demonstrating that text difficulty level affects students' ability to generalize word reading across texts. A similar investigation by Daly, Bonfiglio, Mattson, Persampieri, and Foreman-Yates (2005) produced a somewhat different finding. Daly, Bonfiglio, et al. (2005) also investigated text difficulty level. In this study, however, all three participants displayed greater improvement in the harder passages than in the easier passages. In addition, one participant's performance actually reached higher absolute levels in the harder rather than the easier passages. The contradiction in results is more apparent than real, however. Students in the Daly, Bonfiglio, et al. (2005) study were reading significantly more fluently than those in the Daly, Martens, et al. (1996) study. Both of these studies suggest that there is an optimal range at which students benefit from oral reading fluency instruction, but that the range probably differs according to students' current skill level. Unfortunately, too little research has been conducted in this area to identify what those ranges are at different levels of oral reading fluency proficiency. But it is nonetheless essential to choose texts that are not too difficult or too easy if benefits are to be maximized for students.

Most often, schools depend on commercially prepared reading programs for teaching students. These reading programs contain the instructional texts used by teachers and are referred to as *core reading programs* because the curriculum is supposed to be delivered to all students in the school, even when other reading programs are used for supplemental interventions, as in an RTI program. Core reading programs contain both reading materials and teaching activities, and therefore constitute a reading package to be delivered to every student as the foundation of reading instruction. A recent study by Crowe, Connor, and Petscher (2009) compared five commercially available core reading programs used as a part of the state of Florida's Reading First initiative. Crowe and colleagues examined the oral reading fluency growth of more than 30,000 students in first through third grade in Reading First schools that contained high proportions of students from lower-socioeconomic-status backgrounds and generally weaker academic achievement. All five core reading programs contained decodable passages (i.e., a high proportion of phonetically regular words) with multiple levels, but varied in the amount of explicit instruction given to students and the degree of specificity of teaching activities.

Reading Mastery (http://www.mcgraw-hill.co.uk/sra/readingmastery.htm) outperformed the other curricula in general in producing the greatest increases in oral reading fluency growth (measured as monthly increases in correctly read words per minute), and students in Reading Mastery met or exceeded achievement benchmarks more often than students in the other curricula. Reading Mastery has scripted lessons and uses a direct-instruction approach while emphasizing strategic sequencing of skills and multiple practice opportunities with text as a part of each lesson, among other things.

The results of this study led Crowe et al. (2009) to point to the importance of explicit instruction with students with weaker skills. Therefore, the core curriculum also has a significant effect on a student's progress. A stronger core reading curriculum may decrease the need for supplemental instruction for those students who are at risk for reading difficulties.

Active Treatment Ingredients That Make Interventions Effective

A strong intervention is obviously more likely to be effective than a weak intervention. But, intervention strength does not just refer to magnitude along some dimension of time or intensity. For psychosocial interventions, Yeaton and Sechrest (1981) point out that conceptual relevance is what influences treatment strength. *Conceptual relevance* refers to the presumed active treatment ingredients based on prior theory and research. The ingredients that make a treatment effective should be specified in advance so that appropriate decisions can be made about when and where to apply the treatment. Selecting an effective intervention hinges on choosing ingredients (i.e., treatment components) that suit the needs of the one receiving treatment. Two heuristics have proved themselves to be extremely useful for conceptualizing treatment strength for academic interventions, which guide how to match intervention components to students' proficiency levels. Lentz (1988) has been credited with making popular the distinction between performance and skill deficits. For a performance deficit, low levels of academic responding can be attributed to ineffective reinforcement contingencies. Making the contingencies stronger by using more powerful reinforcers or changing some other dimension of reinforcement (e.g., reducing delay, reducing response effort, and/or increasing magnitude) leads to an immediate increase in academic responding for the child who has the skill but fails to display it under current instructional arrangements. School psychologists should recommend mix-and-match intervention components to meet the students' instructional needs. Thinking in terms of performance and skill deficits is very helpful in this regard.

For a skill deficit, low levels of academic responding can be attributed to an instructional deficit and not simply to poorly arranged reinforcement contingencies. The student needs instruction to increase accurate responding. The instructional hierarchy model (Haring & Eaton, 1978) is a vintage behavior analytic model that has been successfully and repeatedly applied to a wide variety of types of academic deficits (Ardoin & Daly, 2007). Daly, Lentz, and Boyer (1996) used it to identify the active treatment ingredients in reading interventions and showed how it can explain divergent patterns of results across reading intervention studies.

According to the instructional hierarchy model, skill proficiency progresses from a behavioral deficit (no or very low levels of responding) to accuracy (slow but correct responding) to fluency (rapid, correct responding) to generalization (use of the skill in new contexts and under different conditions). Effective teachers vary instruction according to a student's proficiency level, using modeling, prompting, and error correction to improve accuracy, practice (opportunities to respond) and positive reinforcement for improved rate of fluency building, and varying contexts for skill use (e.g., practice across diverse instructional items) to improve generalized responding. These heuristics complement one another and can guide the practitioner in generating testable hypotheses about reasons for academic performance deficits. If the student has a performance deficit, then positive reinforcement contingencies should be applied. When a performance deficit is not present, the practitioner should examine whether the student has an accuracy, fluency, and/or generalization problem and should adapt instruction accordingly. The specifics of how to use this model in practice for oral reading fluency interventions will be outlined in the next section.

BEST PRACTICES IN ORAL READING FLUENCY INTERVENTIONS

The number of intervention options for oral reading fluency problems is limited, but the interventions themselves can be quite effective when appropriately applied according to the student's skill level. The interventions to be described in this chapter appear in Table 8.1. Interventions are listed as "components" in the table because they can be combined to create an intervention package that is best suited to the needs of the learner. For example, listening passage preview (a

modeling strategy) can be carried out before repeated readings (a fluency strategy), while error correction can be applied after each passage reading. Positive reinforcement and performance feedback can be combined with repeated readings such that the contingencies are described before passage reading, and feedback and reinforcement are delivered after the last reading.

Critical Factors in Selecting Intervention Components

Two factors are critical to creating an effective intervention: matching the intervention to the student's instructional needs and adapting the intervention to the instructional context so that it can be readily carried out as frequently and accurately as planned. An effective intervention model must balance both considerations. Daly, Witt, Martens, and Dool (1997) proposed a functional assessment model for school psychologists' use that accounts for both students' instructional needs (relying on and combining the skill versus performance deficit distinction and the Instructional Hierarchy model) and the contextual need in schools for efficiency. With respect to the latter, school psychologists should recommend simpler interventions when possible because they are easier to implement.

Daly et al. (1997) described five common reasons for poor academic performance that can be used to generate academic interventions based on a student's current pattern of responding to instruction. The common reasons are organized in terms of ease of use, with the earlier explanations requiring simpler and less intrusive interventions than the latter reasons. Table 8.2 presents an application of the functional assessment model to oral reading fluency strategies. This intervention framework relies on careful observation of the learner's responding to identify the most probable common reason and promising oral reading fluency interventions. A school psychologist should tailor the assessment through interviews and observations to decide which pattern best characterizes the student's current performance. The common reasons outline testable hypotheses that can guide functionally appropriate instructional and/or motivational components, which school psychologists can recommend to the teacher or incorporate as a part of a Tier 2 or Tier 3 protocol in an RTI program. Each common reason, current student reading pattern, and recommended intervention is described below to assist school psychologists with how to prioritize and combine strategies.

Table 8.1. Oral Reading Fluency Interventions

Intervention Component	How to Use It
Positive reinforcement with performance feedback	1. Place one or more rewards in front of the child and say, "You will have a chance to earn one of these rewards for reading this story. Choose one of things you would like to work for." Rewards can be activities (helping the teacher) or tangibles (small trinkets). For activities, a symbolic representation (a picture or word on a flashcard) should be used. 2. Place the reward in front of the child, but beyond his or her reach. 3. Say, "First, we will practice reading the story. You can earn a reward for doing well. In order to earn the [reward], you have to read [number of words] with no more than three errors." 4. Have the child read the story while tracking correct words and errors. 5. Calculate the score. Say, "That time, you read ____ words and made ____ errors." 6. If the student met the goal, then provide the reward. If the student did not meet the goal, then do not provide the reward.
Repeated readings with performance feedback	1. Say, "You are going to read this passage aloud three times. If you do not know a word, I will say it so you can keep reading. At the end of each reading, I will tell you how many words you read and the number of words you missed. Please try your best." 2. Say, "Start," and begin the timing once the student reads the first word in the passage. 3. Follow along as the student is reading, highlighting errors. After 3 seconds, say the missed word to the student. 4. After the first minute of reading, draw a bracket around the word the student incorrectly read and write the number that corresponds to the current trial (e.g., 1, 2, or 3) but have the student finish the entire passage. 5. After the student completes the entire passage, calculate the total number of words read and subtract from this number the total number of errors. Say, "You read ____ words correctly per minute and had ____ errors." 6. Say, "Please read the passage aloud again." 7. Repeat Steps 2–5. 8. Say, "Please read the passage aloud one last time." 9. Repeat Steps 2–5.
Listening passage preview	1. Say, "I am going to read the passage aloud while you follow along with your finger and read the words to yourself." 2. Read the entire passage to the student at a pace of approximately 130 words per minute.
Phrase drill error correction	1. Have the student read the passage aloud. 2. As the student is reading, highlight errors on your copy of the story. After 3 seconds, highlight the error word and say it to the student. 3. After the student completes the passage, say, "We are going to practice all of the words that you read incorrectly." 4. Point to the first highlighted word in the passage and say, "This word is ____," and instruct the student to repeat the word. Point to the beginning of the sentence that contains the highlighted word and say, "Please read this sentence aloud three times." 5. Repeat Step 4 for all of the highlighted words.
Syllable segmenting and blending error correction	1. Say, "We are going to practice the words you read incorrectly." 2. Point to an error word, cover all but the first syllable with an index card, and say, "These letters say ____. Now you say it." Say, "Good," if the student responds correctly. If not, then repeat this step for the missed syllable. 3. Repeat Step 2 for all syllables in the word, successively exposing each one until the student practices all syllables in the word. Complete this process for all error words. 4. Return to the first error word, cover all but the first syllable, and say, "Now say the sounds and then say the word." Expose the first syllable and have the student say the sound. Do this for each syllable, and then say, "Say the word." If the student makes an error, then say, "No. The word is ____. Say it. Good."

Table 8.2. Selecting Oral Reading Fluency Strategies

Five Common Reasons for Poor Academic Performance	Current Student Reading Pattern	Intervention
"They don't want to do it."	If you see variable fluency rates and higher rates of responding under reward contingencies ...	... set up a positive reinforcement program for improving reading fluency and/or use performance feedback.
"They have not spent enough time doing it."	If you do not see the student practicing reading aloud and/or his or her fluency is poor ...	... increase practice through repeated readings.
"They have not had enough help to do it."	If you see high errors but reasonable fluency ...	... use error correction.
	If you see high errors and poor fluency ...	... use listening passage preview and error correction.
"They have not had to do it that way before."	If you see poor fluency in novel texts following instruction ...	... train in context and across passages by using repeated readings and use positive reinforcement for generalized improvements.
"It is too hard."	If you see poor fluency and high errors despite use of modeling and error correction ...	... change text difficulty level.

They Don't Want to Do It

Some students demonstrate low oral reading fluency rates because "they don't want to do it," meaning that they have a performance deficit. Students with a performance deficit may not be uniformly low fluency when reading. Rather, they may be variable; that is, some days they do well and other days they do poorly. This is usually a clue that existing reinforcement contingencies are not strong enough to maximize student responding. There is a simple way to test for a performance deficit. Daly et al. (1997) presented a protocol that takes very little time (see the appendix in Daly et al., 1997). Accordingly, a preferred item (e.g., a tangible reward) or activity is offered for meeting a prespecified criterion level of responding. If the student meets or exceeds the criterion, then school psychologists should recommend and develop a reinforcement plan for the teacher.

The protocol in Table 8.1 outlines how to use positive reinforcement for an oral reading fluency problem. For example, Daly, Persampieri, McCurdy, and Gortmaker (2005) allowed students to choose a tangible reward from a bag contingent on exceeding the students' previous oral reading fluency score by 30%. Both of the elementary-age students demonstrated oral reading fluency gains in the reward condition. Offering reinforcement for improved performance is simple and requires little teacher supervision. The student should be placed on a regular and predictable schedule (e.g., once or twice a week) of progress checks. Providing the

student with a choice of reinforcers prior to the progress check (Daly et al., 1997) or using a token economy for performance improvements (Ayllon & Roberts, 1974) can boost performance.

The best method for selecting reinforcers is to conduct a stimulus-preference assessment. We recommend the Multiple-Stimulus Without Replacement method. Daly et al. (2009) demonstrated that simple, school-based activities (e.g., access to computer) selected based on the preference results can be effective at improving academic performance. Alternately, if the teacher currently has a token economy in place for other things, the intervention plan can be linked to that. We recommend that school psychologists check performance under unreinforced conditions from time to time as well. For example, school psychologists can alternate assessments between reinforced and nonreinforced conditions to evaluate whether intervention effects are being generalized to nonreinforced conditions (Daly, Persampieri, et al., 2005).

Another motivational strategy that may also help to address performance-deficit problems is to provide performance feedback. With performance feedback, the teacher provides feedback on correctly read words per minute and/or errors immediately after a passage is read (Eckert, Dunn, & Ardoin, 2006). Performance feedback is also included in Table 8.1. Interestingly, Eckert et al. (2006) found that providing feedback on errors had a larger effect on oral reading fluency than providing feedback on correctly read words per minute, but that both were effective relative to a control condition. As such, school psychologists might consider recommending that the teacher provide feedback on both correct words and errors. Performance feedback can be made more interesting for the student by having the student graph reading scores, which has been shown to further improve intervention effects (Therrien, 2004).

Regardless of whether programmed reinforcers or performance feedback or both are used, the teacher should stress with the student just how important it is to practice and to do his or her best. Clear reminders should be given about the contingencies for improvement in future sessions. The student might be told that practicing will probably help him or her get the reward in the next session. As noted earlier, testing for responsiveness to positive reinforcement contingencies is simple and efficient. If the test does not produce an immediate increase in performance, then a more complex, skill-based intervention is needed.

They Have Not Spent Enough Time Doing It

If the student has a skill deficit, then the school psychologist should observe the amount of time the student is actively reading, as well as the student's oral reading fluency. A student with a fluency problem needs more frequent practice. The National Reading Panel (2000) recommends guided oral reading practice as a routine instructional practice. The most common form of oral reading fluency practice is the method of repeated readings. The protocol in Table 8.1 outlines how to do it. The student reads the same passage aloud a predetermined number of times or until a certain criterion level of performance is reached (Begeny, Krouse, Ross, & Mitchell, 2009). Repeated readings has been shown to improve fluency, accuracy, and comprehension in both elementary- and secondary-level students (Chard, Vaughn, & Tyler, 2002; Freeland, Skinner, Jackson, McDaniel, & Smith, 2000; Therrien, 2004). Chard et al. (2002) described it as "the most documented approach to improving fluency" (p. 403) and recommended that repeated readings should be a core component of all reading fluency interventions. They also recommended frequent repetition of text reading with different people (e.g., teacher, parent, other students) and with progressively more difficult texts, while providing feedback and error correction.

Daly, Martens, Barnett, Witt, and Olson (2007) emphasized the importance of using *sequentially matched materials*, meaning that texts should be of appropriate difficulty level, and that there should be frequent, brief opportunities to repeatedly practice reading passages, regular monitoring, and performance goals to establish when to move on to harder materials.

They Have Not Had Enough Help to Do It

Some skill deficits require more assistance than repeated practice. Daly et al. (1997) recommend increasing feedback and using strategies that target accuracy. A student who has high error rates will need error correction and possibly modeling. If fluency is fine, then error correction will probably be sufficient. If fluency is low and error rate is high, then modeling and error correction should be used. The error correction strategies that appear in the research literature all include modeling of the error word and most include response prompting of some type. They differ in the prompting strategy that is used. O'Shea, Munson, and O'Shea (1984) compared three common error correction strategies: word supply, word drill, and phrase drill. For word supply, the teacher modeled correct reading of an error word. For word drill, the teacher modeled correct reading of an error word and had the student repeatedly read the error word. For phrase drill, the teacher modeled correct reading of an error word and had the student repeatedly read the entire phrase containing the error word three times. Word drill improves on word supply by including prompted practice of the error word. Phrase drill improves on the other two conditions by prompting practice of the error word in the context of connected text. O'Shea et al. (1984) found that phrase drill error correction was the most effective strategy. Phrase drill error correction appears to be more effective because it has the student practice reading the error word in text, which is the natural context for responding (Chard et al., 2002; Daly, Lentz, et al., 1996).

The protocol in Table 8.1 outlines how to implement phrase drill error correction. More recently, Daly, Bonfiglio, et al. (2005) and Daly et al. (2006) used what they called *syllable segmentation error correction* (Table 8.1) for repeated errors that had previously been corrected with phrase drill error correction. Syllable segmentation breaks the error word down into syllables and has the student practice reading and blending the syllables following the teacher's modeling of each syllable.

For the student who displays a high error rate and poor fluency, multiple strategies should be used to improve accuracy. Listening passage preview should be added to error correction because the teacher's modeling of accurate and fluent reading will help to reduce errors before they occur, making the student's subsequent practice more efficient and effective (Chard et al., 2002; Daly, Lentz, et al., 1996). During listening passage previewing, the student follows along silently as a skilled reader (e.g., a parent, teacher, or recording) reads the passage aloud (Begeny et al., 2009). In this way, the skilled reader serves as a model for the student, demonstrating what fluent reading sounds like and helping the student to learn new words that appear in the passage. The protocol in Table 8.1 outlines how to do it. Passage previewing has been shown to be effective for increasing the reading fluency and accuracy of students with reading difficulties and learning disabilities (e.g., Rose & Beattie, 1986; Skinner, Cooper, & Cole, 1997). Of the various ways in which passage previewing can be carried out, it appears to be best to have a live model (e.g., a teacher or tutor) read the passage to the student (Daly & Martens, 1994; Rose & Beattie, 1986; Therrien, 2004).

They Have Not Had to Do It That Way Before

Students with accuracy and fluency problems may have difficulty using the skill in natural contexts (Daly et al., 1997). Generalizing a newly acquired response to untrained conditions is difficult and often requires explicit programming (Stokes & Baer, 1977), especially for students with learning difficulties (Howell & Nolet, 2000). If the student does not improve with instruction in new texts at the same grade level, then the student may have a generalization problem. Thus, even though the student may read instructional texts better after each reading, it is critical to check for progress in novel texts at the same difficulty level. The best way to do this is to examine their growth in CBM progress monitoring data. A lack of growth over time in spite of short-term improvements suggests a generalization problem. For oral reading fluency, four strategies have been shown to affect students' ability to generalize: (a) controlling the difficulty level of the texts (Daly, Martens, et al., 1996); (b) practicing reading in connected text, the natural context for reading (Daly & Martens, 1994); (c) systematically varying the texts (Martens et al., 2007); and (d) using programmed reinforcement for generalized improvements (Daly, Bonfiglio, et al., 2005).

Ideally, school psychologists should recommend combining multiple strategies into a multicomponent intervention. Fortunately, each of these strategies requires little time, and a single intervention session can be carried out in about 20 minutes. Generalization strategies are of two broad types: (a) those that involve using instructional content that will help the learner outside of instruction, and (b) positively reinforcing occurrences of generalized responding (improved

reading in novel texts) outside of training conditions (Miltenberger, 2012). Controlling the text difficulty level, prescribing practice in connected text, and systematically varying texts are examples of the former category of generalization strategy, while reinforcing instances of generalization is an example of the latter.

Manipulating the instructional content involves controlling what is presented and how it is presented. The role of difficulty level in promoting generalization was discussed earlier. Intervention starts with selecting texts of appropriate difficulty level (Daly, Martens, et al., 1996; Martens et al., 2007). Intervention sessions should include repeated readings, which provide the kind of practice in reading connected text that is called for with a generalization problem. Using texts with overlapping words will probably have a greater effect than texts without overlapping words (Hiebert, 2005; Hiebert & Fisher, 2005; Rashotte & Torgesen, 1985). Using a phonetically regular curricular series makes it more likely that word overlap will be controlled. Repeated readings can be further strengthened in several ways if necessary and feasible.

In his meta-analysis of oral reading fluency interventions, Therrien (2004) found that generalized improvements with repeated readings may be even greater if (a) the intervention is carried out by an adult (rather than a peer), (b) the adult models fluent reading first, (c) corrective feedback is given, (d) performance criteria are used, (e) comprehension questions are asked, and (f) student performance is graphed. Martens et al. (2007) improved second- and third-grade students' generalized oral reading fluency levels by having them repeatedly practice reading passages until they met a performance criterion of 100 correctly read words per minute as the basis for moving on to the next passage. The passages were taken from a grade level at which the participants could read at least 50 correctly read words per minute. The repeated readings sessions also included listening passage previewing at the beginning of the session and phrase drill error correction following each passage reading.

Although the instructional strategies just described constitute a strong intervention, they will probably not be sufficient to promote generalized improvements. Reinforcing instances of generalization has been shown to be effective at improving students' oral reading fluency in novel texts (Daly, Bonfiglio, et al., 2005; Gortmaker, Daly, McCurdy, Persampieri, & Hergenrader, 2007). In these studies, instruction included listening passage preview, repeated readings, phrase drill error correction, and performance feedback, after which the experimenters offered programmed reinforcement for improvement in texts that had many of the same words as the original training text but were written as a different story (passages with high content overlap). Therefore, training was offered in one set of passages and reinforcement in different (i.e., high content overlap) passages.

Setting up a program to offer an incentive for improving performance and reinforcing the student for meeting performance goals may increase the student's motivation to practice and benefit from intervention sessions, and the reinforcement for reading trained words across contexts should improve their ability to read those words when they appear in other texts (Daly, Bonfiglio, et al., 2005). Again, progress should be monitored in both reinforced and unreinforced conditions to gauge the degree to which the student's oral reading fluency is improving under natural conditions.

It Is Too Hard

The issue of difficulty level has already been discussed at length. Here, the original point made by Daly et al. (1997) is reiterated. When all else fails, consider moving the student down in the curriculum. This strategy is placed last in terms of priorities because it will often be difficult for a teacher to individualize a student's reading program in this way. The student is usually already a part of a reading group, and moving the student to another group—or, if there are no other students in the classroom being instructed a whole grade-level lower than his or her current instructional level, providing individualized instruction—may not be feasible. The previously presented strategies require fewer modifications and should be attempted first. If the student benefits from these, then there is no need to move the student down in the curriculum. Yet, some students' skills are so poor that it will be necessary to place them at a lower level in the curriculum before true growth will occur.

SUMMARY

The two most important things to keep in mind are that (a) oral reading fluency is an important instructional target that should be included as a routine part of reading instruction, and (b) interventions should be adapted to the individual learner's skill level. Oral reading fluency was neglected for far too long as something that teachers should actively work on. Fortunately, times are changing and educators are now seeing its importance. Recognizing its role and place in the developmental sequence of literacy skills will go a long way toward helping struggling learners become readers. More specifically, school psychologists should evaluate students' mastery of prerequisite skills and their oral reading fluency as a routine part of monitoring student educational performance.

Guidelines have been provided for interpreting students' reading patterns as a basis for selecting interventions. Of all the strategies presented, repeated readings is the most important. Just as with any skill, practice is the key ingredient to making progress. This practice can be made more effective when appropriate contingencies are used to improve motivation and adjustments are made based on whether the student needs modeling, error correction, and/or adjustments with instructional materials. The interventions presented in this chapter can be used to supplement current instruction, either as a part of regular core instruction or as supplemental interventions in response-to-intervention programs. Each is easy to administer and takes a brief amount of time.

REFERENCES

Adams, M. J. (1990). *Beginning to read: Thinking and learning about print.* Cambridge, MA: MIT Press.

Ardoin, S. P., & Daly, E. J., III. (2007). Introduction to the special series: Close encounters of the instructional kind: How the instructional hierarchy is shaping instructional research 30 years later. *Journal of Behavioral Education, 16,* 1–6.

Ayllon, T., & Roberts, M. D. (1974). Eliminating discipline problems by strengthening academic performance. *Journal of Applied Behavior Analysis, 7,* 71–76. doi:10.1901/jaba.1974.7-71

Ball, E., & Blachman, B. (1991). Does phoneme awareness training in kindergarten make a difference in early word recognition and developmental spelling? *Reading Research Quarterly, 26,* 49–66.

Begeny, J. C., Krouse, H. E., Ross, S. G., & Mitchell, R. C. (2009). Increasing elementary-aged students' reading fluency with small-group interventions: A comparison of repeated reading, listening passage preview, and listening only strategies. *Journal of Behavioral Education, 18,* 211–228. doi:10.1007/s10864-009-9090-9

Chard, D. J., Vaughn, S., & Tyler, B. J. (2002). A synthesis of research on effective interventions for building reading fluency with elementary students with learning disabilities. *Journal of Learning Disabilities, 35,* 386–406. doi:10.1177/00222194020350050101

Crowe, E. C., Connor, C. M., & Petscher, Y. (2009). Examining the core: Relations among reading curricula, poverty, and first through third grade reading achievement. *Journal of School Psychology, 47,* 187–214.

Daly, E. J., III, Bonfiglio, C. M., Mattson, T., Persampieri, M., & Foreman-Yates, K. (2005). Refining the experimental analysis of academic skill deficits, Part I: An investigation of variables affecting generalized oral reading performance. *Journal of Applied Behavior Analysis, 38,* 485–498.

Daly, E. J., III, Bonfiglio, C. M., Mattson, T., Persampieri, M., & Foreman-Yates, K. (2006). Refining the experimental analysis of academic skill deficits, Part II: An investigation of the use of brief experimental analysis for identifying reading fluency interventions. *Journal of Applied Behavior Analysis, 39*, 323–331.

Daly, E. J., III, & Kupzyk, S. (2012). Teaching reading. In G. J. Madden (Ed.), *The APA handbook of behavior analysis* (pp. 405–423). Washington, DC: American Psychological Association.

Daly, E. J., III, Lentz, F. E., & Boyer, J. (1996). The instructional hierarchy: A conceptual model for understanding the effective components of reading interventions. *School Psychology Quarterly, 11*, 369–386.

Daly, E. J., III, & Martens, B. K. (1994). A comparison of three interventions for increasing oral reading performance: Application of the instructional hierarchy. *Journal of Applied Behavior Analysis, 27*, 459–469. doi:10.1901/jaba.1994.27-459

Daly, E. J., III, Martens, B. K., Barnett, D., Witt, J. C., & Olson, S. C. (2007). Varying intervention delivery in response-to-intervention: Confronting and resolving challenges with measurement, instruction, and intensity. *School Psychology Review, 36*, 562–581.

Daly, E. J., III, Martens, B. K., Kilmer, A., & Massie, D. (1996). The effects of instructional match and content overlap on generalized reading performance. *Journal of Applied Behavior Analysis, 29*, 507–518. doi:10.1901/jaba.1996.29-507

Daly, E. J., III, Persampieri, M., McCurdy, M., & Gortmaker, V. (2005). Generating reading interventions through experimental analysis of academic skills: Demonstration and empirical evaluation. *School Psychology Review, 34*, 395–414.

Daly, E. J., III, Wells, J. N., Swanger-Gagne, M., Carr, J. E., Kunz, G. M., & Taylor, A. M. (2009). Evaluation of the Multiple-Stimulus Without Replacement stimulus preference assessment method using activities as stimulus events. *Journal of Applied Behavior Analysis, 42*, 563–574. doi:10.1901/jaba.2009.42-563

Daly, E. J., III, Witt, J. C., Martens, B. K., & Dool, E. J. (1997). A model for conducting a functional analysis of academic performance problems. *School Psychology Review, 26*, 554–574.

Deno, S. L. (1989). Curriculum-based measurement and special education services: A fundamental and direct relationship. In M. R. Shinn (Ed.), *Curriculum-based measurement: Assessing special children* (pp. 1–17). New York, NY: Guilford Press.

Eckert, T. L., Dunn, E. K., & Ardoin, S. P. (2006). The effects of alternate forms of performance feedback on elementary-aged students' oral reading fluency. *Journal of Behavioral Education, 15*, 149–162. doi:10.1007/s10864-006-9018-6

Eldredge, J. L. (2005). Foundations of fluency: An exploration. *Reading Psychology, 26*, 161–181. doi:10.1080/02702710590930519

Freeland, J. T., Skinner, C. H., Jackson, B., McDaniel, E., & Smith, S. (2000). Measuring and increasing silent reading comprehension rates: Empirically validating a repeated readings intervention. *Psychology in the Schools, 37*, 415–429. doi:10.1002/1520-6807(200009)37:5<415::AID-PITS2>3.0.CO;2-L

Fuchs, L. S., Fuchs, D., Hosp, M. K., & Jenkins, J. R. (2001). Oral reading fluency as an indicator of reading competence: A theoretical, empirical, and historical analysis. *Scientific Studies in Reading, 5*, 203–210. doi:10.1207/S1532799XSSR0503_3

Good, R. H., III, & Jefferson, G. (1998). Contemporary perspectives on curriculum-based measurement validity. In M. R. Shinn (Ed.), *Advanced applications of curriculum-based measurement* (pp. 61–88). New York, NY: Guilford Press.

Gortmaker, V. J., Daly, E. J., III, McCurdy, M., Persampieri, M. J., & Hergenrader, M. (2007). Improving reading outcomes for children with learning disabilities: Using brief experimental analysis to develop parent tutoring interventions. *Journal of Applied Behavior Analysis, 40*, 203–222. doi:10.1901/jaba.2007.105-05

Haring, N. G., & Eaton, M. D. (1978). Systematic instructional procedures: An instructional hierarchy. In N. G. Haring, T. C. Lovitt, M. D. Eaton, & C. L. Hansen (Eds.), *The fourth R: Research in the classroom* (pp. 23–40). Columbus, OH: Merrill.

Hiebert, E. H. (2005). The effects of text difficulty on second graders' fluency development. *Reading Psychology, 26*, 183–209. doi:10.1080/02702710590930528

Hiebert, E. H., & Fisher, C. W. (2005). A review of the National Reading Panel's studies on fluency: The role of text. *The Elementary School Journal, 105*, 443–460.

Hintze, J. M., & Silberglitt, B. (2005). A longitudinal examination of the diagnostic accuracy and predictive validity of R-CBM and high-stakes testing. *School Psychology Review, 34*, 372–386.

Hofstadter, K. L., & Daly, E. J., III. (2011). Improving oral reading fluency using a peer-mediated reading intervention. *Journal of Applied Behavior Analysis, 44*, 641–646. doi:10.1901/jaba.2011.44-641

Howell, K. W., & Nolet, V. (2000). *Curriculum-based evaluation: Teaching and decision making* (3rd ed.). Belmont, CA: Wadsworth.

Hudson, R. F., Pullen, P. C., Lane, H. B., & Torgesen, J. K. (2009). The complex nature of reading fluency: A multidimensional view. *Reading and Writing Quarterly, 25*, 4–32. doi:10.1080/10573560802491208

Jenkins, J. R., Fuchs, L. S., van den Broek, P., Espin, C., & Deno, S. L. (2003). Sources of individual differences in reading comprehension and reading fluency. *Journal of Educational Psychology, 95*, 719–729.

Kazdin, A. E. (2011). *Single-case research designs: Methods for clinical and applied settings* (2nd ed.). New York, NY: Oxford University Press.

Kuhn, M. R., & Stahl, S. A. (2003). Fluency: A review of developmental and remedial practices. *Journal of Educational Psychology, 95*, 3–21.

Lane, H. B., Hudson, R. F., Leite, W. L., Kosanovich, M. L., Strout, M. T., & Fenty, N. S. (2009). Teacher knowledge about reading fluency and indicators of students' fluency growth in reading first schools. *Reading and Writing Quarterly, 25*, 57–86. doi:10.1080/10573560802491232

Lentz, F. E. (1988). Effective reading interventions in the regular classroom. In J. L. Graden, J. Zins, & M. J. Curtis (Eds.), *Alternative educational delivery systems: Enhancing instructional options for all students* (pp. 351–370). Washington, DC: National Association of School Psychologists.

Martens, B. K., Eckert, T. L., Begeny, J. C., Lewandowski, L. J., DiGennaro, F. D., Montarello, S. A., ... Fiese, B. H. (2007). Effects of a fluency-building program on the reading performance of low-achieving second and third grade students. *Journal of Behavioral Education, 16*, 39–54.

McGlinchey, M. T., & Hixson, M. D. (2004). Using curriculum-based measurement to predict performance on state assessments in reading. *School Psychology Review, 33*, 193–203.

Miltenberger, R. G. (2012). *Behavior modification: Principles and procedures* (5th ed.). Belmont, CA: Wadsworth, Cengage Learning.

National Association of School Psychologists. (2010). *Model for comprehensive and integrated school psychological services.* Bethesda, MD: Author. Retrieved from http://www.nasponline.org/standards/2010standards/2_PracticeModel.pdf

National Reading Panel. (2000). *Teaching children to read: An evidence-based assessment of the scientific research literature on reading and its implications for reading instruction.* Rockville, MD: Author. Retrieved from http://www.nationalreadingpanel.org

O'Shea, L. J., Munson, S. M., & O'Shea, D. J. (1984). Error correction in oral reading: Evaluating the effectiveness of three procedures. *Education and Treatment of Children, 7,* 203–214.

Pikulski, J. J., & Chard, D. J. (2005). Fluency: Bridge between decoding and reading comprehension. *Reading Teacher, 58,* 510–519. doi:10.1598/RT.58.6.2

Rashotte, C. A., & Torgesen, J. K. (1985). Repeated reading and reading fluency in learning disabled children. *Reading Research Quarterly, 20,* 180–188.

Rose, T. L., & Beattie, J. R. (1986). Relative effects of teacher-directed and taped previewing on oral reading. *Learning Disability Quarterly, 9,* 193–199. doi:10.2307/1510464

Samuels, S. J. (2006). Toward a model of reading fluency. In S. J. Samuels & A. E. Farstrup (Eds.), *What research has to say about fluency instruction* (pp. 24–46). Newark, DE: International Reading Association.

Shinn, M. R. (1989). *Curriculum-based measurement: Assessing special children.* New York, NY: Guilford Press.

Shinn, M. R., Good, R. H., III, Knutson, N., Tilly, W. D., III, & Collins, V. L. (1992). Curriculum-based measurement of oral reading fluency: A confirmatory analysis of its relation to reading. *School Psychology Review, 21,* 459–479.

Skinner, C. H., Cooper, L., & Cole, C. L. (1997). The effects of oral presentation previewing rates on reading performance. *Journal of Applied Behavior Analysis, 30,* 331–333. doi:10.1901/jaba.1997.30-331

Snow, C., Burns, S., & Griffin, P. (1998). *Preventing reading difficulties in young children.* Washington, DC: National Research Council.

Speece, D. L., & Ritchey, K. D. (2005). A longitudinal study of the development of oral reading fluency in young children at risk for reading failure. *Journal of Learning Disabilities, 38,* 387–399.

Stokes, T. F., & Baer, D. M. (1977). An implicit technology of generalization. *Journal of Applied Behavior Analysis, 10,* 349–367. doi:10.1901/jaba.1977.10-349

Therrien, W. J. (2004). Fluency and comprehension gains as a result of repeated reading. *Remedial and Special Education, 25,* 252–261. doi:10.1177/07419325040250040801

Yeaton, W. H., & Sechrest, L. (1981). Critical dimensions in the choice and maintenance of successful treatments: Strength, integrity, and effectiveness. *Journal of Consulting and Clinical Psychology, 49,* 156–167.

Best Practices in Delivering Intensive Academic Interventions With a Skill-by-Treatment Interaction

Matthew K. Burns
University of Minnesota
Amanda M. VanDerHeyden
Education Research and Consulting
Anne F. Zaslofsky
University of Minnesota

OVERVIEW

The goals of school psychology are to improve competencies for all students and to build capacities of systems to address student needs (Ysseldyke et al., 2006). Emphasizing systemic solutions and intervening with a single struggling student are not mutually exclusive activities, and addressing the intense academic needs of individual students will always be the responsibility of school psychologists. This chapter will describe a framework for selecting effective academic interventions for individual students that relies on direct measurement of student skills. We will discuss basic considerations for intensive academic interventions, present the aspects of effective academic interventions, describe a system in which data from measures of student skill are used to identify appropriate academic interventions, and provide an example for reading and one for math. Readers will be able to implement a model that relies on a skill-by-treatment interaction to identify intensive academic interventions for individual students.

The chapter aligns with the National Association of School Psychologists (NASP) *Model for Comprehensive and Integrated School Psychological Services* (NASP, 2010) domain of Interventions and Instructional Support to Develop Academic Skills. Moreover, school psychological services are best delivered through a multitiered model

(Ysseldyke et al., 2006), and the skills discussed in this chapter are most relevant for services provided at Tier 3.

Response-to-intervention (RTI) decision-making frameworks have reinvigorated an interest in academic interventions among school psychologists. Most instructional and intervention decisions at Tiers 1 and 2 are made by grade-level teams and classroom teachers. School psychologists are actively involved in identifying interventions for students with significant academic deficits (Tier 3). Thus, school psychologists need to be knowledgeable in research regarding systems change, but also need a strong working knowledge of evidence-based assessment and intervention practices for individual students.

For decades, educators relied on popular academic interventions that had intuitive appeal but little empirical support. Historically, school psychologists attempted to identify interventions with an aptitude-by-treatment interaction in which instructional strategies for individual students were selected based on measured characteristics of the students (e.g., a student with poor cognitive process xyz would be provided with an intervention for xyz that would result in improved performance of all tasks that involve cognitive process xyz; Cronbach, 1957). For example, interventions for children with learning difficulties in the 1960s, 1970s, and early 1980s focused on various approaches to perceptual training, intervening with psycholinguistic skills (e.g., receptive and expressive language, association, and sequential memory), and matching the modality of instruction with the preferred learning style, all of which led to small effects (Kavale, 2007). Thus, after an entire career of research, the architects of the original aptitude-by-treatment interaction approach concluded that cognitive abilities alone did not explain individual differences in intervention effectiveness and recommended that such an approach to intervention selection be summarily abandoned (Cronbach & Snow, 1977).

Moreover, recent meta-analytic research of 23 studies that involved interventions for working memory found effect sizes for word reading and math that were close to zero. Researchers concluded that "there was no convincing evidence of the generalization of working memory training to other skills (nonverbal and verbal ability, inhibitory processes in attention, word decoding, and arithmetic)" (Melby-Lervag & Hulme, 2013, p. 270).

Burns, Codding, Boice, and Lukito (2010) found that math interventions that relied on modeling and explicit instruction were more effective for students who were in the frustration level of the specific skill than for students who demonstrated an instructional level for the skill. They called this a *skill-by-treatment interaction*, which was defined as the process of selecting academic interventions based on student functioning in the specific skill rather than by underlying aptitudes, and presented it as a framework for making intervention decisions for students receiving a Tier 3 intervention. Below we will discuss this framework within the larger context of effective academic interventions for individual students.

BASIC CONSIDERATIONS

To review the intervention literature in school psychology would exceed the scope of this chapter, but several meta-analyses have identified effective intervention practices. We simultaneously searched EBSCO, Education Full Text, and PsycINFO databases in September 2013 with the terms *meta-analysis* and *reading intervention* (58) or *math intervention* (45) or *writing intervention* (65) to identify relevant meta-analytic research. We found 168 unique meta-analyses, 22 of which were relevant to K–12 education published in a research journal since 1999. Thus, there does not appear to be any shortage of recent research regarding effective intervention practices for academic deficits. Those meta-analyses for which the researchers found a large effect,

which we define as $d = .80$ for group designs and $d = 2.80$ for single-case design research (Burns & Wagner, 2008), are listed in Table 9.1. We also include specific interventions for individual academic skills for which a small effect was found.

In the following sections we will detail the five research-supported characteristics of effective, intensive academic interventions: explicit instruction, appropriate level of challenge, frequent opportunities to respond, correctly targeted using a skill-by-treatment interaction approach, and immediate feedback. Thus, school psychologists should critically examine any academic intervention to determine if the five components described below are present. If they are not present, then school psychologists should be especially skeptical about the proposed intervention.

Explicit Instruction

Explicit instruction is characterized by systematic scaffolds, which include high levels of modeling, guided and independent practice, and structured feedback (Archer & Hughes, 2011). Procedures are modeled, examples of correct and incorrect responses are provided, and students are afforded frequent opportunities to respond through guided and independent practice. Finally, student performance is monitored, and corrective feedback is provided as needed (Archer & Hughes, 2011). Research has found explicit instruction to be an effective instructional approach for students with severe learning difficulties (Gersten et al., 2009; Graham, McKeown, Kiuhara, & Harris, 2012; Kavale, 2007).

Instructional Level or Appropriate Level of Challenge

To be successful, the intervention or instruction should provide an appropriate level of challenge. An appropriate level of challenge is achieved when there is a match between the required task's difficulty and the student's performance. If the task is too easy, then the student is not actively engaged and is not learning much new material. Thus, the student does not need to practice the material in order to master it and motivation will be reduced. If the task is too difficult, then the student lacks the prerequisite knowledge and the new knowledge cannot be learned easily and integrated into prior knowledge, so the student will be frustrated.

The concept of instructional level, or appropriate level of challenge, was first presented by Betts (1946),

Table 9.1. Effective and Ineffective Academic Intervention Practices Based on Meta-Analyses of Intervention Research

Age Group	Reading	Writing	Math
Elementary: Practices with large effects	• Repeated reading • Using easier reading material • Immediate performance feedback • Direct instruction • Phonemic awareness instruction • Explicit phonics instruction	• Strategy instruction for planning, editing, and paragraph structure • Peer-assisted writing • Setting clear and specific goals	• Drill techniques • Practice with modeling • Explicit instruction • Student verbalizations of mathematical reasoning • Include a broad range of examples • Cross-age tutoring • Concrete–representational–abstract • Speed-based intervention
Practices with small or negative effects	• Whole language approaches • Sentence combining	• Grammar instruction	• Problem structure representation
Adolescent: Practices with large effects	• Comprehension strategies • Reciprocal teaching • Teaching vocabulary • Semantic organizers • Concept maps	• Self-regulation strategy development • Strategy instruction • Summarization • Setting product goals	• Teach to use visual representations of problems • Self-monitor problem solving • Self-reflect on problem-solving process
Practices with small or negative effects	• Fluency interventions	• Studying models of writing • Teaching grammar	• Technological enhanced instruction

Note. References for the meta-analyses on which this table is based are available from the first author upon request.

who introduced the concepts of frustration, instructional, and independent levels of challenge during instruction. These levels were based on the observation that reading comprehension began to decline rapidly when unknown words comprised more than approximately 5% of the text, and students experienced no difficulties in reading and comprehension when unknown words comprised 2% or less of the text. Frustration, instructional, and independent levels continue to be used today when discussing levels of challenge, but have been more clearly operationalized. The independent level is above 97% known words, the instructional level contains between 93% and 97% known words, and the frustration level is below 93% known words (Gravois & Gickling, 2008). Further research has shown that for rehearsal, practice, and drill (e.g., math facts, flashcards, spelling, phonemic awareness), any approach that contained at least 50% known items led to a mean large effect, but 85–90% known led to the largest effects (Burns, 2004a).

Whereas accuracy criteria may be used to judge the challenge level of a task, there are also general rules of thumb for fluency scores for math at different grade levels

of material. Burns, VanDerHeyden, and Jiban (2006) studied fluency criteria for math instructional levels and recommended 14–31 digits correct per minute for second- and third-grade students and 24–49 digits correct per minute for fourth- and fifth-grade students. Thus, school psychologists can conduct single-skill fluency assessment probes for 2–4 minutes and compare the resulting data to these criteria in order to identify an instructional level.

A second component of the instructional level should be considered when preparing an appropriately challenging learning task. Determining an optimal pace of instruction is critical to effective planning, and the pace of instruction relies on the rate with which children learn. Therefore, the rate of acquisition of skills should be considered and is the second component of the instructional level. Rate of acquisition represents the amount of information that an individual child can successfully rehearse, retain, and use at a later time (Burns & Parker, 2014). It is important to consider the number of new items that students can learn at any one time, because if the total number of new words exceeds the student's acquisition rate, then the task can be too challenging and can result in student frustration.

Research indicates that learning is enhanced when learning tasks are appropriately matched to the instructional level (i.e., level of challenge). Percentages of task completion, task comprehension, and on-task behavior were all consistently high for students when assignments were at the instructional level, but all three were low when materials were at the frustration level (task too hard). There was a high percentage of off-task behavior observed when materials were at the independent level (task too easy) of challenge (Treptow, Burns, & McComas, 2007).

Frequent Opportunities to Respond

Practice helps students retain newly learned information. Some teachers associate practice with drill procedures and have argued against the importance of effective practice, but providing more student opportunities to respond by increasing the number of presentations while rehearsing new items leads to improved academic engagement, learning, and retention of the newly learned items. In fact, comparisons of various instructional approaches (e.g., computer-assisted instruction and flashcard methods) found that the increased opportunities to respond was the aspect of the intervention that was most directly related to the outcomes (Szadokierski & Burns, 2008).

Targeted Based on Student Skill

To address a child's unique learning needs, the school psychologist must understand what skills the child needs to be able to complete (i.e., develop a skill hierarchy), measure the child's performance in goal and prerequisite skills, characterize the child's performance (accuracy and speed), and design the intervention to improve performance as needed on a given skill in the hierarchy. The instructional hierarchy (Haring & Eaton, 1978) represents the dynamic interface between instructional activity and student competence and provides the basis for selecting the right level of challenge for the instructional materials that will be used during intervention (Burns et al., 2010).

Student competence develops as target skills progress through the following phases: (a) acquisition, (b) proficiency, (c) generalization, and (d) adaptation (Haring & Eaton, 1978). A student's performance at the acquisition stage is characterized by low accuracy and subsequent dysfluency. Effective acquisition interventions include modeling, guided practice, frequent feedback, and activities designed to increase the salience of the correct discrimination to be learned. After acquiring the skill, students exhibit fluency-building stage performance that is more accurate but still dysfluent, and corresponding interventions should enhance fluency in skill performance. Effective fluency-building interventions emphasize independent timed practice, multiple opportunities to respond, and use of small rewards or privileges for improved performance. Most academic deficits involve these first two stages, but students operating in the generalization or adaptation stages may require interventions such as guided application of fluent skills under novel conditions and use of learned skills to solve more complex or different tasks.

Feedback

It is useful to think of the series of interactions that occur in a classroom or within an intervention session as a series of learning trials that can be quantified as (a) an instructional cue or prompt to respond, (b) a student response, and (c) teacher-provided or material-provided feedback. Feedback is the component of instruction that ensures that the student acquires the target skill or that stimulus control is established. In other words, the function of feedback is to ensure that, in response to a certain instructional cue (e.g., $8 + 5$), the correct response (i.e., 13) is reinforced and nothing else. Incomplete learning trials occur when an instructional cue is provided, a student responds, and feedback is either absent or incorrect. Where incomplete learning trials are prevalent, learning suffers.

BEST PRACTICES IN DELIVERING INTENSIVE ACADEMIC INTERVENTIONS WITH A SKILL-BY-TREATMENT INTERACTION

The specific interventions outlined in Table 9.1 have been demonstrated to be effective based on meta-analytic research. Thus, school psychologists interested in academic interventions could begin by implementing the interventions listed in the table. However, we also reviewed the interventions for which there was a large effect to determine what the interventions had in common and, as described above, found that each included (a) explicit instruction, (b) learning of materials that represented an instructional level, (c) frequent opportunities to respond, (d) interventions targeted to student skill, and (e) corrective feedback. Below we will discuss best practices for incorporating each of these five criteria into interventions.

Explicit Instruction

From an intervention perspective, explicit instruction involves modeling the skill first ("I do"), completing the task with the student so as to provide immediate feedback and scaffolding ("we do"), then having the student complete the task on his or her own ("you do") with corrective feedback that moves from immediate to delayed as student proficiency improves. Of course, there is much more to explicit instruction than the simple "I do, we do, you do" format, but modeling the skill first is critically important for interventions.

It is not unusual to see teachers and school psychologists ask the students to attempt a task with little support before beginning an intervention. For example, imagine working with a student on spelling. The first step is often to have the student attempt the word first and then direct the student in a method to determine the correct spelling as he or she struggles to spell the word. Unfortunately, asking the student to struggle as the first step in the intervention creates an opportunity for failure, and the student is already familiar with that experience. Of course, asking a student to complete a task that he or she may not be able to complete could be an important part of the assessment process in order to determine where the intervention should focus, but the intervention should begin with success. Therefore, the school psychologist should instead orally present the word that needs to be spelled while the school psychologist is spelling it correctly (I do), ask the student to copy the correct spelling of the word (we do), and then have the student write the word from memory with immediate feedback on the accuracy (you do).

Other examples include completing a math problem for the student first while describing the thought processes out loud and leaving it as a model, asking the student to complete a similar problem while looking at the model and getting immediate feedback on every step, and then having the student compete additional problems on his or her own. Another example is showing a student a letter, saying the sound that corresponds to the letter, asking the student to then say the corresponding sound, and then having the student provide the sound for the letter as the student finds it in print three consecutive times.

Instructional Level

School psychologists should think of the level of challenge as the "Goldilocks rule" and should incorpo-

rate measurement of instructional match into decision making when whole classes and individual children show high rates of off-task behavior and/or low rates of learning. At the whole-class level, task difficulty should be roughly matched to the skill level of the median-performing student. At the individual intervention level, intervention tasks should be aligned with the individual student's skill proficiency, which may require working on tasks that are below grade level.

It would go beyond the scope of this paper to describe how to assess the instructional level for reading, math, and writing, and readers are referred to other publications (e.g., Burns & Parker, 2014; Gravois & Gickling, 2008). An instructional level is determined by having the student engage in the skill with the materials used for instruction and record the number and percentage of items in which the student responded correctly (e.g., read words correctly, gave the correct letter sound) in order to determine appropriately challenging material for intervention. For example, reading is determined by having the student read for 1 minute, recording the number of words read correctly and incorrectly, and then dividing the number read correctly by the total number of words to find the percentage of words read correctly. The student should be able to correctly read 93–97% of the words. Thus, repeated reading would be conducted with passages in which the student could read 93–97% of the words. Math involves having the student complete a math task for 2 minutes in a single skill (e.g., a probe of single-digit multiplication facts) and computing the number of digits correct per minute. An instructional level for math would be 14–31 digits correct per minute for second and third graders and 24–49 digits correct per minute for fourth and fifth graders (Burns et al., 2006).

In addition to percentage of words known, school psychologists should also consider the acquisition rate when designing interventions. As described above, the acquisition rate is the amount of new information that a student can be taught, rehearse, and use at a later time. In practice, an acquisition rate is easily identifiable because students begin to make frequent errors while rehearsing a new item. For example, if a school psychologist were helping a student to learn math facts, and attempted to teach six facts but the student's acquisition rate was only four, then the student would learn the first four with little difficulty, but would start making frequent errors while rehearsing the fifth fact, would exhibit more time off task, and would not recall the fact at a later time. *Frequent* is operationally defined as making three errors while rehearsing a new item, and any time the student does not correctly respond within

2 seconds, it is considered an error (e.g., no response, incorrect response, or correct response after 2 seconds).

School psychologists should consult with teachers and other personnel about continuing to teach new items until the student makes three errors while learning one new item, and then stopping because the acquisition rate will have been reached. This number is often smaller than most people would predict. In fact, it is not unusual for young students with learning difficulties to demonstrate an acquisition rate of only one or two items (Burns, 2004b), and it would be better to teach only one or two items than to spend time teaching additional items that the student would not retain. Moreover, students exhibit higher rates of off-task behavior when learning items after they have exceeded their acquisition rate.

Opportunities to Respond

Although opportunities to respond are important for student learning, especially for students with academic deficits, most classroom teachers seem to lack effective methods to provide the necessary repetition. Paired peer practice is an effective approach for groups of students, and drill flashcard methods can be effective for individual students. Paired peer practice strategies involve structured practice with peer assistance, scripted answer checking and corrective feedback, and timed independent practice. The effectiveness of paired peer practice has been consistently supported (VanDerHeyden, McLaughlin, Algina, & Snyder, 2012).

Effective drill methods for individual students involve interspersing new items to be rehearsed within previously learned ones at a ratio including at least 50% known, but 85–90% known would be preferable (Burns, 2004a). Incremental rehearsal is a flashcard technique used to rehearse items that need to be memorized to automaticity. The procedure, outlined in Table 9.2, involves folding in unknown items (e.g., words, letter sounds, math facts, spelling words) with known items using a high ratio of known items. Previous research has found incremental rehearsal to be effective with a variety of topics and student populations (Burns, Zaslofsky, Kanive, & Parker, 2012).

Targeted Based on Student Skill

School psychologists can use the learning hierarchy to target interventions by assessing accuracy of performance and fluency of performance on a given task to determine whether a student needs acquisition, fluency

Table 9.2. Steps in Incremental Rehearsal

1. Present first unknown letter
   - Present first known letter
2. Present first unknown letter
   - Present first known letter
   - Present second known letter
3. Present first unknown letter
   - Present first known letter
   - Present second known letter
   - Present third known letter
4. Present first unknown letter
   - Present first known letter
   - Present second known letter
   - Present third known letter
   - Present fourth known letter
5. Present first unknown letter
   - Present first known letter
   - Present second known letter
   - Present third known letter
   - Present fourth known letter
   - Present fifth known letter
6. Present first unknown letter
   - Present first known letter
   - Present second known letter
   - Present third known letter
   - Present fourth known letter
   - Present fifth known letter
   - Present sixth known letter
7. Present first unknown letter
   - Present first known letter
   - Present second known letter
   - Present third known letter
   - Present fourth known letter
   - Present fifth known letter
   - Present sixth known letter
   - Present seventh known letter

Note. After completing the rehearsal sequence with the first letter, that first unknown letter is then treated as the first known, the previous final (seventh) known is removed, and a new unknown letter is introduced. Thus, the number of flash cards always remain constant (eight).

building, or generalization support during intervention. The school psychologist can assess accuracy by examining samples of student performance on particular problematic tasks (e.g., mathematics and writing). Timed assessments are required to determine the fluency of the skill. If the student is inaccurate, then acquisition instruction is needed. If the student's performance is accurate but below a fluency criterion, then the student needs fluency-building instruction. Once the school psychologist has determined whether the student needs acquisition support or fluency-building support, the school psychologist can use functional assessment procedures to test the effect of instructional supports on student learning.

As stated above, the first step in intervening for students with severe academic difficulties is to correctly target the intervention focus. The areas examined by the National Reading Panel (National Institute of Child Health and Human Development, 2000) could be conceived as a developmental framework for a reading intervention selection model. One of the first acts of the National Reading Panel was to divide reading into major topic areas, including alphabetics (phonemic awareness and phonics instruction), reading fluency, and comprehension (including vocabulary instruction and text comprehension instruction). These areas represent a general progression of reading skill development among struggling readers (Berninger, Abbott, Vermeulen, & Fulton, 2006). For example, a struggling student often must first develop phonemic awareness. Then that student can successfully decode words and can read with fluency, which eventually leads to an improved reading vocabulary and comprehension. It should be noted that proficient readers may not always follow this same progression, but struggling readers seem to more consistently require this sequence of skill development.

Math is based on objectives, which can be used to identify intervention targets. Essentially, practitioners can assess student skills in specific math objectives to determine the appropriate starting point for intervention. Each objective within a grade-level curriculum could be individually assessed and compared with the instructional-level criteria of 14–31 digits correct per minute for second and third graders and 24–49 digits correct per minute for fourth and fifth graders. Practitioners would administer single skill probes until the task that represents an instructional level is identified for students, and the intervention would directly target that skill. The Common Core State Standards (National Governors Association Center for Best Practices & Council of Chief State School Officers, 2010) provide an excellent sequence of expected learning outcomes by content area that have been (or are being) adopted in most states for instructional planning.

Feedback

Assuming that the correct antecedent variables have been arranged and the occasion has been set for the student to actively respond, then there are several characteristics of feedback that influence effectiveness. These components are frequency, immediacy, and content or accuracy. Each of these components will be described below relative to the student's stage of learning.

Feedback is important at all stages of learning (acquisition of the skill, fluency building, and generalization). When children are first learning a skill (acquisition stage of learning), responses will be hesitant and sometimes incorrect. It is imperative at this stage of learning that feedback be immediate. Hence, during this stage of learning, independent practice of the skill is counterproductive and actually gives the student a chance to practice the skill incorrectly. Guided practice is the ideal form of instruction whereby a peer or teacher monitors each student response and provides immediate corrective feedback. The content of the feedback at this stage should be correct, quick (i.e., interrupting the incorrect response), and combined with antecedent strategies such as cuing or prompting correct responses when the teacher anticipates an incorrect response is likely. At this stage, delayed error correction will be inefficient and ineffective. Effective teachers have a system for tracking student responding when they are teaching a new skill and for ensuring that students have made the correct discrimination before moving into independent work.

Once a skill has been established (i.e., the student can accurately perform the skill), then fluency-building intervention is the optimal choice. At this stage, feedback can be delayed and should be tied to motivating contingencies to maximize growth and learning. Reinforcing faster performance and blocking reinforcement for slower performance is the guiding principle. At this stage, feedback should not interrupt responding (because it interferes with fluency and is unnecessary). Content aspects of feedback are important at this stage, too. Feedback must still be correct, but also it can be less elaborate. The key is to provide feedback after short intervals of practice where students are working to improve their performance. Feedback also generally may be brief rather than elaborate while preserving instructional time and maintaining a brisk pace of instruction. At this stage, overcorrection may be an effective consequence-based strategy that can be combined with delayed feedback. When corrective feedback is provided, the student is then asked to provide the correct response three times in quick succession.

Once the student can perform the skill accurately and quickly (i.e., fluently), then generalization-level instructional strategies are appropriate. At this stage of learning, feedback can be delayed and in most cases should be elaborate. That is, feedback should occur frequently, and it should provide information about why (or what aspects of) the response was incorrect and prompt expanded thinking and connection to new skills and understanding. Critically, students should be given an opportunity to correct their mistakes. This level of work may be ideal for homework or independent practice because delayed feedback is effective for learning at this stage.

Examples

An effective intervention will likely include the aspects listed above and should be linked to measures of student skill. Below we will provide two examples of using data to determine appropriate interventions that include the five components described above.

Reading

A demonstration of a reading intervention involves a second-grade student named John who was referred for consultation due to reported difficulties in reading. John was enrolled in a class where universal screening indicated that the majority of his classmates were performing at a level that predicted future reading success. John read 20 words correctly per minute on a grade-level passage. He read 22 words correctly per minute on an equivalent grade-level passage when offered a reward to beat his score. His error rate was also high, with only 70% and 75% of the words read being read accurately. The school psychologist followed up this assessment by directly assessing John's decoding skills with a pseudoword (nonsense word) measure, and John's skills fell between the 15th and 25th percentile.

The data presented above suggest that John is struggling with reading decoding. He demonstrated difficulty with reading fluency because he read only 20 or 22 words correctly per minute, but his low accuracy (i.e., less than 93%) and decoding skills below the 25th percentile suggest that he does not successfully decode unknown words. Thus, the school psychologist decided to target reading decoding because it was the more fundamental skill of the two (fluency or decoding). The school psychologist then administered a standardized assessment of phonemic awareness and determined that John demonstrated sufficient phonemic awareness.

Next, the school psychologist administered a decoding inventory to determine what sounds the student needed to be taught. John correctly identified the sounds for 65% of the letters and letter combinations. This low level of accuracy indicated that although decoding was the appropriate target, John was inaccurate and demonstrated skills that fell within the acquisition phase

of learning, which suggests the need for high modeling with explicit error correction to increase accuracy.

The school psychologist consulted with the classroom teacher about using incremental rehearsal to intervene with John. As described above, incremental rehearsal (Table 9.2) involves folding in unknown words with known words using a high ratio of known items, which addresses the opportunities to respond and instructional-level criteria of an effective intervention. Moreover, specific tasks can be targeted based on student need, as in this example, and can be explicitly taught by first modeling the sound for the letter on the card, asking the student to state the sound, and then practicing it with little feedback. Corrective feedback can be provided as needed for each incorrect response and should be at an adequately dense schedule to ensure correct responding during intervention.

In this example, one unknown item (e.g., the sound /sh/) was presented for every seven knowns (e.g., the sounds /t/, /s/, /m/, /r/, /f/, /v/, and /a/) during daily peer tutoring sessions for approximately 5–15 minutes each morning. The peer tutor was another student in the class who was a higher-performing student but still demonstrated relative difficulty with reading. Sounds were selected to be taught by examining the reading material for that day's instruction to identify sounds and words in the text that contained unknown sounds.

John's progress was monitored once each week with two different curriculum-based measures (CBM). Nonsense word fluency was used to monitor progress in decoding, and oral reading fluency was used as a general outcome measure. A goal of at least 57 sounds per minute for nonsense word fluency was established because that was the criterion for the spring benchmark of first grade. A criterion of 80 words per minute was also established by the winter benchmark on the oral reading fluency measure. The final baseline point was obtained on October 18, and the intervention began shortly thereafter.

As shown in Figure 9.1, John's CBM data points continued on a trend toward the goal, and the final criterion for nonsense word fluency was reached on November 22. After demonstrating two more consecutive data points above the criterion, the intervention stopped. John correctly identified the sounds of 99% of the letter and letter combinations in the subsequent assessment, and the school psychologist concluded that the intervention target should switch to fluency. At that time, a daily repeated reading intervention began, which

Figure 9.1. John's Weekly Curriculum-Based Measurement Scores for Nonsense Word Fluency and Oral Reading Fluency

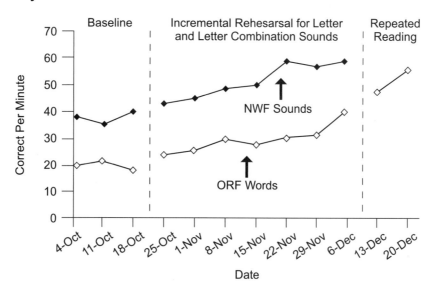

Note. NWF = nonsense word fluency; ORF = oral reading fluency.

resulted in an immediate increase in words read correctly per minute.

Mathematics

A second-grade child, Joan, was referred to the school psychologist because the teacher was concerned about Joan's ability to perform expected grade-level math tasks successfully. The first step was for the school psychologist and teacher to select a worksheet that could be administered class-wide and represented a skill that the average student ought to be able to complete at that time of year given the program of instruction at that school. Importantly, the school psychologist should be aware of the state content standards for mathematics, a computational skill should be selected, and the skill should be one that students must be able to do to benefit from continued general education instruction in that classroom. So for this case, the school psychologist selected a mixed probe of addition and subtraction facts 0–20 in the fall of the school year.

The median score for the class fell within the instructional range (Burns et al., 2006), but Joan had the lowest score in the class, which fell within the frustration range. Thus, Joan will likely struggle to perform multidigit addition and subtraction with and without regrouping (skills that appear in the second-grade standards) and will struggle to successfully solve more complex or novel problems that require the computation of addition or subtraction facts 0–20.

The second step was to target the intervention more specifically for Joan. Thus, the school psychologist next administered a series of probes to identify which skills Joan could perform and which skills required acquisition instruction. Joan scored within the instructional level range for subtraction 0–5, but not within subtraction 0–20. Incentives did not improve performance for the more advanced subtraction skills (see VanDerHeyden & Witt, 2008). Hence, the school psychologist developed an intervention to build fluency starting with subtraction 0–10, then increasing task difficulty to 0–15, then to 0–20 based on mastery at each stage.

The school psychologist trained a peer tutor in Joan's class to conduct the intervention, which consisted of the following components. Joan practiced flashcards of the target skill for 3 minutes. The peer tutor was taught specifically how to effectively present and pace flashcards, to immediately and briefly correct student errors, and to set aside any missed items for additional practice. When the timer rang, the daily timed practice sheet was taken out of the intervention folder, the timer was set for 2 minutes, and Joan worked to beat the score from the previous day. When the timer rang, the peer tutor and Joan scored the worksheet; they wrote the number of digits correctly completed in 2 minutes at the top; and Joan corrected each error, explaining to the peer tutor how she was correcting the error. The entire intervention required only 10 minutes to implement each day and provided Joan with multiple opportunities to respond, immediate but brief feedback during practice, and delayed feedback following the timed test. This intervention was appropriate for Joan because she could accurately perform the skill; she did not need acquisition-level instructional strategies, but instead needed to build fluency in the skill quickly so that she could benefit maximally from the general education instructional program for second grade.

Each week the school psychologist graphed Joan's performance, evaluated and addressed implementation integrity concerns, and administered a mixed probe of addition and subtraction facts 0–20. When Joan reached mastery for subtraction 0–10, materials were changed to increase task difficulty to subtraction 0–15, and then again to subtraction 0–20. Within 3 weeks, Joan performed in the mastery range on a mixed probe of addition and subtraction 0–20, which was a level of performance that was similar to Joan's peers. The school psychologist shared graphed results each week with the teacher and at the end of the intervention discussed what types of instructional strategies would be appropriate to promote generalization of the trained skill. In a collaborative and collegial fashion, the school psychologist also cued the teacher to use instructional strategies

that would most effectively establish new skills, such as multidigit addition and subtraction without regrouping (i.e., acquisition-level strategies).

Developmental Differences

School psychologists should consider several developmental factors when engaging in intensive academic interventions, most of which are discussed above. For example, the developmental level of the student would help determine how many new items (e.g., letter sounds, math facts, spelling words, sight words) to teach. Students in preschool and kindergarten should probably be taught a small number of new items (e.g., 1 or 2), and the number would increase for most students to three items for first grade, five for third grade, and seven for fifth grade (Burns, 2004b).

The appropriate target should be assessed for every student, but reading, math, and writing skills follow a general developmental trend, described in Table 9.3. Table 9.1 describes effective intervention practices, and Table 9.3 describes potential targets for intervention and instruction for most children. Of course, school psychologists should use assessment data to identify intervention targets for individual students, but the

Table 9.3. Targets for Intervention Efforts by Developmental Level

Developmental Age	Reading	Writing	Math
Early childhood: Preschool and kindergarten	• Concepts of print • Phonemic awareness	• Alphabet knowledge • Letter writing	• Number sense
Early elementary: Grades 1–2	• Phonological awareness (phonemic awareness and decoding)	• Text production • Transcription	• Addition and subtraction of whole numbers
Upper elementary: Grades 3–5	• Decoding • Fluency • Comprehension	• Text structure by genre • Creativity/imagery • Text production	• Multiplication and division of whole numbers • Fractions and decimals • Perimeter and area of triangles and quadrilaterals
Middle school: Grades 6–8	• Fluency • Vocabulary • Comprehension	• Text structure • Self-regulated strategies • Metacognition • Summarizing	• Multiplication and division of fractions and decimals • Operations with positive and negative integers • Percent, ratio, rate, and proportionality • Two- and three-dimensional shapes (e.g., perimeter, area, surface, and volume)
High school: Grades 9–12	• Vocabulary • Comprehension	• Text genre • Self-regulated strategies	• Quantifying attributes of interest • Solving algebraic equations • Geometry • Statistics and probability

information in Table 9.3 may provide potential starting points for those assessments.

Meta-analytic research by the National Reading Panel (National Institute of Child Health and Human Development, 2000) suggested that interventions should target phonemic awareness for kindergarten students, phonological awareness (phonemic awareness and phonics instruction) for most students in first and second grade, reading fluency for most students in third and fourth grades, and comprehension (including vocabulary instruction and text comprehension instruction) for older students. Of course, these are general trends that do not necessarily apply to individual students.

Graham et al. (2012) summarized several effective writing strategies and developmental trends for writing. Early intervention should focus heavily on transcription, such as forming the letters correctly, and production. However, more advanced writers need to learn how to self-regulate their writing and how to format writing for different genres. There is considerable guidance for targets of math instruction and intervention based on meta-analytic research by Gersten et al. (2009) and the National Mathematics Advisory Panel (2008), along with the Common Core State Standards. As shown in Table 9.3, intervention efforts with young children should focus on number sense, and intervention efforts for older students should focus on algebraic concepts.

Multicultural Competencies

Academic interventions, much like effective school psychology practice, need to be rooted in multicultural competency. Thus, school psychologists should display open empathy, caring, flexibility, and involvement with the social relations of the students with whom they work (Cartledge & Kourea, 2008). However, students from diverse backgrounds are also less likely to experience quality instruction and may develop sustained academic difficulties as a result. Thus, culturally competent instruction for students with academic difficulties should also include high levels of student academic responding, appropriate pacing, timely feedback, and recognizing of the individual strengths and needs of students (Cartledge & Kourea, 2008). High levels of responding can be achieved with frequent opportunities to respond, appropriate pacing happens when school psychologists consider students' acquisition rates, and targeting the intervention for each student recognizes the needs of an individual student. In other words, the components of an effective academic intervention as outlined above are at the very core of multicultural competence.

Evaluation of Outcomes

School psychologists should monitor the progress of a student receiving an intervention at least once each week, and should consider both the level at which the student is functioning and the rate of growth. CBM is ideally suited to monitor the progress of students receiving interventions.

Shapiro and Clemens (2009) provide a conceptual framework for evaluating RTI models that examines different data for different decisions. The interventions described here are most applicable for Tier 3 interventions, which are evaluated by assessing the number of students who move to a less intense tier (i.e., Tier 2), the average rate of progress compared with a target group such as students not receiving intervention, and the percentage of students referred for special education evaluations who are actually identified with a disability. Weekly CBM data can be aggregated into a numeric slope with the SLOPE function in Microsoft Excel or with one of numerous online slope calculators. Those data can then be used to compare the rate of growth to the rate of growth for the population based on the season benchmark standards for the given grade. Shapiro and Clemens (2009) also discussed using the percentage of students referred for special education being identified with a disability as a criterion because only students with the most severe difficulties should be referred. They did not provide a criterion for the percentage, but it seems that at least 90% of students referred for special education should be identified with a disability.

SUMMARY

Implementing or guiding the implementation of effective academic interventions for individual students is an important task for school psychologists (Ysseldyke et al., 2006), and school psychologists are frequently involved in making decisions about Tier 3 interventions. Research suggested that effective interventions consistently involved the following five components: (a) correctly targeted with the instructional hierarchy, (b) appropriately challenging based on the individual student's instructional level, (c) explicitly taught, (d) containing frequent opportunities for student response, and (e) followed by feedback appropriate for the student's phase of learning. The combination of accuracy and fluency data can identify the stage of learning at which the student is functioning, which can then be used to identify interventions within a skill-by-treatment interaction paradigm, and the interventions should then address the other areas listed above.

School psychologists are practically bombarded with interventions that all claim to be research based. School psychologists should know how to critically evaluate interventions to determine if the interventions are worth attempting, and the five criteria listed here could help with that role. If the five components described here are not present, then school psychologists should be skeptical about the proposed intervention. Some interventions might address some aspects of an effective intervention better than others, but all five should be present to some degree.

As the role of school psychologists shifts to that of instructional ally and consultant in the classroom, school psychologists have a unique opportunity to enhance system capacity to promote learning by all students through more effective and individualized intervention and instruction. Moreover, using the skill-by-treatment paradigm outlined here would allow school psychologists to improve decision making about Tier 3 interventions for individual students, which would likely increase the outcomes for the students.

AUTHOR NOTE

Disclosure. Matthew Burns has a financial interest in books he authored or coauthored that are referenced in this chapter.

REFERENCES

Archer, A., & Hughes, C. (2011). *Explicit instruction: Effective and efficient teaching.* New York, NY: Guilford Press.

Berninger, V. W., Abbott, R. D., Vermeulen, K., & Fulton, C. M. (2006). Paths to reading comprehension in at-risk second-grade readers. *Journal of Learning Disabilities, 39*, 334–351.

Betts, E. A. (1946). *Foundations of reading instruction.* New York, NY: American Book.

Burns, M. K. (2004a). Empirical analysis of drill ratio research: Refining the instructional level for drill tasks. *Remedial and Special Education, 25*, 167–175.

Burns, M. K. (2004b). Age as a predictor of acquisition rates as measured by curriculum-based assessment: Evidence of consistency with cognitive research. *Assessment for Effective Intervention, 29*(2), 31–38.

Burns, M. K., Codding, R. S., Boice, C. H., & Lukito, G. (2010). Meta-analysis of acquisition and fluency math interventions with instructional and frustration level skills: Evidence for a skill-by-treatment interaction. *School Psychology Review, 39*, 69–83.

Burns, M. K., & Parker, D. C. (2014). *Curriculum-based assessment for instructional design: Using data to individualize instruction.* New York, NY: Guilford Press.

Burns, M. K., VanDerHeyden, A. M., & Jiban, C. (2006). Assessing the instructional level for mathematics: A comparison of methods. *School Psychology Review, 35*, 401–418.

Burns, M. K., & Wagner, D. (2008). Determining an effective intervention within a brief experimental analysis for reading: A meta-analytic review. *School Psychology Review, 37*, 126–136.

Burns, M. K., Zaslofsky, A. F., Kanive, R., & Parker, D. C. (2012). Meta-analysis of incremental rehearsal: Using phi coefficients to compare single-case and group designs. *Journal of Behavioral Education, 21*, 185–202.

Cartledge, G., & Kourea, L. (2008). Culturally responsive classrooms for culturally diverse students with and at risk for disabilities. *Exceptional Children, 74*, 351–371.

Cronbach, L. J. (1957). The two disciplines of scientific psychology. *American Psychologist, 12*, 671–684.

Cronbach, L. J., & Snow, R. E. (1977). *Aptitudes and instructional methods: A handbook for research on interactions.* New York, NY: Irvington.

Gersten, R., Chard, D. J., Jayanthi, M., Baker, S. K., Morphy, P., & Flojo, J. (2009). Mathematics instruction for students with learning disabilities: A meta-analysis of instructional components. *Review of Educational Research, 79*, 1202–1242.

Graham, S., McKeown, D., Kiuhara, S., & Harris, K. R. (2012). A meta-analysis of writing instruction for students in the elementary grades. *Journal of Educational Psychology, 104*, 879–896.

Gravois, T. A., & Gickling, E. E. (2008). Best practices in curriculum-based assessment. In A. Thomas & J. Grimes (Eds.), *Best practices in school psychology V* (pp. 885–898). Bethesda, MD: National Association of School Psychologists.

Haring, N. G., & Eaton, M. D. (1978). Systematic instructional technology: An instructional hierarchy. In N. G. Haring, T. C. Lovitt, M. D. Eaton, & C. L. Hansen (Eds.), *The fourth R: Research in the classroom* (pp. 23–40). Columbus, OH: Merrill.

Kavale, K. A. (2007). Quantitative research synthesis: Meta-analysis of research on special education needs. In L. Florian (Ed.), *The SAGE handbook of special education* (pp. 207–221). Thousand Oaks, CA: SAGE.

Melby-Lervag, M., & Hulme, C. (2013). Is working memory training effective? A meta-analytic review. *Developmental Psychology, 49*, 270–291.

National Association of School Psychologists. (2010). *Model for comprehensive and integrated school psychological services.* Bethesda, MD: Author. Retrieved from http://www.nasponline.org/standards/2010standards/2_PracticeModel.pdf

National Governors Association Center for Best Practices & Council of Chief State School Officers. (2010). *Common Core State Standards.* Washington, DC: Author.

National Institute of Child Health and Human Development. (2000). *Report of the National Reading Panel: Teaching children to read: An evidence-based assessment of the scientific research literature on reading and its implications for reading instruction: Reports of the subgroups* (NIH Publication No. 00-4754). Washington, DC: Author.

National Mathematics Advisory Panel. (2008). *Foundations for success: The final report of the National Mathematics Advisory Panel.* Washington, DC: U.S. Department of Education.

Shapiro, E. S., & Clemens, N. H. (2009). A conceptual model for evaluating systems of effects of response to intervention. *Assessment for Effective Intervention, 35*, 3–16.

Szadokierski, I., & Burns, M. K. (2008). Analogue evaluation of the effects of opportunities to respond and ratios of known items within drill rehearsal of Esperanto words. *Journal of School Psychology, 46,* 593–609.

Treptow, M. A., Burns, M. K., & McComas, J. J. (2007). Reading at the frustration, instructional, and independent levels: The effects on students' reading comprehension and time on task. *School Psychology Review, 36,* 159–166.

VanDerHeyden, A., McLaughlin, T., Algina, J., & Snyder, P. (2012). Randomized evaluation of a supplemental grade-wide mathematics intervention. *American Educational Research Journal, 49,* 1251–1284.

VanDerHeyden, A. M., & Witt, J. C. (2008). Best practices in can't do/won't do assessment. In A. Thomas & J. Grimes (Eds.), *Best practices in school psychology V* (pp. 131–140). Bethesda, MD: National Association of School Psychologists.

Ysseldyke, J. E., Burns, M. K., Dawson, M., Kelly, B., Morrison, D., Ortiz, S., … Telzrow, C. (2006). *School psychology: A blueprint for the future of training and practice III.* Bethesda, MD: National Association of School Psychologists.

10 Preventing Academic Failure and Promoting Alternatives to Retention

Mary Ann Rafoth
Susan W. Parker
Robert Morris University (PA)

OVERVIEW

Academic failure, often defined as occurring when students perform significantly below grade benchmarks on standardized tests and typically associated with nonpromotion to the next grade, is a national concern. Student underachievement and the status of America's students on international rankings of reading and math continue to garner attention. The Obama administration's Race to the Top program (http://www2.ed.gov/programs/racetothetop/index.html) aims to improve teaching and learning, increase achievement, and close the achievement gap between minority and mainstream students.

The issue of student retention in grade, which came to national attention when President Bill Clinton called for an end to social promotion in his 1998 State of the Union address, remains a natural part of the discussion. If there is a national call to stop sending students who do not meet specific standards on to the next grade, many infer that there must also be a national mandate to retain those unprepared students at their current grade level.

Every year approximately 2.4 million U.S. students are held back in school. Ethnic minority youth and boys, especially if they live in poverty and their parents did not finish high school or lack a college education, are more frequently retained; that is, over half of African American males and 49% of Hispanic males are old for grade by age 14 (National Center for Education Statistics, 2012). At least 20–50% of all students have been retained at least once before the ninth grade. African American students are about twice as likely to be retained as Caucasian students and boys twice as likely to be retained as girls (National Center for Education Statistics, 2012). Twenty percent of students with mothers with less than a high school education were retained compared with just 3% of children whose mothers held a bachelor's degree or higher (National Center for Education Statistics, 2012).

The passage of the No Child Left Behind (NCLB) legislation in 2001 led to a significant increase in student retention over the last decade. For example, Florida's institution of mandatory retention based on high-stakes testing practices led to the retention of 28,028 third-grade students in 2003. A similar plan in New York City schools could have affected as many as 15,000 third graders. A high-stakes testing and retention policy was also implemented in the Chicago city schools in 1996. In total, nine states and three large urban school districts adopted mandatory retention policies based on standardized assessments, affecting about 30% of all public school students. However, large school districts found that retaining all the students who did not measure up on standardized tests caused backlogs of students in the lower grades and that having large numbers of students repeat a whole grade of school is costly. The cost of effective prevention and remediation are far less than the estimated $11,467 a year cost per child of retention (or almost $20 billion nationally per year) or the cost of socially promoting a child without needed skills (National Center for Education Statistics, 2012).

For example, Ohio has recently established an intensive assessment and intervention program for students in grades K–3 with the Third Grade Reading Guarantee, which requires assessment of every student's reading skill by September 30 of each school year, determination of whether or not a student is on track to meet benchmark standards in third grade, and development of an intervention plan for each student who is off track (see http://education.ohio.gov). Beginning in 2013–2014, students who do not meet benchmark test scores on the Ohio Achievement Assessment must be retained unless they have been identified as limited English proficient students and have been enrolled in U.S. schools for less than 2 years, are students identified for special education services whose Individualized Education Programs (IEP) specifically exempt them from the guarantee, or have been receiving intensive remediation for 2 years and have already been retained in grades K–3. A student in the latter situation must receive intensive reading instruction in fourth grade. The guarantee requires districts to advance the student to the next grade whenever third-grade competency is reached even if it is the middle or end of a school year or during the summer. In addition, beginning in 2013–2014, school districts must provide a teacher with specific training and credentialing in reading to each retained student on an improvement and monitoring plan. This approach seems to blend research-based interventions with retention in such a way that the costs of retaining a student are heightened by requiring both additional intervention and a highly credentialed teacher.

As this approach in Ohio illustrates, effective interventions before students experience serious failure in the classroom are more easily talked about than put into place. Even though retaining students is unlikely to be beneficial, states and school districts, particularly large urban centers (e.g., New York, Chicago, Detroit, and Houston), continue to institute policies that are destined to increase the number of students who are retained or who drop out of school. These changes took place even after 2 decades of analysis of research and debate had largely concluded that retention was a costly and ineffective intervention. The inclusion of retention in the Ohio model, which otherwise emphasizes early intervention and intensive remediation, is testimony to the inability of educators to let the concept go.

The plan in Florida noted earlier included mandated intensive academic remediation for retained students. However, while retention was associated with positive academic outcomes a year later in Florida, fewer than half of the students who had been retained were considered proficient readers after intervention. Moreover, many schools with state mandates to retain in the basis of standardized assessment results have no programs in place to provide students with a different educational experience in the retained year or do not receive additional funding to meet the needs of those students.

The National Association of School Psychologists (NASP) has argued that any intervention that attempts to fit a one-size-fits-all formula on students will fail (see NASP Position Statements: *Grade Retention and Social Promotion*, http://www.nasponline.org/about_nasp/positionpapers/GradeRetentionandSocialPromotion.pdf, and *Appropriate Academic Supports to Meet the Needs of All Students*, http://www.nasponline.org/about_nasp/positionpapers/AppropriateAcademicSupport.pdf). Retention is one such intervention. Only accurate and effective diagnosis of student learning problems will lead to effective intervention and increased achievement. For this reason, school psychologists are frequently involved in making individual retention decisions or influencing the policies of their school districts to provide alternatives to retention.

While retention is of questionable educational benefit with negative effects on achievement, self-concept, school dropout rates, and high-risk behaviors in adolescence, the general public and even many teachers continue to believe in its efficacy. Many teachers and school administrators continue to see retention as a positive practice that acts to lessen daily school failure and to motivate students to work harder. Many teachers and school administrators still believe that early retention, especially, helps children. The conflict between this belief system and the research evidence is often frustrating and confusing for parents. Parent Internet Listservs are replete with back and forth exchanges between parents and teachers often discussing retention in a positive light.

This chapter provides the school psychologist with a brief review of the research on student retention as well as discussion of the main causes of academic failure that lead to retention at different points in a student's school career. The concluding section will address the roles that school psychologists may play in helping school districts move to systemic problem-solving approaches to preventing academic failure through differentiating services based on degree of need in accord with the Intervention and Instructional Support domain of the NASP *Model for Comprehensive and Integrated School Psychological Services* (NASP, 2010).

Of the many professionals involved either in developing district-wide retention policies or in making retention decisions about individual students, the school psychologist is uniquely qualified to act as a consultant in generating alternatives via an evidence-based problem solving approach. School psychologists should help to evaluate the reasons for school failure, plan appropriate instructional programs for the following year whether or not the child is retained, and act as consultants both to parents faced with retention decisions and to the school districts in developing programs that are viable alternatives.

Best practices regarding nonpromotion center on a thorough understanding of the research and careful consideration of the needs of the individual student. Best practices regard avoiding academic failure center around systemic responses to the main sources of failure for students at key grades: failure to learn to read in the primary grades; inability to organize, study efficiently, and learn independently in middle school; and loss of motivation in high school.

BASIC CONSIDERATIONS

Retention or nonpromotion is the practice of requiring a child to repeat a particular grade or requiring a child of appropriate chronological age to delay entry to kindergarten or first grade. With the introduction of graded schools in the 19th century, retention emerged as a response to the problem of students unprepared for the academic demands of the next grade. Concern about possible negative effects of retention has been expressed since the 1930s. Little research exists to validate the effectiveness of retention (Holmes & Matthews, 1984; Jimerson, 1999; Moser, West, & Hughes, 2012). Only one major study (Alexander, Entwisle, & Dauber, 1994) appeared to support the use of retention, at least in the higher grades, but only in the finding that continuous skill degradation among low-achieving students appeared to have been halted by retention.

Additionally, research published in the medical literature in the 1990s found that adolescents who are old for grade are at much greater risk for a variety of problem behaviors including smoking, chewing tobacco, drinking alcohol, driving with someone who is drinking, using alcohol or other drugs before sexual intercourse, and using drugs (Byrd, Weitzman, & Doniger, 1996). Similarly, Byrd, Weitsman, and Auinger (1997) and Resnick et al. (1997) investigated students who were old for grade (regardless of reason). Both studies found that higher rates of behavior problems were reported in this group. Statistical techniques such as meta-analysis and causal modeling has helped overcome the weaknesses of individual studies and the use of larger databases have established more definitive relationships between retention and later achievement and social growth and identifying being old for grade as a risk factor in itself.

Kindergarten and Elementary Level

Children are often recommended for retention at the kindergarten level because they have failed to acquire basic readiness skills and are not progressing in reading. Sometimes these determinations are made because of poor performance on a readiness test administered before entry into kindergarten or at the end of the year. Failure to display skills, particularly in reading in the classroom, coupled with low achievement scores, is often the reason a child is suggested as a candidate for retention after completing a year of kindergarten or first grade.

Some children enter kindergarten with little exposure to academics, the school routine, or prerequisite skills, such as letter and number recognition, which are typically taught in most preschools. Children from home backgrounds in which such exposure is limited may find themselves candidates for delayed entry into kindergarten or retention. Again, most likely to be retained in kindergarten are African American or Hispanic boys who are chronologically young for grade, display poor readiness skills, and who are living in poverty (Cadima, McWilliam, & Leal, 2010).

Delayed entry or retention at the kindergarten level also occurs because some children are judged to be developmentally immature, a generic term that may be indicative of a wide variety of delays. Likewise, children who are physically small or relatively young compared with their peers (because of cutoff dates for school entry) are often candidates for delayed entry or retention. Many parents and teachers believe that the extra year will allow the child, especially if the child is a boy, to compete more effectively with peers the following year. This practice is often referred to as academic red-shirting. Finally, as was noted earlier, delayed entry has also been associated with a higher rate of involvement in high-risk behaviors in adolescence.

While late birth date children who are retained or held out of school for a year initially may do better than those enrolled in first grade at the prescribed age, longitudinal studies show that initial achievement gains do not hold up over time or remain very slight (Jimerson et al., 2006). Research suggests that retention in kindergarten or first grade may be associated with poorer academic and social functioning throughout the elementary grades and even into young adulthood (Alexander et al., 1994; Jimerson et al., 2006). Differences in achievement related to age exist to some extent in elementary school but tend to diminish and even disappear by middle school. Profiles of children who are retained in kindergarten indicate that they have multiple deficits and needs, making it unlikely that simple exposure to the same curriculum would be an effective intervention. Wilson and Hughes (2006) found similar patterns in the retention of Hispanic children in first grade. Poor reading skills, being young at entrance to first grade, and teacher–child relationships are often cited as reasons for early retention. Retention in kindergarten or first grade often presents the most difficult decision for school officials and parents.

Large-Scale Studies of Retention

Multiple intervening factors may account for both the continued prevalence of retention and the subsequent ramifications associated with the practice. A landmark study on the effects of retention was conducted by Holmes and Matthews (1984). They conducted a meta-analysis of 44 studies, calculating 575 effect sizes to determine the effects of retention on a variety of factors, such as achievement, personal adjustment, and self-concept. Meta-analysis has become a popular way to aggregate a large number of studies that investigate a common research question. All the studies selected by Holmes and Matthews compared a group of retained students with a group of promoted students. Thirty-three of the studies investigated achievement effects. Those studies yielded an overall effect size that indicated that retained students scored significantly lower than promoted students on achievement measures. While teachers believe that retention in kindergarten through third grade is not harmful, when Holmes and Matthews (1984) analyzed the data by the grade levels in which the retention took place (grades 1–6), they found negative effects at all grade levels. This calls into question the commonly held belief that the earlier a student is retained the greater the likelihood that retention will produce positive effects.

Similarly, while the relationship to retention and dropping out of high school is stronger for later retentions than earlier retentions, retention at any age remains a powerful predictor of dropping out. Silberglitt, Jimerson, Burns, and Appleton (2006) examined the impact of timing of grade retention on reading growth trajectory and found that the impact of retention in grades K–2 on reading progress were comparable to those retained in grades 3–5. While proponents of retention maintain that promoting children when they are not ready for the demands of the next grade can have a harmful effect on personal adjustment, the bulk of the research does not support this contention.

In addition to achievement effects, Holmes and Matthews (1984) also calculated effect sizes on personal adjustment measures taken from 21 studies. They found negative effects for social adjustment, emotional adjustment, and behavior, as well as self-concept. Anderson, Whipple, and Jimerson (2005) found that sixth-grade students rated retention as a more stressful life event than either loss of a parent or blindness. Smith and Shepard (1989) reported that clinical interviews with retained students indicate these students saw their retention as flunking and as punishment. In this same study, parents of retained kindergartners reported that their children experienced teasing and adjustment problems because of their nonpromotion.

Jimerson (2000) summarized studies on retention between 1990 and 1999, systematically reviewing 19 studies that met a standard set of criteria for inclusion (published in a professional journal, addressed the impact of early grade retention on achievement, socioemotional development or other factors, and included an identifiable comparison group of promoted students). A meta-analysis was conducted with these studies examining academic achievement and socioemotional development. The study measured the degree of either benefit or harm of the intervention between the retained and comparison group across studies. Results examining achievement differences were very similar to the results of the Holmes and Matthews (1984) meta-analysis. Of 173 analyses that explored academic achievement, 9 found that retained students outperformed the comparison group of promoted students, 70 found that the comparison group outperformed the retained students, and 94 yielded no statistical differences at all. Only three of the nine analyses favoring retained students considered outcomes beyond the repeated year. Results examining socioemotional and behavioral outcomes were explored in 16 studies yielding 127 analyses. Of these, 108 yielded no significant differences between the retained and the matched comparison group. Thirteen significantly favored the comparison group, while six favored the group of students who were retained. Effect size for emotional adjustment was much higher than the Holmes and Matthews (1989) meta-analysis for the retained group while effect size for the social and behavior adjustment was similar. The retained group had overall lower ratings of adjustment, lower ratings of self-concept, and lower school attendance. Overall, 12 of the 19 study authors drew negative conclusions about the efficacy of retention. Four study authors drew favorable conclusions. However, these authors agree that retained children were still not successful at school—seeing retention as a way of lessening incompetence, at least temporarily, and not creating competence—and all argue for additional remedial strategies.

Another study (Wu, West, & Hughes, 2010) of the impact of grade retention in first grades on psychosocial outcomes found that children who had been retained showed some short-term and long-term gains in regard to teacher ratings of activity level and engagement levels. Short-term gains in peer-related liking and school belongingness were also found. However, these gains tended to decrease rapidly after the retained year ended. A similar pattern was noted in math and reading achievement; that is a short-term boost followed by a rapid decline· relative to nonretained age mates. The authors warn of the potential long-term negative impact of this struggle-succeed-struggle cycle in succeeding grades.

In summary, no authors conclude that early retention alone can solve the problem of academic failure and most conclude that it will not benefit students and may actually harm them.

Secondary Level

The secondary level (i.e., middle school, junior high school, and high school) students are most often retained for two reasons: (a) a lack of sufficient credits to be promoted to the next grade level or to graduate from high school or (b) a failure to pass mandated minimum competency exams. The sources of these failures lie in either the student's failure to learn to read effectively in the primary grades; a student's inability to develop the organizational, metacognitive, and study skills necessary for success in the upper grades; or a devastating combination of the two. Gains made in the retained year are temporary, and students fall behind without sustained services. Alternative education is often not provided to these students, and, for many, life outside of school becomes more important.

Research on retention at the secondary level has generally examined the relationships between grade retention and attendance, suspension, and self-concept, with an emphasis on the correlation between retention and dropout rates (Jacob & Lefgren, 2009; Smith & Shephard, 1989). Retention rates at the high school level are related to attendance and suspension rates. Generally, students who are failing do not attend school on a regular basis. In addition, students who have been retained prior to the secondary level are less likely to attend school on a regular basis in junior and senior high school. Additionally, regardless of the grade in which retention occurs, secondary students who have

been retained often exhibit low self-esteem. in a follow-up study of high school students with a history of grade retention, Hagborg, Masella, Palladino, and Shepardson (1991) found that retained students scored lower on a number of variables, including achievement, intelligence, and grades, and were more often absent from school and scored lower on a measure of self-esteem than did nonretained peers. Students retained later in their educational careers displayed even lower grades, less positive school attitudes, more discipline problems, lower self-control, and a more externalized locus of control. Retained graduates are significantly less likely to enroll in postsecondary education than normally promoted graduates. In addition, the later the retention the less likely they were to pursue postgraduation education.

The majority of the research on retention at the secondary level has also focused on the relationship between retention and dropping out of school. Smith and Shephard (1989) reported that students who drop out are five times more likely to have repeated a grade than students who eventually graduate. Studies that conclude that retention is associated with dropping out are numerous (Jacob & Lefgren, 2009). Being retained twice virtually guarantees a student will drop out of school, and grade retention alone has been identified as the single most powerful predictor of dropping out. This relationship can be explained by two competing hypotheses: (a) Repeating a grade may increase the risk of dropping out or (b) poor achievement may account for both retention and dropping out. In many early studies undertaken to analyze the relationship between retention and dropping out of school, the achievement variable was not controlled.

However, in a number of studies (e.g., Jimerson, 1999) the achievement variable was adjusted in order to focus only on the relationship between retention and dropping out. The dropout rate of overage students (retainees) is appreciably higher than the dropout rate of regularly promoted students when reading achievement scores are equivalent for the two groups. Even in high-socioeconomic school districts, where students are less likely to leave school, a significant increase in dropout rates has been found for retained students. Jimerson (1999) found that retained students had a greater probability of poorer educational and employment outcomes in late adolescence when compared with low-achieving but promoted students, including levels of academic adjustment by eleventh grade, dropping out by age 19, receiving a diploma by age 20, enrolling in a postsecondary education program, receiving low educational employment status ratings, being paid less per hour, and receiving poor competence employment ratings at age 20.

Some Children Benefit From Retention

Children who make academic and social gains after repeating first grade have not experienced serious academic deficits in the year prior to retention, have strong self-esteem and social skills, and show signs of difficulty in school because of high absenteeism, illness, or frequent family moves rather than low ability. These same factors predict success with retained students in the upper grades. The fact that relatively high achievement and high self-concept prior to retention correlated with positive outcomes implies that the most successful retainees are those who need it the least. Even the most successful retainees are no better than promoted controls on a variety of outcome measures at the end of first grade. While there may be individual children who benefit from retention, it cannot be predicted who they are. Students who benefit from retention are more likely to have had additional educational interventions such as after-school tutoring and a specific remedial plan beyond simple retention. Because these additional interventions were not provided for matched groups, it is difficult to ascertain whether the retention or the interventions produced positive effects.

Relationship Between Retention and Special Education

Retention and special education have had a complicated and dynamic relationship during the years following passage of the 1975 Education for All Handicapped Children Act. The nature of this relationship has received little attention in the literature. As retention decisions vary widely across states and districts, so does the relationship between these decisions and the referral of students for evaluation of eligibility for special education. Examination of this complex relationship is further complicated by the lack of required transparent reporting regarding these practices (Gaffney & Zaimi, 2003). In addition to the past practice employed by some schools of using retention to delay referral to special education, the current era of high-stakes testing, with required achievement benchmarks for promotion, has resulted in a resurgence of the practice of grade retention despite continued research proving its lack of efficacy. The rate of placement in special education is higher for students who were previously retained than it was for low-performing students never retained.

Retained students may be students with undiagnosed learning disabilities.

Retained students may be identified for special education after retention fails to correct an achievement lag. Students who have been retained may be referred to special education to allow them an exemption from the policy requiring general education students to meet the criteria in standardized state tests. Retention can delay a student's entry into the high-stakes assessment pool in hopes of having more time to reach minimum proficiencies (Allington & McGill-Franzen, 1997). When retention is unsuccessful, referral for special education services may be the next approach adopted. NASP and others have long advocated for early intervention of learning difficulties in lieu of retention for students struggling academically. School administrators from six districts, with significantly increasing numbers of young children enrolled in special education programs and retained in grade, were interviewed by Allington and McGill-Franzen (1997). Because administrators viewed both retention and gift-of-time options (late initial entrance to school) as either free or low-cost responses to a student's lack of readiness or progress is telling. The administrators held to these perceptions, even though there is a wealth of research reflecting the lack of success of these alternatives in accelerating academic achievement, as well as significant costs associated with the practice of retention.

Special education students in Texas were retained at about two times the rate of their nonidentified peers *(IDRA Newsletter,* 1999). McLeskey and Grizzle (1992) studied grade retention of students with learning disabilities in Indiana and found 58% of these students had been retained before being labeled. Similar to the Texas statistics, approximately twice as many identified students in Indiana were retained as students without disabilities. Roderick and Nagaoka (2005) found the same pattern among retained students in Chicago. School psychologists must actively work to ensure that retention is not used to delay special education identification in their schools or districts.

Davey (2005) provided a glimpse into the personal ramifications a student may experience as a result of these practices. Davey reported on a student from the south side of Chicago who repeated the third grade three times due to her inability to pass the required test. In the spring of her final year in third grade, she was evaluated and found to have a mild cognitive impairment providing her eligibility for special education. The following fall she was placed in the seventh grade, where her teacher described her as seriously frightened and stressed. When comparing the reported statistics for the percentage of children meeting the standards, analyses suggests an increasing use of special education placements and retention before the third grade produces misrepresentative reports regarding student achievement and school effectiveness (Allington & McGill-Franzen, 1997).

Similarly, Buslinger-Clifford (2004) studied 179 elementary schools in the Miami-Dade Public Schools in Florida and examined the practices of retention and referral to special education. Noting the two ways to eliminate scores on high-stakes test reports are through retention and referral to special education, significant increases in each were reported following the implementation of high-stakes testing in Florida. Beebe-Frankenberger, Bocian, Macmillian, and Gresham (2004) found that more than 50% of special education students in 22 elementary schools in three urban southern California school districts had been retained by the end of second grade prior to being eligible for special education services. In these districts, retention appears to be utilized as an intervention and often a precursor to being identified for special education.

BEST PRACTICES IN REDUCING ACADEMIC FAILURE AND REDUCING RETENTION

School psychologists' involvement with retention practices can occur on several levels. It can range all the way from designing alternative interventions and follow up to influencing school or district-wide retention policies to lobbying for change on a state level through the collective efforts of a state school psychology association. An important effort at each of these levels should be to promote systemic approaches to reduce academic failure and the use of alternatives to retention that will not put students even more at risk by making them old for grade. This same caveat may be applied to the grade placement of older internationally adopted students as well. The educational needs of the student should be balanced against the risks of being old for grade when schools are determining appropriate grade placement.

Promoting Systemic Solutions

The only real solution to the retention/social promotion debacle is to eliminate the most serious academic failures before they occur. This can only happen when the problem is attacked from a system-wide approach with careful attention to developmental issues and the findings of research on the efficacy of various forms of intervention.

The use of screening assessments in preschool and kindergarten to identify students who may be at risk for academic failure, particularly in the area of phonemic awareness, has been shown to be a sound method of predicting which children will have difficulty learning to read. Similarly, reading interventions that provide intensive, early, and individualized help that targets a child's specific weaknesses (e.g., Success for All, Reading Recovery, Direct Instruction) have been shown to be effective in reducing early reading failure. The use of learning strategies instruction has been shown to be very effective in improving study skills and performance in middle school students. The inability to organize and study independently is often a key factor in academic failure at this level (Forness, Kavale, Blum, & Lloyd, 1997). Inability to read effectively and to learn to study independently often leads to failure at the elementary and middle school levels and creates profound motivation problems at high school that contribute to dropping out, the ultimate school failure.

Systemic approaches to solving the problem of serious academic failure must target each of these areas from a developmental perspective that seeks to increase academic success at each major educational level (elementary, middle, and high school) by ensuring that more students are able to meet major academic task demands.

Individual Retention Decisions

School psychologists can be important participants when decisions are made about retaining students in their schools. They should help evaluate the reasons for school failure by looking at the children's school and developmental histories, the effectiveness of the instruction the children have received, and the remediation strategies or programs available to the children. The school psychologist should help plan an appropriate instructional program for retained students and should act as a consultant both to parents and to school personnel to help them make better retention decisions. The case discussions that follow illustrate the part the school psychologist can play in making retention decisions for a variety of students.

Case Studies

Ekaterina: A young girl, Ekaterina, adopted from Russia at age 8 ½, arrived in the United States halfway through her third grade year. However, prior to coming to the United States she had little formal schooling although she could read and write in Russian. Additionally, she had experienced neglect and trauma in her early life resulting in her removal from her biological parents at age 5 and placement in an orphanage.

After much research and discussion with medical doctors, social workers, and other families who had adopted older children, her adoptive parents decided to place her with her same-age peers in the third grade instead of in second grade as some had suggested. The elementary school had an excellent reputation. However, the makeup of the student body was predominantly White middle to upper middle class suburban families, and the staff had little experience with students requiring services for English language learners (ELL) or emotional support services. Within a month Ekaterina had a command of fundamental English phrases. Her ability to read Russian also helped to facilitate her communication as she would use a Russian to English dictionary to express basic wants and needs. Her parents were thrilled with her progress and were surprised and dismayed when one of her teachers called them to a meeting in which she demanded that she be removed from her math class. The teacher said that Ekaterina should be immediately put back into the second grade or possibly tested for special education. The meeting could have become very contentious. However, the school psychologist, who was new to the district after having worked in a large urban metropolitan district for years, shared his viewpoint. He said that he had worked with many students who had been adopted from overseas and had needed ELL supports. It takes time for these students to adjust for a variety of reasons. Additionally, Kat is not a typical ELL student in that she came to this country alone, not with her biological family intact. In those cases, learning English would be the child's main priority. However, Kat had many things she needed to acclimate to, and the school district should provide her with everything possible before any decisions were made. Additionally testing a student like Kat, especially for special education, at this point in time would not provide very reliable results. In the school psychologist's opinion, a discussion about retention or special education was premature at this point in time.

The school psychologist continued to outline what type of supports the school could provide which included instructional support, a combination of ELL services that were both push-in and pull-out, and talking with the school counselor about starting a "lunch bunch" for a small group of students to practice social skills. He also offered to work with a previously identified fifth-grade student, Zoe, who lived on the same street as Kat. Zoe had expressed interest in helping

Kat to adjust. Without any adult prompting, Zoe had taught herself a few Russian phrases and had helped Kat to find her locker, the lunch room, and so on. With the school psychologist's support, a more formal peer-mentoring program was put in place to help Kat. Additionally, the majority of the other teachers and staff were more than willing to attempt the accommodations and supports suggested by the school psychologist. Kat remained in the third grade with her same-age peers in the school until fifth grade. She continued to learn English and adjust to her new family and life.

As required by the state she resided in, she took part in formalized testing in third grade and as expected scored below basic in both reading and math. However, by the fifth grade she scored basic in reading and although still scoring below basic in math she had made great gains in the area and was very close to a basic score.

Kat is now in eighth grade and continues to thrive and grow. She still receives ELL services but is on the cusp of testing out of services halfway through her eighth-grade year. She has a large group of friends and is involved in a variety of extracurricular activities. Without the expertise and experience of the school psychologist Ekaterina would have had a very different outcome.

Greg: A teenage boy, Greg, was diagnosed with anxiety and depression near the end of ninth grade. He had an IEP in place for a number of years as his parents and school personnel both realized he needed extra supports in place in order to succeed. However, without a diagnosis or clear understanding of why he was struggling, his family and educational team members were often frustrated as some things worked well and others did not and all involved (including Greg) struggled to understand why. Prior to his diagnosis and their subsequent understanding of his issues, his parents and teachers were concerned about his inability to focus, his constant trips to the nurse's office due to stomachaches and headaches, and missed school for other issues and illnesses (in retrospect, all anxiety related) that caused him to miss course content.

The diagnosis of anxiety and depression, although saddening for his parents on one hand, also provided some relief as they felt they now had a framework from which to operate and could finally start to address the necessary issues to help their son to move in a positive direction. They connected with both the school psychologist and an outside therapist. They changed medication and worked through adjusting dosage. They met with the IEP team and other pertinent faculty members at the high school. All of these steps seemed to help Greg to move forward, and by providing an understanding of depression and anxiety, his family and teachers felt more equipped to support him. Although his tenth-grade year was not perfect, overall Greg seemed to be improving. He was attending class more often, not calling his parents to pick him up halfway through the day, making new friends and reconnecting with old ones. Overall, he maintained a low B/high C average with the exception of biology. Greg failed the second semester of biology. However, he was able to take and pass the final exam, but because he received an F for the second semester of the course, Greg and his parents were informed he would have to repeat the class as a junior. They were also told due to his noncompletion of the required sophomore curriculum he would technically still be considered a sophomore. This sophomore designation would force him to attend a few other elective courses that were mainly sophomore courses and potentially his lunch period would be predominantly sophomores.

This caused great angst for Greg and his family for a variety of reasons. In addition to feeling that he had worked hard in so many areas, he was still being penalized because of his mental health issues. To further complicate the situation, Greg's younger sister was a sophomore and he would be in one class with her, a cause for embarrassment for both him and his sister. His parents were also upset because they had seen such vast improvement with Greg as he dealt with anxiety around attending school and they were afraid a setback such as being retained for a course would significantly damage the progress he had made. Moreover, because he had an IEP, his parents questioned why he had fallen so far behind in the first place. Shouldn't supports have been in place when his teacher first recognized he was struggling?

All of these issues were discussed at a team meeting at the end of Greg's sophomore year. Greg's parents felt that the majority of the team members did not adequately understand Greg's mental health issues and just how far he had come by being able to function in a large suburban school setting. They provided letters from his private therapist stating that forcing Greg to remain a sophomore would likely harm his fragile self-image. Other meetings were held and the options on the table included taking biology during an 8-week summer school session that would allow him to begin the following school year as a junior.

This situation presents a typical secondary scenario where retention is largely punitive and it is difficult to bend rules even when promotion is clearly in the best interest of the student. The school psychologist can be a key team leader in these cases.

Jack: In another case that illustrates a common scenario with young children, Jack, a first grader whose teacher recommended retention, was referred by his parents to the school psychologist for testing to rule out the possibility of a learning disability. The teacher reported that Jack was having difficulty getting beyond the primer level in reading, his attention span seemed somewhat short, he had some trouble completing work independently, and he also seemed to be exhibiting some behaviors the teacher felt were immature such as fidgeting in his seat and putting his fingers in his mouth. Jack was assessed as having average intelligence with achievement commensurate with his ability. The school psychologist met with Jack's teacher and parents. The school psychologist reviewed the test results and then led a discussion about retention and summarized the research, stressing that there is little evidence that it helps over the long term. The school psychologist indicated that initially students who are retained in first grade show some improvement over similar students who are not retained, but that these gains tend to disappear by third grade. The school psychologist noted that Jack's teacher was trying to make the best decision for Jack as she could precisely because she was worried about the child's progress in the coming year, thereby lending support to the teacher without necessarily endorsing the teacher's recommendation.

The school psychologist reported that while some children do seem to benefit from retention, at present educators lack the ability to predict reliably just which children will benefit. Therefore, the school psychologist stressed to Jack's parents that it would be important that they feel comfortable with whatever decision they made, since undoubtedly Jack would sense his parents' comfort or discomfort with the decision. This statement was emphatically echoed by Jack's teacher. The decision was left in the parents' hands. The mother later reported to the school psychologist that she had decided not to have her son retained. The mother indicated that as a child his father had matured at a young age and she was worried that the same would happen to her son. While the mother decided to have her son continue on to second grade, she wanted to be sure he would be able to get supplemental reading services and that his teachers would continue to monitor his progress in reading. The importance of these interventions was critical to whether or not the student was retained.

Summary

All of these cases illustrate in different ways the importance of the school psychologist's training in the development of both academic and behavioral interventions. School psychologists are also in a position to provide follow-up plans as student progress is monitored. Most parents and educators are unaware of the research on retention. The school psychologist should be willing to share this research to help schools and parents make informed decisions. This information should not be imparted dogmatically or in a way that impairs working relationships with colleagues or parents.

In some cases, this may mean recognizing that schools will make decisions to retain children when the school psychologist feels it is not in the best interest of those children. Especially in these cases, it will be important for the school psychologist to participate in developing a specific plan of action by which the student's skills deficits can be remediated.

Christenson and Picklo (2005) found that, despite the NCLB legislation's focus on improving student performance, viable instructional options that serve both as alternatives to retention and complementary practices when a child is retained are not used with high frequency. Their study examined the availability of instructional options for struggling students based on three characteristics: retention practices, awards/sanctions, and level (elementary versus middle/junior high school). Ninety-nine schools across 19 states were used to draw 249 participants who were regular education teachers, special education teachers, and school psychologists. Instructional options included cooperative learning strategies, group work, one-to-one tutoring, smaller class sizes, multiage grouping, flexible scheduling, use of curriculum-based measurement to make frequent instructional adjustments, within-class ability grouping, small group instruction, looping, intensive remedial help, before or after school homework programs, coordinated home–school interventions, instructional consultation, peer-assisted learning strategies, and instructional support from paraprofessionals or volunteers.

Teachers and school psychologists may be using the same interventions to assist all students without considering the needs of individual students. School psychologists are encouraged to gather follow-up data on children who have been retained and of children of comparable achievement levels who are not retained to help their school districts better understand the outcomes of retention decisions and to help teams make more individualized recommendations.

Especially in these cases, it will be important for the school psychologist to participate in developing a specific plan of action by which the student's skills deficits can be remediated.

School District/System Level

School psychologists' participation at a school district or system level can take many forms. As within their own schools, school psychologists can publicize the research on retention to help guide the development of informed policies. They can also serve an evaluative role, using district-wide data to assess the outcomes of retention decisions. They can also monitor the progress of students to ensure that problems are identified and addressed early before retention becomes a consideration.

School psychologists can also promote the development of effective alternatives to retention at all grade levels, from preschool through high school. These can include both developing programmatic interventions that address the needs of failing students and expanding the capabilities of classroom teachers to meet the needs of students at different skill levels. Increasing academic engagement and achievement for all students by improving instructional practice by grounding it in data-driven decision making will reduce academic failure and the need to retain. By meeting the needs of most students in the regular classroom, resources can be freed up to work with students who begin to fall behind the general student population. They need targeted interventions to prevent failure and avoid retention with specifically designed academic, social and/or emotional support and interventions. These are students like Jack and to a large degree even Ekaterina. Intensive intervention is designed to address those remaining students who continue to demonstrate needs following targeted interventions such as Greg.

Programmatic Interventions

Programmatic interventions may include developing screening programs to identify children at risk for school failure and to ensure early access to programs already available in the school or community, such as Head Start. Borman and Hewes (2002) found that students in the program Success for All completed eighth grade at earlier ages, had better achievement outcomes, had fewer special education placements, and fewer retentions.

While school psychologists may also work with the school system to develop intervention programs such as after-school tutoring or summer school courses, such programs may not be sufficient to make up serious deficits in short amounts of time and cannot take the place of preventive, systemic approaches. At the secondary level, school psychologists should encourage the development of reentry programs for dropouts and alternative education programs, such as ones that combine teaching skills with job training. Successful programs at the high school level often have two characteristics: (a) one or more individuals who develop relationships with students and monitor their progress carefully and (b) some mechanism to allow students who have failed courses and lost credits to regain these credits in quicker than normal time, allowing for graduation at the expected time. Simply put, successful programs must address the motivational issues that have developed by adolescence and the lack of academic achievement identity typically present in students who drop out of school. Because unsuccessful middle and high school students often lack basic strategic learning skills, intervention programs should also target these areas.

The instructional technology that enables classroom teachers to meet the needs of students of different skill levels is already available, but in many cases teachers do not have access to that technology. School psychologists can assist their school districts in learning about this technology and arranging for inservice programs to bring this information into the classroom. Instructional approaches such as mastery learning, team teaching, cooperative learning, peer tutoring, and curriculum-based assessment are all methods that have been shown to produce academic gains in students of all achievement levels. For instance, many school districts have responded to high numbers of retentions in the early grades by implementing a curriculum-based assessment and remediation program such as DIBELS to correct basic reading problems. Similarly, many school districts have adopted curriculums with embedded strategy instruction to foster metacognitive awareness and learning strategies in students.

To be taught and implemented effectively, programs must have a commitment to providing sufficient inservice training. School psychologists are often effective lobbyists for such continuing professional development. In making arguments for such training, school psychologists should help school administrators recognize the economic benefits of reducing retention rates. Given the annual cost of retaining a child (an average of $11,467 per year per student; National Center for Education Statistics, 2012), if a school

district, for instance, retains 30 students annually, adding a year to those students' school careers will cost districts or state educational agencies about $343,000 each year. There is no doubt that quality training for teachers and many specific interventions can be obtained at a far lesser cost.

State Education Agencies

As advocates for children, school psychologists can often be most effective when they move beyond the realm of their own schools and school districts to work at a state level to bring about change. The discrepancy between what is known about retention and what is practiced is great enough to warrant action at a higher level. While a school psychologist acting alone cannot influence state policies and practices, change can occur through the efforts of a state school psychology association. School psychology associations are encouraged to share the research on retention with their state education agencies and with other professional education associates (such as state principal and superintendent groups). They are also encouraged to use the lobbying resources available to them to influence legislation, including funding for alternative services delivery and legislation that affects policy, such as decreasing the rigidity of minimal competency requirements.

The NASP Advocacy Roadmap (http://www.nasponline.org/advocacy/roadmaps/practice-model/index.aspx) provides school psychologists with a set of tools to plan and execute grassroots advocacy by lobbying for an effective understanding of contemporary school psychology; to promote school psychological services for children, families, and schools; and to provide a foundation for the future of school psychology. There is probably no other topic as closely aligned with these goals as the prevention of school failure and the development of alternatives to retention. Use of NASP position statements and research summaries are essential tools in advocating for support at the state level to provide the resources for children to succeed in school.

The cost of retention is acutely felt at the state level because the additional costs of providing another year of school comes mostly from the state to the local school district. Yet, state legislators largely fail to make this connection and fail to redirect funds into more effective interventions. Connecting the cost of retention to its lack of success and outlining effective use of funds is a clear priority for school psychologists who want to influence practice at the state level.

SUMMARY

Research suggests that there are no clear benefits to retaining students and that the practice can have deleterious effects on students' achievement, self-concept, attitudes, and high-risk behavior. It can also increase the likelihood of dropping out of school. Although it is possible that a small percentage of students retained may benefit, it is impossible to predict which students those will be. Delayed entry into kindergarten is no more effective than retention and whatever initial benefits may be derived from retention after kindergarten or first grade appear to be washed out by the end of third or fourth grade. Meanwhile, there are dangerous correlations between retention and many high-risk behaviors for students who are old for grade.

School psychologists should assist in making retention decisions about individual students and should promote effective alternatives to retention. Most important, school psychologists must press for systemic solutions that target early reading deficits, independent learning skills, and motivational problems from a developmental perspective. Working to change school practices in the area of retention will require sharing the research on retention with educators, conducting evaluations on the outcomes of retention decisions at the local level, and lobbying at the state level to promote changes in policy and to advocate for alternative service delivery systems that more effectively meet the needs of students experiencing school failure.

REFERENCES

Alexander, K., Entwisle, D., & Dauber, S. (1994). *On the success of failure: A reassessment of the effects of retention in the primary grades.* New York, NY: Cambridge University Press.

Allington, R. L., & McGill-Franzen, A. (1997). How administrators understand learning difficulties. *Remedial and Special Education, 18,* 223–243.

Anderson, G. E., Whipple, A. D., & Jimerson, S. R. (2005). *Grade retention: Achievement and mental health outcomes.* Bethesda, MD: National Association of School Psychologists.

Beebe-Frankenberger, M., Bocian, K. M., Macmillan, D. L., & Gresham, F. M. (2004). Sorting second-grade students: Differentiating those retained from those promoted. *Journal of Educational Psychology, 96,* 204–215. doi:10.1037/0022-0663.96.2.204

Borman, G. D., & Hewes, G. M. (2002). *The long-term effects and cost effectiveness of Success for All Educational Evaluation and Policy Analysis, 24,* 243–266.

Buslinger-Clifford, S. L. (2004). *Retention and special education referral practices before and after the implementation of high-stakes testing* (Unpublished doctoral dissertation). University of Florida, Gainesville.

Byrd, R. S., Weitzman, M., & Auringer, P. (1997). Increased behavior problems associated with delayed school entry and delayed school progress. *Pediatrics, 100,* 654–661.

Byrd, R. S., Weitzman, M., & Doniger, A. S. (1996). Increased drug use among old-for-grade adolescents. *Archives of Pediatric and Adolescent Medicine, 150,* 470–476.

Cadima, J., McWilliam, R. A., & Leal, T. (2010). Environmental risk factors and children's literacy skills during the transition to elementary school. *International Journal of Behavioral Development, 34,* 24–33. doi:10.1177/0165025409345045

Davey, M. (2005, January 16). A child held behind. *New York Times* (pp. 31–37).

Forness, S. R., Kavale, K. A., Blum, I. M., & Lloyd, J. W. (1997). Meta-analysis of meta-analyses: What works in special education and related services. *Teaching Exceptional Children, 29,* 4–9.

Gaffney, J. S., & Zamia, E. (2003, November). *Grade retention and special education: A call for a transparent system of accountability* Paper presented at the annual meeting of the Teacher Education Division of the Council for Exceptional Children, Biloxi, MS.

Hagborg, W. J., Masella, G., Palladino, P., & Shepardson, J. (1991). A follow-up study of high school students with a history of grade retention. *Psychology in the Schools, 28,* 310–316.

Holmes, C. T., & Matthews, K. M. (1984). The effect of non-promotion on elementary and junior high school pupils: A meta-analysis. *Review of Educational Research, 54,* 225–236.

IDRA Newsletter. (1999, February). Failing our children. San Antonio, TX: Author. Retrieved from http://www.idra.org/IDRA_Newsletter/February_1999_Celebrating_25_Years_1973_-_1998/Failing_Our_Children/

Jacob, B., & Lefgren, L. (2009). The effect of grade retention on high school completion. *American Economic Journal: Applied Economics, 1*(3), 33–58. doi:10.1257/app1.3.33

Jimerson, S. R. (1999). On the failure of failure: Examining the association between early grade retention and education and employment outcomes during late adolescence. *Journal of School Psychology, 37,* 243–272.

Jimerson, S. R. (2000). *Grade retention review 2000: New directions for research and practice in the 21st century.* Paper presented at the annual meeting of the National Association of School Psychologists, New Orleans, LA.

Jimerson, S. R., Pletcher, S. M., Graydon, K., Schnurr, B. L., Nickerson, A. B., & Kundert, D. K. (2006). Beyond grade retention and social promotion: Promoting the social and academic. *Psychology in the Schools, 43,* 85–98. doi:10.1002/pits.20132

McLeskey, J., & Grizzle, K. L. (1992). Grade retention rates among students with learning disabilities. *Exceptional Children, 58,* 548–554.

Moser, S. E., West, S. G., & Hughes, J. N. (2012). Trajectories of math and reading achievement in low-achieving children in elementary school: Effects of early and later retention in grade. *Journal of Educational Psychology, 104,* 603–621.

National Association of School Psychologists. (2010). *Model for comprehensive and integrated school psychological services.* Bethesda, MD: Author. Retrieved from http://www.nasponline.org/standards/2010standards/2_PracticeModel.pdf

National Center for Educational Statistics. (2012). *The condition of education: Grade retention.* Washington, DC: Author. Retrieved from http://0-nces.ed.gov.opac.acc.msmc.edu/pubs2012/2012045_1.pdf

Picklo, D. M., & Christenson, S. L. (2005). Alternatives to retention and social promotion: The availability of instructional options. *Remedial and Special Education, 26,* 258–268.

Resnick, M. D., Bearman, P. S., Blum, R. W., Bauman, K. E., Harris, K. M., Jones, J., … Udry, J. R. (1997). Protecting adolescents from harm: Findings from the National Longitudinal Study on Adolescent Health. *Journal of the American Medical Association, 278,* 823–832.

Roderick, M., & Nagaoka, J. (2005). Retention under Chicago's high-stakes testing program: Helpful, harmful, or harmless? *Educational Evaluation and Policy Analysis, 27,* 309–340. doi:10.3102/01623737027004309

Silberglitt, B., Jimerson, S. R., Burns, M. K., & Appleton, J. J. (2006). Does the timing of grade retention make a difference? Examining the effects of early versus later retention. *School Psychology Review, 35,* 134–141.

Smith, M. L., & Shepard, L. A. (1989). Flunking grades: A recapitulation. In L. A. Shepard & M. L. Smith (Eds.), *Flunking grades: Research and policies on retention.* New York, NY: Falmer.

Wilson, V. L., & Hughes, J. N. (2006). Retention of Hispanic Latino students in first grade: Child, parent, teacher, school, and peer predictors. *Journal of School Psychology, 44,* 31–49.

Wu, W., West, S. G., & Hughes, J. (2010). Effect of grade retention in first grade on psychosocial outcomes. *Journal of Educational Psychology, 102,* 135–152. doi:10.1037/a0016664

11 Best Practices in Services for Gifted Students

Rosina M. Gallagher
Northeastern Illinois University
Linda C. Caterino
Arizona State University
Tiombe Bisa-Kendrick
Miami Dade County (FL) Public Schools

OVERVIEW

Gifted and talented students represent a neglected and underperforming minority in U.S. public schools. Analyzing the student data from the National Assessment of Educational Progress, for example, Loveless, Farkas, and Duffet (2008) found that "the performance of high achieving students was languid" (p. 2). Studying the same data, Plucker, Burroughs, and Song (2010), identified "excellence gaps" for subgroups of students performing at advanced levels. Reviewing the findings of the 2009 Program for International Student Assessment, Fleischman, Hopstock, Pelczar, and Shelley (2010) highlighted the dismal performance of U.S. 15-year-old top students in reading, mathematics, and science literacy compared with their peers across the globe. More recently, Xiang, Dahlin, Cronin, Theaker, and Durant (2011) examined achievement trends of students in reading and mathematics on the Measures of Academic Progress. They found that two out of five students achieving at the 90th percentile in the early grades descended to the 80th percentile in 4 years.

These findings are not surprising, as educators are generally ill-prepared to work with advanced learners. Loveless et al. (2008) report data from the National Teacher Survey by Farkas and Duffett indicating 65% of the teachers surveyed state they had little or no training to teach academically advanced students. Also, while 77% of the teachers agreed to feeling pressured to move struggling students to proficiency, and putting the needs of advanced students on the back seat, 90%

favored more professional development to improve their work with advanced learners. A recent national survey likewise suggests that school psychologists have traditionally not been involved in systematically serving gifted students. Robertson, Pfeiffer, and Taylor (2011) found that 66.2% of responding practicing school psychologists rarely conducted gifted student evaluations, and 94% received little or no training in gifted screening and assessment during their graduate studies. While most school psychology graduate programs require specific coursework on learning disabilities, there is actually a greater percentage of U.S. students identified as academically gifted as there are students identified with learning disabilities: 6% (National Association for Gifted Children, 2010) versus 4.9% (National Center for Education Statistics, 2012). There is clearly a need for school psychologists to become more involved in supporting gifted children and those who teach and care for them.

This chapter provides information to assist school psychologists to better understand and serve gifted children and youth. Specifically, our goals are to (a) review the gifted education trajectory, highlighting research that shows how educational, social, and political factors currently have an impact on the lives of gifted learners; (b) discuss available identification and assessment instruments to serve the heterogeneous gifted population in public schools; and (c) examine proven approaches that support individual talent and healthy psychosocial development. Consistent with the domain of Interventions and Instructional Support to Develop

Academic Skills in the National Association of School Psychologists (NASP) *Model for Comprehensive and Integrated School Psychological Services* (NASP, 2010), throughout the chapter we discuss how the school psychologist can be a valuable resource in identifying giftedness and assisting educators to design, implement, monitor, and evaluate interventions and instructional supports that enable gifted learners to maximize their potential.

BASIC CONSIDERATIONS

Beliefs on what constitutes giftedness are controversial. This section looks at major perspectives that combine intelligence, creativity, and motivation, as well as environmental influences that can inhibit or facilitate high achievement. Included is a discussion of how state policies differ on what services should be provided to gifted students and how the offerings should be funded, as well as a review of national efforts to support the education of gifted and talented learners.

Conceptualizations of Giftedness

Conceptualizations of intelligence and giftedness have evolved over the years. Renzulli (1978) proposed a three-ring model of giftedness: above-average ability (not necessarily superior), creativity, and task commitment. Gardner (1993) developed the well-known theory of multiple intelligences: spatial, linguistic, logical–mathematical, kinesthetic, musical, interpersonal, intrapersonal, and naturalistic intelligence. Sternberg's (2005) successful intelligence includes wisdom, intelligence (academic and practical), and creativity synthesized. Most recently, Pfeiffer (2012) proposes his Tripartite Model of Giftedness: viewing academic giftedness through high intelligence, through outstanding accomplishments, and through the potential to excel. He suggests that the first perspective assesses high intelligence via IQ, the second emphasizes academic performance, and the third focuses on students who have the potential to succeed if provided a stimulating and nurturing environment.

Subotnik, Olszewski-Kubilius, and Worrell (2011) published a landmark monograph that emphasizes the integration of motivation, interest, and personality with high ability in order to nurture talent to the point where an individual can become accomplished in a particular field. They note that eminence should be the goal of gifted education and, more importantly, state that giftedness is not a fixed concept; that is, children may require gifted education services at one point in their

education and not another. Therefore, children should be continually assessed to determine their educational needs.

National Initiatives and Legislation

Gifted education, while based to some extent on theoretical perspectives and academic research, has also been profoundly influenced by legislative and budgetary factors. In 1972, Commissioner of Education Sidney Marland Jr. published a report concluding that gifted and talented students have special needs, and directed the U.S. Office of Education to develop a national strategy to provide for their education. It was recommended that school districts identify at least 3–5% of their student population as gifted, typically based on a cognitive measure. Marland also noted that there were too few culturally and linguistically diverse students and students from low socioeconomic status families represented in gifted programs.

The Education for All Handicapped Children Act of 1975 (P.L.94-142) subsequently required schools to individualize instruction for handicapped students and to provide such education in the "least restrictive environment." Although gifted and talented was not a specific handicapping condition listed in P.L. 94-142, it prompted 17 states to include giftedness as an "area of exceptionality," and to apply many of the same procedures to serve students with disabilities to the gifted, including the development of an individual education plan.

In 2002, No Child Left Behind offered competitive statewide grants to serve students who were traditionally underrepresented in gifted and talented programs, especially economically disadvantaged students, those learning English as a second language, and students with disabilities. All but three states (Massachusetts, New Hampshire, and South Dakota) have a current definition of giftedness. However, eight states do not require local districts to follow the state definition (National Association for Gifted Children, 2010).

Based on information provided by the National Association for Gifted Children, 37 states specifically recognize children who have advanced intellectual skills, 34 recognize achievement, 25 recognize creativity, 20 refer to visual arts or arts and humanities, 15 refer to performing arts (including music and dance), 14 refer to leadership, and 4 refer to motivation or task commitment (Table 11.1). In addition, four states specifically make reference to ethnic or cultural diversity, and two refer to different socioeconomic levels. Other states

Table 11.1. Gifted Domains by State Law

Domain	States
Intellectual ability	AK, AZ, AR, CA, CO, CT, DE, GA, HI, ID, IA, KS, KY, LA, ME, MI, MN, MS, MO, MT, NE, NV, NM, NY, NC, OK (top 3%), OR, RI, SC, TN, TX, UT, VT, VA, WA, WV, WI
Achievement	AL, AZ, CA, CO, CT, DE, HI, ID, IL (top 5% in language arts or math), IA, KS, KY, LA, ME, MI, MN, MS, MT, NE, NV, NM, NY, NC, OK, OR, RI, SC, TN, TX, UT, VT, VA, WV, WI
Creativity	AL, AK, AR, CA, CO, CT, DE, GA, HI, ID, IA, KY, MI, MN, MS, NE, NM, OK, OR, RI, TX, UT, VT, WA, WI
Problem solving	NM
Visual arts	CA, CO, DE, HI, ID, IA, KY, ME, MN, MS, NE, NY, OK, OR, RI, UT
Arts/humanities	MI
Artistic	SC, TX, VT
Performing arts	CA, CO, DE, HI, ID, IA, KY, ME, MN, MS, NY, OK, OR, RI, UT
Music	CO, OR
Dance	OR
Leadership	CA, CO, DE, HI, ID, IA, KY, MN, OK, OR, TX, UT, WA, WI
Motivation	AR, GA, IN
Task commitment	AR
Exceptional gifts	IN
Interests	IN
Reference to twice-exceptional	CO, VA
Reference to socioeconomic status or economically disadvantaged	CO, VA
Reference to ethnicity/cultural background	CO, NC, VA, WA

provide more vague definitions, not referring to any particular domain. (McClain & Pfeiffer [2012] provide slightly different statistics.) Unlike special education, gifted education was not provided funding under P.L. 94-142. Fourteen states have no mandate to identify or provide services for gifted learners, and five states provide no funding at all for these services (National Association for Gifted Children, 2010).

The 2011 TALENT Act (To Aid Gifted and High-Ability Learners by Empowering the Nation's Teachers; S. 512 & H. R. 2338) was reintroduced in both houses of Congress in March 2013. The bill focuses on four key provisions. First, it calls for changes to the assessment and accountability systems. Second, it calls for documentation as to how educators are being trained to identify and serve advanced learners, and by requiring states and districts to include students in their plans for the use of federal Title II funds. Third, Title I schools are expected to describe how they will identify and serve high-ability underserved populations. Fourth, in order to promote research, a competitive grant program designed to include high-ability students not formally identified as gifted will be initiated, and a national research and dissemination center will be established. Should the TALENT Act become law, school psychologists may become more involved in the assessment of gifted children as well as in curriculum planning.

BEST PRACTICES IN SERVICES FOR GIFTED STUDENTS

Best practices in working with gifted and talented learners are consistent with services provided to children with special needs. The school psychologist, as a member of the problem-solving team, can play a pivotal role in each of the service areas outlined in Table 11.2: identification and assessment, educational placement and monitoring of the differentiated education plan, consultation, advocacy, and research. After obtaining a foundational background in the area of giftedness, school psychologists may choose a generalist approach to serving the gifted. However, some school psychologists may decide to acquire additional knowledge and skills in a specific area of interest, such as working with twice-exceptional learners (e.g., children who have exceptional aptitude in math, for example, with difficulties in reading or writing and/or social skills) or with gifted children from culturally and linguistically diverse populations. Others may prefer to focus on intellectual and academic areas, or on supporting the psychosocial development of profoundly gifted learners.

Table 11.2. School Psychologists' Services and Methods to Support Gifted and Talented Students

School Psychologists' Services	Knowledge and Skills	Special Considerations and Methods

Identification and assessment	• Assessment:
	  • Cognitive and academic abilities
	  • Interests
	  • Experiences and opportunities
	• Sensitivity to special populations:
	  • Exceptional abilities and disabilities: Twice-exceptional, visual–spatial learners, profoundly gifted
	  • High-ability, low SES, and culturally and linguistically diverse
		• Use multiple and varied measures, local norms:
		  • Identify strengths and needs
		  • Develop talent or potential, then assess
		  • Value home and life experiences
		  • Use surveys and behavior scales
		  • Assess early and regularly to modify goals
		• Seek input from multiple sources: student, family, peers, community members
		• Ensure multiple entry points and pathways

Educational services and differentiated education plan	• Background on instructional models:
	  • Ability grouping
	  • Acceleration
	  • Enrichment
	  • Cluster grouping
	
	• Monitor personal education plan:
	  • Academic growth
	  • Self-knowledge and self-regulation
	  • Character development
	  • Social skills and civic responsibility
		Promote:
		• Curriculum differentiation
		• Ongoing assessment to modify instruction
		• Flexible grouping within class, across grades
		• Early kindergarten entrance, content compacting, grade skipping, early college
		• Independent study and research
		• Creative products and performances
		• Service learning projects, mentorships
		Use formative measures:
		• Teacher ratings with rubrics
		• Supplement and/or replace curriculum
		• Independent study; courses online; mentorships
		• Portfolios: creative products or performances, contests, collaborative problem solving
		• Leadership activities
		• Student self-assessment
		Use summative measures:
		• Standardized tests with above grade-level ceilings, off-level tests
		• Teacher evaluation and student self-assessment

Consultation and collaboration	• Individual and group counseling • Support teachers • Support administrators • Support families	Foster: • Self-understanding and self-regulation • Interpersonal relationships • Goal setting and decision making • Character development and self-advocacy Support: • Psychosocial curriculum • Training in gifted and multicultural pedagogy • A challenging differentiated curriculum for all • Participate in program and service design • Assist with program and service evaluation • Offer professional development in specialty area • Stay abreast of research on best practices • Lead parent workshops on topics of interest • Promote home–school relationships and networking • Provide resources
Advocacy	• Stay informed on issues that have an impact on high-ability and talented students • Get to know state legislators • Take an active role	• Stay abreast of state and national legislation • Assist in building school–community partnerships • Communicate benefits of gifted education to policy makers at local, district, and state levels
Research	• Conduct needs assessments • Survey areas of interest • Evaluate programs and services	• Participate in state and national organizations that support gifted students • Conduct studies and disseminate findings

Still others may choose research and advocacy to have an impact on public policy at local, state, and national levels.

Identification and Assessment of Gifted Abilities

This section reviews assessment instruments and issues relevant to the identification of giftedness.

Cognitive Assessment

Cognitive ability tests have been the most commonly used measures for the identification of gifted students, as this practice has been shown to predict school performance. Sixteen states mandate that schools use intelligence tests to identify students, but cut-off scores vary by state (e.g., Arizona and Oklahoma require that a student score at the 97th percentile on an approved cognitive test, and Mississippi requires scores at the 90th percentile). Seventeen states require the use of achievement tests, but only 15 states stipulate specific test scores for qualification (ranging from the 90th to the 97th percentile). Thirteen states require the use of teacher or parent nominations, nine require a teacher behavior rating scale, and seven require a behavioral checklist. In addition, nine states require a creativity test and eight states require the inclusion of performance measures (McClain & Pfeiffer, 2012). According to Worrell and Erwin (2011), the most frequently administered individual assessments used in the identification of gifted children are the Wechsler Intelligence Scale for Children-IV, the Stanford-Binet-V, the Differential Abilities Scale II, and the Woodcock-Johnson Test of Cognitive Abilities-III. Other possible cognitive measures include the Kaufman Assessment Battery for Children-Second Edition and the Reynolds Intellectual Assessment Scale. Current practices also include the use of the General Ability Index on the Wechsler scales to limit the influence of the working memory and processing speed scales.

Individual assessments can be costly and time consuming, so many school districts resort to group tests that do not need to be administered by school psychologists. One of the most popular group tests is the Cognitive Achievement Test, which can be used with students K–12. The test yields three scores: verbal, quantitative, and nonverbal. The Otis-Lennon School Ability Test-Eighth Edition is another group test. This test measures five domains (verbal comprehension, verbal reasoning, pictorial reasoning, figural reasoning, and quantitative reasoning) and yields a total score, the School Ability Index. Finally, off-level testing with the SAT and the American College Testing Program has also been used for group talent searches. While group-administered tests are less time consuming and less expensive, critics (e.g., Beal, 1996) have found their accuracy to be lower than that of individual intelligence tests. Group tests may have a lower ceiling and afford the examiner less of an opportunity for behavioral observation.

Assessment of Gifted Students From Diverse Backgrounds

It has long been argued that identification through the use of IQ tests alone fails to identify many gifted children, especially those with nonacademic abilities (e.g., Winner, 2000). Using IQ as the only criteria for the identification of gifted students has also been criticized due to disproportionality. There has been continuous underrepresentation of students of color in gifted programs. Donovan and Cross (2002) found that, although there is considerable variability among states, African American and Hispanic students are less than half as likely to be in gifted programs as Caucasian students, and Native American and Native Alaskan students fall between African American and Caucasian students. Presently, 26 states mandate specific policies for identifying culturally diverse students for gifted programming. Arkansas, for example, requires that the list of "nominated" students be "representative of the entire student population in terms of race, sex, and economic status" (National Association for Gifted Children, 2010).

In order to provide an appropriate assessment of diverse students, school psychologists need to be specifically familiar with the cultural background of their student population. Each ethnic group has unique characteristics and values that need to be taken into consideration. Language issues also need to be carefully considered. Naglieri and Ford (2005) determined that students with developing English language skills are not likely to earn high scores on verbal and quantitative ability measures, regardless of their actual intellectual ability. Naglieri and Ford (2005) further determined that many measures of cognitive ability inadvertently require academic skills to earn high test scores.

Wellisch and Brown (2012) recommend the use of nonverbal tests such as the Naglieri Nonverbal Ability Test 2, the Universal Nonverbal Intelligence Test, and the Raven's Progressive Matrices. Worrell and Erwin (2011) also suggest the use of additional nonverbal tests such as the Leiter International Performance

Scales-Third Edition and the Test of Nonverbal Intelligence-Fourth Edition.

The Bilingual Verbal Ability Test-Normative Update, which measures advanced vocabulary in English and 17 other languages, can be helpful in determining language dominance. If Spanish is a child's dominant language and the school psychologist is fluent in that language, then the Batería III Woodcock-Muñoz may be useful in determining the cognitive abilities of Spanish speakers.

The use of nonverbal tests has been controversial. For example, while the Naglieri Nonverbal Ability Test 2 has been demonstrated to identify gifted students in a more representative way than traditional IQ tests (Naglieri & Ford, 2005), Lohman, Korb, and Lakin (2008) have criticized the use of the Raven's Progressive Matrices for overestimating the number of high-scoring children and the Naglieri Nonverbal Ability Test 2 for overestimating the number of both high- and low-scoring children and for having excessive score variability. Moreover, the exclusive use of nonverbal tests may miss minority students who have better developed verbal than nonverbal skills.

Achievement Tests

In the past, standardized achievement tests such as the Iowa Test of Basic Skills or the Stanford series were routinely given in schools on an annual basis, and the top 3–10% of students were considered for gifted programming. However, since many districts have now moved to statewide achievement tests that have been less researched, the psychometric qualities of these tests may be questionable. In addition, with the move to Common Core State Standards, most states will require the use of a new test, the Partnership for Assessment of Readiness for College and Careers, by the 2014–2015 school year. The use of this assessment method to identify giftedness is yet to be documented.

Off-grade–level testing has also been used in the identification process. For example, students may take standardized achievement test batteries designed for older students, or even the College Board SAT. For example, the SAT has been used to determine eligibility for accelerated summer opportunities for young scholars at many universities across the country.

Creativity Tests

Creativity is listed as a qualifying area for gifted education in many states, but this domain is infrequently used for identification, perhaps because this construct is difficult to define and assess. The Torrance Test of Creative Thinking and its revisions are the most commonly used measure of creative potential (Lemons, 2011). The test measures fluency, elaboration, and originality in figural and verbal tasks.

The Creativity Assessment Packet designed for students in grades 3–12 includes three components: Exercise in Divergent Thinking, Exercise in Divergent Feeling, and the Williams Scale. The Exercise in Divergent Thinking is a drawing test in which students are asked to work on incomplete drawings and create a title. The product is scored on fluency, originality, flexibility, and elaboration. The Exercise in Divergent Feeling is a 50-item self-rating scale of characteristics such as curiosity, imagination, and risk taking. The Williams Scale is a teacher- and parent-rating scale of creative characteristics. Lemons (2011) has noted that the predictive validity of creativity tests tends to be weak, as these measures may not predict future accomplishments.

Parent and Teacher Nomination

Another identification method has been the use of observation and subsequent parent and teacher nomination, sometimes via the use of specific gifted behavior rating scales. Merrick and Targett (2004) suggest that parent nomination may be helpful in that parents have had the opportunity to observe the child over a longer period of time and in a variety of situations, but parents may not have a comparison group and may not always be objective regarding their child's performance.

Merrick and Targett's (2004) parent rating form assesses the following characteristics: quick recall, advanced knowledge regarding specific subjects, advanced vocabulary knowledge, early reading or writing ability, unusually intense interest and enjoyment when learning new things, understanding information well enough to teach others, comfort around adults, leadership abilities, resourcefulness and innovation, and the use of imaginative methods.

Frasier and Passow (1994) identified the following 10 core gifted characteristics that may be evident in gifted children from diverse backgrounds: motivation, intense unusual interests, highly expressive communication skills, effective problem solving, excellent memory, inquiry (curiosity), quick grasp or insight, use of logic and reasoning, imagination or creativity, and ability to convey and pick up humor. However, these characteristics and those assessed in other gifted rating scales, while long thought to indicate giftedness, have not always been subject to stringent validity tests to support their relationship with gifted identification.

The use of teacher nominations has also been advocated (Worrell & Erwin, 2011). Teachers have the opportunity to observe the child in different academic situations and can compare the child to other students. The teacher nomination rubric by Merrick and Targett (2004) includes the following characteristics reportedly indicative of giftedness: unusual alertness, advanced play behavior, exceptional memory, early reading, rapid pace of learning, asking many questions, early development of classifying and investigative skills, exceptional mathematical ability, imagination, early speech, early social interactions, feelings of frustration, heightened sensitivity, social and emotional maturity, and early awareness of difference from others.

Gifted Rating Scales

Specific standardized gifted behavior rating scales include the Scales for Rating the Behavioral Characteristics of Superior Students, first published in 1976, which assessed the following characteristics of gifted students: learning, creativity, motivation, leadership, artistic, musical, drama, communication (precision), communication (expressive), and planning. Four new scales were recently added to the Scales for Rating the Behavioral Characteristics of Superior Students: reading, mathematics, science, and technology. The test manual reports good internal reliability and validity data. The Scales for Identifying Gifted Students, another gifted behavior scale, includes the following seven subscales: general intellectual ability, language arts, mathematics, science, social studies, creativity, and leadership. Both a school version and home version are available. It has good internal consistency, reliability, and validity, and has no gender or ethnic group bias.

The Gifted Evaluation Scale-Second Edition can be used for the screening and identification of children K–12. This teacher rating scale includes five areas: intellectual ability, creativity, specific academic aptitude, leadership, and performing and visual arts, with an optional scale on motivation. The Gifted and Talented Evaluation Scales were also designed to identify gifted students between the ages of 5 and 18. The Gifted and Talented Evaluation Scales asks teachers and parents to rate the child's intellectual ability, academic skills, creativity, leadership, and artistic talent. Finally, the Gifted Rating Scales ask teachers to assess potential gifted students on the following domains: intellectual ability, academic ability, creativity, artistic talent, motivation, and, for first through eighth graders, leadership ability.

The proponents of these rating scales note that these instruments are less expensive and less time consuming than individual assessments. Critics note that teacher nomination is suspect since research has shown teachers to be quite poor identifiers of gifted children (e.g., Moon & Brighton, 2008). This is not surprising when one looks at the findings of the National Association for Gifted Children (2010) report regarding teacher preparation in gifted education. It found that only six states require preservice training for regular classroom teachers on characteristics and needs of gifted students. Moreover, teacher bias has been identified in gifted education referrals, with teachers referring more males than females (Bianco, Harris, Garrison-Wade, & Leech, 2012). In addition, Bianco (2005) found that teachers were less willing to refer students with learning disabilities and behavioral disorders to gifted programs.

Portfolios

The use of portfolios has also been advocated for the identification and progress monitoring of students for gifted programs (Mitra-Itle, 2011). Portfolios include work samples so that evaluators can judge actual work products. However, these samples may not be representative of the student's typical work and may not sample all domains. Unless clear rubrics are developed, the evaluation of portfolios may also be too subjective.

Interest and Aptitude Inventories

Finally, interest and aptitude inventories are also used in gifted identification, as well as in motivating students by personalizing the curriculum. For example, Renzulli's Interest-A-Lyzer (Renzulli, 1997) asks students a series of open-ended questions in order to assess students' present and potential interests in the performing arts, technology, creative writing, business management, athletics, history, social action, science, and fine arts and crafts.

Response to Intervention

Bianco (2010) recommends a model using response to intervention (RTI) for both identification and programming. In Tier 1, all students would be exposed to a "culturally responsive, high-quality curriculum and instruction that nurtures all children's capacity to learn and excel" (p. 323), which provides multiple opportunities for gifted potential to emerge. Tier 1 would also include culturally sensitive universal screening. For Tier 2, the regular education teacher would provide interventions in the general education classroom in collaboration with the gifted education teacher and the child's family. This would involve differentiated instruction and enrichment opportunities to allow the child to explore the core curriculum in greater depth or at an accelerated pace, as well as mentoring and summer internships. Tier 3 interventions would include radical acceleration such as skipping a grade, early advanced placement classes, or early college entrance.

The National Association for Gifted Children (2010) supports the use of an RTI model in gifted identification and intervention. They suggest that the gifted need grade-level core content to be supplemented or replaced through acceleration and/or increased depth and complexity in the curriculum for Tiers 1, 2, and 3. Interventions include additional time and attention from teachers with expertise in content and differentiation. Progress monitoring should document replacement curriculum, mastery, and additional services.

Summary of the Identification Process

The current view of researchers and theorists in gifted education is that, just as in special education, more than one measure should be used to make a determination, especially since most state legislation views giftedness as a multidimensional concept (e.g., Pfeiffer, 2012). Many states advocate the use of multiple criteria in identifying gifted students. A wide variety of identification strategies may lead to a more equitable proportion of gifted children (Merrick & Targett, 2004). Mitra-Itle (2011), for example, suggests the use of a multimethod procedure that includes the use of a cross battery Cattell–Horn–Carroll approach using the Ortiz model for the assessment of diverse students; the use of nonverbal tests such as the Naglieri Nonverbal Ability Test 2; the Raven's Progressive Matrices; the use of non-English tests such as the Wechsler Spanish version; student, parent, and teacher interviews; a portfolio of permanent products; a sociometric questionnaire; observations; performance-based assessments; the Iowa Test of Basic Skills; and the Gifted and Talented Evaluation Scales. Worrell and Erwin (2011) describe an alternative view of the identification process. In their model, a pool of candidates nominated by teachers and parents is screened for high achievement. Students in the top 20% are administered a comprehensive achievement test to find those scoring in the 90th percentile. Specific students are then selected for additional in-depth assessment of cognitive, academic, and psychosocial functioning. These students may then be considered through interest inventories, curriculum-based measures, alternative assessments, portfolios of work samples, and rating scales of gifted behaviors.

Merrick and Targett (2004) view identification as an ongoing process that requires continual assessment to determine evolving needs, as is the case for students in special education. These researchers also recommend that students be tested earlier and more frequently in response to Subotnik's developmental conception of giftedness. This is all the more necessary since we know that IQ scores do not remain stable over time.

To conclude this section, Table 11.3 provides a comparison of different methods that can be used for the identification and assessment of gifted students.

Educational Services

School psychologists should become aware of developmental differences among this population, and develop multicultural competencies to promote the identification of underserved groups.

Addressing Developmental Differences

Gifted children are frequently characterized with *asynchronous development*. That is, they often develop various areas in their life at different rates and/or may not always be in sync with their age peers. For example, a 3-year-old may show literacy and numeracy skills equivalent to those of a 6-year-old, develop physically like a 4-year-old, and exhibit emotional and social behaviors typical of a 3-year-old, the child's chronological age. This asynchronous development may be a challenge to manage for the child and his or her teachers, parents, and other caregivers, and may preclude the use of a common intervention and whole grade acceleration.

This type of acceleration requires that school psychologists, as members of the education team, determine a child's physical, social, and emotional development in addition to his or her cognitive and academic abilities. The Differentiated Education Plan should then afford challenging schoolwork, but still promote the child's socialization with age-level peers.

When considering accelerated placement for middle school students, 12-year-olds are frequently required to take high-power tests like the SAT designed for college-bound students. It is highly recommended that school psychologists counsel these young people and their parents to not be unduly concerned on the possibility of achieving lower scores. These tests cover advanced content and have a high index of difficulty for young teens. Students should be encouraged to do their best in order to discover a more accurate measure of their achievement in targeted areas.

Table 11.3. Comparison of Assessment Measures to Identify Giftedness in Children

Assessment	Advantage	Disadvantage
Group aptitude tests	Standardized, objective; less time consuming; less expensive than individual assessments	Multiple choice; may underestimate potential of children with ADHD or test anxiety; may not be effective for low-income and culturally diverse (low socioeconomic status and *culturally and linguistically diverse* students)
Individual ability tests	More comprehensive; predict academic achievement; standardized; more objective, flexible; one/one format, may reduce anxiety, improve student engagement	Expensive, time consuming; may not be effective for low socioeconomic status and culturally and linguistically diverse students
Nonverbal tests	May increase identification of English learners, disadvantaged, or underrepresented students	May miss students with advanced verbal skills; may overidentify gifted students
Off-level tests	Raise ceiling; may identify student performance above grade level; may identify underachievers that perform better on challenging tasks	May not be as effective for disadvantaged or culturally diverse students; group assessment may underestimate children with ADHD or test anxiety
Parent nomination	Parents have had more time to observe their child in more situations and for a longer period of time	Subjective, may be biased; parents may not have a comparison group
Teacher nomination and teacher rating scales	Teachers can observe the child in different academic situations; teacher can compare the child to other students	Subjective, teachers may not have much experience with gifted children; may underrepresent children with associated disabilities or behavioral problems; may underrepresent females
Portfolios	Evaluation of actual work products; may identify students who have test anxiety but perform well in class	Samples may not be representative of the child's daily work; may not sample all academic domains; subjective
Creativity tests	May identify students who have advanced creativity but may be missed by traditional ability tests	May be less predictive of academic performance
Group achievement tests	Standardized; objective; recognize past learning ability; less time consuming; less expensive	May penalize students from poor academic environments; may penalize students with ADHD or test anxiety
Individual achievement tests	Standardized; objective; recognize past learning ability; may be beneficial for students with ADHD or test anxiety	May penalize students from poor academic environments; expensive; time consuming

Some large urban school districts, for example, provide academic centers for seventh and eighth graders housed in selective enrollment high schools, with a designated counselor for guidance and support. Properly placed, gifted youth generally thrive in these centers. Some graduate in 2 or 3 years, while others opt for Advanced Placement courses and online independent learning programs or college courses, allowing them to still graduate with high school friends.

Developing Multicultural Competencies

In addition to being familiar with the assessment instruments and processes, school psychologists should become particularly familiar with the cultural background of the students enrolled in the schools they serve. Each group has unique characteristics and values to be considered, understood, and appreciated. Pursuing

professional development to gain general awareness of a specific culture can be helpful in developing and implementing educational interventions. However, it is more important that school psychologists actively reach out to families, engage the families in meaningful school activities, and gain a better understanding of values and resources that may help the families accept recommendations for advanced academic programming.

Instructional Approaches

Proven instructional models include acceleration, ability grouping, enrichment, and cluster grouping. Acceleration, previously discussed, is the process of advancing students to reach competencies commensurate with their readiness levels and potential. Colangelo, Assouline, and Gross (2004) have reported on 18 types of acceleration, including early admission to kindergarten or first grade, self-paced instruction in a content area, curriculum compacting or extracurricular programming, participation in Advanced Placement or honors courses, and early admission to high school or dual enrollment in high school and college. The Iowa Acceleration Scale-Third Edition can be used as an objective guide in making radical acceleration decisions. The Iowa Acceleration Scale guides a child study team composed of educators, parents, and others through a discussion of the academic and social characteristics of the child. It requires consideration of assessment information, as well as information regarding the child's motivation, school attendance, and relationships with teachers and peers.

A second educational model is ability grouping, the practice of organizing students based on competency in certain content areas and adjusting the curriculum to meet specific ability levels and interests. Ability grouping can occur within a specific class (e.g., reading instruction) or across grade levels. Offering algebra, laboratory science, or computer programming has become part of the middle school curriculum for advanced learners in many school districts. Ability grouping should not be confused with tracking, the largely abandoned practice of placing students permanently in vocational, general, or academic tracks from middle school and beyond.

Enrichment interventions are generally well-structured activities that extend a challenging curriculum and are designed to develop creative thinking and problem solving or nurture talent and cultivate character and leadership. Activities can vary from conducting independent research, creating artistic products, or implementing service learning experiences to working with an established mentor in the field to a full-blown program such as the nationally recognized School-Wide Enrichment Model developed by Renzulli and Reis (1985).

Cluster grouping is an inclusion model that allows identified gifted students to receive services in their areas of academic strength or on a daily basis. A group of four to six gifted students are clustered in a mixed ability classroom with a teacher who has training in gifted pedagogy. Proponents of the cluster model (e.g., Winebrenner & Brulles, 2008) list the following benefits of this approach: Gifted students feel accepted, may share similar interests and challenge each other to exceed learning standards, teachers come closer to providing better educational services to all students, high achievers welcome the opportunity to assume leadership roles, and administrators find the model cost effective and may allow for the accommodation of few or many students even at a school-wide level. Responding to

critics, researchers recommend not including special needs students with a gifted cluster, making training in differentiation and gifted education available to all teachers so anyone can have the option of teaching a gifted cluster on a rotating basis, and assuring nongifted students have the opportunity to be cycled into a cluster classroom over their school years.

Differentiated Education Plan for the Gifted and Talented

Similar to the Individualized Education Program for special education students, the Differentiated Education Plan is based on assessment data and includes intervention goals and techniques. Currently, only 10 states plus the District of Columbia require a Differentiated or Personal Education Plan for the gifted and talented (Alabama, Florida, Kansas, Kentucky, Louisiana, New Mexico, Oklahoma, Pennsylvania, Virginia, West Virginia). The Personalized Education Plan by the Johnston Community Schools Extended Learning Program in Iowa is a high school model that includes five sections: student identification and needs assessment with recommended modifications, an outline of services to be provided ranging from extended studies, Advanced Placement classes and competitions, counseling mentoring or service learning, and documentation. This plan includes six goals with performance measures: skills in the affective domain, growth in self-directed learning, inquiry and research skills, critical thinking and reasoning, creative thinking, and communication skills.

To help develop a Differentiated or Personal Education Plan, school psychologists will need additional background in differentiated instruction and a better understanding of factors that uniquely have an impact on the psychosocial development of this population. Moreover, if the TALENT Act becomes law, federal, state, and local education agencies will be responsible for demonstrating how they are identifying, serving and assessing the annual growth and progress of advanced and gifted learners. Data from such plans can certainly be used to support the effectiveness of interventions and services provided by school staff, including school psychologists.

Case Study: A Budding Scientist

Providing appropriate services to students regardless of their educational placement requires the judicious collaboration of teachers, clinicians, and family; that is, the full education support team. A brief case study illustrates how a young child with promising potential can be helped to develop leadership skills and an aptitude and interest in science.

Colin, a 2-year-old African American male was enrolled in day care. He impressed his day care caregiver with above-average language development and insatiable curiosity, but marked difficulty in relating to peers and complying with instructions. Unless given undivided attention, Colin's high energy was disruptive to the day care environment. After years, this behavior pattern eventually led to a psychological evaluation that found him eligible for behavioral interventions through the emotional and behavior disorders program at the end of first grade. Distressed at this recommendation, his mother transferred Colin to a different public school.

Midway through the second grade, his teacher noted that Colin achieved above-grade–level scores on the annual state assessment battery, and rated his background knowledge and performance on science projects exceptional. Usually the first to complete classroom tasks, Colin insisted on helping others to finish their work so they would join him to draw bugs for his collection. The teacher eventually consulted with the school psychologist and presented a portfolio of Colin's work with drawings, list of books read, sample stories, and anecdotal records of disruptive incidents.

After reviewing school records, the school psychologist administered cognitive and academic measures, an interest survey, and the Gifted Rating Scales. The school psychologist also observed Colin building an animal habitat in the classroom, explaining to peers why they should eat their fruits and vegetables at lunch, and looking for insects at recess. An interview with Colin's mother revealed that Colin learned to read prior to entering kindergarten, had an interest in collecting things, fought with siblings to watch the Discovery Channel, and was generally able to keep siblings "in line."

Upon reviewing all case study findings, the educational team concluded that Colin was eligible to enroll in the gifted program. Colin's Differentiated Education Plan included activities such as creating an interest center on insects for the class, an independent project to study butterfly behavior at the Butterfly Pavilion of the Natural History Museum, and a social skills program to help Colin develop self-awareness, self-regulation, and interpersonal skills.

Promoting Psychosocial Development

Colin's case study highlights the importance of monitoring the development of gifted children, as recommended by researchers such as Wellisch and Brown (2012). However, the psychosocial competencies of the gifted have been a source of controversy. Some studies suggest that gifted children are at risk for social and emotional difficulties, and others propose that the gifted possess protective factors that enhance their interpersonal skills and place them at a social advantage over typical peers. Janos and Robinson (1985) stated that 20–25% of gifted children experienced social and/or emotional difficulties at a rate that is about twice that of nongifted students. More recently, Peterson and Ray (2006) have reported that in elementary school, gifted students frequently experience teasing about their intelligence or academic prowess beginning in kindergarten and peaking in sixth grade.

Other studies have found no significant difference between gifted and nongifted children in rates of depression, anxiety, suicidal ideation, neuroticism, behavior problems, and difficulty with peer relationships. Neihart, Reis, Robinson, and Moon (2002) concluded that there was "no evidence that gifted children or youth—as a group—are inherently any more vulnerable or flawed in adjustment than any other group" (p. 268). In a more recent study, Wellisch et al. (2011) studied 80 families in New Zealand and Australia and found that parents did not report any significant difference in internalizing or externalizing behavior problems between children with IQs at or over 120 and children with IQs below 120.

School psychologists interested in counseling this population may want to explore factors that uniquely affect gifted and creative students. For example, gifted young children (as well as their parents, caregivers, and teacher) need help to understand and accept that they may have exceptional abilities in some areas but not in others. School psychologists may work closely with parents and teachers to develop a Differentiated Education Plan for children who manifest attention deficit hyperactivity, outlining structured as well as spontaneous self-selected classroom activities.

For gifted children prone to maladaptive anxiety, perfectionism, and explosive behavior, school psychologists can assist these children to set realistic goals and carefully manage steps to start and complete specific objectives. Individual and group counseling may help curb tendencies to being critical of self and others, and to build social skills and develop friendships. Positive psychology tenets may be beneficial in teaching young people to identify and capitalize on their signature strengths and develop the social virtues such as gratitude, perseverance, and kindness, which can increase student enjoyment and engagement in school and improve academics as well as social relationships.

Another stress for gifted young people is career planning. Since young gifted students frequently have the potential to succeed in different areas (multipotentiality), they may have difficulty deciding on a specific career track. School psychologists may want to facilitate group sessions where young people explore the value of pursuing their passions versus practical or arbitrary career paths.

Supporting Families

School psychologists can also help to promote home–school–community relationships by facilitating parent workshops and providing resources such as the National Association for Gifted Children's *Mile Marker Series,* a CD-ROM that maps out a wealth of information to better understand and nurture the gifted child. Another resource, the Illinois State Board of Education Gifted Education Seminar Parent Module, guides parents to discuss topics like perspectives on giftedness, motivation, relationships, discipline, stress management, and advocacy. Participants conclude the module by drafting a personal action plan to guide a gifted child. Those interested in further information may contact the Illinois State Board of Education.

Supporting families may include guiding parents to enroll their children in charter or university schools or even home schooling. School psychologists can provide varied resources and counsel parents through the process. Home schooling might be considered under varied circumstances: when a child's academic and emotional development are at extremes, when high levels of intensity and perfectionism require the understanding of patient adults able to research and discuss areas of interest at will, and when a child thinks in divergent and creative ways with unbridled curiosity and intense drive. Profoundly intellectually gifted and multitalented youth with a diagnosed medical or behavioral condition may be better served through independent learning experiences. It is important to remember that families pay taxes and are entitled to appropriate support services from the public school.

Consulting With Teachers

School psychologists can also support teachers by evaluating academic interventions, enrichment and service learning experiences, or promoting appropriate classroom behavior. Some gifted children can be rambunctious, impulsive and opinionated, or introverted, and capable of intense focus in areas of interest and thus resist transitions in the regular classroom. These behaviors can be confused with symptoms for attention deficit, autism spectrum, and conduct and obsessive–compulsive disorders (Webb et al., 2005). School psychologists knowledgeable about giftedness in children can help determine the need for appropriate educational and/or behavioral interventions or referral for medical consultation. Carefully designed and evaluated, these interventions can potentially improve classroom practices and add to badly needed research in the field of gifted education.

Consulting With Administrators

School psychologists can become critical members of the district gifted identification and curriculum team by participating in activities such as conducting needs assessments and interviewing stakeholders, designing inclusive and equitable identification practices, implementing instructional models that serve the "whole child," systematically evaluating programs and services, and staying abreast of federal reform initiatives to ensure they include the gifted.

Expanding Professional Knowledge

If school psychologists choose to develop a specialty in gifted education, they may need to expand their knowledge base by participating in university courses and attending state and national conferences, special workshops, or webinars by organizations such as the National Association for Gifted Children (http://www.nagc.org) and its state affiliates or Supporting Emotional Needs of the Gifted (http://www.sengifted.org). Another option might be participating in the Gifted Education Seminar series, developed and piloted by the Illinois State Board of Education in 2010 and 2011.

Promoting Advocacy and Research

School psychologists may choose to become involved in gifted organizations to stay abreast of national legislative issues and how these may have an impact on gifted students. For example, they should be aware that the Common Core State Standards are insufficient to meet the needs of gifted learners. According to the National Association for Gifted Children, gifted students still require supplementary activities and materials, if not replacement of the curriculum through independent learning experiences, mentorships, or apprenticeships.

School psychologists are in a position to promote and contribute to needed research in the field of gifted identification and assessment. Potential areas for further study include defining innovative ways to identify high-ability learners with atypical learning profiles and those from diverse home and life experiences, researching the comparative efficacy of various instructional models, exploring the impact of the independent learning movement on our public schools, researching the role of mentoring and internships, and studying the social and emotional development of gifted youth.

Evaluating Effectiveness of Services

The NASP Practice Model (NASP, 2010) includes standards that school psychologists can use to evaluate their services. They can formulate questionnaires to survey levels of satisfaction from various stakeholders: the students, teachers, administrators, and families. Questionnaires may include items such as: Do we implement prevention-oriented services that promote a positive school climate in which gifted and talented learners are respected and valued? Do we support teacher efforts to extend or replace the curriculum for gifted learners through mentorships or apprenticeships? Do we collaborate with the administration in the design and evaluation of gifted programming and related services? Do we participate in professional development to stay informed of best practices and policies that have an impact on gifted students? Do we maintain current resources for families to support their children as they transition from primary to intermediate grades, through high school, and beyond? Do we advocate for policies and funding to ensure gifted and talented students have a right to equitable educational services? Focus groups can also be conducted. Once the data are analyzed, school psychologists can report the findings and recommendations orally and in print to appropriate stakeholders.

SUMMARY

Recent studies confirm the existence of "excellence gaps" or languishing progress among top students across our nation's public schools. Reasons for this untenable situation vary from a traditional democratic focus on helping struggling students achieve basic competency levels and limited understanding or misunderstanding of giftedness in children and confusion on how to best meet their needs, to sporadic national legislation and insufficient funding to support an inchoate system to educate our most able learners. The tide is changing, however, and educators, community leaders, policy makers, and the general public are becoming increasingly aware that, to ensure growth and national security in a competitive global society, the United States must see that *all* children, including the gifted, have equal opportunity to fulfill their potential.

School psychologists are uniquely poised to support this population with additional individual study and professional development. The NASP Practice Model (NASP, 2010) provides a framework that outlines five service areas. The present chapter has described the knowledge, skills, and special methods to be acquired or developed to service high aptitude learners. Giftedness exists in all groups of students regardless of race, ethnicity, and socioeconomic background. But school psychologists need to become sensitive to how giftedness is manifested in special populations, including those with exceptional abilities and diverse home and life experiences. In general, the use of multiple measures, local norms, and input from varied sources are recommended to identify gifted learners from minority groups.

School psychologists interested in proven instructional methods may want to look further into ability grouping, acceleration, enrichment, and cluster grouping. As part of the RTI process and problem-solving team, school psychologists can be instrumental in guiding, monitoring, and evaluating curricular and enrichment interventions. Acceleration, the process of advancing students to reach competencies commensurate with their readiness levels and potential, for example, has widespread research support as an effective and economical approach to serve academically talented students. The more recent, cost-effective, school-wide, cluster-grouping model has also been found to challenge the gifted in peer groups, but also to motivate high achievers to assume leadership roles in the absence of gifted classmates.

With increased knowledge and sensitive awareness of the characteristics and unique needs of gifted, creative, and talented learners, school psychologists already possess basic background and competencies to promote their social and emotional development. School psychologists acutely recognize that intellectual ability and achievement are not sufficient to bring about personal fulfillment and success in life. They can thus be instrumental in creating opportunities for gifted students to develop self-knowledge, self-regulation, and effective social skills to become responsible decision makers.

Finally, school psychologists who are knowledgeable about gifted education and choose to stay current on trends, policies, and initiatives for educational reform can play a pivotal role as consultants to teachers, administrators, and families, but also as advocates and researchers to promote best practices in the education of gifted students.

REFERENCES

Beal, A. L. (1996). A comparison of WISC-III and OLSAT-6 for the identification of gifted students. *Canadian Journal of School Psychology*, *11*, 120–129.

Bianco, M. (2005). The effects of disability labels on special education and general education teachers' referrals for gifted programs. *Learning Disability Quarterly*, *28*, 285–293.

Bianco, M. (2010). Strength-based RTI: Conceptualizing a multi-tiered system for developing gifted potential. *Theory Into Practice*, *49*, 323–330.

Bianco, M., Harris, B., Garrison-Wade, D., & Leech, N. (2012). Gifted girls: Gender bias in gifted referrals. *Roeper Review*, *33*, 170–181.

Colangelo, N., Assouline, S. G., & Gross, M. U. M. (2004). *A nation deceived: How schools hold back America's brightest students*. Iowa City, IA: University of Iowa.

Donovan, S., & Cross, C. (2002). *Minority students in special and gifted education*. Washington, DC: National Academies Press.

Fleischman, H. L., Hopstock, P. J., Pelczar, M. P., & Shelley, B. E. (2010). *Highlights from PISA 2009: Performance of U.S. 15-year-old students in reading, mathematics and science literacy in an international context*. Washington, DC: National Center for Education Statistics.

Frasier, M., & Passow, A. H. (1994). *Toward a new paradigm for identifying talent potential* (RM94112). Storrs, CT: University of Connecticut, National Research Center on the Gifted and Talented.

Gardner, H. (1993). *Multiple intelligences: The theory in practice*. New York, NY: Basic Books.

Janos, P. M., & Robinson, N. M. (1985). Psychosocial development in intellectually gifted children. In F. Horowitz & M. O'Brien (Eds.), *The gifted and talented: Developmental perspectives* (pp. 149–195). Washington, DC: American Psychological Association.

Lemons, G. (2011). Diverse perspectives of creativity testing: Controversial issues when used for inclusion into gifted programs. *Journal for the Education of the Gifted*, *34*, 742–772. doi:10.1177/0162353211417221

Lohman, D., Korb, K., & Lakin, J. (2008). Identifying academically gifted English-language learners using nonverbal tests: A comparison of the Raven, NNAT, and CogAT. *Gifted Child Quarterly*, *52*, 275–296. doi:10.1177/0016986208321808

Loveless, T., Farkas, S., & Duffet, A. (2008). *High-achieving students in an era of NCLB: Report of National Assessment of Educational Progress*. Washington, DC: National Center for Education Statistics.

McClain, M., & Pfeiffer, S. (2012). Identification of gifted students in the United States today: A look at state definitions, policies, and practices. *Journal of Applied School Psychology*, *28*, 59–88.

Merrick, C., & Targett, R. (2004). *Gifted and talented education: Professional development package for teachers: Module 2*. Sydney, New South Wales, Australia: GERRIC. Retrieved from https://www.det.nsw.edu.au/mediaLibrary/Docs/1/db47f089-37c9-461c-bf28-5ac086ff2407.pdf

Mitra-Itle, N. (2011). *Ethical considerations for gifted assessment and identification of diverse students*. Bethesda, MD: National Association of School Psychologists. Retrieved from http://www.nasponline.org/conventions/2011/handouts/pa/Ethics%20and%20Gifted%20Identification.pdf

Moon, R. R., & Brighton, C. M. (2008). Primary teachers' conceptions of giftedness. *Journal for the Education of the Gifted*, *31*, 447–480.

Naglieri, J. A., & Ford, D. Y. (2005). Increasing minority children's participation in gifted classes using the NNAT: A response to Lohman. *Gifted Child Quarterly*, *49*, 29–36.

National Association for Gifted Children. (2010). *State of the states in gifted education: National policy and practice data 2008–2009*. Washington, DC: Author. http://www.nagc.org/uploadedFiles/Advocacy/State%20definitions%20(8-24-10).pdf

National Association of School Psychologists. (2010). *Model for comprehensive and integrated school psychological services*. Bethesda, MD: Author. Retrieved from http://www.nasponline.org/standards/2010standards/2_PracticeModel.pdf

National Center for Education Statistics. (2012). *Digest of education*. Washington, DC: Author.

Neihart, M., Reis, S. M., Robinson, N. M., & Moon, S. M. (Eds.). (2002). *The social and emotional development of gifted children: What do we know?* St. Paul, MN: Prufrock Press.

Peterson, J. S., & Ray, K. E. (2006). Bullying and the gifted: Victims, perpetrators, prevalence, and effects. *Gifted Child Quarterly*, *50*, 148–168.

Pfeiffer, S. I. (2012). *Serving the gifted: Evidence-based clinical and psychoeducational practice*. New York, NY: Routledge.

Plucker, J., Burroughs, N., & Song, R. (2010). *Mind the (other) gap! The growing excellence gap in K–12 education*. Bloomington, IN: Center for Evaluation and Education Policy.

Renzulli, J. S. (1978). What makes giftedness? Reexamining a definition. *Phi Delta Kappan*, *60*, 180–184.

Renzulli, J. S. (1997). *Interest-a-Lyzer family of instruments: A manual for teachers*. Waco, TX: Prufrock Press.

Renzulli, J. S., & Reis, S. (1985). *School-Wide Enrichment Model: Executive summary*. Storrs, CT: University of Connecticut. Retrieved from http://www.gifted.uconn.edu/sem/semexec.html

Robertson, S., Pfeiffer, S., & Taylor, N. (2011). Serving the gifted: A national survey of school psychologists. *Psychology in the Schools*, *48*, 786–799. doi:10.1002/pits.20590

Sternberg, R. J. (2005). The WICS model of giftedness. In R. J. Sternberg & J. E. Davidson (Eds.), *Conceptions of giftedness* (2nd ed., pp. 327–342). New York, NY: Cambridge University Press.

Subotnik, R. F., Olszewski-Kubilius, P., & Worrell, F. C. (2011). Rethinking giftedness and gifted education: A proposed direction forward based on psychological science. *Psychological Science in the Public Interest*, *12*, 3–54.

Webb, J. T., Amend, E. R., Webb, N. E., Goerss, J., Beljan, P., & Olenchak, F. R. (2005). *Misdiagnosis and dual diagnoses of gifted children and adults*. Tucson, AZ: Great Potential Press.

Wellisch, M., & Brown, J. (2012). An integrated identification and intervention model for intellectually gifted children. *Journal of Advanced Academics, 23*, 145–167. doi:10.1177/1932202X12438877

Wellisch, M., Brown, J., Taylor, A., Knight, R., Berresford, L., Campbell, L., & Cohen, A. (2011). Secure attachment and high IQ: Are gifted children better adjusted? *The Australasian Journal of Gifted Education, 20*, 24–33.

Winebrenner, S., & Brulles, D. (2008). *The cluster grouping handbook: How to challenge gifted students and improve achievement for all.* Minneapolis, MN: Free Spirit.

Winner, E. (2000). The origins and ends of giftedness. *American Psychologist, 55*, 159–169.

Worrell, F., & Erwin, J. (2011). Best practices in identifying students for gifted and talented education programs. *Journal of Applied School Psychology, 27*, 319–340.

Xiang, Y., Dahlin, M., Cronin, J., Theaker, R., & Durant, S. (2011). *Do high flyers maintain their altitude? Performance trends of top students.* Washington, DC: Thomas B. Fordham Institute.

12 Best Practices in Planning for Effective Transition From School to Work for Students With Disabilities

Fred Jay Krieg
Sandra S. Stroebel
Holly Bond Farrell
Marshall University (WV)

OVERVIEW

Transition planning involves preparing students to leave high school and enter the workforce. Effective transition planning for students with disabilities is essential for these students to have a high quality lifestyle, including successful employment. Schools must collaborate with local businesses and community agencies to develop a true working relationship that includes on-the-job training for these students. School psychologists, with their unique skills, knowledge of federal law, awareness of current trends in education, relationships within the community, and familiarity with disabilities are in a key position to facilitate this collaboration and help students make the transition from school to work.

The National Association of School Psychologists (NASP) *Model for Comprehensive and Integrated School Psychological Services* (NASP, 2010) domain of Interventions and Instructional Support to Develop Academic Skills defines the skills and expectations for school psychologists to practice. In this role, school psychologists help develop appropriate goals for students, enhance home–school collaboration, and encourage data-based decision making related to school-to-work transition. Specifically, this chapter will provide information concerning how school psychologists can support the transition services in their schools, including roles of school psychologists in transition planning, legal foundations of transition planning requirements, key members of transition teams and their responsibilities, a best practices model for transition planning, and skills required for students with disabilities to transition successfully into the world of work.

The need for effective transition planning is clearly evident. Lack of successful transition planning has resulted in high rates of unemployment and underemployment for students with disabilities. As reported by the National Council on Disability (2007), students with disabilities have lower rates of employment (38% of adults with disabilities are employed compared to 63% of the general population) and are underrepresented in high growth fields. The majority of adults with disabilities are employed in service and blue-collar sectors. Only 17% of people with severe disabilities (those who need help with self-care and going outside of the home) are employed. There is also a wage gap between workers with disabilities and those without (National Council on Disability, 2007). Students with more severe disabilities have been found to earn less than those with more moderate disabilities (Estrada-Hernandez, Wadsworth, Nietupski, Warth, & Winslow, 2008). The cost to society is enormous and the need to reverse these trends is evident.

What the Laws Mandate

There are several laws that have provided the foundation for transition planning in schools. These laws and their requirements are outlined in Table 12.1.

Table 12.1. Laws Affecting Transition Services

Law/Regulation	Date	Requirements for Transition Planning
Americans with Disabilities Act	1990	• Mandates equal access to employment for individuals with disabilities • Requires workplace modifications for individuals with disabilities • Prohibits discrimination of individuals with disabilities in hiring
School-to-Work Opportunity Act	1994	• Establishes relationships between secondary and postsecondary education institutions • Provides work experience and planned programs of job training • Utilizes workplace mentoring
No Child Left Behind Act	2002	• Requires documentation of successful outcomes for students with disabilities
Individuals with Disabilities Improvement Act	2004	• Requires schools to provide transition services to students with disabilities • Encourages outcome-oriented goals • Focuses on student needs and preferences • Includes instruction in the development of employment and postschool living skills • Requires services to begin no later than 16
Carl D. Perkins Vocational and Applied Technology Education Act; Carl D. Perkins Career and Technical Education Act	2006	• Provides for assistance in entry to vocational education programs for students with disabilities • Assesses individual needs of students • Specifies that supplementary services and modifications be provided for students with disabilities • Provides career counseling for students

Relationship to Problem-Solving Model

School psychologists implement transition services using a decision-making model. To be effective, schools must develop relationships with businesses and community agencies to provide optimal transition services for students. However, often agencies and businesses that collaborate with schools are not familiar with this decision-making model used by school psychologists. Even when familiar, the appropriate daily usage of the model may be lacking in schools or businesses. To ensure proper implementation, a continuous improvement process needs to be implemented. This process includes a coherent definition of the problem, appropriate data collection, clearly articulated goals, identification of barriers, research-based interventions, and alignment of resources to needs. The data presented should justify the identified plan of action. Last, the plan must include an evaluation plan to complete the loop of continuous improvement.

Transition and the Three Tier Model

Transition planning is a Tier 3 activity. Transition services are designed for special education students to give them extra assistance with post high school plans. According to the Individuals with Disabilities Improvement Act (IDEIA), transition needs should be adopted into the Individualized Education Program (IEP) starting at age 16. Since the introduction of a three-tiered instructional model, special education students have more often than not been trained within the regular classroom setting. As a result they tend to view themselves as being more capable than did previous generations of students with disabilities. As students move into secondary education, the differentiation between students with mild disabilities who have the potential for postsecondary education and those for whom that possibility does not exist becomes clearer. As a result, transition planning requires specifically defined interventions that are high quality, scientifically based, and matched to student needs. Well-integrated transition plans will coordinate school services with the efforts and practices of business and community agencies.

The best school-to-work programs are developmental as well as comprehensive in nature, and are designed to begin at the elementary level, giving children increasingly complex knowledge about the world of work, even for children without disabilities (Thomas & Dykes, 2010). These school-wide Tier 1 services continue to be expanded with early career planning, which include interest inventories and career awareness activities in later elementary and middle school. Students need to gain an understanding of their interests and abilities as well as an understanding of the world of work. Tier 2 activities will focus on those students who do not appear to be college bound, are in need of extra assistance in planning and require additional support services, and who are not identified as special education students.

BASIC CONSIDERATIONS

Effective transition services for students with disabilities result in stable full-time employment including benefits. In order to achieve this, a collaborative team process rather than a cooperative relationship is essential. Members of the team must understand the difference between being cooperative, where each agency maintains its own goals and objectives, and being collaborative, where the transition team develops a common goal and has shared responsibility and mutual accountability (Gostick & Elton, 2010). The transition team should consist of a small number of people with complementary skills who are equally committed to the common purpose of employing students with disabilities. The team must hold each member mutually accountable for successful transitions (Hartman, 2009). The school psychologist is uniquely equipped to foster the collaborative relationship between case workers, parents, students, administrators, and agency representatives.

The process of planning for the transition from student to adult life cannot be successful without the student being a key member of the transition team. Students must be involved in data gathering and problem solving to ensure that the transition plans are realistic, meaningful, and student centered. Successful transition cannot be accomplished solely by professional team members; it must include family involvement and student self-determination (Wehmeyer, Field, & Thoma, 2012). School psychologists are in a unique position to advocate for families.

If transition plans are not realistic and meaningful, then the desired result of successful employment and engagement in adult life is unlikely to be achieved. The implementation of transition teams that focus on realistic planning and student support are likely a contributing factor in the decrease in dropout rates for students with disabilities.

The National Center for Educational Statistics (2013) reports that in 2009 the dropout rate for students with disabilities was not significantly different from the dropout rate for students without disabilities. According to the U.S. Department of Education (2011b), successful dropout prevention programs for students with disabilities feature consistent monitoring of students including attendance rates, detentions, and suspensions and include a focus on academic performance. Additional best practices in this area consist of providing additional academic support, using in-depth problem solving to address obstacles, and coordination with community support services to help prevent students with disabilities from dropping out.

BEST PRACTICES IN PLANNING EFFECTIVE SCHOOL-TO-WORK TRANSITION

Within the transition literature, research has not clearly identified the best model for effective transition services. The What Works Transition Research Synthesis Project of Colorado State University (http://www.nsttac.org/content/what-works-transition-research-synthesis) reviewed and synthesized 20 years of research and advancements in the area of transition for youth with disabilities. However, there were not enough studies with methodological adequacy to assess collaborative service delivery or program structures (Cobb & Alwell, 2009).

Based on our experiences working in schools, the following model is proposed. (See Figure 12.1.) In order to implement the model, two separate but integrated teams need to be established. The internal team is the school transition team, which consists of school personnel whose role is to teach students the prerequisite employment skills and the necessary social skills to be successful in the workplace. A second team, the external team (external to the school system but not the school environment), is responsible for developing the community commitment, relationships, and resources to be used by students as they prepare to transfer to outside employment. Although the development and implementation of the transition IEP rests within the school system, it cannot be successfully executed without an effective external team.

A transition coordinator, employed by the school system, must chair both teams and serve as a link between the two. Given the practice model that delineates the knowledge and skills of a school psychologist, it is apparent that the school psychologist is the ideal person to serve as the transition coordinator. However, owing to the shortage of and the need for school psychologists to serve in many other capacities of critical need deemed more valuable than transition planning, a survey of transition coordinators found an overwhelming number were not school psychologists but more frequently special education teachers. When this occurs, the role of the school psychologist becomes that of a consultant, another position for which the school psychologist is well trained. As consultant, the school

Figure 12.1. Transition Process

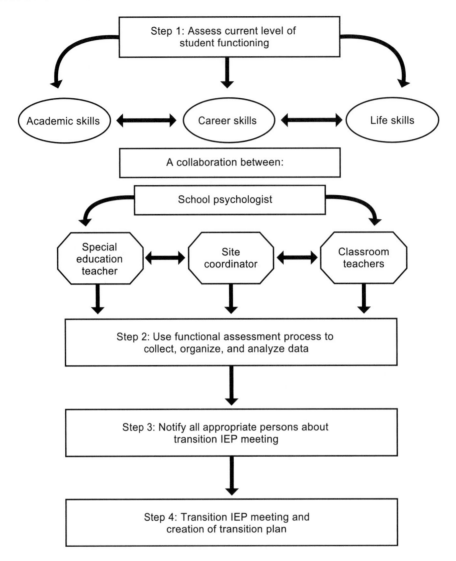

psychologist must work closely with the transition coordinator to ensure that data-based decision making, involvement of the family, communication with the community-based agencies, and evaluation of services are occurring.

Transition Coordinator

The key to having the two teams, internal and external, working collaboratively is the careful selection of the person for the transition coordinator position. This person could be the school psychologist, the director of special services, or a special education teacher. Depending on the size of the school district, this position can be full or part time. The transition coordinator must possess excellent interpersonal skills, leadership qualities, knowledge of community resources, and understanding

of handicapping conditions. Transition team development, program organization, and direct services to students are the foremost responsibilities of the transition coordinator. The individual in this role acts as a liaison between the school, the home, and community involved in the transition process.

A school site mentor, who works in a manner similar to a case manager, is a professional employed at the school who is designated as the advocate for a particular student and who consults with classroom teachers, counselors, related services personnel, and the employer of the student to design and monitor the progress of the student's plan. Interviews of students have shown the desirability of having a mentor to provide guidance (Trainor, Carter, & Swedeen, 2012). There is remarkable similarity in the job descriptions of the school site mentor and the transition coordinator. However, each site mentor manages only a few cases whereas the transition coordinator has the overriding responsibility of the entire transition process. The transition coordinator serves as the supervisor of the school site mentors.

If the transition team program is new to the school district, then the transition coordinator will have the important role of forming the teams. If teams are already in place, then the coordinator will be responsible for filling vacancies. As the team begins to create the service delivery system that will meet the needs of the student population in the community, the transition coordinator will be responsible for coordinating these services. A long-range plan needs to be developed by the transition coordinator that should include the following objectives:

- Prioritize concerns identified by needs assessments.
- Identify and evaluate existing programs and resources.
- Coordinate planning between local school agency, vocational agencies, and postschool institutions.
- Develop jobs.
- Arrange on-site visits to successful programs.
- Create ideas for innovative, alternative programs.
- Establish and evaluate time lines within the high school curriculum for vocational interest and aptitude assessments, career exploration with job experiences, and individual vocational assessments.
- Establish a system for following students after they leave high school to determine the effectiveness of transition planning.
- Consider interagency agreement with other agencies regarding evaluation and assessment of students so that efforts are not duplicated.
- Provide leadership and inservice training in transition for staff of local school agencies, community agencies, and the business community.
- Maintain a high level of knowledge regarding transition research, funding sources, materials, technology resources, and best practices.

In addition, the transition coordinator should ensure that meaningful work experiences and employment are readily available when students begin considering their job search. With the assistance of the school site mentors and various businesses, the link between student and employer must be established in a manner that is mutually beneficial for all. The skills needed for a job, from assessment to specific IEP goals, need to be developed in conjunction with the postsecondary site in order to ensure a successful transition. The transition coordinator ensures that each student has developed appropriate skills as indicated previously and is ready to use those skills to the benefit of the receiving business. The earlier a plan is in place, the more likely the student will stay in school, use the transition services developed through the IEP, and have a favorable outcome. The goal is the successful completion of the IEP, which, if executed properly, should result in successful transition. Finally, the transition coordinator monitors the district's compliance with state and federal regulations (Luecking & Buchanan, 2012).

Transition coordinators are also responsible for the evaluation of the program they supervise. Transition program evaluation is the key to a successful program and can be advantageous for numerous reasons. Program evaluation helps meet legislation requirements by documenting progress toward student goals and objectives. By locating strengths and weaknesses in the transition program, evaluation can help determine curriculum effectiveness and required changes necessary to address community needs. By tracking students that leave secondary school, vital information can be gained in order to design, improve, and/or revise transition services. These data must be shared with both the internal and external transition teams.

If the school psychologist is not the transition coordinator, then the role of the school psychologist is to use the practice model skills of program evaluation to assist the transition coordinator in determining if the organization as a whole is working and includes the appraisal of the school and work community. Program evaluation should be both formative and summative and should influence the development and implementation of future transition planning. It should also have an impact on the education policies related to the system as a whole, in the short term as well as the long term. The ultimate goal is to determine the efficiency and effectiveness of current programs (Posavac, 2010).

School-Linked Services

Once the two teams are formed, schools must nurture the school community relationship by permitting outside agencies access to the school when students are present. A collaborative relationship between schools, community agencies, and local businesses is fostered by inviting partners into the school to provide their services to students who are readily accessible during the school day. The recent Supreme Court decision to uphold the Patient Protection and Affordable Care Act (ACA) provides an example of how mental health services can be delivered to students within the school setting. The ACA authorized new funding for school-based health clinics, which serves as a model for school-linked services. An office in the school building can be provided for use by external agencies. Students will know that on a particular day a representative of a given agency will be in the building and they can arrange their schedule accordingly. This easy access of students to outside agencies and vice versa helps to strengthen the collaborative relationship. The desired outcome is to extend the relationship developed in the school into the youth's adult life.

Decisions about which agencies and what services to provide are made by the transition coordinator with input from both the internal and external transition teams. Bringing agencies into schools in this manner strengthens relationships, facilitates the use of services, decreases stigmatization, and improves integration of services.

Stages for IEP

The second step is development and implementation of the transition IEP, which unfolds in four main stages. The first stage is the procurement of basic information about the student's levels of functioning in academic skills, life skills, and career skills. This stage is done at the pre-IEP meeting, which is attended by the school mentor, classroom teachers, transition coordinator, the school site mentor, and the special education teacher. In the second stage any assessment data are collected. In the third stage, notifications of all persons and agencies invited to attend the meeting are made. The transition coordinator, knowledgeable about students' needs and the community and business resources, is able to link these two by inviting the appropriate parties. The fourth stage is composed of the IEP meeting where the student's transition needs are addressed and integrated into the transition IEP.

Assessment Strategies

To develop an appropriate transition IEP, students need to be assessed for their strengths and weaknesses. Student skills necessary for successful transition into employment are outlined in Table 12.2. The teaching of these skills requires a shift in educational focus for these students at the secondary level. The focus of their secondary education becomes employment skills, replacing the remedial education focus of the past. In addition to employment skills, the student with disabilities will require extensive instruction in social and personal skills in order to enhance employability and social competencies. School psychologists should guide the school system in developing a plan to teach social competence, self-responsibility, and interpersonal skills.

Table 12.2. 21st Century Skills Needed for Successful Employment

Academic Skills	Life Skills	Career Skills
Core academic subjects • Language arts • Math • Science • Art • History	*Personal awareness* • Self-esteem • Interpersonal relations • Self-responsibility • Self-advocacy	*Career assessment and abilities* • Interests • Limitations • Ethics/values • Accommodations • Needs
Content skills • Global awareness • Civic literacy • Economic literacy • Business literacy	*Skills of daily living* • Appropriate dress • Social rules • Personal productivity • Health and wellness awareness	*Career planning* • Interest assessment • Career exploration • Vocational training
Learning and thinking skills • Critical thinking • Problem solving • Collaboration	*Social skills* • Communication skills • Flexibility/adaptability • Personal productivity • Self-direction • People skills	*Career skills* • Leadership • Personal productivity • Social responsibility • Collaboration
Information media and technology skills • Computer and Internet skills • Work technology		

Within this context, school teams should work collaboratively with personnel from local, state, and federal agencies to merge resources and develop the supports essential for students with disabilities to make a positive and successful transition from school to work and into the community (Kellems & Morningstar, 2010).

Assessments must measure the areas identified in Table 12.2 through standardized testing, as well as competency-based testing (Partnership for 21st Century Skills, 2011). Assessment results help teachers, parents, and students make decisions about curriculum needs and aid the team members in developing IEP goals and objectives. The assessment data also provide guidance as to which placement in the community or business will most likely be beneficial and successful. The customized IEP developed through this process must be consistent with the stated objectives and desires of the student and his or her family (Test, 2012).

Functional Assessment

Functional assessment appraises the difficult-to-quantify cognitive aspects, such as the ability to learn and solve problems, and allows the evaluator the opportunity to observe how an individual uses knowledge and problem-solving skills. Furthermore, a functional assessment identifies and targets the obstacles to goal accomplishment in the context of the demand placed on the individual in a real-life situation. Constructing the assessment so that the student is required to perform a task in a natural or simulated setting rather than on paper in the classroom is what defines the functional nature of the assessment.

Interest Surveys

IDEIA requires that transition planning consider the student's interests when selecting vocational placements. Information from a student interest survey can be used to get information on work experience, current employment or career goals, interests in vocational activities, and participation in community programs and services. Vocational interest tools include the Self-Directed Search, the Strong Interest Inventory, the Career Key, Career Decision-Making System-Revised, IDEAS: Interest Determination Exploration and Assessment System, and the Occupational Aptitude Survey and Interest Assessment-Second Edition.

Self-Determination

Self-determination is linked to successful postsecondary outcomes (Cobb, Lehmann, & Newman-Gonchar, 2009). Instruments are available to identify students' strengths

and limitations with regard to self-determination. The Arc's Self-Determination Scale (adolescent version) is a 72 item instrument that assesses autonomy, self-regulation, psychological empowerment, and self-realization. The Self-Determination Assessment Battery consists of five instruments, one of which is a 37-item scale to assess the student's cognitive knowledge of self-determination skills. There are also parent and teacher perception scales and an observation checklist.

Vocational Evaluations

Vocational evaluations provide the student with an increased awareness of career options and a better understanding of his or her own personal abilities, capacity, and potential. Included in a vocational evaluation is a work exploration experience that exposes the student to different environments and job tasks and helps the student determine his or her preferences (Condon & Callahan, 2008). Available instruments include the Differential Aptitude Test and the Armed Services Vocational Aptitude Battery.

The following objectives are generally met in a vocational evaluation: (a) acquire knowledge of a student's work personality, (b) estimate the impact of a student's disability on his or her performance, (c) determine change possibilities of the work personality, (d) estimate training capacity (ability to benefit from formal learning, informal learning, or experimental learning in a work setting), and (e) project future levels and types of work activities.

Vocational Personality Types

Holland (1997) developed a theory to predict the characteristics of people and environments that lead to positive or negative vocational outcomes, as well as the characteristics that lead to vocational permanence. His theory was based on the idea that vocational career choice is an expression of an individual's personality. Thus, people within an occupation are similar. According to this theory, people can be categorized as belonging to one or more personality types: realistic, investigative, artistic, social, enterprising, and conventional. Each type of personality is thought to display a particular set of skills and values, as well as predict preferences for particular activities. Within this theory, environments were also categorized based on the vocational personality type of the preponderance of people within that work setting. The person and the environment connect when there is harmony between the person and the environment and when people are placed in positions where their skills can be utilized and their values expressed. Although Holland's work is more than 15 years old, its relevance to the vocational assessment process cannot be ignored, as congruence between personality and environment is a contributing factor in job satisfaction (Holland, 1997).

Interviews

Interviews give insights into the student's thoughts and preferences. Also, information about how a disability affects the student's daily living and the types of problems the disability may cause in the workplace can be obtained. Areas addressed during the interview include medical problems, family history, developmental background, social and leisure activities, educational background, work experience, career and job awareness, potential barrier to achieving goals, learning styles and preferences, vocational interests and goals, and oral communication ability. School psychologists are well trained in interviewing techniques and can perform this task for the team.

Assessment Tools and Methods

Portfolio development is becoming a common practice in education and has several applications in the transition process. Portfolios can be a marketing tool when offered to prospective employers or when self-employment is the goal; that is, it helps to outline self-employment alternatives with appropriate supports (Condon & Callahan, 2008). Portfolio development is also an excellent tool for promoting self-advocacy.

Other assessment tools are available including task analysis, comprehensive vocational evaluations (for students with more severe disabilities), and behavior rating scales. Instruments need to be selected that provide information to aid in transition IEP planning. When tailoring a school-to-work program, a variety of assessment methods and approaches should be evaluated and applied to situations where they best fit (Condon & Callahan, 2007).

Notification for Transition IEP Meeting

Once the transition teams have been formed, and all of the vital assessment information is collected, the formal IEP process can begin. Notification will allow all concerned parties an opportunity to prepare for the IEP meeting. As discussed earlier, part of the job description of the transition coordinator will be to know which people and agencies to invite to attend the IEP meeting and to make the necessary notifications.

The participation of the external team in the IEP meeting serves to provide opportunities for the enhanced development of the student's transition IEP. School-linked services and the opportunity for students to interact with employers in actual work situations helps the IEP team develop a more practical and viable IEP. A practical IEP guides the students training within the secondary school and results in a process that is less theoretical and more practical.

According to IDEIA, the student must be invited. If the student chooses not to attend, then his or her preferences must be documented and taken into consideration in keeping with federal law. Student interests can be obtained through an interest survey or interview. This procedure not only keeps the IEP in compliance with the law, but it also encourages the student to become involved in the decision-making process and affords an opportunity for the student to commit to the transition plan (Thoma & Wehman, 2010).

Under IDEIA, the IEP "must include a statement of transition services ... including, if appropriate, a statement of each public agency's and each participating agency's responsibilities or linkages, or both, before the student leaves the high school" (Section 300.346). Concerning agency participation, current law (Section 300.321) modifies previous regulations: Public agencies are still required to invite other agencies that are likely to be responsible for providing or paying for transition services to the student's IEP team meeting. However, if the invited agency does not send a representative, public agencies are no longer required to take additional steps to obtain the participation of those agencies in the planning of transition as required under former Section 300.344(b)(3)(ii).

Transition IEP Meeting

IEP development drives the transition planning process. Incorporating transition plans into the IEP requires listing goals and objectives to be mastered for the next year and must be chosen based on current levels of performance as well as potential future postsecondary options. The subskills and goals targeted on the student's IEP can be used to generate the coordinated set of activities mandated by IDEIA. This set of activities can be constructed by asking five fundamental questions as shown in Table 12.3. Plans to address goals or subskills that have not been mastered are addressed in the IEP with a projected date for mastery. These goals are written on the transition IEP and the student's transition profile.

The last step in the IEP meeting is assigning responsibilities for the transition services. The internal transition team will review the existing IEP to make sure

Table 12.3. Key Questions for IEP Development

Question	Activity
What instruction will the student need to master the target skills and realize projected adult outcomes?	Design instruction to match recognized areas of need.
What community experiences can be included in the plan to help the student master skills and achieve projected adult outcomes?	Develop community experiences that include targeted programs and services.
What objectives should be *developed* for employment and other postschool living settings?	Design objectives that will help the student to complete postschool living outcomes.
Does the student need a structured program to acquire daily living skills that will be required as an adult?	Develop individualized objectives and design activities that will help the student attain daily living skills.
Does the student require a functional vocational evaluation?	Create vocational assessment experiences in natural settings.

that progress is occurring toward achievement of the stated goals and objectives. Oversight is the responsibility of the school site mentor and ultimately the transition coordinator. The resultant transition IEP is then added to the student's current IEP. The transition IEP can be integrated into the regular IEP or it can be a separate document.

In addition to the IEP, IDEIA requires schools to complete a Summary of Performance and specifies that "a public agency must provide the child with a summary of the child's performance which shall include recommendations on how to assist the child in meeting the child's postsecondary goals" (Section 300.305(e)(3)). This document is separate from the IEP and describes the student's disability and how it affects school work and activities. Students are encouraged to describe which supports and accommodations have been helpful. The Summary of Performance is a bridge from special education services in high school to community agencies in the workplace, yet many schools are not using the form effectively.

It is even more critical now that some school districts are limiting the use of traditional psychoeducational evaluations in favor of response-to-intervention assessments. This practice may result in outdated documentation of disabilities (Shaw, Dukes, & Madaus, 2012). Agencies require current documentation of disabilities, the impact of the disability, and the need for accommodations. The Summary of Performance can provide agencies with this information and facilitates the continuity of services (U.S. Department of Education, 2011a).

Student/Parent Involvement

By law, students are required to be part of the transition process. The research demonstrates that the more the student participates in the process, and exercises decision making when appropriate, the better the outcome and the secondary gain of increasing self-advocacy skills is accomplished (Posavac, 2010). Students may require some training and preparation to ensure their comfort in a room full of adults. A balance must be reached between the personal interests, preferences, and actual skills necessary to accomplish the stated goal. However, students with disabilities often lack self-awareness of their strengths and weaknesses, as well as their need for accommodations. As described earlier, school-linked services increase the likelihood that students will continue to obtain support from community resources. It is crucial that students with disabilities develop the needed self-advocacy skills sooner rather than later (Trainor, 2007). The transition process is an excellent vehicle for developing self-determination. During the entire transition planning process, students should be encouraged to articulate and discuss their concerns, preferences, and conclusions about their options (Cobb et al., 2009).

The link between parent involvement and postsecondary success is as well established as the role of parents in school success (Test et al., 2009). Parents know their child better than anyone, and their accumulated personal experience with their child will provide team members with unique insights. Parents must support increased self-determination by their child by stepping back and allowing their child to advocate for himself or herself.

For some students with disabilities, parents have been an integral part of their lives, protecting them from a harsh world and working to educate others on the nature of their child's disability in order to provide the best accommodations and supports for their child. Many times the parents became the voice for their child. The child may have become excessively reliant on this, and may be either unable or unwilling to speak for and advocate for himself or herself. This outcome is likely due to the safety and comfort derived from the parent taking care of things or the fear of trying it out on his or her own. Likewise, after many years of taking care of their child's every need, it can be difficult for many parents to let go and allow the child to take care of some of his or her own needs. Parents may need emotional support as they move through the process of creating and fostering independence in their child. By encouraging parents to become involved in the school-to-work process, team members can educate parents on the importance of helping their child become a self-advocate.

School psychologists and other team members need to be sensitive to cultural factors that may influence parental beliefs about student participation, as well as their own ability to participate freely in the transition process. Schools may need to obtain interpreters to communicate with parents. It is important that the parents' cultural differences are respected. In some cases, parents may need training to participate effectively in the transition process. Computer-based instruction is available, and research has demonstrated that the use of this technology increases parental knowledge of post–high school services available (Rowe & Test, 2010).

Barriers to Transition Services

Barriers to providing transition services are numerous, as shown in Table 12.4. It is suggested that schools can overcome some of these barriers by partnering with other schools and area businesses. Most states have regional structures that provide support to schools. Area schools need to become aware of resources available through these organizations. Another resource that is underused is the family. Parents can play a role in networking in the community (Collet-Klingenberg & Kolb, 2011).

Case Study

Jason is 18 years old and attends a large suburban high school. Jason is moderately mentally impaired and has received some form of special education since he was 4 years old. He continues to receive speech and language services to improve his ability to speak and understand language. Jason receives all of his instruction in the special education classroom. Jason's mainstream experiences are limited to participation in homeroom and lunch. He is currently receiving instruction in reading and basic math skills, physical education, home economics, and industrial arts. Jason reads at approximately the third-grade level and has mastered only the very basic math skills. He

Table 12.4. Barriers to Transition

Barrier	Potential Solution
Lack of funding	• Obtain grants from government • Secure funds from local businesses • Partner with other schools to pool resources
Lack of parent involvement	• Provide evening functions • Use technology to reach busy parents • Make home visits
Lack of community involvement	• Invite community leaders to school functions • Set up lunches with community representatives • Hold a transition fair each year
Lack of transportation	• Obtain grants from the government • Explore public transportation options • Partner with other schools to pool resources
Few options in community	• Encourage job creation in students • Explore parent networking
Lack of coordination between agencies, which often results in competitive and duplicative efforts	• Facilitate meetings between agencies • Invite relevant partners to the IEP meeting
Confusion among parents and youth about what programs and services are available	• Improve communication through technology • Hold a transition fair each year • Distribute printed materials
Lack of career exploration programs in middle schools	• Use a tiered system to present vocational experiences to students

travels independently in his neighborhood by bicycle and takes the bus to and from school each day.

Transitional needs were discussed at the annual review held at the end of his sophomore year. It was decided that a vocational assessment would be completed. The assessment indicated that Jason had a variety of vocational interests, good eye–hand coordination, the ability to follow two-step verbal directions, and sufficient on-task behavior.

The transition plan was initiated in the fall of Jason's junior year during his IEP meeting. Jason and his parents agreed to the idea of a community vocational experience for Jason for a half of each school day. The purpose of the experience was to further assess career interests, to identify employment skills and training needs, and to develop the skills and attitudes necessary for paid employment.

Jason's parents would like for him to have more than one kind of work experience. Jason's teachers feel he needs a job coach to be with him when he travels in the community and when he is on the job. The speech therapist is concerned about Jason's communication skills in the workplace. The IEP was written to address these concerns. Jason has goals for communication, social skills, and self-efficacy.

A job coach is found for Jason, and through the activities of the transition team a community vocational experience at the local grocery store is arranged. He works with his job coach two afternoons a week at the grocery store, stocking shelves and bagging groceries. The job coach helps Jason learn the tasks of his job, and assists Jason in becoming acclimated to the work environment. Jason and his job coach take breaks with the other employees, where the job coach helps Jason learn appropriate ways to converse with his coworkers. As Jason becomes more comfortable in his job, his job coach gradually assists Jason less and less with Jason's work assignments.

Several months into the community vocational experience, the transition team meets again to discuss how it is going. Jason and his parents are both pleased with the experience, and the transition teams feels the experience is a successful one. It is decided that Jason will continue to work at the grocery store with his job coach for the remainder of the school year, at which point the team will meet again to consider other potential vocational placements for Jason.

SUMMARY

Schools are required to prepare students to be productive citizens, an increased challenge for students with disabilities. A complex technological infrastructure resulting in a new global economy has increased the difficulty of competitive survival for students with disabilities. One model for successful transition services is the development of an internal team of school professionals and an external team composed of community agencies and businesses. Collaboratively they will develop a transition IEP for students with disabilities by age 16 as required by special education law. Essential to the success of this endeavor is a school transition coordinator who bridges the gap between these teams and provides the link to build and deliver transitional services.

School psychologists, with their knowledge of assessment of intellectual ability and personality, dynamics of parental involvement, adolescent development, mental health counseling, legal rights and ethical issues, data collection, and program design and evaluation, are best positioned to make sure transition services are beneficial for students. Consistent with the NASP Practice Model (NASP, 2010), school psychologists need to be proactive in applying their skills to enhance the transition process. Having this knowledge and bringing it to the IEP and transition team meetings can provide greater understanding about the student to those helping plan the student's life after school.

It is also vital to have active parents, who facilitate their child becoming a self-advocate while fostering independence. Both the internal and external teams use a collaborative problem-solving model to develop the transition IEP, which is designed as an integrated agreement between the community, including local businesses and schools. Only when all of these components are in place can the transitioning of students from school to outside employment be successful.

AUTHOR NOTE

Disclosure. Fred Jay Krieg has a financial interest in books he authored or coauthored referenced in this chapter.

REFERENCES

Cobb, B., & Alwell, M. (2009). Transition planning/coordinating interventions for youth with disabilities: A systematic review. *Career Development for Exceptional Individuals, 32,* 70–81.

Cobb, B., Lehmann, J., & Newman-Gonchar, R. (2009). Self-determination for students with disabilities: A narrative metasynthesis. *Career Development for Exceptional Individuals, 32,* 108–114.

Collet-Klingenberg, L. L., & Kolb, S. M. (2011). Secondary and transition programming for 18–21 year old students in rural Wisconsin. *Rural Special Education Quarterly, 30*(2), 19–27.

Condon, E., & Callahan, M. (2008). Individualized career planning for students with significant support needs utilizing the discovery and vocational profile process, cross-agency collaborative funding and Social Security work incentives. *Journal of Vocational Rehabilitation, 28*, 85–96.

Estrada-Hernandez, N., Wadsworth, J. S., Nietupski, J. A., Warth, J., & Winslow, A. (2008). Employment or economic success: the experience of individuals with disabilities in transition from school to work. *Journal of Employment Counseling, 45*, 14–24.

Gostick, A., & Elton, C. (2010). *The orange revolution*. New York, NY: Free Press.

Hanley-Maxwell, C., & Izzo, M. (2012). Preparing students for the 21st century workforce. In M. L. Wehmeyer & K. W. Webb (Eds.), *Handbook of adolescent transition education for youth with disabilities* (pp. 162–178). New York, NY: Routledge.

Hartman, M. A. (2009). Step by step. *Teaching Exceptional Children, 41*(6), 6–11.

Holland, J. L. (1997). *Making vocational choices: A theory of vocational personalities and work environments* (3rd ed.). Odessa, FL: Psychological Assessment Resources.

Kellems, R., & Morningstar, M. (2010). Tips for transition. *Teaching Exceptional Children, 43*, 60–68.

Luecking, R. G., & Buchanan, L. A. (2012). Job development and placement in youth transition education. In M. L. Wehmeyer & K. W. Webb (Eds.), *Handbook of adolescent transition education for youth with disabilities* (pp. 11–31). New York, NY: Routledge.

National Association of School Psychologists. (2010). *Model for comprehensive and integrated school psychological services*. Bethesda, MD: Author. Retrieved from http://www.nasponline.org/standards/2010standards/2_PracticeModel.pdf

National Center for Educational Statistics. (2013). *Public school graduates and dropouts from the common core of data: School year 2009–2010*. Washington, DC: Author. Retrieved from http://nces.ed.gov/pubsearch/pubsinfo.asp?pubid=2013309rev

National Council on Disability. (2007). National disability policy: A progress report. November 1, 1998–November 19, 1999. Washington, DC: Author. (ERIC Document Reproduction Service No. ED442240)

Partnership for 21st Century Skills. (2011). *Framework for 21st century learning*. Washington, DC: Author. Retrieved from http://www.p21.org/overview/skills-framework

Posavac, E. (2010). *Program evaluation: Methods and case studies* (8th ed.). Chicago, IL: Loyola University of Chicago.

Rowe, D. A., & Test, D. W. (2010). The effects of computer-based instruction on the transition planning process knowledge of parents of students with disabilities. *Research and Practice for Persons With Severe Disabilities, 35*, 102–115.

Shaw, S. F., Dukes, L. L., III, & Madaus, J. W. (2012). Beyond compliance using the summary of performance to enhance transition planning. *Teaching Exceptional Children, 44*(5), 6–12.

Test, D. W. (2012). *Evidence-based instructional strategies for transition*. Baltimore, MD: Brookes.

Test, D. W., Mazzotti, V., Mustian, A., Fowler, C., Kortering, L., & Kohler, P. (2009). Evidence-based secondary transition predictors for improving post-school outcomes for students with disabilities. *Career Development for Exceptional Individuals, 32*, 160–181.

Thoma, C. A., & Wehman, P. (2010). *Getting the most of of IEPs*. Baltimore, MD: Brookes.

Thomas, S. B., & Dykes, F. (2010). Promoting successful transitions: What can we learn from RTI to enhance outcomes for all students? *Preventing School Failure, 55*, 1–9.

Trainor, A. A. (2007). Perceptions of adolescent girls with LD regarding self-determination and post-secondary transition planning. *Learning Disability Quarterly, 30*, 31–45.

Trainor, A. A., Carter, E. W., & Swedeen, B. (2012). Community conversations: An approach for expanding and connecting opportunities for employment for adolescents with disabilities. *Career Development for Exceptional Individuals, 35*, 50–60.

U.S. Department of Education. (2011a). *Questions and answers on secondary transition*. Washington, DC: Author. Retrieved from http://idea.ed.gov/explore/view/p/root,dynamic,QaCorner,10

U.S. Department of Education. (2011b). *Trends in high school dropout and completion rates in the United States: 1972–2009. Compendium report*. Washington, DC: Author. Retrieved from http://www.eric.ed.gov/PDFS/ED524955.pdf

Wehmeyer, M., Field, S., & Thoma, C. (2012). Self-determination and adolescent transition education. In M. L. Wehmeyer & K. W. Webb (Eds.), *Handbook of adolescent transition education for youth with disabilities* (pp. 165–181). New York, NY: Routledge.

13

Best Practices in Facilitating Transition to College for Students With Learning Disabilities

Raymond Witte
Miami University (OH)

OVERVIEW

The purpose of this chapter is to examine the transition issues and practices that are crucial for students with learning disabilities in college settings. Moving from the high school to the college setting represents a truly unique educational conversion. School psychologists as well as other school team members must be knowledgeable and skilled in this key transformation process. All need to follow an effective general problem-solving model in order to address the multitude of issues and corresponding decisions that inevitably emerge with this system shift.

Facilitating the transition process directly relates to the practice domains outlined in the National Association of School Psychologists (NASP) 2010 *Model for Comprehensive and Integrated School Psychological Services* (NASP, 2010) but especially to Interventions and Instructional Support to Develop Academic Skills and School-Wide Practices to Promote Learning. The domain of Interventions and Instructional Support to Develop Academic Skills reflects student-level services where "[s]chool psychologists have knowledge of biological, cultural, and social influences on academic skills; human learning, cognitive, and developmental processes; and evidence-based curricula and instructional strategies" (p. 5). The domain of School-Wide Practices to Promote Learning involves more system-level services and requires that school psychologists "have knowledge of school and systems structure, organization, and theory; general and special education; technology resources; and evidence-based school practices that promote learning and mental health" (p. 5). That extensive knowledge base and corresponding skill sets are continuously utilized through the ongoing problem solving that is necessary in addressing the multitude of academic and system issues that exist as a student prepares for the college environment. The school psychologist needs to demonstrate and model this problem-solving capacity throughout a student's educational journey. This essential skill must also be taught to, and demonstrated by, the students with special learning needs so that they can make effective and independent decisions throughout their college career.

Every Student Has a Story

Justin is a senior in high school. He was first identified with a reading disability in third grade and also received a clinical diagnosis of attention deficit hyperactivity disorder. Reading instruction and support, primarily in the area of reading comprehension, was provided for Justin as part of his Individualized Education Program (IEP) throughout his elementary school experience. Considerable progress was demonstrated to the extent that he was able to maintain comparable academic growth with his grade peers. Support services were continued into middle and high school. However, minimal direct service was required, and only indirect progress-monitoring services were maintained. For his attention issues, Justin was placed on medication and responded well to that approach. In addition, as part of his daily classroom instruction, he received printouts of class/lecture material in order to aid his understanding and retention of the covered content. Also, during tests he received extra time in class to complete and hand in his work.

Now, as a senior, and due to several issues (e.g., college adjustment, lower tuition fees), Justin has decided to attend a regional campus of a major university during his first and second year. He hopes to transfer prior to his junior year to the main campus and complete the rest of his undergraduate courses there. He believes that the regional campus environment will provide him an opportunity to adjust to the college setting while providing him with smaller class sizes and less distractions than would exist on the main campus. He also wants to pump up his grade point average before he transfers to the main campus.

Justin's story is not that different from many other young people who have special learning needs and are trying to successfully transition to college. As a result of professional training in a variety of areas including academic intervention and engagement, problem solving, general advocacy, as well as other life management and organizational skills, school psychologists are able to help facilitate the collection of skills and learning opportunities that are needed to help students with learning disabilities effectively transition and succeed at the college level.

Transition as a Functional Process

All intervention tiers and corresponding support(s) can be used for transition instruction. That starts at the Tier 1 level where, along with effective core academic instruction, students can also obtain specific information about college programs, academic requirements, and future careers. In addition, embedding within the classroom curriculum education survival skills (time management, study strategies, use of technology, research skills) can be done as well as providing more focused small group learning opportunities (Tier 2 level) for selected students who evidence slower learning progress and require more intensive learning opportunities. Also, students with limited exposure and/or background regarding college and future career opportunities may need more absorption time and repeated learning activities. For students who do not respond to Tier 3 academic intervention and evidence qualities consistent with a learning disability and qualify for special education services, academic preparation must still continue to focus on acquiring the strongest academic skill base possible and thereby increase the possibility of academic success at the college level. In particular, the development and continued refinement of each identified student's IEP becomes essential in focusing the instruction and learning that is required to

prepare students with essential transition skills and knowledge.

Transition as a functional process can be found and experienced throughout the educational career of a student. However, the movement from the K–12 setting to the college setting represents one of the most significant educational transition events for a student. The school psychologist is in a unique position to be able to support teachers and schools in the instructional process of students throughout their entire educational career. That support can include providing direct and indirect services to other professionals and the systems that support those students. For that reason school psychologists need to be available to assist in bridging and connecting the K–12 and college settings. This can be accomplished by facilitating effective instructional and programming connections and providing professional support/collaboration services regarding the diverse learning needs of identified students while maintaining and strengthening school-to-college partnerships. This content and professional service has immediate relevance and importance for school psychologists at the middle and high school levels. However, school psychologists who serve the elementary level also need to know and understand transition as preparation for the college setting starts at kindergarten and is maintained throughout a student's entire K–12 school career.

BASIC CONSIDERATIONS

In order to promote the transition services and experiences for students with learning disabilities who are transitioning to the college setting, school psychologists must possess knowledge and understanding of this complex process, the trends, and the potential issues and obstacles students can encounter.

Higher Education Trend

Given the ever-increasing expectations and need for a more educated workforce, the necessity of pursuing a college education has never been greater for students, including those with special learning needs (Eckes & Ochoa, 2005; Floyd, 2012). Consequently, a substantial and growing number of identified students continue to seek out and pursue higher education opportunities (Kurth & Mellard, 2006; Stodden, Conway, & Chang, 2003). According to Wagner, Newman, Cameto, Garza, and Levine (2005) approximately 23% of high school graduates with learning disabilities who graduate from high school transition to institutions of higher education. Furthermore, owing to economic factors (e.g., rising tuition costs) and general accessibility, 2-year institutions serve a large percentage of students with special needs (National Center for Educational Statistics [NCES], 2011).

In the NCES report (NCES, 2011), the Postsecondary Education Quick Information System survey—based on the results of 2-year and 4-year institutions for the 2008–2009 academic year—found that more 700,000 students with disabilities were enrolled in postsecondary institutions, with about half being served in public 2-year colleges. In particular, approximately one third of the enrolled students reported a diagnosis of a specific learning disability. Consequently, with greater admissions numbers, the need to provide a variety of effective services to a larger number of students has increased as well (Floyd, 2012).

Planning for Transition Success

The educational conversion from the secondary to the college setting requires a skilled team as well as purposeful planning and implementation. Given this educational reality, school psychologists at the middle and high school levels, can help direct and facilitate an effective transition process for identified students. However, college preparation and readiness are not limited to the junior or senior years. The process really starts at the elementary level by making sure that students are held to the highest academic standards (e.g., Common Core), that they acquire and meet the same or comparable learning outcomes as their nonidentified peers, and that their skill development is on track so that they are ready and able to handle a college curriculum upon graduation from high school. In fact, positive postschool outcomes are more likely for students with special learning needs when they receive instruction in the general education classroom (Landmark, Ju, & Zhang, 2010; Williams-Diehm & Benz, 2008). Therefore, positive school outcomes require longitudinal academic planning over the entire K–12 career of a student. If a student with a learning disability is going to be able to attend and, more importantly, succeed in college, then the focus and direction of the instruction to meet that goal must start at the beginning of his or her academic career.

In addition to facilitating academically prepared students, a school psychologist must have expertise in serving as a liaison between the K–12 and the postsecondary settings. The understanding of the

systems, their operating procedures, and their interaction practices is essential for a successful transition. School psychologists are uniquely positioned to assist in several key areas of the transition process. In particular, disability assessment and qualification procedures along with effective remedial and accommodation work in the classroom set the important foundation and groundwork for later progress. As students approach graduation, the knowledge and command of federal law, personal management, self-advocacy, and higher education issues (e.g., institutional support services, developmental course offerings) become vital in providing effective high school-to-college services. Also, the liaison work and collaboration/coordination between the high school and college settings is essential and serves as the primary professional link between those two educational systems.

Student Focus

Each student with a learning disability is recognized as possessing a unique collection of strengths and challenges, daily needs, skill sets, experiences, and necessary instructional supports (Skinner & Lindstrom, 2003; Sparks & Lovett, 2009). With that understood, Vogel and Reder (1998) found that adults with learning disabilities experience learning difficulties in at least one of six primary areas: oral language, reading, written language, mathematics, study skills, and attention problems. These challenges, in addition to production problems such as organizing work and adhering to deadlines (DaDeppo, 2009; Heiman & Precel, 2003) and problems with focused attention (Mayes, Calhoun, & Crowell, 2000), further exacerbate the learning difficulties of identified students who are admitted into colleges and universities.

When academic distress occurs and limited academic success is evidenced, personal issues such as student self-esteem and personal self-confidence can also be affected. Furthermore, adults with learning disabilities are at risk for more significant psychological factors such as social isolation, depressive conditions, general anxiety, and the potential for chemical dependency (Vogel & Reder, 1998).

Setting Focus

Individual student issues are certainly not the only significant factors in the transition process. An entirely different learning environment is encountered at the postsecondary level (Brinkerhoff, Shaw, & McGuire, 1992; Cawthon & Cole 2010). Consequently, the college setting and its parameters must also be understood owing to the dynamic interplay between the student and his or her learning environment. Substantial environmental variations exist between the high school and college settings, and for that reason it is imperative that identified students are aware of these key differences before they arrive on campus (see Table 13.1).

BEST PRACTICES IN FACILITATING TRANSITION TO COLLEGE FOR STUDENTS WITH LEARNING DISABILITIES

It is important for all school team members, including school psychologists, to view transition as more than just a particular event but as a long-term problem-solving process that requires clear planning and implementation of effective instruction for every student, but especially students with learning disabilities.

Planning and Student Advocacy

As Wiggins (1998) aptly stated, "The only way we can properly judge where we are is relative to where we want to be" (p. 1). Intended outcomes guide the important experiences, tasks, and orchestrated opportunities that need to occur during the entire acquisition process. This is transition planning in its most essential form. What becomes critical is the acquisition of the required skill and knowledge sets that are necessary to master those intended educational goals. For instructional purposes, this requires a backward design

mapping process whereby all essential prerequisite steps, skills, and requirements are identified and become instructional targets over the course of the student's K–12 educational career so that progress can be maintained and extended to the college level.

One, if not the key, difference between the K–12 and the postsecondary setting is the movement away from (and reliance on) a team-centered approach and toward an individual student approach. At the college level, each identified student, as opposed to the IEP team, bears the sole responsibility for maintaining and refining the transition plan and making sure it is implemented (Cawthon & Cole, 2010). All official contact as well as confirmation of provided services falls on the student as an independent self-advocate. Given this reality, every student must seize the opportunity during the middle and high school years to develop and refine his or her transition commitment, which should take the form of attending scheduled progress meetings as well as participating in academic and course planning decisions. Identified students must be provided these opportunities in order to practice implementing effective problem-solving strategies in regards to school career decisions.

Academic Preparation

Given the reality and challenges of the college setting, high school students with learning disabilities need to enter college as prepared as possible and that includes all academic and life management areas. The intent should be to have each student competent in all basic

Table 13.1. Educational Differences Between High School and College Settings for Students With Disabilities

High School Setting	College Setting
• The IEP is recognized as the primary factor in a student's instructional delivery plan • Support/school team reviews a student's academic process and contributes to educational decisions • Academic standards guide classroom instruction	• Individual courses and academic programs drive instruction; individualized instruction is rare • Each individual student reviews and pursues his or her academic decisions • Professional standards and requirements guide individual programs of study
• Individual one-on-one teacher–student contact time is typically high	• Individual one-on-one professor–student contact time may be limited and graduate students may be responsible for providing out-of-class support
• Smaller classroom enrollments (e.g., 25 students or less) are common • Daily review of classwork/homework is common	• Larger classroom enrollments are common, especially for large lecture formatted classes • High expectation for out-of-classroom work, reading, and general preparation
• In-class work time to complete assignments and/or review previous work is not uncommon • A strong support network has typically developed by the time a student reaches high school	• In-class work time is rare and the pace and coverage of material varies with each professor • A support network (e.g., friends, college resources) must be reestablished

academic domains (e.g., reading, math, writing) and functioning at the highest grade level possible. Along with strong learning skills, support skills (e.g., work scheduling, time management, test review procedures) are needed. Given the importance of the whole student, functional life skills involving effective mental and physical health management (e.g., adequate sleep, exercise, friend and family support) also need to be in place and utilized. A complete preparation package is absolutely necessary, and this preparation should remain the focus throughout a student's educational career.

A tiered approach is quite effective when organizing and providing transition training and services to all students, including those with learning disabilities. At every tier level, the assets and abilities of each student along with family resources must be carefully considered when building each student's transition foundation. Providing systematic and effective instruction, monitoring of student progress and development, along with organized planning helps to address the needs of all students who aspire to continue their education beyond high school. Across all the intervention and support levels, a school psychologist must utilize continuous problem solving, effective data-based decision making, system-focused practices, evidence-based intervention, and collaboration/cooperation practices and policies.

Tier 1

At the Tier 1 level, the focus is on the provision of useful and relevant content and skills that prepare all students to be functional and independent learners, capable of examining a multitude of issues and using a varied and appropriate array of resources to address various problems or questions. Students need to possess a deep and broad knowledge base along with the capacity for higher thinking skills that encompass the entire continuum of Bloom's revised taxonomy. Regarding this goal, school psychologists can and should advocate for a robust curriculum that provides ample opportunities for those skills to be obtained. Opportunities to embed specific transition-related information and/or skills can also be pursued. For example, teaching and practicing academic support skills such as time management or the effective use of a planner could be part of the primary curriculum within the regular classroom. These and other important skill topics (e.g., stress management) can be covered, and school psychologists are in the unique position to help in the delivery of that material.

In particular, professional support can take a variety of forms and can include acting as consultants, providing research support, or even serving as instructional partners to teachers. All of these are possible and should be considered given the particular needs and issues of your school(s). Additional support opportunities for school psychologists can involve community outreach and consultation. For example, speaking engagements (e.g., community centers, religious groups) highlighting college planning and transition can be provided. That outreach would be especially helpful for special parent groups (e.g., Children and Adults With Attention Deficit Hyperactivity Disorder). If well designed instructional opportunities are provided in the regular classroom, students can obtain and maintain a strong academic skill base. This foundation is essential for all future learning and that includes transitioning to higher education.

Tier 2

Effective instruction at the Tier 1 level in the regular classroom is important yet may not be enough for some students. Thus, additional time, instruction, and practice may be necessary for particular skill sets to be developed and refined. Consequently, more intensive, small group-formatted instruction is provided for students identified as at risk for academic difficulty. Beyond the academic support that is provided for at-risk students as part of Tier 2 intervention, transition information can be provided to students who are pursuing college but may lack resources and family supports. In particular, first-generation college-bound students may have limited knowledge and/or understanding about the college preparation and selection process. School psychologists, in combination with other professionals such as guidance counselors, can provide concentrated and focused instruction on specific college issues. A school psychologist can also serve as a school coach or mentor to these students and provide guidance and personal attention relative to their college aspirations and plans. That help and support can also be extended to the student's family.

Tier 3

Tier 3 is designed to provide intensive and individualized support to those students who are identified as exhibiting the most severe of learning and/or behavioral difficulties and who demonstrate minimal response to high-quality and well-delivered Tier 1 and 2 interventions. If Tier 3 intervention proves to be ineffective, special education resources and services are available and the IEP provides the framework and instructional delivery for a student's individualized academic program. As was mentioned earlier in the chapter, it is necessary for a student with a learning disability to obtain the strongest possible academic foundation. This provides the greatest opportunity for a successful graduation from high school as well as an effective college transition.

Secondary Preparation

For students with learning disabilities, the standard preparation and planning for college starts at the middle school and proceeds through the high school years. To that end, Brinckerhoff (1996) identified basic transition goals for every year of high school. For example, starting with the freshman year and moving into the sophomore year, critical issues such as disability awareness, knowledge of legal rights, selection of appropriate college preparatory courses, and career exploration constitute the transition focus. These areas continue to be important and receive attention during the junior and senior years; however, more specific goals are identified, which can include active exploration of postsecondary options and institutions as well as more formal test preparations (e.g., SAT, ACT) and special testing issues that may need to be documented (e.g., additional test completion time). In addition, throughout the 4 years of high school, an emphasis on functional independence, planning, and self-determination (i.e., self-advocacy and goal-setting behavior) is needed (Skinner & Lindstrom, 2003).

In order to further facilitate the transition process, a summary of performance (SOP) is required by law (according to the 2004 reauthorization of the Individuals with Disabilities Education Act [IDEA]) for any student identified with an educational disability. The SOP is completed in the student's final year prior to graduation, and contains a summary of the student's academic achievement and general functional skills along with the accommodations and modifications that have been provided to the student (Floyd, 2012). It must also list specific recommendations directed toward the transition to postsecondary goals that may include college. More importantly, college personnel are looking for this SOP and its content to potentially help a student with special learning needs in the transition process. Therefore, the summary of performance serves as a critical connector and bridge for the student who is moving from high school to college.

Qualifying for Services in College

At the postsecondary level, the student with special learning needs is in the driver's seat when it comes to documenting his or her disability. This includes applying for appropriate accommodations and ensuring the approved classroom accommodations are provided. The protection and coverage afforded under IDEA does not extend to students with identified disabilities once they enter college (Reilly & Davis, 2005). There is no legal mandate or requirement that an appropriate education plan designed to meet specific individual student needs must be provided to any student identified with a disability. In higher education, a range of support services are typically available, but the student bears the responsibility of providing evidence of the disability and then seeking appropriate services and accommodations to meet his or her individual needs under the protective legislation of the Americans with Disabilities Act (ADA).

Passed in 1990, the ADA is federal civil rights law that protects students with disabilities from being discriminated against in postsecondary and work settings. The ADA guarantees for all people with disabilities equal opportunity for employment and equal access to all programs, including college (Cawthon & Cole, 2010). The ADA Amendments Act of 2008 (which took effect January 1, 2009) refined the law and clarified issues such as identifying and defining a disability consistent with previous federal legislation (e.g., Section 504 of the Rehabilitation Act of 1973).

The Rehabilitation Act of 1973 provides general guidelines for disability identification for students who move on to postsecondary settings. According to this federal law, a student must show evidence of a physical or mental impairment that substantially limits one or more major life functions such as caring for one's self, walking, seeing, hearing, speaking, breathing, working, performing manual tasks, and learning (U.S. Department of Health and Human Services, 2006) and the student must be recognized as demonstrating an impairment that substantially limits those life functions in order for the disability qualification to be made.

Documentation of a Learning Disability

In order to receive accommodations in the college classroom setting, documentation must confirm a student's learning disability and be reviewed by the appropriate college personnel. While no universal set of criteria is used in the confirmation of a learning disability at the college level, the most common approaches that are followed include pattern of strengths and weaknesses (e.g., aptitude–achievement discrepancy), response to intervention (RTI), and low achievement performance (Sparks & Lovett, 2009). Although still recognized, major limitations with the aptitude–achievement discrepancy model have been acknowledged and low achievement alone is not considered adequate for a learning disability determination (Francis et al., 2005; Machek & Nelson, 2007; Sternberg & Grigorenko, 2002). The RTI model continues to receive increased interest and support as an appropriate model of learning disability identification (Fletcher, Denton, & Francis, 2005).

Non-ability–based evaluations such as RTI are increasingly common in the K–12 setting. Consequently, more intervention-based reports are making their way to the postsecondary level (Oifesh, 2006). Since these reports reflect actual student classroom performance data, they contain information that is critical to the transition process. Evidence of effective learning accommodations is available and can be directly integrated into the college classroom. These data exceed information that is typically generated from formal testing as they inform the team of what works in the classroom in regard to the instructional process. The documentation of the learning disability is still provided in this type of report (usually demonstrated by achievement that falls well below expected grade-level performance). However, the important information on the relative effectiveness of the intervention for a student is also provided. The utility of the data-based intervention report is becoming more recognized and appreciated at the college level, although the specific, and sometimes restricted, academic intervention focus (e.g., reading fluency) consistent with RTI does not always align well or easily translate to broader college curriculum goals and instruction (Sparks & Lovett, 2009).

A standard psychoeducational evaluation completed during high school can serve as a formal verification document of a student's disability in college (Sparks & Lovett, 2009), and much of the collected data in that document can help identify the necessary accommodations and services that would be needed for the identified student. As part of the evaluation process, a disability is typically identified through the use of formal achievement and cognitive test data as a demonstrated discrepancy between an individual's capacity to learn and perform compared to his or her actual performance and functioning level in a particular area such as reading or math. Many college admissions/disabilities offices require that if a psychoeducational evaluation is completed that it be current and the evaluation be conducted no later than a year prior to a student's arrival on campus. Therefore, families sometimes request an updated evaluation during the senior year of high school although a school district is not obligated to provide that service in order to satisfy college entrance or eligibility requirements.

Disclosing the Disability

When a student with special learning needs goes to college, it is not enough to document the existence of a disability and/or the interventions that have been developed and implemented to address his or her learning needs. It must be demonstrated that the impairment also has a direct impact on the individual's life and general functioning (Hatzes, Reiff, & Bramal, 2002). For that reason this information needs to be contained in the individual report or evaluation that the student brings to campus. The disabilities coordinator, the official contact person who receives, reviews, and identifies potential accommodations in the classroom, will specifically search in the report for information and written verification of the disabling condition, as well as the intervention strategies that have been implemented in order to confirm its impact on the student upon his or her entrance into college. What is reported, and also what is not reported, is critical to the potential services and accommodations that can and will be provided to an identified student.

As reported in the work of Hatzes et al. (2002), all postsecondary institutions must follow federal guidelines and most adhere to the learning disability documentation guidelines advocated by the Association on Higher Education and Disability (AHEAD). For submitted reports, several AHEAD criteria must be met:

- Credentials of the evaluator(s)
- Diagnostic statement identifying the disability
- Description of the diagnostic methodology used
- Description of the current functional limitations
- Description of the expected progression or stability of the disability
- Description of current and past accommodations, services, and/or medications
- Recommendations for accommodations, adaptive devices, assistive services, compensatory strategies, and/or collateral support services

Entering college students shoulder the responsibility of disclosing their disability and seeking out necessary academic accommodations in the college classroom

(Floyd, 2012). Unlike IDEA where the school possesses the legal responsibility to confirm the disability and provide services, in the college setting the identified student must disclose his or her disability and provide documentation of that disability. This is critical since not all students self-disclose. In fact, it has been reported that only "40% of postsecondary students with disabilities identify themselves as having a disability and have informed their postsecondary schools of that disability" (Wagner et al., 2005, p. 15). For students who disclose their disability status, postsecondary institutions are required to provide accommodations throughout the campus, including the classroom, to ensure that students are not discriminated against because of their disability. These accommodations can be related to course delivery (e.g., audio recording classes, being provided with note takers, obtaining instructor's outlines or lecture notes), classroom support materials (e.g., audio textbooks), and to course requirements themselves (e.g., extra time to complete tests).

As the protections under IDEA cease at the postsecondary level, the change in the legal status of an identified student has significant implications. In particular, students must understand that the college and its representatives will only be working with them in regard to official business. All primary educational issues such as disability confirmation, assessment and verification, disability disclosure, instructional programming, general advocacy, as well as academic progress review fall under the direct responsibility of the entering student (Brinckerhoff et al., 1992). This represents a significant shift from high school, and students must be ready and prepared for this responsibility.

Effective Transition

A successful transition for students with learning disabilities from high school to college requires a well-developed and executed plan. Clearly, the work and focus of the IEP and the transition team, which should include the school psychologist, sets the educational foundation and potential for success. Getting accepted into college and qualifying for services is just the beginning of the postsecondary journey.

What components and actions need to be taken to increase the chances of both college acceptance and academic success? Consider the following actions that need to be initiated during the middle school years and completed during the high school years.

Transition plan as a functioning document: The transition plan within the IEP needs to exist as a functioning

document starting at least by middle school. College plans/actions can precede this (e.g., elementary level) and the school psychologist is in a key position to push for that goal, especially if a student (parent) voices interest in attending college. Existing transition plans are required by the age of 16 for all identified students under IDEA, and a statement of transition services is required. However, some states (e.g., Ohio) require plans to be in place by the age of 14. In addition, a summary of performance is required for all students who qualify for special education services and must be present during their final year of high school. This document helps form the bridge between the secondary and college settings and should be shared with the college disabilities coordinator as soon as possible, preferably at least a semester before admittance (Floyd, 2012).

Members of the support team: Starting at the eighth grade, the guidance counselor should be a part of the support team in order to ensure that the transition plan is focused on selecting appropriate college preparatory courses and obtaining the necessary number of credits in all core areas (e.g., English, math, science, foreign language). Also, acquisition and refinement of learning support skills (e.g., study skills, note taking, testing skills/preparation, self-assessment/progress monitoring) should be emphasized and the school psychologist can be most helpful in the instructional process of these support skills.

Private tutoring and/or school support during the summer months: In high school, private tutoring and/or school support during the summer months (if offered within the school district) to minimize academic skill regression should be a consideration. Students should be encouraged to take or retake classes (if necessary) during summer school. Maintaining a lighter academic load (fewer core subject courses) during the academic year can be especially helpful. This provides a good opportunity to obtain and maintain the highest grade point average possible. This approach can be particularly helpful for athletes with special learning needs. Given the training and participation time demands placed upon athletes during their playing season, a more manageable academic load provides them with an even greater chance of academic success in the classroom (Dalke & Schmitt, 1987; Vogel & Adelman, 1992).

Updated academic profile during the senior year: Generating an updated academic profile during the senior year of high school is important. Current test performance data, along with aptitude results if provided, are important sources of information that may be used for the documentation of potential services at the postsecondary level.

Finding potential colleges early: Identifying potential colleges early is important. This can happen as soon as the sophomore year. As students and families explore potential colleges, schools that have a good track record in supporting students with special learning needs should be identified. Several colleges need to be identified and then visited, if possible, no later than the student's junior year. Students and their families need to inquire as to the learning assistance services available and meet with the appropriate service personnel. Calling before a visit to set up an appointment is highly recommended. Students should get all their questions answered before making any decisions. Also, simply having a disability coordinator on campus does not ensure exemplary service and support for the student. Differences in resources exist among schools, and it is important to identify those differences (Madaus, 2005).

Legal adult status: If the matriculating student is 18 years of age or older, legal adult status is recognized and all contact information is directed to the student. Parents can be involved and informed only if consent by the student is given. Given this reality, prior to his or her eighteenth birthday, it is good practice for the student to take on the responsibility of setting up visits, making contact arrangements, confirming schedules, or whatever else needs to be done.

Taking summer courses: To help with the transition process, ask the college disability coordinator if it is advisable to take a course or two over the summer, prior to the start of the academic school year. Also, the disability coordinator would also be aware of other learning opportunities that might help ease a new student into the college environment such as developmental courses or study skills/time management classes (Turnberger, 2008).

College professors vary in knowledge of required accommodations: Students need to be aware that college professors will vary in their knowledge of and general response to required accommodations (e.g., effective implementation, attitude toward accommodations) for students with special learning needs (Katsiyannis, Zhang, Landmark, & Reber, 2009). It is recommended that a student visit professors during office hours so that the nature of the student's disability is understood as well as the approved accommodations.

Possessing high school transcripts: Students should have several copies of their updated high school transcripts in their possession. The transcripts should contain a complete listing of courses taken in core academic areas, credits earned, as well as any special aspects to those classes (e.g., advanced placement courses taken with AP credit received, skill remediation courses).

Rights, protections, and procedural safeguards: Prior to coming to college, students need to be fully informed regarding their rights, protections, and procedural safeguards afforded to them through the legislative safeguards of the ADA and the Rehabilitation Act of 1973 (Brinckerhoff et al., 1992; Madaus, 2005).

Self-disclose to a college official: As mentioned earlier, students with special needs must self-disclose (i.e., officially indicate they have an identified disability) to a designated college official in order to be eligible for special services/accommodation at the postsecondary level (Lynch & Gussel, 1996). A disclosing letter accompanied by a professional evaluation is typically presented during that initial meeting.

Disabilities coordinator: Every college is required to have a designated disabilities coordinator who serves as the official contact person for identified students and helps to coordinate and oversee rendered services. Once accepted at a college, the disabilities coordinator becomes a very important resource and contact person. Students need to know and be familiar with the disabilities coordinator, and how to reach him or her whenever academic issues or concerns arise.

Understanding the necessity of self-advocacy: Students with special learning needs must understand the necessity of self-advocacy, as this skill along with disability knowledge and effective support services increases the likelihood of successful postsecondary transitions (Milsom & Hartley, 2005). The responsibility falls on each individual student to seek out appropriate contacts, necessary services, and other relevant educational supports.

College-supported counseling services: College-supported counseling services are usually available on most campuses. Students may need to talk to someone about college pressures and stressors, as well as seek general support as they pursue their academic studies. In addition, support groups/associations can also help provide emotional and personal support (Cosden & McNamara, 1997; Finn, 1997). School psychologists are in a key position to be able to help students and their families identify and connect with potential support groups.

Institutional expectations: Both 2- and 4-year colleges require a professional evaluation and report along with the necessary documentation of a learning disability, evidence of school-based intervention, and how the conditions directly have an impact on the daily life and functioning of the student. School psychologists need to make sure that a student's evaluation is complete and will meet all college requirements. However, differences in admission criteria can exist between 2- and 4-year colleges. Some 2-year colleges have more of an open door admissions policy with fewer academic requirements that must be met before the student is admitted or placed in a particular program of study. In addition to less stringent admission standards, these 2-year colleges usually offer developmental courses centered on skill review and enhancement. This kind of preparation may be desirable and necessary if a student graduated from a high school with limited course offerings or is particularly weak in certain core content areas/skills. However, developmental courses rarely, if ever, are recognized for credit toward a degree or program. For example, a developmental math course may be needed and necessary for skill development for a student and credit hours may be obtained, but it will likely not meet the math requirements for a specific program of study or degree. Also, 4-year colleges may have more selective admissions and/or program requirements. For example, a higher grade point average, specific courses taken and passed in high school, service work in the community, as well as additional requirements may be expected for admission. Consequently, an automatic acceptance should not be assumed, even if success at a 2-year college has been demonstrated. Admissions criteria should be identified and carefully reviewed for each college considered.

Transition Responsibilities

School psychologists bring many skills to the transition table as they are in a special position to help students with learning disabilities proceed from the K–12 setting to the college setting. As transition teams are configured within your school district (at all levels: elementary, middle, and high school), consider the following:

- At a minimum, school psychologists need to be present on transition teams at the middle school level. This is necessary in order to ensure that well-developed plans and a firm foundation and structure for future goals are established. School psychologists serving on teams at the high school level need to carefully review the folders of students who move from the middle school. The team must ensure that course/credit requirements are met and academic skill proficiencies are as strong as possible so that admission to college continues to be a viable option for identified students.

- Consistent with the NASP (2010) Practice Model focus on developing and improving student competencies, school psychologists can help provide services (both direct and indirect) that are focused on functional skill areas such as academic foundation skills, executive processing and planning, academic support skills, mental health and wellness, and problem-solving/coping skills along with other life-long competency skills.

- Consultation services for transitioning students are essential. The high school team (e.g., student, guidance counselor, school psychologist, college contact person, teachers, parents) must develop a detailed postsecondary plan complete with a time line, documented support services, and an updated evaluation with information on the student's present academic performance and instructional needs in the classroom to ensure a smooth transition from high school to college.

- Success in any classroom is dependent upon identifying the necessary skills and performances that are required to complete classroom assignments, projects, and tests. In 2002, Deno acknowledged a functional learning discrepancy as "the difference between the level of performance required to meet environmental demands and the level of performance emitted by the individual" (Deno, 2002, p. 42). The concept of a functional discrepancy certainly applies to any learning activity in a college classroom. Identifying classroom demands and making sure the student has the skills, provides the effort, and receives the support resources that are required in each class is paramount. This is where the expertise of the school psychologist can help in identifying effective and necessary accommodations that are needed and appropriate in the college classroom setting.

- Identifying professional contacts and developing relationships with local universities, especially with the disability coordinators, are important for the future success of transitioning students. In particular, the more knowledge a school psychologist possesses in regards to the college environment, the more help and assistance can be offered to high school students and their families. The acculturation of the student and the family to college life and its challenges is critical. The school psychologist can serve as an information resource (e.g., college tutoring services, program requirements) and a helpful contact person in that process.

- Given the importance of self-advocacy and self-determination for identified students in college (Field,

Sarver, & Shaw 2003), providing information and role-play practice sessions for high school juniors and seniors is very important. These students need to be given opportunities to develop personal reliance and autonomy. In addition, they must also possess the skills and confidence to face the variety of classroom challenges that will certainly arise during their college years.

SUMMARY

As students with learning disabilities continue to seek out higher education opportunities, school psychologists, particularly at the middle and secondary school levels, need to be key members of transition teams. Critical transition issues, from disability documentation and qualification to actual classroom accommodations and skill training, exist for identified students, and the successful resolution of these challenges requires the talents of many professionals including those of the school psychologist. With early planning, persistent focus, and periodic monitoring of progress, successful transitions can be achieved. Moreover, the breadth and depth of preparation is important given the demands of the college setting. As reported in Landmark et al. (2010, p. 173) "transition is a results-oriented process" and for that reason every student with a learning disability must be as academically prepared and organizationally competent as he or she can be. In particular, proficiency in basic areas including academics, learning, and academic planning, as well as mental health management, are essential, and the school psychologist is in a key role to provide much of this assistance and training.

School psychologists play an essential role in ensuring that required transition components and plans are in place. In accordance with federal mandates, a transition plan needs to be in place by the time a student is 16. The summary of performance is also required and must be completed during a student's final year of high school (Madaus & Shaw, 2006). These requirements need to be met so that identified students receive the necessary adjustments and supports to continue their success at the college level. In addition to documentation functions, school psychologists can serve as consultants to provide training in several key areas such as federal law, self-determination, and general advocacy skills.

Successfully transitioning students with learning disabilities into college requires the long-term planning and action of individuals throughout the career of each identified student. School psychologists are central to that process and for that reason must continue to advocate for the needs of these students and the services they require. To a great extent, the successful conversion and adjustment to the college setting is the desired end game for these students. Effective transition services are essential in assisting students with learning disabilities to continue on with their lives, and school psychologists play a key role in that important life process.

REFERENCES

Brinckerhoff, L. C. (1996). Making the transition to higher education: Opportunities for student empowerment. *Journal of Learning Disabilities, 29*, 118–136. doi:10.1177/002221949/602900202

Brinckerhoff, L. C., Shaw, S. F., & McGuire, J. M. (1992). Promoting access, accommodations, and independence for college students with learning disabilities. *Journal of Learning Disabilities, 25*, 417–429. doi:10.1177/002221949/202500702

Cawthon, S. W., & Cole, E. V. (2010). Postsecondary students who have a learning disability: Student perspectives on accommodation access and obstacles. *Journal of Postsecondary Education and Disability, 23*, 112–128.

Cosden, M. A., & McNamara, J. (1997). Self-concept and perceived social support among college students with and without learning disabilities. *Learning Disability Quarterly, 20*, 2–12.

DaDeppo, L. M. W. (2009). Integration factors related to the academic success and intent to persist of college students with learning disabilities. *Learning Disabilities Research & Practice, 24*, 122–131. doi:10.1111/j.1540-5826.2009.00286.x

Dalke, C., & Schmitt, S. (1987). Meeting the transition needs of college-bound students with learning disabilities. *Journal of Learning Disabilities, 20*, 176–180. doi:10.1177/002221948702000306

Deno, S. L. (2002). Problem solving as "best practice." In A. Thomas & J. Grimes (Eds.), *Best practices in school psychology IV* (pp. 37–55). Bethesda, MD: National Association of School Psychologists.

Eckes, S., & Ochoa, T. (2005). Students with disabilities: Transitioning from high school to higher education. *American Secondary, 33*(3), 6–20.

Field, S., Sarver, M. D., & Shaw, S. F. (2003). Self-determination: A key to success in postsecondary education for students with learning disabilities. *Remedial and Special Education, 24*, 339–349. doi:10.1177/07419325030240060501

Finn, L. L. (1997). *Critical support services for college students with learning disabilities.* Retrieved from ERIC database. (ED412712)

Fletcher, J. M., Denton, C., & Francis, D. J. (2005). Validity of alternative approaches for the identification of learning disabilities: Operationalizing unexpected underachievement. *Journal of Learning Disabilities, 38*, 545–552. doi:10.1177/00222194050380061101

Floyd, K. (2012). Postsecondary students with learning disabilities: Can we do more? *Journal of Special Education Apprenticeship, 1*(1), 1–13.

Francis, D. J., Fletcher, J. M., Steubing, K. K., Lyon, G. R., Shaywitz, B. A., & Shaywitz, S. E. (2005). Psychometric approaches to the identification of LD: IQ and achievement scores are not sufficient. *Journal of Learning Disabilities, 38*, 98–108. doi:10.1177/00222194050380020101

Hatzes, N. M., Reiff, H. B., & Bramel, M. H. (2002). The documentation dilemma: Access and accommodations for post-secondary students with learning disabilities. *Assessment for Effective Intervention, 27,* 37–52. doi:10.1177/073724770202700304

Heiman, T., & Precel, K. (2003). Students with learning disabilities in higher education: Academic strategies profile. *Journal of Learning Disabilities, 36,* 248–258. doi:10.1177/002221940303600304

Katsiyannis, A., Zhang, D., Landmark, L., & Reber, A. (2009). Postsecondary education for individuals with disabilities: Legal and practice considerations. *Journal of Disability Policy Studies, 20,* 35–45. doi:10.1177/1044207308324896

Kurth, N., & Mellard, D. (2006). Student perceptions of the accommodation process in postsecondary education. *Journal of Postsecondary Education and Disability, 19,* 71–84.

Landmark, L. J., Ju, S., & Zhang, D. (2010). Substantiated best practices in transition: Fifteen plus years later. *Career Development for Exceptional Individuals, 33,* 165–176. doi:10.1177/0885728810376410

Lynch, R. T., & Gussel, L. (1996). Disclosure and self-advocacy regarding disability-related needs: Strategies to maximize integration in postsecondary education. *Journal of Counseling & Development, 74,* 352–357. doi:10.1002/j.1556-6676.1996.tb01879.x

Machek, G. R., & Nelson, J. M. (2007). How should reading disabilities be operationalized? A survey of practicing school psychologists. *Learning Disabilities Research & Practice, 22,* 147–157. doi:10.1111/j.1540-5826.2007.00239.x

Madaus, J. W. (2005). Navigating the college transition maze: A guide for students with learning disabilities. *Teaching Exceptional Children, 37*(3), 32–37.

Madaus, J. W., & Shaw, S. F. (2006). The impact of the IDEA 2004 on transition to college for students with learning disabilities. *Learning Disabilities Research & Practice, 21,* 273–281. doi:10.1111/j.1540-5826.2006.00223.x

Mayes, S. D., Calhoun, S. L., & Crowell, E. W. (2000). Learning disabilities and ADHD: Overlapping spectrum disorders. *Journal of Learning Disabilities, 33,* 417–424. doi:10.1177/002221940003300502

Milsom, A., & Hartley, M. (2005). Assisting students with learning disabilities transitioning to college: What school counselors should know. *Professional School Counseling, 8,* 436–441.

National Association of School Psychologists. (2010). *Model for comprehensive and integrated school psychological services.* Bethesda, MD: Author. Retrieved from http://www.nasponline.org/standards/2010standards/2_PracticeModel.pdf

National Center for Education Statistics. (2011). *Students with disabilities at degree-granting postsecondary institutions: First look* (NCES Publication No. 2011-018). Washington, DC: U.S. Department of Education. Retrieved from http://nces.ed.gov/pubs2011/2011018.pdf

Ofiesh, N. (2006). Response to intervention and the identification of specific learning disabilities: Why we need comprehensive evaluations as part of the process. *Psychology in the Schools, 43,* 883–888. doi:10.1002/pits.20195

Reilly, V. J., & Davis, T. (2005). Understanding the regulatory environment. In E. E. Getzel & P. Wehman (Eds.), *Going to college: Expanding opportunities for people with disabilities* (pp. 25–48). Baltimore, MD: Brookes.

Skinner, M. E., & Lindstrom, B. D. (2003). Bridging the gap between high school and college: Strategies for successful transition of students with learning disabilities. *Preventing School Failure, 47,* 132–137. doi:10.1080/10459880309604441

Sparks, R. L., & Lovett, B. J. (2009). College students with learning disability diagnoses: Who are they and how do they perform? *Journal of Learning Disabilities, 42,* 494–510. doi:10.1177/0022219409338746

Sternberg, R. J., & Grigorenko, E. L. (2002). Difference scores in the identification of children with learning disabilities it's time to use a different method. *Journal of School Psychology, 40,* 65–83.

Stodden, R. A., Conway, M. A., & Chang, K. (2003). Findings from the study of transition, technology, and postsecondary supports for youth with disabilities: Implications for secondary school educators. *Journal of Special Education Technology, 18*(4), 29–44.

Turnberger, S. (2008). *Assisting college students with learning disabilities by evaluating community college student development courses.* Fairfax, VA: George Mason University. Retrieved from http://hdl.handle.net/1920/3068

U.S. Department of Health and Human Services, Office of Civil Rights. (2006). *Your rights under Section 504 of the Rehabilitation Act.* Washington, DC: Author. Retrieved from http://www.hhs.gov/ocr/civilrights/resources/factsheets/504ada.pdf

Vogel, S. A., & Adelman, P. B. (1992). The success of college students with learning disabilities: Factors related to educational attainment. *Journal of Learning Disabilities, 25,* 430–441. doi:10.1177/002221949202500703

Vogel, S. A., & Reder, S. (Eds.). (1998). *Learning disabilities, literacy, and adult education.* Baltimore, MD: Brookes.

Wagner, M., Newman, L., Cameto, R., Garza, N., & Levine, P. (2005). *After high school: A first look at the postschool experiences of youth with disabilities. A report from the National Longitudinal Transition Study-2 (NLTS2).* Menlo Park, CA: SRI. Retrieved from http://www.nlts2.org/reports/2005_04/nlts2_report_2005_04_complete.pdf

Wiggins, G. (1998). *Educative assessment: Designing assessment to inform and improve student performance.* San Francisco, CA: Jossey-Bass.

Williams-Diehm, K. L., & Benz, M. R. (2008). Where are they now? Lessons from a single district follow-up study. *Journal for Vocational Special Needs Education, 30*(2), 4–15.

Section 2

Interventions and Mental Health Services to Develop Social and Life Skills

Best Practices in Applying Positive Psychology in Schools

Terry M. Molony
Philadelphia College of Osteopathic Medicine and Cherry Hill (NJ) Public Schools
Maureen Hildbold
AIM Academy (PA)
Nakeia D. Smith
Upper Darby (PA) Public Schools

OVERVIEW

Across the world, schools face serious obstacles in their mission to educate the "whole child" in addition to pressures such as school accountability and high stakes testing. Positive psychology is a universal approach that can be applied in schools to promote students' development of academic, social, and behavioral skills, as well as to prevent and address mental health challenges. Positive psychology is defined as the scientific study of strengths and virtues that enable individuals and communities to flourish with its focus on positive emotions, positive individual traits, and positive institutions (Seligman, 2002).

Since the late 1990s, research has concentrated on components of positive psychology and the development of programs and interventions to foster well-being and prevent psychological distress (Fredrickson, 2009). Most of this research has been centered on adults. However, more recently the research has extended to adolescents and younger children in schools (e.g., Froh, Fan, Emmons, Bono, Huebner, & Watkins, 2011; Marques, Lopez, & Pais-Ribero, 2011). As positive psychology practices for schools continue to develop, school psychologists will be equipped with powerful tools to find creative ways to help children, teachers, parents, and schools to thrive.

Positive psychology's emphasis on strengths is closely aligned with the National Association of School Psychologists (NASP) *Model for Comprehensive and Integrated School Psychological Services* (NASP, 2010) under the Intervention and Mental Health Services domain specifically to enhance the learning and mental health of all children and youth. Within this domain, school psychologists can use a positive psychology approach directly at the student level and by collaborating with teachers and parents to provide a continuum of developmentally appropriate, strength-based supports for students, including programs that promote factors such as gratitude, character strengths, and optimistic problem solving. A positive psychology approach can be used individually or in small groups through counseling and coaching of students. Because of the universal significance of themes such as courage, persistence, grit, humor, and humanity, positive psychology provides opportunities for school psychologists to collaborate and consult with teachers, school staff, and parents in many different ways to develop a strengths-based lens to view students. School psychologists can also guide the development of academic and other assignments (e.g., art projects, performances, structured discussions, writing assignments, and reflections) around comprehensive themes of positive psychology to increase students' self-awareness as well as to enhance student learning.

On a systems level, school psychologists can demonstrate and encourage the daily use of positive psychology practices to foster a healthy school climate, prevent problems, and encourage work satisfaction for professionals, thereby enabling schools to flourish. In addition, school psychologists can use positive psychology themes to enhance family–school collaboration services, such as through presentations and information-sharing sessions with parents at PTA meetings or mental health fairs.

This chapter will review the major research findings about positive psychology in schools, spotlighting many important components of positive psychology including positive affect, character strengths, gratitude, flow, optimism, and hope. In addition, this chapter will highlight and discuss school psychologists' best practices in applying positive psychology principles to enhance the well-being of children, families, and school personnel.

Positive Psychology's Orientation

Based on its emphasis on strengths and self-awareness, positive psychology is closely related to fostering student resilience, social skills, social and emotional learning, positive behavior supports, and positive youth development. Positive psychology can be distinguished from traditional school initiatives because of its impetus to create a pathway to well-being instead of simply removing a negative factor or characteristic (Fredrickson, 2009). For instance, a school's character education program could promote a bully prevention program to reduce incidences of bullying. In contrast, a school completely immersed in a culture of positive psychology would cultivate school-wide positive emotions and interactions through the ongoing practice of gratitude and meaningful relationships. This would create a climate of positive relationships where bullying would not occur.

Brief History

Historically, the mission of psychology has been three-fold: curing mental illness, helping to make the lives of people more fulfilling and productive, and identifying and nurturing excellence and talent (Seligman, 2002). However, after World War II, psychology's focus narrowed to a treatment approach based on the disease or medical model. Although the deficit-focused, medical model has resulted in many benefits, including successful psychological and medical treatments for emotional distress, researchers in positive psychology suggest that an overemphasis on the treatment of disorders has detracted from the other missions of psychology, such as making lives better, nurturing excellence, and developing prevention programs (Seligman, 2002). In addition, supporters of a positive psychology approach point out the benefits of studying people who flourish, providing a more balanced and complete view of the human experience from a scientific perspective (Fredrickson, 2009).

The positive psychology movement can be traced to writings of ancient scholars, philosophers, and spiritual leaders, as well as to humanistic psychology (Peterson & Seligman, 2004). Positive psychology has been successfully applied in many different settings and contexts including healthcare, business, therapy, and now schools (Seligman, 2002). With the worldwide mission of education to develop the whole child, positive psychology's emphasis on well-being, character development, and meaningful engagement for students can powerfully support and complement important goals in schools.

Criticisms of Positive Psychology

Despite lofty goals, positive psychology has not been embraced by the entire psychological community. Most of the criticism about positive psychology is based on an incorrect perception that positive psychology is simply about positive thinking. Researchers in positive psychology (e.g., Aspinwall & Tedeschi, 2010) indicate that these criticisms are due to a misunderstanding of the premise of positive psychology because the interpretation of the popular culture oversimplifies the scientific evidence and conclusions of the research.

BASIC CONSIDERATIONS

Positive psychology fits into a multitiered service, problem-solving model primarily as a prevention approach. The basic premise of positive psychology in schools is a universal practice that would be nurtured and cultivated on a daily basis (Seligman, Ernst, Gillham, Reivich, & Linkins, 2009). At the selected or targeted level of intervention, vulnerable students, or those at risk, might require small group interventions that would allow for more individual connections and deeper reflection. Although research in using a positive psychology approach in counseling is in its infancy, school psychologists can broaden their toolbox by incorporating positive psychology constructs with other evidenced-based orientations (Harris, Thoresen, & Lopez, 2007). For students who require a more intense approach, such as those students with anxiety, depression, or other emotional distress, school psychologists can integrate and individualize the general strategies discussed in the chapter.

Therefore, school psychologists can use the techniques of positive psychology on a universal level, formally and systematically when working with individuals or groups, and in everyday interactions, as well as with targeted students with higher level needs. As school psychologists learn more about the essential ingredients of positive psychology, school psychologists will likely find that they can have a positive impact on a variety of interactions and situations (Harris et al., 2007).

Applications Across Age and Developmental Levels

As with any therapeutic, academic, or social skill intervention, consideration of the level of skills and needs of the child is always necessary to implement strategies appropriately. Many interventions based on positive psychology require a level of cognitive awareness or sophistication and may not be appropriate for very young children (Froh, Fan, et al., 2011). Research has supported positive psychology techniques with children from late elementary school throughout adulthood (e.g., Froh, Fan, et al., 2011; Marques et al., 2011; Seligman et al., 2009). Since research findings for the use of positive psychology with adolescents in schools is promising, school psychologists can use their expertise in child development to translate the more sophisticated concepts into language that is child friendly and begin to introduce topics to young children or those with developmental challenges.

Diverse Populations

Some critics of positive psychology have suggested that it is a western convention, since values like optimism and hope are predominant in western culture. However, positive psychology appears to be an international phenomenon. Worldwide research on well-being suggests that it is an important construct across cultures, although the values and traditions of the cultures may define well-being differently (Ponterotto, Mendelowitz, & Collabolletta, 2008). Positive psychology seems to transcend most cultures with its strong emphasis on meaningful engagement and connections to others as the basis for enduring happiness and well-being. In particular, character strengths, based on the writings of various ancient religions and cultures, seem to harmoniously blend important East and West characteristics and values (Peterson & Seligman, 2004). Most of the applications of positive psychology require a personal approach, based on the individual's unique strengths and values that allow for differentiation across cultures (Ponterotto et al., 2008).

However, research in applying positive psychology in schools cites the lack of diverse groups as a limitation in the studies. One program, the Penn Resiliency Project, reports consistent positive outcomes across various ethnic groups and regions (Seligman et al., 2009).

School psychologists are urged to consider guidelines from research regarding cultural proficiency and multicultural issues when introducing the topic of positive psychology to different ethnic groups, acknowledging individual differences, values, and interests.

Implications for Schools

One of the goals of positive psychology is to help institutions thrive, and centers of learning, such as schools, are key organizations for its fundamental practice. A school that is based on principles of positive psychology would emphasize a positive school climate in which students are ready to learn. These schools would have relevant and engaging learning activities. Students' strengths would be emphasized. Students themselves would set challenging yet realistic goals, and they would have high hope for achievement. Teachers would have high levels of satisfaction with their work. Teachers would be role models of optimism and would encourage effort and hard work and treat everyone with respect. Schools emphasizing positive psychology would have strong character education and social and emotional learning programs as active components of educational goals, as well as a significant focus on positive youth development (Seligman et al., 2009).

In 2008, Geelong Grammar School, in Victoria, Australia, partnered with the Positive Psychology Center of the University of Pennsylvania to develop a positive education approach, which immerses positive psychology in the classroom (Seligman et al., 2009). Geelong, with 1,500 students enrolled in four campuses, uses a whole school approach that, along with direct classroom instruction, integrates five domains essential to flourishing: positive purpose, positive relationships, positive emotions, positive health, and positive engagement (Seligman et al., 2009). In 2013, Geelong began a 3-year research project with the University of Melbourne and Monash University and the results will likely provide more guidance regarding best practices in positive psychology for schools.

Measuring Outcomes

Since the late 1990s, the positive psychology research community has developed several measurement tools that have been refined to validly and reliably measure gratitude, well-being, life satisfaction, and other constructs in adults. More recently, the research has extended to determine if the tools are valid and reliable for children of diverse populations and cultures (Park, Huebner, Laughlin, Valois, & Gilman, 2004) and for special populations, such as individuals with disabilities (Gilman, Easterbrooks, & Frey, 2004). However, there remains a scarcity of definitive research regarding appropriate instruments to measure various constructs of positive psychology in children, and this is an area that continues to be researched.

Students' strengths are seldom measured in schools, although there are many measures for problems, including, for example, the number of office discipline referrals, detentions, and missed recesses. Portfolios demonstrating students' strengths, surveys of life satisfaction, gratitude scales, and school climate surveys are suggested as possible positive measures of individual and system-wide well-being. In the future, school report cards might report the level of flourishing for a school, as well as traditional academic measures.

BEST PRACTICES IN APPLYING POSITIVE PSYCHOLOGY IN SCHOOLS

A large focus of positive psychology research has been centered on happiness and well-being. Although Americans currently possess better living conditions, greater wealth, general comfort, and daily conveniences than they did 40 years ago, they do not report themselves as happier (Seligman, 2011). Lyubomirsky, Sheldon, and Schkade (2005) suggest a formula for sustainable happiness that includes three factors: 50% set by genetics, 10% determined by life circumstance, and 40% determined by intentional activity. The fact that 40% of happiness can be influenced by how people voluntarily deal with adversity suggests that school psychologists, based on a positive psychology approach, can promote direct teaching of healthy ways to solve problems.

Another conceptualization of long lasting well-being, is the PERMA model (Seligman, 2011), which includes five essential elements: savoring positive emotions, engaging in absorbing activities, developing support systems through positive relationships, finding meaning through connections with others and issues that transcend oneself, and accomplishments through learning new skills and achieving goals. School psychologists can demonstrate, teach, and communicate these elements to students, teachers, and parents through encouragement of daily practice, consultation, small group interventions, and presentations. A wealth of positive psychology research with adults indicates that people with high levels of well-being experience health

benefits (Fredrickson, 2009) engage in community participation, are more liked by others, live longer, and perform better at work (Veenhoven, 2005) than those who do not. Therefore, it seems imperative for schools, as well as school psychologists, to foster well-being at an early age in children.

Positive Affect and Resiliency

Research on positive psychology links positive affect, or being in a good mood, with resiliency (Fredrickson, 2009; Seligman, 2002). Fredrickson (2009) suggests that a three to one daily ratio of positivity to negativity determines a person's level of flourishing. Fredrickson's Broaden and Build Theory is important for school psychologists because it suggests that positive emotions help people become more interested in learning new skills that build enduring personal and social resources over time. Fredrickson (2009) further suggested that positive emotions can provide an undoing effect of negative feelings and that introducing positive affect, even after someone experienced a high level of negative emotion, led to a more relaxed state.

Resiliency is reported to be positively correlated with life satisfaction, optimism, and tranquility, while being negatively correlated with depression (Fredrickson & Kurtz, 2011). Positive feelings associated with gratitude, hope, kindness, leadership, love, spirituality, and teamwork were determined to be part of the healing process during tragedies such as the 9/11 attacks (Peterson & Seligman, 2004). With violence, shootings, and other school crises, school psychologists can emphasize strengths and positive emotions to provide a break or respite to enhance students' coping efforts and replenish needed resources that have been depleted by stress (Peterson & Seligman, 2004).

Academic benefits of positive psychology also have been documented. Isen (2005) reviewed the literature that supports the benefits of positive affect in decision making in a range of settings, age groups, and professions. Benefits of positive affect include a broader scope of attention and range of behavioral responses, as well as an increase in creativity, especially intuitive ability and creative problem solving (Isen, 2005). Schools that provide numerous opportunities for positive emotions can be thriving institutions that encourage students and teachers to engage in innovative and creative paths to solving problems. It is likely that activities to increase positive affect might have favorable impact on performance in high stakes testing, but additional research needs to be conducted.

School psychologists can help children recognize, cultivate, and explore positive feelings to develop new skills, competencies, and ways of thinking about their experiences and their futures. For example, school psychologists can consult with teachers about the use of positive affect as a possible tool to prevent anxiety that many children experience with high-stakes testing (Fredrickson, 2009), as well as with selected students with anxiety disorders, who might require a more intensive intervention. Cultivating positive experiences in schools may improve overall school climate so that schools can be places to thrive. See Table 14.1 for a list of activities that school psychologists can model or teach to children and emphasize in collaboration with teachers and parents to increase positive emotions and foster well-being of students. These simple strategies to infuse daily interactions with positive affect have significant implications for school psychologists to use with children in schools.

Lens of Strengths

Although school psychologists typically emphasize a strengths-based orientation, they often find themselves using a deficit model in schools or identifying children's problems. Fortunately, positive psychology widens the point of entry in working with students through identifying and tapping into children's unique perspectives, strengths, talents, and interests, thereby leading to strategies that enhance learning. New information can be organized according to students' personal, meaningful, and relevant connections based on specific interests and strengths. A strengths-based approach can be applied to diverse children and adults from different populations, age groups, developmental levels, and disabilities. Therefore, school psychologists can apply principles of positive psychology by focusing on what is right about students and bringing that awareness to teachers, administrators, and parents.

Example: Helping teachers and parents find strengths in students. Ms. Tanzoli, a third-grade teacher, consulted with her school psychologist about Robbie, who was generally inattentive and not productive in class. During a meeting, Ms. Tanzoli and Robbie's mother described all the things Robbie did wrong. As the discussion progressed, the school psychologist pointed out that Robbie was a very creative thinker, although the school psychologist acknowledged that Robbie often did not follow Ms. Tanzoli's instructions. Bringing Robbie's creativity to the attention of Ms. Tanzoli and Robbie's mother led to an optimistic intervention approach. Ms. Tanzoli made use of Robbie's personal connections, using his interests and experience with the subject matter to make learning more relevant for him. In addition, Robbie reported that he felt acknowledged instead of reprimanded for his creative thinking, and he responded by taking more ownership of the need to actively engage. Therefore, the school psychologist discarded a deficit model and replaced it with a strengths-based model.

Example: Helping low performing students identify their strengths. Throughout elementary school, Jasmine demonstrated an extremely slow work pace and rarely completed her schoolwork or homework. Her teachers were disappointed and frustrated with Jasmine because they felt she did not respond to their efforts to help her. In fourth grade, things got worse for Jasmine when her grandmother, who was her primary caregiver, died. Jasmine became depressed. She almost always seemed on the verge of tears and produced even less academic work. Jasmine had limited family supports, and counseling was recommended but not pursued. In school, none of the students wanted to work with her in groups. It was commonly stated by the students and teachers that Jasmine did not do her share of the work. In addition, Jasmine was frequently late for school because she often missed the bus. On these occasions, Jasmine walked more than a mile to school. No one at school recognized her motivation to come to school, but instead Jasmine received frequent punishments because she was late.

The school psychologist began to work with Jasmine and learned that Jasmine had a beautiful singing voice. The school psychologist asked Jasmine to perform at the monthly school assembly and everyone was impressed with her talent. As a result, the teachers and students

Table 14.1. Activities to Enhance Positive Affect

- Create a positivity portfolio, a collection of items related to a positive emotion, and use these items to elicit feelings of relaxation or well-being at times of stress (Fredrickson, 2009)
- Watch a movie or read a book that is uplifting and inspiring
- Be mindful of positive experiences
- Plan time to savor positive feelings

began to respond to her more positively. Although Jasmine continued to have a slow work pace, she felt valued and became more hopeful and more invested in her schoolwork. She put in the time to learn to type, which substantially improved her work output. In addition, she realized that if she used songs to help her to remember things, she was much more successful in mastering academic concepts.

Character Strengths

Peterson and Seligman (2004) comprehensively investigated the construct of well-being by defining and classifying positive traits found in the writings of ancient spiritual leaders, moral philosophers, and educators, as universal virtues that existed across historical time periods and cultures. Peterson and Seligman (2004) identified six core virtues: courage, humanity, justice, temperance, transcendence, and wisdom, which they used to develop a more comprehensive list of character or signature strengths. Character strengths are clearly distinguished from general talents and abilities, because character strengths are directed for the benefit of others and society.

School psychologists can help children to flourish by working with them, as well as with their teachers and parents, to identify and develop character strengths. Scales, Benson, Leffert, and Blyth (2000) found that character strengths are associated with positive outcomes including school success, kindness, altruism, leadership, the ability to defer gratification, and a greater appreciation for diversity. Evidence suggests that hope, kindness, social intelligence, self-control, and perspective taking can buffer negative effects of stress and trauma and help youth thrive (Park & Peterson, 2009). In addition, Scales et al. (2000) reported that character strengths are associated with a reduction in substance and alcohol abuse, depression, suicidal ideation, and violence in youth. An emphasis on character strengths provides an alternative to a deficit focus because character encompasses a constellation of positive traits, not simply the absence of problems. Character strengths provide the foundation for positive youth development, can have a positive impact on school climate, and can be used as a basis for antibullying and other prevention programs.

Park, Peterson, and Seligman (2004) report that character strengths of love, hope, and zest are related to positive life satisfaction consistently across age levels. Park and Peterson (2009) reported that for very young children, the most prevalent strengths were love,

kindness, creativity, curiosity, and humor. For older youth, love, gratitude, hope, and zest were the strongest predictors of life satisfaction. Park and Peterson (2009) also reported that youth who possessed character strengths of hope, zest, and leadership demonstrated fewer internalizing problems (depression and anxiety), whereas youth possessing the character strengths of persistence, honesty, prudence, and love demonstrated fewer externalizing behaviors (aggression). Thus, research strongly suggests that many character strengths are inversely related to various types of emotional and behavioral challenges.

Park and Peterson (2009) reported that grade point averages (GPAs) were better predicted by the character strengths of perseverance, fairness, gratitude, honesty, hope, and perspective than by IQ. They further reported that high levels of love, hope, and zest at the beginning of the school year were related to increases in the levels of satisfaction at the end of the year (Park & Peterson, 2006). The importance of developing character strengths at an early age is emphasized by these findings, suggesting that present levels of happiness or satisfaction might be related to future happiness or satisfaction.

Research also suggested that self-regulation of parents did not strongly correlate to the parents' own life satisfaction; however, parents' self-regulation was strongly related with their child's life satisfaction, providing evidence for the importance of a stable home environment (Park & Peterson, 2006). Findings such as these encourage school psychologists to engage in family–school collaboration to support parents in supporting children.

School psychologists can provide innovative services to families through individual consultation and group presentations to promote development of strengths including children's self-regulation and school survival skills. School psychologists might find that parents are more likely to attend programs about developing students' strengths, in contrast to programs describing students' problems. Since life satisfaction is critical for health, good relationships, success, and well-being across all ages (Lyubomirsky, King, & Diener, 2005), cultivating character strengths provides an important pathway to thriving and mental health for children.

School psychologists can assist teachers in weaving the theme of character strengths throughout the academic curriculum by structuring book discussions around characters displaying or lacking various character strengths. Many books on required classroom reading lists can be used as the vehicle for academic assignments. For example, the characters in Louisa May

Alcott's *Little Women* can be used to illustrate several character strengths, including Jo's zest, Beth's courage, and Marmee's humanity. Table 14.2 provides some activities that school psychologists can suggest to students and teachers to increase awareness and cultivate character strengths. Promoting others to draw on their character strengths throughout their everyday lives can help to foster students' academic achievement, happiness, sense of self-efficacy, gratitude, and improve school climate (Park & Peterson, 2009).

Example: Collaborating with teachers about character strengths. The school psychologist asked the art teacher, Mr. Davis, to collaborate on a project integrating character strengths in an art unit on self-portraits. Mr. Davis was pleased to collaborate, and he invited the school psychologist to visit the sixth-grade art classes to introduce the idea of character strengths. The school psychologist developed a list of questions to define and describe character strengths in child-friendly language and presented the information to the class. The students were excited about the project, and they decided to incorporate their strongest character strength in the self-portraits. A great deal of conversation was generated throughout the school when the self-portraits were hung to decorate the hallways. Students and teachers across the school asked for more information about character strengths. As a result, other classes did similar projects.

Example: Teaching children about character strengths. A school psychologist facilitated a positive psychology club for fifth graders. During a club meeting, the students discussed their signature strengths and how they might use them every day. The students seemed especially interested in transcendence, but no one seemed to truly understand the concept. At the next week's meeting, Jason proudly proclaimed that he had felt transcendence. Jason said, "I noticed the sun setting as I was riding my bike home for dinner last night. All of a sudden I realized how beautiful it was. It made me feel so peaceful, relaxed, and happy."

The other students were intrigued and wanted to experience transcendence too. Many of them sought out transcendent experiences to describe in future group meetings, such as watching the sun set, noticing the beauty of nature while taking a hike, and paying attention to a deep blue sky or soft puffy clouds on a sunny day.

Gratitude

Gratitude is a powerful positive emotion and is associated with high levels of well-being (McCullough, Kilpatrick, Emmons, & Larson, 2001). Feelings of well-being when experiencing gratitude include feeling affirmed and valued, as well as a heightened awareness of social supports, which increases positive feelings (McCullough & Emmons, 2003). Research by Froh, Emmons, Card, Bono, and Wilson (2011) suggested that grateful adolescents enjoyed more social integration and higher life satisfaction, earned higher GPAs, and were less depressed or anxious than less grateful adolescents. They also suggest that positive affect may be a moderator of gratitude in children, and found that children with low levels of positive affect prior to a gratitude intervention responded with higher levels of gratitude and positive affect after the intervention than children with higher initial levels of positive affect (Froh, Emmons, et al., 2011).

Researchers believe that feelings of gratitude gradually emerge when children are between 7 and 10 years old, suggesting the importance for adults to give specific feedback to young children explaining the reasons why they are grateful (Froh, Fan, et al., 2011). Additional research investigating precursors of gratitude, such as prosocial behavior, perspective taking, and empathy is suggested to determine interventions that might promote the development gratitude (Froh, Fan, et al., 2011).

There are abundant opportunities to practice gratitude given all of the interactions occurring in schools. A common gratitude practice for all ages, keeping a

Table 14.2. Using Character Strengths in Schools

- Identify signature strengths online at http://www.authentichappiness.com
- Develop new character strengths and try them out in different situations
- Use strengths every day and pay attention to how it feels
- Use strengths in academics through writing assignments and discussions
- Use strengths in art, performances, and other projects
- Use strengths to improve school climates by noticing and appreciating others' strengths
- Use strengths to facilitate transitions by enhancing student confidence and providing strengths-based information to staff at the new setting
- Use strengths to enhance service learning projects
- Display strengths on bulletin boards

gratitude journal, has been has been demonstrated to increase positive affect and well-being in children (Froh, Sefick, & Emmons, 2008). School psychologists can encourage students, teachers, and parents to keep a gratitude journal to notice and savor feelings of gratitude on a daily or less regular basis. Another powerful gratitude intervention for adolescents and adults is a gratitude visit. For a gratitude visit, an individual writes and hand delivers a letter to someone who had been especially kind (Seligman, 2002). Both the writers of the letters and recipients of the visits report overwhelming positive emotions and well-being (Seligman, 2002).

In addition to gratitude programs for students, school psychologists can encourage gratitude programs for teachers and parents. At faculty meetings or parent presentations, school psychologists can suggest that the teachers and parents keep a gratitude journal or make a gratitude visit and then reflect on the experience. By combining strengths-based supports with gratitude, school psychologists can promote teachers finding characteristics they appreciate about children, especially children whom they may find challenging. It is very likely that the dynamics between students and teachers would change for the better if teachers are able to authentically experience positive emotions and express them to students (McCullough et al., 2001). Teachers who express gratitude frequently and intensely create cultures of caring and can have significant impact on school climate (McCullough et al., 2001). See Table 14.3 for activities about gratitude that school psychologists can use with children, teachers, and parents.

Example: Informal expressions of gratitude. A school psychologist interested in gratitude handed out Post-it notes in a variety of shapes, sizes, and colors for students to surprise others with messages of gratitude. Many teachers, students, office staff, and bus drivers pleasantly discovered a Post-it note in their work area with a specific message from a student. The recipients of the Post-it notes reported positive feelings and subsequently left surprise notes for others. Thus, additional prosocial benefits of expressing gratitude were achieved.

Flow and Student Engagement

Creation of learning environments that engage learners is central to a positive psychology approach in education and is captured in the concept of flow. Csikszentmihalyi (1997) describes the state of flow as the successful match between the level of challenge of a task and the level of skill of an individual. Through research using experience sampling, students were given beepers that signaled intermittently during the day and were asked to record what they were doing and how engaged they were in the task (Csikszentmihalyi, 1997). From this research, the following conditions for flow were delineated: (a) the task must be challenging but controllable, (b) the individual is able to concentrate, (c) goals are clear, (d) feedback is immediate, (e) the individual has a sense of control over actions, (f) the sense of self disappears, and (g) the sense of duration of time is altered (Csikszentmihalyi, 1997).

Csikszentmihalyi (1997) compares and contrasts the level of challenge with the level of skill required for a task and suggests that a low challenge task that requires little skill is considered boring (e.g., repetitious busy work at school), whereas a low challenge task that requires some skill can be relaxing (e.g., reading a fun book). In contrast, a high challenge task for which one does not have the skills can be anxiety provoking (e.g., a student with a reading problem taking a difficult multiple choice test), whereas a high challenge task for which one has strong skills creates flow (e.g., a student with strong math skills doing challenging math calculations). The same activity, such as doing math problems for homework, can produce flow, anxiety, boredom, or another state depending on the perceived difficulty of the task and the level of the person's skill.

Table 14.3. Gratitude Activities for Students, Teachers, and Parents

- See NASP's Gratitude Works program for several ideas at http://www.nasponline.org/communications/spawareness/2009_gratitudeworks.aspx
- Gratitude visit
- Gratitude journal
- Count your blessings: Before falling asleep, think of three positive events that occurred during the day for which you are thankful
- Notice and express gratitude when you see it in others
- Display gratitude messages on bulletin boards
- Informal expressions of gratitude: Use Post-it notes or other cards to write short messages of gratitude to surprise others
- Encourage teachers to be role models of gratitude

Frequent complaints from teachers about students not completing homework or independent class work is often explained by a lack of flow experience for the child, based on a mismatch between the level of skill and level of challenge of the task, as well as insufficient feedback about progress toward the goal for the child. It is disturbing to acknowledge that little flow experience occurs during a typical school day (Shernoff, Csikszentmihalyi, Schneider, & Shernoff, 2003), in contrast to how much flow is experienced through videogame playing. The popularity of videogames is convincing evidence for the importance of flow and how people, even children, seek flow experiences.

See Table 14.4 for a list of activities about the flow experience that school psychologists can promote for children. School psychologists can consult with teachers about flow, as well as share the information through presentations to teachers and parents. Teachers might be encouraged to present lessons in different ways or to offer a variety of options for assignments so that students can choose the one that best meets their unique combination of levels of challenge and skills.

Example: Flow and football. A school psychologist was teaching flow to a group of fourth graders and Dayshawn was the first to understand the concept. He said, "When I was learning to play football, I had to think about everything at once: the rules, what I was supposed to do, where the other players are and stuff like that. Now I'm good at football and as soon as the game starts, I don't really think about it. I'm in the flow, just playing. Then when the whistle blows at the end, I can't believe we played the whole game." When he spoke about his experience in those terms, other children began to understand flow. As the discussion continued most students reported that homework was not a flow experience for them; however, Tahjay said she was in the flow when she did division homework because it was fun and easy for her.

Example: Flow and academic assignments. Melissa, a student with a reading problem, said that she has more of a flow experience when she does a project as opposed to taking a test. She said, "When I take a test, I get really nervous and forget everything. I remember things better when I work on a project and I even got an A on my project about whales. I really learned a lot. In fact, I think I might want to be a marine biologist."

Optimism

The theory of optimism and pessimism is based on 30 years of research about how people explain everyday events that occur in their lives (Seligman, 2002) and has significant implications for schools. Research suggests that people who demonstrate an optimistic attribution style also experience positive psychological and physical health outcomes, with optimists being active problem solvers as opposed to being in denial (Aspinwall & Brunhart, 2000). Seligman (2002) suggests that pessimistic people view negative events as global, stable, and internal, and they view positive events as specific, unstable, and external. To the pessimist, bad events occur in most aspects of life, all the time, and because of personal characteristics or flaws. Negative attributions lead to people feeling hopeless and drained of motivation. Pessimists also believe that positive events occur rarely, only in specific situations, and simply because of luck. In contrast, optimists view negative events as seldom occurring, only in certain domains of their lives, and not due to their own actions. A more flexible optimistic attribution for negative events inspires problem solving because optimists believe things can change. Optimists have a rosy view of positive events, which they believe occur frequently, in many aspects of their lives, and because of their own merits.

Formal School-Based Optimism Curriculum

The Penn Resiliency Program (Seligman et al., 2009), a school-based curriculum to increase the daily resiliency skills of adolescents, has been well researched for more than 20 years with diverse samples, including individuals from various racial/ethnic backgrounds; rural, urban, and suburban communities; and different countries,

---

Table 14.4. Strategies to Increase Flow for Children

- Teach children about the concept of flow to increase their awareness
- Teach children to make scales for different dimensions of experience such as flow, boredom, relaxation, frustration, and anxiety so they can learn to differentiate between them
- Have children identify activities in which they are in the flow both in and out of school
- Have children design flow experiences for school that might enhance their learning, and design projects to demonstrate what they know
- Teach children to appropriately advocate with teachers for flow experiences
- Have children self-monitor during tasks to increase awareness

including the United States, United Kingdom, Australia, China, and Portugal. The Penn Resiliency Program teaches the skills of optimism using assertiveness, decision making, creative brainstorming, and relaxation training activities. The curriculum is delivered in group sessions 60–90 minutes each. Lessons are presented through stories, skits, role-plays, and other formats in which the participants actively practice the skills and reflect on the activities. Findings, based on the body of research from 2,000 children ranging in ages from 8 to 15, suggest that the Penn Resiliency Program can reduce and prevent symptoms of depression, anxiety, behavior problems, and hopelessness for children of diverse ethnic backgrounds (Seligman et al., 2009).

Although a formal curriculum can make it easy to work with children to change their attributions, it is not necessary. Once school psychologists learn about the optimistic and pessimistic attribution styles, they will find ways to teach them to students, teachers, and parents. See Table 14.5 for some activities for school psychologists to use in schools to help children develop the skills of optimism. These activities can be modified for use with teachers and parents.

Example: Teaching optimism to children. A school psychologist was teaching a group of fifth graders about optimism, and Samir spoke up. He said that learning about optimism and pessimism helped him one day when he became upset because he forgot to do his homework, and subsequently had to miss recess. Samir said, "I kept getting angrier and angrier thinking about how I always get in trouble. I was so mad that I almost got into a fight with Joey. Then all of a sudden I remembered about optimism. It was really hard because I was so mad and I really wanted to go out to recess. But I tried to think differently. I told myself it's only one day I'm missing recess and if I keep cool and do the work fast during recess, I could probably go outside for the last 10 minutes."

Optimism in Consultation With Teachers

Teaching attributions about optimism and pessimism can be especially helpful when school psychologists consult with teachers because optimistic teachers create optimistic classrooms. School psychologists can first present the topic of optimism to teachers using examples that are not school related and therefore are not threatening to teachers. A goal of the discussion should be to reinforce the idea that flexibility in thinking about a problem leads to a multitude of solutions. The school psychologist can advise teachers to pay attention to when they say "always" and "never" and recognize that words such as these can limit teachers' flexibility. When teachers discover for themselves that they are engaging in a pessimistic approach, they often are willing to shift their mindset.

Example: Promoting teacher optimism. A first-grade teacher, Ms. Jones, was very frustrated with Claudia, a student whom Ms. Jones described as always uncooperative. During a discussion with the school psychologist, Ms. Jones acknowledged that she reinforced Claudia's negative attention-seeking behaviors by creating power struggles with the student. However, Ms. Jones also stated that she did not think a behavior plan would work because she did not think that Claudia could change. During the consultation, the school psychologist reflected in a neutral, nonjudgmental tone some of the negative attributions that Ms. Jones had made. "So Claudia is only six years old and there is already no hope that she can change." When Ms. Jones heard her own statements reflected, she realized how rigid she had been. This led to flexibility in thinking.

The school psychologist also helped motivate Ms. Jones by recognizing her strengths as a teacher. She affirmed Ms. Jones' obvious past success in working with many students in difficult situations and suggested that her frustration (i.e., negative affect) was actually interfering with her excellent problem-solving skills. Ms. Jones suddenly seemed energized by the challenge and suggested a behavior plan. They devised one based on Claudia's strengths, including her love of learning, to increase intrinsic motivation. Claudia earned points throughout the day to do extra reading on the computer under Ms. Jones' supervision. Claudia was very successful with the plan. She received additional positive

Table 14.5. Activities to Develop Optimism in Children

- Teach children about the optimistic and pessimistic attribution style
- Provide common scenarios for positive and negative events
  - Play games like thumbs up/thumbs down to practice recognizing pessimistic or optimistic attribution styles
  - Change attributions from pessimistic to optimistic, while keeping it realistic
  - Role-play scenarios and discuss the related attributions
- Ask the students to pay attention to their own attributions and discuss

attention from her teacher, which improved their relationship, and also improved her academic skills. Ms. Jones learned that through collaboration her concerns could be heard, her frustrations could be expressed, and, with a focus on optimism and strengths, a positive outcome could be reached.

Hope

Many times students stuck in negative patterns of behavior feel little or no hope. They cannot find pathways out of the problem or are unable to mobilize their energy to believe they can change things. Hope theory provides some guidance to help students in these situations (Snyder, Rand, & Sigmon, 2005). Marques et al. (2011) reviewed research on hope and reported that hope is positively associated with well-being, self-worth, life satisfaction, academic achievement, compliance with medical regimes, athletic success, and social competence. Hope predicted academic achievement beyond what would be expected based on personality, intelligence, and previous academic achievement (Day, Hanson, Maltby, Proctor, & Wood, 2010). Gilman, Dooley, and Florell (2006) indicated that adolescents who reported significantly high hope also reported significantly high levels of global life satisfaction and personal adjustment.

Programs based on hope theory in schools focus first on guiding children to set realistic goals that are intrinsically motivating (Snyder et al., 2005). Sometimes setting realistic goals is difficult because hopeless students often use pessimistic attributions. When this occurs, the school psychologist is advised to start at the student's level of motivation and not impose a goal on the student. With encouragement and gentle probing, students often can define a basic goal, as simple as wanting to get through the school day to go home to play videogames. The school psychologist can use that rudimentary goal to demonstrate that the student has some power or control over his or her day and then facilitate moving on to more important goal setting in the future.

Another strategy to help define goals is to link future goals with past goals (Snyder et al., 2005). School psychologists can help students remember what worked in the past, even if unrelated to school, because past accomplishments remind students of strengths that could be used in the future. For instance, a child's successful basketball performance was probably due to a great deal of practice, which reinforces the idea that practice helps to improve most skills. Table 14.6 provides some suggestions for enhancing hope and goal setting in schools (Marques et al., 2011).

Marques et al. (2011) developed Building Hope for the Future, a 5-week hope-based curriculum for middle school students. The program integrates strategies of cognitive behavior, narrative and solutions-focused approaches, and offers psychoeducation, structured activities, role-plays, social skills instruction, and guided discussions. Marques et al. (2011) reported that the intervention increased hope, self-worth, and life satisfaction in middle school children, although results did not support significant changes in mental health or academic achievement.

Example: Positivity portfolios and strengths. A school psychologist working at a high school used a positivity portfolio intervention with Keisha, a young woman who felt hopeless about getting into college. Keisha had performed poorly on her SATs after many attempts, despite doing very well throughout high school. Keisha stated that all her life she thought that people viewed her as not intelligent because she was African American. She said, "I always worried I wasn't good enough and doing poorly on the SATs proves it." The school psychologist suggested that Keisha develop a positivity portfolio based on pride in her accomplishments. She asked Keisha to place artifacts in the portfolio representing her academic honors and success throughout her education.

At first, Keisha was put off by the word "pride" because of religious reasons but was comfortable using the term "confidence." Keisha stated that a positivity portfolio seemed silly but she agreed to put one together based on her previous academic accomplishments. Keisha brought her confidence positivity portfolio to the next session and presented and discussed it with the school psychologist. During the 2 weeks before the

Table 14.6. Strategies for Enhancing Hope and Goal Setting

- Use stories that illustrate how hope helps people get through difficult times.
- The stories should be at an appropriate developmental level for the age level of the child.
- Start with short-term goals. Later chain short-term goals to develop long-term goals.
- Focus on goals that are intrinsically motivating and refrain from imposing goals on a child.
- Monitor progress. Celebrate as the goal is reached or modify if the child gets off track.

SATs, Keisha was instructed to spend 10 minutes each day concentrating on the items in the portfolio and eliciting the positive feelings that she initially experienced when she had received the honors and certificates. The day before the test, Keisha said that she felt serene and relaxed after using the positivity portfolio. Weeks later when Keisha received her test results, she had significantly improved her scores and ultimately was accepted at the college of her choice. Despite her initial reluctance, Keisha attributed her success on the SATs to the use of her portfolio that allowed her to believe in herself, relax, and think more clearly as she took the test.

Applications at the Top Tier: Working With Troubled Youth

Although positive psychology is a universal, preventive approach for working with all students in schools, it also can be used more intensely with targeted individuals. School psychologists and other mental health professionals are cautioned to recognize that while the strategies, such as hope and optimism might seem simple, they can be powerful tools to be used carefully. For instance, often students with severe depression and anxiety are not experiencing positive emotions and they might respond negatively to a basic suggestion to count their blessings. Troubled students or students experiencing academic difficulties might firmly believe that they have no blessings to count. The role of school psychologists is not to use positive psychology to convince students to feel happy but instead to empathize, reframe the negative thoughts, or expand the thinking to discover more flexible options. For example, if the student is unable to think of three positive things that happened that day, perhaps he or she could think of a good thing that happened last year or at some other point in life. Finding that positive event could lead to positive emotions to build on for future problem solving. Another strategy would be to expand the individual's thinking of what a positive event involves. Although the troubled student might not be able to think of an extremely positive event, perhaps as a starting point, he or she can think of a small event that was mildly positive, resulting in a small increase in positive feelings.

Example: Positive affect and a lonely student. Isabel, a high school student, said she felt sad and lonely because she had no friends. She could think of nothing positive about her interactions with others and felt that no one was nice to her. The school psychologist asked Isabel if she would be willing to do an experiment and Isabel

agreed. The school psychologist asked Isabel to pay closer attention to how people interacted with her during the week. At the next session, Isabel said that she had never noticed before that another student, Sara, always held the door for her before algebra class and saved her a seat. Isabel said, "I probably took it for granted and didn't think about it as something nice. But when I noticed, it did make me feel good." Isabel said that she realized she might be discounting other little positive things in her life too. That small intervention to increase Isabel's positive affect began to open the door to problem solving.

Example: School refusal. Suddenly in March, Molly, a first grader, began to cry and refuse to leave her mother to come to school for no apparent reason. After a week of Molly's crying and missing school despite interventions by the teacher, principal, and guidance counselor, the school psychologist was asked to help. The school psychologist collaborated with the parents and teacher to develop a plan combining three themes of positive psychology. First, the school psychologist used character strengths and talked with Molly about her bravery in leaving her mother. Molly responded to this strategy and throughout the day would repeat to herself, "I'm a very brave girl." Second, the school psychologist developed a relationship based on trust by keeping in touch with Molly's parents during school so they felt that Molly's needs were being compassionately met. Therefore, they agreed with the school psychologist's request to bring Molly to her classroom 10 minutes early every day and to leave immediately, even if Molly cried. Last, recognizing the need to undo the negative emotions and increase positive affect, the school psychologist played a game with Molly in her classroom during the 10 minutes before school. Within 3 days Molly completely stopped crying, and on the fifth day she got in line with the other students instead of playing the game before school. For the rest of the school year, Molly usually gave the school psychologist a big smile and wave as they passed in the hallway each morning.

SUMMARY

Principles of positive psychology research have provided information that can be applied to schools to help them become flourishing centers of learning. In contrast to a deficit model, positive psychology focuses on positive emotions, positive traits, and positive institutions. Applications for positive psychology in schools are based on research using scientific techniques that test theories, as opposed to positive thinking and denial.

School psychologists can use positive psychology to implement, demonstrate, and cultivate strategies to foster well-being in children, teachers, and parents. School psychologists can communicate the benefits of increasing positive affect, identifying and using character strengths, expressing gratitude, engaging in flow activities, learning the skills of optimism, and enhancing hope to increase individual well-being, as well as to improve school climate. School psychologists can integrate knowledge of child development and other psychological orientations when applying positive psychology strategies to various age groups, developmental levels, and diverse populations. A positive psychology approach can be used individually or with groups of children, in collaboration with teachers, and through presentations and information sharing with parents. Although primarily a prevention approach to be used universally, positive psychology can be used with selected or targeted students in a more individualized manner to address the needs of troubled youth. As research on the application of positive psychology in schools continues to evolve, school psychologists will learn new ways to identify and nurture a greater variety of positive emotions, such as creativity, courage and curiosity to enhance the lives of children and help school communities to thrive.

REFERENCES

Aspinwall, L., & Brunhart, S. (2000). What I do know won't hurt me: Optimism, attention to negative information, coping and health. In J. Gillham (Ed.), *The science of optimism and hope.* (pp. 163–200). Radnor, PA: Templeton Foundation Press.

Aspinwall, L., & Tedeschi, R. (2010). The value of positive psychology for health psychology: Progress and pitfalls in examining the relation of positive phenomena to health. *Annals of Behavioral Medicine, 39,* 4–15. doi:10.1007/s12160-009-9153-0

Csikszentmihalyi, M. (1997). *Finding flow: The psychology of engagement with everyday life.* New York, NY: Basic Books.

Day, L., Hanson, K., Maltby, J., Proctor, C., & Wood, A. (2010). Hope uniquely predicts objective academic achievement above intelligence, personality, and previous academic achievement. *Journal of Research in Personality, 44,* 550–553. doi:10.1016/j.jrp.2010.05.009

Fredrickson, B. (2009). *Positivity: Groundbreaking research reveals how to embrace the hidden strength of positive emotions, overcome negativity, and thrive.* New York, NY: Crown.

Fredrickson, B., & Kurtz, L. (2011). Cultivating positive emotions to enhance human flourishing. In S. Donaldson, M. Csikszentmihalyi, & J. Nakamura (Eds.), *Applied positive psychology: Improved everyday life, health, schools, work, and society.* (pp. 35–48). New York, NY: Psychology Press.

Froh, J. J., Emmons, R. A., Card, N. A., Bono, G., & Wilson, J. A. (2011). Gratitude and the reduced costs of materialism in adolescents. *Journal of Happiness Studies, 12,* 289–302. doi:10.1007/s10902-010-9195-9

Froh, J. J., Fan, J., Emmons, R. A., Bono, G., Huebner, E. S., & Watkins, P. (2011). Measuring gratitude in youth: Assessing the psychometric properties of adult gratitude scales in children and adolescents. *Psychological Assessment, 23,* 311–324. doi:10.1037/a0021590

Froh, J. J., Sefick, W. J., & Emmons, R. A. (2008). Counting blessings in early adolescents: An experimental study of gratitude and subjective well-being. *Journal of School Psychology, 46,* 213–233. doi:10.1016/j.jsp.2007.03.005

Gilman, R., Dooley, J., & Florell, D. (2006). Relative levels of hope and their relationship with academic and psychological indicators among adolescents. *Journal of Social and Clinical Psychology, 25,* 166–178. doi:10.1521/jscp.2006.25.2.166

Gilman, R., Easterbrooks, S., & Frey, M. (2004). A preliminary study of multidimensional life satisfaction among deaf/hard of hearing youth across environmental settings. *Social Research Indicators, 66,* 143–164. doi:10.1023/B:SOCI.0000007495.40790.85

Harris, A., Thoresen, C., & Lopez, S. (2007). Integrating positive psychology into counseling: Why and (when appropriate) how. *Journal of Counseling and Development, 85,* 3–13. doi:10.1002/j.1556-6678.2007.tb00438.x

Isen, A. (2005). A role for neuropsychology in understanding the facilitating influence of positive affect on social behavior and cognitive processes. In C. Snyder & S. Lopez (Eds.), *Handbook of positive psychology.* (pp. 528–540). New York, NY: Oxford University Press.

Lyubomirsky, S., King, L., & Diener, E. (2005). The benefits of frequent positive affect: Does happiness lead to success? *Psychological Bulletin, 131,* 803–855. doi:10.1037/0033-2909.131.6.803

Lyubomirsky, S., Sheldon, K., & Schkade, D. (2005). Pursuing happiness: The architecture of sustainable change. *Review of General Psychology, 9,* 111–131. doi:10.1037/1089-2680.9.2.111

Marques, S., Lopez, S., & Pais-Ribero, J. (2011). Building hope for the future: A program to foster strengths in middle-school students. *Journal of Happiness Studies, 12,* 139–152. doi:10.1007/s10902-009-9180-3

McCullough, M., & Emmons, R. (2003). Counting blessings versus burdens: An experimental investigation of gratitude and subjective well-being in daily life. *Journal of Personality and Social Psychology, 84,* 377–389. doi:10.1037/0022-3514.84.2.377

McCullough, M., Kilpatrick, S., Emmons, R., & Larson, D. (2001). Is gratitude a moral affect? *Psychological Bulletin, 127,* 249–266. doi:10.1037//0033-2909.127.2.249

National Association of School Psychologists. (2010). *Model for comprehensive and integrated school psychological services.* Bethesda, MD: Author. Retrieved from http://www.nasponline.org/standards/2010standards/2_PracticeModel.pdf

Park, N., Huebner, S., Laughlin, J., Valois, R., & Gilman, R. (2004). A cross-cultural comparison of the dimensions of child and adolescent life satisfaction reports. *Social Research Indicators, 66,* 61–79. doi:10.1023/B:SOCI.0000007494.48207.dd

Park, N., & Peterson, C. (2006). Character strengths and happiness among young children: Content analysis of parental descriptions. *Journal of Happiness Studies, 7,* 323–341. doi:10.1007/s10902-005-3648-6

Park, N., & Peterson, C. (2009). Strengths of character in schools. In R. Gilman, E. Huebner, & M. Furlong (Eds.), *Handbook of positive psychology in schools.* (pp. 65–76). New York, NY: Routledge.

Park, N., Peterson, C., & Seligman, M. (2004). Strengths of character and wellbeing. *Journal of Social and Clinical Psychology, 23*, 603–619. doi:10.1521/jscp.23.5.603.50748

Peterson, C., & Seligman, M. (2004). *Character strengths and virtues: A handbook and classification*. Washington, DC: American Psychological Association.

Ponterotto, J., Mendelowitz, D., & Collabolletta, E. (2008). Promoting multicultural personality development: A strengths-based, positive psychology worldview for schools. *Professional School Counseling, 12*, 93–99. doi:10.5330/PSC.n.2010-12.100

Scales, P. C., Benson, P. L., Leffert, N., & Blyth, D. A. (2000). Contribution of developmental assets to the prediction of thriving among adolescents. *Applied Developmental Science, 4*, 27–46. doi:10.1207/S1532480XADS0401_3

Seligman, M. (2002). *Authentic happiness: Using the new positive psychology to realize your potential for lasting fulfillment*. New York, NY: Free Press.

Seligman, M. (2011). *Flourish: A visionary new understanding of happiness and well-being*. New York, NY: Free Press.

Seligman, M., Ernst, R., Gillham, J., Reivich, K., & Linkins, M. (2009). Positive education: Positive psychology and classroom interventions. *Oxford Review of Education, 35*, 293–311. doi:10.1080/03054980902934563

Shernoff, D. J., Csikszentmihalyi, M., Schneider, B., & Shernoff, E. S. (2003). Student engagement in high school classrooms from the perspective of flow theory. *School Psychology Quarterly, 18*, 158–176. doi:10.1521/scpq.18.2.158.21860

Snyder, C., Rand, K., & Sigmon, D. (2005). Hope theory: a member of the positive psychology family. In C. Snyder & S. Lopez (Eds.), *The handbook of positive psychology*. (pp. 257–276). New York, NY: Oxford University Press.

Veenhoven, R. (2005). Is life getting better? How long and happily do people live in modern society? *European Psychologist, 10*, 330–343. doi:10.1027/1016-9040.10.4.330

Best Practices in Social Skills Training

Jennifer R. Frey
The George Washington University (DC)
Stephen N. Elliott
Cindy Faith Miller
Arizona State University

OVERVIEW

Schools are social and dynamic places. Learning, working, and playing are highly social processes, and children who acquire and use skills that allow them to interact effectively and avoid problems with peers and adults have advantages as learners, workers, and players. Such skills commonly are referred to as social skills. Teachers classify several social skills as critical for students' classroom success: following directions and rules, paying attention to instructions, controlling temper, managing conflict, and interacting well with others (Frey, Elliott, & Kaiser, 2013; Lane, Givner, & Pierson, 2004; Lane, Stanton-Chapman, Jamison, & Phillips, 2007). Researchers also have documented that some of the most socially important outcomes for children and youth include peer, teacher, and parent acceptance (Gresham, 2002).

Parker and Asher's (1987) classic review showed that children who had difficulties in peer relationships often demonstrated an antisocial and/or aggressive behavior. Without effective interventions, this behavior pattern is likely to continue (Elliott, Frey, & DiPerna, 2012). Children's social behaviors also have a meaningful and predictive relationship with their long-term academic achievement. As a result, school social skills typically are viewed as academic enablers (DiPerna & Elliott, 2002). Researchers of a longitudinal study frequently cited to support this perception of social skills as academic enablers found that social skills of 500 third graders, as assessed by teachers, were slightly better predictors of these students' academic achievement in eighth grade than their achievement test results in third grade (Caprara, Barbaranelli, Pastorelli, Bandura, & Zimbardo, 2000). Other investigators have reported similar findings, thus highlighting that social skills are vitally important social and academic enablers for children in schools.

This chapter addresses the domain of Interventions and Mental Health Services to Develop Social and Life Skills of the National Association of School Psychologists (NASP) *Model for Comprehensive and Integrated School Psychological Services* (NASP, 2010). This chapter specifically focuses on methods for teaching and helping children improve key social skills. The assessment concepts and intervention strategies presented address fundamental competencies for school psychologists concerning methods for enhancing the development and well-being of all students, data-based decision making, and multitiered intervention services. After reading this chapter, school psychologists will have several powerful conceptual organizers for analyzing social skills, knowledge of key social skills to consider for improvement, a framework for cultural considerations, and a systematic six-step process for teaching and improving social skills.

BASIC CONSIDERATIONS

Social skills are multidimensional, interactive, and context specific behaviors. There are four common features of social skills (Elliott et al., 2012): (a) social skills facilitate the initiation and maintenance of positive relationships, (b) social skills promote peer acceptance and friendship development, (c) social skills are related to positive school outcomes, and (d) social skills help individuals adapt and adjust to their social environments.

Often when we first think of social skills we think of skills such as sharing, conversational turn-taking, cooperating with others, initiating or responding to peers or adults, or social problem solving. Findings from factor analyses and reviews of the social skills intervention research suggest social skills can be classified into the following seven areas of social behavior: cooperation, communication, assertion, responsibility, empathy, engagement, and self-control (see Gresham & Elliott, 2008). Behaviors in each of these response classes can be assessed reliably, and they have been targets of universal (Tier 1), targeted (Tier 2), and intensive (Tier 3) social skills interventions for students of all ages.

Top 10 Social Skills

Gresham and Elliott (2008) researched teachers' ratings of the social skills most critical to students' classroom success. From preschool through early adolescence, the following 10 skills were identified as most critical: listening to others, following directions, following classrooms rules, ignoring peer distractions, asking for help, taking turns in conversations, cooperating with others, controlling temper in conflict situations, acting responsibly with others, and showing kindness to others. These top 10 social skills potentially are the socially important behaviors to target in universal or prevention-based social skills training programs because they are the skills most frequently rated by teachers as critical for successful classroom experiences (Gresham & Elliott, 2008).

Students participating in universal or prevention-based social skills programs should be screened on these top 10 skills to determine if they need more intensive social skills instruction. For students who may need more support, their social skills should be assessed, and intensive or targeted interventions should be developed (or modified from existing to curricula) to meet their needs (Tier 2 and/or Tier 3 social skills interventions). The social skills addressed in these Tier 2 and Tier 3 intervention programs may go beyond the top 10 social skills and include other skills such as paying attention to others, paying attention to your work, standing up for others, respecting people's things, introducing yourself to others, and making compromises (see Elliott & Gresham, 2008). The Social Skills Improvement System (Gresham & Elliott, 2008) provides screening tools, ratings scales, a universal intervention program

addressing the top 10 social skills, and an intervention guide designed for small group (Tier 2) selected intervention with materials for teaching 20 social skills to students in small groups. School psychologists may find this system useful for assessing social skills and planning interventions.

How Children Learn Social Skills

Often children acquire social skills without systematic training. They learn these skills from watching friends, siblings, and adults and through talking with their parents and teachers. Some children, however, need to be taught specifically how to perform a social behavior and/or when (in what context) to use the skill. Social skills can be taught using approaches grounded in social (Bandura, 1977), operant (Skinner, 1953), and cognitive–behavior (Weissburg, 1985) learning theories.

Given the context-specific nature of social skills, an important distinction in the performance of social behaviors is between social skills acquisition deficits and social skills performance deficits (Gresham & Elliott, 1990, 2008). Sometimes children do not perform desired social behaviors because they do not know how to perform these behaviors. When a child cannot demonstrate a skill, the behavior is considered an acquisition deficit. Acquisition deficits (or can't do behaviors) need to be explicitly taught and reinforced. Sometimes students have a desired social behavior within their repertoire, but they do not perform the behavior consistently or at desired levels. These behaviors are classified as performance deficits (or won't do behaviors). Performance deficits are due to motivational or performance issues and not to issues with learning the skill. During the assessment process, school psychologists should determine if the absence of a skill is due to an acquisition deficit or a performance deficit to determine how the skill needs to be taught and reinforced.

BEST PRACTICES IN SOCIAL SKILLS TRAINING

Before social skills can be taught, school psychologists and teachers need to know what skills to teach and which students might need additional support. Therefore, social skills assessment is a necessary component of best practices in social skills training. Social skills assessment should be used to monitor progress during social skills programs, to identify children for whom universal intervention is insufficient, and to determine which social skills to teach. In this section, we describe common methods in and recommendations for social skills assessment, discuss selection of intervention targets, present a six-step process for teaching social skills, and discuss cultural and gender considerations when planning social skills instruction.

Social Skills Assessment

To design and implement effective social skills interventions, there must be an assessment system that provides the necessary information for such intervention planning. Assessment of social skills must include measurement of (a) a broad range of prosocial behaviors (e.g., communication, cooperation, self-control) and antisocial behaviors (e.g., externalizing behaviors, internalizing behaviors), (b) specific behaviors within each of the categories of social behaviors (e.g., initiating to peers, responding to peers, following directions, resolving conflicts with peers and adults) for identification of possible intervention targets, (c) a method for determining acquisition and performance deficits and social skills strengths, and (d) the social validity of intervention targets. School psychologists have central roles in using or supporting the use of social skills assessments through administration of the assessments and/or supporting teachers and parents in interpreting and understanding assessment results.

Assessment Methods

Several methods exist for assessing students' social skills: direct observation, parent/teacher/child interviews, peer sociometric ratings, and social behavior rating scales. Ratings scales are the most frequently used method for assessing students' social skills (Crowe, Beauchamp, Catroppa, & Anderson, 2011; Humphrey et al., 2011), and they can be used across settings by multiple informants (e.g., teachers, parents, students) and over time to provide information about performance on a range of behaviors. Rating scales are useful to school psychologists, teachers, and parents because they summarize raters' characterizations of their experiences with students and their recent observations of students' behaviors. In a review of measures of social–emotional skills, Humphrey et al. (2011) determined the three most frequently used social behavior rating scales were the Diagnostic Analysis of Nonverbal Accuracy (Nowicki & Duke, 1989); the Social Competence and Behavior Evaluation Scale (LaFreniere & Dumas, 1990); and the Social Skills Rating System and its revision, the Social Skills Improvement System–Rating Scales (Gresham & Elliott, 1990, 2008).

With that said, the use of rating scales to measure performance of social behaviors has been criticized by some investigators. For example, a consistent finding across rating scales completed by multiple informants is that there is moderate to low cross-informant agreement (e.g., Gresham, Elliott, Cook, Vance, & Kettler, 2010). That is, the ratings provided by a parent, for example, and the ratings provided by a teacher for the same child generally are only moderately correlated. Yet in the case of social skills assessment, even little to moderate agreement across raters is informative. By gathering ratings from multiple informants, a child's behavior can be understood across situations and settings. Low agreement across raters can inform school psychologists and teachers about which behaviors may occur only in one setting (e.g., home or school), while moderate to high agreement might inform school psychologists and teachers about behaviors that are occurring across a variety of situations and contexts. This information is useful for determining acquisition and performance deficits, strengths, and intervention targets.

Another concern with the use of rating scales is that they are indirect observational measures. The information yielded by a rating scale is different from the data collected through direct observation of specific, often discrete, behaviors. Ratings scales generally are more global measures with behaviors aggregated into response classes or subscales (e.g., the discrete, observable behavior of initiating to a peer may be one of the behaviors included in the class of communication behaviors on a rating scale). However, more behaviors can be measured on a rating scale than can be measured during direct observation.

Even with limitations, rating scales are an effective and efficient method for assessing social skills and should be utilized by school psychologists as part of the overall assessment process for identifying students who may need additional support in learning social skills and/or for planning and monitoring social skills interventions.

Multiple Measures

Recommended practice is to use multiple methods and to gather information from multiple sources. By using multiple measures and methods, a more complete picture of a student's skills and needs can be created. More specifically, we recommend school psychologists (a) conduct multiple direct observations of the target student with his or her peers across routine settings; (b) interview teachers and caregivers, and potentially the target student, to gather more information about any concerns and when either low performance of desired social behaviors or increased performance of problem behaviors is observed; and (c) have teachers and, when possible, parents complete rating scales (preferably norm-referenced rating scales) for performance of social skills, externalizing, and internalizing behaviors. The exact assessments used and behaviors observed should be based on the purpose of the assessment: identification, intervention planning, or progress monitoring.

Identification of Target Behaviors

Owing to the context-specific nature of social skills, it is important to not only identify what social skills are in a student's repertoire but also which skills are important for students to learn and use in what situations. From a social validity perspective, the behaviors selected for intervention should be behaviors that parents, teachers, and peers feel are socially important, adaptive, and functional in a given context. Therefore, it is important to gather information from multiple informants (e.g., parents, teachers, students) about which skills are necessary for successful, positive experiences in various settings (e.g., home, school, community) before deciding what skills need to be taught and where these skills should be taught (Frey et al., 2013).

To address the issue of social validity, Gresham and Elliott introduced the use of social skills importance ratings on the Social Skills Rating Scales (Gresham and Elliott, 1990) and the Social Skills Improvement System–Rating Scales (Gresham and Elliott, 2008). On these rating scales, parents and teachers not only rate how often they have observed a target child performing a behavior, but they also rate how important that behavior is for success in their classrooms (teachers) or for their children's development (parents). Using this model, frequency and importance ratings for each social skill item are considered together to identify and prioritize skills that should be targeted in intervention. Specifically, social skills items with low frequency ratings (behaviors that have never or seldom been observed by the rater) and high importance ratings are socially important skills that are either an acquisition or performance deficit for the child and therefore should be included as targets of a social skills intervention for that child. School psychologists, teachers, and parents should discuss in which contexts or settings and with whom a child can perform a specific skill. If a child can perform the skill in some contexts, then parents and specialists should continue to reinforce that skill when they observe it and create more opportunities for the child to practice the skill. If the team learns the child cannot perform the skill in any settings, then that skill

may need to be taught through direct instruction, modeling, and coaching. In the absence of importance ratings, school psychologists should discuss with teachers and parents which social behaviors are most important to them prior to selecting which social skills to teach.

Teaching and Supporting Social Skills

Social skills are most effectively taught through modeling desired social behaviors, providing opportunities to practice new skills, providing corrective feedback and reinforcement in the moment, and discussing or reviewing social skills after students have an opportunity to practice these skills. Across all ages, six identified components of effective social skills programs are: tell, show, do, practice, monitor progress, and generalize (Elliott & Gresham, 2008). Using these six components, the school psychologist should first provide a learning objective, define the target skill, discuss why that skill is important, and give step-by-step information about how to perform the skill (the tell phase). Next, the school psychologist should model examples and nonexamples of the target behavior and engage the students in a role-play of performing the behavior (the show phase). After students have had an opportunity to learn and observe the skills, the school psychologist should ask students to define the skill and explain why it is important, state the steps required to accomplish the skills, discuss in which situations it would be appropriate or important to perform the skill, and then the students should model the target skill for the school psychologist (the do phase). Then the school psychologist should create opportunities for the students to practice the target skill in functional contexts and situations (the practice phase). During this part of the training, the school psychologist should prompt the use of the target behavior, as needed, and naturally observe and reinforce students for performing the target behavior and provide corrective feedback as needed. Over time, the school psychologist also should ask the students to think about how they are doing performing the skills and, when appropriate, self-evaluate their performance (the monitor progress phase). School psychologists should plan or coordinate for students to practice the skill outside of the primary intervention setting and with other interaction partners (the generalize phase). In addition, school psychologists should discuss with parents what skills children are practicing at school and, if appropriate, provide support and strategies for parents to help their children practice these skills in home and community settings as well. When these six components are incorporated into social skills interventions, students acquire new social behaviors, increase the rate and consistency of performance of these new behaviors, and, because of the generalize component, students should be able to use the new skills across appropriate contexts (Elliott et al., 2012).

Multiple intervention packages and systems already exist for teaching and supporting all students in a classroom (universal intervention) and for teaching social skills in targeted or intensive intervention settings, and school psychologists are encouraged to reference Elliott et al. (2012) and the Collaborative for Academic, Social, and Emotional Learning *Guide for Effective Social and Emotional Learning Programs* (http://casel.org/guide) for a review of common social skills instruction programs. Table 15.1 provides a brief comparison of selected evidence-based social skills intervention programs based on the review work of Elliott et al. (2012) and the Collaborative for Academic, Social, and Emotional Learning. In determining what socials skills intervention strategy or package to use, the challenge is in selecting an appropriate intervention that matches the needs of the students and the values of the teachers and families, having the resources and time to implement the intervention, and having effective support and feedback for intervention implementation.

Teachers are in a unique position to serve as effective social skills trainers. They spend extensive time with children across multiple contexts and have in-depth knowledge of the unique characteristics, strengths, and limitations of the students in their classroom. The role of teachers also allows them to take advantage of teachable moments by teaching, monitoring, and reinforcing skills in naturally occurring situations, thereby promoting generalization. Despite the advantages of having teachers function as social skills trainers, teachers often do not receive adequate training on selecting and implementing social–emotional curricula and might feel uncomfortable or burdened when asked to "add one more thing" to their already demanding responsibilities and schedules. Therefore, school psychologists should be mindful of supportive strategies they can utilize when working with teachers on implementing social skills interventions.

First, teachers might be more receptive and comfortable implementing social skills interventions if they are involved in the process of selecting and planning for the interventions. Second, it is essential that teachers are provided with training on how to effectively implement the program selected for their classroom and that they are given ample time to plan for how to incorporate the program into their schedule. During the training,

emphasize the key role that social skills plays in academic success, so teachers are able to recognize how their efforts contribute to short- and long-term achievement. Once teachers begin implementing a social skills intervention program, it is important to provide ongoing support to assist them with teaching and monitoring students' progress. School psychologists might consider team teaching some lessons with teachers and/or scheduling regular consultative meetings to troubleshoot issues and discuss progress. Third, it is important that school psychologists advocate for the importance of implementing social skills interventions by seeking administrative support and resources for teachers. Teachers will be more likely to successfully meet the social and emotional needs of students when they are in a supportive and positive school environment.

Cultural and Gender Considerations

The acquisition and performance of social skills occurs within a cultural context that includes the cultural traditions and social norms that each child has learned from his or her family and the cultural milieu and social expectations of the school environment. During the 2009–2010 school year, approximately 45% of students enrolled in public elementary and secondary schools were from ethnic or racial minority backgrounds (Chen, 2011). Regarding the level of ethnic diversity in educators, reports indicated that approximately 83% of public school teachers (in 2007–2008; U.S. Department of Education, 2012) and 91% of school psychologists (in 2009–2010; Curtis, Castillo, & Gelley, 2012) were from Caucasian backgrounds. These statistics illustrate the high level of cultural incongruity between educators and the students they serve.

The diversity in students' backgrounds and the lack of diversity within educators has important implications for efforts directed at teaching social skills effectively. It is important to consider that children learn and enact social skills within the context of the peer group. However, children within the peer group may value different social behaviors, and this difference may be especially true when children are from different cultural backgrounds or gender groups. Therefore, school psychologists need to be aware of cultural/gender differences and have the skills to help children negotiate cultural misunderstandings.

School psychologists also need to be aware of cultural differences between students and the school environment. The culture of most schools tends to be consistent with the values, expectations, and norms of the dominant

Table 15.1. Comparison of a Sample of Common, Evidence-Based Social Skills Intervention Programs

Program	Target Grades	Primary Goal	Target Skills/Behaviors	Format	Intervention Monitoring	Student Data Forms	Website
Good Behavior Game	1–6	Reduction of classroom disruption, aggression, and shyness	Talking or verbal disruption; aggression/physical disruption; out-of-seat behavior; noncompliance	Interdependent group contingency teams	No	No	http://goodbehaviorgame.com
The Incredible Years	Pre-K–2	Teach understanding/recognition of feelings; problem solving; anger management; and friendship making skills	Peer aggression and disruption; social skills and cooperation; understanding of feelings; conflict management skills; academic engagement	Classroom-wide curriculum; 64 lessons taught through explicit instruction	Yes	No	http://www.incredibleyears.com
PATHS Curriculum	K–6	Facilitate self-control, emotional awareness, and interpersonal problem-solving skills	Improvement of self-control; conflict resolution strategies; decision making; emotion regulation; promote empathy	Daily class curriculum; 40–52 lessons per grade taught through explicit skills instruction	Yes	Yes	http://www.channing-bete.com/prevention-programs/paths/paths.html
Positive Action Program	Pre-K–12	Promote character development and socioemotional skills; reduce disruptive and problem behaviors.	Self-concept; positive actions for mind/body; managing self responsibly; getting along with others; honesty with self and others; continuous self-improvement	Scripted lessons, role-plays, and activities; 140 lessons per grade taught through explicit skills instruction	Yes	Yes	http://www.positiveaction.net
Second Step	Pre-K–8	Instruction in social and emotional learning	Empathy; emotion management; friendship skills; problem solving	Brain builder games; weekly theme activities; reinforcing activities; home links; 22–28 weekly topics with explicit skills instruction	Yes	Yes	http://www.secondstep.org
Social Skills Improvement System—Class-Wide Intervention Program	Pre-K–8	Learn and apply social skills; enable academic achievement and enhance interpersonal relationships	Cooperation; assertion; responsibility; empathy; self-control	Ten sequenced units on social skills; weekly lessons organized into a six-phase instructional approach	Yes	Yes	http://www.pearsonassessments.com/HAIWEB/Cultures/en-us/Productdetail.htm?Pid=PAaSSISclass

Note. Based on information from Elliott, Frey, and DiPerna (2012) and from the Collaborative for Academic, Social, and Emotional Learning (2012).

culture. This culture can be problematic for students from ethnic and racial minorities who might have been socialized in ways that are inconsistent with the expectations of their school culture and who might then be misunderstood or punished at school for behaving in ways that are socially acceptable at home. To effectively address this concern, school psychologists need to recognize the difference between social skills acquisition or performance deficits and cultural differences that exist between students and the school environment. Furthermore, when cultural differences arise, it needs to be considered whether the differences can be respected in the school environment or whether it is necessary for students to alter their behaviors so they can be successful in social and academic situations at school. Establishing strong school–family partnerships is key for school personnel to understand the social norms in students' homes and for parents to understand the social expectations at school. Ultimately, differences in social expectations and practices may exist. If so, learning to discriminate when different expectations are in effect becomes a major intervention outcome.

Developing and maintaining the skills to be a culturally competent school psychologist is a challenging task; that is, school psychologists are encouraged to commit to a long-term learning process where they identify gaps in their skills and participate in cross-cultural training opportunities. A key ingredient to implementing culturally competent social skills training is for school psychologists to be aware of their own gender/cultural identity and to continually reflect on how their biases may have an impact on their perceptions of and interactions with students. There are many resources available to school psychologists who are interested in increasing their cultural competencies (e.g., Lopez & Rogers, 2007). The goal of the following sections is to briefly introduce school psychologists to issues that are important to consider when specifically implementing culturally competent social skills training focusing on the social categories of gender and ethnicity.

Gender and Ethnic Differences in Social Skills

A number of studies have identified gender and ethnic differences in social skills. Regarding gender differences in social behaviors, girls have been found to be more prosocial (Romer, Ravitch, Tom, Merrell, & Wesley, 2011), talkative (Leaper & Smith, 2004), and better at decoding others' emotions (Hall, Carter, & Horgan, 2000) when compared to boys. Moreover, observational studies on aggression have consistently found that boys are more aggressive than girls. It is important to note, however, that there is considerable within-group variability and many more similarities than differences between groups. Furthermore, it is important to keep in mind that differences in behaviors are not necessarily due to biological differences between groups. Rather, group differences are often explained by a multitude of factors (e.g., biological, social, cognitive, situational) that interact with each other in complex ways.

Intergroup Attitudes, Interactions, and Miscommunications

The differences in the values, norms, and communication styles between individuals from different groups have the potential to lead to intergroup miscommunications or conflict. Although there has been limited research directly addressing how children's gender or cultural differences cause miscommunications, studies on children's intergroup attitudes and interactions suggest that miscommunications likely occur between groups. For instance, research on children's other-gender attitudes and interactions indicates that girls and boys have more positive feelings toward and feel more comfortable with same-gender peers compared to other-gender peers. Children's same-gender positivity bias is present as early as preschool and is associated with children's expectancies (e.g., likelihood of inclusion and enjoyment) for interacting with same-gender and other-gender peers in fifth grade (Zosuls et al., 2011). Furthermore, research suggests that children have more positive interactions when working with same-gender than other-gender peers. Strough, Swenson, and Cheng (2001) found that, compared to mixed-gender dyads, same-gender dyads reported greater friendship, enjoyment expectations, and perceptions of affiliation. Similarly, findings from observational studies have suggested that children are more collaborative and affiliative when working with same-gender than other-gender peers (e.g., Leman, Ahmed, & Ozarow, 2005).

Similar to the research on other-gender relationships, studies examining cross-ethnic attitudes and interactions suggested that children feel more positive about and comfortable with peers who are members of their ethnic group compared to peers who are not members of their ethnic group. Research on intergroup ethnic attitudes has suggested that when children are asked to indicate their preferences, allocate rewards, or make trait attributions, they tend to make decisions that favor same-ethnic peers over other other-ethnic peers (see Nesdale, 2007).

Role of Self-Segregation

The role of segregation has long been implicated as a key factor in children's intergroup relationships. The premise pertaining to social skills development is that spending time in predominantly same-gender and same-ethnic peer groups leads to the development of gender- and ethnic-typed interaction styles that become more strengthened and rigid throughout development. The prevalence of gender and ethnic segregation is a concern when considering the potential consequences for peer relationships. Gender development researchers believe that the pervasive nature of gender segregation leads girls and boys to have vastly different socialization experiences that strengthen gender-typed behaviors and, in turn, contribute to cross-gender communication and interpersonal problems in adolescence and adulthood (Underwood & Rosen, 2009). Studies examining ethnic segregation also suggest implications for peer relationships. Recent research with African American and European American fourth and fifth graders found that ethnic segregation predicted declines in cross-ethnic acceptance (Wilson & Rodkin, 2012). Taken together, research suggests that gender and ethnic segregation can be detrimental to intergroup interactions and relationships.

Promoting Positive Cross-Gender and Cross-Ethnic Interactions

Concerns regarding intergroup biases and segregation have led researchers and practitioners to develop and implement strategies to promote more positive intergroup relationships. These strategies include the promotion of intergroup contact, teaching key relationship skills, and increasing awareness of gender/cultural biases. A description is provided of a recently developed school-based program that incorporates these strategies to promote positive gender and peer relationships.

Intergroup Contact

The negative outcomes associated with segregation have prompted researchers to consider the potential benefits of promoting intergroup contact. A meta-analysis of 515 studies found that intergroup contact reduces prejudice between groups and that effects are stronger when approaches are structured to meet Allport's (1954) four optimal conditions: equal status between the groups in the situation, common goals, intergroup cooperation, and support of institutional authorities (Pettigrew & Troop, 2006). The most widely documented school-based strategy consistent with Allport's intergroup contact theory is the use of cooperative learning techniques. Cooperative learning involves placing students in small groups to work together to accomplish shared goals. Key features to establishing effective cooperative learning groups include positive interdependence, promotive interaction, individual accountability, interpersonal skills, and group processing (see Gillies, 2007). When cooperative learning groups incorporate these key features, they promote improved academic achievement and positive social relationships, support the formation of cross-ethnic friendships, and improve intergroup attitudes (Slavin & Cooper, 1999).

While cooperative learning techniques traditionally have been implemented in classrooms to accomplish academic learning goals, they also can be used effectively as a tool for providing culturally competent social skills training. When students are placed in diverse cooperative learning groups (mixed-sex and mixed-ethnic groups), they will have opportunities to practice and generalize social skills with peers who are both similar and different from them. These opportunities may assist students with recognizing their own and others' perspectives and unique styles of interacting and may allow them to apply their knowledge and skills in supportive and culturally meaningful contexts.

Providing students with experiences to learn and practice social skills with diverse peers should not be limited to the primary intervention setting. It is important that students have ongoing chances to generalize what they learned during the intervention to their daily interactions. This goal can be accomplished by intentionally planning opportunities for students to interact with diverse peers throughout the school day. Importantly, creating consistent opportunities for students to interact with mixed-sex and mixed-ethnic peers communicates to students that diversity is valued and supported in their school.

Key Relationship Skills

Evidence-based social skills interventions incorporate a variety of different skills to facilitate students' academic achievement and interpersonal relationships. However, certain social skills may be especially important for the development of positive intergroup relationships. For instance, social skills that help students recognize different perspectives, resolve disagreements, and increase self-awareness are critical to the establishment of positive mixed-sex and mixed-ethnic relationships. These skills include empathy, communication, and problem-solving skills. While many social skills programs include activities to teach these core skills, school psychologists may need to incorporate additional elements into their lessons to ensure that culturally competent learning objectives are being met. In addition, school psychologists need to be mindful of potential gender and cultural differences in utilizing communication and problem strategies so they can help students enact these skills in ways that are meaningful to the students.

School psychologists should consider implementing interventions to assist students with becoming aware of how their gender and cultural biases have an impact on their peer interactions. A large body of evidence suggests that children's gender cognitions (e.g., stereotypes, attitudes) affect their personal preferences and social behaviors (e.g., Miller, Martin, Fabes, & Hanish, 2013). Thus, children would benefit from participating in activities that assist them with developing the skills to critically evaluate their own biases and the stereotyped messages they encounter in the environment (e.g., from peers, family, and the media).

Sanford Harmony Program

The Sanford Harmony Program is a recently developed universal, teacher-led program designed to promote positive gender and peer relationships for children in preschool through fifth grade (Miller et al., 2012). This program is based on the premise that inclusive school communities, where all children feel accepted and valued, are essential to the social and academic success of students. The conceptual model guiding the program draws from theories and research on intergroup contact, social cognition, and gender socialization. Taken together, the goals of the program are to promote diverse positive peer contact and to teach students the social and cognitive skills needed to facilitate successful interactions between diverse peers (e.g., other-sex interactions).

The Sanford Harmony Program incorporates a multicomponent approach to promote positive gender relationships. The first step of the program is to provide sustainable professional development training to teachers and school staff to assist them with increasing their awareness of biases and the importance of promoting inclusion in the classroom. During this training, the teachers participate in a series of experiential exercises and are given multiple opportunities to practice the strategies they will use in the program. Furthermore, teachers are provided with access to an online platform where they participate in ongoing professional development activities and receive continued support and guidance in implementing the program.

The curriculum features include two overlapping components. The first component includes a series of relationship-building activities designed to introduce students to fundamental ideas and skills for successful peer relationships. The activities are organized into five core units: diversity and inclusion, critical thinking, communication, problem solving, and peer relationships. In the early childhood program (preschool to second grade), the concepts are introduced through engaging storybooks and then the students participate in hands-on, interactive activities to support and practice what they learned from the stories. In the intermediate program (third to fifth grade), the students learn and practice skills by participating in interactive games, hands-on activities, role-plays, and discussions. The overall approach guiding the development and implementation of the activities is that students learn by doing and by participating in experiences that enable them to discover information and ideas for themselves while also receiving guidance from teachers and peers.

The second component includes four embedded school practices that provide ongoing opportunities for students to engage with diverse peers and practice skills during everyday interactions. The four embedded experiences are Meet Up, Buddy Up, Scramble Up, and Team Up. During Meet Up, teachers create a weekly forum where students gather as a whole classroom to establish and monitor expectations for how to treat one another, exchange ideas, share experiences, and solve problems. Buddy Up is a peer buddy system that creates opportunities for children to get to know and learn with an other-sex peer. Scramble Up provides a structure for students to engage in positive interactions with peers during the lunch period. Students are placed in mixed-sex lunch bunches once a week and are provided with brief activities to support positive interactions. Finally, Team Up is a structured cooperative learning experience designed to provide students with the support needed to effectively communicate and collaborate in mixed-sex and diverse peer groups. Students learn to monitor group functioning to ensure that all members are contributing to the process and meeting their goals.

The initial pilot evaluations of the Sanford Harmony Program's components have demonstrated its effectiveness in establishing positive peer relationships (Miller et al., 2012). Moreover, feedback and process data collected from teachers implementing Sanford Harmony components also has been positive. Teachers reported the activities are engaging and meaningful and that the program fosters a positive classroom community and more positive gender relationships.

Key Challenges

Beyond cultural and gender considerations, three key challenges exist to implementing social skills training programs and understanding intervention effects. These challenges are (a) monitoring change during the intervention and not just after treatment; (b) monitoring delivery of the training program or social skills instruction; and (c) programming for and measuring generalization of newly learned skills across contexts, settings, and persons.

Progress Monitoring

Throughout social skills training, regardless of the training program, data should be collected to determine if students are performing the skills targeted in intervention in both the primary intervention setting and settings where generalization is expected and appropriate. If performance of the targeted skill is not increasing, then the instructional strategies may need to be modified to better meet the learning needs of the students. If students are demonstrating acquisition and generalization of a target skill, then that skill should continue to be reinforced, but a new target skill can be introduced. Goal attainment scaling, progress-monitoring records, reliability change indexing, and a combination of visual and statistical analyses are possible methods for monitoring progress during intervention and evaluating change after completion of the intervention (Elliott, Roach, & Beddow, 2008). Some social skills intervention programs, such as the Social Skills Improvement System, provide progress-monitoring materials aligned with their assessments and the skills taught during the program for school psychologists and teachers to use to collect data about students' progress. Software for iPads and tablets also is available for collecting observational data on specific, discrete behaviors.

Monitoring Intervention Implementation

Monitoring intervention implementation or treatment fidelity—the degree to which the intervention is implemented as intended—is a critical component of evaluating intervention effectiveness. If an intervention is not implemented as designed, then it is impossible to discern whether students are not making progress or increasing their performance of desired social behavior because the intervention is not working or because they are not receiving the intended instruction and

reinforcement. Based on a review of the methodological quality of school-based social skills interventions for preschoolers, Frey and Kaiser (2012) found that few studies reported treatment fidelity data when describing and interpreting their interventions and results. It is essential to monitor intervention implementation before evaluating intervention effectiveness. Again, some intervention packages, such as the Social Skills Improvement System, include intervention integrity checklists and rating scales for implementation of each teaching strategy for each skill. If school psychologists are planning to use a social skills curriculum, then they should determine whether that curriculum provides materials for monitoring intervention implementation. In the absence of preprepared intervention monitoring materials, school psychologists can monitor intervention implementation by team teaching, observing social skills lessons taught by others, and/or by asking teachers to complete intervention monitoring forms about what they taught and how they taught it.

Generalization

A consistent limitation reported across social skills intervention studies is that newly learned social skills often do not generalize from trained to untrained contexts, such as from the classroom to the playground or to home or other community settings (e.g., Maag, 2006). It is unclear, however, if lack of generalization has been because children did not in fact generalize their newly acquired skills or if generalization was not sufficiently measured during and after intervention. Frey and Kaiser (2012) found that the majority of preschool social skills intervention studies they reviewed did not measure generalization, and when generalization was measured, the researchers did not intentionally program for generalization in their intervention models.

As previously mentioned, generalization is a key component of effective interventions. Interventionists should intentionally program for generalization when teaching social skills. Students need opportunities to practice skills with multiple interaction partners and across contexts and activities for which that skill is appropriate. In addition, interventionists should assess whether students are generalizing the skills, and, if students are not, more intensive instruction or alternate instructional methods should be used to ensure generalization of skills.

Seven generality facilitators have been identified (Elliott et al., 2008). Interventionists should (a) target behaviors that will be maintained by natural reinforcement contingencies; (b) train across different behaviors, settings, and persons; (c) train loosely; (d) systematically withdraw or fade interventions; (e) reinforce performance of target behaviors; (f) include peers in social skills training; and (g) provide intervention booster sessions. Incorporating as many of these facilitators as possible into a social skills training program should increase the probability that newly learned skills will generalize to other appropriate settings and with other people (Elliott et al., 2008).

SUMMARY

Social skills matter in the social, emotional, and academic lives of children. Many parents and educators help advance the development and use of social behaviors that involve listening, turn-taking, helping, and self-control. Some children, however, need more explicit support and more opportunities to practice using their social skills. Some children also have co-occurring problem behaviors that interfere with desired social behavior. For these two groups of students, social skills interventions can be effective. There are a number of approaches to social skills intervention and resources to facilitate school psychologists' intervention efforts. Regardless of the specific social skills resources used, research supports the use of a six-step process—tell, show, do, practice, monitor progress, and generalize— for teaching social skills. With this information and sensitivity to issues of individual differences and diversity of background and situations, school psychologists should be helpful collaborators with teachers who wish to conduct universal social skills training in their classrooms or more intensive interventions for smaller groups of children who need more support. Successful social skills interventions contribute to safer, healthier, and high-achieving schools and equip children with important skills that will advance their relationships with others and enhance their sense of personal self-respect.

AUTHOR NOTE

Disclosure. Stephen N. Elliott has a financial interest in books he authored or coauthored referenced in this chapter. Cindy Faith Miller is a co-developer of the Sanford Harmony program, and there is potential for this program to generate revenue.

REFERENCES

Allport, G. W. (1954). *The nature of prejudice.* Cambridge, MA: Perseus.

Bandura, A. (1977). *Social learning theory.* Englewood Cliffs, NJ: Prentice-Hall.

Caprara, G. V., Barbaranelli, C., Pastorelli, C., Bandura, A., & Zimbardo, P. F. (2000). Prosocial foundations of children's academic achievement. *Psychological Science, 11,* 302–306.

Chen, C. (2011). *Public elementary and secondary school student enrollment and staff counts from the common core of data: School year 2009–10.* (NCES 2011-347). Washington, DC: U.S. Department of Education. Retrieved from http://nces.ed.gov/pubs2011/2011347.pdf

Collaborative for Academic, Social, and Emotional Learning. (2012). *Effective social and emotional learning programs: Preschool and elementary school edition.* Chicago, IL: Author. Retrieved from http://casel.org/guide

Crowe, L. M., Beauchamp, M. H., Catroppa, C., & Anderson, V. (2011). Social function assessment tools for children and adolescents: A systematic review from 1988 to 2010. *Clinical Psychology Review, 31,* 767–785. doi:10.1016/j.cpr.2011.03.008

Curtis, M. J., Castillo, J. M., & Gelley, C. (2012). School psychology 2010: Demographics, employment, and the context for professional practices: Part 1. *Communiqué, 40*(7), 28–30.

DiPerna, J. C., & Elliott, S. N. (2002). Promoting academic enablers to improve student achievement. *School Psychology Review, 31,* 293–298.

Elliott, S. N., Frey, J. R., & DiPerna, J. C. (2012). Promoting social skills: Enabling academic and interpersonal successes. In S. E. Brock & S. R. Jimerson (Eds.), *Best practices in school crisis prevention and intervention* (2nd ed., pp. 55–78). Bethesda, MD: National Association of School Psychologists.

Elliott, S. N., & Gresham, F. M. (2008). *Social Skills Improvement System: Intervention guide.* Minneapolis, MN: Pearson Assessments.

Elliott, S. N., Roach, A. T., & Beddow, P. (2008). Best practices in preschool social skills training. In A. Thomas & J. Grimes (Eds.), *Best practices in school psychology V.* (pp. 1531–1546). Bethesda, MD: National Association of School Psychologists.

Frey, J. R., Elliott, S. N., & Kaiser, A. P. (2013). Social skills intervention planning for preschoolers: Using the SSiS-Rating Scales to identify target behaviors valued by parents and teachers. *Assessment for Effective Intervention.* Advanced online publication. doi: 10.1177/1534508413488415

Frey, J. R., & Kaiser, A. P. (2012). *Effects of school-based social skills interventions on the social behaviors of preschoolers: A meta-analysis.* Manuscript submitted for publication

Gillies, R. M. (2007). *Cooperative learning: Integrating theory and practice.* Thousand Oaks, CA: SAGE.

Gresham, F. M. (2002). Teaching social skills to high-risk children and youth: Preventive and remedial approaches. In M. Shinn, H. Walker, & G. Stoner (Eds.), *Interventions for academic and behavior problems II: Preventive and remedial approaches.* (pp. 403–432). Bethesda, MD: National Association of School Psychologists.

Gresham, F. M., & Elliott, S. N. (1990). *Social Skills Rating System.* Circle Pines, MN: American Guidance Service.

Gresham, F. M., & Elliott, S. N. (2008). *Social Skills Improvement System– Rating Scales.* Minneapolis, MN: Pearson Assessments.

Gresham, F. M., Elliott, S. N., Cook, C. R., Vance, M. J., & Kettler, R. J. (2010). Cross-informant agreement for social and problem behavior ratings: An investigation of the Social Skills Improvement System Rating Scales. *Psychological Assessment, 22,* 157–166.

Hall, J. A., Carter, J. D., & Horgan, T. G. (2000). Gender differences in nonverbal communication of emotion. In A. H. Fischer (Ed.), *Gender and emotion: Social psychological perspectives.* (pp. 97–117). New York, NY: Cambridge University Press.

Humphrey, N., Kalambouka, A., Wigelsworth, M., Lendrum, A., Deighton, J., & Wolpert, M. (2011). Measures of social and emotional skills for children and young people: A systematic review. *Educational and Psychological Measurement, 71*, 617–637. doi:10.1177/0013164410382896

LaFreniere, P. J., & Dumas, J. E. (1996). Social competence and behavior evaluation in children ages 3 to 6 years: The short form (SCBE-30). *Psychological Assessment, 8*, 369–377.

Lane, K. L., Givner, C. C., & Pierson, M. R. (2004). Teacher expectations of student behavior: Social skills necessary for success in elementary school classrooms. *Journal of Special Education, 38*, 104–110.

Lane, K. L., Stanton-Chapman, T., Jamison, K. R., & Phillips, A. (2007). Teacher and parent expectations of preschoolers' behavior: Social skills necessary for success. *Topics in Early Childhood Special Education, 27*, 86–97.

Leaper, C., & Smith, T. E. (2004). A meta-analytic review of gender variations in children's language use: Talkativeness, affiliative speech, and assertive speech. *Developmental Psychology, 40*, 993–1027. doi:10.1037/0012-1649.40.6.993

Leman, P. J., Ahmed, S., & Ozarow, L. (2005). Gender, gender relations, and the social dynamics of children's conversations. *Developmental Psychology, 41*, 64–74. doi:10.1037/0012-1649.41.1.64

Lopez, E., & Rogers, M. R. (Eds.). (2007). *Handbook of multicultural school psychology: An interdisciplinary perspective.* Mahwah, NJ: Erlbaum.

Maag, J. W. (2006). Social skills training for students with emotional and behavioral disorders: A review of reviews. *Behavioral Disorders, 32*, 155–172.

Miller, C. F., Gaertner, B., Kochel, K. P., Martin, C. L., Fabes, F. A., Hanish, L. D., … Foster, S. A. (2012, November). *The Sanford Harmony Program: Promoting positive relationships between girls and boys.* Paper presented at the International Video Conference on Peer Relations, Concordia University, Montreal, Canada.

Miller, C. F., Martin, C. L., Fabes, R. A., & Hanish, L. D. (2013). Bringing the cognitive and social together: How gender detectives and gender enforcers shape children's gender development. In M. R. Banaji & S. A. Gelman (Eds.), *Navigating the social world: What infants, children, and other species can teach us.* New York, NY: Oxford University Press.

National Association of School Psychologists. (2010). *Model for comprehensive and integrated school psychological services.* Bethesda, MD: Author. Retrieved from http://www.nasponline.org/standards/2010standards/2_PracticeModel.pdf

Nesdale, D. (2007). The development of ethnic prejudice in early childhood: Theories and research. In O. Saracho & B. Spodek (Eds.), *Contemporary perspectives on social learning in early childhood education.* (pp. 213–240). Charlotte, NC: Information Age.

Nowicki, S., Jr., & Duke, M. P. (1989). *A measure of nonverbal social processing ability in children between the ages of 6 and 10.* Paper presented at the annual meeting of the American Psychological Society, Alexandria, VA.

Parker, J. G., & Asher, S. R. (1987). Peer relations and later personal adjustment: Are low-accepted children at risk? *Psychological Bulletin, 102*, 357–389.

Pettigrew, T. E., & Troop, L. R. (2006). A meta-analytic test of intergroup contact theory. *Journal of Personality and Social Psychology, 90*, 751–783. doi: 10.1037/0022-3514.90.5.751

Romer, N., Ravitch, N. K., Tom, K., Merrell, K. W., & Wesley, K. L. (2011). Gender differences in positive social-emotional functioning. *Psychology in the Schools, 48*, 958–970. doi:10.1002/pits.20604

Skinner, B. F. (1953). *Science and human behavior.* New York, NY: Macmillan.

Slavin, R. E., & Cooper, R. (1999). Improving intergroup relations: Lessons learned from cooperative learning programs. *Journal of Social Issues, 55*, 647–663. doi: 10.1111/0022-4537.00140

Strough, J., Swenson, L. M., & Cheng, S. (2001). Friendship, gender, and preadolescents' representations of peer collaboration. *Merrill-Palmer Quarterly, 47*, 475–499. doi:10.1353/mpq.2001.0025

Underwood, M. K., & Rosen, L. H. (2009). Gender, peer relations, and challenges for girlfriends and boyfriends coming together in adolescence. *Psychology of Women Quarterly, 33*, 16–20. doi:10.1111/j.1471-6402.2008.01468.x

U.S. Department of Education. (2012). *Digest of education statistics, 2011.* (NCES 2012-001). Washington, DC: Author.

Weissberg, R. P. (1985). Designing effective social problem-solving programs for classrooms. In B. H. Schneider, K. H. Rubin, & J. E. Ledingham (Eds.), *Children's peer relations: Issues in assessment and intervention.* (pp. 225–242). New York, NY: Springer.

Wilson, T. M., & Rodkin, P. C. (2012). Children's cross-ethnic relationships in elementary schools: Concurrent and prospective associations between ethnic segregation and social status. *Child Development.* Advance online publication. doi:10.1111/cdev.12020

Zosuls, K. M., Martin, C. L., Ruble, D. N., Miller, C. F., Gaertner, B. M., England, D. E., & Hill, P. (2011). "It's not that we hate you": Understanding children's gender attitudes and expectancies about peer relationships. *British Journal of Developmental Psychology, 29*, 288–304. doi:10.1111/j.2044-835X.2010.02023.x

16 Best Practices in Fostering Student Resilience

Amity L. Noltemeyer
Miami University (OH)

OVERVIEW

Maria's family experienced poverty that prevented them from accessing healthy food and securing stable living arrangements. Brian lost his mother to a drug overdose last year, and his father is serving a life sentence in prison. Ahmed spent the first 4 years of his life in a war zone and came to the United States as a refugee at age 12. Amber's parents recently divorced following 7 years of domestic violence. Marcus experienced intense, pervasive bullying throughout his school years.

Although the life experiences of each of these children are vastly different, each of these circumstances constitutes a potential risk factor for future social–emotional maladjustment. As a result of our training in mental health, coupled with our access to all children in schools, school psychologists are ideally poised to help foster the positive development of children experiencing these types of risks.

Children who have been exposed to circumstances like these have experienced adversity. Adversity is a term used to describe events that have the potential to disrupt normal development and pose a threat to positive functioning. Although adversity may place students at an increased risk for undesirable outcomes, children and youth who experience similar risk factors may exhibit markedly different responses and outcomes.

Why do some children fare better in the face of these risk factors than others, perhaps even evidencing normal developmental trajectories? These children are said to be resilient, experiencing positive adaptation in the face of adverse situations.

Resilience is an important consideration for school psychologists, considering its ties to several frameworks guiding school psychological practice. Although relevant to many of the 10 domains outlined by the National Association of School Psychologists (NASP) *Model for Comprehensive and Integrated School Psychological Services* (NASP, 2010a), social–emotional resilience is particularly central to understanding and implementing the domain of Interventions and Mental Health Services to Develop Social and Life Skills. Specifically, this domain specifies that "[s]chool psychologists have knowledge of biological, cultural, developmental, and social influences on behavior and mental health, behavioral and emotional impacts on learning and life skills, and evidence-based strategies to promote social–emotional functioning and mental health" (p. 5). This knowledge can be applied through direct and indirect services provided within a problem-solving framework. These services should be aligned with a multitiered system of support, in which children are provided with different types and intensities of supports based on their unique risk and protective factors.

This chapter will provide school psychologist practitioners with the fundamental knowledge necessary to develop these types of effective resilience-enhancing supports. School psychologists will learn basic considerations about resilience, risk, and protection; specific ways that they can foster student resilience within a comprehensive three-tiered approach; developmental, individual, and cultural considerations relevant to the resilience discourse; and methods for evaluating services and outcomes. After reading this chapter, it is hoped that school psychologists will be better equipped to plan and implement resilience-building strategies in their schools.

BASIC CONSIDERATIONS

In order to provide effective resilience-promoting services, school psychologists first must acquire knowledge to sufficiently understand the mechanisms underlying resilience, risk, and protection.

Resilience

Resilience is a term that refers to patterns of desirable adaptation in situations where adversity has threatened normal development (Masten, Cutuli, Herbers, & Reed, 2002). Although not directly measured, resilience is inferred based on measurement of risk and adaptation (Luthar & Zelazo, 2003). Resilient students are often described as having "beat the odds," "bounced back," or "risen above their circumstances." The story of Dawn Loggins, who worked relentlessly to improve her life and was ultimately accepted to Harvard University following experiences of neglect, poverty, bullying, transiency, parental drug abuse, abandonment, and homelessness (Kuo, 2012), is one of many publicized examples of resilience.

Resilience is different from resiliency; whereas *resiliency* refers to a personality trait within a child that allows him or her to adapt positively, *resilience* refers to a dynamic process of maintaining positive adaptation in the face of adversity (Masten, 1994). Although resiliency can certainly serve a protective role for individuals facing adversity, thus promoting resilience, resiliency reflects personal attributes such as resourcefulness and flexibility that do not necessarily assume the presence of adversity (Luthar, Cichetti, & Becker, 2000). This is a subtle distinction, revealing that although fostering resiliency warrants discussion, there are also other processes and protective factors outside of the child that can be supported to enhance resilient outcomes. Also, although the notion of resilience includes coping, resilience is also a much broader construct than coping. Resilience and coping are active processes, but coping is an individual process whereas resilience also recognizes the importance of social influences and context (Rutter, 2012). In fact, recent conceptualizations of resilience have stressed this ecological and context-dependent nature (e.g., Ungar, 2008), implying that factors that promote resilience in one setting or population may differ from those in other settings or populations.

Because many children enter U.S. schools having experienced a variety of adversities, schools represent an ideal environment in which to foster student resilience. Furthermore, because resilience is believed to be a socially and contextually influenced process, the notion of resilience offers a sense of optimism to educators regarding their ability to effectively reach students entering their classrooms with a history of risk or adversity (Esquivel, Doll, & Oades-Sese, 2011). However, despite the utility of resilience as a construct and its promising applications in schools, Doll, Jones, Osborn, Dooley, and Turner (2011) also caution against the overgeneralization of resilience research to school mental health practices for several reasons, including the immutability of many of the risk factors, the relatively small proportion of variance in school success predicted by school factors (as opposed to individual, family, and community factors), and the fact that individual students may differ from findings on resilience derived from population-based statistics. Considering this line of reasoning, it is important for school-based professionals to prevent and reduce those risks that are amenable to change, build assets, institute supports that recognize the importance of multiple contexts on a child's development, and appreciate dynamic and situational aspects of resilience.

Risk Factors

To subsequently be characterized as resilient, a child must experience one or more risk factors that threaten his or her developmental outcomes. When specifically considering negative mental health outcomes, there are a variety of such risk-inducing factors that exist across a continuum of ecological systems. Although some of these are inherent within the child and/or are relatively immutable, others represent specific preventable experiences that a child is exposed to in the form of adversity. An exhaustive list of risk factors is well beyond the scope of this chapter; however, several salient examples that are particularly relevant for school psychologists are reviewed (see Figure 16.1).

- *Individual:* Within the individual, for example, resistant temperament (Deater-Deckard, Dodge, Bates, & Pettit, 1998), substance abuse (Hallfors, Waller, Bauer, Ford, & Halpern, 2005), major illness or accident (Turner & Lloyd, 1995), and preterm birth (Bhutta, Cleves, Casey, Cradock, & Anand, 2002) are a few of the factors that may serve as obstacles to the realization of typical social–emotional development.
- *Family:* Within the family, youth who have been maltreated or abused (Turner & Lloyd, 1995), have an absentee parent (Deater-Deckard et al., 1998), or have permissive parents (e.g., Schaffer, Clark, & Jeglic, 2009) experience a heightened risk for subsequent social–emotional difficulties.
- *Schools:* Schools can also serve as ecologies that contribute to child and adolescent risk. For example,

Figure 16.1. Risk and Protective Factors at the Individual, Family, School, and Community Levels

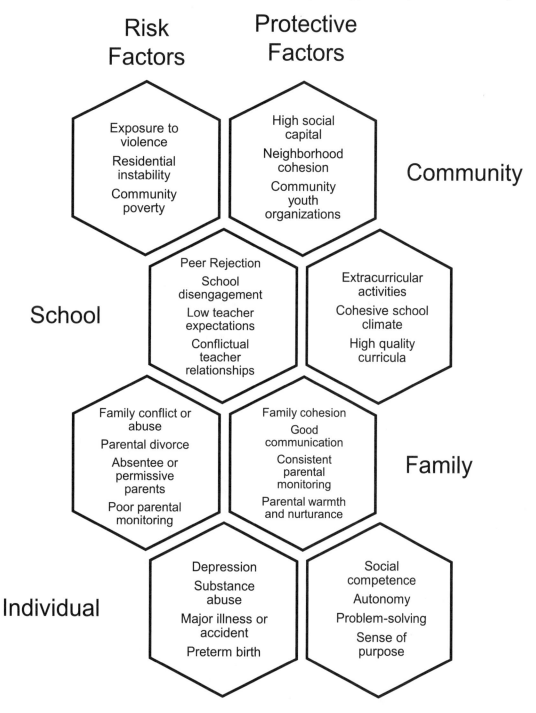

research suggests that school disengagement (Henry, Knight, & Thornberry, 2012), conflictual teacher relationships (Silver, Measelle, Armstrong, & Essex, 2005), and peer rejection at school (e.g., Deater-Deckard et al., 1998) are problematic.

- *Community:* Communities that experience high levels of violence (see Margolin & Gordis, 2000) and poverty (see Leventhal & Brooks-Gunn, 2000) are

more likely to produce negative mental health sequelae, and children experiencing residential/community instability experience similarly increased risk (see Leventhal & Brooks-Gunn, 2000).

Studies examining the prevalence of such risk factors among children and adolescents have unfortunately painted a grim portrait of the obstacles facing today's youth. For example, as of 2010, nearly one in five U.S. children lives in poverty, and these rates have been increasing (Federal Interagency Forum on Child and Family Statistics, 2010). Furthermore, 12.3% of infants born in the U.S. are affected by preterm birth and 8.18% experience low birth weight (Martin et al., 2010). Not only have 9.8% of children and adolescents witnessed an assault in their family, but 18.6% report having been victims of maltreatment themselves during their lives (Finkelhor, Turner, Ormrod, & Hamby, 2009). Regarding community violence, 28.7% of children and youth report having witnessed some form of community assault during their lives (Finkelhor et al., 2009). These are merely a few indicators of a complex and risk-laden environment where children and adolescents may reside.

Although many studies consider the effect of exposure to these types of single traumatic adverse experiences, it is also important to note that risk factors often co-occur in a series of events, leading many researchers to shift their attention from single risk indicators to the notion of cumulative risk (see Masten & Powell, 2003). As a testament to the impact of cumulative risk, Sameroff, Gutman, and Peck (2003) documented a very large decline in social–emotional and academic outcomes associated with an increased number of risks experienced by youth. Similarly, Turner and Lloyd (1995) found particularly clear and significant relationships between cumulative traumatic experiences in childhood and psychological disorders in adulthood. Consequently, it is important to identify the total quantity of risk factors present in addition to the types.

Protective Factors

Many supports can help buffer children experiencing adversity from negative social–emotional and mental health outcomes. Given the context-dependent nature of resilience, these may differ based on a variety of individual, family, school, community, and cultural factors. However, within each of these systems, several protective factors have been shown to mitigate the effects of adversity (see Figure 16.1 for examples).

- *Individual:* Within the individual, four general domains of personal assets may serve a protective role (see Bernard, 2004, for a review of each): social competence (e.g., communication, empathy, compassion), problem solving (e.g., critical thinking, flexibility, resourcefulness), autonomy (e.g., internal locus of control, self-efficacy, positive identity), and sense of

purpose (e.g., achievement motivation, optimism, goal direction).
- *Family:* Family factors that may protect children from risk include family cohesion, good communication, consistent parental monitoring (i.e., tracking children's activities), and parental warmth and nurturance (see Noltemeyer & Bush, 2013).
- *School:* In the school, children who participate in extracurricular activities (Schmidt, 2003), those who attend schools with a cohesive school climate (Loukas & Murphy, 2007), and those who are exposed to a high quality curriculum (Hall et al., 2009) are more likely to experience success.
- *Community:* Community protection may be enhanced by higher social capital, neighborhood cohesion, and opportunities for involvement in community youth organizations (see Noltemeyer & Bush, 2013).

The exact mechanisms by which protective factors exert their effects remain an area of dispute. However, the popular interactive model contends that resilience emerges when the relationship between a risk factor and negative developmental outcomes is weakened by the existence of protective factors (Fraser, Kirby, & Smokowski, 2004). In other words, protective factors modify the effects of adversity on child outcomes (Masten et al., 2002). For example, the existence of an active, strong, and caring extended family network may mitigate some of the potentially negative effects of parental incarceration on a child's well-being. This differential effect of adversity at various protective levels may occur either because the protective factor (a) prevents a risk factor, (b) buffers a risk factor, or (c) interrupts a risk chain through which the effects of a risk factor are exerted (Fraser et al., 2004).

There also has been an interest in understanding these mechanisms across multiple ecological levels. For example, in dynamic systems models, risk and protective factors are represented at multiple levels of analysis (e.g., cellular, individual, family, school, cultural; Masten et al., 2002). This type of systemic approach is consistent with research suggesting that resilience is a process of navigating one's way through tensions using a combination of individual, family, and community strengths (Ungar, 2008). Despite advances in understanding the role of protective factors as resilience promoters, further research is needed to elucidate how they interact with risk factors at each of these levels to produce outcomes (Masten et al., 2002).

Together, the extant knowledge about resilience, risk, and protection reveal salient implications for school psychologists and their work with students. For example, considering the important goal of school psychologists to maximize the social–emotional functioning of all students, school psychologists should strive to (a) minimize students' exposure to risk factors; (b) increase students' access to protective resources, particularly for the vulnerable or at-risk students; and (c) develop supports that recognize and incorporate the various ecologies in which students function.

BEST PRACTICES FOSTERING STUDENT RESILIENCE

School psychologists can utilize a tiered approach to conceptualize services designed to foster student resilience. Within each tier, it is important to consider how the assets of the individual, school, family, and community systems can be harnessed to support positive adaptation and minimize risk for maladaptive behaviors (also, within Tier 1, it is important to work toward minimizing exposure to adversity and risk altogether). Supporting multiple systems of influence like these simultaneously and in a mutually supportive way is important for strengthening outcomes (Esquivel et al., 2011). Implementation of three tiers across these systems should be systematic and well aligned, and may occur within the scope of a larger school reform initiative such as school-based mental health programming or school-wide positive behavior support. Across all tiers, high quality professional development, data-based decision making, culturally responsive practices, evidence-based intervention, and collaboration must be essential features. The individual-focused supports may focus on developing personal resiliency skills within students, whereas the school, family, and community supports aim to enhance the protective function of these settings that have an impact on students. A review of key resilience-enhancing supports within each of the three tiers is provided (see Figure 16.2 for an overview).

Tier 1 (Primary or Universal Supports)

In Tier 1, a primary goal is to enhance protective factors for the general school population. To this end, school psychologists can be advocates for the selection and implementation of a curriculum that promotes the development of skills linked to resilient and positive social–emotional and behavioral outcomes, such as social competence, problem solving, autonomy, and sense of purpose. When selecting a social–emotional curriculum, school psychologists can access several

resources that house systematic reviews and descriptions of curricula, such as the Collaborative for Academic, Social, and Emotional Learning (http://casel.org). What follows are some examples of such curricula that target at least one of the previously mentioned areas and have some evidence to support their use: (a) Promoting Alternative Thinking Strategies (Kam, Greenberg, & Kusche, 2004), (b) Caring Community (Schaps, Battistich, & Solomon, 2004), (c) 4Rs (Brown, Jones, LaRusso, & Aber, 2010), and (d) I Can Problem Solve (Shure, 1992).

In addition to a formal social–emotional curriculum, school psychologists can work collaboratively with teachers to increase awareness of resilience promotion and structure their individual classrooms in ways that will enhance healthy social–emotional functioning. As only a few examples of their more comprehensive model for developing resilient classrooms, Doll, Zucker, and Brehm (2004) discuss teachers' need to support the following:

- Teacher–student relationships by establishing sensitive rapport, creating an ethos of caring in the classroom, providing constructive and encouraging feedback, and establishing weekly classroom meetings
- Peer relationships by organizing social interactions so that the tasks are developmentally and individually appropriate, encouraging students to work together and solve problems in a positive way, providing frequent and relevant opportunities for friendships to emerge, and exposing less socially adept peers to their more competent counterparts through small group or partner work
- Home–school relationships by sharing home-based practices that parents can use to support their child's classroom work, encouraging students to share responsibility for increased parental communication about school, providing parents with opportunities to provide input or be involved in the school, communicating honestly and respectfully, and collaborating with parents
- Behavioral self-control by developing behavioral expectations with students early in the school year; teaching expectations through examples, role play, practice, and feedback opportunities; utilizing self- or peer-management interventions; and using instructional practices that are engaging and well paced

There are many additional ways that school psychologists can help institute or strengthen protective factors for students. For example, school psychologists should

Figure 16.2. Key Resilience-Enhacing Supports Within a Three-Tiered Model

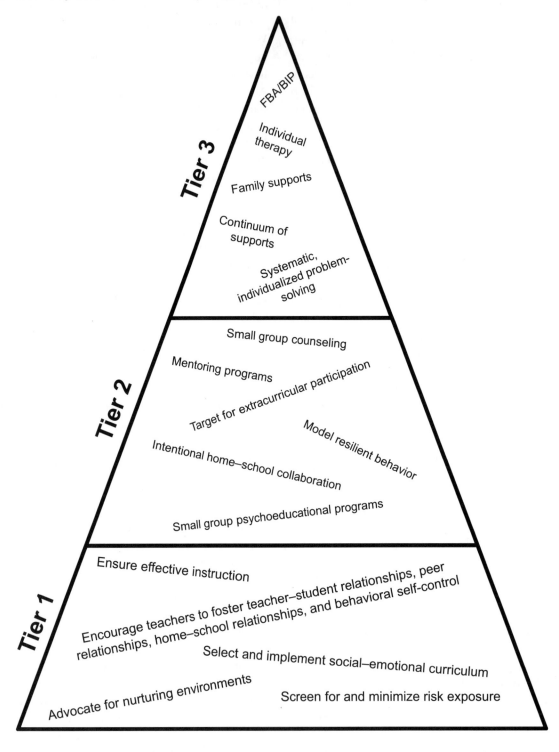

work as effective instructional consultants to ensure a high-quality core curriculum that is implemented with fidelity, establish effective means for collaborating with families and community members, and promote a positive school climate, all of which may mitigate risk. Overall, school psychologists should strive to create nurturing environments that minimize exposure to biologically or psychologically toxic events (Biglan, Flay, Embry, & Sandler, 2012). These environments involve teaching, promoting, and reinforcing prosocial behavior while concurrently limiting opportunities for problem behavior and fostering psychological flexibility

(Biglan et al., 2012). Although these strategies are recommended for all children, not just those exposed to adversity, they are likely to be particularly influential for at-risk children.

In addition to enhancing protective factors, school psychologists can strive to minimize student exposure to risk and adversity. Although these services may not be considered resilience enhancing—since the term resilience implies the presence of risk factors—they certainly can have a positive impact on students and align well with the goal of the profession. When designing these types of preventive services, school psychologists should consider initiatives related to those risk factors that are particularly prevalent within their school context. For example, in communities with high levels of poverty, school psychologists might work with social service providers to make all families aware of resources available to help with food insecurity and access to medical care.

Tier 2 (Secondary, Selective, or Strategic Supports)

Although school psychologists can strive to prevent or reduce exposure to major adversities, children experience adversity in many ways large and small. Consequently, not all adversity can or even should be prevented (e.g., everyday small challenges that help students grow and develop). Therefore, in addition to prevention programming, school psychologists need to harness protective resources when children have experienced adversity. Tier 2 involves supporting youth who have experienced some degree of adversity, which may be transient, mild, or recent, and/or has not had a significant impact on their developmental outcomes. Consistent with research findings documenting the benefits of early intervention for youth experiencing adversity (e.g., Reynolds & Ou, 2003), the goal of this tier is to intervene early and decisively to prevent the risk-inducing experiences from contributing to negative outcomes.

In this tier, school psychologists should be involved in designing, and possibly implementing, supplemental intervention for students who are identified as experiencing some degree of adversity. This supplemental intervention should be informed by the nature of the adversity experienced, the current functioning of the child, and the protective resources that can be capitalized or built upon. Small group counseling and psychoeducational programs for youth experiencing a variety of risk factors have shown promise for preventing and/or reducing the behavioral correlates of various risk factors, and are well aligned with school psychologists' training and expertise. What follows are some examples: (a) Coping Cat (Kendall, Gosch, Furr, & Sood, 2008), (b) Children of Divorce Intervention Program (Pedro-Carroll, 1997), (c) Cognitive Behavioral Intervention for Trauma in Schools (Jaycox, Kataoka, Stein, Langley, & Wong, 2012), and (d) The Incredible Years Dina Dinosaur Child Training Programs (Webster-Stratton, & Reid, 2003).

When implementing small group counseling or psychoeducational programs to ameliorate risk and build competencies of students, there are several important considerations for school psychologists including methods for determining who will participate, group size, scheduling, structure, techniques, and evaluation methods.

Mentoring programs have also shown promise for improving student outcomes, particularly for at-risk students. For example, Big Brothers Big Sisters is a community-based program that matches youth with adult mentors who serve as role models, build relationships, and enhance positive youth development. Other community-based programs also can be considered within this targeted tier, including community-based after-school programs. Also, the Behavior Education Program involves a student having twice daily brief meetings with an adult at school to receive feedback and reinforcement on their daily goals (Crone, Hawken, & Horner, 2010). When developing or implementing any school-based mentoring program, it is important for school psychologists to consider the quality of the program to ensure the experience has its intended positive effects. MENTOR has a variety of resources available to help program planners design and implement mentoring programs effectively. As one example, their *Elements of Effective Practice for Mentoring* (MENTOR, 2009) provides research-based standards and benchmarks for six critical dimensions of mentoring program operations (i.e., recruitment, screening, training, matching, monitoring and support, and closure) along with specific ideas related to program planning, implementation, and evaluation.

In the absence of, or in addition to, formal mentoring programs, school psychologists can strive to ensure that each at-risk child builds a strong relationship with one staff member in the school. For example, if a student has naturally developed a positive relationship with his or her science teacher, then that teacher may be targeted to check in with the student informally, and the student may be reassured that he or she can see that teacher in times of need. In addition to role models and mentors, at-risk children may be targeted for specific encouragement to participate in activities that may protect them from the negative outcomes of adversity. For example, these students can be encouraged to participate in extracurricular or community activities in which they can develop an informal support network of both adults (e.g., coaches or club advisors) and peers.

In addition to these student-focused supports, more intentional efforts toward home–school collaboration are warranted in Tier 2. Although home–school collaboration is necessary for every student, this is particularly true for at-risk students. If the source of adversity originated in the family setting, then school psychologists should collaborate with families to help them obtain the supports necessary to reduce these risks. For example, Winslow, Sander, and Wolchik (2005) review several specific parent programs that can be used to counteract conditions of adversity such as divorce, poverty, premature birth, and death. Also, through consultative work or parent trainings, school psychologists can help parents to model resilient behaviors themselves. Children and adolescents' attitudes about setbacks may be influenced by the way they observe others deal with them. For example, a comment like, "One bad thing after another happens to our family. Our luck will never change," may make a child feel very differently about his or her ability to overcome a difficult situation than a comment like, "Even though we are going through a rough time right now, we are strong enough to make it through this together." School psychologists should also consider ways to strengthen parental competencies through group training or psychoeducational programs. As an example, Borden, Schultz, Herman, and Brooks (2010) recommend offering the Incredible Years parent training program at the selective level to families with identifiable risk factors, such as groups at schools serving low-income families.

At this level it is also important to acknowledge and appreciate those adults—whether family members, educators, or community members—who serve a protective function for at-risk children and adolescents. These individuals may not fully realize the important function they serve, and acknowledging their efforts can serve to reinforce a further commitment to a child's resilience. During her term as NASP president, Rhonda Armisted initiated a Resilience Builders program whereby NASP members could formally acknowledge individuals who contribute to student resilience in their schools with a certificate and posting of their name on the NASP website

(Armisted, 2007). Similar programs can be considered for implementation within any school.

Finally, although appropriate at any of the tiers, it is important to intentionally teach at-risk children about resilience, introducing them to the concepts and exposing them to others who were resilient in similar situations. For example, age-appropriate fictional books or movies with characters who have overcome adversity can be used to guide discussion and foster a connection to a child's life. In addition to these types of books, there are age-appropriate nonfiction books (e.g., Jones, 2007) that youth can read to learn more about how to resile in difficult situations.

Tier 3 (Tertiary, Indicated, or Intensive Supports)

Tier 3 is designed to provide intensive and individualized supports to the even smaller proportion of students exhibiting notable difficulties adapting to adversity. Students may be identified for Tier 3 services due to inadequate response to high-quality, well-implemented Tier 1 and Tier 2 supports. For example, a student who has experienced familial dysfunction and is exhibiting increasingly intense anxious behavior that is now interfering with his or her educational outcomes, despite participation in the Coping Cat program at Tier 2, may require more intensive supports. Other students, however, may progress to Tier 3 services by exhibiting such extreme levels of risk or adversity that more intensive supports were immediately warranted to facilitate effective and safe functioning and coping. For example, a student whose immediate family was killed in a car accident and who is having suicidal thoughts and extreme difficulty reintegrating into the school setting would need immediate Tier 3 supports until the situation stabilizes.

At this tier, it is essential that a continuum of integrated and coordinated services be designed to support the student. This will necessitate the collaboration of many professionals, both within and beyond the school setting. At this level, it is recommended that a school-based team meet at regular intervals to engage in a systematic and individualized problem-solving process in an attempt to maximize protective resources, minimize risk factors, and minimize the negative outcomes that have already manifested.

School psychologists are well poised to facilitate this team, given their training in problem solving, resilience, mental health, effective interventions, and progress-monitoring strategies. Families should be included in the problem-solving process to the greatest degree possible, with alignment between home and school incorporated into planning and implementation efforts. In addition, school psychologists can use this opportunity to offer personalized resources and strategies to families. Within this tier, school psychologists may provide individualized parenting training on home issues that are directly related to school problems. In addition, school psychologists can refer families to community supports and perhaps even participate in these supports. For example, school psychologists may be involved in the National Wraparound Initiative, an intensive community-based team approach that brings together diverse community, school, and family stakeholders to develop and monitor a plan to meet the child's and family's needs (see Walker, Bruns, Conlan, & LaForce, 2011).

The specific supports provided to the student should be highly individualized based on that student's needs, risk factors, and protective factors. Because significant maladaptive behaviors have often already emerged at this tier, a functional behavior assessment and behavior intervention plan are warranted to more specifically identify the function of these behaviors and develop a plan based on the antecedents and consequences maintaining the behavior. Although the presence of adversity and absence of protective factors are likely contributing factors that should be documented and built into such a plan, there also may be some setting-specific antecedents and consequences that can be identified through a systematic functional behavior assessment as intensifying or aggravating the behaviors above and beyond the effect of the adversity alone. The resulting behavior intervention plan should be implemented as planned and should be monitored for effectiveness.

Schools should also be prepared to respond to acute crises that may have a marked impact on students. Implementation of a solid crisis plan in these situations is critical. However, beyond the acute phase, students who have experienced trauma that has interfered with their ability to progress educationally may benefit from brief solution-focused therapy or cognitive–behavioral therapy as part of their school intervention plan to help them cope and alter irrational cognitions that may be interfering with their school performance. However, it may also be determined through the problem-solving process that the student requires intensive therapeutic supports that extend beyond the parameters of the school psychologist's service provision. For example, a student experiencing years of psychological and physical abuse and abandonment affecting many life functions will require more than the limited counseling services available within a school setting. In these cases, it is necessary to provide an appropriate referral to a capable and competent community-based mental health service provider who can extend work being initiated in the school setting. Additionally, in some cases, the families of children experiencing such profound adversity may themselves be overwhelmed or under an extraordinary amount of stress either directly through the effects of the adversity also affecting the child, or indirectly by the stress the child has experienced from the adversity. In these cases, child-focused services may be necessary but not sufficient to promote adaptive functioning, and referral to family-based mental health services is warranted.

Considerations for Different Populations

When developing interventions to support and enhance resilience, it is necessary to consider developmental and individual differences that may influence risk, protection, and resilience. For example, children who have been exposed to adversity at earlier developmental periods are more likely to experience negative sequelae than their older peers (Keiley, Howe, Dodge, Bates, & Pettit, 2001). In addition, children who have experienced multiple adversities are more likely to experience negative outcomes than those exposed to an isolated adversity (e.g., Sameroff, Seifer, Baldwin, & Baldwin, 1993). Together, these findings suggest that prevention and early intervention services, provided soon after an initial identification of risk rather than after the emergence of negative behavioral patterns, may serve an important role. School psychologists are well poised to help identify these risks and determine the appropriate levels of initial support needed.

Also, because resilience is context-dependent, it is important to be cognizant of cultural influences in school psychologists' work to promote resilience. For example, risk exposure may vary for children of different cultural and racial backgrounds. Whereas racial discrimination may be a salient risk factor for some African American and Latino children, it may not be for Caucasian children. Also, variables that serve a protective function in one setting or culture may not assume the same function in another. For example, in Latino communities, the values of familismo (familism), personalismo (personalism), and respeto (respect) may serve a protective function (Reyes & Elias, 2011) unique to that culture. School psychologists must not only be aware of how values and norms like these may contribute to resilience differently for students with diverse backgrounds, but must harness this knowledge to develop interventions that are well aligned with the needs and characteristics of the students they serve.

Evaluation of Services

When developing supports to enhance student resilience, it is important to collect information that can fill the dual role of informing intervention service delivery and evaluating intervention outcomes. The types and extent of data collection will heavily depend on context-specific risk factors, protective factors, and supports, thereby precluding an exhaustive discussion of this topic. In addition, this is an emerging topic that will likely be refined and informed by future research. However, it is clearly important for schools to establish a method of identifying educationally relevant risk, so that prevention and intervention can be targeted appropriately. Despite the utility of assessing for risk factors, it is also important to consider and assess protective factors that may serve to mitigate risk when it is present. When such assets are available, they can be used as resources in strengthening intervention supports for students; when they are absent, knowledge of their absence can serve as an impetus for developing an intervention plan that incorporates these types of supports. In addition, promoting these assets in students who have not experienced adversity but nonetheless exhibit behavior or emotional concerns may enhance student outcomes (although not considered resilience, because adversity was not experienced).

Screening for social–emotional risks and protective factors at Tier 1 may include informal interviews, checklists, teacher nominations, universal screening rating scales, or other teacher- or parent-provided information about key factors relevant to school functioning. These sources of information may be used to inform which students need additional supports and what types of supports they need. Some adversities are educationally relevant and may be included on a school parent questionnaire or enrollment form (e.g., major illness, divorce/custody status), and others may be available from extant school data (e.g., peer rejection, conflictual teacher relationships). However, others are highly specific and may emerge from individual consultation or discussions with parents (e.g., recent victimization in the community, exposure to violence). A school-based team should work to develop the most appropriate methods for identifying risk at Tier 1 and informing the need for Tier 2 supports, making the procedures clear to all teachers who might become aware of significant student risks.

Students who begin receiving Tier 2 should be monitored to assess the degree that social–emotional manifestations of their risk are (or are not) expressed. The exact behaviors monitored will depend on the child and circumstances, and the frequency and extent of data collection will depend on the intensity of services. However, it is likely that some combination of observation, permanent products, direct behavior ratings, or progress-monitoring rating scales may be used. Students who are not progressing as would be expected, based on criteria established at the school level, may progress to Tier 3 supports.

Within Tier 3, more detailed information may be collected about the risk factors, protective factors, and behavioral manifestations the students are experiencing. This may be accomplished through more extensive interviews, observations, checklists, or rating scales. Further guidance on assessment of risks, protective factors, and social–emotional competencies—including comparison of various instruments and assessment methods—is provided by the National Center for Mental Health Promotion and Youth Violence Prevention and Collaborative for Academic, Social, and Emotional Learning (2011). When collecting information about risk or social–emotional competence factors at any tier, in order to avoid potential ethical violations or dilemmas, schools should (a) avoid having teachers routinely compile detailed background histories for all children, as sensitive information may be included that is unnecessary to service provision; (b) notify parents prior to any mental health screening and provide them with the opportunity to remove their child from such screening (Armisted et al., 2012); and (c) follow all guidelines from the NASP *Principles for Professional Ethics* (NASP, 2010b).

In addition to using data to inform intervention supports, school psychologists should also be intentional about evaluating the effectiveness of asset and resilience-promoting interventions that are instituted. At Tier 1, this may involve examining school-wide indicators (e.g., office disciplinary referrals, risk or protection indicators, achievement data) before and after implementation. At Tiers 2 and 3, this evaluation will likely involve the application of single-subject design research methodologies to examine trends in growth compared to peer norms or predetermined standards. It also may involve tracking the number of students served and aggregating findings across students. Across all tiers, school psychologists can also consider collecting stakeholder data on perceptions of their own professional functioning in an effort to inform improvements in the types of school psychological services provided.

SUMMARY

Resilient children and adolescents exhibit positive development despite exposure to adversity. Resilience is a socially and contextually influenced phenomenon generally thought to exert its influence through protective factors that weaken the relationship between risk factors and negative outcomes. School psychologists are ideally poised to foster student resilience through direct and indirect efforts delivered through a tiered model of support. Universal supports—designed to build all students' capacity for resilience while concurrently minimizing risks—include a strong social–emotional learning curriculum, classrooms structured to maximize healthy social–emotional development, effective instruction and professional development offerings, and nurturing environments. Strategic supports, characterized by early intervention to prevent risk or adversity from exerting a negative influence, include small group psychoeducational or counseling programs, high-quality mentoring opportunities, and systematic home–school collaboration. Finally, intensive supports for those students exhibiting notable difficulties adapting to adversity consist of a continuum of integrated and highly coordinated services such as functional behavioral assessment, individualized behavioral intervention plans, and referrals to community mental health providers. When developing and implementing supports across these tiers, school psychologists should consider developmental, individual, and cultural differences that may have an impact on risk and protection. Additionally, consistent with the scientist-practitioner model, a plan for evaluating resilience-related service provision and outcomes should be developed and implemented. Overall, school psychologists should be intentional, comprehensive, and systematic in their resilience-promoting role in order to maximize positive social–emotional development.

REFERENCES

Armistead, L. A., Jacob, S., Provenzano, F., Madigan, J., Pearrow, M., & Klose, L. (2012, February). *From the ethics committee inbox.* Presented at the annual convention of the National Association of School Psychologists, Philadelphia, PA.

Armisted, R. J. (2007). President's message: A blueprint for building resilience. *Communiqué, 36*(1), 2.

Bernard, B. (2004). *Resiliency: What we have learned.* San Francisco, CA: WestEd.

Bhutta, A. T., Cleves, M. A., Casey, P. H., Cradock, M. M., & Anand, K. J. S. (2002). Cognitive and behavioral outcomes of school-aged children who were born preterm: A meta-analysis. *Journal of the American Medical Association, 288*, 728–737. doi:10.1001/jama.288.6.728

Biglan, A., Flay, B. R., Embry, D. D., & Sandler, I. N. (2012). The critical role of nurturing environments for promoting human well-being. *American Psychologist, 67*, 257–271. doi:10.1037/a0026796

Borden, L. A., Schultz, T. R., Herman, K. C., & Brooks, C. M. (2010). The Incredible Years parent training program: Promoting resilience through evidence-based prevention groups. *Group Dynamics: Theory, Research, and Practice, 14*, 230–241. doi:10.1037/a0020322

Brown, J. L., Jones, S. M., LaRusso, M. D., & Aber, J. L. (2010). Improving classroom quality: Teacher influences and experimental impacts of the 4Rs program. *Journal of Educational Psychology, 102*, 153–167. doi:10.1037/a0018160

Crone, D. A., Hawken, L. S., & Horner, R. H. (2010). *Responding to problem behaviors in schools: The behavior education program.* New York, NY: Guilford Press.

Deater-Deckard, K., Dodge, K. A., Bates, J. E., & Pettit, G. S. (1998). Multiple risk factors in the development of externalizing behavior problems: Group and individual differences. *Developmental Psychopathology, 10*, 469–493. doi:10.1017/S09545794980011709

Doll, B., Jones, K., Osborn, A., Dooley, K., & Turner, A. (2011). The promise and the caution of resilience models for schools. *Psychology in the Schools, 48*, 652–659. doi:10.1002/pits.20588

Doll, B., Zucker, S., & Brehm, K. (2004). *Resilient classrooms: Creating healthy environments for learning.* New York, NY: Guilford Press.

Esquivel, G. B., Doll, B., & Oades-Sese, G. V. (2011). Introduction to the special issue: Resilience in schools. *Psychology in the Schools, 48*, 649–651. doi:10.1002/pits.20585

Federal Interagency Forum on Child and Family Statistics. (2010). *America's children in brief: Key national indicators of well-being, 2010.* Washington, DC: U.S. Government Printing Office.

Finkelhor, D., Turner, H., Ormrod, R., & Hamby, S. L. (2009). Violence, abuse, and crime exposure in a national sample of children and youth. *Pediatrics, 124*, 1411–1423. doi:10.1542/peds.2009-0467

Fraser, M. W., Kirby, L. D., & Smokowski, P. R. (2004). Risk and resilience in childhood. In M. W. Fraser (Ed.), *Risk and resilience in childhood: An ecological perspective* (2nd ed.; pp. 1–12). Washington, DC: National Association of Social Workers.

Hall, J., Sylva, K., Melhuish, E., Sammons, P., Siraj-Blatchford, I., & Taggart, B. (2009). The role of pre-school quality in promoting resilience in the cognitive development of young children. *Oxford Review of Education, 35*, 331–352. doi:10.1080/03054980902934613

Hallfors, D. D., Waller, M. W., Bauer, D., Ford, C. A., & Halpern, C. T. (2005). Which comes first in adolescence: Sex and drugs or depression? *American Journal of Preventative Medicine, 29*, 163–170. doi:10.1016/j.ampre.2005.06.002

Henry, K. L., Knight, K. E., & Thornberry, T. P. (2012). School disengagement as a predictor of dropout, delinquency, and problem substance use during adolescence and early adulthood. *Journal of Youth and Adolescence, 41*, 156–166. doi:10.1007/s10964-011-9665-3

Jaycox, L. H., Kataoka, S. H., Stein, B. D., Langley, A. K., & Wong, M. (2012). Cognitive behavioral intervention for trauma in schools. *Journal of Applied School Psychology*, *28*, 239–255. doi:10.1080/15377903.2012.695766

Jones, J. L. (2007). *Bouncing back: Dealing with the stuff life throws at you.* New York, NY: Franklin Watts.

Kam, C. M., Greenberg, M. T., & Kusche, C. A. (2004). Sustained effects of the PATHS curriculum on the social and psychological adjustment of children in special education. *Journal of Emotional and Behavioral Disorders*, *12*, 66–78. doi:10.1177/10634266040120020101

Keiley, M. K., Howe, T. R., Dodge, K. A., Bates, J. E., & Pettit, J. S. (2001). The timing of child physical maltreatment: A cross-domain growth analysis of impact on adolescent externalizing and internalizing problems. *Developmental Psychopathology*, *13*, 891–912.

Kendall, P. C., Gosch, E., Furr, J. M., & Sood, E. (2008). Flexibility within fidelity. *Journal of the American Academy of Child and Adolescent Psychiatry*, *47*, 987–993. doi:10.1097/CHI.0b013e31817eed2f

Kuo, V. (2012, June 8). *From scrubbing floors to Ivy League: Homeless student to go to dream college.* Atlanta, GA: CNN. Retrieved from http://www.cnn.com/2012/06/07/us/from-janitor-to-harvard/index.html

Leventhal, T., & Brooks-Gunn, J. (2000). The neighborhoods they live in: The effects of neighborhood residence on child and adolescent outcomes. *Psychological Bulletin*, *126*, 309–337. doi:10.1037//0033-2909.126.2.309

Loukas, A., & Murphy, J. L. (2007). Middle school student perceptions of school climate: Examining protective functions on subsequent adjustment problems. *Journal of School Psychology*, *45*, 293–309. doi:10.1016/j.jsp.2006.10.001

Luthar, S. S., Cicchetti, D., & Becker, B. (2000). The construct of resilience: A critical evaluation and guidelines for future work. *Child Development*, *71*, 543–562. doi:10.2307/1132374

Luthar, S. S., & Zelazo, L. B. (2003). Research on resilience: An integrative review. In S. S. Luthar (Ed.), *Resilience and vulnerability: Adaptation in the context of childhood adversities* (pp. 510–549). New York, NY: Cambridge University Press.

Margolin, G., & Gordis, E. B. (2000). The effects of family and community violence on children. *Annual Review of Psychology*, *51*, 445–479. doi:10.1146/annurev.psych.51.1.445

Martin, J. A., Hamilton, B. E., Sutton, P. D., Ventura, S. J., Mathews, T. J., & Osterman, M. J. K. (2010). Births: Final data for 2008. In, *National Vital Statistics Reports* (vol. 59, no. 1). Hyattsville, MD: National Center for Health Statistics. Retrieved from http://www.cdc.gov/nchs/data/nvsr/nvsr59/nvsr59_01.pdf

Masten, A. S. (1994). Resilience in individual development: Successful adaptation despite risk and adversity. In M. C. Wang & E. W. Gordon (Eds.), *Educational resistance in inner-city America: Challenges and prospects* (pp. 3–25). Hillsdale, NJ: Erlbaum.

Masten, A. S., Cutuli, J. J., Herbers, J. E., & Reed, M. G. J. (2002). Resilience in development. In C. R. Snyder & S. J. Lopez (Eds.), *Handbook of positive psychology* (pp. 74–88). New York, NY: Oxford University Press.

Masten, A. S., & Powell, J. L. (2003). A resilience framework for research, policy, and practice. In S. S. Luthar (Ed.), *Resilience and vulnerability: Adaptation in the context of childhood adversities* (pp. 1–25). New York, NY: Cambridge University Press.

MENTOR. (2009). *Elements of effective practice for mentoring.* Alexandria, VA: Author. Retrieved from http://www.mentoring.org/downloads/mentoring_1222.pdf

National Association of School Psychologists. (2010a). *Model for comprehensive and integrated school psychological services.* Bethesda, MD: Author. Retrieved from http://www.nasponline.org/standards/2010standards/2_PracticeModel.pdf

National Association of School Psychologists. (2010b). *Principles for professional ethics.* Bethesda, MD: Author. Retrieved from http://www.nasponline.org/standards/2010standards/1_%20Ethical%20Principles.pdf

National Center for Mental Health Promotion and Youth Violence Prevention. (2011). *Strategies for social and emotional learning: Preschool and elementary grade student learning standards and assessment.* Waltham, MA: Author. Retrieved from http://www.promoteprevent.org/webfm_send/2306

Noltemeyer, A. L., & Bush, K. R. (2013). Adversity and resilience: A synthesis of international research. *School Psychology International*, *35*, 474–487. doi:10.1177/0143034312472758

Pedro-Carroll, J. (1997). The children of divorce intervention program: Fostering resilient outcomes for school-aged children. In G. W. Albee & T. P. Gullotta (Eds.), *Primary prevention works: Issues in children's and families' lives* (pp. 213–238). Thousand Oaks, CA: SAGE.

Reyes, J. A., & Elias, M. J. (2011). Fostering social-emotional resilience among Latino youth. *Psychology in the Schools*, *48*, 723–737. doi:10.1002/pits.20580

Reynolds, A. J., & Ou, S. (2003). Promoting resilience through early childhood intervention. In S. S. Luthar (Ed.), *Resilience and vulnerability: Adaptation in the context of childhood adversities* (pp. 436–459). New York, NY: Cambridge University Press.

Rutter, M. (2012). Resilience: Causal pathways and social ecology. In M. Ungar (Ed.), *The social ecology of resilience: A handbook of theory and practice* (pp. 33–42). New York, NY: Springer.

Sameroff, A., Gutman, L. M., & Peck, S. C. (2003). Adaptation amount youth facing multiple risks: Prospective research findings. In S. S. Luthar (Ed.), *Resilience and vulnerability: Adaptation in the context of childhood adversities* (pp. 364–391). New York, NY: Cambridge University Press.

Sameroff, A. J., Seifer, R., Baldwin, A., & Baldwin, C. (1993). Stability of intelligence from preschool to adolescence: The influence of social and family risk factors. *Child Development*, *64*, 80–89. doi:10.1111/j.1467-8624.1993.tb02896.x

Schaffer, M., Clark, S., & Jeglic, E. L. (2009). The role of empathy and parenting style in the development of antisocial behaviors. *Crime & Delinquency*, *55*, 586–599. doi:10.1177/0011128708321359

Schaps, E., Battistich, V., & Solomon, D. (2004). Community in school as key to student growth: Findings from the child development project. In J. E. Zins, R. P. Weissberg, M. C. Wang, & H. J. Walberg (Eds.), *Building academic success on social and emotional learning: What does the research say?* (pp. 189–205). Thousand Oaks, CA: SAGE.

Schmidt, J. A. (2003). Correlates of reduced misconduct among adolescents facing adversity. *Journal of Youth and Adolescence*, *32*, 439–452. doi:10.1023/A:1025938402377

Shure, M. B. (1992). *I can problem solve: An interpersonal cognitive problem-solving program.* Champaign, IL: Research Press.

Silver, R. B., Measelle, J. R., Armstrong, J. M., & Essex, M. J. (2005). Trajectories of classroom externalizing behavior: Contributions of child characteristics, family characteristics, and the teacher-child relationship during the school transition. *Journal of School Psychology, 43*, 39–60. doi:10.1016/j.jsp.2004.11.003

Turner, R. J., & Lloyd, D. A. (1995). Lifetime traumas and mental health: The significance of cumulative adversity. *Journal of Health and Social Behavior, 36*, 360–376. doi:10.2307/2137325

Ungar, M. (2008). Resilience across cultures. *British Journal of Social Work, 38*, 218–235. doi:10.1093/bjsw/bcl343

Walker, J. S., Bruns, E. J., Conlan, L., & LaForce, C. (2011). The National Wraparound Initiative: A community of practice approach to building knowledge in the field of children's mental health. *Best Practices in Mental Health, 7*(1), 26–46.

Webster-Stratton, C., & Reid, M. J. (2003). Treating conduct problems and strengthening social and emotional competence in young children: The Dina dinosaur treatment program. *Journal of Emotional and Behavioral Disorders, 11*, 130–143. doi:10.1177/10634266030110030101

Winslow, E. B., Sandler, I. N., & Wolchik, S. A. (2005). Building resilience in all children. In S. Goldstein & R. B. Brooks (Eds.), *Handbook of resilience in children* (pp. 337–356). New York, NY: Springer.

17 Best Practices in Assessing and Promoting Social Support

Michelle K. Demaray
Christine K. Malecki
Northern Illinois University

OVERVIEW

Social support is a crucial construct in the lives of youth. Social support refers to general and specific supportive behaviors from people that enhance a youth's functioning and/or may buffer him or her from negative outcomes (Malecki & Demaray, 2002). Thus, social support may be a sense of feeling loved or cared for by parents or teachers. It can also consist of supportive behaviors, such as helping a child with homework. Important sources of social support for children and adolescents are typically parents, teachers, classmates, and friends.

A large literature base has demonstrated that social support is consistently linked to positive outcomes for youth for a wide range of outcomes, including both externalizing and internalizing behaviors (Suldo & Shaffer, 2008). In general, children and adolescents who have low levels of perceived social support are more likely to have symptoms of depression, anxiety, and other internalizing problems (Stice, Ragan, & Randall, 2004). In addition, low levels of perceived social support are associated with problem behaviors including conduct problems (Rockhill, Vander Stoep, McCauley, & Katon, 2009). Both theory and research support the notion that at times social support may benefit all youth regardless of risk. However, sometimes it is more influential for youth at risk and, in turn, may buffer them from negative outcomes.

The construct of social support provides an important framework to conceptualize prevention and intervention efforts at multitiered levels in schools. School psychologists may use the framework provided in this chapter in a problem-solving methodology to determine if there is sufficient social support at the individual, group, and school level. The construct of social support is closely tied to the domain of Interventions and Mental Health Services to Develop Social and Life Skills in the National Association of School Psychologists (NASP) *Model for Comprehensive and Integrated School Psychological Services* (NASP, 2010). It is important for school psychologists to have knowledge of constructs that are relevant to the mental health of children in order to promote prevention and intervention efforts. Social support plays an important role in the mental health of children and adolescents (Suldo & Shaffer, 2008).

This chapter will briefly review theories and research on the construct of social support. It will also provide practical information on how school psychologists can assess social support both school-wide and with individual students. The chapter will present information on both prevention and intervention strategies aimed at promoting social support in the lives of youth in schools.

BASIC CONSIDERATIONS

When most people think of social support, they think about the emotional support provided by important people in their life. For example, in regards to social support for children and adolescents, one may think about how peers can encourage one another and how parents show they care for their children. However, social support is a broader construct than just emotional support, and social support is provided from a vast array of sources.

Social Support Models and Theories

The most comprehensive model of social support that is helpful for practitioners and researchers was proposed by Tardy (1985). Tardy's model defines five important aspects of social support. The first aspect is the *direction* of social support. Direction refers to whether supportive behaviors are given or received from an individual. Often overlooked, but very important, is the *disposition* of the supportive behaviors. Disposition refers to social support being simply available versus actually enacted by an individual. It may be that simply knowing that support is available is helpful, even if he or she does not act on or utilize that support. At other times, knowing there is support available may not be enough and it may have to be enacted to be helpful. For example, knowing a teacher makes himself or herself available to support a student may provide a sense of support even if the student does not have to utilize that support. Additional aspects of social support especially relevant to measurement of the construct are *description* and *evaluation*. Description has to do with assessing social support in terms of how frequently it is available or enacted upon, and evaluation has to do with how important that support is to someone. For example, an individual may be receiving significant amounts of social support (description) but not really value those supportive behaviors or find them important (evaluation). The *content* of social support is often referred to as types of social support. The most common types of social support assessed are emotional support (i.e., caring behaviors), informational support (i.e., providing needed information and advice), instrumental/operational support (i.e., providing time and resources), and appraisal support (i.e., providing feedback). Finally, the social support *network* refers to the sources of support in someone's life. Some examples of important sources of support for children and adolescents are parents, teachers, classmates, and friends.

Although Tardy (1985) provides an excellent framework for labeling and defining the different aspects of social support, his model does not describe the functions of social support nor the relations among social support and important outcomes for children and adolescents. Social support is proposed to function in two broad ways represented by the main effect model or the stress buffering model. The main effect model proposes that social support is important for all youth regardless of any prior stressor. For example, it might be predicted that a school with high levels of teacher support would benefit all students. In much of the research, social support has been found to be beneficial for all children and adolescents: the more social support a child has, the better his or her outcomes. Conversely, it has also been shown that the less social support a child has, the worse

his or her outcomes. This overall relation among social support and outcomes represents the main effect model (Cohen, Gottlieb, & Underwood, 2000).

However, there are some outcomes whereby the relations among social support and outcomes are less all encompassing. This is explained by the stress buffering model. The stress buffering model suggests that for some outcomes, social support is only beneficial for students who are at risk or under some stressor (Cohen et al., 2000; Cohen & Wills, 1985). The stress buffering model suggests that social support benefits those who need it the most and is less crucial for those not at risk or under stress. For example, social support may not be related to better academic outcomes in the general student body, but it may be related to better academic outcomes for students who are from a lower socioeconomic status. Thus, social support in this scenario was not beneficial for all students, just students who could be considered at risk due to low socioeconomic status.

It is important to note that the main effect and stress buffering models are not necessarily competing models. Both models may be appropriate and relevant for the relation between social support and a particular outcome. Imagine a situation where social support is related to lower anxiety for all students (i.e., having social support is related to less anxiety generally), but for students whose parents are going through a divorce having a strong social network may be particularly beneficial, even over and above the main effect role of social support. Both the main effect and stress buffering models are relevant in this scenario. School psychologists should be aware that although social support may be beneficial for all students, there may be students at risk for a variety of reasons (e.g., divorce, low socioeconomic status) and social support may be especially important during those times or for those students.

Social Support and Outcomes

The child and adolescent research literature is starting to catch up to the vast literature base surrounding adult social support. What researchers have learned is that social support seems, at times, to be related to virtually everything important in children's and adolescents' lives. This chapter does not have the space to comprehensively review this vast literature, but a brief summary is given here to provide a snapshot of the evidence of the importance of social support in the lives of children and adolescents.

In general, research has demonstrated significant relations among social support and internalizing problems, externalizing problems, and academic performance. For example, students with higher levels of social support tend to have lower levels of internalizing symptoms of depression and anxiety (Demaray, Malecki, Davidson, Hodgson, & Rebus, 2005). Social support is also related to higher levels of positive social emotional outcomes such as self-esteem, self-concept, social skills, and relationships with parents, teachers, and peers (Demaray et al., 2005). Regarding externalizing problems, higher levels of appropriate social support are related to lower levels of conduct problems, drug use, bullying behaviors, behavior referrals, and violence (Davidson & Demaray, 2007). Finally, although the evidence is less clear, there is some evidence that higher social support is at least indirectly, or for certain groups of students, related to stronger academic performance (Malecki & Demaray, 2006). Clearly, social support has been found to be an important construct in the lives of youth.

When school psychologists want to understand the context of students' lives, it may be important to assess students' perceptions of social support. School psychologists are often responsible for school-wide social–emotional screening or individual assessment of a student's social–emotional status. Below are some strategies and considerations for school psychologists in the best practice assessment of social support within a multitiered model.

BEST PRACTICES IN ASSESSING AND PROMOTING SOCIAL SUPPORT

Assessment is an important first step prior to implementing strategies to promote social support. School psychologists are in the ideal role to assess social support at the individual, group, and school level. Some core recommendations for assessment of social support based on Tardy's (1985) framework are provided below. School psychologists should: (a) Consider the student's perceptions of social support. It is the student's view that is important. For example, a teacher may think he or she is providing support to the student but the student may not perceive that behavior as supportive. (b) Consider both the frequency and importance of social support (Tardy's description versus evaluation aspects). For example, if a student does not deem a particular supportive behavior as important, that would not be an important target behavior for intervention. (c) Consider the various types of social support a student is receiving and/or lacking (e.g., emotional, instrumental, informational, appraisal). (d) Consider all of the sources a child is

receiving support from in his or her network. Is a child lacking support from a particular source?

Assessment of Social Support

Assessment approaches for social support may have different purposes and can be aligned with a multitiered model. Given the importance of social support in creating a sense of connectedness to school and as a protective factor for at-risk youth, the first purpose of assessment is focused on screening student perceptions of social support school-wide to aid in planning Tier 1 prevention and behavioral support efforts. Social–emotional screening is becoming an increased focus for schools and school psychologists (NASP, 2009). A school needs to decide what important social–emotional constructs it wants to screen for. If a school decides not to screen for social support school-wide, the staff could target its social support assessments toward at-risk groups or individuals. Thus, a second purpose of assessment is to assess targeted groups of students or individual students to determine their perceptions of social support to aid in planning group or individualized intervention efforts at Tiers 2 and/or 3.

There are three basic methods in the assessment of social support: (a) measurement of network size and social integration, (b) rating scales, and (c) interviews. A description of each of these strategies is presented below along with a discussion of appropriate use (e.g., screening, individual assessment). A multiple-gated methodology could be used to assess social support across the tiers or an individual strategy could be used by a school psychologist for a specific purpose. A discussion of how to use a multiple-gated procedure to the assessment of social support will be presented after a description of each of the techniques.

Network analysis involves having a student simply identify individuals whom the student can go to for support, with the number of individuals the student lists as a rough estimate of support in his or her life. Additional information may be gathered by asking students to identify everyone in their list who knows each other by placing a mark next to these names. This is referred to as a social integration method. The connections among the supportive people identified are intended to demonstrate how dense a network is for that student. A denser network is assumed to be more supportive (Gottlieb, 2000). Some social integration measures also ask students to identify the different sources or types of relationships a student has in his or her life (e.g., coach, mentor, parent; Brissette, Cohen, &

Seeman, 2000). Asking about the types of relationships that provide support to a child provides more information than just a count of the people available. For example, one child could list 10 people available for support that are all friends and another child could list 10 different types of supportive relationships such as a coach, friend, parent, teacher, and so on.

Both network analysis and social integration measures are ideal as screeners because of their brevity. This information is quick and easy to collect and score, even if the school psychologist is collecting these data from all students in a school. A disadvantage of this tool is that it is a more crude measure of social support as no information is collected about the quality of support that is provided to students. For example, a student may provide a long list of supportive individuals who are not actually providing quality support to the child/adolescent. Another disadvantage of the social network measure is that one does not necessarily know what sources of support a child is identifying since the tool does not categorize the source of support unless that is part of the assessment. Thus, a student could report a high number of people as supportive but all of these supportive individuals could be located in the student's neighborhood and the student may not identify anyone at school. For screening purposes, however, students who are identified as having few supportive individuals

in their life via this tool could then be assessed more thoroughly via other assessment strategies to more closely examine supportive relationships. Of course, determining if someone has enough supportive individuals in his or her life may depend on the individual's own preferences. For example, some students may feel like one supportive friend is enough and others may require more. The problem of interpretation could be solved by asking students a global question about their satisfaction with their support.

There are several rating scales available to assess students' perceptions of social support. See Table 17.1 for detailed information on six rating scales that may be used to assess social support. One advantage of using rating scales in universal screening is that more in-depth information could be collected compared to network analysis data because information is collected about social support across the various sources (e.g., parents, teachers, classmates, and friends) and, in some cases, types of supportive behaviors (e.g., emotional, appraisal). More descriptive data gathered via rating scales may aid in Tier 1 intervention planning. For example, if there are a significant number of students who perceive low levels of teacher support, a school-wide strategy to increase teacher–student relations may be implemented. Furthermore, a school psychologist could utilize a subscale focused on peer support to identify students

Table 17.1. Rating Scales to Assess Social Support

Scale and Author	Items and Response Format	Subscales Based on Source
Child and Adolescent Social Support Scale[a] (Malecki, Demaray, & Elliott, 2000)	120 items; 12 each of frequency and importance items on a Likert-type scale for each source	Parent, teacher, classmate, close friend, school; total/global support
Network of Relationships Inventory[b] (Furman & Buhrmester, 1985)	241 items on a Likert-type scale; 29 items for each of 8 relationship figures plus 9 general questions	Mother, father, sibling, relative, boy/girl friend, same-sex friend, other-sex friend, other
Multidimensional Scale of Perceived Social Support[c] (Zimet, Dahlem, Zimet, & Farley, 1988)	12 items on a Likert-type scale	Family, friend, significant other; total/global support
Social Support Questionnaire[c] (Sarason, Levine, Basham, & Sarason, 1983)	27 items used to determine network density as well as satisfaction that is based on a 6-point Likert scale	Overall network; family network; overall support satisfaction score
Perceived Social Support Scale[c] (Procidano & Heller, 1983)	40 items (20 items for family, 20 items for friend) using agreement ratings (yes, no, do not know)	Friend, family
Social Support Scale for Children[c] (Harter, 1985)	36 items using two-part answer strategy	Parent, teacher, classmate, friend subscales; total/global support

Note. [a]Provides additional scores based on four types of social support: emotional, instrumental, informational, and appraisal. [b]Provides subscales based on eight types of social support: companionship, instrumental, aid, intimacy, nurturance, affection, admiration, and reliable alliance. [c]Does not provide subscales based on social support type.

who report low peer support and provide a group intervention focused on social skills or peer relations. A disadvantage of utilizing rating scales for universal screening is that the length of the measures adds to the needed time and effort to administer, score, interpret, and summarize the data, which may be costly as well.

Social support rating scales are ideal at the individual assessment level because it allows for school psychologists to gather more in-depth information across the various sources, types, and frequency of social support for an individual student. This information may drive particular intervention strategies with a group of students or an individual student. Some of the items from rating scales could also be modified to progress monitor intervention efforts.

Interviewing is also a technique that could be utilized in conjunction with a rating scale or alone. Used in conjunction with a rating scale, the interviewer could follow up with the individual student about areas or relationships that were identified as having low levels of support. For example, if a student rated most of the questions about peer and teacher support with low frequency, the school psychologist could follow up with an interview about peer and teacher relationships, probing more about what the student is currently experiencing and what the student has done, if anything, to try to increase support from these individuals. In addition, an interview allows the school psychologist to determine if the lack of support from a particular source is problematic for the student. For example, the student may report low levels of peer support but say that this does not bother him or her. See Table 17.2 for example questions that may be asked during an interview to assess current levels of social support.

Multitiered Assessment

When used alone, measures of social network size and social integration measures are more suited to school-wide screening and prevention and intervention planning at Tier 1. Brief rating scales could also be appropriate tools for school-wide screening. When assessing individual student's or small groups of students' perceptions of social support, the use of rating scales and/or interviews are most ideal. A multiple-gated procedure could be used to screen school-wide via measures of social network size and/or social integration. Students who are flagged as having small networks via these tools could then complete more thorough assessments such as rating scales. Students who still score low via rating scales could be interviewed to aid in intervention planning. Data at all of these levels

Table 17.2. Sample Questions to Assess Social Support Questions Through an Interview

Who are the people who most care about you?
- How important is it that these people care about you?
- Is there anyone that you wish would care more about you?

Who are the people who give you advice and help you when you need it?
- How important is it that these people help you?
- Is there anyone that you wish would help you more?

Who are the people who tell you whether or not you did a good job on something?
- How important is it that these people give you feedback?
- Is there anyone who you wish would give you more feedback?

Who helps you get the things you need or teaches you the things you need to know?
- How important is it that these people give you things or information that you need?
- Is there anyone who you wish would give you more information?

Which of these people do you spend the most time with?
- Is there anyone you wish you could spend more time with?

Who do you feel most comfortable talking to if you have a problem about something? Why?

Do you feel like there are enough people in your life who would help you if you needed it?

could guide problem solving around school-wide prevention, group, and individual intervention efforts.

Developmental Considerations

One consideration that should be made when assessing and planning for socially supportive interventions should be the age of the student, as perceptions of social support have been found to vary by these characteristics. For example, research has found that children and early adolescents report parents and friends as similarly supportive, but teens 16 and older report their friends as more supportive than their parents (Bokhorst, Sumter, & Westenberg, 2010). Regarding support from teachers, younger students tend to perceive more support from their teachers than older students, with adolescents perceiving lower levels of support from their teachers as they progress through school (Demaray & Malecki, 2002). These considerations regarding the age of the student might influence school psychologists to involve peers in interventions more often for adolescents and reach out to parents and teachers for younger students. This can help capitalize on the already existing developmental trend.

Cultural Considerations

Culture is another important consideration for school psychologists as they conceptualize the role of social support in the lives of students in their schools. Research has indicated that there are variations among perceptions of support and relations to outcomes for different ethnic groups, including Caucasian, African American, Asian American, and Latino groups (Kim & McKenry, 1998). For example, one study investigated cultural differences in willingness to utilize social support among Asians, Asian Americans, and European Americans. These researchers found that Asians and Asian Americans were less likely to seek social support than European Americans (Taylor et al., 2004). Thus, school psychologists may, at times, be working with groups of individuals who are not likely to seek social support on their own based on cultural expectations. Summarizing all the research on cultural differences is beyond the scope of this chapter. School psychologists should be aware of any potential cultural influences when problem solving around providing additional social support to youth.

Promoting Social Support

Once a school psychologist has identified school-wide (Tier 1) needs for increasing social support, targeted needs (Tier 2), or individual student needs (Tier 3), interventions must be implemented to address those concerns. Using Tardy's (1985) framework, the needs have to be identified and addressed based on the sources of support necessary and the types of support needed. For example, do the data suggest there is a lack of informational support (what is expected of them) from adults in the school as a Tier 1/school-wide issue? Do the data suggest that a few students have serious lack of social support of all types from important sources in their life and they may need individual counseling or another individualized intervention? If so, these needs can be addressed in many ways.

One helpful framework that can help school psychologists think about intervening with social support is the mnemonic "AEIO-you": appraisal support, emotional support, informational support, and operational support (also known as instrumental support). School psychologists can examine the data and determine how he or she can promote all types of social support (AEIO) for all students school-wide, groups of students, or individual students, and can focus on which of the types are necessary as indicated by the data. We will identify some potential interventions and illustrate

how AEIO-you might play out as a helpful framework in each.

Tier 1 Strategies

It is important to note that many Tier 1 interventions are not directly focused on increasing social support. However, social support is often embedded as part of the intervention. Although not always specifically stated, social support may also be the mechanism by which some interventions are effective. For example, a positive behavioral supports approach has as a foundation making clear the behavioral expectations of a building (informational support). If students do not know what is expected of them, they will not be as likely to perform and will feel less grounded. It certainly is important to note that there is not one intervention or one approach that is appropriate for all schools and for all students. School psychologists must identify the needs at his or her particular school and implement evidence-based interventions accordingly. Social support is related to many constructs such as resilience and engagement in school. Thus, staff should think about universal strategies that intentionally build connections with others or that build perceptions of support students perceive from individuals in the school (teachers, staff, and peers). There are also strategies that can attempt to increase parental support for students and increase parents' connection with the school.

A preventive strategy to improve the mental health of all students includes an emphasis on social–emotional learning in the core curriculum of schools. Social and emotional learning is "the capacity to recognize and manage emotions, solve problems effectively, and establish positive prelateships with others" (Zins & Elias, 2006, pg. 1; see the Collaborative for Academic, Social, and Emotional Learning website [http://casel.org] for more information on social–emotional learning). Historically, educational systems and mental health systems have been considered two independent systems with the educational system focused on academic performance and the mental health system focused on a wide range of mental health outcomes (Merrell & Gueldner, 2010). The movement to include social–emotional learning in schools is trying to bring these two systems together by incorporating social–emotional content into school curriculum. The goal of social–emotional learning is to teach emotional skills in schools just like schools teach reading and math. The focus is on universal prevention of problems by promotion of positive social and emotional behaviors. Social–emotional learning itself is not a program, but a philosophy of educating children on social and emotional factors. However, there are curricula available that focus on social–emotional learning. Some of these curricula are reviewed below as possible Tier 1 efforts to increase social support.

There are five key components of effective social–emotional learning: self-awareness, social awareness, responsible decision making, self-management, and relationship skills (Zins & Elias, 2006). In this section, a few key examples of packaged, evidence-based, school-wide programs or approaches are described with attention drawn to their inclusion of how elements of social support (AEIO-you) are built into these programs or approaches. It should be noted that one good first step for school psychologists is to examine Tier 1 social–emotional interventions and approaches that are already being implemented, ensure they are being implemented with integrity, and to potentially increase the intensity with which any social support components are implemented.

CHAMPS. CHAMPS (Sprick, 2009) is an acronym for conversation, help, activity, movement, participation, and success, and this approach is based on Sprick's STOIC model (structure, teach behavioral expectations, observe and supervise, interact positively with students, and correct fluently). CHAMPS does not explicitly describe social support among its components, but several types of support can be seen in the CHAMPS approach including appraisal, emotional, and informational. Students are provided informational support as a foundation. The behaviors that are expected in the school are explicitly communicated, reviewed, and assessed frequently. Students feel more grounded with this informational support. They know what is expected of them and they understand what consequences will arise if they do not behave according to these expectations. Instructional and behavioral routines are some of the vehicles of this informational support that are part of the CHAMPS approach. Using CHAMPS, teachers and school personnel are expected to provide students with fluent or immediate feedback on their behavior. This appraisal support is crucial for reinforcing appropriate behavior and for allowing (and expecting) students to immediately correct negative behavior. Building positive relationships through this appraisal support and through celebrations for positive behavior is another way that relationship building and emotional support is made explicit in the CHAMPS approach. The prosocial behavior theory is apparent within this approach with clear behavioral principles and an

acknowledgement and flexibility for diverse students and environments. CHAMPS can be an excellent approach to use because it is neither a set curriculum nor program. It is a customizable approach that can be tailored to meet the needs of any school setting and population of students. School psychologists are in a position to drive the professional development, setup, and implementation of CHAMPS.

Caring School Community. It is easy to see how Caring School Community (Schaps, 2009) reflects social support in its approach given that creating a caring community within the school is a major aim. Building the perception of and availability of emotional support is key to this approach. The objectives of Caring School Community are to develop a sense of community (emotional), to set classroom norms (informational), to apply positive social value to social interactions, to address classroom issues positively (appraisal), and to help students with transitions. It uses activities such as team building, playground check-ins (to address positives and challenges), and cross-age mentoring in the classroom, home-side activities to activate parent involvement at home, and school-wide community building to link students, parents, teachers, and others as a community unit (all operational support). Thus, Caring School Community addresses all of the AEIO-you types of support: appraisal, emotional, informational, and operational. The Caring School Community curriculum relies on the social–exchange theory, encouraging mutually beneficial emotionally supportive exchanges between students, students and teachers, and teachers and families. Again, school psychologists can help educate teachers about Caring School Community and can lead the cross-age mentoring and school-wide aspects of this intervention while teachers lead the classroom lessons and practices.

Strong Start / Strong Kids / Strong Teens. Another example of a Tier 1 program that promotes social support school-wide is the Strong Start/Strong Kids/Strong Teens curriculum (Merrell, Carrizales, Feuerborn, Gueldner, & Tran, 2007). The objectives of this set of programs are to teach social and emotional skills, promote resilience, strengthen existing assets, and increase coping skills. The Strong Start/Strong Kids/Strong Teens curricula provide informational support by explicitly teaching awareness of and managing of emotions including anger, happiness, worry, social skills, and social problem solving. Emotional support seems inherent in the managing of, identifying of, and responding to others' feelings. Although the emotional and informational supports are apparent from the AEIO-you framework, other aspects may be present and could be emphasized if needed. Teachers are able to present the lessons and are in an ideal position to emphasize and review the concepts into daily classroom life, but many school psychologists also present the lessons in classrooms.

This has been a list of a few evidence-based school-wide interventions that promote socially supportive environments through the lens of our AEIO-you framework. School psychologists who have not adopted a specific program or curriculum could think about the AEIO-you framework of social support to determine what might be needed to bolster a socially supportive environment for the staff and students at their school. In general, school psychologists should reflect on the types of support being provided at their school. In addition, social support needs to be reciprocal and cross-source (teacher–parent, parent–child, teacher–child, teacher–teacher).

Is communication across the social support network adequate? That is, is informational support provided to allow parents, teachers, and students to feel they are grounded with the information they need? Is emotional support apparent in the respect staff shows one another, the care shown toward students, and the level of welcoming of parents in the school? Do teachers have the time and resources they need to do their job effectively? This operational support (time and resources) is key for successful implementation of any intervention in schools. It is important to build and promote a socially supportive environment to set the context of caring and to provide the necessary environment for learning to occur most optimally. However, even if a supportive environment is created and maintained, there may be students who need more targeted or intensive support and strategies in the form of Tier 2 and Tier 3 interventions.

Tier 2 and 3 Strategies

Some students may still lack social support despite school-wide prevention and intervention efforts aimed at promoting social support. Of course the reasons that students may perceive low social support are highly varied. Taking a broad ecological perspective, the reasons for low support may have to do with the student (e.g., temperament, lack of social skills to access social support) or may have to do with the environments he or she is involved with ranging from immediate environments (e.g., family transitions at home) to more removed

environments (e.g., parent's work stress). Many Tier 2 and 3 interventions that will be targeted at problems associated with low social support (e.g., school disengagement, lack of social skills) and may not target low social support directly. However, many potential Tier 2 and 3 interventions have components that will lead to increased social support.

The assessment section of this chapter discussed several methods that might be used to target students who may be at risk of low social support. This assessment information can be used to plan appropriate interventions, or to identify what types of support (using the AEIO-you framework) and what sources of support (e.g., parent, peer) may need to be promoted. It is also important to determine if there is actually lower support available to this student or is it just perceived that way by the individual. If there seems to be adequate support being provided to the individual, there could be a mismatch between what the student needs and what is being provided. For example, the student's parents may be providing him or her with information about what to do about being bullied but may not be providing much emotional support in terms of empathy. Additionally, a child may have support from a particular source but not be able to perceive it due to cognitive distortions and this may need to be addressed. For example, a student who is depressed may not be able to perceive supportive behaviors that actually are available due to his or her depression.

In the case of actual lower levels of social support, it is important to acknowledge that low levels of support may be due to a variety of reasons. For example, it may be a skill deficit, such as a social skills deficit that is keeping the student from engaging with others in an appropriate manner and thus building social support resources. Or, the student may lack the skill of accessing available social support as a coping mechanism when needed. There also may be interfering factors associated with the lack of perceived social support. For example, a child may be rejected by his or her peers due to aggressive behaviors and thus the child is not receiving support from his or her peers. It is critically important to match the Tier 2 or 3 intervention with the needs of the students in order to aid in eventually building up social support resources. There are a wide range of Tier 2 or 3 interventions that may potentially increase perceived social support. A few potential Tier 2 interventions that also have a social support component are reviewed below.

Check & Connect and other mentoring.
Check & Connect was developed to "promote student

engagement with school though relationship building, problem solving, and persistence'' (Anderson, Christenson, Sinclair, & Lehr, 2004, p. 97). The program provides at-risk students a mentor, called a monitor, who collects data on indicators of student disengagement (e.g., absences, grades) and then connects through building relationships with students, families, and school personnel. There are several aspects of AEIO-you in Check & Connect. For example, the monitor develops a relationship with the student (emotional support) and focuses on the goal of keeping the student engaged in school by way of weekly meetings and parent communication (informational and instrumental support). This intervention has been shown to improve attendance and reduce dropout rates (Sinclair, Christenson, Evelo, & Hurley, 1998). Interestingly, there is evidence that one of the key factors of the Check & Connect intervention is the monitor–student relationship. One study found it was the monitor–student relationship that was significantly related to academic engagement (Anderson et al., 2004). Thus, this program is focused on increasing the adult social support in the students' lives through the provision of a mentor.

There are other mentoring programs that may be utilized to increase social support from other adults in students' lives. Building supportive positive relationships with adults is key to helping students become resilient. At-risk students can be assigned a mentor who meets with them on a scheduled basis and focuses on goals and progress toward those goals. There are many different mentoring programs. However, it is important to note that research has demonstrated a modest or small effect for typical youth (DuBois, Holloway, Valentine, & Cooper, 2002). Through a meta-analysis that included 55 studies, DuBois and colleagues concluded that the results of the mentoring programs are stronger when they are based on theory or utilized empirically based strategies and when a strong relationship is developed between the mentor and mentee. In addition, they noted that mentoring may be more beneficial for children at risk due to environment factors (e.g., poverty) and not personal factors (e.g., mental illness). Similar to Check & Connect, any mentoring program is focused on fostering a supportive relationship (i.e., building emotional support) with a mentor and thus increasing overall social support. It was noted by research on Check & Connect and the Dubois mentoring meta-analysis that the relationship with the monitor is a key component in mentoring interventions.

A school psychologist can be, and often is, the mentor in these student–mentor interventions. Having some flexibility in his or her schedule can allow for a school psychologist to make time to check in with mentored students throughout the week. A school psychologist can also facilitate the relationship between other adult mentors (teachers, staff) and students by monitoring and facilitating the use of the AEIO-you framework via the mentoring relationship.

Training students to foster supportive relationships with others. Students may be lacking effective social problem-solving or cognitive skills to develop and foster positive supportive relations with others. Groups focused on development of social skills or coping with social situations may help a student to foster important relationships. Given that students will need to be able to function well in groups, this intervention may be more appropriate for Tier 2 interventions versus Tier 3. These interventions can also be utilized school-wide in classrooms as part of Tier 1 planning. Certainly the informational support is key in social skills training and problem-solving training. Students need to learn these skills (informational), have the opportunity to practice them (operational), and get feedback on the use of the skills (appraisal).

Recent meta-analytic research has documented a small effect size for classroom-wide social skills interventions (January, Casey, & Paulson, 2011). There are numerous social skills curricula that could be utilized with groups of students needing social skills interventions. For example, meta-analysis research has documented effects of social skills training with both antisocial youth and students with learning disabilities (Kavale & Mostert, 2004). For some students, focusing on social skills may help them to better access social support resources and develop supportive relationships. School psychologists have the training and tools needed to provide these interventions in schools.

Individual counseling. Students with low support may benefit from individual or group counseling. Research has identified that during difficult times having someone identified who cares about them was vital (Langaard & Toverud, 2009). School psychologists may provide counseling with the ultimate goal to provide additional support and sense of caring to this individual from another adult source in school. The entire AEIO-you framework can come into play with a therapeutic relationship. Additionally, the focus of counseling may be to increase students' perceived social support from other adult and peer sources, focusing on whichever types of support are lacking. Various social skills intervention techniques or social problem-solving strategies may also be utilized in the counseling setting to increase access to and participation in social support. The research is varied depending on technique and methodology but there is great promise. A recent study found that African American elementary-age students who participated in a group counseling program reported significant increases in connectedness to school (Lemberger & Clemens, 2012). Thus, there are several ways individual and group counseling can be utilized to increase social support for a student in need, and school psychologists are best positioned to use evidence-based approaches matched to their assessed need.

SUMMARY

Social support is a crucial construct in the lives of children and adolescents. It is not only associated with overall positive outcomes for youth, but may have the ability to buffer some at-risk youth from negative outcomes. This makes social support an important focus of prevention and intervention efforts for school psychologists. Perceptions of social support can be assessed school-wide or at an individual level via social network and integration measures, rating scales, and interviews. If social support is deemed a problem school-wide, there are Tier 1 strategies (e.g., social–emotional learning) and programs that may help increase students' perceptions of social support and foster positive relationships in schools. For students who, despite prevention efforts, still have lower levels of social support, school psychologists can focus on group and or individual interventions that boost social support.

REFERENCES

Anderson, A. R., Christenson, S. L., Sinclair, M. F., & Lehr, C. A. (2004). Check & Connect: The importance of relationships for promoting school engagement. *Journal of School Psychology, 42*, 95–113. doi:10.1016/j.jsp.2004.01

Bokhorst, C. L., Sumter, S. R., & Westenberg, P. M. (2010). Social support from parents, friends, classmates and teachers in children and adolescents aged 9 to 18 years: Who is perceived as most supportive? *Social Development, 19*, 417–426. doi:10.1111/j.1467-9507.2009.00540.x

Brissette, I., Cohen, S., & Seeman, T. E. (2000). Measuring social integration and social networks. In S. Cohen, L. Underwood, & B. Gottlieb (Eds.), *Measuring and intervening in social support*. New York, NY: Oxford University Press.

Cohen, S., Underwood, L. G., & Gottlieb, B. H. (2000). *Social support measurement and intervention: A guide for health and social scientists*. New York, NY: Oxford University Press.

Cohen, S., & Wills, T. A. (1985). Stress, social support, and the buffering hypothesis. *Psychological Bulletin, 98*, 310–357. doi:10.1037//0033-2909.98.2.310

Davidson, L. M., & Demaray, M. K. (2007). Social support as a moderator between victimization and internalizing/externalizing behaviors from bullying. *School Psychology Review, 36*, 383–405.

Demaray, M. K., & Malecki, C. K. (2002). Critical levels of perceived social support associated with student adjustment. *School Psychology Quarterly, 17*, 213–241. doi:10.1521/scpq.17.3.213.20883

Demaray, M. K., Malecki, C. K., Davidson, L. M., Hodgson, K. K., & Rebus, P. J. (2005). The relationship between social support and student adjustment: A longitudinal analysis. *Psychology in the Schools, 42*, 691–706. doi:10.1002/pits.20120

DuBois, D. L., Holloway, B. E., Valentine, J. C., & Cooper, H. (2002). Effectiveness of mentoring programs for youth: A meta-analytic review. *American Journal of Community Psychology, 30*, 157–197.

Furman, W., & Buhrmester, D. (1985). Children's perceptions of the personal relationships in their social networks. *Developmental Psychology, 21*, 1016–1024. doi:10.1037/0012-1649.21.6.1016

Gottlieb, B. H. (2000). Selecting and planning support interventions. In S. Cohen, L. G. Underwood, & B. H. Gottlieb (Eds.), *Social support measurement and intervention: A guide for health and social scientists* (pp. 195–220). New York, NY: Oxford University Press.

Harter, S. (1985). *Manual for the Social Support Scale for Children*. Denver, CO: University of Denver.

January, A. M., Casey, R. J., & Paulson, D. (2011). A meta-analysis of classroom-wide interventions to build social skills: Do they work? *School Psychology Review, 40*, 242–256.

Kavale, K. A., & Mostert, M. P. (2004). Social skills interventions for individuals with learning disabilities. *Learning Disabilities Quarterly, 27*, 31–43. doi:10.2307/1593630

Kim, H. K., & McKenry, P. C. (1998). Social networks and support: A comparison of African Americans, Asian Americans, Caucasians, and Hispanics. *Journal of Comparative Family Family Studies, 29*, 313–334.

Langaard, K., & Toverud, R. (2009). Caring involvement: A core concept in youth counseling in school health services. *International Journal of Qualitative Studies on Health and Well-Being, 4*, 220–227.

Lemberger, M. E., & Clemens, E. V. (2012). Connectedness and self-regulation as constructs of the student success skills program in inner-city African American elementary school students. *Journal of Counseling and Development, 90*, 450–458. doi:10.1002/j.1556-6676.2012.00056.x

Malecki, C. K., & Demaray, M. K. (2002). Measuring perceived social support: Development of the Child and Adolescent Social Support Scale. *Psychology in the Schools, 39*, 1–18. doi:10.1002/pits.10004

Malecki, C. K., & Demaray, M. K. (2006). Social support as a buffer in the relationship between socioeconomic status and academic performance. *School Psychology Quarterly, 21*, 375–395. doi:10.1037/h0084129

Malecki, C. K., Demaray, M. K., & Elliott, S. N. (2000). *The Child and Adolescent Social Support Scale*. DeKalb, IL: Northern Illinois University.

Merrell, K. W., Carrizales, D. C., Feuerborn, L., Gueldner, B. A., & Tran, O. K. (2007). *Strong teens–Grades 9–12: A social-emotional learning curriculum*. Baltimore, MD: Brookes.

Merrell, K. W., & Gueldner, B. (2010). *Social and emotional learning in the classroom: Promoting mental health and academic success*. New York, NY: Guilford Press.

National Association of School Psychologists. (2009). *Appropriate behavioral, social, and emotional supports to meet the needs of all students.* (Position Statement). Bethesda, MD: Author. Retrieved from http://nasponline.org/about_nasp/positionpapers/appropriatebehavioralsupports.pdf

National Association of School Psychologists. (2010). *Model for comprehensive and integrated school psychological services.* Bethesda, MD: Author. Retrieved from http://nasponline.org/standards/2010standards/2_PracticeModel.pdf

Procidano, M. E., & Heller, K. (1983). Measures of perceived social support from friends and from family: Three validation studies. *American Journal of Community Psychology, 11,* 1–24. doi:10.1007/BF00898416

Rockhill, C. M., Vander Stoep, A., McCauley, E., & Katon, W. J. (2009). Social competence and social support as mediators between comorbid depressive and conduct problems and functional outcomes in middle school children. *Journal of Adolescence, 32,* 535–553. doi:10.1016/j.adolescence.2008.06.011

Sarason, I. G., Levine, H. M., Basham, R. B., & Sarason, B. R. (1983). Assessing social support: The Social Support Questionnaire. *Journal of Personality and Social Psychology, 44,* 127–139. doi:10.1037/0022-3514.44.1.127

Schaps, E. (2009, March/April). Creating caring school communities. *Leadership,* 8–11.

Sinclair, M. F., Christenson, S. L., Evelo, D. L., & Hurley, C. M. (1998). Dropout prevention for high-risk youth with disabilities: Efficacy of a sustained school engagement procedure. *Exceptional Children, 65,* 7–21.

Sprick, R. (2009). *CHAMPS: A proactive and positive approach to classroom management* (2nd ed.). Eugene, OR: Pacific Northwest Publishin.

Stice, E., Ragan, J., & Randall, P. (2004). Prospective relations between social support and depression: Differential direction of effects for parent and peer support. *Journal of Abnormal Psychology, 113,* 155–159.

Suldo, S. M., & Shaffer, E. J. (2008). Looking beyond psychopathology: The dual-factor model of mental health in youth. *School Psychology Review, 37,* 52–68.

Tardy, C. (1985). Social support measurement. *American Journal of Community Psychology, 13,* 187–202. doi:10.1007/BF00905728

Taylor, S. E., Sherman, D. K., Kim, H. S., Jarcho, J., Takagi, K., & Dunagan, M. S. (2004). Culture and social support: Who seeks it and why? *Journal of Personality and Social Psychology, 87,* 354–362.

Zimet, G. D., Dahlem, N. W., Zimet, S. G., & Farley, G. K. (1988). The Multidimensional Scale of Perceived Social Support. *Journal of Personality Assessment, 52,* 30–41. doi:10.1207/s15327752jpa5201_2

Zins, J. E., & Elias, M. J. (2006). Social and emotional learning. In G. G. Bear & K. M. Minke (Eds.), *Children's needs III: Development, prevention, and intervention* (pp.1–13). Bethesda, MD: National Association of School Psychologists.

18 Best Practices in Classroom Discipline

George G. Bear
University of Delaware
Maureen A. Manning
Towson University (MD)

OVERVIEW

Many school psychologists may have little involvement in matters of school discipline other than manifestation determination meetings. Given its close connection to the social, emotional, and behavioral development of students, and the practices that foster such development, school discipline provides ripe opportunities for the services of school psychologists. Such services fit nicely within the National Association of School Psychologists (NASP) *Model for Comprehensive and Integrated School Psychological Services* (NASP, 2010). Among the model's guiding principles are that school psychologists draw from theories, models, and research in psychology and education in both "creating and maintaining safe, supportive, fair, and effective learning environments" and helping "students succeed academically, socially, behaviorally, and emotionally" (NASP, 2010, p. 3). Furthermore, school psychologists' involvement in preventing and correcting behavior problems represents an opportunity to use a problem-solving approach in consultation and to advocate for comprehensive and multitiered services for students.

Educators have long recognized two meanings, and aims, of discipline in the context of schooling (Bear, 2005). The most common refers to the correction and management of student behavior typically for the sake of order, safety, and student compliance, often with the additional goal of preventing behavior problems. This has generally entailed the use of various forms of punishment, and threats thereof, including classroom rules and school-wide codes of conduct linked to punitive consequences for violations. Punishment ranges from mild to harsh, with suspensions, expulsions, and corporal punishment being common. For example, each year approximately 3 million students in the United States are suspended from school (Losen & Gillespie, 2012). Likewise, more than 200,000 students are spanked each year in school in the 19 states that continue to allow the use of corporal punishment (Center for Effective Discipline, 2013). The zero tolerance approach to school discipline is consistent with this meaning of school discipline. Violations of rules are corrected, or punished, immediately, often without consideration of the circumstances involved. Although serious acts of misbehavior, such as fighting, drugs, and weapons, are generally targeted for suspensions and expulsions, too often minor acts of noncompliance are also included.

As noted by Kauffman and Brigham (2000), zero tolerance has come to mean "something stupid—getting tough on little things without allowing discretion in what to do about them" (p. 278). However, not all zero tolerance policies and practices involve "bad judgment" (Kauffman & Brigham, 2000, p. 277). That is, as opposed to a pervasive zero tolerance approach, many schools use clear and fair behavioral expectations, classroom rules, and school policies to communicate that behaviors harmful to others are not tolerated. This includes imposing punishment as a consequence for behaviors such as drugs, weapons possession, bullying, and acts of violence, but only after consideration of the circumstances involved. When zero tolerance is utilized in this manner, it constitutes one part of a more comprehensive, rational, and positive approach to managing and correcting behavior and preventing behavior problems.

Such a comprehensive approach is seen in most models of classroom management and school discipline, including the recently popular school-wide positive behavior interventions and supports approach (SWPBIS; Sugai et al., 2010), with which many school psychologists are likely familiar if not involved. SWPBIS and zero tolerance share the same aims: management, correction, and prevention of behavior problems. However, SWPBIS achieves those aims with much greater emphasis on prevention over correction, while also emphasizing use of positive reinforcement instead of punishment. In this manner it is certainly the more positive of the two approaches. Nevertheless, often SWPBIS's aim is the same, as seen in reduced office disciplinary referrals and suspensions being the primary outcome cited in support of its effectiveness (Bear, 2010).

Educators often overlook the second meaning and aim of discipline, although the importance of self-governance in a democracy has been recognized by educators since the onset of education in the United States (Bear, 2005). School discipline also refers to educators developing self-discipline; that is, developing within students the cognitions, emotions, and behaviors associated with socially and morally responsible behavior. This is seen in behavior that is self-regulated and not determined primarily by the salience of punishment and rewards controlled by others. In combination with the use of teacher-centered techniques to manage and correct misbehavior in the short term, student-centered techniques are used to achieve what is recognized as the more important and long-term aim of developing self-discipline. Student-centered techniques include class meetings, individual and group problem-solving discussions, service learning, and the active involvement of students in curriculum lessons and in classroom and school-wide activities designed to develop social and emotional skills. As shown later, the social and emotional learning (SEL) approach to prevention and school discipline (see Durlak, Gullotta, Domitrovich, Goren, & Weissberg, in press) is most consistent with this meaning and aim of school discipline.

As noted earlier, school psychologists have many opportunities to become involved in classroom and school discipline, and there are several domains within the NASP (2010) Practice Model that are consistent with school psychologists' involvement. The first domain is that of Interventions and Mental Health Services to Develop Social and Life Skills. As stated in the NASP Practice Model, interventions and mental health services in the school should include curricula designed to help students develop self-regulation, empathy, and healthy decision making. These interventions may be delivered at any of the three tiers of intervention. For example, school psychologists may teach social and emotional skills to an entire classroom of students, to small groups, or to individual children. Related domains include (a) Consultation and Collaboration, (b) School-Wide Practices to Promote Learning (under which the area of discipline is specifically referenced), and (c) Preventive and Responsive Services. For example, school psychologists may consult and collaborate with individual teachers and school teams in planning, implementing, and evaluating a comprehensive approach to classroom and school discipline, which may include the review and selection of a school-wide curriculum (i.e., Tier 1). School psychologists are also likely to be involved in planning, implementing, and evaluating individual behavior intervention plans for students at Tier 2 and Tier 3. A major challenge to educators and school psychologists is creating classrooms and schools in which the dual meanings and aims of the term *discipline* are appreciated and achieved.

The purpose of this chapter is to present a summary of evidence-based strategies and techniques of classroom discipline that are consistent with the dual meanings and aims of school discipline. Instead of advocating one particular model or approach of school discipline, we recommend evidence-based strategies and techniques found across various models and approaches, particularly the popular SEL and SWPBIS approaches. This would include strategies and techniques found in both of those approaches that were derived from earlier research following the ecological and process–product approaches to classroom management (see Bear, in press). The SEL and SWPBIS approaches differ greatly in their philosophical and theoretical roots and in the emphasis placed on teacher-centered strategies for managing and correcting student behavior versus student-centered strategies for developing self-discipline (for a review see Osher, Bear, Sprague, & Doyle, 2010). Together, however, they offer a wide range of evidence-based strategies and techniques for the effective management, correction, and prevention of behavior problems and for the development of self-discipline.

BASIC CONSIDERATIONS

Effective classroom discipline demands an understanding of the multiple factors that influence children's social–emotional functioning and mental health. Because many teachers have limited knowledge of children's mental health, collaboration with school psychologists is essential. School psychologists must be aware of research and theory in developmental psychology, especially of various cognitive, emotional, developmental, biological, cultural, home, peer, school, and community factors that interact in an ongoing and transactional fashion in determining the prosocial and antisocial behavior of children and adolescents. School psychologists should also be knowledgeable about theory and research in educational psychology on teacher, classroom, and school characteristics and processes that influence student behavior inside and outside of school. Research in applied behavior analysis on functions of behavior and how these functions are related to environmental antecedents and consequences is also critical.

To ensure that reasonable expectations for student behavior are established, school psychologists must understand, and help teachers and administrators understand, behavior that is developmentally appropriate. For example, secondary school teachers may occasionally benefit from refreshers on adolescent development and behaviors that are common during this period.

During manifestation determination reviews, it is also helpful for school psychologists to provide information to Individualized Education Program teams to assist them in determining whether students' behaviors were linked directly to the students' disabilities or perhaps represented behaviors typical of the students' age group.

School psychologists must also have an understanding of the multiple risk factors and protective assets commonly targeted in classroom and school-wide discipline programs, as well as in programs designed more specifically to prevent bullying and aggression and to promote prosocial behavior (see Bear, 2012b). Programs that focus primarily, if not exclusively, on a single dimension of behavior, such as student compliance, values, self-esteem, social problem solving, moral reasoning, peer influences (e.g., peer mediation), or observable antecedents and consequences of behavior, are inconsistent with research and contemporary models of psychology and are likely to fail (Durlak, Weissberg, Dymnicki, Taylor, & Schellinger, 2011; Ttofi & Farrington, 2011).

Another important consideration, especially when school psychologists consult and collaborate with teachers and others, is that one size does not fit all. At the classroom and school-wide levels, strategies and techniques should be based on one's primary aim (Bear, 2012a), which, in turn, should be based on the population's needs. To pinpoint those needs, a needs assessment is recommended, such as use of student surveys at the classroom level and comprehensive school climate surveys at the school-wide level. Used in combination with other indicators of the need for change (e.g., office disciplinary referrals, suspensions, absences), class and school climate surveys (preferably completed by students but also teachers/staff and parents) should assess such areas as teacher–student relationships, student–student relationships, home–school communication, respect for diversity, safety, and the clarity and fairness of expectations and rules. Such indicators should be used not only for needs assessment but also to monitor and measure program effectiveness.

In developing interventions and programs, preference should be given to strategies and techniques that target risk factors and protective assets shown in theory and research to be linked to important outcomes, particularly to those strategies and techniques shown to lead to actual improvements in the behaviors targeted for change. Consideration should be given to avoiding and overcoming potential barriers to implementation and the lack of fidelity of implementation. In a recent federal report, it was estimated that approximately 44% of all research-based curriculum prevention programs implemented in schools meet minimal standards for overall fidelity of implementation (U.S. Department of Education, 2011). The report also found that only 7.8% of prevention programs meet minimal standards of being research based. Only 3.5% of prevention programs in schools were found to be both research based and well implemented.

Among the barriers to implementation that school psychologists should be aware of is whether or not teachers and staff perceive a need for change and are ready for change, when needed. Resistance should be expected when strategies and techniques are not based on the identified needs of the teacher, classroom, school, or targeted student and when they conflict with the philosophy, training, or educational aims of the teacher or school. As such, these and other factors associated with resistance and lack of fidelity need to be considered (see Bear, 2013; Durlak et al., 2011).

Finally, it is important that school psychologists and educators be knowledgeable of current federal and state laws and regulations pertaining to various aspects of school discipline. These include the special disciplinary provisions of the 2004 Individuals with Disabilities Education Act (IDEA) pertaining to children, federal and state legislation on school violence and bullying, and prevention-oriented legislation in many states, such as those requiring social and emotional learning programs, character education, and bullying prevention programs.

Consulting and collaborating with administrators and teachers regarding self-discipline and methods of discipline necessarily entail a host of multicultural competencies, a review of which is beyond the scope of this chapter. At a minimum, however, school psychologists need to be aware of the discipline gap that exists in many schools, whereby patterns of discipline (including office referrals, suspensions, and expulsions) vary by gender, race, socioeconomic status, and disability status. For example, males, African Americans, and students with low socioeconomic status are suspended and expelled at rates much higher than their peers (American Psychological Association Zero Tolerance Task Force, 2008). School psychologists can assume a leadership role by guiding educators to examine the disparity in discipline referrals in their school and by facilitating "courageous conversations" in which educators examine their assumptions and biases (e.g., about race and disability) and explore factors that may contribute to the disparity. School psychologists should also be aware of cultural differences in parenting styles and behavior, and must examine their own assumptions and biases. For example, research indicates that the majority of parents, especially African American parents, spank their young children (Sorkhabi & Mandara, 2013). White school psychologists whose parents used a different method of discipline might make the assumption that this is a harmful practice based on their own Eurocentric views. However, research has not generally found mild, nonabusive spanking to result in negative outcomes for children, especially when used in the context of parental warmth and support (Sorkhabi & Mandara, 2013). School psychologists are encouraged to increase their multicultural competencies and to work on a school-wide, district-wide, or statewide level to advocate for training in cultural proficiency for all educators.

BEST PRACTICES IN CLASSROOM DISCIPLINE

A comprehensive approach to classroom management and school discipline aligns with a multitiered system of supports for students. A comprehensive approach combines strategies for managing and correcting student behavior with those for developing self-discipline. In addition, it includes strategies for preventing behavior problems. Preventive strategies serve the above two aims, but they are intended more specifically to minimize the need to correct misbehavior. In a multitiered system, these strategies generally apply to the universal level (i.e., Tier 1). A fourth component applies more at the school-wide than classroom level: the provision of more intensive interventions and supports for students deemed at risk of or currently exhibiting serious or chronic behavior problems. In a multitiered system, these interventions may be found at all tiers, but they are most common at the targeted and intensive levels (i.e., Tier 2 and Tier 3).

A comprehensive approach, especially the first three components, is supported by extensive research on the authoritative style of discipline, a style of discipline first supported by Diana Baumrind's theory and research in the area of parenting or child rearing (for a review see Larzelere, Morris, & Harrist, 2013). An authoritative style is associated with a host of favorable social, emotional, and academic outcomes, especially when compared to styles of discipline that are overly harsh, strict, and less responsive to children's social and emotional needs (i.e., authoritarian style), more lax and laissez-faire (i.e., permissive style), or neglecting.

The authoritative approach is characterized by two general qualities: high demandingness and high responsiveness. High demandingness refers to adults having clear and consistently high behavioral expectations, closely monitoring and supervising their children's behavior, and using discipline, where appropriate, in a rational, fair, firm, and consistent manner to correct student behavior. Responsiveness refers to adults demonstrating warmth, acceptance, and caring; communicating openly and clearly while emphasizing persuasion rather than one's authority to manage and correct student behavior; and being responsive to each student's social, emotional, physical, and cognitive needs. Although the bulk of the research on authoritative discipline has been conducted with parents, more recent research has found that this style characterizes the most effective teachers and schools. That is, the most effective teachers and schools provide a balance of demandingness (also referred to as structure) and responsiveness (also referred to as support). This is supported by research in classroom management, school-wide discipline, school climate, and bullying prevention (Bear, in press).

In the remainder of this chapter we present evidence-based strategies and techniques that follow from authoritative styles of discipline and that integrate the SWPBIS and SEL approaches. Whereas a major strength of SWPBIS is demandingness or structure, a major strength of SEL is responsiveness or support, especially social and emotional support. The strategies and techniques are grouped under three components of comprehensive classroom discipline noted above: (a) developing self-discipline, (b) preventing behavior problems, and (c) correcting behavior problems (see Figure 18.1). The fourth component of comprehensive discipline, remediating and responding to chronic and serious behavior problems, is not covered owing to space limitations. Remediation of chronic behavior problems entails services and supports that extend beyond what classroom teachers alone can provide, and corresponds most closely with Tier 2 and Tier 3 of interventions.

Few of the strategies and techniques presented below are specific to any one of the four components, or to any one of the three tiers of the mental health model of prevention and intervention. For example, consistent with authoritative discipline, many of the techniques for developing self-discipline, such as social problem solving and perspective taking, also serve to prevent behavior problems, and vice versa, and should be applied during the correction of behavior problems. Grouping various strategies and techniques into a particular component is somewhat arbitrary, done for heuristic purposes, and is based on the relative emphasis of the strategies, techniques, and primary aims of each component.

Best Practices for Promoting Self-Discipline

School psychologists play a valuable role in promoting student self-discipline through their consultations with teachers and other staff members. Given the tendency of many schools to be reactive and to focus on short-term measures to control behavior, school psychologists can help educators shift their focus to the long-term development of self-discipline, thereby fulfilling education's mission of teaching children to be responsible citizens. In doing so, school psychologists also help prevent behavior problems in both the short term and long term. Self-discipline reflects *internalization*, which is defined as "taking over the values and attitudes of society as one's own so that socially acceptable behavior is motivated not by anticipation of external consequences but by intrinsic or internal factors" (Grusec & Goodnow, 1994, p. 4). Consistent with a large body of research in developmental psychology, self-discipline denotes that behavior is linked to certain cognitions and emotions, which develop with age and are intricately and reciprocally related to environmental events. Finally, it signifies that the ultimate indicator of the

Figure 18.1. Components of Comprehensive School Discipline

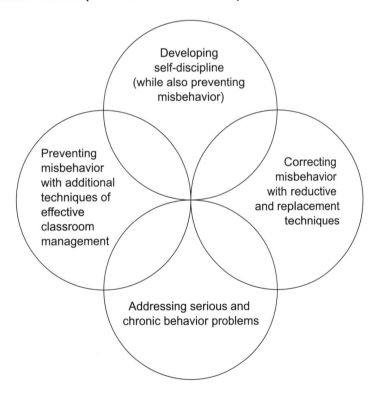

Note. Adapted from *Developing self-discipline and preventing and correcting misbehavior*, by G. G. Bear (with A. Cavalier & M. Manning), 2005, Boston, MA: Allyn & Bacon.

effectiveness of classroom discipline (and school-wide discipline) is not how many students are referred to the office or how well students behave under close adult supervision, but the extent to which students act responsibly when supervision is minimal and when external rewards and punishment are not salient.

A focus on promoting social and emotional competencies associated with self-discipline is found in three national initiatives in education: SEL (Durlak et al., in press), character education (Nucci & Narvaez, 2008), and positive psychology (see Bear & Manning, 2014). Each has more similarities than differences, and for this reason the latter two are often subsumed under the more general umbrella of SEL (Osher et al., 2010). SEL refers to "the process of acquiring and effectively applying the knowledge, attitudes, and skills necessary to recognize and manage emotions; developing caring and concern for others; making responsible decisions; establishing positive relationships; and handling challenging situations capably" (Zins & Elias, 2006, p. 1). In line with this definition, SEL programs target five key competencies: self-awareness, social awareness, responsible decision making, self-management, and relationship skills (Durlak et al., 2011).

When developing school-wide, classroom-level, or student-level interventions to promote student self-discipline, school psychologists should take heed of the following four general strategies commonly found in SEL programs (for elaboration, see Bear, Whitcomb, Elias, & Blank, in press; Durlak et al., in press).

Teach social, emotional, and behavioral competencies by implementing well-designed, developmentally appropriate, evidence-based lessons: As noted by the acronym SAFE, lessons should be sequenced (step-by-step lessons are taught within and across school years), active (students play an active, rather than passive, role in learning), focused (sufficient time is devoted to skill development), and explicit (goals are clearly articulated; Durlak et al., 2011). Themes such as empathy, emotion regulation, respect, and responsibility connect the lessons together. In order to promote generalization, lessons and skills should be integrated into the curriculum and throughout the school day. School psychologists can serve a vital role in assisting school teams with the selection of evidence-based curricula and may wish to refer to the 2013 CASEL guide for a review of social and emotional learning programs (Collaborative for Academic, Social, and Emotional Learning, 2012) or the Illinois state standards for social and emotional learning (http://www.isbe.state.il.us/ils/social_emotional/standards.htm).

Provide frequent opportunities for students to apply social and emotional learning skills, including social and moral problem solving, emotion regulation, and responsible behavior: Opportunities for such teachable moments abound in schools. Many opportunities arise naturally each day and others can be part of planned activities. Examples include class meetings, student government and service learning activities, conflict resolution, peer mediation, cooperative learning, sports, and extracurricular activities. As discussed below (and under the component of correction), disciplinary encounters also provide excellent opportunities for students to apply skills of social and moral problem solving and responsible behavior.

Promote a positive classroom and school climate, with educators modeling the same SEL skills that children are learning: A wealth of research supports the importance of a caring, connected community at school in preventing or reducing behavior problems (see Gerlach & Hopson, 2013). Improving relationships between teachers and students is of utmost importance. An important part of this process includes teachers learning, and demonstrating, the same skills of emotional competence that students learn. As noted by Powell and Kusuma-Powell (2010), "the way to improve school culture" is "by enhancing teacher emotional intelligence" (p. 132). After learning and being encouraged to apply skills such as self-awareness, emotion regulation, and empathy, educators may reflect more often upon their behavior, become more aware of how their moods influence their perceptions, take a few moments to calm themselves before responding impulsively to a discipline infraction, and be more likely to discuss a problem with students rather than assert their power and demand compliance (Powell & Kusuma-Powell, 2010). Additional aspects of school climate that should be targeted include student–student relationships, family–school–community relationships, safety, clear and fair expectations and rules, appreciation for diversity, and student engagement (see http://www.delawarepbs.org for free and validated school climate surveys that measure these aspects).

Provide additional supportive systems and services: School psychologists can play an important role in providing additional supports and services when the elements listed above are not sufficient for preventing and correcting behavior problems. This includes services at Tier 2 and Tier 3, such as individual and small-group counseling, booster sessions from the curriculum, additional social skills or anger management training, consultation with teachers, crisis intervention, and supports for parents. Some of these services may be provided by other mental health specialists, such as school counselors, school social workers, and/or therapists working outside or in conjunction with the school system. In such cases, school psychologists serve a valuable consultative role.

Prevention of Discipline Problems With Additional Techniques of Effective Classroom Management

School psychologists also can play an important role in helping teachers manage their classrooms more effectively. The most common behavior problems in classrooms are minor ones, in the sense that they are less likely than more major behavior problems to result in a student being sent to the office or suspended. Although minor behavior problems disrupt learning (of self or others), they rarely harm others. Minor behavior problems commonly observed or reported by teachers are students getting out of their seat, talking to others without permission, distractibility, hyperactivity, immature or silly behavior, and rushing through assignments (Harrison, Vannest, Davis, & Reynolds, 2012).

In a study of office discipline referrals reported by 1,510 schools in 43 states, Spaulding et al. (2010) found that the most common major problem behaviors resulting in office discipline referrals included (among others) defiance and disruptive behavior. Across grade levels, defiance led to the most referrals, representing 29% of office discipline referrals in elementary schools, 31% in middle schools, and 24% in high schools. Defiance and disruptive behavior are typically considered classroom-managed behaviors, that is, behaviors that teachers can be taught to manage within their classrooms, with the intention of increasing teacher authority and student instructional time.

Developing self-discipline is widely recognized as one part of effective classroom management, with the other part being the use of teacher-centered techniques for establishing order, safety, and cooperation (Bear, in press). Teachers who are most effective in both aspects of classroom management are authoritative in their approach, that is, high in both demandingness and responsiveness (Brophy, 1996). In demonstrating demandingness, or structure, authoritative teachers prevent behavior problems by setting high standards and holding high expectations and enforcing rules and standards in a firm, fair, and consistent manner. Although authoritative teachers use punitive and reactive strategies when needed, they focus more on the use of positive, proactive techniques of prevention for increasing the likelihood that students will exhibit

appropriate behavior willingly rather than grudgingly (Brophy, 1996). Additional techniques that are associated with this dimension of authoritative discipline and are commonly found in most evidence-based books on classroom management include (a) creating a physical environment that is conducive to teaching and learning, (b) establishing predictable procedures and routines and fair rules and consequences, (c) frequently monitoring student behavior and responding immediately to signs of misbehavior, (d) providing academic instruction and activities that motivate learning, and (e) establishing and maintaining close communication with each student's parents or caregivers and working hard to garner their support.

In demonstrating responsiveness, authoritative teachers prevent behavior problems by creating caring, respectful, and supportive teacher–student relationships that help motivate students to comply with teachers out of respect for them rather than simply out of fear of punishment or the desire to earn tangible rewards. Authoritative teachers are responsive to students' basic needs of competence, belongingness, and autonomy (Ryan & Deci, 2000). Positive teacher–student relationships have a significant effect on student achievement, motivation, and behavior (for a review see Sabol & Pianta, 2012). These relationships prevent many behavior problems and promote social and emotional development. Not only do effective teachers develop positive relationships with students, but they also promote positive relationships and a sense of community among the students themselves. Such positive student–student relationships are associated with a number of academic and social–emotional outcomes, including greater academic initiative, academic achievement, liking of school and self-esteem, and fewer delinquent and aggressive behaviors (Brand, Felner, Shim, Seitsinger, & Dumas, 2003). In sum, authoritative teachers create a classroom (and often school-wide) climate in which students follow norms for appropriate behavior not only out of respect for the teacher but also out of respect for one another.

In helping to develop positive relationships, as well as achieve other valued outcomes, authoritative teachers use praise and rewards, a practice of much controversy in recent years. However, in recognition of their limitations, praise and rewards, and especially rewards, are used strategically and sparingly. Perhaps foremost among the limitations are that the effects often are not maintained after intervention ends and seldom generalize outside the setting in which praise and rewards are systematically applied (Landrum & Kauffman, 2006).

Furthermore, many students, especially adolescents, prefer not to be praised or rewarded publicly (Bear, 2013), as often practiced in SWPBIS programs. Most controversial among the limitations of the use of rewards, as frequently cited in the literature, is that praise and especially rewards harm intrinsic motivation. That limitation has been the subject of ongoing debate, which is beyond the scope of this chapter (see Bear, 2010).

In short, research shows that praise and rewards are generally effective in increasing desired behavior. However, research also shows that tangible rewards may be detrimental to intrinsic motivation under some, albeit limited, circumstances. The most likely circumstances are when students perceive rewards to be used in a controlling (rather than informational) manner and when social comparisons are emphasized.

As with other techniques of classroom management and socialization, praise and rewards have their limitations, but they can largely be minimized or avoided by using the techniques in a wise and strategic fashion. Best practices in the use of rewards, as reviewed by Bear (2010), are displayed in Table 18.1. School psychologists are advised to consult Bear (2010) when incorporating praise and rewards into classroom or individual intervention plans.

Best Practices for Correcting Misbehavior

School psychologists can be instrumental in recommending research-based strategies for correcting student misbehavior. These strategies can be used at any of the tiers of intervention; that is, these strategies may be included in the school (and/or district) code of conduct, may be written into a classroom teacher's discipline ladder, and may be incorporated into an individual student's behavior intervention plan. It should be noted that many of the same techniques used to prevent misbehavior and to develop self-discipline are used to correct misbehavior. For example, clear and high expectations, positive reinforcement, and caring and supportive relationships continue to be critical. However, correcting misbehavior necessitates the use of additional techniques that are more specific to the immediate and pressing need to stop or decrease behaviors that interfere with teaching and learning or that otherwise are harmful to an individual student or others.

In general, techniques more specific to correction fall into two categories: reductive techniques and replacement techniques. Punishment with aversives, response cost, and extinction are the most common reductive techniques. Positive and negative reinforcement are the most common replacement techniques. These five behavioral techniques, which exist in multiple forms and under various terms, can be found in nearly all classrooms (Landrum & Kauffman, 2006). Punishment ranges in restrictiveness from physical proximity and removal of privileges to suspension and corporal punishment. Corporal punishment is the one form of punishment that most professional organizations in

Table 18.1. Best Practices in the Use of Rewards

- Use tangible rewards only occasionally, if at all, when reinforcing behavior that is intrinsically motivated.
- Adopt the following strategies to increase the effectiveness of praise and rewards and to help reduce the likelihood that rewards will be perceived as controlling:
  - Emphasize the informational aspect of the reward and the importance of intrinsic motivation (e.g., "The reason for giving you a surprise free-time period is that all of you have demonstrated that you care about others in the class.").
  - Highlight the value or usefulness of the behavior that is praised or rewarded.
  - Highlight the student's specific achievement or the skills and effort demonstrated toward the achievement.
  - Allow the student to play an active role in determining the reward (e.g., giving the student choices) and the behavior or criteria necessary to earn it.
  - Administer rewards in an unexpected, or surprise, fashion.
- Do not promise rewards that you do not plan to, or cannot, deliver.
- Use praise and tangible rewards in a sincere, credible, and timely manner.
- Recognize that students' interpretation of praise depends not only on the actual words said, but also on the manner by which the words are communicated.
- Make praise and rewards contingent upon success or effort.
- Rely less on public praise and more on private praise, especially with adolescents.
- Do not hesitate to use tangible rewards to motivate behavior that is not intrinsically motivated.
- Always use praise and rewards more often than punishment. When punishment is used, always combine it with the use of praise and rewards.
- Praise and reward not only desired behaviors but also prosocial reasoning and emotions that underlie the behaviors.

psychology and education oppose, including the American Psychological Association, NASP, and the National Education Association.

The limitations of punishment in schools are well known and covered extensively elsewhere (see Bear, 2010). A brief summary of the arguments in favor of and against punishment is presented in Table 18.2. Because this is such a controversial issue, school psychologists should be aware that there is no research indicating that the use of punishment should be eliminated. Indeed, research shows that the most effective parents, teachers, and schools rely on the fair and judicious use of high behavioral expectations, sanctions, and mild forms of punishment. Furthermore, punishment can help foster self-discipline. This is especially true when punishment is combined with techniques for preventing misbehavior and for developing self-discipline and when implemented in a caring, yet firm, fair, and judicious manner. When used in this manner, punishment is likely to reduce the interfering behavior in the short term and also convey the longer term message that the misbehavior is socially or morally unacceptable. In sum, the use of punishment per se is not a primary problem. The problem is that too many schools overly rely on its use and fail to place greater emphasis on alternative positive techniques that prevent behavior problems and develop self-discipline. School psychologists should play an important role in communicating this message to educators and ensuring the implementation of positive techniques that promote long-term development.

In order to correct, and reduce, misbehavior, effective adults utilize reductive behavioral techniques, such as punishment, as well as behavioral replacement techniques. Behavioral replacement techniques serve the purpose of reducing undesired behavior by increasing desired behaviors that are incompatible with the undesired behavior (e.g., reinforcing students for raising their hands rather than or in combination with punishing them for calling out). Replacement techniques typically include some form of positive reinforcement, and to a lesser extent negative reinforcement, used singly or in combination with reductive techniques, particularly punishment or extinction. Common among these techniques are contingency contracts, daily report cards, Mystery Motivator, group contingencies (e.g., Good Behavior Game), and self-management.

Evidence-based reductive and replacement techniques for correcting mild, moderate, and severe behavior problems are presented in Tables 18.3, 18.4, and 18.5, respectively. It is recommended that school psychologists familiarize themselves with these techniques to enhance their consultations and the development of behavior intervention plans. The techniques are drawn from research reviews of discipline in parenting (e.g., Larzelere et al., 2013), from reviews of teaching (e.g., Emmer et al., 2008), and from popular textbooks on classroom management and school discipline that emphasize evidence-based practices (e.g., Emmer & Evertson, 2012; Weinstein & Novodvorsky, 2011). The techniques are grouped, albeit somewhat arbitrarily, hierarchically indicating that educators should generally use the techniques appearing early in the hierarchy before using those appearing later.

In practice, during disciplinary encounters the above techniques and strategies would be applied in the context of a two-part problem-solving process for correcting misbehavior (Bear, 2010). Part 1 is student centered, focusing on altering the student's behavior and the cognitions and emotions that underlie the targeted behavior problem. This approach includes building assets and addressing deficits. The adult assumes a guiding, yet directive, role while helping the student engage in problem solving and developing a plan of action. Four steps are suggested, with the adult helping

Table 18.2. A Balanced View of Punishment

Supporting Its Use	Limitations
• School codes of conduct and state and federal laws require punishment for certain undesired behaviors (e.g., bullying, aggression, possession of drugs) • Punishment is effective in decreasing undesired behavior • Effective teachers and schools use high behavioral expectations, sanctions, and mild forms of punishment fairly and judiciously (and in combination with positive techniques) • Sanctions and punishment serve as deterrents • Punishment can help foster self-discipline	• Teaches students what not to do, but not what to do • Effects often are short term and not lasting • Fails to address the multiple factors that typically contribute to a student's behavior • Models punishing others • In certain forms (e.g., suspension), reinforces avoidant and escape behavior • May produce undesirable side effects • Frequent use contributes to a negative classroom and school climate

Table 18.3. Techniques for Correcting Mild Behavior Problems

Use for minor acts of misbehavior by the student, such as not attending, not raising his or her hand to talk, passing notes, talking to others, and getting out of his or her seat. The techniques below are most appropriate, and effective, when the targeted behavior first begins to appear and has not become frequent. See Table 18.4 for techniques to use when such behaviors demonstrate resistance to the techniques below.

Ignore the Misbehavior (Use Extinction)

- This works best when the teacher's attention is reinforcing the target behavior; other techniques are more appropriate when the target behavior disrupts learning or harms others.
- When used, combine with reinforcement of appropriate behavior.
- Expect the target behavior to become worse before it gets better and to quickly return to its previous state when reinforced in the future.

Redirect the Student

Monitor the student's behavior closely, and when the behavior problem is first observed, or anticipated, use nonverbal or verbal redirection to stop or prevent the behavior (and group contagion).

Nonverbal redirection

- Establish eye contact.
- Move near the student (i.e., use physical proximity).
- Give a facial expression that expresses that you are aware of the behavior and it is to stop (e.g., a harsh stare).
- Use a hand signal or other nonverbal cue (snap fingers) to prompt appropriate behavior.

Verbal redirection

- Simply state the student's name or incorporate the student's name into the lesson.
- Direct the student to participate in the lesson.
- Remind the student (and/or others around the student) what that student should be doing and/or remind that student and others of the respective rules (foreshadowing).
- Remind the student of previously good behavior.
- Warn the student of the negative consequences of the behavior.

Make Deliberate Efforts to Reinforce Appropriate Behavior and Enhance the Teacher–Student Relationship

This serves not only to prevent future misbehavior, but also to correct misbehavior by increasing the frequency of replacement behaviors.

- Reinforce the desired behavior, particularly those behaviors that are incompatible with the targeted behavior. As a rule of thumb, try to reinforce the student at least three times for every one negative correction. Follow recommendations on the use of praise and rewards presented in this chapter.
- While the targeted student is observing, praise other students, especially those valued by the targeted student, for appropriate behavior.
- In general, increase time spent in positive interaction with the student (e.g., Banking Time; see Driscoll & Pianta, 2010).

Alter the Physical Environment

- Change seating such that the student is near good role models, away from distractors, or closer to the teacher.

Hold a Class Meeting

This is most appropriate when the problem behavior is shown by students in addition to the targeted student.

- Focus on the impact of the behavior on the student and other students, ways to avoid its reoccurrence, and alternative desired behaviors.

Contact the Home and Garner the Support of Parents

- Because the behavior problem is minor, give a gentle message that their child's behavior has recently been resistant to the above interventions, and you would appreciate their support.
- Send positive messages home about improved behavior.
- Note to the parents that more systematic interventions will be implemented if the misbehavior continues and that a parent conference will be requested.

---

the student to (a) identify the problem behavior and explore why it occurred; (b) reflect upon why the behavior is a problem (e.g., its impact on others); (c) assume responsibility for one's own actions, including accepting the consequences and fixing the problem, when appropriate; and (d) plan how the behavior might not happen again and, as appropriate, to commit to a plan of action.

Part 2 of the problem-solving process is more teacher centered, focusing on the teacher's and school's responsibility to (a) directly support the student's problem-solving action plan and (b) address environmental factors, especially classroom and school factors that influence the targeted behavior. This would include modifying current preventive and corrective practices, where appropriate. Because many educators may be unfamiliar with, or unsure how to conduct, these problem-solving discussions, particularly the student-centered format, school psychologists may provide

Table 18.4. Techniques for Correcting Moderate Behavior Problems

Use for behavior problems such as a first-time offense of nonviolent fighting, minor theft, or continued behavior problems despite use of the techniques above, especially when the behavior disrupts learning.

Hold a Private Problem-Solving Conference With the Student

This would entail Part 1 of the problem-solving process described in the chapter and should always be used in combination with Part 2, with the latter focusing more on the actions and support of adults.

- Meet when the student is calm, not angry. Avoid arguing; be firm, yet respectful of the student's thoughts and feelings.
- Focus on how the behavior is to improve. Use optimism that it will improve and offer support.
- Use a social problem-solving approach that includes induction (messages that promote empathy and responsibility): Identify the problem, its consequences, and the student's personal goals (including self-regulation); challenge the student to consider feelings and thoughts of others; think of alternatives; try a plan and then evaluate it.
- Use scaffolding or dialoguing, applying as much guidance and assistance as is developmentally needed to help the student through the problem-solving process.

Require a Written Self-Examination of the Problem Behavior

This might involve social problem solving and induction and be combined with a contingency contract.

Use Positive Reinforcement Techniques in a Planned and Systematic Approach With or Without a Contingency Contract

This might include various forms of differential reinforcement (e.g., differential reinforcement of omission of behavior, differential reinforcement of incompatible behavior, and differential reinforcement of lower rates of behavior).

- Follow general guidelines on the effectiveness of different schedules of reinforcement. For example, at first, reinforce desirable behaviors contingently, consistently, and immediately. Once the behavior is established, reinforce intermittently. Also, follow recommendations presented in this chapter on the general use of praise and rewards.
- Use the Premack Principle (i.e., reward the student with a preferred activity but only after the student has completed a nonpreferred task).
- Use rewards in a game-like, motivating manner (e.g., Mystery Motivator).
- Provide opportunities for the desirable behaviors to be exhibited and reinforced in a variety of realistic settings. Reinforce with a variety of reinforcers.
- Use a recording system (e.g., point card, homework log) to monitor changes in behavior and earning of rewards.
- Involve parents in the reinforcement, where feasible. For example, call, e-mail, text a message to parents, or send a positive note home. Use a daily report card, if needed.

Implement a Behavioral Self-Management Technique

- Self-recording is a technique in which the student records the frequency of specific identified behaviors in a behavioral diary or on a data recording sheet.
- Self-evaluation is a technique in which the student self-records the behavior but also evaluates the behavior against a specific criterion.
- Self-reinforcement is a technique in which the student self-records, self-evaluates, and self-reinforces.

Develop a Contingency Contract

- Include techniques listed above (and below), as appropriate.
- Define the behavior in clear and concise terms. Behaviors should be easy to monitor and record.
- Make sure that the contract is fair, clear, and positive.
- Include an easy way to record the behavior.
- Start small with respect to goals.
- Include the student in planning the contract. Allow for negotiation.
- Include the following in the written contract:
  - Statement of the goals of the contract
  - Clearly specified responsibilities of the student (and the teacher)
  - Times/days the contract is in effect
  - Consequences for successful completion
  - Consequences if the student fails to fulfill his or her responsibilities
  - Starting and renegotiation dates
  - Signatures of all parties concerned (student, teacher, parent)
- Be sure to follow up on the student's progress on both a short- and long-term basis.
- Modify and change the contract, when needed.

Implement the Good Behavior Game or Another Group Contingency to Reward Group and/or Individual Behavior

This is most appropriate when several students exhibit the targeted behavior problems.

Continued

Table 18.4. Continued

- Consider using a group contingency technique within the format of motivational gaming, as done in the empirically supported Good Behavior Game (Van Lier, Muthén, van der Sar, & Crijnen, 2004), in which students play a game that rewards appropriate behavior of the group (see Bear, 2010, for a review of research on the Good Behavior Game and for specific implementation steps).

Use Response Cost

- Contingent upon misbehavior, take away previously earned or acquired rewards or privileges, such as recess or the student sitting where he or she prefers.

Use Overcorrection

- Have the student fix the problem (i.e., restitutional overcorrection).
- Have the student repeatedly practice the correct behavior (i.e., positive-practice overcorrection; for example, as a consequence of writing on the desk the student has to wash all of the desks in the classroom).

Use Time-Out From Reinforcement

This includes time-out in or near the classroom as well as time-out that is out of the room, such as in-school suspension and detention.

- Recognize that time-out is not effective for students who want to be removed from the classroom (i.e., an environment that presents a negative climate, with few reinforcers of appropriate behavior), resulting in negative reinforcement (however, also recognize that student removal for disruptive behavior may serve the purpose of helping others learn).
- Use after the above techniques have failed (unless otherwise required by the code of conduct).
- Make clear when and why the procedure will be used.
- Use an appropriate setting (safe, monitored by an adult, no attention, no reinforcers).
- Be firm and calm, and simply state the problem and the related rule.
- Do not argue or lecture before, during, or after time-out.
- Be consistent and keep it short (e.g., use a timer). Add time if the student is noncompliant during time-out.
- Combine with techniques presented previously, especially reinforcement of appropriate behavior, response cost, and a problem-solving approach.

Hold a Teacher–Parent–Student Conference

- Develop a formalized behavior intervention plan that specifies interventions to be implemented and responsibilities of the school, home, and student.

---

ongoing training and consultation to interested teachers and staff.

The choice of techniques, when they are to be used (including at what point in the hierarchy), and how intensely and frequently, should be determined by a variety of considerations. These considerations include (a) the behavior's severity (e.g., its impact on the learning of others, harm to self or others); (b) the student's developmental level; (c) the student's response to previous interventions; (d) cognitive, emotional, and environmental factors contributing to the behavior; (e) the teacher's acceptance of and skills in the use of various techniques; and (f) a host of practical and situational factors (e.g., immediacy of addressing the problem, time available to devote to the behavior, supports and resources available, students' and parents' acceptance of the intervention, school policies). It is important to note that each technique in the tables is intended to be used in combination with one or more of the other techniques listed. Each should also be used in combination with 12 general strategies presented below.

Balance demandingness and responsiveness: Although authoritative adults would rather guide than externally control students, these adults understand that the latter

might be necessary when a student is defiant or noncompliant. In correcting misbehavior, authoritative adults are confrontive rather than coercive; they are demanding, firm, and goal-directed, but not overly controlling and punitive, intrusive, or undermining of the student's sense of autonomy; and they monitor behavior closely. It is the greater use of coercive behavioral control that most clearly differentiates authoritarian from authoritative discipline. Whereas the immediate aim of authoritative adults might be compliance, and they prefer confrontive over coercive control to obtain it, their long-term aim is self-discipline. Authoritative adults understand that to develop self-discipline, and to elicit willing instead of grudging compliance (Brophy, 1996), they need to provide support that is developmentally appropriate and responsive to students' social and emotional needs. As in preventing behavior problems and developing self-discipline, in correcting misbehavior authoritative adults recognize that close teacher–student relationships are a critical part of responsiveness. In demonstrating responsiveness, authoritative adults are sensitive to cultural differences, respecting the feelings, thoughts, and dignity of all students and their families. Authoritative adults also recognize that what is generally

Table 18.5. Techniques for Correcting Serious or Chronic Behavior Problems

Use for serious violations of school rules that cause a great deal of classroom disruption, such as continual noncompliance or defiance and physical or verbal aggression toward peers or teachers. Note that a school's code of conduct, and many state laws, dictate the consequences for serious and chronic misbehavior.

Use a Combination of the Techniques in Tables 18.3 and 18.4 in a More Intensive, Planned, Systematic, and Sustained Approach

- Place increased emphasis on fidelity of implementation.

Use Physical Restraint

- Use only when necessary, appropriate, and consistent with ethical and legal guidelines.
- Be familiar with, and trained where appropriate, in procedures for deescalating aggression and preventing violence.

Refer to Support Staff and/or School Intervention Team for Consultative Assistance and Support Services

- Develop a comprehensive individual intervention plan, guided by a comprehensive, formalized, broad-based functional behavior assessment that examines both proximal and distal factors (including environmental, cognitive, emotional, and medical) that influence the student's behavior, with an emphasis on those that services can affect.

Refer for Direct Services Provided by Mental Health Specialists Inside or Outside of the School Setting

- Mental health specialists may be school psychologists, school counselors, social workers, and clinical psychologists, as needed.
- Services might entail special education, counseling, social skills training, anger management training, parent management training/family therapy, and medical intervention (e.g., medication), as needed. These services should be addressed in the student's individual intervention plan.

Suspend the Student Out of School

- Suspend the student only when necessary and as a last resort (or as required by the code of conduct).
- Place the student at home (not recommended for long-term suspension).
- Place the student into an interim alternative education setting.
- Place the student in an alternative education program, or other restricted educational and/or mental health setting, as needed.
- Be aware of special provisions in IDEA governing the removal of students with disabilities for more than 10 school days.

Expel From School

- Expel the student as required in the code of conduct for serious offenses such as possession of weapons or drugs.
- Where feasible (and as required for students with disabilities), continue to provide educational and related services.

effective in correcting behavior problems (as well as in preventing these behaviors and developing self-discipline) is not specific to race, ethnicity, or culture (Kauffman, Conroy, Gardner, & Oswald, 2008; Sorkhabi & Mandara, 2013).

View disciplinary encounters as educational opportunities: Authoritative adults understand that behavior problems, especially minor ones, are normal and vary with developmental level. Authoritative adults understand that these problems still require correction. They view disciplinary encounters not merely as situations that may require correction, or punishment, but as opportunities to teach appropriate behavior and develop self-discipline. This method requires patience, recognizing that, as in academic subjects, the learning of social and emotional competencies takes time and mistakes are often made along the way. These mistakes provide opportunities to develop SEL skills. Thus, unlike authoritarian adults, authoritative adults do not act as prosecutors seeking criminal justice, but as educators striving to develop skills of self-discipline.

Gottman (1997) uses the term *emotion coach* to describe the function that effective parents serve when disciplinary events occur, and others (e.g., Powell & Kusuma-Powell, 2010) have suggested the need for teachers to adopt an emotion coaching role as well. The five steps of emotion coaching described by Gottman (1997) and supported by substantial parenting research are (a) recognize the child's feelings; (b) recognize the opportunity to express empathy, build intimacy with the student, and teach self-discipline; (c) listen to the child's viewpoint and validate his or her feelings; (d) label the child's feelings using age-appropriate vocabulary; and (e) set limits on the child's behavior and help him or her problem-solve the situation. Thus, emotion coaching is similar to an authoritative discipline style and results in similar outcomes. Research suggests that children who have been emotionally coached by their parents are more academically, socially, and emotionally competent and display greater self-discipline (Gottman, 1997).

Be firm and fair, but not too lenient and not too harsh: Punishment should fit the crime and be consistent. Consistency refers to treating students the same for the same misbehavior and under the same circumstances. Judicious refers to responding in a fair, sensible, and expedient fashion. When punishment is not used in this manner, students are less likely to respond favorably to the consequence, and are unlikely to internalize the values that adults might be trying to communicate in their disciplinary actions (other than punishment for the sake of correction). Moreover, when consequences for rule violations are not perceived by students to be fair, school climate and safety are likely to suffer.

Examine the factors that help explain or contribute to the misbehavior, especially those most directly related to the misbehavior: School psychologists are often involved in conducting functional behavior assessments, or in training teachers and staff how to conduct them. Examining antecedents and consequences that might prompt and reinforce behavior, as well as other contributing factors, helps educators gain insight as to why the misbehavior is occurring. Unlike in traditional functional behavior assessments, however, the factors examined should not be limited to observable environmental factors (e.g., classroom, instructional, school, peer, and home) but should also include intra-individual factors that are not always observed (e.g., social cognitive processes). Particular attention should be given to those factors that have the most direct influence on the target behavior. The major purpose, however, is to identify and target those factors that are malleable, that is, factors that might likely be changed to improve behavior.

Adhere to the principle of minimal sufficiency: This principle refers to using the least amount of external pressure necessary to change behavior. Underlying this principle are four concepts: (a) students are less likely to accept the punitive consequence, and internalize the message, if it is perceived as too harsh or overly controlling; (b) harsher interventions, especially those perceived to be unfair, often are no more effective than milder ones (e.g., 10 days of out-of-school suspension is likely to be no more effective than 1 day of in-school suspension); (c) in general, the limitations of punishment apply more to harsher forms of punishment than milder ones; and (d) with the exception of addressing the most serious and chronic behavior problems shown to be resistant to intervention, teachers tend to prefer interventions that are positive, are of brief duration, and are easy and inexpensive to implement.

Recognize that there's a right time and a wrong time for confrontation and social problem solving: Behavior that disrupts the classroom should be responded to immediately. However, it may not always be appropriate to immediately confront the student's behavior, such as challenging the student's excuses and engaging in social problem solving. Confrontation is especially ill advised when students are overly angry or upset, or in a public forum. Not only might this make the situation worse, but the student also is unlikely to process the message intended, focusing instead on the punishment. Thus, where feasible, confrontation and social problem solving should occur when the student and adult are calm and can discuss the situation privately.

When punishment is used, always combine it with positive techniques for increasing desired behaviors and maintaining supportive relationships: Perhaps chief among the many limitations of punishment noted previously is that punishment does not teach what should be done, and its widespread use creates a negative classroom and school climate. These limitations can be avoided by combining punishment with positive techniques for teaching, increasing replacement or desired behaviors, and maintaining positive teacher–student and student–student relationships.

Emphasize the impact of the student's behavior on others, and additional reasons why the behavior is wrong other than the adverse consequences for the perpetrator: Induction serves this purpose. Induction is a disciplinary technique shown to foster empathy, a sense of responsibility, and moral behavior (Hoffman, 2000), and it is widely used in SEL programs that focus on caring and responsibility, such as Responsive Classrooms (Charney, 2002), Caring Schools Community (Watson & Battistich, 2006), and Restorative Justice (Morrison & Vaandering, 2012). Through induction, greater attention is directed to the impact of the behavior on others than on the consequences to oneself. Induction should be used in the context of a social problem-solving approach not only to help students reflect upon and fix a behavior problem, but also to help them develop self-discipline. Examples include helping students understand why their behavior is problematic, generate and evaluate alternative solutions to be used in the future, accept the consequences of their behavior, repair any harm to relationships that resulted from the misbehavior, and develop a plan and a commitment to implement it.

Induction should also be used as a supplement to punishment, to help students understand the reasoning behind the rule that was broken and the punishment that is applied. When students' attention is narrowly focused on rules and punishment, educators may unintentionally foster simplistic or self-focused (i.e., hedonistic) reasoning. Students may verbalize that a behavior is "wrong" or "against the rules," and that it will result in negative consequences for themselves, but such knowledge does not seem to deter them from misbehavior (e.g., Manning & Bear, 2011). Similarly, research indicates the ineffectiveness of the lecture or law-related approach to education, such as that used in drug education programs (e.g., Drug Abuse Resistance Education). Simply telling students what to do, or what not to do, is insufficient. What does seem more effective is stimulating empathy for others, as inductions do.

Encourage acceptance of responsibility: Perceptions of autonomy, self-control, and choice are critical to self-discipline, and thus are emphasized in the SEL approach and many popular models of classroom management (e.g., William Glasser's models). Disciplinary encounters present an excellent opportunity for students to learn that they largely determine their own behavior, and its impact on others, by the decisions and choices they make.

Tactfully challenge students' denials and excuses used to avoid responsibility: A substantial body of research shows that individuals frequently avoid assuming responsibility for their behavior, as well as feelings of empathy, by denying what they did or giving excuses for their behavior (e.g., Bandura, Caprara, Barbaranelli, Pastorelli, & Regalia, 2001). Such denials, excuses, and blaming should be confronted directly, which is a strategy commonly used in several popular models of classroom management, including Glasser's models, Positive Discipline (Nelsen, Lott, & Glenn, 2000), Love and Logic (Fay & Funk, 1995), and the more evidence-based Aggression Replacement Training (Glick & Gibbs, 2011). School psychologists can review this literature and help teachers tactfully challenge students' excuses without damaging relationships.

Encourage students to accept the consequences of their misbehavior and to repair any harm to others or in the relationship with others: This strategy also is included in the models cited above, especially Restorative Justice (Morrison & Vaandering, 2012). It is guided by theory and research on the role of self-perceptions of autonomy, competence, and belongingness in behavior and emotional well-being. In learning to assume responsibility for their behavior and understanding that their behavior is influenced by their decisions and choices, students admit their mistakes and accept the consequences of their actions. Where applicable, to maintain positive relationships with others, this also entails repairing harm to others and restoring relationships that were harmed.

Seek support from others: Collaboration with others, especially parents, should be facilitated when dealing with many behavior problems, especially recurrent and serious ones. Support from peers also often is warranted, as is more intensive support from mental health specialists and school personnel.

SUMMARY

The area of student discipline provides many opportunities for school psychologists, who can be involved at the school, classroom, and individual student level. Discipline has two purposes when applied to schools: (a) the prevention, management and correction of student misbehavior and (b) the development of self-discipline in students. Many schools have implemented short-term, reactionary (both punitive and positive) strategies to preserve safety, order, and compliance while largely neglecting the long-term social and emotional development of their students. School psychologists are in an ideal position to help administrators and teachers consider the limitations of punishment, especially a pervasive zero tolerance approach to discipline, and the shortcoming of compliance-oriented practices.

To inform the collaboration that school psychologists conduct with teachers, administrators, and school teams, this chapter presented evidence-based strategies for preventing and responding to behavior problems, as well as for developing self-discipline. Knowledge of these strategies, and the research that supports them, will help school psychologists when consulting on individual behavior plans, assisting a teacher with classroom management, or helping to refine codes of conduct for a school or district. Consistent with a focus on prevention and universal interventions, this chapter paid significant attention to the authoritative style of classroom management. By emphasizing the effectiveness of a balanced approach of responsiveness and demandingness (and using other techniques presented in the chapter when necessary), school psychologists can help educators prevent many misbehaviors from occurring (or recurring), and can help promote students' self-discipline.

AUTHOR NOTE

Disclosure. George G. Bear has a financial interest in books he authored or coauthored referenced in this chapter.

REFERENCES

American Psychological Association Zero Tolerance Task Force. (2008). Are zero tolerance policies effective in the schools? An evidentiary review and recommendations. *American Psychologist, 63,* 852–862. doi:10.1037/0003-066X.63.9.852

Bandura, A., Caprara, G. V., Barbaranelli, C., Pastorelli, C., & Regalia, C. (2001). Sociocognitive self-regulatory mechanisms governing transgressive behavior. *Journal of Personality and Social Psychology, 80,* 125–135. doi:10.1037/0022-3514.80.1.125

Bear, G. G. (with Cavalier, A., & Manning, M.). (2005). *Developing self-discipline and preventing and correcting misbehavior.* Boston, MA: Allyn & Bacon.

Bear, G. G. (2010). *School discipline and self-discipline: A practical guide to promoting prosocial student behavior.* New York, NY: Guilford Press.

Bear, G. G. (2012a). Both suspension and alternatives work, depending on one's aim. *Journal of School Violence, 2,* 174–186. doi:10.1080/15388220.2012.652914

Bear, G. G. (2012b). Self-discipline as a protective asset. In S. Brock & S. Jimerson (Eds.), *Best practices in crisis prevention and intervention in the schools* (2nd ed., pp. 27–54). Bethesda, MD: National Association of School Psychologists.

Bear, G. G. (2013). Teacher resistance to frequent rewards and praise: Lack of skill or a wise decision? *Journal of Educational and Psychological Consultation, 23,* 318–340.

Bear, G. G. (in press). Preventive classroom management. In E. T. Emmer & E. J. Sabornie (Eds.), *Handbook of classroom management* (2nd ed.). Mahwah, NJ: Erlbaum.

Bear, G. G., & Manning, M. A. (2014). Positive psychology and school discipline. In R. Gilman, E. S. Huebner, & M. Furlong (Eds.), *Handbook of positive psychology in schools* (2nd ed., pp. 347–364). New York, NY: Routledge.

Bear, G. G., Whitcomb, S., Elias, M., & Blank, J. (in press). SEL and School-Wide Positive Behavioral Interventions and Supports. In J. Durlak, T. Gullotta, C. Domitrovich, P. Goren, & R. Weissberg (Eds.), *Handbook of social and emotional learning.* New York, NY: Guilford Press.

Brand, S., Felner, R., Shim, S., Seitsinger, A., & Dumas, T. (2003). Middle school improvement and reform: Development and validation of a school-level assessment of climate, cultural pluralism, and school safety. *Journal of Educational Psychology, 95,* 570–588. doi:10.1037/0022-0663.95.3.570

Brophy, J. E. (1996). *Teaching problem students.* New York, NY: Guilford Press.

Center for Effective Discipline. (2013). *U.S.: Corporal punishment and paddling statistics by state and race.* Canal Winchester, OH: Author. Retrieved from http://www.stophitting.com/index.php?page=statesbanning

Charney, R. S. (2002). *Teaching children to care: Classroom management for ethical and academic growth, K–8* (Rev. ed.). Greenfield, MA: Northeast Foundation for Children.

Collaborative for Academic, Social, and Emotional Learning. (2012). *2013 CASEL guide: Effective social and emotional learning programs: Preschool and elementary school edition.* Chicago, IL: Author. Retrieved from http://www.casel.org

Driscoll, K. C., & Pianta, R. C. (2010). Banking time in Head Start: Early efficacy of an intervention designed to promote supportive teacher-child relationships. *Early Education and Development, 21,* 38–64. doi:10.1080/10409280802657449

Durlak, T., Gullotta, C., Domitrovich, P., Goren, & Weissberg, R. (Eds.) (in press). *Handbook of social and emotional learning.* New York, NY: Guilford Press.

Durlak, J. A., Weissberg, R. P., Dymnicki, A. B., Taylor, R. D., & Schellinger, K. B. (2011). The impact of enhancing students' social and emotional learning: A meta-analysis of school-based universal interventions. *Child Development, 82,* 405–432. doi:10.1111/j.1467-8624.2010.01564.x

Emmer, E. T., Epstein, M., Atkins, M., Cullinan, D., Kutash, K., & Weaver, R. (2008). *Reducing behavior problems in the elementary school classroom: A practice guide* (NCEE #2008-012). Washington, DC: National Center for Education Evaluation and Regional Assistance, Institute of Education Sciences, U.S. Department of Education. Retrieved from http://ies.ed.gov/ncee/wwc/publications/practiceguides

Emmer, E. T., & Evertson, C. M. (2012). *Classroom management for middle and high school teachers* (12th ed.). New York, NY: Pearson.

Fay, J., & Funk, D. (1995). *Teaching with love and logic: Taking control of the classroom.* Golden, CO: Love and Logic Press.

Gerlach, B., & Hopson, L. M. (2013). Effective methods for improving school climate. In C. Franklin, M. B. Harris, & P. Allen-Meares (Eds.), *The school services sourcebook: A guide for school-based professionals* (pp. 13–24). New York, NY: Oxford University Press.

Glick, B., & Gibbs, J. C. (2011). *Aggression replacement training: A comprehensive intervention for aggressive youth* (3rd ed.). Champaign, IL: Research Press.

Gottman, J. (1997). *The heart of parenting: Raising an emotionally intelligent child.* New York, NY: Simon & Schuster.

Grusec, J. E., & Goodnow, J. J. (1994). Impact of parental discipline methods on the child's internalization of values: A reconceptualization of current points of view. *Developmental Psychology, 30,* 4–19. doi:10.1037/0012-1649.30.1.26

Harrison, J. R., Vannest, K., Davis, J., & Reynolds, C. (2012). Common problem behaviors of children and adolescents in general education classrooms in the United States. *Journal of Emotional and Behavioral Disorders, 20,* 55–64. doi:10.1177/1063426611421157

Hoffman, M. L. (2000). *Empathy and moral development: Implications for caring and justice.* New York, NY: Cambridge University Press.

Kauffman, J. M., & Brigham, F. J. (2000). Editorial: Zero tolerance and bad judgment in working with students with emotional or behavioral disorders. *Behavioral Disorders, 25,* 277–279. doi:10.1177/0741932510362509

Kauffman, J. M., Conroy, M., Gardner, R., & Oswald, D. (2008). Cultural sensitivity in the application of behavior principles to education. *Education and Treatment of Children, 31,* 239–262. doi:10.1353/etc.0.0019

Landrum, T. J., & Kauffman, J. M. (2006). Behavioral approaches to classroom management. In C. M. Evertson & C. S. Weinstein (Eds.), *Handbook of classroom management: Research, practice, and contemporary issues* (pp. 47–71). Mahwah, NJ: Erlbaum.

Larzelere, R. E., Morris, A. S., & Harrist, A. W. (Eds.) (2013). *Authoritative parenting: Synthesizing nurturance and discipline for optimal child development.* Washington, DC: American Psychological Association. doi:10.1037/13948-002

Losen, D. J., & Gillespie, J. G. (2012). *Opportunities suspended: The disparate impact of disciplinary exclusion from school.* Los Angeles, CA: Civil Rights Project. Retrieved from http://civilrightsproject.ucla.edu/resources/projects/center-for-civil-rights-remedies/school-to-prison-folder/federal-reports/upcoming-ccrr-research

Manning, M. A., & Bear, G. G. (2011). Moral reasoning and aggressive behavior: Concurrent and longitudinal relations. *Journal of School Violence, 11,* 258–280. doi:10.1080/15388220.2011.579235

Morrison, B. E., & Vaandering, D. (2012). Restorative justice: Pedagogy, praxis, and discipline. *Journal of School Violence, 11,* 138–155. doi:10.1080/15388220.2011.653322

National Association of School Psychologists. (2010). *Model for comprehensive and integrated school psychological services.* Bethesda, MD:

Author. Retrieved from http://www.nasponline.org/standards/2010standards/2_PracticeModel.pdf

Nelsen, J. D., Lott, L., & Glenn, H. S. (2000). *Positive discipline in the classroom: Developing mutual respect, cooperation, and responsibility in your classroom* (3rd ed.). New York, NY: Three Rivers Press.

Nucci, L., & Narvaez, D. (2008). *Handbook on moral and character education*. Oxford, UK: Routledge.

Osher, D., Bear, G. G., Sprague, J. R., & Doyle, W. (2010). How can we improve school discipline? *Educational Researcher, 39*, 48–58. doi:10.3102/0013189X09357618

Powell, W., & Kusuma-Powell, O. (2010). *Becoming an emotionally intelligent teacher*. Thousand Oaks, CA: Corwin.

Ryan, R. M., & Deci, E. L. (2000). Self-determination theory and the facilitation of intrinsic motivation, social development, and well-being. *American Psychologist, 55*, 68–78. doi:10.1037/0003-066X.55.1.68

Sabol, T. J., & Pianta, R. C. (2012). Recent trends in research on teacher-child relationships. *Attachment and Human Development, 14*, 213–231. doi:10.1080/14616734.2012.672262

Sorkhabi, N., & Mandara, J. (2013). Are the effects of Baumrind's parenting styles culturally specific or culturally equivalent? In R. E. Larzelere, A. S. Morris, & A. W. Harrist (Eds.), *Authoritative parenting: Synthesizing nurturance and discipline for optimal child development* (pp. 113–135). Washington, DC: American Psychological Association. doi:10.1037/13948-006

Spaulding, S. A., Irvin, L. K., Horner, R. H., May, S. L., Emeldi, M., Tobin, T. J., & Sugai, G. (2010). School-wide social-behavioral climate, student problem behavior, and related administrative decisions: Empirical patterns from 1,510 schools nationwide.

Journal of Positive Behavior Interventions, 12, 69–85. doi:10.1177/1098300708329011

Sugai, G., Horner, R. H., Algozzine, R., Barrett, S., Lewis, T., Anderson, C., … Simonsen, B. (2010). *School-wide positive behavior support: Implementers' blueprint and self-assessment*. Eugene, OR: University of Oregon. Retrieved from http://www.pbis.org

Ttofi, M. M., & Farrington, D. P. (2011). Effectiveness of school-based programs to reduce bullying: A systematic and meta-analytic review. *Journal of Experimental Criminology, 7*, 27–56. doi:10.1007/s11292-010-9109-1

U.S. Department of Education. (2011). *Prevalence and implementation fidelity of research-based prevention programs in public schools: Final report*. Washington, DC: Author.

van Lier, P. A. C., Muthén, B. O., van der Sar, R. M., & Crijnen, A. A. M. (2004). Preventing disruptive behavior in elementary schoolchildren: Impact of a universal classroom-based intervention. *Journal of Consulting and Clinical Psychology, 72*, 467–478. doi:10.1037/0022-006X.72.3.467

Watson, M., & Battistich, V. (2006). Building and sustaining caring communities. In C. M. Evertson & C. S. Weinstein (Eds.), *Handbook of classroom management: Research, practice, and contemporary issues* (pp. 253–279). Mahwah, NJ: Erlbaum.

Weinstein, C., & Novodvorsky, I. (2011). *Middle and secondary classroom management*. New York, NY: McGraw-Hill.

Zins, J. E., & Elias, M. J. (2006). Social and emotional learning. In G. G. Bear & K. M. Minke (Eds.), *Children's needs III: Development, prevention, and intervention* (pp. 1–13). Bethesda, MD: National Association of School Psychologists.

19 Best Practices in Assessing and Improving Executive Skills

Peg Dawson

Center for Learning and Attention Disorders, Portsmouth, NH

OVERVIEW

School psychologists who have been in the field beginning a decade or two prior to the turn of the century have had the opportunity to observe an evolving conceptualization of how to meet the needs of students who underperform and underachieve. We have gone from the refer–test–place model, to an emphasis on mainstreaming, and, most recently, to a model that provides a graduated set of interventions based on the severity of the need and student response to already attempted interventions. This approach employs a multitiered model that begins with high quality instruction in the regular classroom, moves to more intensive small group interventions, and, finally, if previous efforts fail, to a more intensive level of support, where an individualized intervention is designed.

While school psychology and special education were focusing on an evolving understanding of how best to meet the needs of problem learners, within the broader education community a parallel movement was taking place. This began with *A Nation at Risk* (National Commission on Excellence in Education, 1983), was followed by the No Child Left Behind Act, and most recently has led to a call for states to embrace a more uniform curriculum that would emphasize the kind of analytical thinking and problem solving necessary for students growing up in an information age. As of 2013 we are now on the threshold of adopting the Common Core State Standards, developed by the National Governors Association and the Council of Chief State School Officers.

Underlying school success, however, is a set of skills that has been neglected both in thinking about the needs of problem learners and in thinking about what it will take for a challenging curriculum such as the Common Core State Standards to be implemented effectively. Traditionally, educators think about what students need to know and what they need to be able to do. For instance, we teach children the difference between fiction and nonfiction and we teach them how to produce both kinds of writing. Neglected, however, are a set of foundational skills students need to have to make possible both kinds of learning (content area knowledge and academic skills).

These are skills—commonly referred to as *executive skills* or *executive functions*—that students must bring to bear on every learning task they confront in order to master it. There is not a complete consensus on the definition of executive skills (see Barkley, 2012b, for a discussion), but, broadly speaking, the term refers to the brain-based skills required to execute tasks. Although there is also no agreement regarding how many different executive skills there are, nor the appropriate terminology for individual skills, the term executive function is generally considered to be an "umbrella construct that includes a set of interrelated functions that are responsible for purposeful, goal-directed problem-solving behavior" (Gioia, Espy, & Isquith, 1996, p. 1). Executive function encompasses the skills that drive behavior regulation, such as controlling emotions, managing impulses, and dealing with situations requiring cognitive flexibility, as well as a set of metacognitive skills, such as initiating tasks, sustaining attention, keeping track of what needs to be done, planning and organizing tasks, and monitoring behavior based on feedback from the environment or the reactions of others.

Frankly, there is no task we ask students to perform, from as young as preschool through postsecondary education and beyond, that does not require some level of executive functioning. Furthermore, there is evidence to show that performance on measures of executive functioning very early on (as young as preschool) is a better predictor of later academic performance than either cognitive ability or family characteristics, both of which are commonly understood to influence academic outcomes (Jacobson, Williford, & Pianta, 2011).

And yet no one is charged with teaching these skills. As a result, students who are advantaged either by heredity or environment with strong executive skills tend to be far more successful in school than those who lack those advantages. Without a clear understanding of the role executive skills play in learning, when school psychologists assess learning problems or design interventions to overcome them, school psychologists are likely to have an incomplete understanding of why students fail, and how to help students overcome failure.

This chapter will provide a brief introduction to executive skills, including definitions of terms and how these skills manifest themselves within a developmental context, from early childhood through adolescence. Best practice guidelines for assessment of executive skills will focus on sources of information school psychologists should consider during the evaluation process as well as how to interpret the results and make decisions regarding the need for services. The chapter will conclude with a discussion of interventions, both those geared to individuals as well as interventions that can be implemented on a class-wide or school-wide basis.

The National Association of School Psychologists (NASP) *Model for Comprehensive and Integrated School Psychological Services* (NASP, 2010) is a framework for service delivery. Because executive skills encompass both behavior regulation and metacognition, the domains of Interventions and Instructional Support to Develop Academic Skills as well as the domain of Interventions and Mental Health Services to Develop Social and Life Skills have associated executive skill components. Furthermore, when schools fully grasp the central role executive skills play in academic success, school psychologists can help schools put in place strategies to promote executive skill development as a critical component of a school dropout prevention program, thus incorporating the NASP domain of Preventive and Responsive Services. Executive skill development is not within the purview of schools alone, and school psychologists can play a role in helping parents understand these skills and how they can support their development in the home, using the NASP domain of Family–School Collaboration Services. Finally, all school psychology service delivery is built on two foundational domains: an assessment

process that is based on Data-Based Decision Making and Accountability and a process using Consultation and Collaboration with students, families, educators, and allied service providers. Knowing how to assess executive skills, design measurable interventions, and communicate findings and recommendations with appropriate individuals are key skills school psychologists should possess to meet the needs of underperforming and underachieving students.

While the material in this chapter should be useful for school psychologists as they assist in designing interventions for individual students with executive skill weaknesses, it is our hope that they will move beyond an individual child focus and consider how to promote executive skill development at a system's level, or at a universal (Tier 1) general education level by designing whole-class and whole-school supports and training models to ensure that by the time students graduate from high school, they have what they need to be successful in college or in the workplace.

It is a rare employer who asks an employee to solve an algebraic equation or outline the economic and cultural factors that led to the Civil War. On a daily basis, however, employers ask their employees to use planning, organization, and time-management skills, as well as all the other executive skills featured in this chapter. These same skills are necessary to function as responsible adults in the home and all other venues. By targeting executive skills, schools can more effectively prepare students for life beyond school.

BASIC CONSIDERATIONS

Infants are not born with executive skills, but the mechanism for executive skill development is hard wired into the brain, much the way language acquisition is. These skills develop slowly, primarily within the prefrontal cortex, beginning shortly after birth and not reaching full maturation in typically developing brains until the middle of the third decade of life (De Luca & Leventer, 2008).

The growth of the prefrontal cortex, and the brain more broadly, occurs through the generation of neurons (nerve cells) that communicate with each other through branching structures called axons and dendrites. These form the so-called gray matter of the brain. These branches connect at junctures called synapses. When skills are learned and practiced, neurons fire, and with each firing, insulating material called myelin encircles the nerve cells in the form of a fatty sheath (white matter), increasing the speed with which nerve signals are conducted. The faster the impulse travels, the better the skill. In the early years, there is tremendous growth in the number of nerve cells and synaptic connections.

In order for skills to work efficiently, however, a process called *pruning* reduces the number of neurons and synapses, winnowing the brain of excess nerve cells so that those that remain can work in a more streamlined fashion. Pruning takes place at two points of development, first during the preschool years and then throughout the course of adolescence.

Brain research has shown that executive skills reach maturation at different points in age. The earliest executive skill to develop is inhibition, followed soon after by working memory around 7–8 months of age. *Shifting*, or attentional flexibility, appears to be another early developing skill (Best & Miller, 2010). Although questions have been raised about whether these skills are independent of each other, a unity and diversity viewpoint has been proposed (Miyake et al., 2000) that states that executive skills form a set of interrelated but distinct components. Among the later developing executive skills are planning and goal setting (De Luca & Leventer, 2008). The pruning that takes place in adolescence allows for more complex executive skills, such as metacognition, to emerge and develop (Chapman, Gamino, & Mudar, 2012).

Definition of Terms

As noted previously, researchers differ in how they define individual executive skills. This has led to a proliferation of definitions and constructs, with one researcher (Eslinger, 1996) identifying 33 different executive skills. Dawson and Guare (2009) have identified 11 executive skills that they believe are most associated with school success and are listed in Table 19.1, in roughly the order in which they emerge and mature, along with a brief definition and descriptions of how the skills manifest themselves at the younger and older end of the developmental period.

Impact on School Performance

While a discussion of brain development and how executive skills emerge and mature over time can be complicated, the critical information for school psychologists is that in typically developing individuals the skills emerge slowly, take lengthy practice to perfect, and do not reach full maturation until around age 25. Full maturation occurs even later in those with attention

disorders or other developmental disorders. Executive skills can be affected by a wide range of environmental factors and psychological disorders. The consensus is that attention deficit hyperactivity disorder (ADHD) is fundamentally a disorder involving executive skills, particularly task initiation, sustained attention, and response inhibition, as well as goal-directed persistence (Barkley, 1997; Willcutt, Doyle, Nigg, Faraone, & Pennington, 2005). Experts also agree that individuals with autism spectrum disorders, in addition to impairments in the social and communication domains and restricted, repetitive, and stereotypic behaviors, have profound executive skill weaknesses (Hume, Loftin, & Lantz, 2009), including weaknesses in initiation, planning, and metacognition. Children born with fetal alcohol syndrome have been shown to have impairments in attention, spatial working memory, planning, set shifting, and strategy use as a result of prenatal exposure to alcohol (Green et al., 2009). Traumatic brain injury can also have an impact on executive function (Ewing-Cobbs, Levin, & Fletcher, 1998). And there is also evidence that sociocultural factors, such as poverty and low socioeconomic status, can have an impact on executive skill development (Blair & Ursache, 2011; Lucas & Buchanan, 2012).

As children progress through school the demands on executive skills increase. Students with vulnerable executive skills may function adequately in the lower grades, but as they are expected to complete seatwork independently, produce larger quantities of writing, and manage more complex tasks, such as long-term assignments or studying for unit tests or midterms, they often struggle, and academic performance declines. For many, middle school is the tipping point (Jacobson et al., 2011). Having to juggle multiple classes with teachers who do not necessarily coordinate homework load and assignment deadlines, combined with the fact that the social life of middle schoolers is more time consuming, requiring children to manage a daily schedule with competing demands, is more than many students with weak executive skills can handle. By the time students reach high school, what leads to failing grades often has less to do with poor academic skills or weak cognitive ability, and more to do with executive skill development that has failed to keep pace with demands.

Particularly at this stage, if school psychologists who become involved in assessing or designing interventions for failing students do not consider the role played by executive functions, they are likely to fall short in their efforts to keep underperforming and underachieving students in school and on track for graduation.

Table 19.1. Executive Skills Definitions

Executive Skill	Definition	Examples
Response inhibition	The capacity to think before you act. This ability to resist the urge to say or do something allows the child the time to evaluate a situation and how his or her behavior might impact it.	A young child can wait for a short period without being disruptive. An adolescent can accept a referee's call without an argument.
Working memory	The ability to hold information in memory while performing complex tasks. It incorporates the ability to draw on past learning or experience to apply to the situation at hand or to project into the future.	A young child can hold in mind and follow one- or two-step directions. The middle school child can remember the expectations of multiple teachers.
Emotional control	The ability to manage emotions to achieve goals, complete tasks, or control and direct behavior.	A young child with this skill can recover from a disappointment in a short time. A teenager can manage the anxiety of a game or test and still perform.
Flexibility	The ability to revise plans in the face of obstacles, setbacks, new information, or mistakes. It relates to an adaptability to changing conditions.	A young child can adjust to a change in plans without major distress. A teenager can accept an alternative such as a different job when the first choice is not available.
Sustained attention	The capacity to keep paying attention to a situation or task in spite of distractibility, fatigue, or boredom.	For a younger child an example is completing a 5-minute chore with occasional supervision. A teenager can pay attention to homework, with short breaks, for 1–2 hours.
Task initiation	The ability to begin projects without undue procrastination, in an efficient or timely fashion.	A young child is able to start a chore or assignment right after instructions are given. A teenager does not wait until the last minute to begin a project.
Planning/prioritization	The ability to create a roadmap to reach a goal or to complete a task. It also involves being able to make decisions about what is important to focus on and what is not important.	A young child, with coaching, can think of options to settle a peer conflict. A teenager can formulate a plan to get a job.
Organization	The ability to create and maintain systems to keep track of information or materials.	A young child can, with a reminder, put toys in a designated place. A teenager can organize and locate sports equipment.
Time management	The capacity to estimate how much time one has, how to allocate it, and how to stay within time limits and deadlines. It also involves a sense that time is important.	A young child can complete a short job within a time limit set by an adult. A teenager can establish a schedule to meet task deadlines.
Goal-directed persistence	The capacity to have a goal, follow through to the completion of the goal, and not be put off by or distracted by competing interests.	A first grader can complete a job to get to recess. A teenager can earn and save money over time to buy something of importance.
Metacognition	The ability to stand back and take a bird's-eye view of oneself in a situation, to observe how to problem solve. It also includes self-monitoring and self-evaluative skills (e.g., asking How am I doing? How did I do?).	A young child can change behavior in response to feedback from an adult. A teenager can monitor and critique performance and improve it by observing others who are more skilled.

Note. From *Smart But Scattered: The Revolutionary "Executive Skills" Approach to Helping Kids Reach Their Potential*, by P. Dawson and R. Guare, 2009, New York, NY: Guilford Press. Copyright 2009 by Guilford Press. Adapted with permission.

BEST PRACTICES IN ASSESSING AND IMPROVING EXECUTIVE SKILLS

As with any domain likely to have a significant impact on learning and behavior, executive skills are best assessed using multiple measures rather than relying on a single source of information or data. This is in part because environments support executive skills to a greater or lesser degree, and hence the impact of an executive skill weakness will vary depending on the setting. For instance, schools generally provide more structure than is available in the home, and thus executive skills may look less problematic at school than at home. On the other hand, schools place more demands on students to use executive skills, in which case executive skills may appear weaker at school than at home. Because of the disparities in environmental demands and supports, any assessment of executive skills should include gathering information from both parents and teachers.

Assessment of Executive Skills

At a minimum, an assessment of executive skills should include parent, teacher, and/or student interviews and behavior checklists. Parent interviews, in particular, provide useful information because parents can provide a developmental context and a longer term perspective than is available to teachers. In the home, executive skill weaknesses manifest themselves in three primary contexts: daily routines, chores, and homework.

Interviews

When interviewing parents, school psychologists should ask how independently children are able to engage in any of those three activities. If parents report difficulties in any of those domains, then further questioning should bring to light which executive skills are affected. For example, children who struggle with homework may do so because they forget to bring home needed materials (working memory), delay starting homework (task initiation), quit before the work is done (sustained attention), give up at the first obstacle (emotional control), or be at a loss for how to actually do the assigned work (which may involve planning, organization, or metacognition).

When interviewing teachers, school psychologists should focus on understanding the specific problem areas of greatest concern to teachers, bearing in mind that classroom performance may not correlate well with standardized test performance. A student may be able to produce a piece of writing in a testing situation, in part because the evaluator is sitting with the student and making sure the student spends the allotted time working. In the classroom, however, when a teacher assigns a writing task, a student may struggle because the task is not being closely supervised or is more open ended than the writing prompt given to the student in the testing situation. By carefully interviewing teachers, school psychologists can understand what environmental factors either mitigate or exacerbate executive skill weaknesses.

Student interviews can also provide useful information, but caution is urged in interpreting student self-reports. Students often lack insight into their own behavior and misjudge their own strengths and weaknesses. If they are looking for an excuse for poor school performance, they may exaggerate their weaknesses. This is sometimes the case when students believe that taking a stimulant medication will make school easier for them, and hence they report that their attentional difficulties are more pronounced than they actually are. On the other hand, if they mistakenly equate an attention disorder or any other executive skill weakness with "stupidity," they may underreport genuine problems. The more specific school psychologists can be in the questions they ask, the more likely they are to obtain useful information. Both the adolescent version of the Brown Attention-Deficit Disorder Scales and the structured student interview developed by Dawson and Guare (2010) include items and questions that reach a useful level of specificity.

Behavior Rating Scales

Behavior rating scales provide a norm-referenced assessment of executive skills so that school psychologists can compare the performance of the student in question with others of the same age. Examples of rating scales designed to assess executive skills in students are the Behavior Rating Inventory of Executive Function (Gioia, Isquith, Guy, & Kenworthy, 2000), the Barkley Deficits in Executive Function Scale–Children and Adolescents (Barkley, 2012a), and the Comprehensive Executive Function Inventory (Naglieri & Goldstein, 2012). Whenever possible, obtaining both parent and teacher ratings is useful (Barkley's rating scale only has a parent version), since executive skills manifest themselves differently at home and at school.

In addition to rating scales focused explicitly on executive skills, the assessment process should also include a more broad-band social–emotional rating scale such as the Behavior Assessment System for

Children–Second Edition (Kamphaus & Reynolds, 2007) or the Achenbach scales (Child Behavior Checklist, Teacher Report Form; Achenbach, 1991a, 1991b). As noted previously, executive skill weaknesses are often associated with an array of psychological disorders, and hence it is important to understand the skill weaknesses within a wider context of social–emotional functioning. Elevated levels of internalizing problems, such as anxiety or obsessive–compulsive disorder, are often associated with weaknesses in a number of executive skills, including emotional control, flexibility, and task initiation. Similarly, youngsters with elevated externalizing problems often struggle with response inhibition, sustained attention, and emotional control.

Classroom Observations

Other components that are often included when assessing executive skills are classroom observations and the administration of formal tests. While both may provide useful information, there are limitations to each. When an observer enters a classroom, his or her very presence alters the dynamics of that classroom. People generally behave differently when they know they are being observed, and children are no different. Most commonly, they put on their best behavior, and it is the rare student who cannot maintain a higher level of performance for at least the short amount of time during which the observation is taking place. If the observer is in and out of the classroom frequently, such that he or she is seen as part of the daily classroom structure, then the observation is more likely to yield an accurate picture. Even then, steps should be taken to ensure that the observation is occurring during an activity in which the problem behavior is likely to occur. If a child has difficulty remembering to raise his or her hand before speaking out, then a circle time activity may be a good time to schedule an observation. If a child has a great deal of difficulty getting started on writing tasks, then the observation should be scheduled during independent seatwork when the class is working on a writing assignment.

Formal Tests

There are a number of commercially available tests that are designed to assess executive skills, such as the Delis-Kaplan Executive Function System (Delis, Kaplan, & Kramer, 2000) or the NEPSY-II (Korkman, Kirk, & Kemp, 2007). Unfortunately, the results obtained from formal measures of executive functioning do not always correlate well either with parent or teacher reports or

with behavior rating scale results. There are a number of reasons for this, but a primary one is because the way standardized tests are constructed reduces the need for the test taker to access executive skills to perform the tasks. For instance, problems with task initiation are difficult to observe when the evaluator is sitting across from the child and signaling when to start the task. Sustained attention is difficult to assess when most formal tests present the child with tasks that can be completed within a short time frame.

Furthermore, even when a test purports to measure a particular executive skill, how that skill is assessed in a formal testing situation may be very different from how the skill is applied in a real-life context. For instance, the Rey Osterrieth Complex Figure is assumed to assess, among other things, planning skills. But the planning required to copy a complex geometric drawing is substantially different from the planning required to carry out a long-term project or set up a study schedule for preparing for final exams, two real-world applications of planning skills that are critical to school success. For a more detailed discussion of the shortcomings of tests of executive function, the reader is referred to Barkley (2012b).

What formal tests allow for is direct observation of the child engaged in a variety of cognitive tasks, and this may have some utility in understanding how executive skill weaknesses manifest themselves. This may most usefully be done when the psychologist knows in advance what to look for. For example, an in-depth interview with parents may bring to light the fact that their daughter has problems with situations requiring cognitive flexibility. She may throw tantrums when unexpected changes in plans arise, or she may be unable to accept her parents' explanation of how to do her math homework when it differs from the way the teacher explained it. Cognitive inflexibility may show up on cognitive measures in a variety of ways; that is, difficulty adjusting to the greater level of abstraction required to complete more challenging puzzles (e.g., Block Design on the Weschler Intelligence Scale for Children-Fourth Edition [WISC-IV] or Triangles on the Kaufman Assessment for Children-Second Edition), or difficulty shifting set when the most obvious answer to a question is not the right one (often seen on the Picture Concepts subtest of the WISC-IV). Inflexible children also have difficulty generating more than one answer to questions when multiple responses are called for, as is the case with a number of questions on the Comprehension subtest of the WISC-IV. When school psychologists know what to look for, they may be able to pick up on more subtle manifestations of the problem, even if the subtest score by itself does not signal a significant weakness.

The reason for assessing executive skills is to understand the role executive skills may play in academic or behavior problems. In some cases executive skills are the primary reason for the problem at hand, while in other cases these skills are contributing factors. When designing interventions, understanding the role played by executive skills increases the likelihood that the intervention targets the appropriate behavior, thereby increasing the likelihood that the intervention will be successful.

Designing Interventions for Executive Skill Weaknesses

Research on expertise (Eriksson, 1996) concludes it takes 10,000 hours of deliberate practice to develop expertise. Interventions to address executive skill weaknesses are most effective when these weaknesses are viewed more as habit change rather than as short-term strategies to change isolated behaviors. As a result, those who work with students to improve executive functioning are well served by taking a long view; that is, by setting long-term goals and building in ongoing training and practice as well as progress monitoring to mark improvement. If executive skill development is seen as a slow acquisition of habits of mind, then those who work with children are likely to be patient, thoughtful, and deliberate in their approach, recognizing that more often than not progress is measured in years and not months, a mantra that is worth repeating to parents and teachers who may become exasperated with the slow pace of change or improvement.

Role of the School Psychologist

School psychologists who work directly with students (e.g., as therapists, behavior specialists, or coaches) can incorporate the strategies described below into their own interactions with students. Because practice on a daily basis is the most effective way to acquire new skills, however, school psychologists are usually not in the best position to be the direct agents of behavior change. They are typically limited in the amount of time they spend with either individual students or groups of students. However, they are in a position to provide instruction, training, and coaching to those who can provide ongoing direct intervention, particularly parents and teachers. Thus, realistically, the role school psychologists can play in implementing the suggestions

in this chapter will be indirect rather than direct; that is, through consultation and advocacy. To perform these roles, school psychologists will need a solid grounding both in executive skills and in the range of intervention options available to improve executive functioning.

Examples of ways school psychologists can share this expertise are:

- Through working with parents and teachers on individual students with executive skill weaknesses on a case consultation basis
- Providing inservice training for teachers to help teachers understand executive skills and to help teachers implement classroom-based strategies for creating supportive environments for students with executive skill weaknesses as well as teaching strategies to help improve executive functioning
- Providing presentations or ongoing seminars for parents on executive skills and how parents can support executive skill development at home
- Leading study groups for parents or teachers on the topic (this differs from the suggestions above in that in this context the school psychologist acts less as an expert on the topic but as a group member taking the lead in helping either parents or teachers better understand the topic and to apply the lessons learned)
- Leading seminars for middle or high school students to help these students assess their own executive skill strengths and weaknesses, to understand how executive skills have an impact on school performance, and to learn strategies for strengthening executive skills in the context of classroom behavior and study skills
- Setting up coaching programs and peer coaching programs at the middle and high school level; that is, school psychologists are ideally situated to organize and train coaches, either peer coaches or adult volunteers, and as a systems-level intervention this approach could reap tremendous benefits to struggling students and academic underachievers, especially those students who may not qualify for special education supports
- Consulting at the systems level by working with school administrators to understand the critical role executive skills play in school success.

Intervention Design

There are two ways of thinking about interventions to address executive skill weaknesses: the focus can be on the needs of individual students, identified through the assessment process described above, or on designing classrooms and schools that simultaneously provide accommodations and supports for immature executive skills and that foster executive skill improvement in a developmentally appropriate fashion. This way of thinking corresponds nicely to the NASP Practice Model (NASP, 2010), which identifies the domains of Student-Level Services and Systems Level Services. It also fits a multitiered model of service delivery, with its underlying premise that interventions begin at a whole-class or whole-school level before moving on to more intensive interventions for students who need them.

While school psychologists are most commonly charged with designing interventions to meet the needs of individual students, in the process of doing so patterns often emerge that show how schools may be failing large numbers of students in predictable ways. School psychologists may be well positioned to help schools tackle these systems-level issues in a way that reduces the number of students in need of intensive or individualized interventions.

What follows are general principles for thinking about interventions that should be familiar to school psychologists since they fit in an A-B-C model (antecedent-behavior-consequence). Whether a school psychologists is operating at an individual child level or at a classroom or school level, there are two options available. If the goal is to help students with executive skill weaknesses be more successful in school, then school psychologist can either target the surrounding environment or the school psychologist can target the student.

Environmental Modifications

Environmental modifications operate at the antecedent level and are designed to improve the goodness of fit between task demands and the child's current level of functioning and may include modifications such as changing the physical or social environment, modifying the tasks children are asked to perform, or changing the way adults interact with students to increase the likelihood that the students will use or practice weak executive skills. These modifications may be geared toward individual students (e.g., making tasks shorter so that children with weak sustained attention are not expected to complete the same amount of work as their peers with longer attention spans) or can be implemented as whole-class strategies (e.g., asking the whole class to complete a proofreading checklist before handing in a writing assignment). Examples of each are provided below:

Change the physical or social environment: Classrooms can be structured to reduce the impact of weak or immature executive skills. Preschool classrooms, for instance, are designed to reduce the temptation to run inside by placing furniture in such a way that children cannot run very far before they run into something. In the elementary classroom, children who have difficulty initiating tasks or sustaining attention are placed near the teacher so they can be cued and monitored. Teenagers who are susceptible to distractions may be allowed to listen to music on a mobile device while taking tests. Children whose poor impulse control gets them in trouble on the playground may be assigned to a structured activity led by a playground aide as an alternative to free play.

Modify the tasks students are asked to perform: Students with short attention spans are asked to do shorter tasks, or breaks are built in so that they are not overwhelmed by how long they think the task will take to accomplish. Students with problems with weak flexibility who do not respond well to surprises or uncertainty benefit from a visible daily schedule so they can see how their day will go when they arrive at school each day. These same students often have trouble with open-ended tasks, so they may be asked to do a closed-ended task instead (e.g., writing their spelling words 10 times each rather than composing sentences with the spelling words). Students who struggle with goal-directed persistence are given choices to make tasks more appealing to them.

Change the way adults interact with students: This may mean providing prompts, cues, or supervision for students who have weak working memory or poor organization (e.g., reminding them to hand in homework, making sure they have written down their homework assignments, or watching them place their homework in the homework folder rather than stashing it randomly in their backpack). It may mean rehearsing with a child how the child will handle a challenging situation (e.g., for a child with weak emotional control, it may mean role playing how the child will handle it when assigned some math work that the child thinks he or she cannot do). Another way adults can alter responses to students with weak executive skills is to go out of their way to notice when students use a weak skill or show improvement. Through the use of specific praise, students learn what is valued, which increases the likelihood the student will produce the response in the future. Statements such as, "I saw you really trying to control your temper" or "I like the way you thought about that and figured out a good solution to the problem" provide this kind of specific feedback. Finally, when adults who work with children embed metacognitive questions into their conversations, this will prompt students to access their own executive skills. Examples of these kinds of questions are: What are three things you can do if you start your math homework and realize you don't remember how to do it? How long do you think it will take you to finish the poster you have to do for health class? When are you planning on starting it? What can you do if you realize you're about to lose your cool in the lunchroom?

School psychologists who work directly with students (e.g., as therapists, behavior specialists, or coaches) can incorporate these suggestions into their own interactions with students. More broadly, however, they can share these strategies with both parents and teachers; that is, the adults who come into contact with children on a daily basis and have the greatest likelihood of intervening effectively.

Teaching Executive Skills

Environmental modifications have limitations, the most obvious being that if the focus is exclusively on this strategy, every environment the child encounters will have to be modified (the home, the sports field, religious institutions, and shopping malls) as well as every single school setting the child enters (playground, cafeteria, gym, classroom, corridors). This is not only unrealistic, it does not prepare the student for a world in which he or she is expected to function independently without modifications. Thus, the child must be targeted directly, either by teaching the child the weak skill or providing motivation for the child to practice the weak skill to make it stronger.

Teaching a skill means operating directly on the behavior of concern (i.e., the missing or weak executive skills) and involves the following process: (a) describe the problem behavior; (b) set a goal related to the problem behavior; (c) establish a procedure or a set of steps the child will follow to reach the goal; (d) turn the steps into a written list, checklist, or short set of rules to follow (with very young children, pictures can be used in place of words); (e) prompt the child to use the list when it is needed; (f) evaluate the process and make changes if necessary; and (g) fade the supervision. For example, a child with weak working memory who is learning to write sentences may continually forget to begin each sentence with a capital letter and end it with a period. A two-step checklist could be created (Start every sentence with a capital letter. End every sentence with a period). The child could be prompted to complete the checklist each time a writing assignment is completed. When the child is able to use the checklist effectively, the teacher can fade the process by asking the child to check the work without using a checklist and to place a small checkmark next to his or her name to signal that he or she has done so. Eventually, the checkmark can be dropped as well. For other examples of teaching procedures for common home and school problems associated with executive skill weaknesses, the reader is referred to Dawson and Guare (2009, 2010).

Some students have executive skills at their command but choose not to employ these skills because it takes too much time, feels burdensome or effortful, or they do not believe that using the skill makes a difference for the final outcome. For example, a student may well be capable of developing a plan for writing a paper or completing a chemistry project, but may feel that the quality of the work does not suffer if the planning phase is omitted. In these cases, the best intervention strategy may be to work with consequences; that is, create an incentive for using the skill. This may be in the form of a daily home–school report card targeting specific behaviors, such as, for the child with weak response inhibition, raising a hand to speak rather than calling out or keeping hands to himself or herself when walking in line. While positive incentives are generally preferable to negative consequences, there are times when penalties work well, such as, for a student who fails to do homework because of weak task initiation or sustained attention, having that student remain after school on days he or she fails to hand in homework can be effective.

For students with significant executive skill weaknesses, incorporating all three strategies (environmental modifications, skill instruction, and the use of motivators or incentives) should be considered. A planning form that can be used for designing individual interventions is shown in Figure 19.1. This planning form can be used at all levels of a multitiered system to design interventions ranging from those that could be incorporated into whole class instruction or daily routines to those that might be considered Tier 2 or Tier 3 strategies. The role of the school psychologist in this planning process may vary from school to school, but in many schools it is the school psychologist who provides a leadership role in designing interventions and monitoring progress.

Research Support for Intervention Strategies

Empirical evidence supporting the efficacy of interventions for improving executive skills is limited by a number of practical and methodological considerations. First, intervention research tends to focus on interventions

Figure 19.1. Checklist for Designing Interventions

Intervention Steps

1. Establish the behavioral goal.

   Problem behavior: _____

   Goal behavior: _____

2. What environmental supports will be provided? (Check all that apply.)

   ☐ Change physical or social environment (e.g., add physical barriers, reduce distractions, provide organizational structures, reduce social complexity).

   ☐ Change the nature of the task (e.g., make shorter, build in breaks, give something to look forward to, create a schedule, build in choice, make the task more fun).

   ☐ Change the way adults interact with the child (e.g., rehearsal, prompts, reminders, coaching, praise, debriefing, feedback).

3. What procedure will be followed to teach the skill?

   Who will teach the skill/supervise the procedure?

   What steps will the child follow?
   1. _____

   2. _____

   3. _____

   4. _____

   5. _____

   6. _____

4. What incentives will be used to encourage the child to learn, practice, or use the skill? (Check all that apply.)

   ☐ Specific praise

   ☐ Something to look forward to when the task (or a piece of the task) is done

   ☐ A menu of rewards and penalties

   Daily reward possibilities:_____

   Weekly reward possibilities:_____

   Long-term reward possibilities:_____

Note. From *Smart But Scattered: The Revolutionary "Executive Skills" Approach to Helping Kids Reach Their Potential*, by P. Dawson and R. Guare, 2009, New York, NY: Guilford Press. Copyright 2009 by Guilford Press. Adapted with permission.

of brief duration (i.e., weeks or months), while, as noted earlier, months or years are more often needed for interventions to bear fruit. Second, it is easier to design an intervention using simple laboratory tasks (e.g., computer games for improving working memory) than it is to design an intervention to be implemented in vivo directed at real-world tasks requiring executive functions (such as remembering to bring to and from school all the materials needed to complete and hand in homework assignments). Third, effective interventions are often complex, involving multiple components. When this is the case, it is challenging, if not impossible, to unpack the intervention to determine which components were critical to success.

Nonetheless, executive function intervention studies are becoming prevalent enough to enable some conclusions to be drawn about efficacy, using a combination of meta-analyses, single case studies, and small case series. For an extensive review of the extant literature, see Slomine, Locascio, and Kramer (2010), which groups interventions by the specific executive skill targeted, focusing on attention, working memory, initiation, problem solving, and inhibitory control. Many of the studies Slomine et al. (2010) cite employ one or more of the three strategies emphasized in this chapter and described above. For instance, studies aimed at improving initiation typically use cueing strategies, such as verbal prompts, visual cues (pictures or reminder notes), or physical prompts, but efforts have also been made to teach subjects to self-prompt, using smartphones or other electronic devices (e.g., DePompei et al., 2008; Gillette & DePompei, 2004).

Transferring the prompting function to the children themselves is an example of teaching the skill. Another example of efforts to teach students skills have focused on teaching a problem-solving strategy to children and teenagers impaired in this function due to an acquired brain injury (Gureasko-Moore, DuPaul, & White, 2006; Suzman, Morris, Morris, & Milan, 1997; Wade, Walz, Carey, & Williams, 2008). Direct instruction in executive skill strategies has also been shown to be effective within the context of academic skills, most notably the work of Graham and Harris (2002), who developed an approach to teaching writing that includes goal setting, self-instruction, self-monitoring, and self-reinforcement.

Interventions designed to treat symptoms associated with ADHD are extensive and provide the greatest empirical support for the efficacy of practices to enhance executive functioning. In a recent review, DuPaul, Eckert, and Vilardo (2012) classified the kinds of interventions into three categories that match the three intervention strategies described in this chapter: (a) academic interventions, focusing "primarily on manipulating antecedent conditions" (p. 391); (b) contingency management, defined as "an intervention that uses reinforcement (e.g., praise, tangibles) or punishment (e.g., corrective feedback, response cost)" (p. 391) to effect behavior change; and (c) cognitive–behavioral approaches designed to improve self-control by teaching strategies such as cognitive rehearsal, self-instruction, and self-management. DuPaul et al. (2012) concluded that all three intervention practices were associated with positive effects for both academic and behavioral outcomes. Since the symptoms associated with ADHD

represent a subset of the executive skills described in this chapter, this suggests that similar efforts to tackle other executive skill deficits may be equally promising.

One study that went beyond the executive skill weaknesses traditionally associated with ADHD attempted to improve organizational skills in ADHD students (Abikoff et al., 2013). This study is also unique in that it compared a strategy that focused on teaching deficient executive skills (Organizational Skills Training) with one that employed a motivational strategy that primarily relied on the use of reinforcers to improve organization (Parents and Teachers Helping Kids Organize). Although both groups improved more than controls on most of the nine outcomes measured, a head-to-head comparison of the two interventions demonstrated the superiority of the skills training intervention over the contingency management intervention, particularly when looking at gains in academic proficiency.

While it is likely unrealistic to expect school psychologists to conduct formal outcome studies of their own as they begin to implement the strategies described in this chapter, responsible intervention design must include identifying ways to assess efficacy. Whenever possible, naturally occurring records can serve as outcome measures. These might include reduced discipline referrals (as measures of improved response inhibition or emotional control), increased homework completion rates (as measures of improved working memory, task initiation, and sustained attention), and improved grades on long-term projects (as measures of improved planning and time management skills). Checklists, rubrics, and goal-setting strategies can also be created to measure outcomes objectively. Dawson and Guare (2012) provide a discussion of progress monitoring for executive skill development that spells out these strategies with more specificity.

Cultural Considerations

It becomes quickly evident in looking at cultural influences on executive skill development that different parenting styles and cultural values have an impact on the development of traits commonly associated with both temperament and personality. There is considerable overlap, particularly when considering traits associated with temperament and those commonly defined as executive skills. For example, Garstein et al. (2006) define temperament as "individual differences in reactivity an self-regulation, which are constitutionally based and influenced over time by heredity, maturation, and experience" (p. 146). They note that the specific traits associated with self-regulation and reactivity are attention, behavioral inhibition, arousability of affect, and self-soothing. Child-rearing patterns in different cultures are felt to reflect the values of those cultures. For instance, Eastern cultures are felt to promote collectivist attitudes, while Western cultures emphasize individualistic attitudes.

Delineating cultural differences in executive skill development is well beyond the scope of this chapter. Studies have shown, for instance, that motivational beliefs and self-regulated learning vary when comparing early adolescents in the United States to those in China (Wang & Pomerantz, 2009) and that self-report of adolescent procrastination is greater in Singapore than Canada (Klassen et al., 2009). A study comparing Finnish and American students found differences in both attentional control and inhibitory control (Gaias et al., 2012), while another study found that whereas there is a gender gap between boys and girls when it comes to self-control in young children in America (with girls exhibiting more self-control than boys), no gender gap in self-control development is evident in Asian cultures (Wanless et al., 2013).

While it is unrealistic to expect school psychologists to fully understand how child-rearing practices influence executive skill development in children from different cultures, it is reasonable for school psychologists to be sensitive to cultural differences and to avoid imposing their own values on families from different cultural backgrounds. It is therefore incumbent on school psychologists to elicit from the parents the values and behavioral expectations those parents may import from their own cultures. School psychologists also should avoid sounding judgmental when they work with parents to help parents understand things they can do at home to promote the kind of executive skill development that will be most likely to further academic success.

Case Examples

One case example is focused on an elementary-age student with problems with behavioral excesses associated with those executive skills most closely tied to problems with behavior regulation. The second case example features a middle school student with executive skill weaknesses associated with behavioral deficits (i.e., poor time management, working memory, task initiation, sustained attention).

Case Example 1

Max is a third-grade student who, when given an assignment requiring some kind of production (math,

writing), acts in one or more of the following ways more than half the time: complains loudly or refuses to do the task ("I don't know how to do this!" "I'm not doing this stupid paper!"), pushes the paper off the desk or crumples it, or roams around room and does not respond to teacher directions. The problem behaviors occur whether or not the task is within Max's independent ability, but the more difficult the task, the more disruptive the behavior.

A multipronged approach is developed to help Max learn to handle his weak emotional control, inflexibility, and response inhibition. Elements of the intervention include (a) a social story describing how he feels and what his options are for helping himself; (b) the creation of a hard-times board (see Dawson & Guare, 2009, for more detailed instructions) that identify triggers, can't do's (behavior Max was not allowed to exhibit), and coping strategies; (c) shorter tasks with check-in breaks at the end of each section with the teacher or paraprofessional; (d) immediate check-ins following the presentation of the task instructions to make sure Max understands the task or to offer help; (e) Max's agreement that if he begins to get upset and does not remember to use his hard-times board, he will accept a cue from an adult to make a choice from it; (f) a rule that if his behavior disrupts class, Max will take an out-of-class break for at least 2 minutes and whatever time after that until he is able to resume his in-class plan; (g) Max's agreement that uncompleted work will be finished during free time or, if needed, at the end of school; and (h) an incentive system allowing him to earn points that he can use to buy computer time, a highly preferred activity, at the end of the morning and at the end of school.

The components of the plan are rehearsed with Max in the classroom with the paraprofessional and teacher modeling how the plan would be implemented and then walking Max through the procedure with cues until he can independently demonstrate how it would work. He and the paraprofessional and teacher agree on a starting time for the plan, and, at the beginning of the day and on returning from lunch, the plan is reviewed by his reading the social story. Over time, Max becomes better able to manage his emotions in the context of the kind of written work that he found aversive.

Case Example 2

Kevin is a bright middle school student with ADHD whose academic performance is inconsistent, with grades on nightly homework assignments, tests and quizzes, and long-term assignments ranging from A to F, depending on the amount of effort he puts into studying and whether or not he remembers to do the work or to hand it in on time. His parents employ punitive measures (such as removing access to video games), and he is frequently prevented from participating in sports (his school has a policy that prohibits student athletes from participating in sports events in any given week if they have earned grades of C or less on any graded work the week before). These measures have not been successful, and his parents are looking for a more effective approach to improving Kevin's study habits and working memory. Together, the school psychologist, Kevin, and his parents design an incentive system that allows Kevin to earn points engaging in behaviors that increase the likelihood of academic success, including using an assignment book on a daily basis to record homework assignments, handing in his homework on time, completing homework with at least 80% accuracy, and earning grades of B- or better on tests and quizzes (with more points earned the higher the grade). When Kevin earns 500 points, he can trade the points in for a smartphone, which his parents have agreed to let him purchase.

The incentive system is designed so that it would take Kevin a minimum of 10 weeks to earn the phone, but by tallying points each week and graphing the total, he can objectively measure his progress toward his goal. The plan has built in some ground rules: Kevin agrees to start homework at 7:00 p.m. except on nights when he has a basketball game; Kevin is willing to accept one reminder from his parents to start homework; and Kevin and his mother or father meet to compute points together once a week, usually on Friday to allow him to see his progress toward his smartphone goal. It is understood that at these weekly check-ins, both Kevin and his parents will focus on the positives, with each person stating at least one positive thing about the process at the time they calculate points.

Once implemented, Kevin earns the smartphone within the time frame established. More importantly, he brings his grades up in all subjects, and the plan allows Kevin to practice habits such as writing down assignments, remembering to hand in homework, and studying for tests more thoroughly and effectively, all executive skills that are critical to long-term school success.

Promoting Executive Skill Development Within a Multitiered Model

In designing a multitiered system of supports for students with executive skill weaknesses, the emphasis should be on Tier 1, universal supports. There are two primary ways to support executive skills in a regular classroom. First, classroom teachers can build in daily routines, such as a routine for collecting homework or creating a list of classroom behavior rules that are reviewed regularly with the whole class. These routines correspond to environmental modifications. Second, teachers can incorporate components of executive skill instruction into the subject matter being taught. For instance, when long-term projects are assigned, teachers can teach students how to break down complex assignments into subtasks and time lines. As time goes on, teachers can transfer more and more of the planning process to the students themselves (e.g., by requiring the students to develop a plan as part of the project itself).

Not all students respond to whole-class supports and instructional strategies. For these, either Tier 2 or Tier 3 strategies will be necessary. Table 19.2 provides examples of the kinds of strategies that are appropriate at all three levels.

For a three-tiered model to work effectively, target behaviors must be defined explicitly and rules for success at any given level must be agreed upon. It is beyond the scope of this chapter to describe in detail how this can be done, but readers are referred to other chapters as well as to Dawson and Guare (2010) for examples of how decisions are made within a three-tiered model.

Systems Level Models

As noted previously, executive skill proficiency in young children is a better predictor of later academic success than either cognitive ability or family characteristics. Schools have limited ability to affect directly either intelligence or family traits, but they can have an impact on the development of executive skills by creating classrooms that support training these skills in a developmentally appropriate fashion. Since this a variable that schools can have some control over, making it a target of systems level intervention should be a strategic use of school district resources in terms of time, money, and manpower.

While this is in no way intended to represent the universe of options available to school districts, some ways they might tackle the problem are described below.

Make executive skills a component of school district strategic planning: By making executive skill development an explicit goal, districts can then identify the tactics, strategies, and resources needed to achieve measureable results. When new initiatives are proposed, school administrators often argue that their plates are already full and they have no capacity to take on more work. In

Table 19.2. Strategies for Executive Skill Development at Three Levels

Intervention Tier	Environmental Modifications	Instructional Supports	Motivational Strategies
Tier 1 (universal): Systems-level or classroom-level supports directed at all students and designed to meet the needs of most students.	• Establish classroom routines to manage things such as using an assignment book, handing in homework, planning for long-term assignments, maintaining notebooks • Teach classroom rules for behavior (post prominently, review regularly, and practice for mastery) • Set up school-wide monitoring/feedback systems (such as Power School or TeacherEase)	*Teach:* • Study skills necessary to meet course requirements: how to study for tests, how to break down long-term assignments into subtasks and time lines • Organizational/working memory skills: how to maintain an assignment book, how to organize notebooks, how to remember important things such as due dates, permission slips • Homework skills: how to plan homework sessions, strategies for getting started, screening out distractions, persisting until completion, avoiding temptation, solving problems	• Use group contingencies to meet specific criteria • Build in fun activities following effortful classroom tasks • Make liberal use of effective praise targeted to executive skill development
Tier 2 (targeted): Somewhat more intensive interventions to meet the needs of the 10–15% of students for whom universal supports are insufficient	• Modify assignments to increase likelihood of success (shorten, build in choice, make more closed ended) • Set up after school homework clubs • Provide weekly progress reports to inform parents of missing assignments, upcoming deadlines	• Set up small group coaching for at-risk students to teach them how to make and follow homework plans and provide closer monitoring to students with working memory deficits or planning or organizational problems • Institute peer tutoring programs or train volunteer tutors • Contact parents to develop a simple plan to address the problem (e.g., arranging for progress reports)	• Home–school incentive systems (daily or weekly report cards) • Require students to use free time or after school time to complete unfinished work
Tier 3 (intensive): For the 1–7% of students with chronic and more severe problems	• At this level an effective intervention involves working collaboratively with parents, teachers, and students to develop an individual support plan	*Elements of an effective intensive intervention:* • Target behavior is well defined and includes criteria for success • Specific environmental modifications are identified • The skill is explicitly taught, modeled, and rehearsed regularly • Someone is assigned to check in with the student at least daily • The student is given a visual reminder of expectations; the student's independent use of the skill is monitored over time so that progress can be measured	

Note. From *Executive Skills in Children and Adolescents: A Practical Guide to Assessment and Intervention* (2nd ed.), by P. Dawson and R. Guare, 2010, New York, NY: Guilford Press. Copyright 2010 by Guilford Press. Used with permission.

fact, by infusing executive skills into daily classroom practices, other goals become easier to achieve. The Common Core State Standards, for instance, can only be successfully implemented if the foundational executive skills are strong enough to support them.

Identify grade level expectations for executive skills, along with the environmental supports and teaching strategies necessary to meet those expectations: We know that executive skills emerge gradually. This means that it is reasonable to identify key executive skills to target at different age levels and to create a gradually diminishing system of supports based on developmentally appropriate expectations. In the lower elementary years, for instance, schools might target task initiation, sustained attention, emotional control, flexibility, and response inhibition. Moving into upper elementary years, targeted expectations for working memory, planning, and organization can be added. Given the often dramatically increased demands at the middle school level, these three skills should continue to be targeted, along with the addition of time management. At the high school level, an emphasis should be placed on goal-directed persistence and metacognition, along with advanced level training for the other executive skills.

Make executive skills a focus of home–school collaboration efforts: Executive skills develop through practice, and students are well served when both parents and educators have a role to play. Parent–teacher conferences, school open house events, and PTA activities can all be used to help parents understand executive skills, why these skills are important, and steps parents can take to ensure that their children have an opportunity to practice these skills at home. Parents do not always appreciate the role that chores, daily routines, and homework play in helping children develop good work habits. Once parents understand the connection, they are often motivated to do their part.

Create a system of coaching interventions to support students with executive skill weaknesses: Coaching (Dawson & Guare, 2012) is a versatile strategy designed to help students improve executive skills. It has been shown to be an effective way to help elementary-age students with ADHD improve peer relationships (Plumer, 2007; Plumer & Stoner, 2005), to help middle school students improve homework completion (Merriman, 2010), and to improve academic skills at the high school level (Merriman & Codding, 2008). While this strategy can be used on an ad hoc basis as a Tier 2 or Tier 3 intervention, it can be employed more effectively by establishing it as a service available to students in need in the same way that some schools offer check-in/check-out procedures as a dropout prevention program or provide weekly progress reports to parents to help their children stay on top of their homework. A cadre of adults and peers can be trained to provide this service under the supervision of a school psychologist, following procedures outline by Dawson and Guare (2012).

Remove barriers to providing special education supports for students with severe executive skill weaknesses: All too often students are denied access to the services they need because scores on standardized achievement tests are used as evidence that they are acquiring academic skills at a rate commensurate with their peers. For many of those students, the issue is not input (i.e., acquisition of information or knowledge) but one of output (i.e., ability to demonstrate that knowledge in a format that is acceptable to teachers). When this occurs at the high school level, students are often seen as unmotivated and this is seen as the barrier preventing them from doing the expected work.

Given what is known about executive skills and the impact on behavior and academic performance, it is incumbent on schools to address these skill weaknesses when these weaknesses can be shown to be a primary factor causing students to fail classes or grades. The best way to do this is through a response-to-intervention model, and it is hoped that schools will increasingly adopt this model as the way to meet the needs of students with disabilities.

Where this model is not implemented, however, students with executive skill deficits are often denied services because it is felt they do not have a recognized disability. Many, but not all, students with significant executive skill weaknesses also have ADHD or an autism spectrum disorder, and can access special education through these classifications. For those who do not have ADHD or an autism spectrum disorder, a case can be made that they have a specific learning disability. The Learning Disabilities Association of America (n.d.) defines the disorder in this way: "A learning disability is a neurological condition that interferes with a person's ability to store, process, or produce information." With this in mind, there can be little argument that when executive skill weaknesses are causing students to fail classes or grades, their weaknesses would qualify as a learning disability.

School psychologists have many demands on their time, and school districts vary in terms of how they deploy school psychological services. Whether school psychologists are involved primarily with individual case studies, consultation to teachers around classroom-based concerns, or establishing school-wide interventions, the stronger grounding they have in executive skills and their impact on learning and behavior, the better they will be able to meet the needs of the students they are charged with helping.

SUMMARY

Executive skills are brain-based skills shown to be strong predictors of school achievement. Executive skills emerge slowly and are dependent on brain maturation and practice to become fully operational. When students struggle in school, the assessment process should include an evaluation of executive functioning, primarily through the use of interviews and norm-referenced rating scales. Interventions to address executive skill weaknesses fall into three categories: (a) environmental modifications to improve fit between task demands and the student's current level of functioning, (b) teaching strategies to help students develop more competent executive skills, and (c) incentives or other forms of reinforcement designed to motivate students to use or practice skills that they have but that they find effortful or tedious to employ. A three-tiered response-to-intervention model is well suited to meeting the needs of students with executive skill weaknesses. Universal supports include establishing classroom routines and whole-class teaching strategies that are likely to be effective with the vast majority of students. For students for whom whole-class supports are insufficient, more intensive small group interventions can be used to teach executive skills more explicitly and to provide more direct supervision to ensure students practice the skills being taught. Finally, intensive one-on-one interventions can be designed for students who need a more individualized approach. These typically involve a collaborative effort on the part of teachers and specialists, parents, and the students themselves. School psychologists are also encouraged to address executive skill development at a systems level, for example, by helping schools identify grade-level expectations along with environmental supports and teaching strategies that are developmentally appropriate, by providing guidance to parents about how the parents can support executive skill development in the home, and by developing systems of interventions, such as coaching, to meet the needs of underachieving and underperforming students.

AUTHOR NOTE

Disclosure. Peg Dawson has a financial interest in books she authored or coauthored referenced in this chapter.

REFERENCES

Abikoff, H., Gallagher, R., Wells, K. C., Murray, D. W., Huang, L., Feihan, L., & Petkova, E. (2013). Remediating organizational functioning in children with ADHD: Immediate and long-term effects from a randomized control trial. *Journal of Consulting and Clinical Psychology, 81,* 113–128. doi:10.1037/a0029648

Achenbach, T. M. (1991a). *Child Behavior Checklist.* Burlington, VT: University of Vermont.

Achenbach, T. M. (1991b). *Teacher report form.* Burlington, VT: University of Vermont.

Barkley, R. A. (1997). *ADHD and the nature of self-control.* New York, NY: Guilford Press.

Barkely, R. A. (2012a). *Barkley Deficits in Executive Function Scale–Children and adolescents.* New York, NY: Guilford Press.

Barkley, R. A. (2012b). *Executive functions: What they are, how they work, and why they evolved.* New York, NY: Guilford Press.

Best, J. R., & Miller, P. H. (2010). A developmental perspective on executive function. *Child Development, 81,* 1641–1660. doi:10.1111/j.1467-8624.2010.01499.x

Blair, C., & Ursache, A. (2011). A bi-directional model of executive functions and self-regulation. In R. F. Baumeister & K. D. Vohs (Eds.), *Handbook of self-regulation: Research, theory, and applications* (pp. 300–320). New York, NY: Guilford Press.

Chapman, S. B., Gamino, J. F., & Mudar, R. A. (2012). Higher order strategic gist reasoning in adolescence. In V. F. Reyna, S. B. Chapman, M. R. Dougherty, & J. Confrey (Eds.), *The adolescent brain: Learning, reasoning and decision making* (pp. 123–151). Washington, DC: American Psychological Association.

Dawson, P., & Guare, R. (2009). *Smart but scattered: The revolutionary "executive skills" approach to helping kids reach their potential.* New York, NY: Guilford Press.

Dawson, P., & Guare, R. (2010). *Executive skills in children and adolescents: A practical guide to assessment and intervention* (2nd ed.). New York, NY: Guilford Press.

Dawson, P., & Guare, R. (2012). *Coaching students with executive skills deficits.* New York, NY: Guilford Press.

De Luca, C. R., & Leventer, R. J. (2008). Developmental trajectories of executive functions across the lifespan. In V. A. Anderson, P. Jacobs, & P. Anderson (Eds.), *Executive functions and the frontal lobes: A lifespan perspective* (pp. 23–55). New York, NY: Taylor & Francis.

Delis, D., Kaplan, E., & Kramer, J. (2000). *Delis-Kaplan Executive Function Scale.* San Antonio, TX: Psychological Corporation.

DePompei, R., Gillette, Y., Goetz, E., Xenopoulos-Oddsson, Bryen, D., & Dowds, M. (2008). Practical applications for use of PDAs and smartphones with children and adolescents who have traumatic brain injury. *NeuroRehabilitation, 23,* 487–499.

DuPaul, G. J., Eckert, T. L., & Vilardo, B. (2012). The effects of school-based interventions for attention deficit hyperactivity disorder: A meta-analysis. *School Psychology Review, 41,* 387–412.

Eriksson, K. A. (Ed.). (1996). *The road to expert performance: Empirical evidence from the arts and sciences, sports, and games.* Mahwah, NJ: Erlbaum.

Eslinger, P. J. (1996). Conceptualizing, describing, and measuring components of executive function: A summary. In G. R. Lyon & N. A. Krasnegor (Eds.), *Attention, memory, and executive function* (pp. 367–395). Baltimore, MD: Brookes.

Ewing-Cobbs, L., Levin, H. S., & Fletcher, J. M. (1998). Neuropsychological sequelae after pediatric traumatic brain injury: Advances since 1985. In M. Ylvesaker (Ed.), *Traumatic brain injury rehabilitation: Children and adolescence* (2nd ed., pp.11–26). Boston, MA: Butterworth-Heinemann.

Gaias, L. M., Räikkönen, K., Komsi, N., Garstein, M. A., Fisher, P. A., & Putnam, S. P. (2012). Cross-cultural temperamental differences in infants, children and adults in the United States of America and Finland. *Scandinavian Journal of Psychology, 53,* 119–128.

Garstein, M. A., Gonzalez, C., Carranza, J. A., Ahadi, S. A., Ye, R., Rothbart, M. K., & Yang, S. W. (2006). Studying cross-cultural differences in the development of infant temperament: People's Republic of China, the United States of America, and Spain. *Child Psychiatry and Human Development, 37,* 145–161.

Gillette, Y., & DePompei, R. (2004). The potential of electronic organizers as a tool in the cognitive rehabilitation of young people. *NeuroRehabilitation, 19,* 233–243.

Gioia, G. A., Espy, K. A., & Isquith, P. K. (1996). *Behavior Rating Inventory of Executive Function–Preschool version.* Odessa, FL: Psychological Assessment Resources.

Gioia, G. A., Isquith, P. K., Guy, S. C., & Kenworthy, L. (2000). *Behavior Rating Inventory of Executive Function.* Odessa, FL: Psychological Assessment Resources.

Graham, S., & Harris, K. R. (2002). Prevention and intervention for struggling writers. In M. Shinn, G. Stoner, & H. Walker (Eds.), *Interventions for academic and behavior problems II: Preventive and remedial techniques* (pp. 589–610). Bethesda, MD: National Association of School Psychologists.

Green, C. R., Mihic, A. M., Nikkel, S. M., Stade, B. C., Rasmussen, C., Munoz, D. P., & Reynolds, J. N. (2009). Executive function deficits in children with fetal alcohol spectrum disorders (FASD) measured using the Cambridge Neuropsychological Tests Automated Battery (CANTAB). *Journal of Child Psychology and Psychiatry, 50,* 688–697.

Gureasko-Moore, S., DuPaul, G. J., & White, G. P. (2006). The effects of self-management in general education classrooms on the organizational skills of adolescents with ADHD. *Behavior Modification, 30,* 159–183.

Hume, K., Loftin, R., & Lantz, J. (2009). Increasing independence in autism spectrum disorders: A review of three focused interventions. *Journal of Autism and Developmental Disorders, 39,* 1329–1328.

Jacobson, L. A., Williford, A. P., & Pianta, R. C. (2011). The role of executive function in children's competent adjustment to middle school. *Child Neuropsychology, 17,* 255–208.

Kamphaus, R. W., & Reynolds, C. R. (2007). *Behavior Assessment System for Children-Second edition.* San Antonio, TX: Psychological Corporation.

Klassen, R. M., Ang, R. P., Chong, W. H., Krawchuck, L. L., Huan, V. S., Wong, I. Y. F., & Yeo, L. S. (2009). A cross-cultural study of adolescent procrastination. *Journal of Research on Adolescence, 19,* 799–811. doi:10.1111/j.1532-7795.2009.00620.x

Korkman, M., Kirk, U., & Kemp, S. (2007). *NEPSY-II.* San Antonio, TX: Psychological Corporation.

Learning Disabilities Association of America. (n.d.). Defining learning disabilities. Pittsburgh, PA: Author. Retrieved from http://www.ldanatl.org/new_to_ld/defining.asp

Lucas, M., & Buchanan, C. (2012). The Tinker Toy Test as a measure of the dysexecutive syndrome in those from differing socioeconomic backgrounds. *South African Journal of Psychology, 42,* 381–388.

Merriman, D. E. (2010). *The effects of group coaching on the homework completion of secondary students with homework problems* (Unpublished doctoral dissertation). New York, NY: City University of New York.

Merriman, D. E., & Codding, R. S. (2008). The effects of coaching on mathematics homework completion and accuracy of high school students with ADHD. *Journal of Behavioral Education, 17,* 339–355.

Miyake, A., Friedman, N. P., Emerson, M. J., Witzki, A. H., Howerter, A., & Wager, T. D. (2000). The unity and diversity of executive functions and their contributions to complex "frontal lobe" tasks: A latent variable analysis. *Cognitive Psychology, 41,* 49–100.

Naglieri, J., & Goldstein, S. (2012). *Comprehensive Executive Function Inventory.* Toronto, ON, Canada: Multi-Health Systems.

National Association of School Psychologists. (2010). *Model for comprehensive and integrated school psychological services.* Bethesda, MD: Author. Retrieved from http://www.nasponline.org/standards/2010standards/2_PracticeModel.pdf

National Commission on Excellence in Education. (1983). *A nation at risk: The imperative for educational reform.* Washington, DC: U.S. Department of Education.

Plumer, P. J. (2007). Using peers as intervention agents to improve the social behaviors of elementary-aged children with attention deficit hyperactivity disorder: Effects of a peer coaching package. *Dissertation Abstracts International: Section A. Humanities and Social Sciences, 68*(7-A), 2813.

Plumer, P. J., & Stoner, G. (2005). The relative effects of classwide peer tutoring and peer coaching on the positive social behaviors of children with ADHD. *Journal of Attention Disorders, 9,* 290–300. doi: 10.1177/1087054705280796

Slomine, B., Locascio, G., & Kramer, M. (2010). Empirical status regarding the remediation of executive skills. In S. J. Hunter & E. P. Sparrow (Eds.), *Executive function and dysfunction: Identification, assessment, and treatment* (pp. 209–231). New York, NY: Cambridge University Press.

Suzman, K. B., Morris, R. D., Morris, M. K., & Milan, M. A. (1997). Cognitive-behavioral remediation of problem solving deficits in children with acquired brain injury. *Journal of Behavior Therapy and Experimental Psychiatry, 28,* 203–212.

Wade, S. L., Walz, N. C., Carey, J. C., & Williams, K. M. (2008). Preliminary efficacy of a web-based family problem-solving treatment program for adolescents with traumatic brain injury. *Journal of Head Trauma Rehabilitation, 23,* 369–377. doi:10.1097/01.HTR.0000341432.67251.48

Wang, Q., & Pomerantz, E. M. (2009). The motivational landscale of early adolescence in the United States and China: A longitudinal investigation. *Child Development, 80,* 1272–1287.

Wanless, S. B., McClelland, M. M., Lan, X., Son, S., Cameron, C. E., Morrison, F. J., … Sung, M. (2013). Gender differences in behavioral regulation in four societies: The United States, Taiwan, South Korea, and China. *Early Childhood Research Quarterly, 28,* 621–633.

Willcutt, E. G., Doyle, A. E., Nigg, J. T., Faraone, S. V., & Pennington, B. F. (2005). Validity of the executive function theory of attention-deficit hyperactivity disorder: A meta-analytic review. *Biological Psychiatry, 57,* 1336–1446.

20 Best Practices in Solution-Focused, Student-Driven Interviews

John J. Murphy

University of Central Arkansas

OVERVIEW

It's a lot better when you ask a person what they want to do.
—Molly, 10-year-old student

As the coordinator of school psychological services in an urban school district, I was no stranger to irate phone calls. But the one I received several years ago from a school principal named Carol left a lasting impression. "I just asked my school psychologist to talk to a student with behavior problems, and I was told that school psychologists can consult with teachers and parents but aren't trained to work directly with kids for anything other than testing. How can you call yourself a school psychologist if you can't sit down and talk with a student about a school problem?"

Good question, and one that is as relevant now as it was then. I continue to hear similar concerns from administrators, teachers, and school psychologists themselves, along with a steady stream of requests to conduct training workshops for school psychologists who are asked to provide therapeutic intervention for individual students who require intensive, Tier 3 services.

In light of the growing emphasis on indirect services that reach many students, it is unlikely that counseling and other intensive therapeutic services will ever become a major role for school psychologists. But this does not mean, as Carol bluntly points out, that we should entirely avoid such services. The need for school psychologists' involvement in the full continuum of school-based mental health services—from universal, school-wide Tier 1 strategies through the provision of Tier 3 counseling and other direct mental health services for individual students—is clearly stated in the National Association of School Psychologists (NASP) *Model for Comprehensive and Integrated School Psychological Services* (NASP, 2010) and in NASP's position statement, *The Importance of School Mental Health Services* (NASP, 2008). These documents affirm that good mental health enhances children's overall success and that school psychologists are well positioned to provide a wide range of mental health services, from prevention through individual counseling. Regardless of personal opinions about school psychology's role in offering therapeutic services, the steady growth of mental health programs in schools will increase the demand for school psychologists to provide such services (Fagan & Wise, 2007).

This chapter offers step-by-step guidelines and strategies for conducting solution-focused, student-driven interviews with individual students. Student-driven interviewing is a therapeutic intervention for school problems that invites students to take an active role in every aspect of their care, from formulating goals through evaluating the usefulness of services (Murphy, 2013). The ideas and techniques in this chapter will enhance school psychologists' efforts to implement two key areas of the Interventions and Mental Health Services to Develop Social and Life Skills domain in the NASP Practice Model: (a) provision of developmentally appropriate mental health services, including individual counseling, and (b) evaluation of mental health interventions for individual students. This chapter will help school psychologists implement the positive, strengths-based aspects of the problem-solving approach and the individualized, intensive therapeutic services associated with Tier 3 of the multitiered model of student support.

Following a discussion of what works in helping people change, the key tasks and strategies of student-driven interviewing are described and illustrated through real-life conversations involving a variety of students and problems. It is my hope that this chapter will enhance school psychologists' ability to, in Carol's words, "sit down and talk with a student" in competent, change-focused ways.

BASIC CONSIDERATIONS

Helping people change is the essence of the school psychology profession. Whether consulting a teacher or counseling a student, change is the ultimate goal. Simply put, the professional usefulness of a school psychologist rests largely on their ability to help people change.

What Works in Helping People Change

Outcome research in psychotherapy and counseling provides valuable hints about how change occurs in helping relationships. This research forms the empirical basis of student-driven interviewing. Based on scientific analyses of hundreds of studies involving a variety of clients, helpers, and settings, researchers have proposed that successful therapeutic outcomes result mainly from the operation of a few core ingredients (Asay & Lambert, 1999; Wampold, 2010). These ingredients are common to all helping relationships regardless of the practitioner's treatment model or theoretical orientation, and hence the term *common factors of change* applies. These factors are

displayed in Figure 20.1 along with the extent to which (as a percentage) each factor contributes to successful outcomes.

Client Factors

Client factors are the most potent of all ingredients in the change process (accounting for 40% of change). This category includes everything that students bring to the table when they meet with school psychologists: life experiences, cultural traditions, strengths, values, special interests and talents, resilience, social support systems, influential people, and other "natural resources" in their lives. In a review of research, Bohart and Tallman (2010) concluded that the client's capacity for self-healing is the most powerful element of change in helping relationships. Others have reported that focusing on people's strengths and resources is a prerequisite of effective outcomes (Gassman & Grawe, 2006). These findings urge school psychologists to help students recognize and apply their unique strengths and resources to school solutions.

Client factors are available in every student and every situation. Students just need to be asked about them. Unfortunately, students with problems are often viewed as having little to contribute toward solutions. In contrast to diagnostic interviews that focus on what is wrong and missing in students' lives, student-driven interviews seek out students' strengths, successes,

Figure 20.1. Common Factors of Change in Helping Relationships and Their Percentage Contributions to Successful Outcomes

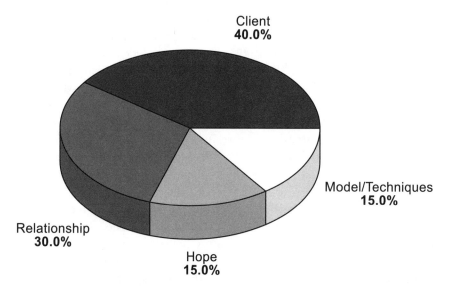

Note. From "The Empirical Case for Common Factors in Therapy: Quantitative Findings," by T. P. Asay and M. J. Lambert (p. 31), in *The Heart and Soul of Change: What Works in Therapy,* by M. A. Hubble, B. L. Duncan, and S. D. Miller (Eds.), Washington, DC: American Psychological Association. Copyright 1999 by the American Psychological Association. Adapted with permission.

feedback, preferences, and other student factors that can be applied toward school solutions.

Relationship Factors

Relationship factors are the second most important ingredient in the change process (accounting for 30% of change). These factors include the student's experience of acceptance, empathy, respect, accommodation, collaboration, validation, and encouragement from the school psychologist. Research has repeatedly verified the strong and reliable link between intervention outcomes and client perceptions of the therapeutic relationship (Horvath, Del Re, Fluckiger, & Symonds, 2011; Norcross, 2010). While many such studies have involved adults, recent reviews have indicated that the therapeutic relationship is equally important when working with children and adolescents (Shirk, Jungbluth, & Karver, 2012). Student-driven interviewing translates empirical research on relationship factors into practical methods for (a) inviting students to take an active role in shaping the goals and content of intervention services; (b) obtaining regular student feedback on the relationship, goal attainment, and usefulness of services; and (c) adjusting services based on student feedback.

Hope Factors

Hope plays a key role in effective outcomes (accounting for 15% of change), though its influence is relatively smaller than that of client and relationship factors. Hope factors include students' self-efficacy, that is, the belief in one's ability to resolve problems and reach goals (Bandura, 2006). Students who connect their improvements and progress to their own actions are more likely to sustain such efforts in the future (Molden & Dweck, 2006).

The last thing struggling students need from school psychologists is a reminder of what is wrong with them. Students need a strong dose of hope. Student-driven interviewing enhances students' hope by acknowledging their strengths and resources, focusing on future goals and possibilities, and connecting their accomplishments—no matter how small—to their own efforts through questions such as, "What did you do differently to get your work done today?" and "How did you muster up the energy to make it happen?"

Model/Technique Factors

This category consists of the practitioner's theoretical model of intervention and techniques associated with the model. Theoretical ideas and techniques provide useful structure and direction to the helping process. The impact of these theoretical ideas and techniques on

outcomes, however, is relatively small compared to the combined impact of the other common factors (accounting for 15% of change; Wampold, 2010). The effectiveness of a school psychologist's intervention ideas and techniques depends largely on the student's acceptance of these ideas and techniques, which helps to explain why no single treatment model has proved superior to others in overall effectiveness with children (S. D. Miller, Wampold, & Varhely, 2008). These findings urge school psychologists to (a) hold lightly to their favorite ideas and techniques instead of marrying them so that they can let go of them if they are not working for a particular student and (b) tailor their approach to each student instead of fitting the student to their approach.

This discussion is not meant to criticize intervention techniques or to minimize their value. The more ideas and techniques that school psychologists know, the better able school psychologists will be to match them with specific students. The point here is not to discard intervention models or techniques, but to put them in their proper perspective with the other common factors of change, and to use them in flexible ways based on the student's response and feedback.

Student-driven interviewing translates the research on common factors of change into practical strategies that help school psychologists to do the following:

- *Client factors:* Explore students' strengths and resources
- *Relationship factors:* Build therapeutic partnerships that invite students to become actively involved in every aspect of their care
- *Hope factors:* Promote hope for a better future
- *Model/technique factors:* Select and flexibly apply therapeutic ideas and techniques that accommodate each student's preferences, resources, and feedback

Practical Assumptions of Student-Driven Interviewing

Student-driven interviews are designed to activate the common factors of change from the very first moments of contact with students. With common factors as an empirical foundation, the following practical assumptions about students guide the interviewing process. (see Table 20.1)

Cooperation Promotes Change

Student-driven interviewing is a cooperative approach that builds strong alliances with students by treating them as collaborators and by recruiting and cooperating with their strengths, preferences, and feedback. Students are more likely to accept suggestions and interventions that accommodate their opinions and strengths compared with interventions that are imposed on them. If school psychologists want students to cooperate with them, school psychologists need to cooperate with students. After all, school psychologists work for students, and not the other way around.

Every Student Offers Strengths and Resources That Can Be Incorporated Into School Interventions

This assumption is consistent with the growing emphasis on positive psychology within the school psychology profession. Whereas traditional interviews and interventions focus primarily on what is wrong or missing with students, student-driven interviews expand problem-solving options by inviting students to apply what is right and working in their lives toward school solutions. Since every student brings a unique set of strengths and resources to the table, customized interventions are developed one student at a time based on his or her natural resources. The customized practice of fitting interventions to students instead of the other way around is consistent with NASP recommendations that school psychologists show "respect for human diversity" and promote "effective services, advocacy, and social justice for all children" (NASP, 2010, p. 3). In addition to improving outcomes, building interventions from students' unique strengths and resources ensures culturally competent practice (Sue & Sue, 2013).

It Is More Useful to Focus on Future Possibilities Than Past Problems

Students referred for services are usually well aware of their shortcomings, which is why they often welcome the opportunity to focus on future possibilities and seem to experience a renewed sense of hope and energy as a result. People generally prefer to discuss what they can do to make things better rather than what they have done to make things worse. Student-driven interviews honor this preference by inviting students to envision a

Table 20.1. Practical Assumptions of Solution-Focused, Student-Driven Interviewing

- People are capable and resourceful.
- Cooperation promotes change.
- Every student offers strengths and resources that can be incorporated into school interventions.
- It is more useful to focus on future possibilities than past problems.
- Small changes lead to bigger changes.
- Language shapes reality.

preferred future and encouraging them to explore times in which the problem is absent or less noticeable.

Small Changes Lead to Bigger Changes

Big problems do not always require big solutions. The systemic idea that one small change can lead to larger improvements is encouraging to school psychologists who have limited time to conduct elaborate interventions for every problem. Student-driven interviews invite students to focus on attainable goals and small steps toward larger improvements.

Language Shapes Reality

Talking with students is only one of several ways to change a problem, but it is an important one given that students are the primary focus of school interventions. What school psychologists say and how they say it shape students' perceptions of themselves and their prospects for change. Conducting student-driven interviews requires that school psychologists use language in mindful, deliberate ways that enhance students' hope, involvement, and cooperation.

BEST PRACTICES IN CONDUCTING STUDENT-DRIVEN INTERVIEWS

This section describes key tasks and strategies of student-driven interviewing, which are summarized in Table 20.2. The focus of discussion is on the nuts and bolts of how

Table 20.2. Tasks and Strategies of Solution-Focused, Student-Driven Interviewing

Task	Strategies
Create a culture of collaboration	Arrange environment in respectful ways; use icebreakers; orient students; obtain feedback
Discuss problems in solution-focused ways	Acknowledge and prioritize concerns; describe changeable problems; explore environmental factors, problem influence, and solution attempts
Develop goals that matter	Link students' values to school-related goals; ask miracle and scaling questions; incorporate students' language and perceptions into goals
Build interventions from what is right with students	Build interventions from exceptions, strengths, and other student resources

to conduct student-driven interviews, practical strategies that school psychologists can apply in their everyday work with students of all ages and circumstances. Short excerpts of dialogue, adapted from Murphy (2013), are used to further illustrate the techniques of student-driven interviewing.

Task 1: Create a Culture of Collaboration

School psychologists can create a culture of collaboration with students at the very outset of services by (a) arranging the physical setting in respectful ways, (b) using icebreakers and small talk, (c) orienting students to the helping process, and (d) obtaining student feedback. Each of these strategies is described in greater detail below.

Arrange the Physical Setting in Respectful Ways

The physical setting in which a school psychologist meets a student is less important than the conversation that occurs, but it is still important because it can affect the student's first perceptions of the school psychologist. To the extent possible, the school psychologist should arrange the environment in ways that convey respect for the student and that promote the student's comfort and cooperation. When students meet with an adult, they may automatically assume a passive role and expect to be told what to do. Seating arrangements may subtly reinforce this assumption and work against students' involvement in the conversation. Consider the situation in which the school psychologist sits in a large, overstuffed chair behind a big desk while the student sits in a plain chair across the office. Seating arrangements that blatantly portray the school psychologist as "the leader" and the student as "the follower" are inconsistent with the student-driven notion that students are essential contributors to school solutions. The following strategies may also help to promote a respectful, collaborative relationship with students:

- Maintain a clear line of vision to the student and reduce any visual barriers such as plants, telephones, or books.
- Sit at or below the student's eye level when possible; that is, sit in the same size chair as the student, let the student take the big chair, or sit on the floor with the student.
- Conduct the conversation while taking a walk, tossing a ball, playing a board game, or eating lunch with the student.

Use Icebreakers and Small Talk

Given that many students have never experienced a helping relationship and are understandably suspicious when they meet a school psychologist the first time, the school psychologist needs to approach the student in ways that are as comfortable and nonthreatening as possible. One way to do this is to ask questions that convey respect for the student's preferences, perceptions, and resources. Questions about hobbies and interests, community events, and how long the student has lived in the neighborhood can serve as positive, nonthreatening icebreakers that help the student ease into the conversation instead of being immediately subjected to interrogations about the school problem. These short exchanges also reveal strengths, interests, or other student resources that can be incorporated into subsequent interventions. Listening closely to what students say during the opening moments of the interview helps to clarify their overall frame of reference and communication style.

As an example, ask students for their permission to take notes during the meeting, adding that they are free to look at the notes any time during the meeting and photocopy them. This type of transparency strengthens trust and reduces any mystery about the content and purpose of the notes. In addition to starting the first session with some nonthreatening questions and small talk, request students' help with a simple task such as moving a chair or table or helping hang a picture on the wall. These requests provide safe opportunities for students to be successful on their very first task in the relationship, which helps them to ease into the school-related conversation with positive momentum.

Orient Students to the Helping Process

After a couple minutes of small talk, it is important to explain—in clear and simple language—the overall approach and format of the helping process. Here is a quick example involving a 12-year-old student:

School psychologist: "I need you to teach me what you want school to be like and what I can do to help, so I'll need to ask you some questions about what you want and what might help make things better for you at school. We might come up with some ideas right away, or it might take us a while. Either way, I'll need to check with you each time we meet to see how things are going in school and how our meetings are working for you. I'll need your help on that, okay? Do you have any questions?"

Orienting students to the helping process enhances intervention outcomes by preparing them for what lies ahead, increasing their expectancy of change (Constantino & DeGeorge, 2008), and strengthening the therapeutic alliance (Shirk, Karver, & Brown, 2011).

Obtain Student Feedback

In addition to promoting collaboration and student involvement, obtaining systematic client feedback can dramatically improve service outcomes in the helping professions (Gillaspy & Murphy, 2012; Lambert & Shimokawa, 2011). School psychologists can use two simple tools to obtain ongoing feedback on the usefulness and fit of their services to students: the Session Rating Scale (Johnson, Miller, & Duncan, 2000) and the Outcome Rating Scale (S. D. Miller & Duncan, 2001). Figures 20.2–20.5 display both scales along with their child versions: the Child Outcome Rating Scale (Duncan, Miller, & Sparks, 2003) and the Child Session Rating Scale (Duncan, Miller, Sparks, & Johnson, 2003). These measures assess research-identified elements of therapeutic outcome and alliance. Changes in the areas assessed on the Outcome Rating Scale—personal distress, interpersonal well-being, social relationships,

Figure 20.2. Outcome Rating Scale

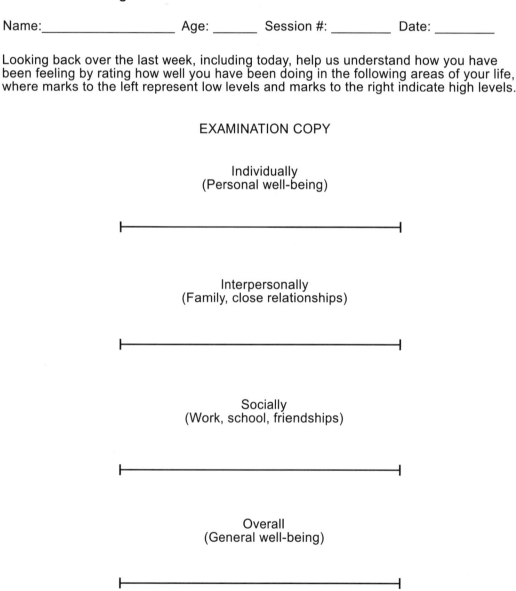

Name:_____ Age: _____ Session #: _____ Date: _____

Looking back over the last week, including today, help us understand how you have been feeling by rating how well you have been doing in the following areas of your life, where marks to the left represent low levels and marks to the right indicate high levels.

EXAMINATION COPY

Individually
(Personal well-being)

Interpersonally
(Family, close relationships)

Socially
(Work, school, friendships)

Overall
(General well-being)

Note. From *Outcome Rating Scale*, by S. D. Miller and B. L. Duncan, 2001, Chicago, IL: Author. Copyright 2001 by the authors. Reprinted with permission from B. L. Duncan and the Heart and Soul of Change Project.

Figure 20.3. Child Outcome Rating Scale

Name:_____ Age: _____ Session #: _____ Date: _____

How are you doing? How are things going in your life? Please make a mark on the scale to let us know. The closer to the smiley face, the better things are. The closer to the frowny face, things are not so good.

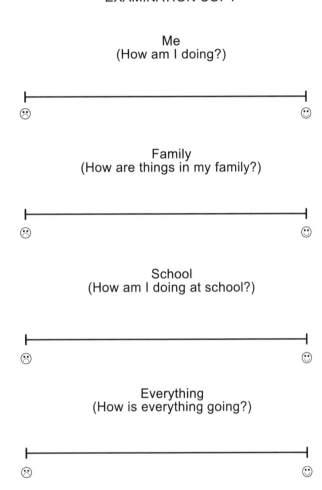

EXAMINATION COPY

Me
(How am I doing?)

Family
(How are things in my family?)

School
(How am I doing at school?)

Everything
(How is everything going?)

Note. From *Child Outcome Rating Scale*, by B. L. Duncan, S. D. Miller, and J. A. Sparks, 2003, Fort Lauderdale, FL: Author. Copyright 2003 by the authors. Reprinted with permission from B. L. Duncan and the Heart and Soul of Change Project.

and overall well-being—are widely considered to be reliable and valid indicators of successful outcome. The Session Rating Scale assesses the client's perception of key aspects of strong alliances and effective counseling sessions; that is, respect and understanding, relevance of goals and topics, and student–school psychologist fit. The Outcome Rating Scale is administered and discussed at the beginning of each meeting and the Session Rating Scale at the end. The systematic use of these measures—both of which have been well researched—supports the NASP Practice Model's

(NASP, 2010) recommendation that school psychologists use valid and reliable assessment techniques to measure students' progress toward behavioral goals, responses to interventions, and outcomes. (See Figures 20.2 and 20.3.)

Both scales use a visual analog format of four 10-centimeter lines, with instructions to place a mark on each line with low estimates to the left and high estimates to the right. The four 10-centimeter lines add to a total score of 40. The score is simply the summation of the marks made by the client to the nearest millimeter

Figure 20.4. Session Rating Scale

Name:_____ Age: _____ Session #: _____ Date: _____

Please rate today's session by placing a hash mark on the line nearest to the description that best fits your experience.

EXAMINATION COPY

Relationship

I did not feel heard,
understood, and ⊢————————————————————————⊣ I felt heard,
respected.   understood,
    and respected.

Goals and Topics

We did not work
on or talk about
what I wanted to ⊢————————————————————————⊣ We worked on
work on or talk   and talked about
about.   what I wanted to
    work on and talk
    about.

Approach or Method

The therapist's
approach is not ⊢————————————————————————⊣ The therapist's
a good fit for me.   approach is a
    good fit for me.

Overall

There was
something missing ⊢————————————————————————⊣ Overall, today's
in the session today.   session was right
    for me.

Note. From *Session Rating Scale (version 3.0)*, by L. D. Johnson, S. D. Miller, and B. L. Duncan, 2000, Chicago, IL: Author. Copyright 2000 by the authors. Reprinted with permission from B. L. Duncan and the Heart and Soul of Change Project.

on each of the four lines, measured by a centimeter ruler or template. The Outcome Rating Scale and Session Rating Scale contain only four items and can be administered in less than a minute, a very appealing feature for busy school psychologists. The Session Rating Scale provides immediate feedback that allows the school psychologist to detect and correct alliance problems as soon as problems occur. For example, when a student rates an item below 9 on the 10-centimeter scale—say, the Approach or Method scale—the school psychologist can follow up by asking, "What can I do differently to make our next meeting better for you?"

When scores remain unchanged or decline on the Outcome Rating Scale, school psychologists can ask students what needs to change to make things better: "Based on your marks, it looks like things haven't changed much over the last couple weeks. How willing are you to try something different to make things better?"

The use of the Outcome Rating Scale and Session Rating Scale at every meeting gives students an ongoing voice in their care and lets them know that school psychologists are willing to adapt the helping process based on their feedback. The results of these measures

Figure 20.5. Child Session Rating Scale

Name:_____ Age: _____ Session #: _____ Date: _____

How was our time together today? Please put a mark on the lines below to let us know how you feel.

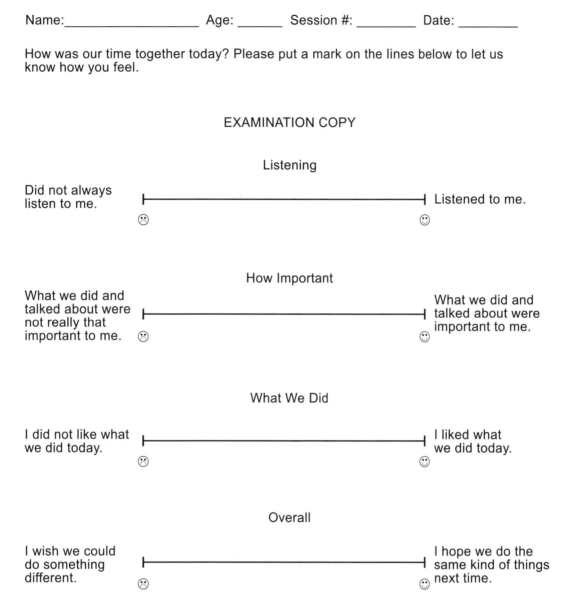

Note. From *Child Session Rating Scale*, by B. L. Duncan, S. D. Miller, J. A. Sparks, and L. D. Johnson, 2003, Fort Lauderdale, FL: Author. Copyright 2003 by the authors. Reprinted with permission from B. L. Duncan and the Heart and Soul of Change Project.

can be charted and graphed to provide a visual snapshot of students' response to intervention. These measures can also be combined with other evaluation methods such as classroom observations, grades, teacher/parent interviews, behavior rating scales, and discipline records.

In addition to benefiting students, collecting formal feedback is an excellent way for school psychologists to systematically increase their cultural competence and accountability. Obtaining and discussing student feedback in the manner described above requires school psychologists to request, respect, and accommodate the

goals and perceptions of students, all of which are hallmarks of culturally competent practice (Sue & Sue, 2013). Collecting outcome and alliance feedback communicates genuine interest in the student's perceptions of the helping relationship and willingness to give the student a voice and choice in the content and delivery of services. Collecting feedback promotes egalitarian student–practitioner relationships and encourages the school psychologist to approach every student as a unique individual regardless of his or her race, ethnicity, gender, and other cultural attributes, all of which enhance school psychologists' cultural competence (McAuliffe & Associates, 2013).

Collecting feedback also enables school psychologists to systematically evaluate their effectiveness over a prolonged period of time. For example, maintaining Session Rating Scale data across several different students may indicate specific areas of relationship building—such as listening or developing goals—that require more attention and improvement on the part of the school psychologist. The Outcome Rating Scale scores provide school psychologists with a cumulative record of service outcomes as perceived by the students. Additional information about using these measures to evaluate and adjust one's own school psychological services and practice is outlined in Murphy and Duncan (2007).

Summary of Task 1

Student-driven interviews promote a culture of collaboration in which students are viewed as capable contributors to school solutions. Inviting student input and feedback enhances outcomes by increasing student involvement in the change process. The strategies in this section—arranging the physical setting, using ice-breakers, orienting students, and collecting feedback—help school psychologists set the stage for effective problem solving by creating a culture of collaboration and accountability from the very outset of services. (See Figures 20.4 and 20.5.)

Task 2: Discuss Problems in Solution-Focused Ways

Discussing problems in solution-focused ways involves (a) validating and prioritizing students' concerns; (b) describing changeable problems; and (c) exploring environmental factors, problem influence, and solution attempts.

Validate and Prioritize Students' Concerns

School problems rarely come in neat little packages, as most referrals involve a combination of social, behavioral, and academic components. It is important to acknowledge all concerns while exploring the ones that are most pressing from the student's perspective. The following questions help students prioritize their concerns:

- Of all these concerns, which one is most important to you?
- If we could change just one of the things you mentioned, which one would make the biggest difference in your school life?

- *[Pointing to the student's completed Outcome Rating Scale]* Which of these areas is most important to you?

Consider the following conversation with Jeremy, a 10-year-old student who mentioned several concerns about school.

School psychologist: "So, you get in trouble for talking in class, arguing with other students, and not turning in homework. Which of these do you want to work on first?"

Jeremy: "I guess homework."

School psychologist: "Okay. Why is the homework important to you right now?"

Jeremy: "My mom and teachers are always getting onto me about it."

School psychologist: "So you're getting it at school and home."

Jeremy: "Yes."

School psychologist: "Let me see if I understand this. When you start to turn in more homework, life will be better at home and school because your mom and teacher won't bug you as much. Is that it?"

Jeremy: "Yes."

School psychologist: "That makes sense. I can see why you want to work on the homework first."

Helping students prioritize problems serves to boost their hope by narrowing a wide range of problems into a specific and manageable focus. Hope is also enhanced through the school psychologist's use of future-focused language such as "*when* you turn in more homework" and "life *will* be better."

Describe Changeable Problems

Once the student prioritizes his or her concerns, the school psychologist then can determine exactly what a particular concern or problem looks like. For example, if the student says that he or she has a "bad attitude," the school psychologist needs to find out specifically what that means and looks like from the student's perspective. Everyday language is full of abstract words that mean different things to different people (immature, disrespectful, spacey, unmotivated, attention deficit hyperactivity disorder). The only way to determine what these words mean to a person is to obtain specific descriptions.

Consider the example of Sherese, a 16-year-old student who told the school psychologist that her biggest problem was "being disorganized." When asked what she did or did not do that reflected disorganization, she was able to describe several changeable behaviors that she wanted to work on: making a to-do list each day, spending less time playing video games, and cleaning her room at least once a week. Sherese became more energized as the conversation shifted from the unchangeable trait of disorganization to the description of specific, changeable actions.

When students use vague terms to describe problems, school psychologists can ask questions that elicit concrete descriptions such as, "If I videoed this problem, what would I see and hear?" and "If we were watching a movie of this problem, what would we see first? Then what?"

Explore Environmental Factors, Problem Influence, and Solution Attempts

Exploring environmental factors related to the problem can provide useful clues for changing it. This includes clarifying the factors such as when and where the problem behavior usually occurs, who is around, what occurs right before and after the behavior, and possible functions of the behavior for the student. Exploring problems in this manner is part of functional behavior assessment (an area that is familiar to many school psychologists and therefore will be given minimal attention here). This is an important aspect of student-directed interviews because small environmental changes can lead to significant improvements in students' school performance and behavior.

In addition to clarifying environmental factors related to the problem, school psychologists can also ask the following types of questions to explore the extent and manner in which the problem influences the student:

- On a scale of 0–10, where 0 is no problem and 10 is serious problem, how would you rate this situation?
- How does this problem affect your life at school and home?
- How does it affect your relationship with your friends, teachers, or parents?
- How would your life be different without the problem?

These questions prevent school psychologists from jumping to conclusions about the meaning of a school problem for a student. These questions also encourage the student to stop and think about how the problem affects his or her life. Students often become more motivated to resolve a problem when they reflect on its influence in their lives.

Exploring solution attempts also helps to provide direction for intervention. Students typically struggle with a problem for a long time before being referred to school psychologists for services. In the course of the struggle, it is easy to become entranced by the problem and overlook potential solutions. Exploring attempted solutions helps school psychologists to (a) discover and apply what has already worked in addressing the problem or similar problems (successful attempts) and (b) discover and avoid what has not worked (unsuccessful attempts). The following questions are useful in exploring the nature and effectiveness of solution attempts:

- What types of things have you already tried? How did they work?
- Of all the things that have been tried, what has worked the best?
- How have you handled similar challenges, and how could that help you with the problem you are having now?
- What have other people done to help you? How did it work?

For students who have received prior counseling or intervention services, they can also be asked, "What did the counselor do that worked well (or not so well) for you?" and "What was most helpful/least helpful in your previous counseling experiences?" Exploring solution attempts invites students to stop and think about what they have already done—or might do differently—to address the problem.

Summary of Task 2

By the time students are referred to school psychologists, many of them are fatigued and discouraged by their struggle with a problem. There is a big difference between talking about a problem and becoming bogged down by it. When interviewing students, it is important to discuss problems in solution-focused ways, that is, ways that acknowledge and explore the problem while instilling a sense of hope for resolving it. School psychologists can do this by validating and prioritizing students' concerns; encouraging students to describe concrete and changeable problems; and exploring relevant environmental factors, problem influence, and solution attempts.

Task 3: Develop Goals That Matter

In conducting student-driven interviews, school psychologists can encourage students to think about what matters most to them and to develop school-related goals that support students' deepest values. Involving students in the development of their own goals enhances their motivation (W. R. Miller & Rollnick, 2013) and honors the recommendation of multicultural experts to invite all clients to play a major role in formulating their therapeutic goals (Sue & Sue, 2013). Sadly, students are often excluded from the goal-building process. Excluding or minimizing student input is like rowing a boat with one paddle instead of two. Like a boat with one paddle, school psychologists' work with students will turn in circles unless students are invested in school-related goals. Student-driven strategies for formulating clear and meaningful goals include (a) linking students' values to school-related goals, (b) asking miracle and scaling questions, and (c) incorporating students' language and perceptions into goals.

Link Students' Values to School-Related Goals

The most important aspect of a school-related goal is its personal significance to the student. Unfortunately, this consideration sometimes takes a back seat to the preferences of school psychologists, teachers, parents, administrators, everyone except the student. Regardless of what others think, a school goal must mean something to students in order to engage their investment and motivation. For some students, school performance holds little intrinsic value or interest. Lacking a personal reason to invest in school, students may understandably adopt a "what's the use?" or "why should I even try?" position. School psychologists can promote student-driven goals by exploring what matters most to students—their deepest values—and linking these values to school-related goals. The following questions help link students' values to their school performance:

- Let's forget about school for a few minutes. If you could be just the kind of person you most want to be, what kind of person is that?
- Pretend that you are 50 years old and that your life has turned out just the way you wanted it to be. Now imagine picking up a book called *Michelle's Life*, and reading your life story at age 50. What are the most important parts of the story?
- What do you want your life to stand for? What small step are you willing take at school next week to move you a little bit closer to the life you want?

- If it were possible for you to have a better life, would you be willing to change some things at school to make it happen?

Ask Miracle and Scaling Questions

The miracle question, a core strategy of solution-focused brief therapy (Franklin, Trepper, Gingerich, & McCollum, 2012), is a playful way to boost hope and formulate goals by inviting people to envision and describe a problem-free future. Here are a few variations of this strategy that school psychologists can use in conversations with students:

- Let's say a miracle happens while you are sleeping tonight and this problem is completely solved. What would be different at school tomorrow? What would your teachers notice and how would they react?
- Imagine that we are looking into a crystal ball at a time in the future when this problem no longer occurs at school. What do you see?
- Imagine that there are two movies about your life. Movie 1 is about your life with the problem, and Movie 2 is about your life without the problem. I already know a lot about Movie 1. Tell me what Movie 2 would look like. Who would be in it? What would they be doing?

As illustrated next with Charice—an 11-year-old student referred for classroom behavior problems—it is helpful to follow up on the miracle question by obtaining specific details and behavioral commitments from students.

School psychologist: "Suppose a miracle occurred one night while you were sleeping and this problem vanished. What would be different at school?"

Charice: "I'd be paying more attention in class and taking notes and doing more work."

School psychologist: "Which one of these things would you be willing to work on first, even just a little, during the next couple days at school?" *[This question keeps Charice in the driver's seat by asking for her opinion on what to work on first. The phrase "even just a little" invites her to focus on small changes instead of the more overwhelming task of changing everything all at once.]*

Charice: "I guess taking notes because it would help my grades."

School psychologist: "That makes sense. What is one small thing you could do next week to get closer to where you want to be on taking notes?" *[This question encourages Charice to commit to a small, specific action related to her goal.]*

As seen with Charice, miracle questions promote a hopeful, student-driven context for developing small, specific goals. The opportunity to focus on a better future can be a breath of fresh air for students who are burdened by ongoing problems at school. Most students enjoy the playful aspect of the miracle question, but no single technique works with every student. Some may view the miracle question as impractical or silly. When that happens, the school psychologist can simply accept the student's response and move on to other goal development strategies.

The following scaling questions offer another avenue for helping students develop small, specific goals:

- On a scale of 0–10, with 10 being the best that things could be in science class and 0 being the worst, where would you rate things in science class now? What would the next higher number look like?
- What will you do differently at school when it moves from a 3 to a 3.5 or 4? How will your teachers be able to tell you moved up a little?
- *[Pointing to the student's mark on the school item of the Child Outcome Rating Scale]* You marked 3.4 on the school scale. What will a 3.5 look like?

The following excerpt illustrates the use of a scaling question with Natalie, a high school student referred to the school psychologist for classroom behavior problems:

School psychologist: "On a scale of 0–100, where 100 is the very best that things can be at school and 0 is the very worst, where are things in school now?"

Natalie: "I'd say about 20."

School psychologist: "How will things be different at school when it moves to a 25?"

Natalie: "My social studies teacher and I won't be getting into it all the time."

School psychologist: "Okay. What else?"

Natalie: "My attitude will be a little better."

School psychologist: "If I videoed you with a better attitude, what would I see you doing differently at school?"

For students who are more comfortable with numbers than words, scaling provides a good way to explore their goals. Scaling strategies also add a novel and playful element, which is always a welcome addition when working with young people. Whatever the reason, many students respond better to the miracle and scaling questions than they do to more direct, traditional questions about their goals.

Incorporate Students' Language and Perceptions Into Goals

School-related goals should reflect key words, phrases, and perceptions of the student whenever possible. This point applies to every student and every circumstance, but this discussion addresses situations that are particularly challenging for school psychologists, that is, when students do not want to participate in services and when they perceive that their goals and preferences take a back seat to the wishes of teachers, parents, or others.

Students are keenly aware of situations in which adults ignore their opinions. Instead of calling students resistant or otherwise discounting their perspectives, school psychologists can meet them where they are by integrating their language and perceptions into goal-related conversations. In working with a student who wants to get out of having to attend counseling every week, the school psychologist can ask the student, "What needs to happen for you to get out of having to come here?" The following questions invite so-called reluctant students to develop goals that accommodate their language and perceptions:

- I know you would rather not be here, so maybe we could work on getting you out of having to do that. Are you interested?
- On a scale of 1–100, where 1 is I won't do anything and 100 is I'll do anything to get out of coming here, how would you rate your willingness to take action that helps you get out of counseling as soon as possible?
- Would you be interested in finding ways to keep your parents or teachers off your case about school?
- What would convince your teachers and parents that you no longer need counseling?
- I already know what your teachers and parents want to change, but what do you want to change?

Summary of Task 3

Students are capable of amazing changes when they are working toward goals that matter to them. In conducting student-driven interviews, school psychologists can facilitate goals that matter by linking students' values to school performance, asking miracle and scaling questions, and incorporating students' language and perceptions into goals. Once school-related goals are in place, school psychologists can encourage students to apply their strengths and resources toward reaching those goals. Practical strategies for doing so are discussed next.

Task 4: Build Interventions From What Is Right With Students

Most people are well aware of what is wrong by the time a student meets with a school psychologist. With all the attention on students' problems and deficiencies, it is easy to overlook what is right in their lives: small successes, strengths, and other resources that can be used to build student-driven interventions. Unlike traditional approaches that focus on remediating problems and correcting deficits, student-driven interviews encourage students to recognize and apply what is right and working in their lives. This is done by constructing interventions from (a) exceptions to the problem and (b) other student-related resources.

Build Interventions From Exceptions to the Problem

Students, caregivers, and school psychologists can become so saturated and discouraged by the problem that they are unable to notice nonproblems or exceptions to the problem. Exceptions refer to times and situations at school in which the problem is absent or less noticeable. Exceptions are mini-solutions that are already happening, just not as often as desired. And they are there for the asking. No problem occurs all the time, even though it may seem that way to students and others. Because exceptions often fall under the radar at first glance, school psychologists need to do some digging to find those exceptions. The following questions—some of which can also be used with teachers and parents—are helpful in identifying exceptions:

- When is the problem less noticeable?
- What is your best class at school?
- Tell me about a time in the past few days or weeks that you made it through the whole morning without getting kicked out of class.

Once exceptions are discovered, the conditions can be explored under which the exceptions occurred in much the same way conditions can be explored surrounding problem occurrences:

- What did you do to make it happen [*referring to the exception*]?
- Who was around when it happened? How did they respond? What was that like for you?
- What else was different about that time?

Clarifying the details and circumstances associated with exceptions lays the groundwork for designing exception-based interventions. For example, details about a class in which the student behaves well can be used to design interventions that incorporate elements of the exception class into other classes:

- How could you make this happen more at school?
- What will it take to do more of what you're doing in math class in one or two of your other classes?
- I wonder what would happen if you conducted a secret experiment where you did this [*referring to the exception behavior*] in one of your other classes and then carefully observed your teacher to see if anything changed between the two of you.

The following conversation briefly illustrates the initial process of discovering and exploring exceptions with Carlos, a 15-year-old student referred for classroom behavior problems.

School psychologist: "When have things been a little better for you in school this week?"

Carlos: "Never. I get in trouble all the time."

School psychologist: "That must be really hard for you. Which class do you get in trouble a little less in?"

Carlos: "Probably science class."

School psychologist: "How would you explain that? What is it about science class—or your approach to it—that helps you behave better and get in less trouble?"

After obtaining specific details about how science class differed from Carlos' other classes—he arrived to class on time, sat closer to the teacher, took more notes, and occasionally did homework—the school psychologist and Carlos explored how he might replicate one or more of these exception-related conditions and behaviors in another class.

Sometimes the best way to resolve a problem is to build on nonproblems, that is, to identify and expand on times in which the problem is absent or less noticeable.

In addition to interviewing students, school psychologists can interview teachers and parents, review educational records, and conduct classroom observations with an eye toward discovering exceptions. The theme of resolving school problems by building on what is right with students is continued in the next strategy.

Build Interventions From Students' Natural Resources

This section describes strategies for identifying and applying naturally occurring internal and external resources of students, such as special interests, talents, cultural experiences, resilience, courage, solution ideas, and influential people. The integration of student resources into school interventions is supported by a growing body of research on the benefits of incorporating as much of the client as possible in the helping process (Bohart & Tallman, 2010; Gassman & Grawe, 2006).

The process of building school-based interventions from students' natural resources is similar to that of building on exceptions. School psychologists can discover student resources by listening for hints of those resources in the students' comments and by asking the following types of questions:

- *Special interests and talents:* What do you enjoy doing outside of school?
- *Influential people:* Who do you respect the most in your life? What would he or she advise you to do about this problem?
- *Solution ideas:* What do you think might help turn things around at school?
- *Courage and resilience:* How have you managed to hang in there without completely giving up?

Once a resource is discovered, then how it might be incorporated into school-based interventions can be explored. Consider a brief example involving Kevin, a 10-year-old student referred for oppositional behaviors, most of which occurred in the afternoons. At one point during the first meeting, the school psychologist discovered that Kevin loved playing baseball. Kevin knew the names, positions, and batting averages of several players on the city's major league baseball team. After a few minutes of baseball talk, the school psychologist wondered aloud if Kevin's current school challenges were similar in any way to the challenges of baseball. For example, they talked about how long the baseball season (school year) is and how important it is to not allow a losing streak (several bad days in a row

at school) ruin the entire year. The school psychologist asked Kevin if he was willing to try a short experiment in which he applied a baseball approach to his classes. He decided to step up to the plate each day and do his best even though he might occasionally strike out and make mistakes. Things improved over the next couple weeks and Kevin's teacher commented on his impressive turnaround. The intervention emerged directly from a readily available, naturally occurring resource in Kevin's life: his love of baseball. As a result, Kevin accepted the intervention and did his best to make it work.

My most memorable lessons about resilience were taught to me by the students and families I served in one of the most economically depressed communities in the United States. The following story is one of many such lessons on students' ability to bend—but not break—under extremely challenging circumstances.

Angela was halfway into her senior year when she was referred for failing two classes and periodically skipping school. Her teachers said that she was capable of passing all of her classes if she would apply herself and take school more seriously.

Angela discussed numerous challenges during the first meeting. Her father moved away when she was an infant. Throughout much of her childhood Angela felt that no one wanted her because she was "a financial burden." She moved between her mother's and uncle's house six separate times and attended eight different schools since kindergarten. Her mother and uncle were investigated several times by social services because of neglect and abuse charges. Angela was currently working 30 hours a week at a restaurant to support herself and her mother. She often worked from midnight to morning and went directly to school after her shift. The following exchange took place at the start of the second meeting.

School psychologist: "I've thought about our discussion last week, and I just have to ask you, with all the hardships you've had to deal with in your life, how have you resisted the urge to give up on school altogether and quit?"

Angela: "Why would I do that? I've got everything ahead of me and I'm in my senior year. I've made it this far and I'm sure not stopping now."

School psychologist: "Sounds like you have a lot to look forward to."

Angela: "I do. I mean, I'm sure I'll have problems. Everybody does. But I've had it worse than a lot of kids, so I know something about how to handle problems."

School psychologist: "I know you do."

Angela: "I almost gave up 2 or 3 years ago. I wanted to quit school and live somewhere else. But I stayed, and I'm glad I did."

School psychologist: "What's different about the new Angela compared to the old Angela?"

She went on to describe differences between the new Angela and old Angela, all of which revolved around her desire to "make something of her life." Various aspects of her resilient approach to life were incorporated into practical interventions for improving her school attendance and grades. These interventions were designed in collaboration with Angela and included (a) using self-talk strategies to remind herself how difficult it has been to get this far in school and how important it is to stay at it through the second half of the school year, (b) asking her teachers if she could occasionally tutor younger students in science because she wanted to become a teacher and science was one of her better classes, and (c) asking her boss about adjusting her work hours so that she had more time on Thursdays to prepare for tests on Friday. Angela seemed to enjoy the rare opportunity to discuss what was right with her and to build on her personal strengths and assets. Despite some ongoing difficulties at home and school, she passed all of her classes, graduated in May, and made plans to attend a local community college.

Building interventions from students' resilience and other natural resources does not minimize the seriousness and pain of problems such as child abuse, unmet nutritional needs, and other challenges in the lives of students. In the midst of these challenges, however, students are always doing something to survive and cope. In other words, they are being resilient and strong. Helping students to recognize and apply these strengths is a key aim of student-driven interviewing. The practice of fitting interventions to students instead of the other way around is consistent with NASP recommendations that school psychologists show "respect for human diversity" and promote "effective services, advocacy, and social justice for all children" (NASP, 2010, p. 3). In addition to improving outcomes, building interventions from students' unique strengths and resources ensures culturally competent practice (Sue & Sue, 2013).

The success of resource-based interventions rests largely on the student's ability to make sense of these interventions and to apply these interventions in personally meaningful ways (Bohart & Tallman, 2010). In addition to engaging students' attention and energy, resource-driven interventions are more culturally sensitive than practitioner-driven interventions that may bear little resemblance to students' everyday lives. Behavioral improvements that result from resource-based interventions have a good chance of being maintained because they are based on natural elements of the student's life, elements that were there before school psychologists arrived on the scene and will remain there after they leave. In addition to improving intervention outcomes by tapping powerful client factors in the lives of students, the process of discovering and applying students' natural resources is one of the most enjoyable aspects of student-driven interviewing.

Summary of Task 4

Every student has something (resources) and is doing something (exceptions) that can be used to construct positive interventions for school problems. Building solutions from exceptions and other resources is based on the practical idea that it is more efficient to ride a train in the direction it is already going—and to harness what is already available—than it is to turn a school problem completely around or to build solutions from scratch. The strategy of identifying and building on competencies and resources supports the NASP Practice Model's (NASP, 2010) recommendation that school psychologists gain knowledge in assessing student strengths and developing related intervention services. Murphy (2008) provides additional examples of how to partner with students in building interventions from exceptions and other student resources.

Developmental Accommodations

There are several ways that school psychologists can address and accommodate developmental factors when conducting student-driven interviews. The use of simple, jargon-free language is helpful in working with students of all ages, but it is especially important with younger students and those students with cognitive and language difficulties. The format and duration of the meetings with students can be varied. For example, when meeting with a younger student who has a short attention span and a high need for physical movement, the school psychologist can talk for shorter periods of time, take more breaks, or talk with the student while taking a walk around the playground. Like other features of student-driven interviewing, these strategies help school psychologists tailor their approach to each individual student.

(Refer to Murphy [2013] for additional information on developmental considerations in conducting student-driven interviews.)

SUMMARY

Students who experience problems often view themselves as passive players in an adults-only version of school-based intervention. This chapter provides school psychologists with strategies for conducting student-driven interviews, that is, therapeutic, solution-focused conversations aimed at resolving school problems by involving students in every aspect of their care, from setting goals to evaluating the usefulness of school psychology services. This highly collaborative approach is based on a growing body of psychotherapy research suggesting that successful intervention outcomes result largely from structuring services around students' strengths, resources, and feedback. Student-driven interviewing assumes (a) that every student offers strengths and resources that can be incorporated into school-based interventions and that doing so boosts students' self-efficacy, energy, and motivation, and (b) that interviewing students provides a unique opportunity to use the power of language in ways that promote school solutions.

Specific tasks and techniques of this approach include (a) creating a culture of collaboration by arranging the physical setting in respectful ways, using icebreakers to help students ease into the conversation, orienting students to the helping process, and obtaining ongoing student feedback on the usefulness of services; (b) discussing problems in solution-focused ways by validating and prioritizing students' concerns, describing changeable problems, and exploring environmental factors, problem influence, and solution attempts; (c) developing goals that matter by linking students' deepest values to school-related goals, asking miracle and scaling questions, and incorporating students' language and perceptions into goals; and (d) capitalizing on what is right with students by building interventions from exceptions to the problem and from other strengths and resources in the lives of students. School psychologists who are interested in a more detailed description of solution-focused, student-driven interviewing—and dozens of examples involving preschool through secondary students—can refer to Murphy (2013).

AUTHOR NOTE

Disclosure. John J. Murphy has a financial interest in books he authored or coauthored referenced in this chapter. He also has a financial interest in various websites mentioned in this chapter.

REFERENCES

Asay, T. P., & Lambert, M. J. (1999). The empirical case for the common factors in therapy: Quantitative findings. In M. A. Hubble, B. L. Duncan, & S. D. Miller (Eds.), *The heart and soul of change: What works in therapy* (pp. 33–55). Washington, DC: American Psychological Association.

Bandura, A. (2006). Toward a psychology of human agency. *Perspectives on Psychological Science, 1,* 164–180. doi:10.1111/j.1745-6916.2006.00011.x

Bohart, A. C., & Tallman, K. (2010). Clients: The neglected common factor in therapy. In B. L. Duncan, S. D. Miller, B. E. Wampold, & M. A. Hubble (Eds.), *The heart and soul of change: Delivering what works in therapy* (2nd ed., pp. 83–11). Washington, DC: American Psychological Association.

Constantino, M. J., & DeGeorge, J. (2008). Believing is seeing: Clinical implications of research on patient expectations. *Psychotherapy Bulletin, 43,* 1–6.

Duncan, B. L., Miller, S. D., & Sparks, J. A. (2003). *Child Outcome Rating Scale.* Fort Lauderdale, FL: Author.

Duncan, B. L., Miller, S. D., Sparks, J. A., & Johnson, L. D. (2003). *Child Session Rating Scale.* Fort Lauderdale, FL: Author.

Fagan, T. K., & Wise, P. (2007). *School psychology: Past, present, and future* (3rd ed.). Bethesda, MD: National Association of School Psychology.

Franklin, C., Trepper, T. S., Gingerich, W. J., & McCollum, E. E. (Eds.). (2012). *Solution-focused brief therapy: Research, practice, and training.* New York, NY: Oxford University Press.

Gassman, D., & Grawe, K. (2006). General change mechanisms: The relation between problem activation and resource activation in successful and unsuccessful therapeutic interactions. *Clinical Psychology and Psychotherapy, 13,* 1–11. doi:10.1002/cpp.442

Gillaspy, J. A., & Murphy, J. J. (2012). Incorporating outcome and session rating scales in solution-focused brief therapy. In C. Franklin, T. S. Trepper, W. J. Gingerich, & E. E. McCollum (Eds.), *Solution-focused brief therapy: Research, practice, and training* (pp. 73–93). New York, NY: Oxford University Press.

Horvath, A. O., Del Re, A. C., Fluckiger, C., & Symonds, D. (2011). Alliance in individual psychotherapy. In J. C. Norcross (Ed.), *Psychotherapy relationships that work: Evidence-based responsiveness* (2nd ed., pp. 25–69). New York, NY: Oxford University Press.

Johnson, L., Miller, S., & Duncan, B. (2000). *Session Rating Scale (Version 3.0).* Chicago, IL: Author.

Lambert, M. J., & Shimokawa, D. W. (2011). Collecting client feedback. In J. C. Norcross (Ed.), *Psychotherapy relationships that work: Evidence-based responsiveness* (2nd ed., pp. 203–223). New York, NY: Oxford University Press.

McAuliffe, G., and Associates. (2013). *Culturally alert counseling: A comprehensive introduction* (2nd ed.). Thousand Oaks, CA: SAGE.

Miller, S. D., & Duncan, B. (2001). *Outcome Rating Scale.* Chicago, IL: Author.

Miller, S. D., Wampold, B. E., & Varhely, K. (2008). Direct comparisons of treatment modalities for childhood disorders: A meta-analysis. *Psychotherapy Research, 18,* 5–14.

Miller, W. R., & Rollnick, S. (2013). *Motivational interviewing: Helping people change* (3rd ed.). New York, NY: Guilford Press.

Molden, D. C., & Dweck, C. S. (2006). Finding "meaning" in psychology: A lay theories approach to self-regulation, social perception, and social development. *American Psychologist, 61*, 192–203.

Murphy, J. J. (2008). *Solution-focused counseling in schools* (2nd ed.). Alexandria, VA: American Counseling Association.

Murphy, J. J. (2013). *Conducting student-driven interviews: Practical strategies for increasing student involvement and addressing behavior problems.* New York, NY: Routledge.

Murphy, J. J., & Duncan, B. L. (2007). *Brief intervention for school problems* (2nd ed.). New York, NY: Guilford Press.

National Association of School Psychologists. (2008). *The importance of school mental health services* [Position statement]. Bethesda, MD: Author. Retrieved from http://www.nasponline.org/about_nasp/positionpapers/MentalHealthServices.pdf

National Association of School Psychologists. (2010). *Model for comprehensive and integrative school psychological services.* Bethesda, MD: Author. Retrieved from http://www.nasponline.org/standards/2010standards/2_PracticeModel.pdf

Norcross, J. C. (2010). The therapeutic relationship. In B. L. Duncan, S. D. Miller, B. E. Wampold, & M. A. Hubble (Eds.), *The heart and soul of change: Delivering what works in therapy* (2nd ed., pp. 113–141). Washington, DC: American Psychological Association.

Shirk, S. R., Jungbluth, N., & Karver, M. (2012). Change processes and active components. In P. C. Kendall (Ed.), *Child and adolescent therapy: Cognitive-behavioral procedures* (4th ed., pp. 471–498). New York, NY: Guilford Press.

Shirk, S. R., Karver, M. S., & Brown, R. (2011). The alliance in child and adolescent psychotherapy. *Psychotherapy, 48*, 17–24. doi:10.1037/a0022181

Sue, D. W., & Sue, D. (2013). *Counseling the culturally diverse: Theory and practice* (6th ed.). Hoboken, NJ: Wiley.

Wampold, B. E. (2010). The research evidence for the common factors models: A historically situated perspective. In B. L. Duncan, S. D. Miller, B. E. Wampold, & M. A. Hubble (Eds.), *The heart and soul of change: Delivering what works in therapy* (2nd ed., pp. 49–81). Washington, DC: American Psychological Association.

21 Best Practices in Group Counseling

Julie C. Herbstrith
Western Illinois University
Renée M. Tobin
Illinois State University

OVERVIEW

It is estimated that 20–25% of children and adolescents experience mental health problems at some point (Ghandour, Kogan, Blumberg, Jones, & Perrin, 2012). Some of these problems are diagnosable mental health disorders, whereas others are less severe yet still present serious challenges for those who experience them. For some children, particularly those already at risk due to various contextual factors, these circumstances lead to negative outcomes that range from academic failure and behavioral difficulties to psychopathology in adulthood. The heightened awareness about mental health issues in children and adolescents has prompted the emergence of services in the public sector (e.g., government agencies), the private sector, and the education sector (Farmer, Burns, Philip, Angold, & Costello, 2003). Despite the growth in services, most children and adolescents do not receive treatment for mental health problems.

Personnel in school systems are experiencing increased demand to provide services that target both academic and socioemotional issues (Millar, Lean, Sweet, Moraes, & Nelson, 2013; Suldo, Friedrich, & Michalowski, 2010). In addition to learning problems, school psychologists are trained to address behavioral and social–emotional functioning in children and adolescents. Further, school psychologists have a sophisticated understanding of the connection between mental health and learning. School psychologists' unique placement in the school environment allows them to use their skills to help children meet challenges and overcome barriers to achieve healthy outcomes. Moreover, school psychologists report a desire to engage

in mental health service delivery (Suldo et al., 2010). Group counseling is one type of service delivery that is consistent with the National Association of School Psychologists (NASP) *Model of Comprehensive and Integrated School Psychological Services* (NASP, 2010) domain of Interventions and Mental Health Services to Develop Social and Life Skills, which calls for school psychologists to engage in practices that integrate mental health services into other types of services delivered in schools.

This chapter outlines a four-stage model designed to guide school psychologists in the design, implementation, and evaluation of counseling groups. Group counseling interventions are framed within a three-tiered model of service delivery. This chapter also provides helpful information about conducting groups in the school setting, from logistical concerns, such as finding space and time, to potential treatment barriers, such as administrative roadblocks. In addition, this chapter provides the most up-to-date information about existing evidence-based group counseling interventions. Finally, this chapter provides school psychologists with additional resources regarding school-based group counseling.

BASIC CONSIDERATIONS

The role and function of school psychologists is varied, but a common theme for most school-based practitioners is a shortage of time to deliver needed services. Simply put, many school psychologists struggle to fit all of their duties into the school day. As such, efficiency in service delivery is critical. Given the rising demand for mental health services, group counseling is a method of service delivery that has a number of advantages.

Beyond the efficiency of group interventions, there is considerable evidence in the treatment literature that group counseling is effective for both psychoeducational and psychosocial needs (Crespi, 2009). Moreover, there is evidence that group treatment is as effective as individual treatment (DeLucia-Waack, Kalodner, & Riva, 2013). Because of its effectiveness and efficiency, group counseling has become the preferred method of service delivery for many school-based practitioners.

Nature of Groups

In addition to the efficiency and effectiveness of conducting groups in schools, there is another key advantage to this mode of service delivery and that is the nature of groups themselves. A well-established list of therapeutic factors has been documented to facilitate intervention goals (Yalom & Leszcz, 2005). The most relevant therapeutic factors for groups of children and adolescents are universality, group cohesiveness, and feedback on interpersonal skills (Shechtman & Gluk, 2005). Universality is the realization that one's problems are not unique, but that other people also struggle with similar situations or problems. Group cohesiveness is the feeling of support and caring that emanates from the group. This factor is important because it facilitates participation in group activities and it encourages self-disclosure. The third factor, feedback on interpersonal skills, is central to progress toward participant goals that are aimed at interpersonal behavior change. Group counseling gives students multiple opportunities to practice the new skills they acquire during sessions with more than one practice partner. Practicing new social and communication skills in an environment in which students feel safe is important.

School Setting

The school setting has other advantages for group counseling as well. One obvious one is that most children go to school. It is well documented that many children who need services do not receive it because of treatment barriers such as transportation issues, financial limitations, and parents' inability to take time off work (Kazdin & Wassell, 1999). These barriers are readily eliminated when group therapy is offered as part of other school services. Another advantage of group counseling in schools is that the nature of groups is familiar to children, who are socialized to work in groups from the time they enter their school years. Children learn from an early age how to work together

in groups and they are familiar with the idea that groups typically have rules. Therefore, becoming part of a new group would probably not be perceived as unusual.

Group Counseling Within the Multitiered Model

Similar to other types of interventions, group counseling interventions can be conceptualized using a multitiered model of intervention in which the level of service delivery corresponds to the scope of intended members at Tiers 1, 2, and 3. Tier 1 counseling groups are typically prevention focused and are targeted toward large groups of students (often entire classrooms, grades, or even school buildings). In fact, Tier 1 groups are primarily made up of nonreferred group members, as exemplified by groups that target violence prevention and character education.

A primary advantage to a Tier 1 counseling group is the increased likelihood that its members will avoid future problems (Hoag & Burlingame, 1997). A secondary advantage is that Tier 1 groups can be easier than other groups from a logistical standpoint. Ready-made groups, such as a second-grade class, already have group norms and rules in place, and group cohesiveness may already exist as well. These are time saving for the facilitator who can begin the group by targeting the predetermined intervention goals rather than working on introductions and icebreaking activities. A third key advantage is that Tier 1 groups promote positive development for everyone, not just children who are referred. Many children who would benefit from services never receive mental health diagnoses (Farmer et al., 2003), thus Tier 1 interventions reach children who might otherwise not receive services. School psychologists are also able to build capacity with Tier 1 group counseling interventions and thereby reach far more children who could benefit from services.

Tier 2 counseling groups are interventions for children who may be at higher risk than the general population for developing certain problems. Tier 2 groups are sometimes referred to as psychoeducational groups (DeLucia-Waack, 2006), and are often designed to reduce risk factors and build on protective factors. Examples of such groups include those conducted with children and adolescents who struggle with social skills and social problem solving. Although these students may not exhibit a high degree of emotional or behavioral problems, their current levels of social competence are suboptimal and therefore place them at an increased risk to develop more significant problems over time. Groups that target social skills deficits provide students with a safe space to learn and practice new behaviors and strategies.

Tier 2 groups are also a viable choice for children and adolescents who experience a significant life event or change, such as divorce or loss. Although their prior social–emotional status may have been typical, an event or change may put them at increased risk for adjustment problems. A primary advantage of Tier 2 groups in these instances is the presence of the therapeutic factors of universality and group cohesiveness, which may serve to normalize emergent problems.

The third level of the multitiered model includes the most intensive types of group counseling for children and adolescents who are struggling with significant issues such as anxiety or depression. In contrast to other groups, students are referred for services at this level. These students are often identified through building-level team meetings addressing the needs of students who may require special education services. Another important distinction between Tier 3 groups and other tier levels is that services are aimed at remediation. As an example, a Tier 3 group for children with depression often targets irrational thought processes, cognitive distortions, and dysfunctional behavior patterns, much like intensive, individual counseling does (DeLucia-Waack, 2006).

Ethical Practice

As with any type of service delivery, it is important for school psychologists to adhere to ethical guidelines (Crespi, 2009). These guidelines dictate that all services be evidence based and delivered within the realm of the practitioner's competency. In addition, school psychologists recognize and are prepared for instances in which a student's needs exceed the level of services that can be provided at school. In addition, Nicholson, Foote, and Grigerick (2009) identified instances in which group counseling may produce deleterious effects (e.g., scared straight and Project DARE programs). Finally, school psychologists are aware of the importance of establishing collaborative relationships with community agencies. Some children and adolescents who need treatment beyond what can be provided in schools do not receive it, and the likely cause is a weak or nonexistent link between schools and other community agencies and resources (Farmer et al., 2003).

School psychologists recognize that, in addition to meeting academic goals, successful students are able to engage in appropriate behavior in school. Further, as noted by Crespi (2009), they recognize that academic performance is tied to psychological adjustment. Group counseling is a tool that can be used at all three tier levels to help children and adolescents succeed.

Multicultural and Diversity Considerations

School psychologists are committed to multicultural competence in service delivery, including group counseling. As an example that may be relevant to group counseling, some students come from families in which the collective interest, or the good of the community, is more important than any one person's interest (DeLucia-Waack, 2006). On a related note, self-disclosure is often an important part of group work but across cultures there are varying levels of shame, or stigma, related to mental health problems. Therefore, it may be difficult, if not extremely distressing, for some children to disclose that they have problems, particularly in front of peers. Further, family members of these students may find group counseling unacceptable for these reasons. In sum, it is important to consider the cultural background of potential group members so that differences may be addressed in appropriate ways when relevant.

Counseling groups can be conducted with culture as an important contextual variable within the group. That is, group members can be encouraged to think about problems in the context of their own cultures. As an example, students might participate in an activity in which they relate their actions to values they hold. Cultural issues will likely play less of a part in groups with young children than they might in groups with adolescents due to developmental differences. Thus, incorporating a balance of activities that highlight both individuality and the group identity may be beneficial (DeLucia-Waack, 2006).

BEST PRACTICES IN GROUP COUNSELING

We present a four-stage model of best practices for delivering school-based group counseling services. The model is based on the most recent research in school psychology and related fields (e.g., school counseling, school social work, child clinical psychology) and it provides guidelines to assist practitioners in designing, implementing, and evaluating the effectiveness of school-based group counseling.

Stage 1: Group Development

As with other intervention services, the first step in the process is to identify a service need that can be met using a group format. It is critical for the school psychologist to understand the specific needs of youth in the school and to ensure that the intervention meets those needs.

Needs Assessment

In terms of specific approaches, school psychologists should plan to orient teachers, administrators, and parents to group counseling through memos, newsletters, or meetings (e.g., PTA or faculty inservice trainings). Through these means, school psychologists should conduct a needs assessment by asking what kinds of issues the constituents would like to see addressed. As part of a needs assessment, it is possible to assess teacher, parent, and student perceptions of need and explain the basic purposes and benefits of groups during the same meeting. Initial needs assessments serve as the foundation for a systematic program evaluation.

Like other intervention services provided by school psychologists, one key to ensuring a successful group counseling program is communication and collaboration with teachers and administrators (Schmidt, 2014). Collaborative partnerships between school psychologists, teachers, administrators, and other staff members are essential, particularly when schools operate within a three-tiered model that is designed to serve all students at the universal level. The success of group work in schools is enhanced when school faculty members, administrators, and the community (e.g., families) are supportive and cooperative of their implementation (Schmidt, 2014). Once groups have been developed based on the school's needs, school psychologists should announce topics and basic group goals to the faculty and staff. They should consider making regular announcements about upcoming groups that will be conducted and continue to listen for opportunities to meet student needs using group formats.

Determining Level of Intervention

An initial step in implementing a counseling group is to determine what kind of group is needed. This decision depends on the appropriate level of intervention based on the school's needs and the referral concerns. If the school identifies needs that are prevention oriented, then the group probably falls into Tier 1, which means that entire classes, grades, or schools receive the intervention. These types of interventions tend to focus on bolstering students' knowledge or skills in an area. Tier 1 interventions are often provided by teachers and/or other school personnel (e.g., school social workers, school counselors), with a school psychologist playing a supportive, consultative role in their implementation,

especially when introducing an intervention for the first time (Stormont, Thomas, & Van Garderen, 2012). For example, when district or school leaders decide to implement a social–emotional learning curriculum to all students, a school psychologist is well poised to provide consultation, training, and support during the process.

If referral concerns indicate that some students may be at higher risk for certain problems, a group developed to address these risks would fall under Tier 2, a level of intervention that is appropriate for students who are at risk of future problems. As an example, an event in the community (e.g., trauma, natural disaster) may trigger problems in a group of students who had not previously demonstrated problems but who now may be experiencing adjustment issues. These Tier 2 groups may be conducted by a school psychologist or by other school personnel with support and consultation provided by the school psychologist as needed. A group developed in response to referrals, including self-referrals, about specific issues (e.g., depression, anxiety) would fall under Tier 3, the most intensive level of intervention. To reiterate from the previous section, Tier 3 groups tend to form based on referrals that are part of special education decisions. Given the severity of needs and the possibility of special education involvement, school psychologists are a likely to provide these Tier 3 interventions.

Stage 2: Group Logistics

As with any school-based intervention, providing group counseling in a school setting requires advanced planning and other specific considerations. These issues include logistical ones as well as more substantive ones.

Setting the Stage for Group Counseling

Implementing a group intervention requires special attention to issues such as school buy-in, counselor qualifications, participant selection, and intervention choice. Once these issues are addressed, successful group counseling requires attention to logistical issues, such as the identification of an appropriate, available space and a suitable time for the group to meet. Before the group begins, collecting preintervention data is key to determining the effectiveness of the intervention over time.

Selecting Group Facilitators

The knowledge of theoretical approaches required to conduct group counseling is the same as is required to provide individual counseling (Sink, Edwards, & Eppler, 2013; Schmidt, 2014).

Qualifications. School psychologists have training in both education and mental health and therefore they are a logical choice to provide a range of group counseling services (Suldo et al., 2010). That said, it is important to ascertain that practitioners work within their range of competency. Although facilitators with less extensive clinical backgrounds can implement some group counseling interventions, several general skills are necessary for anyone to be an effective facilitator. These skills include demonstrating empathy, listening skills, and the generation of statements that clarify, summarize, and reflect on group members' contributions (Yalom, 1995). Effective facilitators are also skilled at connecting one group member's statement to another event or statement, which facilitates generalization (DeLucia-Waack et al., 2013). In his influential book on group therapy, Yalom (1995) discusses important therapeutic factors like universality and cohesiveness that are central to successful treatment. Effective facilitators must also have the abilities to use appropriate self-disclosure and to model appropriate interpersonal behavior. Facilitators must be able to deliver positive and negative feedback and provide support for group members to engage in these processes as well.

In general, the level of intensity of the intervention dictates the amount of clinical training required to implement a given group (Clarke, Lewinsohn, & Hyman, 1990). Practitioners with limited clinical training can often effectively facilitate Tier 1 universal groups, especially when school psychologists provide support (Stormont et al., 2012). Some universal counseling interventions are available as manualized treatments and can be readily delivered by persons with various professional backgrounds. A note of caution about manualized treatments, however, is that they vary considerably in terms of (a) the degree to which they are evidence based and (b) the extent of empirical support they have as effective interventions for a given population. It is important that school psychologists be good consumers of the available research literature and that they consult with other professionals when needed to verify the suitability of any program (including both self-made and commercially available ones) before implementing it.

As with other forms of intervention, as the intensity of student needs increases so do the qualifications of the practitioner in terms of therapeutic training. This is especially true of Tier 1 and 2 groups. Pérusse, Goodnough, and Lee (2009) suggest that an effective group leader will (a) understand students from multiple developmental perspectives such as age or cognitive ability; (b) be competent in the content area; (c) understand group dynamics; and (d) understand contextual factors about group members such as ethnicity, world view, or sexual orientation.

Ideally, two facilitators will colead counseling groups at all tier levels. In line with best practices, Tier 2 counseling groups must have at least one facilitator with some clinical training and experience conducting groups (Waterman & Walker, 2009). Relative to groups conducted at Tiers 1 and 2, counseling groups at Tier 3 require the greatest level of clinical training. Examples of common group coleaders are social workers, school counselors, other student support services personnel (e.g., tutors, teachers of gifted programs), and teachers and staff members from behavior disorders/emotional disturbances classrooms.

Benefits of coleaders. If feasible, conducting groups with more than one facilitator has several advantages. First, the responsibility for planning and preparing group sessions is shared. Suldo et al. (2010) found that time constraints were one reason that school psychologists do not conduct groups in schools. Sharing responsibilities for preparation and planning reduces the amount of time a practitioner must spend on these activities. Sharing responsibilities also facilitates transitions within group sessions: While one leader is finishing up an activity, the other leader can prepare for the next one so that down time is reduced and structure is maintained.

Group work with children and adolescents often has a degree of structure to it so that it runs smoothly. A pragmatic reason to conduct groups with coleaders is the ability for one leader to continue a group activity even in the event that a behavioral issue arises with a group member that requires the attention of the other group leader. Coleaders are better able to manage the behavior of a group, particularly with young children and children with attention problems. Also, having two leaders allows the group to meet even if a leader is absent due to illness or other circumstances. Efforts should be made, however, to include all group leaders at every session for therapeutic continuity.

Coleaders often provide therapeutic value in group counseling in that they model appropriate social exchanges and communication skills when they interact with each other during groups. For example, group members often learn prosocial behaviors through modeling. Coleaders also work together to facilitate both the content and process of the group. Content consists of the skill areas that are the focus of the group session, whereas process consists of statements that often describe what is happening in the group in terms of both verbal and nonverbal reactions of group members. Process statements often serve to provide interpersonal feedback to group members or to move a stalled group out of silence. When working with a group of active children or adolescents, having two group leaders increases the opportunities to use both types of therapeutic techniques.

Participant Selection

Group counseling is not appropriate for all children and adolescents. As a general rule, students who are in crisis or who are deemed dangerous to themselves or others cannot participate in the group (Ehly & Garcia-Vazquez, 1998; Sink et al., 2013). In these cases, students should be referred for more appropriate, individualized services. Beyond students who are in crisis, however, it is important to consider students who may not be fit for group counseling for other reasons. Nicholson et al. (2009) suggest that serious concerns remain about treating children and adolescents with behavior disorders in groups. Further, they note that students who present with serious aggressive and/or antisocial tendencies should be considered for Tier 2 types of social skills groups with great caution because they tend to show little behavior change and, in fact, may experience negative outcomes. Students who are particularly shy or anxious should probably not participate in group counseling either (Manassis et al., 2002). As previously indicated, these situations warrant referrals to more appropriate services such as individual counseling.

Other considerations for participation in group counseling include cognitive ability and developmental level. Meaningful participation in groups depends on the ability of each member to actively participate in the group. Therefore, children who have difficulties due to factors such as cognitive ability level or symptom severity may not be appropriately suited for group counseling. As an example, children with limited capacity for abstract thinking may make the counseling process more complicated for children who are struggling with grief (Stubenbort & Cohen, 2006). Developmental level should be considered in participant selection as well. School psychologists should use their knowledge of child development to determine whether students are suited for a particular group. Also, most manualized treatments include information that guides practitioners in determining which students make suitable candidates for group counseling.

In general, participants are selected through a screening process. The decision about the type of screening that is needed naturally follows from the decision about the tier at which the intervention fits. For Tier 1 groups, minimal screening is necessary because the group content is usually suitable for all students. For groups that fall under Tiers 2 and 3, however, screening potential group members becomes more important. Although every situation is unique to the presenting referral concerns, there are some general best practice guidelines for participant selection.

Heterogeneity versus homogeneity. Homogeneous groups consist of members with more similarities than differences, whereas heterogeneous groups have members with various backgrounds and issues. Homogeneity can be defined according to same gender, age, grade level, ethnicity, referral concern, or a variety of other classifying factors. In general, less intensive interventions (e.g., universal, prevention) are better suited to heterogeneous populations, whereas more intensive interventions (e.g., Tier 2 or 3) are better suited to homogeneous populations (Ehly & Garcia-Vazquez, 1998).

When making this decision, it is important to consider the specific nature of the group. As an example, developing a psychoeducational group on personal hygiene may be better suited to a group of children of the same sex, whereas a group designed to teach friendship skills may be more effective with a heterogeneous group. It is important to consult the current research literature and other professionals when designing a group-level intervention.

Group size. Counseling groups will vary in size, primarily as a function of the tier level into which it fits. Tier 1 groups are usually larger than groups in other tiers because they are offered as universal interventions for entire classrooms or other naturally occurring groups. The size of the group for Tier 2 and 3 groups typically include 6–10 participants (Waterman & Walker, 2009). This range in size is effective because it facilitates therapeutic factors such as group cohesiveness without being intimidating for students (Yalom, 1995).

Closed versus open groups. Closed groups are usually preferred over open groups because they create structure and predictability for group members. Additionally, successful groups for children and adolescents typically include group rules that are determined early on in group sessions. In fact, many practitioners use the entire first session as an orientation to group structure, rules, and goals (Sink et al., 2013). Therefore, it is important for members not to miss this initial session. Another advantage to closed groups is that they fit better with manualized counseling programs that structure activities and goals over the course of a predetermined number of sessions. Finally, closed groups allow members to develop group cohesiveness, the therapeutic factor that promotes sharing and sympathy (Yalom & Leszcz, 2005).

In contrast to closed groups, open groups allow new members to join the group at any time. Generally, open groups are conducted over long periods of time (i.e., for an entire semester or school year). Psychoeducational or guidance groups may be suitable for an open format because students work on general skill development, problem solving, or communication skills (Association for Specialists in Group Work, 2000). Open group formats are also useful in schools in which students tend to relocate frequently. In this instance, it would be difficult to sustain groups if open membership were not allowed.

Informed consent/assent. School psychologists are legally and ethically bound to obtain informed consent from a parent or legal guardian before providing services to children or adolescents. Informed consent should include information about (a) the nature and purpose of the group, (b) the group facilitator, and (c) the duration of the group. Practitioners should be certain to follow local and state laws carefully.

Manualized Treatments

A manualized treatment program is one that has been developed and published to meet specific treatment goals for a specific population. Manualized treatments typically contain step-by-step instructions for each session. There are preplanned objectives and activities for each session and many, and in some cases all, of the materials needed to conduct each session are provided. High quality manualized treatment programs are often empirically supported as effective interventions when used appropriately. On a cautionary note, it is important to review the data related to the effectiveness of the intervention for treating the targeted population carefully prior to implementing a published manualized treatment. Table 21.1 provides select evidence-based treatment for some disorders along with full references and links to resources, where available. Reputable online resources are also available to ease the task of

evaluating the merits of a particular intervention before investing time and/or money in it.

Scheduling

After constituents' needs, group facilitators, participants, and an appropriate intervention have been identified, several logistical concerns must be addressed to implement a group effectively. Generally, counseling groups meet once per week for 8–12 weeks. Eight sessions may be ideal for school-based groups because they fit cleanly into one school quarter. Eight sessions are also often sufficient for the development of group cohesiveness (Yalom & Leszcz, 2005). One key to a successful group-counseling program is coordinating groups within the school's existing schedule. Ideally, individual session length will match existent time blocks so that group members only miss one academic period, if any. Consistent with this goal, it is critical to incorporate enough transition time before and after the session to reduce disruptions from students walking in and out of the classroom. In addition, a smooth transition increases the amount of time that is actually spent doing group work.

When scheduling a group, it is also important to be considerate of the demands on teachers to meet their curriculum goals. When providing universal interventions, try to match the content of the group to the academic curriculum. For example, the Adolescent Coping with Depression Course, a well-established, manualized treatment for depression, is adaptable for use in entire classrooms as a depression prevention program (Clarke et al., 1990). This topic is likely to match well within a health class curriculum. Coordinating the simultaneous delivery of this group with the health teacher's curriculum provides the teacher with assistance in meeting his or her goals as an educator. This alignment of services is consistent with the commitment of school psychologists to work together with other service providers in the school to enhance children's learning and development.

When planning what time of day to conduct Tier 2 or Tier 3 groups, keep in mind that pulling students from key academic curricula (e.g., math, science) is not recommended because missing what is covered in those courses may be detrimental to student learning. Care must be taken, however, to avoid consistently pulling students from specialty classes such as music, art, or physical education (Sink et al., 2013; Schmidt, 2014). If possible, schedule groups during times when no instruction will be disrupted (e.g., after school, recess, lunch, study hall).

Table 21.1. Select Evidence-Based Group Counseling Programs

Disorder	Program	Reference	Link to Materials
Anxiety	Group CBT[a] FRIENDS[b]	Weissman, Antinoro, & Chu (2008) Barrett (1998)	http://www.friendsinfo.net/
Social phobia	Group CBT[a]	Rapee, Wignall, Hudson, & Schniering (2000)	
	Social Effectiveness Training (SET-C)[a]	Beidel & Turner (1998)	http://www.mhs.com/product.aspx?gr=edu&prod=setc&id=overview
Depression	Penn Prevention Program[a]	Gillham et al. (2007)	http://www.ppc.sas.upenn.edu/prpsum.htm
	Self-control therapy[a] (children only) CBT group[c] (adolescents only)	Stark, Reynolds, & Kaslow (1987) Clark et al. (1995)	
	Adolescents Coping with Depression (CWD-A)[a]	Mufson et al. (2004)	http://www.kpchr.org/research/public/acwd/acwd.html
ODD/CD	Group Anger Control Training[b] Rational-Emotive Mental Health Program[a]	Lochman, Barry, & Pardini (2003) Block (1978)	http://effectivechildtherapy.com/sites/default/files/files/pro_REEmanual.pdf
PTSD	Group CBT[b]	Kataoka et al. (2003)	
Substance abuse	Group CBT[c] (adolescents)	Mackay, Donovan, & Marlatt (1991)	

Note. Interventions are classified according to the guidelines presented in Chambless et al. (1996). CBT = cognitive–behavioral therapy; ODD/CD = oppositional defiant disorder/conduct disorder; PTSD = posttraumatic stress disorder.

[a]Probably efficacious; [b]possibly efficacious; [c]well established.

When facilitating groups for adolescents, it is often impossible to avoid disrupting some academic instruction time because potential group participants are attending different content courses throughout the school day. In these situations, it is worthwhile to consider a staggered schedule (Schmidt, 2014), such that the group meets during a different time period each week, allowing participants to miss a particular class occasionally instead of regularly. For example, a group for adolescent girls with depression may meet on Mondays during first period during the first week, during second period during the second week, during third period during the third week, and so on, before cycling back to first period. Another possibility is to alternate days for the group, particularly in schools with different patterns for each day of the week (e.g., Monday-Wednesday-Friday schedules are different than Tuesday-Thursday ones). A third possibility is to alternate between two to four time periods, so that each class is only missed once every 2 weeks or more. Again, communicating with constituents and problem solving is critical to minimizing disruption and maximizing satisfaction. In all cases, developing a clear system of reminding group members of the next meeting time is essential to success of a group.

Supplies and Space

The supplies and space needed to conduct groups in schools varies according to the age of the group participants, the type of group, and the available resources. Two of the most important factors that guide the decision about location of the group sessions are privacy and lack of distractions. To that end, consider posting a schedule of group sessions on the door of the room in use or send staff members and teachers a list of the scheduled meeting times and place for the group. In addition, posting a "do not disturb" sign during group sessions can also minimize disruptions.

As mentioned previously, all groups should be conducted in a space that is private, clear of distractions, and comfortable for the members and facilitators (Schmidt, 2014). Often school psychologists face limited space availability in their schools, and therefore creativity is sometimes necessary to find an appropriate meeting location. Options should be considered such as the empty cafeteria or the auditorium stage or an administrator may be asked if it is possible to reserve a regular meeting time in a conference room. Sometimes the nature of the group will determine the space requirements. For example, a group that employs recreational activities requires a gymnasium or

playground. In contrast, a group that targets everyone (e.g., a prevention group) may be most easily conducted within the classroom.

The type of equipment and supplies needed to conduct groups varies based on the nature of the group. Many groups require few supplies—paper, pencils, and markers will suffice—whereas other groups may require specific equipment to facilitate group activities. For example, a group designed to increase cooperation among peers might use athletic equipment such as a basketball or jump rope to facilitate an interpersonal activity. Similarly, a group designed to target collaborative problem-solving skills might require several different objects for presentation to participants for use as targets of brainstorming activities.

Tangible rewards or prizes are often necessary supplies to conduct groups successfully. Many groups are designed around behavioral contingencies (e.g., positive reinforcers) so a treasure chest or bag of small prizes may be collected to serve as rewards for positive behaviors. A variety of rewards can be included in the treasure chest, including edible reinforcers like popcorn, juice, candy, fruit, or soda. To maximize positive behavior during group sessions, the school psychologist should consider using part of the first session to conduct a reinforcement assessment. Members should be asked to choose preferred items from a generated list. The list might include tangible items such as food and small prizes (e.g., trading cards, inexpensive games, markers, pencils) and intangible items (e.g., chance to be group leader for 5 minutes, a free pass for extra computer time in class provided there is teacher consent, 5 minutes of group time to chat with their peers or use electronics).

Group contingency rewards are especially helpful in facilitating group counseling. Some groups are designed to elicit group cooperation to complete a specific task, and if the group successfully completes the task, a group prize is awarded. Group prizes may consist of tangible items for each group member or fun activities for the group (e.g., a popcorn party, a trip to the playground). These group-level rewards allow for effective behavior management and add to the cohesiveness of the group. Regardless of the rewards selected, it is crucial that the contingency plan be directly tied to the group rules. Importantly, group rules should be explicit in terms of what students should do with their rewards once they have earned them. One sensible rule is that all tangible prizes must be put away in students' backpacks until they get home from school. In many cases, it is possible to identify reinforcers that can be consumed or completed during group sessions. Efforts to identify nontangible reinforcers pay off financially, socially, and philosophically, making the reinforcement assessment worthwhile in preparing for any school-based intervention.

Precounseling Assessment

Decisions about interventions should be guided by data. Moreover, data collection is continuous in that it should be collected prior to intervention (i.e., baseline), during intervention (i.e., progress monitoring), and postintervention (e.g., treatment evaluation). Group counseling is no exception to this practice. As participants are being selected for participation in a group, baseline data should be collected. Participants should be assessed in terms of their current functioning in the targeted area, and data should be collected from multiple informants across multiple settings.

Tier 1 precounseling assessment may consist of teacher or parent ratings scales designed to assess areas targeted for intervention such as prosocial behavior or communication skills. Since interventions at this tier are often class-wide, it is important to consider the amount of time it takes to complete surveys for each participant. Teachers will appreciate brief scales in these instances. Some manualized treatments have precounseling assessment forms included as part of the package.

In instances where students have been referred for group counseling, the source of the referral should be part of the data collection process. Teachers are often the referral source and therefore play a key role in treatment evaluation (Sportsman, Carlson, & Guthrie, 2010). Some methods of precounseling assessment include record reviews (e.g., behavioral incidents, attendance, tardiness), behavior ratings scales, interviews, and observations. Using a problem-solving model, targeted impairments should be operationally defined and objectively measured at baseline (before the intervention). Functional behavior assessment may be a useful tool, especially in instances of externalizing problems. In addition to collecting data from the referral sources, it is important that group participants provide preintervention self-report data whenever possible.

Stage 3: Group Implementation

Counseling children and adolescents in groups is an activity that requires structure to be efficient and effective. Once a group has been planned in line with the aforementioned guidelines, issues of structuring successful group sessions move to the foreground.

Structure

The first session is critical because it frames the overall tone of the group throughout its duration (Schmidt, 2014). During the first session, leaders typically establish rules and limits of the group and discuss issues of confidentiality. Coverage of these topics at the outset provides structure and support for group members.

Often discussion of confidentiality requires a significant portion of the first meeting session because of its central importance to group members, particularly with groups conducted at Tiers 2 and 3. Similar to providing other types of services, school psychologists are obligated to follow NASP ethical guidelines regarding confidentiality procedures. These guidelines include explaining confidentiality to group members and discussing situations in which it must be breached (e.g., when self-harm or harm to others is indicated). Also related to confidentiality, school psychologists must use caution when discussing group counseling issues with other professionals working the schools. Breaches of confidentiality are a serious matter and the welfare and dignity of the client is of foremost importance. Therefore, school psychologists should be prepared to convey this information to any potential group cofacilitator who may not be aware of these issues.

The discussion of confidentiality with group members often leads to the development of a contract, signed by all group members and the facilitators, that clearly states the goals and rules (including confidentiality) for the group. Establishing the group rules helps to structure the intervention and the behavioral expectations for group members. Once established, group rules should be posted in a conspicuous location to serve as a helpful reminder to group members. To aid in managing the group, these rules often include specific behavioral contingencies, as discussed previously. Early in the intervention, group members usually determine a name for their group, which serves to facilitate group cohesiveness. Finally, group members should have a firm understanding of the duration of the group and adequate preparation for its termination. That is, members need to know how many sessions there will be, what termination is, and when it will occur. As with other counseling methods, discussion of termination increases as the time nears.

General Counseling Strategies

It is of primary importance to consider the developmental needs and limitations of each group member. Some students may be unable to participate in activities that require a high degree of abstract thinking, for example. Generally, the younger the members are, the more structured and less abstract activities they will require. Younger children also require shorter duration for all activities and the overall sessions. A helpful way to plan activities for group counseling involves using the three Ps: person, process, and purpose (Trotzer, 2004).

Process refers to what happens during the group. Activities should be designed to initiate group interaction and facilitate the development of comfort and security within the group. Planned activities for each session provide a sense of structure and reduce the ambiguity for group members who learn to anticipate what will happen during group sessions. Over time, activities should facilitate the degree of risk taken by members. That is, activities should help to develop a group norm for sharing, and group members should be increasingly willing to self-disclose in the group. As stated previously, having coleaders is ideal because one leader can attend to group processes while the other leader manages the planned activity.

The purpose of the group refers to the goals and objectives that are identified at the outset of the group (DeLucia-Waack et al., 2013). In addition to group processes that tend to occur rather naturally through group member interaction, the goals and objectives of the group are achieved through planned group activities. Ideally, activities will work in parallel with group processes by integrating what has occurred during group with the group's goals. As a cautionary note, it is possible to become too dependent on activities and lose sight of the issues and goals for the group (DeLucia-Waack et al., 2013).

In addition to in-session activities, homework is an effective way to help group members meet their goals. Successfully completing homework provides group members feelings of accomplishment. It also fosters the therapeutic factor of group cohesiveness because it provides an opportunity for group members to share in a common experience. Further, homework promotes generalization of new skills to environments beyond the group. Developing homework requires that practitioners consider each group member's cognitive and developmental level. Homework assignments must be achievable for all group members if they are to advance the goals and objectives of the group.

Theoretical orientation. Most school psychologists have had some clinical training and therefore have developed a theoretical orientation or an approach to counseling. A practitioner's theoretical orientation is the lens through which he or she interprets behavior, and it

may play a substantial role in group counseling (Cooley, 2009). One's theoretical orientation often encapsulates a group leader's ideas about how behavior change occurs. Therefore, it underlies the counseling techniques that are used, group structure and activities, and goal setting. A solution-focused theoretical orientation may mesh well with group work in schools because it focuses on building strengths rather than on a disciplinary approach (Cooley, 2009).

It has also been suggested that theoretical orientation does not matter as much as the practitioner's belief in the approach to group counseling. Kehle, Bray, and Pérusse (2009) elaborate by suggesting that school psychologists focus on an overarching goal to promote psychological wellness. They use the acronym RICH to refer to four components of good group counseling: resources, intimacy, competence, and health. According to Kehle et al. (2009), focusing on these components is an equally effective way to deliver group-counseling services in the schools. Regardless of how practitioners define their theoretical orientation, best practices suggest an approach in which practitioners understand how their ideas about behavior change translates into how they deliver group counseling.

Specific Counseling Strategies

Specific group counseling techniques are often tied to the type of problem that is being targeted and are based on the theoretical underpinnings of the treatment. As such, a discussion of all possible strategies and techniques is beyond the scope of this chapter. However, Table 21.1 provides information about select treatment manuals that contain detailed explanations of these strategies. As just one example, adolescents who are struggling with symptoms of depression are more likely to experience impaired peer relations (Allen et al., 2006). Therefore, one component of group therapy for depressed adolescents is social skills development. Specific activities to build social skills include teaching students active listening skills, conversation skills, and conflict resolution. These skills are introduced during group sessions in different ways.

The following example comes from the Adolescent Coping with Depression manualized treatment protocol (Clarke et al., 1990). The objective of this session is to introduce this initial step of conversation starting to group members. In this case, one social skill, starting a conversation, is broken down into discrete steps and explained clearly. In the first step, facilitators teach group members to determine whether it is appropriate to start a conversation in different situations. A group leader would use a whiteboard to make two columns (appropriate and inappropriate). Then the group leader would describe various situations to the group and solicit opinions about whether they are appropriate situations for starting a conversation. Once finished, group leaders might role-play situations and ask members to determine whether the situation is appropriate for starting a conversation. Then, group members participate in their own role-plays, with other group members serving as observers.

As with other manualized treatment protocols, homework often plays a vital role and group members are usually assigned tasks to complete outside of group time. In this example, homework might include asking group members to record their own observations of situations they encounter over the next week and to rate these situations in terms of their appropriateness. When the group reconvenes, the homework serves as a discussion point and, if the group leaders determine that members are ready, the next step in building conversation skills would take place.

Progress Monitoring

School psychologists are aware of the importance of monitoring the effectiveness of interventions. In addition to collecting preintervention and postintervention data, practitioners should monitor progress toward treatment goals that were determined at the outset of the group. Progress monitoring may take many forms and is driven by the identified target behaviors. Data can be collected during the group, where possible, especially when goals include the development and reinforcement of replacement behaviors and when there are behavior-based contingencies. Progress monitoring can also include daily report cards that may be part of a participant's behavior intervention plan, or session check-ins that ask each participant to use a brief checklist or feelings thermometer to report behavioral or affective information (Sportsman et al., 2010). Informal data collection is helpful as well. Referred to as treatment notes, session notes, or case notes, taking a moment after each session to record what happened during group is helpful to co-leaders as they plan or modify future sessions.

Ongoing assessment of effectiveness and satisfaction outside of the treatment sessions is central to its success. It is important to solicit feedback from constituents on the perceived effectiveness of groups on student behavior and, more broadly, the effectiveness of groups on school culture. Efforts should be made to provide opportunities for input from other service providers in the schools. As addressed previously, this form of program evaluation begins with a thorough needs assessment and collection of preintervention measures, and continues past the end of the counseling group with the evaluation of postintervention measures and follow-up data. Questionnaires, structured interviews, and ratings scales are valuable tools for this process. In line with the importance of collaborative school partnerships, it is helpful to include other service providers early on in the planning stages and throughout the rest of the process. Administration, teachers, and other staff are likely to provide excellent suggestions for improvement in terms of scheduling, location, and even session content.

Troubleshooting

No intervention works perfectly all the time, and group counseling is no exception. Similarly, group counseling is also subject to violations of treatment integrity. School psychologists must ascertain that counseling interventions are implemented in a manner that is consistent with the way they were developed. It is useful for co-leaders to provide each other with feedback, including assessments of treatment integrity after each session. Also, group leaders are encouraged to seek out knowledgeable observers, where appropriate, or to seek consultation with peers in school psychology or related disciplines.

The most common types of problems that arise in group work are related to rule violations or inappropriate behaviors such as hostility and attention seeking. Preventive efforts should be taken when the group is initiated to minimize the chances for these types of incidents. Group members often play a part in establishing what the consequences will be for rule violations. Of course, group leaders may have to provide a significant amount of input to ensure that rules and consequences are appropriate. Often, consequences are articulated in a step-wise way: first a reminder of the rule is given, next a warning is issued, and finally the child or adolescent member is excused from the group. Depending on the severity, the child or adolescent group member may be dismissed from the group for a portion of a session, for a full session, or permanently.

It is worth noting here that, in some situations, the ideal solution to a problem within a group is the group itself. As noted by Yalom (1995) and others, group processes can be a powerful change agent. As members become more comfortable in the group environment, they tend to settle into the same behavior patterns exhibited outside of group. Given that this behavior repertoire may include suboptimal behaviors or interpersonal skills, it makes sense that letting group members provide feedback may be more effective than other consequences, such as a reprimand from a group leader or excusing the member from group. It is important to state that the degree to which a group may be successful at solving problems for itself may vary as a function of the group leader's experience. More experienced facilitators will be more comfortable letting this process unfold and will be more skilled at providing guidance when needed than less experienced facilitators. Similarly, more experienced group members and older children will be better at negotiating the problem-solving process than will less experienced and younger children.

Some other common problems encountered when conducting group counseling are nonsharing and silence. As discussed previously, these problems can often be avoided with preventive efforts and group activities. Some group members will participate less than others, but group leaders should actively encourage everyone to engage in activities. Waterman and Walker (2009) recommend making process comments that convey the group's interest, support, and acceptance of each group member. As an example, the group leader may tell a quiet member that the group is interested to hear from him or her whether it be now or later. Or the group leader may wonder aloud if something might be prohibiting the group member's participation. As with other instances, group processes may intervene to engage a silent member. Group members will probably notice when a person is quiet or disengaged and they may be able to provide helpful insight into the situation. Sometimes it may be necessary to allow the group to remain silent for a time, which will increase the likelihood that a member will make a contribution that moves the group along. It is not recommended to end a session early because of nonparticipation because of the risk of reinforcing silence in future sessions.

Stage 4: Group Evaluation

As with other activities of a school psychologist, comparing precounseling and postcounseling assessment data is necessary to determine the effectiveness of the group. Tools that were used to measure targeted impairments before the group began (e.g., ratings scales, structured observations, interviews) should be used to evaluate progress. As with other kinds of interventions, writing a treatment summary of the results and interpretations of group counseling outcomes is beneficial. Additionally, it is important to gather information from students, parents, teachers, administrators, and any

other constituents regarding their satisfaction with the group (Schmidt, 2014). For example, assessing the perceived effectiveness of homework assignments in terms of how well skills generalized from setting to setting informs planning for future activities.

Measuring treatment satisfaction is especially helpful if group counseling is novel to the school because it aids in troubleshooting and serves to improve service delivery. Also, it is an effective way to demonstrate to students, parents, teachers, and administrators that their input is valued and that steps are being taken to ensure the highest quality services.

School psychologists should evaluate their own effectiveness across all areas of service delivery. These data serve multiple purposes. First, they provide evidence of the range of services school psychologists provide in their school system. This information may serve to inform administrative decisions. Second, they provide evidence of the number of students served by school psychologists. Many school psychologists are working to expand the number of students who receive services in their buildings. Using data to demonstrate that engaging in group counseling actually builds the capacity of school psychologists is advantageous for several reasons (Stormont et al., 2012). Taken together with student outcome data, it shows the value of group counseling and enhances the degree of buy-in from teachers, administrators, and the community. Finally, after postintervention data are analyzed, providing the results to constituents in an interactive format allows for a discussion of the benefits and opportunities for improvement for future group interventions.

SUMMARY

The mental health needs of children and adolescents continue to rise (Ghandour et al., 2012) but often the systems that are currently in place do not sufficiently address these needs. School systems—and school psychologists, in particular—are increasingly recognized as ideal mental health service providers because of their training and school-based practice (Suldo et al., 2010). The demands on school psychologists' time and resources have increased, however, making it difficult for them to serve as many students as may be warranted. As a result, some school psychologists have turned to group counseling as an effective method for delivering both psychoeducational and psychosocial support to students (Hoag & Burlingame, 1997). Given that group counseling is more efficient and more cost-effective than individual treatment, it is not surprising that group work has become a method of choice for delivering intervention services.

In spite of this method's growing popularity, many school psychologists feel inadequately versed in the basic methods and best practices for group counseling with children and adolescents. Also, school psychologists may face a number of barriers to this type of service delivery. Examples of treatment barriers include problems that are inherent in schools (e.g., space constraints, scheduling), insufficient administrative support, insufficient time, and role strain. (See Suldo et al., 2010, for a comprehensive review of treatment barriers to group counseling in schools.) With these potential treatment barriers in mind, this chapter provides pragmatic information about how to conduct counseling groups in a school setting.

REFERENCES

Allen, J. P., Insabella, G., Porter, M. R., Smith, F. D., Land, D., & Phillips, N. (2006). A social-interactional model of the development of depressive symptoms in adolescence. *Journal of Consulting and Clinical Psychology, 74*, 55–65.

Association for Specialists in Group Work. (2000). Association for Specialists in Group Work: Professional standards for the training of group workers. *Journal for Specialists in Group Work, 25*, 327–354.

Barrett, P. M. (1998). Evaluation of cognitive-behavioural group treatments for childhood anxiety disorders. *Journal of Clinical Child Psychology, 27*, 459–468.

Beidel, D. C., & Turner, S. M. (1998). *Shy children, phobic adults: Nature and treatment of social phobia*. Washington, DC: American Psychological Association.

Block, J. (1978). Effects of a rational-emotive mental health program on poorly achieving, disruptive high school students. *Journal of Counseling Psychology, 25*, 61–65.

Chambless, D. L., Sanderson, W. C., Shoham, V., Johnson, S. B., Pope, K. S., Crits-Christoph, P., ... McCurry, S. (1996). An update on empirically validated therapies. *The Clinical Psychologist, 49*, 5–18.

Clark, G. N., Hawkins, W., Murphy, M., Sheeber, L., Lewinsohn, P. M., & Seeley, J. (1995). Targeted prevention of unipolar depressive disorder in an at risk sample of high school adolescents: A randomized trial of a group cognitive intervention. *American Academy of Child and Adolescent Psychiatry, 34*, 312–321.

Clarke, G. N., Lewinsohn, P., & Hyman, H. (1990). *Leader's manual for adolescent groups*. Eugene, OR: Castalia.

Cooley, L. (2009). *The power of groups: Solution-focused group counseling in schools*. Thousand Oaks, CA: SAGE.

Crespi, T. D. (2009). Group counseling in the schools: Legal, ethical, and treatment issues in school practice. *Psychology in the Schools, 46*, 273–280. doi:10.1002/pits.20373

DeLucia-Waack, J. L. (2006). *Leading psychoeducational groups for children and adolescents*. Thousand Oaks, CA: SAGE.

DeLucia-Waack, J. L., Kalodner, C. R., & Riva, M. T. (Eds.). (2013). *Handbook of group counseling and psychotherapy* (2nd ed.). Thousand Oaks, CA: SAGE.

Dishion, T. J., McCord, J., & Poulin, F. (1999). When interventions harm: Peer groups and problem behavior. *American Psychologist, 54*, 755–764. doi:10.1037/0003-066X.54.9.755

Ehly, S. W., & Garcia-Vazquez, E. (1998). Groups in the school context. In K. C. Stoiber & T. R. Kratochwill (Eds.), *Handbook of group intervention for children and families* (pp. 9–28). Boston, MA: Allyn & Bacon.

Farmer, E. M. Z., Burns, B. J., Phillips, S. D., Angold, A., & Costello, E. J. (2003). Pathways into and through mental health services for children and adolescents. *Psychiatric Service, 54*, 60–66. doi:10.1176/appi.ps.54.1.60

Ghandour, R. M., Kogan, M. D., Blumberg, S. J., Jones, J. R., & Perrin, J. M. (2012). Mental health conditions among school-aged children: geographic and sociodemographic patterns in prevalence and treatment. *Journal of Developmental and Behavioral Pediatrics, 33*, 42–54. doi:10.1097/ DBP.0b013e31823e18fd

Gillham, J. E., Reivich, K. J., Freres, D. R., Chaplin, T. M., Shatte, A. J., Samuels, B., ... Seligman, M. E. (2007). School-based prevention of depressive symptoms: A randomized controlled study of the effectiveness and specificity of the Penn Resiliency Program. *Journal of Consulting and Clinical Psychology, 75*, 9–19.

Hoag, M. J., & Burlingame, G. M. (1997). Evaluating the effectiveness of child and adolescent group treatment: A meta-analysis review. *Journal of Clinical Child Psychology, 26*, 234–246. doi: 10.1207/s15374424jccp2603_2

Kataoka, S. H., Stein, B. D., Jaycox, L. H., Wong, M., Escudero, P., Tu, W., ... Fink, A. (2003). A school-based mental health program for traumatized Latino immigrant children. *Journal of the American Academy of Child and Adolescent Psychiatry, 42*, 311–318.

Kazdin, A. E., & Wassell, G. (1999). Barriers to treatment participation and therapeutic change among children referred for conduct disorder. *Journal of Clinical Child Psychology, 28*, 160–172. doi:10.1207/s15374424jccp2802_4

Kehle, T. J., Bray, M. A., & Pérusse, R. (2009). Introduction to individual and group counseling in the practice of school psychology. *Psychology in the Schools, 46*, 197–198. doi:10.1002/pits.20363

Lochman, J. E., Barry, T. D., & Pardini, D. A. (2003). Anger control training for aggressive youth. In A. E. Kazdin & J. R. Weisz (Eds.), *Evidenced-based psychotherapies for children and adolescents* (pp. 263–281). New York, NY: Guilford Press.

Mackay, P. W., Donovan, D. M., & Marlatt, G. A. (1991). Cognitive and behavioral approaches to alcohol abuse. In R. J. Frances & S. I. Miller (Eds.), *Clinical textbook of addictive disorders* (pp. 452–481). New York, NY: Guilford Press.

Manassis, K., Mendlowitz, S. L., Scapillato, D., Fisksenbaum, L., Freire, M., Monga, S., & Owens, M. (2002). Group and individual cognitive-behavioral therapy for childhood anxiety disorders: A randomized trial. *Journal of the Academy of Child and Adolescent Psychiatry, 41*, 1423–1430. doi:10.1097/00004583-200212000-00013

Millar, G. M., Lean, D., Sweet, S. D., Moraes, S. C., & Nelson, V. (2013). The psychology school mental health initiative: An innovative approach to the delivery of school-based intervention services. *Canadian Journal of School Psychology, 28*, 103–118. doi:10.1177/0829573512468858

Mufson, L., Dorta, K. P., Wickramaratne, P., Nomura, Y., Olfson, M., & Weissman, M. M. (2004). A randomized effectiveness trial of interpersonal psychotherapy for depressed adolescents. *Archives of General Psychiatry, 61*, 577–584.

National Association of School Psychologists. (2010). *Model for comprehensive and integrated school psychological services*. Bethesda, MD: Author. Retrieved from http://www.nasponline.org/standards/2010standards/2_PracticeModel.pdf

Nicholson, H., Foote, C., & Grigerick, S. (2009). Deleterious effects of psychotherapy and counseling in the schools. *Psychology in the Schools, 46*, 232–237. doi:10.1002/pits.20367

Pérusse, R., Goodnough, G. E., & Lee, V. V. (2009). Group counseling in the schools. *Psychology in the Schools, 46*, 225–231. doi: 10.1002/pits.20369

Rapee, R. M., Wignall, A., Hudson, J. L., & Schniering, C. A. (2000). *Treating anxious children and adolescents*. Oakland, CA: New Harbinger.

Schmidt, J. J. (2014). *Counseling in schools: Comprehensive programs of responsive services for all students* (6th ed.). New York, NY: Pearson.

Shechtman, Z., & Gluk, O. (2005). An investigation of therapeutic factors in children's groups. *Group Dynamics: Theory, Research, and Practice, 9*, 127–134. doi:10.1037/1089-2699.9.2.127

Sink, C. A., Edwards, C. N., & Eppler, C. (2013). *School-based group counseling*. Belmont, CA: Cengage.

Sportsman, E. L., Carlson, J. S., & Guthrie, K. M. (2010). Special article with commentary concerning "service delivery": Lesson learned from leading an anger management group using the "Seeing Red" curriculum within an elementary school. *Journal of Applied School Psychology, 26*, 339–350. doi:10.1080/15377903.2010.518823

Stark, K. D., Reynolds, W. M., & Kaslow, N. J. (1987). A comparison of the relative efficacy of self-control therapy and a behavioral problem-solving therapy for depression in children. *Journal of Abnormal Child Psychology, 15*, 91–113.

Stormont, M., Thomas, C. T., & van Garderen, D. (2012). Introduction to the special issue: Building capacity to improve student outcomes through collaboration: Current issues and innovative approaches. *Psychology in the Schools, 49*, 399–401. doi:10.1002/pits.21605

Stubenbort, K., & Cohen, J. A. (2006). Cognitive-behavioral groups for traumatically bereaved children and their parents. In L. A. Schein, H. I. Spitz, G. M. Burlingame, P. R. Muskin, & S. Vargo (Eds.), *Psychological effects of catastrophic disasters: Group approaches to treatment* (pp. 581–628). New York, NY: Haworth Press.

Suldo, S. M., Friedrich, A., & Michalowski, J. (2010). Personal and systems-level factors that limit and facilitate school psychologists' involvement in school-based mental health services. *Psychology in the Schools, 47*, 354–373. doi:10.1002/pits.20475

Trotzer, J. P. (2004). Conducting a group: Guidelines for choosing and using activities. In J. L. DeLucia-Waak, D. A. Gerrity, C. R. Kalodner, & M. T. Riva (Eds.), *Handbook of group counseling and psychotherapy* (pp. 76–90). Thousand Oaks, CA: SAGE.

Waterman, J., & Walker, E. (2009). *Helping at-risk students: A group counseling approach for grades 6–9* (2nd ed.). New York, NY: Guilford Press.

Weissman, A. S., Antinoro, D., & Chu, B. C. (2008). Cognitive-behavioral therapy for anxiety in school settings: Advances and challenges. In M. Mayer, R. Van Acker, J. E. Lochman, & F. M. Gresham (Eds.), *Cognitive-behavioral interventions for students with emotional/behavioral disorders* (pp. 173–203). New York, NY: Guilford Press.

Yalom, I. D. (1995). *The theory and practice of group psychotherapy* (4th ed.). New York, NY: Basic Books.

Yalom, I. D., & Leszcz, M. (2005). *Theory and practice of group counseling* (5th ed.). New York, NY: Basic Books.

22

Best Practices in Delivering Culturally Responsive, Tiered-Level Supports for Youth With Behavioral Challenges

Robyn S. Hess
Vanja Pejic
Katherine Sanchez Castejon
University of Northern Colorado

OVERVIEW

Every year, 13% of students with disabilities, and 7% of those without, experience significant behavioral challenges that result in suspension or expulsion from public schools (Losen & Gillespie, 2012). While there are many potential reasons why students may act out, the effect of underlying emotional and mental health concerns cannot be underestimated. While it is recognized that many children and adolescents have significant mental health needs, within educational settings fewer than 1% of students are identified as having a *serious emotional disturbance* (U.S. Department of Education, 2011). The discrepancy between community prevalence and school identification may suggest that students' mental health needs are under identified within the schools. Unfortunately, for those students who display aggressive, impulsive, and deviant behavior as part of their mental health symptoms, harsh disciplinary consequences rather than appropriate interventions are the more likely response to their needs. Punitive discipline practices are especially applied to students of color (Losen & Gillespie, 2012).

The purpose of this chapter is to describe ways that school psychologists can effectively meet the needs of youth with serious behavioral challenges through culturally responsive, multitiered systems of support that emphasize prevention and early intervention.

Challenging Behavior and Special Education

School personnel struggle to understand, identify, and intervene with students who demonstrate disruptive behavior patterns. When students experience behavioral challenges and intervention does not seem to reverse these negative trends, school psychologists may consider whether special education services are an appropriate option, typically under the category of serious emotional disturbance. For the most part, states have developed criteria that align with the federal definition of serious emotional disturbance, although 20% have broadened their criteria to be more inclusive (Becker et al., 2011). One of the most controversial aspects of the federal law is the exclusion of students whose behavior is considered to represent social maladjustment and who are not viewed as eligible for special education services. Social maladjustment is "based on the premise that students who have problems in conduct (i.e., social maladjustment) are responsible for their behavior and thus do not have a 'legitimate' disability" (Gresham, 2005, p. 329). Although there is no consistent definition of social maladjustment, students who are identified as such are excluded from special education services if they do not demonstrate evidence of another disability (e.g., serious emotional disturbance, specific learning disability) that would otherwise qualify them for services. This lack of definition has contributed to misunderstanding, confusion, and disagreement over which students qualify as emotionally disturbed, yet all but a few states continue to exclude students based on perceived social maladjustment (Becker et al., 2011).

Disproportionality in Special Education and Disciplinary Outcomes

Whether students are excluded from receiving services due to perceived social maladjustment or inappropriately qualified for special education, both responses might suggest a failure to provide adequate prevention and early intervention. The consequences are especially dire for ethnic minority youth who face considerable disproportionality within special education and the juvenile justice system (Christle, Jolivette, & Nelson, 2005; Skiba et al., 2008). Relative to population estimates, African American students appear to be overrepresented in special education especially in the categories of intellectual disabilities and emotional disturbance (Skiba et al., 2008). In contrast, Asian students appear to be underrepresented in all categories of special education. Although these data are somewhat inconsistent, Latino students appear to be underrepresented in special education overall, and specifically in the serious emotional disturbance category (Skiba et al., 2008). This disproportionality calls into question the validity of identification procedures such that school psychologists may be under or over identifying a number of students based on factors other than their educational and social emotional needs. Little is known about the demographics of students who are considered ineligible for special education because of social maladjustment as there is no requirement for school districts to monitor this information.

All too often, students with externalizing behaviors face harsh discipline practices such as suspensions and expulsions. Unfortunately, discipline policies are not enforced equally. Based on national suspension rates for the 2010–2011 school year, one out of every six (17%) African American children was suspended at least once (Losen & Gillespie, 2012). This rate is two to three times higher than for other ethnic or racial groups (e.g., 1 in 13 [8%] for Native American, 1 in 14 [7%] for Latino, 1 in 20 [5%] for Caucasian, and 1 in 50 [2%] for Asian American students). The discipline gap between students from different ethnic backgrounds increases depending on the school setting, with ethnic minority youth in urban settings experiencing much higher rates of suspension and expulsion than their rural or suburban counterparts (Wallace, Goodkind, Wallace, & Bachman,

2008). Racial disproportionality is evident in the type of discipline students receive as well as the intensity of the punishment, with African American and Latino students being sent to the principal's office more often for less serious behavioral infractions in comparison to their Caucasian classmates (Bradshaw, Mitchell, O'Brennan, & Leaf, 2010; Wallace et al., 2008).

The most distressing fact is that suspension and expulsion have not been found to be a deterrent for future misbehavior. Instead, for many students it serves as a potential risk factor for additional suspension, potential expulsion, dropout, or delinquency (Wallace et al., 2008). Disproportionality in student disciplinary actions and persistent achievement gaps lay the groundwork for a disconnect to occur between students and the educational environment, creating a school-to-prison pipeline (Christle et al., 2005). For culturally diverse students, exclusion from the learning environment increases risk of academic failure, social alienation, and future economic challenges. In other words, their futures have been left at the hands of society's justice systems and schools are left clear of responsibility for these students' academic and social emotional education.

Responding to Disproportionality

Despite federal and state regulations discouraging the use of restrictive discipline policies that mandate suspension and expulsion, these punitive methods are still all too common in many school districts. While these types of policies are not ideal, it is also important to recognize the extent to which emotional and behavioral problems monopolize the limited time and resources of educational personnel. Although fewer than 5% of the student population will have severe emotional and behavioral problems, these students may well account for approximately 50% of teachers' and administrators' time (Sugai, Horner, & Gresham, 2002). Consequently, it is of extreme importance that school psychologists use interventions and tools that prevent and respond to behavioral challenges and that can be implemented with integrity, fidelity, and consistency to benefit students, parents, schools, and society at large.

Multitiered systems of support delivered in a culturally competent manner may represent one solution for addressing the disproportionality in discipline outcomes for youth. Although not widely used for behavioral interventions, multitiered systems could serve as an effective framework for addressing, monitoring, and favorably changing a problem behavior from its baseline levels. Utilizing this model with integrity and accuracy should not only help school psychologists to support early interventions and encourage more structured implementation over time, but also to correctly identify students who are eligible for special education services.

Consistent with the National Association of School Psychologists (NASP) *Model for Comprehensive and Integrated School Psychological Services* (NASP, 2010), the purpose of this chapter is to present best practices in school psychologists' development of these tiered levels of support, an important component of the Interventions and Mental Health Services to Develop Social and Life Skills domain. In short, the implementation of multitiered systems of support for students with behavioral challenges across all ages and intervention intensity levels may enhance the overall school climate, improve student behavioral health outcomes, and decrease inappropriate or disproportionate discipline and labeling practices.

BASIC CONSIDERATIONS

Multitiered systems of support grew out of a public health framework and over the last 20 years have been increasingly applied to school settings. For example, response to intervention (RTI) has been widely promoted as a model that meets student needs because decisions regarding the type and intensity of programming are made based on the learner's responses. If students do not respond to the curriculum or intervention available at a specific tier, additional programming components or modules are added to provide increasingly intensive levels of intervention and support. A shift has occurred where the focus is now on finding the specific form of instruction and/or intervention that will allow an individual to be successful, rather than perpetuating a system that addresses a student's needs only after failure has occurred. This model has been used effectively to address academic concerns and, more recently, has been endorsed as an effective means to address social and behavioral concerns (Cheney, Flower, & Templeton, 2008; Gresham, 2005; Hawken, Vincent, & Schumann, 2008).

To meet the needs of increasingly diverse student populations, not only must there be a continuum of evidence-based interventions and practices, these approaches must be implemented in culturally responsive ways. "Without consideration of culturally responsive instruction, discipline, and interventions within all stages of the RTI decision-making model, there is

continued possibility of misinterpretation of student behavior and emotional well-being as disordered" (Harris-Murri, King, & Rostenberg, 2006, p. 781). The disproportionate rates of disciplinary actions between diverse learners and their majority culture peers calls into question the appropriateness of some school-based strategies designed to address behavioral problems. A culturally responsive model of services recognizes the distinctive characteristics of culturally and linguistically diverse students and actively promotes connections between home, school, and community; culturally responsive instruction; appropriate assessment practices; and ongoing professional development for school staff (Harris-Murri et al., 2006).

In order to stop the school-to-prison pipeline among ethnic minority youth, schools need to focus on early intervention to reduce later negative outcomes. Further, addressing behavioral problems through evidence-based interventions within a culturally responsive lens may bridge the achievement gap between students from different ethnic and racial backgrounds. This framework may be useful in the early identification of students with serious emotional disturbance, as well as identifying potential underlying academic deficits. It is well established that academic achievement and social–emotional health are interwoven and inseparable (Adelman & Taylor, 2000). In order to truly provide children access to education, barriers to learning must be removed. One of the first steps to removing these barriers is to create a school environment that is safe and supportive of all students. More than 800 studies reporting on school discipline issues and challenging behavior problems have identified system-wide behavioral programming, social skills training, and academic curricula modifications as the most effective interventions that result in the largest effect sizes (Luiselli, Putnam, Handler, & Feinberg, 2005). However, if culturally responsive academic and behavioral components are not integrated at each tier, these programs may not adequately address the needs of all students.

BEST PRACTICES IN DELIVERING CULTURALLY RESPONSIVE SYSTEMS OF SUPPORT

While there is a great deal of research on effective strategies for intervening with specific types of behavioral problems, information on the systemic application of culturally responsive school-based practices to address behavioral concerns is much more limited. This chapter presents a summary of the literature based on the perspectives of experts in the field, as well as available empirical evidence to provide school psychologists with strategies for enhancing the cultural responsiveness of their practices in addressing the needs of youth with significant behavioral challenges. Across all tiers of support, there are three broad recommendations that help to ensure that school psychologists are incorporating culturally responsive practices: (a) routinely collecting and disaggregating data across student groups on relevant behavioral indicators, (b) purposefully incorporating consideration of cultural background variables into the problem-solving process, and (c) selecting programming that has support for its use with culturally diverse populations.

Collecting and Disaggregating Data on Behavioral Indicators

There are many types of screening and progress-monitoring strategies, educational practices, and prevention/intervention programs appropriate to address challenging behaviors at different tiers and educational levels (i.e., preschool, elementary, secondary). Unfortunately, not all of these practices have been researched with every potential group of students. Therefore, school psychologists must be able to monitor and adapt their practices based on their knowledge of specific ethnic and cultural groups within their own settings.

Noell, Gilbertson, VanDerHeyden, and Witt (2005) offer a comprehensive ecobehavioral framework for assessment and intervention with culturally and linguistically diverse students that is appropriate to implement across all tiers of service. From their perspective, school psychologists must shift from a reliance on normative tools to assessment and monitoring that relies on local norms, criterion-based outcomes, and individualized student outcomes. For example, when screening students for signs of risk, compare screening information among students of a similar demographic (e.g., students who are African American or English language learners) as well as across all students in the school and the district to determine how students' behaviors compare to their "true" peers as well as all peers (Brown & Doolittle, 2007). Student behavior should be assessed across various settings and times to determine whether there are significant differences in presentation based on subject areas or classroom environments.

Considering Cultural Background Variables

When engaging in a problem-solving process, school psychologists can incorporate questions that consider the potential role of cultural, linguistic, and other background variables that may be having an impact on the student's behavior. For example, Brown and Doolittle (2007) proposed a helpful set of guiding questions for each tier to be used by school teams engaged in a problem-solving process for students who are English language learners. In this chapter, a modified set of questions based on Brown and Doolittle's original work is provided within each of the tiers presented below. School psychologists may find it useful to incorporate these types of questions into their own problem-solving processes in order to ensure a consideration of students' unique backgrounds.

Selecting Appropriate Interventions and Monitoring Outcomes

In selecting interventions designed to reduce challenging behaviors, it is important to assess the cultural match between the specific program or strategy and the demographics of the school. School psychologists can review research supporting the effectiveness of different approaches to determine whether the study included participants who are similar to the school's student population. While this is not a guarantee that the program will be successful, school psychologists can be more confident that not only does the approach have support for its effectiveness, but also that it resulted in positive outcomes for diverse groups of students. Once an intervention has been adopted, school psychologists should continue to disaggregate outcome data by gender, ethnicity, and/or socioeconomic status to determine if the program leads to similar outcomes (e.g., reductions in office referrals, increased attendance) for all students. The following approaches are not meant to be all inclusive, but reflect those strategies that have been frequently cited in the literature and that have support for their use with culturally diverse students.

Tier 1: Prevention and Early Intervention

At a universal prevention level, no students are identified as having special needs or problems. Instead a positive foundation is created that supports the greatest number of youth. In other words, all students are provided with supports or programming through school or district-wide practices and reform. For example, within a school setting, primary prevention would be directed toward creating school environments that support student learning and decrease children's risk for learning and/or behavioral problems. Adelman and Taylor (2000) describe this enabling component as a comprehensive, multifaceted approach for addressing barriers to learning by providing a range of activities that promote healthy development. When universal interventions are delivered appropriately and consistently, approximately 80–90% of the school population will respond (Sugai et al., 2002).

Creating Culturally Responsive School Environments

Culturally responsive practices at Tier 1 are designed to promote positive behaviors and broadly address the underlying factors that are associated with negative behaviors (Sullivan et al., 2009). School psychologists are in a primary position to assist in creating system level changes by helping to implement professional development for school staff to build their knowledge and skill around diversity. Culturally appropriate curricula build on students' culture, motivation, home language, and skills to guide instruction (Harris-Murri et al., 2006). These practices help to ensure that teachers are providing meaningful instruction and linking it to the unique needs of their students. Additional areas of focus might include implementing strategies to bring awareness to and affirming diversity in the school and engaging in conversations around school-wide discipline policies and practices (Harris-Murri et al., 2006; Sullivan et al., 2009). Cultural brokers who represent the various student demographics of the school may also help to promote knowledge about diverse students' needs and assist in building family, school, and community partnerships (Green, 2005). Incorporating culturally responsive practices that target school cultures (i.e., perceptions of race and acceptance of all students), school policies (i.e., referral and assessment procedures), and school staff (i.e., knowledge about diverse populations) are key aspects of promoting positive change (Sullivan et al., 2009). Implementation of these broad strategies helps to create a school climate that supports intervention efforts across all tiers.

Culturally Responsive Universal Programming

School psychologists can collaborate with teachers to promote evidence-based practices and culturally responsive early intervention across all levels (Sullivan et al., 2009). Universal social and emotional learning programs can be successfully implemented by teaching staff, and they can lead to improvements in behaviors and social emotional skills, as well as important academic gains (Durlak, Weissberg, Dymnicki, Taylor,

& Schellinger, 2011). One of the more common universal programs for addressing student behavior is school-wide positive behavioral interventions and supports (Sugai et al., 2002). Although there are many elements to this approach, some of the key aspects of implementation include developing clear, consistent school-wide expectations for behavior. These expectations are explicitly taught to students and clearly defined procedures are implemented to regularly acknowledge students for appropriate behaviors and consistently apply consequences for misbehavior (Sugai et al., 2002).

Unfortunately, even in schools that have implemented school-wide behavioral supports, there is evidence for disproportionality in disciplinary outcomes (e.g., Bradshaw et al., 2010). However, when attention is given to the programmatic aspects discussed above (e.g., increasing knowledge of diversity among staff, incorporating culturally responsive instructional practices, and monitoring disaggregated behavioral and referral data for patterns) these effects may be reduced. Vincent, Randall, Cartledge, Tobin, and Swain-Bradway (2011) reported that their 4-year effort to incorporate culturally responsive practices into positive behavioral supports programming resulted in more similar behavioral and academic outcomes for Latino and non-Latino students.

Screening Behavior and Monitoring Program Outcomes

This example highlights the importance of monitoring the effectiveness of programs across different demographic groups. School psychologists can analyze outcome indicators across student groups to identify any trends that may suggest differing program application, trouble spots in the school environment, or concerning achievement or behavioral gaps that need to be addressed. While program data are helpful in identifying individual students who may need additional supports, these data can also be effective for targeting larger areas of concern. When possible, it is good practice to examine all school and district data across different student groups including measures of attendance, achievement, and behavior, as well as indicators of school climate. This level of analysis can be helpful for targeting larger areas of concern. For example, is there a time of day, a classroom, or an area of school where there are more likely to be referrals for behavior problems? Disaggregated data allows school psychologists to analyze whether there are differential rates of office referrals, harsher punishments, or other inconsistencies that affect one group more so than another. With this knowledge, modifications to training and program components can be implemented to better address the needs of all students.

When the goals of universal programming are well defined, it is easy to monitor expected student outcomes to determine whether the program is having the intended effect. For example, school-wide positive behavioral interventions and supports has incorporated a system of tracking major and minor offenses as a method for screening for students who might benefit from additional behavioral interventions. When screening, consider the behaviors that are most predictive of negative long-term outcomes such as aggressive behavior and peer rejection.

Culturally Responsive Problem-Solving Processes

With careful monitoring of screening data, school psychologists can begin to identify those students who would benefit from additional behavioral supports. Using an adaptation of Brown and Doolittle's (2007) guiding questions and interventions (see Table 22.1), school psychologists can lead their teams through a preliminary analysis of the instructional and environmental factors that may be having an impact on a student's behavior. An example of this application to a diverse student is provided below.

Case Example: Hassan

Hassan has recently arrived in the United States after spending his entire life in a refugee camp in Kenya. He is a bright, social student who seems to have adequate English communication skills. Unfortunately, in the classroom he is constantly out of his chair. No matter the time of day, he is moving around the classroom touching materials, talking with his peers, and looking into cupboards. His teacher is frustrated and finds herself redirecting him multiple times per day. While he is initially compliant and returns to his desk, within moments he is out of his seat again. Prior to referring him to the school's problem-solving team, the teacher invites the school psychologist to discuss her concerns. During their consultation, the school psychologist incorporates questions about Hassan's cultural, linguistic, and background experiences in order to better understand how they may be affecting his behavior. The school psychologist completes an observation to determine whether there are times when the out-of-seat behaviors are more likely to occur. Additionally, the school psychologist observes the classroom climate, the instructional strategies used, and Hassan's appropriate behaviors within the classroom.

While there are no other refugee children in this classroom, the school psychologist is aware that refugee children might demonstrate higher levels of activity due to educational gaps or trauma histories. Through observations, the school psychologist is not able to establish an exact antecedent to the behavior, but it appears to occur during less structured times (e.g., group work, independent seat time). The school psychologist sets up a meeting with Hassan's parents and an interpreter to gather more information on the parents' perspective of the concerns. Through this conversation, the school psychologist and teacher come to understand that Hassan really likes his teacher and that in his culture being helpful is a common way to demonstrate his respect. Therefore, his out-of-seat behavior is his way of being helpful (e.g., retrieving objects, cleaning counters, seeing if other students need help). Furthermore, his education in the refugee camp occurred in a very traditional lecture format for 2–3 hours per day. It is possible that Hassan does not understand that during less structured times that he still needs to follow classroom rules.

Table 22.1. Tier 1 Guiding Questions and Interventions

Guiding questions
- Have specific Tier 1 interventions that are culturally, linguistically, and experientially appropriate been used with fidelity?
- Is instruction targeted to the student's level of English proficiency using culturally responsive strategies?
- Have the ecology of the classroom and school been assessed?
- What socially appropriate behaviors can the student perform and in what settings?
- Have the parents been contacted and their input documented?

Intervention
- All students receive high-quality, research-based, and culturally responsive instruction by qualified staff.
- Culturally sensitive universal screening of academics and behavior of all students to identify those who need close monitoring or intervention.
- Progress monitoring compares student to other "true" peers.
- Culturally responsive interventions are implemented for at least 8–12 weeks and progress is monitored.

With this information, the school psychologist and teacher develop a plan to provide Hassan with assigned chores that he can complete each day. Additionally, the interpreter and teacher meet with Hassan to review the behavioral expectations in the classroom and school to ensure that he understands them. Finally, the school psychologist and teacher develop an easy progress-monitoring system to track out-of-seat behavior, with a plan to follow up in a few weeks. After 2 weeks, the teacher stops the school psychologist in the hall to tell the school psychologist how well the plan is working.

Tier 2 Interventions for Serious Behavioral Concerns

Despite our best efforts, some students will continue to struggle. When prevention and early intervention efforts have not been successful, implementation of more selective interventions is needed. These selective or Tier 2 interventions should include strategies that have been proven effective and can be implemented quickly. Increasing structure and explicitness is the cornerstone of most interventions at this tier. For example, Tier 2 interventions may focus on providing additional instruction and practice around behavioral expectations and goal setting through existing support programs in the school. Too often, schools focus exclusively on decreasing negative behaviors without reinforcing positive behaviors (Gresham, 2005). By providing a high level of practice and reinforcement, school personnel increase the probability that students will experience success and continue to perform the desired appropriate behaviors.

For academic problems, Tier 2 interventions are often delivered in a small group format. This type of approach may not be as appropriate when addressing social–emotional and behavioral concerns because of the difficulty in integrating new group members once a group has started, especially if using a structured, manualized approach. However, general social skill interventions, token systems, behavioral contracts, and self-management strategies are consistent with programming delivered at Tier 2 (Hawken et al., 2008). School psychologists can work with school staff to inventory the types of programs that are available in their settings and develop options to address different types of problem behaviors (e.g., truancy, aggression, disruptive classroom behavior). Through this process, school psychologists can also identify where there are programming gaps and determine whether available programs have support for their use with diverse populations.

Culturally Responsive Selective Programming for Behavior

Schools often adopt one or more formalized programs to address a wide range of behavioral concerns. For example, Hawken et al. (2008) recommended such programs as the Behavior Education Program (a modified check-in/check-out program; Crone, Horner, & Hawken, 2004) or Check & Connect (Sinclair, Christenson, & Thurlow, 2005), or a hybrid of the two (Check, Connect, and Expect; Cheney et al., 2009). These types of programs are ideal for Tier 2 because once the infrastructure has been established students who need extra levels of behavioral instruction and support can begin receiving this assistance very quickly. In each of these programs, students are matched with a supportive adult with whom they have a positive relationship. Students meet daily with mentors to set daily goals, receive feedback on their efforts, and problem solve around continuing concerns. In a 5-year outcome study of the Check & Connect program, Sinclair et al. (2005) found that students identified with emotional and behavioral disabilities demonstrated more persistent attendance and were less likely to drop out of school than participants in the control group. Decreased levels of school dropout applied to both African American students, who represented 64% of the participant group, and Caucasian students. Part of the success of this program may be related to the efforts of the school psychologist who consulted regularly with case managers, disseminated behavior-monitoring forms, oriented staff to the program, and maintained timely case reviews for those students who were struggling.

With the Check, Connect, and Expect program (Cheney et al., 2009), elements of Check & Connect and the Behavior Education Program were combined such that students were expected to check in and out with mentors and received daily progress reports from their teachers. Mentors reviewed and charted weekly data to share with their mentees. With this type of ongoing feedback, mentors were able to determine whether students needed more intensive programming (e.g., Basic Plus) or if they could be moved toward self-monitoring. For students who continued to meet behavioral goals, they were advanced to graduate status. In a 2-year outcome study, Cheney et al. (2009) found that 60% of students graduated from the program and showed greater reductions in both internalizing and externalizing behavior than either the nongraduates or the comparison group. While promising, these authors also cautioned that the majority of program graduates were Caucasian and female, suggesting that adaptations may be needed for students from other ethnic backgrounds and males. This type of specific outcome information allows school psychologists to make decisions regarding application to their own setting. It also may lead to program modifications designed to enhance effectiveness for all students. For example, Cheney et al. (2009) hypothesized that differential outcome rates may have occurred because all of the mentors were Caucasian females. Therefore, recruiting a variety of male and culturally diverse mentors might result in more consistent positive outcomes.

Additional information regarding specific program options for students with significant behavioral concerns are available at websites such as the Substance Abuse and Mental Health Services Administration's National Registry of Evidence-Based Programs and Practices (http://www.nrepp.samhsa.gov) and the Technical Assistance Center on Social Emotional Intervention for Young Children (http://www.challengingbehavior. org). In addition to providing descriptions of programs, there is also information regarding program efficacy with students from diverse demographic backgrounds (e.g., cultural, economic, age, setting).

Screening Behavior and Monitoring Program Outcomes

Preexisting school-wide data can be used to recognize students in need of Tier 2 services. Office discipline referrals, tardies/absences, suspensions, academic performance, and formal screening tools can provide useful data that aide in identifying students and refining the definitions of the behaviors in need of targeted interventions. Moreover, comprehensive evaluation of student data provides insight into co-occurring behavioral and academic problems. For example, if a student is struggling only during one class or on types of tasks, it may indicate an underlying academic deficit. School psychologists can utilize academic and social screening tools in an integrated manner to increase the likelihood of ameliorating the students' difficulties in both areas (Luiselli et al., 2005).

Quite often screening tools can also be used as outcome measures. One tool that is especially effective for targeting students who have the highest levels of behavioral problems is the Systematic Screening for Behavior Disorders (Walker & Severson, 1990). Using this screener, teachers identified students in grades 1–3 with the most significant behavioral concerns in one large urban district where more than 70% of the students were from diverse backgrounds (Walker et al.,

2009). In this study, Walker et al. (2009) described the 4-year process for implementing the First Step to Success program. This program is coordinated by a behavioral coach, delivered over a 3-month period, and includes three core components: screening, school interventions, and parent training. In comparison to matched peers, students who received this program demonstrated significant improvements in their behaviors based on both parent and teacher ratings on the Systematic Screening for Behavior Disorders and the Social Skills Rating System, an earlier version of the Social Skills Improvement System (Elliott & Gresham, 2008). One of the limitations of this study was that it could not be determined whether these students would have ultimately qualified for serious emotional disturbance without intervention. However, the high level of baseline behaviors and resulting improvements suggest that First Step to Success is a promising program.

Culturally Responsive Problem-Solving Processes

School psychologists must consider the culture and resources of their own specific settings in order to make the best decisions for program implementation. Regardless of their own cultural or linguistic background, all school psychologists can become involved in the provision of culturally responsive Tier 2 interventions by modifying these approaches according to the characteristics of their students (e.g., socioeconomic status, ethnicity, acculturation level) and the school. For example, training culturally diverse school personnel to become involved in delivering interventions and engaging children and families of the same culture maximizes existing school resources. If a school does not already have culturally diverse school personnel, the school psychologist can help advocate for partnerships with community agencies and local universities. These partnerships can result in the provision of free or low-cost translators/interpreters, cultural liaisons, snacks and refreshments for family events, as well as long-term collaborative relationships between the school and the greater local community.

Staff members with knowledge of a student's culture, cultural liaisons, and interpreters for parents are all important members of problem-solving teams when developing a behavioral support plan for a student who represents a culturally or linguistically diverse background. These individuals can provide important insights into the student's cultural and background experiences, parents' perspectives on the concerns, and help increase knowledge of resources in the community that may represent additional supports. Again, the Tier 2 guiding questions and interventions model by Brown and Doolittle (2007) can be useful in structuring the types of information that the team gathers as they are developing an intervention plan (see Table 22.2).

Case Study: Willie

Willie is a 15-year-old, ninth-grade African American male in general education. He has displayed significant behavioral problems, and his school performance has fallen drastically since the beginning of the school year. Willie's father has been incarcerated for the last 6 years, and Willie's mother has experienced an ongoing drug and alcohol problem. Willie lives with his mother and two younger siblings, for whom Willie has cared during most of his childhood. In school, Willie becomes physically aggressive when asked to read, does not follow teachers' requests, and often bullies other students in his class. Recently, Willie was caught drinking and smoking in the school parking lot with three other students. In accordance with the school's discipline policy, Willie has been suspended many times this year and is headed toward an expulsion.

Willie is brought to the attention of the school's problem-solving team to determine what interventions may be helpful in reducing his aggressive behaviors and beginning levels of drug and alcohol use. Willie's mother is not able to attend the meeting, but the school psychologist has carefully summarized Willie's educational history including absences, behavioral referrals, test scores, and other relevant data. These data are compared to disaggregated school data, and the team finds that Willie's academic scores, especially in reading, are much lower than the school average and the disaggregated average for African American students in the school. His attendance records also show a history of many missed days both presently and during his early elementary years. Although Willie has failed many courses, he has been moved up in grade level with very few additional academic supports provided. It is also clear that, historically, he did not have any significant behavioral problems until he entered ninth grade. The only pattern that is evident is that Willie is more likely to act out by becoming verbally aggressive with his teachers and other students during classes that require a great deal of reading.

The school psychologist suspects that Willie has many gaps in his knowledge from his earlier years of missing school. Additionally, he may be angry and embarrassed about his academic weaknesses as well as other difficulties in his home environment. In this case, rather than his cultural background, it appears likely that Willie's unique circumstances are playing a significant role in his academic and behavioral difficulties. The team decides that more focused achievement testing may reveal gaps in his learning, and through targeted interventions, these will be addressed. Additionally, Willie will be assigned a mentor through the school's Check & Connect program who will work with him to set daily goals, learn better ways to deal with his frustration, and who can encourage Willie to increase his attendance and effort at school.

After the team assigns each member a different responsibility (e.g., contacting Willie's mother, completing the academic testing, and assigning him a mentor), they decide to meet again in 4 weeks to review his progress to determine whether there are signs of improvement.

Tier 3 Intensive Interventions and Expanded Services

Within the school setting, typically only 1–5% of the student population will require Tier 3 interventions

Table 22.2. Tier 2 Guiding Questions

Guiding questions
- Would interventions delivered in small-group format have a high chance for success?
- Has the student's progress been compared to himself or herself using data collected over time and across settings?
- Is the student responding to any intervention?
- Are research-based programs in place for the target student and consideration given to his or her cultural, linguistic, socioeconomic, and experiential background?

Intervention
- Option of receiving different behavior-based programs from Tier 1 (time and intensity) which would include systematic and explicit instruction with modeling, multiple examples, and feedback.
- The program addresses the student's specific behavior needs and progress is carefully monitored and reported.
- Observations occur across different settings and include various activities/tasks.
- Culturally responsive interventions are implemented for at least 8–12 weeks.

(Sugai et al., 2002). Early intervention is critical because if students' antisocial and problematic behaviors are not addressed by the third grade, these behaviors tend to persist and become chronic conditions (Cheney et al., 2008). Students identified as needing Tier 3 interventions have not responded to universal and selective approaches and are therefore likely to receive targeted programming delivered through small, focused group interventions combined with individualized supports. Students at this third tier demonstrate the most chronic and intense behavioral problems. Intervention at this level is considered to be indicated as it is designed to address symptoms and behaviors that represent the highest levels of risk and/or subclinical presentations of a disorder. Without implementation of interventions that provide appropriate, intensive, and specialized support, such students are at high risk for potential expulsion from the school setting.

Culturally Responsive, Intensive Programming

Programs implemented at this level are time intensive and require greater levels of expertise and effort on the part of the school psychologist. One program that has been found to be effective for young children is Child Parent Relationship Therapy, a widely researched school-based, play-therapy intervention. This program has been shown to increase parental empathy and responsiveness and decrease child behavior problems and parental stress (Ceballos & Bratton, 2010). Using a modified version of this program, Ceballos and Bratton demonstrated the effectiveness of this program with Latino immigrant parents whose children were identified as having clinical levels of behavior problems. Some of the key modifications that enhanced the cultural responsiveness of the program included having a bilingual, bicultural individual lead all sessions in Spanish, serving refreshments and allowing families to bring food from their country of origin to create a sense of *familismo* (familialism), translating the Child Parent Relationship Therapy manual to Spanish and changing all American names to Latino names, making weekly reminder calls to all participating parents to incorporate the Latino value of *personalismo* (personalism), providing materials and childcare free of charge, and allowing time for socialization before each Child Parent Relationship Therapy session. Ceballos and Bratton (2010) found significant decreases in internalizing and externalizing problem behaviors (90% of participating children moved from clinical to normal levels posttreatment) as well as a significant decrease in parental stress.

This study demonstrated how an empirically supported program can be adapted for use with diverse populations and provides insight into the kinds of modifications needed to meet the needs of diverse groups.

For older students, evidence-based, cognitive–behavioral interventions are effective for addressing aggressive and defiant behaviors (Powell et al., 2011). These approaches often include multiple components and incorporate the contextual risk factors of the individuals. Emphasis is placed on addressing those variables that can be altered such as the student's cognitions, behaviors, and classroom environment (e.g., one that uses positive, effective behavioral management). Two examples of these types of programs are Anger Coping and Coping Power. These programs, designed for students in Grades 4–6, can be delivered in individual or small group formats and have well-documented success in reducing conduct problems among youth from diverse backgrounds.

If these interventions are not successful, as demonstrated through intensive monitoring, such students may warrant a comprehensive plan that is contextually designed and includes the home, the school, and the community. A wraparound model provides a useful framework because the primary focus is on building a collaborative network among the student, his or her family, the school, and supports in the community (Eber, Hyde, & Suter, 2011). School psychologists can play an integral role in facilitating these teams, advocating for students and families, and developing connections between school and community resources. The goal of a wraparound process is to highlight the student's strengths and risk factors within each of these domains (i.e., home, school, and community) to guide individualized care plans.

The underlying belief is that through this collaborative planning process, families will be more invested because the resulting plan will address the families' priorities and will more likely reflect realistic strategies for supporting the student in different settings. This type of approach is consistent with culturally responsive practice because it incorporates the student's culture, family, and community environment into plan development. This model involves multiple steps outlined by Eber et al. (2011) who conducted a 3-year study of the use of wraparound integrated into a school-wide positive behavioral support program. They found preliminary evidence to suggest that students who were part of these wraparound teams for at least 6 months decreased their externalizing behaviors, increased their academic performance, and were perceived by staff as being at low risk for school failure.

Referring to Special Education

Persistence of severe and chronic behaviors despite intensive, specialized, and individualized interventions for problem behaviors may ultimately result in a special education referral. Through this specialized programming, students may be able to access a greater level of school services or appropriate alternative placements. Use of a well-defined and comprehensive multitiered process of delivering supports and evaluating outcomes may represent a promising approach for identification and qualification of students with serious emotional disturbance. Gresham (2005) posits that if a student is provided with culturally appropriate interventions at the three different intensity levels (universal, targeted, and indicated), and the student's behavioral difficulties continue to stay at unsatisfactory levels, this failure to respond should make a student eligible for special education services. Utilization of this model could decrease the use of nebulous and subjective eligibility criteria and encourage schools to provide earlier social and emotional interventions and services to all students through the use of universal interventions.

As with all decisions, school psychologists must continually monitor referral and placement decisions to determine whether students of color are being disproportionally placed in special education programming. Additionally, school psychologists may assist in progress monitoring to determine whether programming decisions are allowing students to meet their individualized behavioral goals and resulting in improved outcomes.

Culturally Responsive Problem-Solving Practices

Tier 3 interventions require the school team to conduct an in-depth analysis of the student's records, including data collected at Tiers 1 and 2. When intervention efforts have not been successful, school psychologists can lead teams in conducting a complete functional behavioral assessment to gather information critical to understanding student behaviors (Crone et al., 2004). This in-depth analysis should include a consideration of how the student's cultural background may influence the problem behavior (Harris-Murri et al., 2006). In addition to the questions outlined by Brown and Doolittle (2007) in Table 22.3, questions regarding a student's family history and current living situation (including parental employment, neighborhood), home language, ethnic/cultural identity, sexual identity, history of trauma, and any other unique characteristics should be explored. This information may help the school psychologist and the team to develop a better understanding of the cultural factors that could be playing a role in the student's challenging behavior. As noted elsewhere, school psychologists will need to adapt their practices to be more culturally responsive in order to actively engage diverse students and their families.

The work of Liddle, Jackson-Gilfort, and Marvel (2006) outlines several culturally sensitive strategies that they have implemented in their work with street-involved African American and Hispanic youth. While not specific to a school environment, many of these practices could be incorporated into services provided within the school. For example, Liddle et al. (2006) highlight the importance of attending to the unique cultural influences experienced by diverse adolescent youth (e.g., pressures to behave in certain ways or choose deviant peers), engaging youth to participate in the development of his or her treatment plan and goal setting, incorporating a focus on cultural themes, and linking the adolescent with prosocial peers and role

Table 22.3. Tier 3 Guiding Questions

Guiding questions
- Is there evidence of progress from previous interventions?
- Is the student successful with different programming, teaching approaches, and an individualized setting?
- What are the student's functional, developmental, academic, linguistic, and cultural needs?
- If additional assessments are used, are the instruments technically sound, valid, and used appropriately for the student?
- Are test results interpreted in a manner that considers student's language proficiency in L1 and L2 and level of acculturation?

Intervention
- Programming and instruction address the specific learning and behavioral needs and progress is carefully monitored.
- A standardized cognitive, academic, social–emotional, and adaptive assessment may be conducted at this tier.
- Native language assessment data should be included.
- Any standardized test data must be interpreted within the context of student's language proficiency, culture, and level of acculturation.

models. They note that adolescents may need to be taught certain life skills that will allow them to be successful outside of their antisocial lives. Not only can school psychologists promote these strategies in their own work, but they can also encourage their colleagues to do so. Additionally, school psychologists can create opportunities for bicultural socialization experiences, promote a positive cultural identity in the adolescent, and provide inservices regarding positive parenting techniques (Liddle et al., 2006) to further protect these youth from antisocial influences.

Case Study: Carlos

Carlos is a 13-year-old Latino male who is currently in seventh grade though he was retained in fourth grade because of significant reading problems. Carlos currently lives with his mother who speaks very little English and his 5-year-old brother. At age 11, Carlos' father was deported to Mexico and his mother began working two jobs, one of which requires her to work the night shift. After Carlos' father left, both the school and his mother noticed significant behavioral changes. These behaviors include violent outbursts and threats toward teachers and other peers, getting into physical fights during and after school, skipping school (e.g., 30 unexcused absences since the beginning of the academic year), and using drugs and alcohol. Recently, Carlos was caught with a knife and his teacher's wallet in his backpack and has a court date pending for this behavior. He has been suspended from school for 3 days.

The principal at his school believes that Carlos' behaviors will warrant an expulsion unless the school psychologist can figure out how to help Carlos and his family. The process begins with an in-depth interview with Carlos' mother, Carlos, and a review of his records. As noted, Carlos has struggled throughout his education with reading and appears to have very low motivation toward school. In terms of his reading, he is able to perform best when he is allowed to work one-on-one with an adult (e.g., teacher or volunteer). It is likely that his dual language background has interfered with his academic achievement. Although he was provided bilingual programming, he missed so many days that he has gaps in his English language and in academic concepts. Because of the language difference and many absences, he was never formally referred for a special education evaluation. Behaviorally, he performs better when he is in an individualized setting, although he can be defiant and challenging. Carlos historically got along well with other students although they are starting to avoid him because of how explosive he has become.

Finally, it is clear that Carlos is beginning to align with one of the neighborhood gangs and may equate this affiliation with becoming a "man."

Working together with the team, the school psychologist decides on several different courses of action. Carlos will advance to Tier 2 reading interventions to determine whether he begins making progress with these types of supports. If they are not successful, he will be considered for a special education referral. As part of his intervention, he will attend some of the smaller intensive reading classes. Carlos will also be connected with Mr. Lopez who teaches art and is one of the teachers with whom Carlos has developed a connection. Additionally, the school psychologist is about to start a new group using the Anger Coping program, and Carlos will be invited to attend. He and his mother will be referred to the local mental health center which uses a wraparound model and will help bring together various supports in the community. The team agrees to maintain close communication over the next couple of weeks to see if these interventions begin to make a difference in Carlos' behavior.

SUMMARY

Given the number of students with significant behavioral challenges in our schools, it is critical that school psychologists establish a continuum of culturally responsive programming that will meet the needs of students across different ages and levels of intensity. When possible, interventions should represent continuous and similar approaches that encourage consistent behavioral norms. In the current climate of limited resources, it is important to remember that low-cost efforts such as clear expectations, consistency, solid classroom management, engaging curriculum, and positive reinforcement can go a long way in addressing the behavioral needs for the majority of the student population. The effectiveness of these interventions can be enhanced when the school reflects a safe and welcoming climate for all students and when attention to cultural background variables is integrated into all aspects of service delivery.

One of the goals of this chapter is to highlight the significant gap in our educational and discipline outcomes. Too many students continue to be excluded from educational settings with rates that vary based on gender, ethnicity, and disability. In order to reverse these trends, we must provide early intervention through comprehensive service models. School psychologists are encouraged to advocate for promising research-based practices that promote the development of positive behaviors. Through careful, continuous monitoring, school psychologists working with their school teams can accurately determine the effectiveness of programming for all students.

REFERENCES

Adelman, H. S., & Taylor, L. (2000). Looking at school health and school reform policy through the lens of addressing barriers to learning. Children's services. *Social Policy, Research, and Practice, 3,* 117–132.

Becker, S. P., Paternite, C. E., Evans, S. W., Andrews, C., Christensen, O. A., Kraan, E. M., & Weist, M. D. (2011). Eligibility, assessment, and educational placement issues for students classified with emotional disturbance: Federal and state-level analyses. *School Mental Health, 3,* 24–34. doi:10.1007/s12310-010-9045-2

Bradshaw, C. P., Mitchell, M. M., O'Brennan, L. M., & Leaf, P. J. (2010). Multilevel exploration of factors contributing to the over-representation of Black students in office discipline referrals. *Journal of Educational Psychology, 102,* 508–520. doi:10.1037/a0018450

Brown, J. E., & Doolittle, J. (2007). *A cultural, linguistic, and ecological framework for response to intervention with English language learners.* (NCCRESt Practitioner Brief). Tempe, AZ: NCCRESt. Retrieved from http://www.nccrest.org/Briefs/Framework_for_RTI.pdf

Ceballos, P. L., & Bratton, S. C. (2010). Empowering Latino families: Effects of a culturally responsive intervention for low-income immigrant Latino parents on children's behaviors and parental stress. *Psychology in the Schools, 47,* 761–775. doi:10.1002/pits.20502

Cheney, D., Flower, A., & Templeton, T. (2008). Applying response to intervention metrics in the social domain for student at risk of developing emotional or behavioral disorders. *The Journal of Special Education, 42,* 108–126. doi:10.1177/00224-669-0731-3349

Cheney, D. A., Stage, S. A., Hawken, L. S., Lynass, L., Mielenz, C., & Waugh, M. (2009). A 2-year outcome study of the Check, Connect, and Expect intervention for students at risk for severe behavior disorder. *Journal of Emotional and Behavioral Disorders, 17,* 226–243. doi:10.1177/1063426609339186

Christle, C. A., Jolivette, K., & Nelson, C. M. (2005). Breaking the school to prison pipeline: Identifying school risk and protective factors for youth delinquency. *Exceptionality, 13,* 69–88. doi:10.1207/s15327035ex1302_2

Crone, D. A., Horner, R. H., & Hawken, L. S. (2004). *Responding to problem behavior in schools: The Behavior Education Program.* New York, NY: Guilford Press.

Durlak, J. A., Weissberg, R. P., Dymnicki, A. B., Taylor, R. D., & Schellinger, K. B. (2011). The impact of enhancing students' social and emotional learning: A meta-analysis of school-based universal interventions. *Child Development, 82,* 405–432. doi:10.1111/j.1467-8624.2010.01564.x

Eber, L., Hyde, K., & Suter, J. C. (2011). Integrating wraparound into a school-wide system of positive behavioral supports. *Journal of Child and Family Studies, 20,* 782–790. doi:10.1007/s10826-010-9424-1

Elliott, S., & Gresham, F. (2008). *Social Skills Improvement System: Performance screening guide.* Bloomington, MN: Pearson.

Green, T. D. (2005). Promising prevention and early intervention strategies to reduce overrepresentation of African American students in special education. *Preventing School Failure, 49,* 33–41.

Gresham, F. (2005). Response to intervention: An alternative means of identifying students as emotionally disturbed. *Education and Treatment of Children, 28,* 214–222.

Harris-Murri, N., King, K., & Rostenberg, D. (2006). Reducing disproportionate minority representation in special education programs for students with emotional disturbances: Toward a culturally responsive response to intervention model. *Education and Treatment of Children, 4,* 779–799.

Hawken, L. S., Vincent, C. G., & Schumman, J. (2008). Response to intervention for social behavior: Challenges and opportunities. *Journal of Emotional and Behavioral Disorders, 16,* 213–225. doi:10.1177/1063426608316018

Liddle, H. A., Jackson-Gilfort, A., & Marvel, F. A. (2006). An empirically supported and culturally specific engagement and intervention strategy for African American adolescent males. *American Journal of Orthopsychiatry, 75,* 215–225. doi:10.1037/0002-9432.75.2.215

Losen, D. L., & Gillespie, J. (2012). *Opportunities suspended: The disparate impact of disciplinary exclusion from school.* Los Angeles, CA: The Civil Rights Project. Retrieved from http://civilrightsproject.ucla.edu/resources/projects/center-for-civil-rights-remedies/school-to-prison-folder/federal-reports/upcoming-ccrr-research/losen-gillespie-opportunity-suspended-2012.pdf

Luiselli, J. K., Putnam, R. F., Handler, M. W., & Feinberg, A. B. (2005). Whole-school positive behavior support: Effects on student discipline problems and academic performance. *Educational Psychology, 25,* 183–198. doi:10.1080/0144341042000301265

National Association of School Psychologists. (2010). *Model for comprehensive and integrated school psychological services.* Bethesda, MD: Author. Retrieved from http://www.nasponline.org/standards/2010standards/2_PracticeModel.pdf

Noell, G. H., Gilbertson, D. M., VanDerHeyden, A. M., & Witt, J. C. (2005). Eco-behavioral assessment and intervention for culturally diverse at-risk students. In C. L. Frisby & C. R. Reynolds (Eds.), *The comprehensive handbook of multicultural school psychology.* (pp. 904–927). Hoboken, NJ: Wiley.

Powell, N. P., Boxmeyer, C. L., Baden, R., Stromeyer, S., Minney, J. A., Mushtaq, A., & Lochman, J. E. (2011). Assessment and treating aggression and conduct problems in schools: Implications form the Coping Power program. *Psychology in the Schools, 48,* 233–242. doi:10.1002/pits.20549

Sinclair, M. F., Christenson, S. L., & Thurlow, M. L. (2005). Promoting school completion of urban secondary youth with emotional or behavioral disabilities. *Exceptional Children, 71,* 465–482.

Skiba, R. J., Simmons, A. B., Ritter, S., Gibb, A. C., Rauch, M. K., Cuadrado, J., & Chung, C-G. (2008). Achieving equity in special education: History, status, and current challenges. *Exceptional Children, 74,* 264–288.

Sugai, G., Horner, R. H., & Gresham, F. M. (2002). Behaviorally effective school environments. In M. R. Shinn, H. M. Walker, & G. Stoner (Eds.), *Interventions for academic and behavior problems: Vol. 2. Preventive and remedial approaches.* (pp. 315–350). Bethesda, MD: National Association of School Psychologists.

Sullivan, A. L., A'Vant, E., Baker, J., Chandler, D., Graves, S., McKinney, E., & Sayles, T. (2009). Confronting inequity in special education–Part 2: Promising practices in addressing disproportionality. *Communiqué, 38, 1,* 18–20.

U.S. Department of Education. (2011). *Annual report to Congress on the implementation of the Individuals with Disabilities Education Act, selected years, 1992 through 2006.* Washington, DC: Author. Retrieved from http://nces.ed.gov/programs/digest/d11/tables/dt11_048.asp

Vincent, C. G., Randall, C., Cartledge, G., Tobin, T. J., & Swain-Bradway, J. (2011). Toward a conceptual integration of cultural responsiveness and school-wide positive behavior support. *Journal of Positive Behavior Interventions, 13,* 219–229. doi:10.1177/1098300711399765

Walker, H. M., Seeley, J. R., Small, J., Severson, H. H., Graham, B. A., Feil, E. G., & Forness, S. R. (2009). A randomized control trial of the First Step to Success early intervention: Demonstration of program efficacy outcomes in a diverse urban school district. *Journal of Emotional and Behavioral Disorders, 17,* 197–212. doi:10.1177/1063426609341645

Walker, H. M., & Severson, H. H. (1990). *Systematic Screening for Behavior Disorders: User's guide and technical manual.* Longmont, CO: Sopris West.

Wallace, J. M., Jr., Goodkind, S., Wallace, C. M., & Bachman, J. G. (2008). Racial, ethnic, and gender differences in school discipline among U.S. high school students: 1991–2005. *The Negro Educational Review, 59*(1–2), 47–62.

23 Best Practices in Classroom Interventions for Attention Problems

George J. DuPaul
Lehigh University (PA)
Gary Stoner
University of Rhode Island
Mary Jean O'Reilly
Pittsfield (MA) Public Schools

OVERVIEW

Problems with attention to classroom instruction and schoolwork are among the most common difficulties exhibited by students in the United States. In fact, according to a teacher report, approximately 20% of elementary school children in general education classrooms frequently exhibit a short attention span, while 27% are frequently distracted during academic tasks (Harrison, Vannest, Davis, & Reynolds, 2012). When attention problems are severe and/or are accompanied by developmentally inappropriate levels of impulsivity and overactivity, the psychiatric diagnosis of attention deficit hyperactivity disorder (ADHD) may be used (American Psychiatric Association, 2013). Approximately 3–10% of elementary school-aged children in the United States are diagnosed with this disorder, with boys outnumbering girls at about a 2:1 to 5:1 ratio (Barkley, 2006).

Given that most public school classrooms include 20–30 students, teachers will likely address the needs of at least one student with ADHD per school year. Further, ADHD symptoms typically persist from early childhood through at least adolescence for a majority of individuals (Barkley, Murphy, & Fischer, 2008). Thus, attention and associated behavioral difficulties will affect children's school functioning throughout their educational careers.

Children with attention problems and/or ADHD are at higher than average risk for behavioral difficulties including defiance toward authority figures, poor relationships with peers, and antisocial acts such as lying, stealing, and fighting (American Psychiatric Association, 2013). In addition to these behavioral risks, students with ADHD frequently struggle scholastically, presumably owing to their low academic engagement rates and inconsistent work productivity (DuPaul & Stoner, 2014). The results of prospective follow-up studies of children with ADHD into adolescence and adulthood indicate significantly higher rates of grade retention, placement in special education classrooms, and school dropout relative to their peers as well as significantly lower high school grade point average, enrollment in college degree programs, and socioeconomic status (Barkley et al., 2008). Approximately 30% of children with ADHD are classified as having learning disabilities because of deficits in the acquisition of specific academic skills (DuPaul, Gormley, & Laracy, 2013). Some students with ADHD may receive special education services as a function of being classified in other disability categories, including speech/language impairments, emotional disturbance, and Other Health Impaired (U.S. Department of Education, 2008).

Given the risk for poor academic and social outcomes, school psychologists must design and implement interventions to address not only the attention problems central to ADHD, but also the academic underachievement and aberrant social behavior associated with this disorder. The two primary interventions for ADHD are psychostimulant medication (e.g., methylphenidate) and behavioral strategies (e.g., token reinforcement and response cost; Pelham & Fabiano, 2008). These intervention strategies have been found to enhance rates of academic productivity and accuracy for most students (DuPaul, Eckert, & Vilardo, 2012). Further, some children may require the combination of stimulant medication and behavioral intervention to show improvements in academic functioning. Despite their positive effects, these interventions cannot be applied in a generic fashion without considering the individual needs of specific students with attention problems. Further, given the chronic and pervasive difficulties experienced by students with ADHD, interventions must be implemented across home and school settings for an extended period of time.

The purpose of this chapter is to describe the most effective school-based interventions for attention problems or ADHD. School psychologists can support the implementation of these interventions by teachers, parents, peers, and students with attention problems through consultation and training activities. Throughout this chapter we emphasize several key themes consistent with the National Association of School Psychologists (NASP) *Model for Comprehensive and Integrated School Psychological Services* (NASP 2010) Interventions and Mental Health Services to Develop Social and Life Skills domain. First, to be optimally effective, interventions must be designed based on assessment data gathered before and after interventions are implemented. Informed decisions about treatment cannot be made without assessment data. Second, interventions must be tailored to meet the unique needs of individual students, particularly at the individualized level of a multitier intervention system. The best way to accomplish this is by collecting systematic data about behavioral, social, and academic functioning. Third, a comprehensive approach to intervention is necessary wherein strategies across multiple tiers (universal, targeted, and individualized) are considered for inclusion in each student's treatment plan.

BASIC CONSIDERATIONS

There are several basic considerations that support the use of effective strategies to address the needs of students with attention problems. These considerations include (a) use of evidence-based assessment and intervention techniques, (b) collaborative consultation to plan interventions, (c) identification of cultural factors that may have an impact on assessment and intervention, and (d)

understanding conceptual underpinnings of effective classroom intervention.

Assessment and Intervention

Inherent in the responsibility to design, implement, and evaluate interventions for students with attention problems is an assumption of appropriate professional training and competence consistent with the NASP Practice Model (NASP, 2010). In particular, a wide range of assessment skills and strategies are necessary to serve students with attention problems or ADHD. For example, assessment for diagnostic decisions and progress monitoring includes a variety of psychometrically sound measures.

In schools, students with attention problems often present with difficulties in both the achievement and behavior domains. Thus, school psychologists will need to have training in a wide range of empirically supported intervention strategies. Further, the complexities of assessment, diagnosis, and treatment of students with attention problems or ADHD result in services that will inevitably involve multiple professionals, parents, and other community members. Because the most effective interventions for attention problems will be implemented by teachers and parents at the point of performance, school psychologists must be skilled in the areas of consultation, collaboration, and coordination of persons and programs to ensure that quality services are delivered.

Collaboration and Consultation

The need for collaboration and consultation skills is particularly important when working with parents and physicians around establishing whether medication is necessary and effective in treating attention problems and ADHD symptoms. Many empirical studies have provided strong support for the use of psychotropic medication, especially stimulants (e.g., methylphenidate) in reducing symptoms of inattention, impulsivity, and hyperactivity (Barkley, 2006). Nevertheless, medication may not be necessary for some children with ADHD, and even when necessary there are no a priori guidelines for which medication and dosage will be optimally effective for a given child. Thus, school psychologists need to work closely with physicians and parents to (a) establish whether medication is necessary as an adjunct to educational interventions, (b) assess whether a given medication and dosage leads to successful outcomes with minimal adverse side effects, and (c) regularly reevaluate the need for continued or adjusted medication treatment (DuPaul & Stoner, 2013).

Cultural Factors

School psychologists will find that their professional practices improve with increased knowledge of the ways in which cultural norms may have an impact on school-based assessment of and intervention for attention problems. For example, knowledge of how behavior rating scales may reflect culture or bias is important. At a minimum, awareness that factors beyond the behavior of particular students may have an impact on their ratings and lead to overidentification is essential. Varied ratings across groups may be related to differing cultural expectations between student and rater, the effects of poverty, teacher endorsement of higher levels of related behaviors (such as oppositional behaviors) affecting scores on ADHD scales, as well as teacher tolerance for particular behaviors. Cultural norms can have an impact on teacher interpretation of student behavior, and the school psychologist can be helpful in recognizing situations in which teacher and student norms may conflict in a way that may increase overidentification or underidentification of students for behavioral or academic support services. The comparison of direct observations of behavior to rating scale results is also recommended. Some studies have shown that teachers may be more accurate in reporting behaviors of children from ethnic groups different from their own due to a heightened awareness of cultural differences (see Hosterman, DuPaul, & Jitendra, 2008).

Conceptual Underpinnings of Interventions for Attention Problems

Given that interventions for attention problems are most effective when delivered by teachers and parents at the point of performance (i.e., the time and place when attention difficulties are exhibited), school psychologists are primarily engaged in intervention design, consultation, and progress-monitoring activities. There are several important considerations that underlie best practices in designing interventions for students with attention problems and ADHD-related difficulties. First, we believe that school psychologists should advocate for a balanced approach to intervention wherein both proactive and reactive strategies are employed. Specifically, antecedent events that typically precede inattentive behaviors should be manipulated to prevent problematic interactions from arising. In addition, reactive strategies should not be confined to punitive approaches, but should be heavily weighted toward providing positive reinforcement when attentive and appropriate behaviors occur.

Another guiding principle is for strategies to be implemented as close in time and place as possible to the target behavior. For example, if the behavior of concern is attention to and completion of math work, then the most effective intervention strategies will be those that are used in math class at the time when students are expected to complete math work. The further removed the intervention is from the time and place where the behavior of interest occurs, the less effective that strategy will be.

Intervention strategies for attention problems should be selected on the basis of assessment data and empirical support from the research literature. Rather than choosing interventions on the basis of trial and error, school psychologists should collect systematic data about a student's academic and behavioral functioning as well as the classroom environment in an effort to make informed treatment selections. For example, data regarding the possible environmental functions of inattentive behavior can be used to develop interventions that directly address the putative function of problematic behavior.

For students with attention problems, reviewing behavioral data may be particularly helpful for intervention planning purposes. Data that demonstrate patterns of problem behaviors at particular locations or times of day can help teachers and parents begin to understand and analyze the contribution of alterable environmental factors.

A final guiding principle in designing interventions for students with attention problems is to avoid a one-size-fits-all approach. Interventions, particularly at Tier 3, must be individually tailored to meet the needs of each student despite the fact that students may share a common diagnosis or behavioral profile. This process of individualizing intervention plans should take into account (a) the child's current level of academic and behavioral functioning, (b) the possible environmental functions of their inattentive behavior, (c) the target behaviors of greatest concern to the teacher and/or student, and (d) elements of the classroom and/or teaching style that might limit the effectiveness of some interventions. Individualized interventions should be developed through a consultative problem-solving process using assessment data and collaborative interactions between school psychologists and teachers, parents, and other school professionals.

Interventions for students with attention problems can be mediated by a number of individuals, not just the classroom teacher. Specifically, effective strategies can be implemented by parents, peers, or the students with attention difficulties themselves. When available, computers can be used to enhance attention to academic instruction or the completion of drill-and-practice activities. The overriding principle here is that school psychologists need to go beyond placing an onus on the teacher to address all difficulties related to attention problems.

BEST PRACTICES IN CLASSROOM INTERVENTIONS FOR ATTENTION PROBLEMS

The most important intervention agent in the school building is the teacher. By using effective instructional and behavior management strategies, the teacher can provide children with attention problems and their classmates a learning environment that permits all students to fully participate in classroom activities. These strategies also can help provide the class with more instructional time by reducing the time spent coping with behavioral crises. Using effective strategies as part of a well-designed educational support program can allow a teacher to deliver instruction and evaluate student learning without the continual distractions and interruptions that poorly managed problem behavior can provoke.

Teacher-mediated strategies can be used by any adult participant in the classroom, including teacher aides, substitute teachers, or parent assistants. Although most interventions require that each adult carry them out precisely as planned, the strategies are generally simple in design and easily taught to any adults that may be involved in the classroom. Continuity of strategies across adults in a classroom or school serves to reinforce the desired behaviors and to improve management of student behaviors across settings.

Teacher-mediated strategies can be proactive or reactive. A combination of the two generally provides the best results. Proactive strategies typically involve the entire class and are arranged to prevent academic and behavioral difficulties by altering the classroom conditions that allow problems to arise. Proactive strategies can be used throughout the school building and may involve instructional and support staff. Reactive strategies are used in response to problems that arise in the classroom and may be individually tailored to a particular student's needs.

The strategies presented here are organized by level of prevention/intervention or educational service; that is, universal, targeted, and individualized. Table 23.1 presents effective intervention strategies in the context of academic setting (i.e., elementary versus secondary level) and tier of service delivery. We envision universal and targeted level strategies as sufficient for addressing the academic and behavioral needs of most students with

Table 23.1. Possible Interventions for Attention Problems Across Service Delivery Level and School Setting

Level of Service Delivery	Elementary	Secondary
Universal	• School-wide positive behavior support • Flexible grouping for academic instruction • Progress monitoring of basic academic skills • Instruction in study/organizational strategies	• School-wide positive behavior support • Flexible grouping for academic instruction • Instruction in study/organizational strategies
Targeted	• Systematic academic strategy instruction (e.g., Think Before Reading, Think While Reading, Think After Reading) • Class-wide peer tutoring • Behavior education program • Daily behavior report cards	• Systematic academic strategy instruction • Daily (weekly) behavior report cards • Challenging Horizons program • Self-monitoring
Individualized	• Assessment-based behavioral strategies • Token reinforcement • Response cost • Self-monitoring • Self-evaluation • Individualized academic support (e.g., Collaborative Strategic Reading) • Computer-assisted instruction • Family–School Success program	• Contingency contracting • Self-monitoring • Self-evaluation • Individualized academic support (e.g., Collaborative Strategic Reading)

attention problems. Individualized strategies may be necessary for some students with ADHD, particularly those with more severe symptoms and impairment. As with the organizational framework of proactive and reactive strategies, in our experience improved outcomes for target students can be achieved by having a balanced approach in place. Further, teachers faced with multiple students in need of behavior and/or academic support are likely to be overwhelmed by, and unlikely to meet the demands of, delivering multiple classroom interventions if some level of proactive, preventive strategies are not in place. Finally, data regarding student outcomes (i.e., academic achievement and behavior) must be used to determine when interventions can be withdrawn and/or when students can move from one tier of educational support to another.

The goal of these strategies is to monitor and improve student performance. To achieve this goal, it is essential to clearly communicate expectations and to provide both positive and corrective feedback to students. Both proactive and reactive strategies require that expectations and feedback are communicated on an ongoing basis. To be successful in the classroom, students with attention problems generally require frequent opportunities to actively respond to instruction while receiving continual feedback on their performance (DuPaul & Stoner, 2014).

Universal Level of Primary Prevention

The universal level of prevention practices typically involves the entire class or school and is designed to prevent academic and behavioral difficulties by explicitly teaching expectations and actively acknowledging compliance. In a multitiered system of support, primary prevention of problem behavior includes systematic instruction in the specific behaviors students need to demonstrate in order to achieve school success (Sugai & Horner, 2006). The process of teaching, reviewing, and reinforcing expectations is a particularly critical instructional practice to improve classroom management (Simonsen, Fairbanks, Briesch, Myers, & Sugai, 2008).

Because children with attention problems are likely to be present in every classroom and school setting, comprehensive universal behavioral support requires the active participation of all staff, including teachers, administrators, paraprofessionals, cafeteria workers, playground supervisors, bus drivers, and other support staff. Primary prevention also involves family and community members in supporting prosocial behaviors

(Sugai & Horner, 2006). Active family and community involvement in precisely defining appropriate and inappropriate behaviors may reduce cultural bias. At a minimum it allows for the accommodation of differences in behavioral expectations among home, school, and community settings. Helping to train students, families, and staff in evidence-based practices is an area in which school psychologists can have a lasting positive impact. In addition, school psychologists can evaluate the impact of universal interventions through ongoing monitoring of student academic and behavioral progress.

Universal Interventions to Increase Prosocial Behavior

Effective school-wide and individual plans focus on academically and behaviorally important outcomes that are linked to the larger goals of the school, district, and state, while taking community and cultural values into account. On the universal level, an intervention program such as school-wide positive behavior support (Sugai & Horner, 2006) provides a primary level of behavioral instruction for all students through the teaching of three to five positively stated expectations along with the routines and behaviors that actively demonstrate those expectations. The explicit teaching of routines benefits all students while also providing important opportunities for the rehearsal of socially important behaviors for students with attention problems. A school-wide or classroom acknowledgement system is also a critical factor in successfully implementing a universal level of prevention and educational support. Simonsen et al. (2008) identified five critical features of classroom management, including posting, teaching and reviewing expectations, actively engaging students, and acknowledging appropriate behaviors.

Consistent classroom routines and procedures along with frequent feedback allow students to develop self-management skills within a supportive and effective learning environment. The use of specific praise related to expectations may also have a positive impact on rates of academic engagement (Simonsen et al., 2008). Acknowledgement of compliance or noncompliance with rules is a key factor in increasing student understanding of how the general expectations translate into specific behaviors. School psychologists can support teachers in mastering a range of verbal, nonverbal, and visual cues; prompts; and reminders to more effectively support students to stay on task.

Teachers should be encouraged to actively teach expectations to all students throughout the school year. Scheduling school-wide teaching and modeling of expectations at the point of performance early in the school year helps ensure that every student is exposed to the instruction. Specifically, teachers should:

- Actively teach expectations for student engagement by discussion, modeling, and acknowledging children for following them (i.e., catch students following rules) and ensure academic and nonacademic routines are regularly taught and practiced
- Use active supervision practices, such as frequently scanning and circulating through the classroom while monitoring student attention and behavior
- Remind students about expected engagement behaviors before the start of the activity rather than waiting until after a rule has been broken
- Correct behavioral errors (e.g., lack of attention to task) in a brief, clear, and consistent manner, similar to instructional strategies for correcting academic errors
- Maintain a brisk pace of instruction and use a range of verbal, nonverbal, and visual cues to precorrect and redirect inattentive behaviors so that instruction is uninterrupted
- Frequently communicate expectations about use of class time and task engagement in a clear manner through the use of explicitly taught routines and procedures

In addition to active teaching of classroom rules, teachers should be encouraged to design the classroom environment to allow for more careful monitoring of student activities. Teachers should be encouraged to arrange the classroom so that students with attention problems are more likely to participate in class activities while not restricting opportunities to learn and benefit from instruction. For example, students with attention problems may sometimes be placed in quieter areas of the classroom to decrease potential distractions for the child. Although this can be a successful intervention in some cases, it is important that the student continue to have access to teacher instruction, appropriate peer interactions, and class activities.

Transitions from one area of the school to another are often a trigger for problem behavior. Allowing time to teach, model, and practice efficient transition behaviors can prevent problem behaviors that would otherwise be expected during these times. It is particularly important for children with attention problems to have an opportunity to review expectations and consequences when transitioning to a new or typically problematic setting (Pfiffner, Barkley, &

DuPaul, 2006). Transitions into and out of areas with high numbers of students, such as the cafeteria and hallways, often are particularly problematic and a source of many discipline referrals. Active supervision by adults, including moving around the area, scanning for potential trouble spots, and interacting briefly and positively with a number of students has been shown to decrease problem behaviors in common areas (DuPaul & Stoner, 2014).

Universal Interventions to Enhance Academic Performance

Children with attention problems often benefit from class-wide instructional strategies that provide a direct, teacher-mediated link between assessment and intervention. These strategies may include flexible grouping for academic instruction, continual progress monitoring of basic academic skills, and explicit instruction in study and organizational strategies.

Schools that embed ongoing assessment and intervention practices within the school-wide instructional and behavioral programming provide a framework for the prevention of attention problems. Progress monitoring using dynamic repeated assessments of fluency and accuracy in reading, writing, and math allow teachers to monitor student progress over time and adjust instruction accordingly. The size of instructional groups may also have an impact on on-task behavior, with small group instruction allowing for increased monitoring and feedback.

Study strategies are another important factor in achieving success for children and adolescents with attention problems. These organizational and metacognitive strategies often are embedded in the curriculum and instruction in the classroom; however, students with attention problems may need a more explicit level of instruction that teaches the strategy through modeling and demonstration and allows for practice and rehearsal. Many students with attention problems have weak organizational skills related to time and materials, often losing work, forgetting to complete homework, and failing to study adequately for tests. Langberg, Epstein, Urbanowicz, Simon, and Graham (2008) suggest that failure to write down homework assignments and to organize materials needed for school and home may be two key factors contributing to academic challenges for students with attention problems. These students often need teachers and parents to model and help manage simple, effective organizational systems. Teachers should be encouraged to model organizational skills daily by having instructional and student materials easily accessible and by teaching specific skills related to organizing notebooks or binders, homework folders, and calendars (see Evans et al., 2009).

Parents are often affected by the organizational weaknesses of their children with attention problems and may be spending significant time and effort to support homework completion and study skills. Parents and teachers view homework performance from different perspectives in their respective settings, and both perspectives are helpful in planning interventions. School psychologists may consider providing individual or group-based training to remediate organizational weaknesses as a way to increase school success for students with attention problems. Well-organized binders, backpacks, and lockers and fewer late assignments may help set the stage for improved academic functioning. Because problems with organization can have an impact on long-term outcomes for students with attention problems, with failed classes increasing dropout risk and poor time management and project management skills potentially affecting future employment opportunities, organizational skills are an important area for remediation.

Secondary Prevention (Targeted) Practices

The secondary level of instructional and behavioral supports builds on the strong and necessary foundation created by the universal systems. The secondary level of intervention intensifies the support for small groups of students who may have attention problems that are persistent but not severe and who need higher levels of monitoring, instruction, and reinforcement (Crone, Hawken, & Horner, 2010). In order to use limited resources wisely, targeted interventions may be designed for groups of students with similar behavior that has consistently predictable features (e.g., attention problems). As tiered interventions are designed and implemented, it is important to assess whether culturally or linguistically diverse students are overrepresented in intervention groups at the secondary or tertiary levels, as teacher referrals are typically the basis of data used for entry into these interventions.

Students with attention problems, particularly in middle and high school settings, often require more explicit instruction and well-designed interventions to achieve academic and social goals. To be successful in the classroom, students with attention problems generally require frequent opportunities to actively respond to instruction while receiving continual feedback on

their performance (DuPaul & Stoner, 2014). Thus, the secondary level of educational support typically involves more explicit behavioral instruction and acknowledgement in the classroom environment before a student's inattentive behavior has a chance to occur. If the teacher is able to recognize those situations and cues that are reliably followed by inattentive and disruptive behavior, then an efficient way of handling this is to precorrect (i.e., instructions intended to prevent inattention) rather than waiting to react to the student's behavior.

The most successful strategies at this level of support are both efficient to administer within the course of a typical school day and effective in supporting behavior change. Although this chapter is focused on the needs of students with attention problems and/or ADHD in the classroom setting, the intervention strategies may prove helpful in motivating and engaging many students. School psychologists can evaluate the impact of targeted strategies by monitoring student academic and behavioral progress as well as by assessing the degree to which teachers or other school personnel implement strategies with integrity.

Instructional Strategies

Inattentive behaviors have a negative impact on academic achievement over time as students struggle with school performance and homework management (Langberg et al., 2011). For many children with attention problems associated with ADHD, the two primary classroom situations that prompt inattentive behavior are teacher-directed instruction and the presentation of independent academic work. Accommodations and modifications to schoolwork are frequently used to address the needs of students with attention problems. Although these are often helpful, it is also important to develop student skills and not solely rely on lowering the bar for performance (Owens & Fabiano, 2011). Often interventions selected to enhance student engagement in a lesson will be helpful for other students who experience variable engagement and focus during instruction.

Some students may demonstrate significant levels of inattention and off-task behavior as a function of being exposed to curriculum material that is beyond their instructional level. Curriculum-based measurement data can be an important tool to progress monitor basic skills in conjunction with evidence-based educational practices (Shinn, 2007). In fact, in some cases, an adjustment in instruction based on curriculum-based measurement data can lead to notable improvements in task-related concentration. Most children with attention problems, particularly those with ADHD, will require additional interventions to address their academic and behavioral difficulties. For example, students with ADHD are more likely than typical peers to show deficits in reading ability. These areas of weakness have an impact on student performance across the curriculum. However, the use of systematic strategy instruction may help reduce co-occurring reading deficits. A reading comprehension strategy such as Think Before Reading, Think While Reading, Think After Reading requires students to answer questions prior to reading, use specific strategies while reading, and summarize and retell after reading (Johnson, Reid, & Mason, 2012). Research on this strategy has shown that it can help high school students with ADHD increase their recall of key points from text, an important outcome considering the large amount of reading high school students are typically assigned.

Peer tutoring is another example of an intervention that focuses primarily on academic performance in addition to adjusting curriculum to student instructional level. Peer tutoring is defined as any instructional strategy wherein two students work together on an academic activity with one student providing assistance, instruction, and/or feedback to the other (Greenwood, Maheady, & Delquadri, 2002). Several peer-tutoring models have been developed that differ as to instructional focus (acquisition versus practice), structure (reciprocal versus nonreciprocal), and procedural components (e.g., number of sessions per week, methods of pairing students, type of reward system used). Despite these differences, all models of peer tutoring share instructional characteristics that are known to enhance the task-related attention of students with attention problems including (a) working one-to-one with another individual; (b) instructional pace determined by the learner; (c) continuous prompting of academic responses; and (d) frequent, immediate feedback about quality of performance (Pfiffner et al., 2006).

Class-Wide Peer Tutoring (Greenwood et al., 2002), is one of the most widely used peer tutoring programs to enhance the mathematics, reading, and spelling skills of students of all achievement levels. This approach includes reciprocal tutoring using academic scripts and immediate error correction within a structured system of reinforcement. Tutoring sessions are brief, lasting less than 30 minutes, and peer recognition is the primary reinforcer used. This peer tutoring program has been found to enhance the on-task behavior and academic performance of unmedicated students with attention

problems in general education classrooms, while normally achieving students participating in Class-Wide Peer Tutoring also showed improvements in attention and academic performance (DuPaul, Ervin, Hook, & McGoey, 1998). Peer tutoring is a practical and time-efficient intervention that can be implemented to help all students while also meeting the needs of children with attention problems.

The process of planning academic interventions for students with attention problems should include a focus on evaluating and replacing faulty learning strategies with effective strategies. School psychologists should encourage teachers to present major concepts in a clearly organized way and model simple strategies that can be efficiently applied to many academic tasks in order to enhance student engagement (DuPaul & Stoner, 2014).

The implementation of classroom interventions for adolescents with attention problems is complicated, to some degree, by the need for services to be coordinated across multiple teachers and settings. School psychologists play a critical role in facilitating consistent use of recommended strategies in a feasible, acceptable fashion. For example, school psychologists can meet with the team of teachers to design strategies, adapt these across curricula and classrooms, and plan for sequential introduction of strategies across class periods. Effectiveness may be optimized by first introducing a specific intervention in one or two classrooms where the strategy is viewed as most acceptable and feasible (DuPaul & Stoner, 2014). Once initial implementation difficulties are addressed, then the strategy can be gradually introduced into remaining classes. Self-monitoring and self-management strategies may be particularly helpful at the secondary level given less reliance on teacher time and resources (DuPaul & Stoner, 2014).

Strategies to Increase Prosocial Behavior

Although school-wide expectations and an effective teaching and acknowledgement system will provide enough behavioral support for most students, children and adolescents with attention problems, especially those with ADHD, often need more targeted interventions in order to be successful in school. One evidence-based program is the Behavior Education Program (Crone at al., 2010). This program provides immediate behavioral feedback through a daily progress report and includes a reinforcement system based on earning daily points for following expectations. Parent responsibilities include daily review and signing of the progress report along with feedback to their child. Additional reinforcement at home is optional yet helpful. The Behavior Education Program is designed to allow teachers to summarize weekly performance data for the student, thus continually monitoring the effectiveness of the interventions in place in relation to the goals set by the student, teacher, and parents. Reduced inattentive behavior and more consistent academic engagement are among the positive results of this program.

Several programs designed for children with attention problems use daily report cards as a form of feedback and monitoring. The use of daily report cards in an intervention context has been shown to result in significantly improved target behaviors for children with ADHD or disruptive behaviors (Owens et al., 2012). A comprehensive model such as the Family–School Success program (Power et al., 2012), which includes the use of collaborative problem-solving and daily report cards along with training in homework rituals, time management, and goal setting, provides supports to develop both social and academic skills in children with attention problems. Although the intensity of the program may not be easily replicable in schools, and, indeed Power et al. (2012) recommend adaptation for school settings, it provides a model for programming that may reduce homework avoidance and associated parent–child conflict while improving parent–teacher relationships, a powerful combination likely to produce greater success for children with attention problems. Although the use of a daily report card requires sustained time and effort on the part of teachers and parents, research indicates that daily report cards may be a helpful tool for school psychologists to use when planning interventions for children with attention problems or ADHD at either the targeted or the tertiary level.

Homework completion is often an area in need of improvement for children with attention problems. Functional behaviors that support homework completion include writing down the assignment and bringing relevant materials home. Gureasko-Moore, DuPaul, and White (2007) describe a self-management training program for a small group of middle schoolers that uses limited resources well, requiring only brief periods of student training and monitoring by staff. The use of baseline data collected from home and school along with student checklists and logs provides meaningful measures of actual student performance related to homework and classroom engagement. Gradual fading of adult support is built in and would allow school staff to provide the intervention on a rolling basis as needs arise. Because failing homework grades often lead to course

failure, particularly at the secondary level, interventions that successfully target this area can have a large impact on school performance.

After-school programming can be an effective way to deliver social skills training and academic strategy instruction. The Challenging Horizons Program (Evans, Schultz, DeMars, & Davis, 2011) includes group and individual interventions to improve social problem solving along with academic skills training in study strategies and note taking. Implementing a structured support program such as the Challenging Horizons Program at the beginning of the school year may help prevent declining grades due to inattentive behavior over time.

Educating Parents to Act as Partners With the School

Successfully parenting a child or adolescent with attention problems requires a willingness to learn new skills, implement new strategies, and continually update the prevention and support activities used at home as the child grows and changes. Ideally, parents partner with school psychologists and teachers in order to promote their child's success. Creating a partnership for success takes collaboration and communication on both sides, particularly in adolescence when the effect of parent involvement in supporting treatment of attention problems may be more limited (Evans et al., 2011).

School psychologists can inform parents about support services, provide information on how the symptoms of ADHD may manifest in both the school and home settings, and help the parent advocate for their child in the school setting. In addition, school psychologists can encourage teachers to ensure that their classrooms focus on the development of positive adult and peer relationships for children with attention problems. Helping students to engage with school throughout their academic careers requires ongoing support of academic and behavioral growth, along with relationships that provide positive interpersonal connections.

Tertiary Level (Individualized) Intervention Strategies

Students with ADHD may present with problems that are chronic (i.e., long standing in nature) and/or severe (e.g., as compared to typically functioning peers as well as those with milder attention problems). In these instances it is likely that interventions tailored to the individual student and focused on presenting problems will be warranted. The focus of such interventions will be assisting the student to be successful in the classroom/school, with behavior support, academic support, and support linking the student's home and school, or some combination thereof. School psychologists facilitate the implementation of individualized interventions by consulting with and/or training teachers, parents, and other personnel in evidence-based approaches. Further, the impact of intervention should be assessed through ongoing monitoring of student academic and behavioral progress as well as the degree to which interventions are implemented as intended. Assessment data can then inform changes to intervention over time.

Individualized Behavior Supports

Several strategies have been shown to improve the classroom engagement of individual students with ADHD. These include strategies that focus on the manipulation of behavioral consequences, strategies that focus on linking contingency management to the function of inattentive behavior, and strategies that focus on behavior change through self-management. The intent of these interventions is to minimize the impact of inattentive behavior on a classroom, reduce the frequency of negative interactions between the student and the teacher, and teach the student a more appropriate way to meet his or her needs (e.g., secure teacher attention). A concurrent goal is to arrange the environment to enhance the student's ability to focus on learning and minimize reinforcement of inattentive behavior. Specific aspects of these interventions should be individually designed to fit the needs, contexts, and contingencies present for each student.

Behavior Support With Token Reinforcement and Response Cost

Token reinforcement is a commonly used strategy in which students earn points for meeting behavioral expectations (e.g., attending to task and completing assigned tasks), and the points can be exchanged for activity or tangible reinforcers. One example of this type of strategy is response cost wherein students earn tokens based on identified desirable classroom behavior and also may concurrently lose tokens contingent on inappropriate, inattentive behavior (i.e., the response-cost aspect of the system). Students have the opportunity to earn back lost tokens, thus increasing the probability that they will remain engaged and motivated by the system. Response-cost systems require planning and clear communication at the outset. The rules of the system should be taught and reviewed frequently. The

student should understand when the system will be used, how points may be gained or lost, what reinforcers are available in exchange for points, and how and when points may be exchanged. Maintaining student interest will also require periodic changes to the available privileges and reinforcers. Several studies have supported the use of response-cost strategies for children with attention problems associated with ADHD (see Pfiffner et al., 2006).

Functional Assessment-Linked Strategies

Functional assessment strategies are interviews, observations, and environmental manipulations (e.g., changing a seating arrangement) that help to identify environmental variables that reliably precede or follow inattentive behaviors. From a behavior analytic perspective, and in the case of preceding variables, these variables are hypothesized to prompt or occasion the occurrence of inattentive behavior. In the case of variables reliably following inattentive behavior, these are hypothesized to reinforce or maintain inattention.

Understanding the factors that maintain inattentive behaviors, along with the situations that appear to set the stage for those behaviors, is an essential first step in planning successful interventions. For example, consider a target student's off-task behavior that is reliably occasioned by the teacher's presentation of a class-wide, in-seat math work assignment. In this instance, one potential intervention could involve provision of teacher assistance at the beginning of that assignment to ensure that directions are understood, the student has all necessary materials, and the student is able to independently complete the work assigned. This would be a preventive or proactive strategy.

Alternatively, consider the same student and behavior but a different identified function of the inattentive behavior. In this instance, suppose the student's off-task behavior reliably results in teacher attention (e.g., "Joseph, do you need help with your assignment? Let me look at your work and see if I can help."). Here it would be hypothesized that Joseph's off-task behavior is reinforced via teacher-delivered attention. At least one component of a functional approach to intervention would include behavior management strategies intended to strengthen task engagement that would produce the same type of reinforcement. For example, the teacher might use a strategy that included providing attention contingent upon Joseph working on and completing independent in-seat assignments and withholding attention when inattentive behavior occurs. Alternatively, the teacher might work with Joseph to develop an unobtrusive signal that he can use to readily obtain teacher attention and assistance with challenging academic work.

Behavior Support Based on Self-Management Strategies

Another effective intervention approach to improve attentive behavior involves self-directed activities that require students to monitor and/or evaluate their own attention over time. Collectively, such approaches are based on self-management. Self-management systems involve students in observing or monitoring their own attentive behavior, evaluating that behavior relative to an identified standard, and delivering earned reinforcement. At the same time, the task of identifying specific inattentive behaviors and goals will most likely involve adults (e.g., school psychologists, teachers, and parents) in collaboration with students. When developing interventions that include self-management components, it will be useful to clearly identify which aspects will be teacher controlled and which will be managed by the student and to make decisions about these based on the individual student's needs and abilities.

A self-evaluation system generally allows students to earn points that can be used for privileges. The teacher clearly identifies the target behaviors (e.g., timely completion of assigned tasks) and academic performance expected and provides a written rating scale that states the performance criteria for each rating. The teacher and students separately rate student attentive behavior during an activity. At the end of the activity or time period, the teacher and students compare ratings. If they match exactly, then students keep all points and earn a bonus point. If student ratings are within one point of the teacher rating, then students keep their points. If student ratings are more than one point away from teacher ratings, then students do not receive points for the activity. Eventually, the close teacher involvement is faded and students become responsible for monitoring their own behavior.

Children with ADHD often lack the skill to be accurate judges of their own behavior. Because children with ADHD may have a tendency toward recalling their positive behaviors and not recognizing the inattentive behaviors that affect their ratings, a brief discussion or reminder of the behaviors that led to a lower rating may be useful. Setting up a self-management system in a classroom involves training the child with ADHD in the system, providing clear descriptions of the expected on-task behaviors, and drawing up a list of privileges the child would like to earn. The goal is to eventually teach children to monitor their own attentive behavior in the classroom without constant feedback from the teacher.

For example, Evans et al. (2009) engaged middle school students with ADHD in a project aimed at improving school related organization behaviors. The project specifically focused on student academic binders, and used a monitoring tool called the Organization Assessment Sheet, which contained items referring to assignment notebooks, separate class folders, homework folders, and specific organizational strategies using particular sections of the binder. Students were taught to monitor and evaluate their behavior relative to identified expectations for being attentive and well organized, and reinforcers were delivered contingent upon high rates of demonstrated binder organization.

Individualized Academic Supports

Differentiating instruction for students with ADHD often requires some form of individualized instruction to help them succeed academically. Individualized instruction may focus on the development of basic skills such as reading and mathematics, the development of content area knowledge (e.g., science and social studies), study, and organizational skills (e.g., work completion, task engagement). A thorough review of effective intervention strategies across these areas is beyond our scope, but the reader is directed to other chapters in this *Best Practices* edition for details of a wide range of evidence-based instructional interventions.

It is crucial to note that individualizing instruction successfully for students with ADHD often warrants and requires significant teacher support for designing and delivering interventions. For example, Jitendra, DuPaul, Someki, and Tresco (2008) describe and discuss the use of explicit instruction in phonological awareness and word decoding as well as Collaborative Strategic Reading to support the development of reading and reading comprehension, respectively. In the area of math instruction, Jitendra et al. (2008) also reviewed the use of cover-copy-compare fluency building strategies and schema-based instructional approaches to promote the development of higher order skills in mathematics. Further, DuPaul et al. (2006) provide evidence to support the use of consultation-based academic interventions to support both reading and math achievement for students with ADHD. It is interesting to note that the results of DuPaul et al.'s research found similar, positive outcomes for both a generic collaborative consultation model and a specific problem-solving behavioral consultation model.

Computer-Assisted Instruction

Another promising area of academic support for students with ADHD involves computer-assisted instruction.

Research involving children with ADHD has shown three task-related variables to be related to improved attentive behavior. These variables are novel (as compared with familiar) stimulus conditions, immediate (as compared with delayed) feedback, and a one-to-one teacher–student ratio. Arranging these variables into the instructional conditions of a typical classroom on a regular basis is not feasible when considering the classroom teacher as the intervention agent. However, computer-assisted instruction can indeed deliver instruction infused with these variables (Clarfield & Stoner, 2005).

Thus, a growing evidence base suggests the instructional features of computer-assisted instruction help students to focus their attention on academic stimuli. Although not always the case, computer-assisted instruction presents activities incorporating specific instructional objectives, provides highlighting of essential material (e.g., large print and color), utilizes multiple sensory modalities, divides content material into smaller bits of information, and provides immediate feedback about response accuracy.

Individualized Supports Linking Home and School

In addition to school- and classroom-based supports, students with ADHD also are likely to benefit from well-designed supports that link families and schools in working toward common student goals. As discussed previously, Power et al. (2012) demonstrated, through a randomized clinical trial, the effectiveness of the Family–School Success intervention. This intervention involves a combination of parent group meetings, individualized family therapy, conjoint behavioral consultation, homework interventions, and daily report cards. Power et al. (2012) found Family–School Success to improve family–school collaboration, the quality of the family–school relationship, homework completion, and parenting behaviors.

One component of Family–School Success, the daily behavior report card, is worth noting for its individual merit in supporting home–school communication and enhanced classroom engagement for students with ADHD at both targeted and individualized levels of intervention. Daily behavior report cards consist of a list of target behaviors, along with a rating scale and rubric for scoring, as well as provisions for teacher, parent, and student acknowledgements (see DuPaul & Stoner, 2014). Consistent use of daily reports containing these components, and linked to meaningful reinforcement of attentive behavior meeting performance criteria and goals for improvement, can be a helpful support for students with ADHD.

SUMMARY

Children with attention problems and/or ADHD experience many academic and social difficulties that require a comprehensive approach incorporating strategies across universal, targeted, and individualized levels of intervention. Several principles should guide intervention design with this population. First, educational services need to be considered in the context of the multitier model, as some students will succeed with universal services, other students will require targeted interventions, and still other students will necessitate individualized treatment strategies. Second, intervention planning should be linked directly to assessment data (e.g., functional behavioral assessment and curriculum-based measurement). Third, a consultative problem-solving process should be used to design and modify interventions. Fourth, maximum treatment effects will be obtained when intervention is implemented at the point of performance. Fifth, intervention procedures evolve and are modified on the basis of ongoing assessment data. Sixth, it is insufficient to provide training without appropriate follow-up activities (e.g., modeling, feedback, and ongoing consultation) designed to promote maintenance and generalization of effects. Finally, interventions for children with attention problems should involve mediators (e.g., peers, parents, and the students) in addition to teachers, whenever possible.

AUTHOR NOTE

Disclosure. George J. DuPaul and Gary Stoner have a financial interest in the books they authored or coauthored referenced in this chapter.

REFERENCES

American Psychiatric Association. (2013). *Diagnostic and statistical manual of mental disorders.* (5th ed.). Washington, DC: Author.

Barkley, R. A. (Ed.). (2006). *Attention-deficit hyperactivity disorder: A handbook for diagnosis and treatment.* (3rd ed.). New York, NY: Guilford Press.

Barkley, R. A., Murphy, K. R., & Fischer, M. (2008). *ADHD in adults: What the science says.* New York, NY: Guilford Press.

Barry, L. M., & Messer, J. J. (2003). A practical application of self-management for students diagnosed with attention-deficit/hyperactivity disorder. *Journal of Positive Behavior Interventions, 5,* 238–248. doi:10.1177/10983007030050040701

Clarfield, J., & Stoner, G. (2005). The effects of computerized reading instruction on the academic performance of students identified with ADHD. *School Psychology Review, 34,* 246–254.

Crone, D., Hawken, L., & Horner, R. (2010). *Responding to problem behavior in schools: Second Edition: The behavior education program.* New York, NY: Guilford Press.

DuPaul, G. J., Eckert, T. L., & Vilardo, B. (2012). The effects of school-based interventions for attention deficit hyperactivity disorder: A meta-analysis 1996–2010. *School Psychology Review, 41,* 387–412.

DuPaul, G. J., Ervin, R. A., Hook, C. L., & McGoey, K. E. (1998). Peer tutoring for children with attention deficit hyperactivity disorder: Effects on classroom behavior and academic performance. *Journal of Applied Behavior Analysis, 31,* 579–592. doi:10.1901/jaba.1998.31-579

DuPaul, G. J., Gormley, M. J., & Laracy, S. D. (2013). Comorbidity of LD and ADHD: Implications of DSM-5 for assessment and treatment. *Journal of Learning Disabilities, 46,* 43–51. doi:10.1177/0022219412464351

DuPaul, G. J., Jitendra, A. K., Volpe, R. J., Tresco, K. E., Lutz, J. G., Vile Junod, R. E., … Mannella, M. C. (2006). Consultation-based academic interventions for children with ADHD: Effects on reading and mathematics achievement. *Journal of Abnormal Child Psychology, 34,* 635–648. doi:10.1007/s10802-006-9046-7

DuPaul, G. J., & Stoner, G. (2014). *ADHD in the schools: Assessment and intervention strategies.* (3rd ed.). New York, NY: Guilford Press.

Evans, S., Schultz, B., DeMars, C., & Davis, H. (2011). Effectiveness of the Challenging Horizons after-school program for young adolescents with ADHD. *Behavior Therapy, 42,* 462–474. doi:10.1016/j.beth.2010.11.008

Evans, S., Schultz, B., White, L., Brady, C., Sibley, M., & Van Eck, K. (2009). A school-based organization intervention for young adolescents with ADHD. *School Mental Health, 1,* 78–88. doi:10.1007/s12310-009-9009-6

Greenwood, C. R., Maheady, L., & Delquadri, J. (2002). Class-wide peer tutoring programs. In M. R. Shinn, H. M. Walker, & G. Stoner (Eds.), *Interventions for academic and behavior problems II: Preventive and remedial approaches.* (pp. 611–649). Bethesda, MD: National Association of School Psychologists.

Gureasko-Moore, S., DuPaul, G. J., & White, G. P. (2007). Self-management of classroom preparedness and homework: Effects on school functioning of adolescents with attention deficit hyperactivity disorder. *School Psychology Review, 36,* 647–664.

Harrison, J. R., Vannest, K., Davis, J., & Reynolds, C. (2012). Common problem behaviors of children and adolescents in general education classrooms in the United States. *Journal of Emotional and Behavioral Disorders, 20,* 55–64. doi:10.1177/1063426611421157

Hosterman, S. J., DuPaul, G. J., & Jitendra, A. K. (2008). Teacher ratings of ADHD symptoms in ethnic minority students: Bias or behavioral difference? *School Psychology Quarterly, 23,* 418–435. doi:10.1037/a0012668

Jitendra, A. K., DuPaul, G. J., Someki, F., & Tresco, K. E. (2008). Enhancing academic achievement for children with attention-deficit/hyperactivity disorder: Evidence from school-based intervention research. *Developmental Disabilities Research Reviews, 14,* 325–330. doi:10.1002/ddrr.39

Johnson, J., Reid, R., & Mason, L. H. (2012). Improving recall of high school students with ADHD. *Remedial and Special Education, 33,* 258–268. doi:10.1177/0741932511403502

Langberg, J., Epstein, J., Urbanowicz, C., Simon, J., & Graham, A. (2008). Efficacy of an organization skills intervention to improve the academic functioning of students with ADHD. *School Psychology Quarterly, 23,* 407–417. doi:10.1037/1045-3830.23.3.407

Langberg, J., Molina, B., Arnold, L., Epstein, J., Altaye, M., Hinshaw, S., … Hechtman, L. (2011). Patterns and predictors of adolescent academic achievement and performance in a sample of children with attention-deficit/hyperactivity disorder (ADHD). *Journal of Clinical Child & Adolescent Psychology, 40,* 519–531. doi:10.1080/15374416.2011.581620

National Association of School Psychologists. (2010). *Model for comprehensive and integrated school psychological services.* Bethesda, MD: Author. Retrieved from http://www.nasponline.org/standards/2010standards/2_PracticeModel.pdf

Owens, J., & Fabiano, G. (2011). School mental health programming for youth with ADHD: Addressing needs across the academic career. *School Mental Health, 3,* 111–116. doi:10.1007/s12310-011-9061-x

Owens, J., Holdaway, A., Zoromski, A., Evans, S., Himawan, L., Girio-Herrera, E., & Murphy, C. (2012). Incremental benefits of a daily report card intervention over time for youth with disruptive behavior. *Behavior Therapy, 43,* 848–861. doi:10.1016/j.beth.2012.02.002

Pelham, W. E., Jr., & Fabiano, G. A. (2008). Evidence-based psychosocial treatments for attention-deficit/hyperactivity disorder. *Journal of Clinical Child & Adolescent Psychology, 37,* 184–214. doi:10.1080/15374410701818681

Pfiffner, L. J., Barkley, R. A., & DuPaul, G. J. (2006). Treatment of ADHD in school settings. In R. A. Barkley (Ed.), *Attention deficit hyperactivity disorder: A handbook for diagnosis and treatment.* (3rd ed., pp. 547–589). New York, NY: Guilford Press.

Power, T., Mautone, J., Soffer, S., Clarke, A., Marshall, S., Sharman, J., … Jawad, A. (2012). A family-school intervention for children with ADHD: Results of a randomized clinical trial. *Journal of Consulting and Clinical Psychology, 80,* 611–623. doi:10.1037/a0028188

Shinn, M. R. (2007). Identifying students at risk, monitoring performance, and determining eligibility within response to intervention: Research on educational need and benefit from academic intervention. *School Psychology Review, 36,* 601–617.

Simonsen, B., Fairbanks, S., Briesch, A., Myers, D., & Sugai, G. (2008). Evidence-based practices in classroom management: Considerations for research to practice. *Education and Treatment of Children, 31,* 351–380. doi:10.1353/etc.0.0007

Sugai, G., & Horner, R. H. (2006). A promising approach for expanding and sustaining school-wide positive behavior support. *School Psychology Review, 35,* 245–259.

U.S. Department of Education. (2008). *Thirtieth annual report to Congress: Implementation of the Individuals with Disabilities Act.* Washington, DC: Author.

24 Best Practices in School-Based Interventions for Anxiety and Depression

Thomas J. Huberty
Indiana University

OVERVIEW

Anxiety and depression are two of the most common psychological problems that children experience, and they can have significant short-term and long-term effects on personal, social, and academic functioning. Left untreated, anxiety and depression can persist into adulthood, causing lifetime distress and dysfunction. Because the vast majority of children attend public or private schools, there are many opportunities for early identification, intervention, and prevention of anxiety and depression in the school setting. Thus, the school psychologist must have thorough knowledge of both patterns and how to identify, treat, and prevent them in the school setting. Indeed, schools provide the best opportunity to identify and intervene for anxiety and depression in children and youth. Because many children who have anxiety and depression do not receive treatment, school psychologists may be the primary mental health professionals who can provide services to these students.

Therefore, the purpose of this chapter is to provide information about anxiety and depression in children and adolescents and how school psychologists can work with them in the school setting. The objectives of the chapter are to provide information about (a) the nature, prevalence, and development of anxiety and depression in children and adolescents; (b) the causes of anxiety and depression; (c) the effects of anxiety and depression on academic and social development; (d) assessment, intervention, consultation, and prevention; and (e) implications for special education services. Included is discussion of developmental considerations, evaluation of intervention effectiveness and outcomes, multicultural considerations, and parent involvement. The chapter is linked to the domain of Interventions and Mental Health Services to Develop Social and Life Skills in the National Association of School Psychologists (NASP) *Model for Comprehensive and Integrated School Psychological Services* (NASP, 2010).

Characteristics of Anxiety

Anxiety has been defined as "the product of a multi-complex response system, involving affective, behavioral, physiological, and cognitive components" (Weems & Silverman, 2013, p. 515). Worry is a primary cognitive characteristic of anxiety, which Weems and Silverman describe as a cognitive process that is involved in anticipation of future danger. The major forms of anxiety are *trait anxiety* and *state anxiety*. Trait anxiety is characterized as persistent and pervasive generalized anxiety that is expressed in a variety of settings. State anxiety is shown in specific situations, such as giving a public speech or taking a test. Trait anxiety is shown in the majority of anxiety disorders and is considered to be a stable pattern or personality trait, while state anxiety occurs in more specific situations, although it may be shown in cases of specific phobias. Having state anxiety does not mean that a person will have trait anxiety, although those with trait patterns are more likely to have state anxiety (Huberty, 2008).

Anxiety is shown in three primary ways: (a) cognitive, (b) behavioral, and (c) physiological. Often, these symptoms occur simultaneously when a person feels anxious or distressed. Table 24.1 lists the primary cognitive, behavioral, and physiological symptoms of anxiety. Assessment, intervention, consultation, and

Table 24.1. Characteristics of Anxiety

Cognitive	Behavioral	Physiological
• Concentration problems	• Motor restlessness	• Tics
• Memory problems	• Fidgety	• Recurrent, localized pain
• Attention problems	• Task avoidance	• Rapid heart rate
• Oversensitivity	• Rapid speech	• Flushing of the skin
• Problem-solving difficulties	• Erratic behavior	• Perspiration
• Worry	• Irritability	• Headaches
• Cognitive distortion	• Withdrawal	• Muscle tension
• Cognitive deficiencies	• Perfectionism	• Sleeping problems
• Fear attributional bias	• Lack of participation	• Nausea
• Emotion regulation difficulties	• Failing to complete task	• Vomiting
• Negative emotionality	• Seeking easy tasks	• Enuresis

Note. From "Best Practices in School-Based Intervention for Anxiety and Depression" (p. 1474), by T. J. Huberty. In A. Thomas and J. Grimes (Eds.), *Best Practices in School Psychology V*, 2008, Bethesda, MD: National Association of School Psychologists. Copyright 2008 by National Association of School Psychologists. Reprinted with permission.

prevention must consider all three domains when working with these children.

Prevalence and Developmental Patterns in Anxiety

Merikangas et al. (2010) found that anxiety disorders were the most prevalent of all mental disorders, accounting for 31.9% of the cases, with a median onset of 6 years of age. Approximately 8.3% of the study population was classified as having an anxiety disorder that caused severe impairment. Of the sample, 38.0% of females and 26.1% of males had any anxiety disorder, which reflects a ratio of about 1.5 to 1.0 of females to males.

Causes of Anxiety Disorders

The causes of anxiety disoders are numerous, complex, and often interactive with each other. A summary of the major factors is provided below: (a) genetic and biological factors; (b) cultural, social, and family factors; (c) parental psychopathology and mental health; and (d) parental behavior.

Genetic and Biological Factors

The majority of research evidence suggests that genetics account for about one-third of the variance in creating a general risk factor for anxiety disorders (Gregory & Eley, 2011), with the remainder being associated with shared (family) and unshared (individual) environmental variance. Therefore, a genetic predisposition to anxiety may create a risk factor for specific disorders that develop as a result of biological or environmental factors.

Cultural, Social, and Family Factors

People in all cultures experience anxiety at some time, but the incidence of anxiety disorders varies across groups. Anxiety symptoms tend to occur more often in cultures that are collectivist in nature, value emotional inhibition, show deference to others, and discourage expression of emotions, which may contribute to the development of internalizing disorders (Varela et al., 2004).

Parental Psychopathology and Mental Health

An important correlate of child anxiety problems is maternal anxiety. Costa and Weems (2005) found that maternal anxiety was associated with mothers' anxious attachment beliefs and child anxiety. Conversely, child anxiety was associated with a child's insecure attachment beliefs, a child's perceptions of maternal control, and maternal anxious attachment beliefs. These findings are consistent with a large body of research that maternal anxiety is highly correlated with childhood anxiety, which may be translated into dysfunctional maternal behavior, including being overprotective (Costa & Weems, 2005).

Parenting Behavior

Parents of anxious children, especially mothers who are anxious, tend to be overcontrolling, overprotective of their children's behavior, and are more intrusive. If excessive to the extent that a child does not develop effective coping skills, it may interfere with a child's ability to face fear-producing events and may reinforce anxiety.

Effects of Anxiety on Academic Performance

The effects of high levels of anxiety on classroom performance and evaluation in the school setting can be substantial. Problems associated with anxiety include difficulties with attention, concentration, memory, and problem solving that affect performance (Huberty, 2008).

Effects of Anxiety on Social Development

High levels of generalized and chronic anxiety can have significant effects on social performance and competence, which can also increase anxiety (e.g., Creveling, Varela, Weems, & Corey, 2010). Anxious children are less likely to enter social situations, initiate social contact, feel comfortable with strangers, and participate in group activities. Because they tend to be withdrawn and insecure, they may also become victims of bullying and harassment by other children.

Characteristics of Depression

Although anxiety and depression are considered different conditions and are treated as unique, they are highly comorbid and features of one are seen in the features of the other. Comorbidity exceeds 39% for meeting diagnostic criteria (Costello, Egger, Copeland, Erkanli, & Angold, 2011). If anxiety and depression coexist, then anxiety likely preceded depression in most cases. There are some signs of depression that are characteristic of children with depression (e.g., irritability), but, overall, the symptoms are similar to those of adults, and there is

not a separate category of childhood depression in the fifth edition of the *Diagnosic and Statistical Manual of Mental Disorders* (American Psychiatric Association, 2013). Some of the primary characteristics include sadness, anhedonia, depressed affect, and lack of ability to derive enjoyment from usual activities (American Psychiatric Association, 2013). Adolescents are more likely to report dysphoric mood and hopelessness, while young children do not report these symptoms but may appear more depressed. A summary of depressive symptoms is presented in Table 24.2. When Table 24.1 and Table 24.2 are compared, some of the common symptoms between anxiety and depression are evident, reflecting the high comorbidity.

Prevalence and Developmental Patterns in Depression

Merikangas et al. (2010) reported that 18.3% of adolescent females and 10.4% of adolescent males had a mood disorder, with major depressive disorder accounting for the majority of cases. These findings indicate a ratio of approximately 1.75 to 1.0 of females to males. They reported that 3.3% of females and 2.6% of males had a bipolar disorder, indicating a smaller sex difference than with major depression. Thus, depression is less common in young children, with onset more likely in late childhood and early adolescence.

Table 24.2. Characteristics of Depression

Cognitive	Behavioral	Physiological
• "All or none" thinking • Catastrophizing • Memory problems • Attention problems • Internal locus of control • Negative view of self, the world, and future • Automatic thinking • Negative attributional style • Negative affect • Feelings of hopelessness • Low self-esteem • Problem-solving difficulties • Difficulty making decisions • Rumination • Fear of loss of control • Suicidal thoughts	• Depressed mood • Social withdrawal • Lack of participation in usual activities • Limited affect • Decline in self-care and appearance • Decreased work or school performance • Appears detached from others • Crying for no apparent reason • Inappropriate responses to events • Irritability • Apathy • Uncooperative • Suicide attempts	• Psychomotor agitation or retardation • Somatic complaints • Poor appetite or overeating • Insomnia or hypersomnia • Low energy • Excessive fatigue

Note. From "Best Practices in School-Based Intervention for Anxiety and Depression" (p. 1477), by T. J. Huberty. In A. Thomas and J. Grimes (Eds.), *Best Practices in School Psychology V*, 2008, Bethesda, MD: National Association of School Psychologists. Copyright 2008 by National Association of School Psychologists. Reprinted with permission.

Onset of depression in childhood is uncommon, with the majority showing the greatest onset between ages 11 and 14. In the elementary years, the onset and prevalence for boys and girls are about the same but begin to diverge in early adolescence, with girls reporting much higher rates. The reasons for this sex difference have been discussed in the research literature, and explanations include hormonal differences, exposure to different stressors, differences in social expectations between girls and boys, different coping methods, and that girls are more likely to report symptoms than are boys (Klein, Kujawa, Black, & Pennock, 2013).

Causes of Depression and Mood Disorders

The causes of depression and mood disorders are multiple and complex, often interacting and contributing to problems in social, personal, and academic areas. The causes are discussed in a similar manner to anxiety: (a) genetic and biological factors; (b) cultural, social, and family factors; (c) parental psychopathology and mental health; and (d) parental behavior.

Genetic and Biological Factors

Similar to anxiety, family history is a predictor of depression in children, although distinguishing between genetic and environmental (shared and nonshared) influences is a challenging task. Behavioral genetic studies have found modest heritability of about 30–40%, but the estimates depend upon how the data are gathered. Heritability is associated with adolescent depression, while shared environmental factors are more related to childhood depression (Franić, Middeldorp, Dolan, Ligthart, & Boomsma, 2010)

Some of the biological factors involved in anxiety are implicated in depressive disorders. In particular, the *hypothalamic–pituitary–adrenal axis* is involved in regulation of mood and emotions, and the reader is referred to the prior discussion. Depressed children and youth are more likely to have higher basal cortisol levels that are resistant to being lowered (Lopez-Duran, Kovacs, & George, 2009).

Cultural, Social, and Family Factors

Depression exists in all cultures, although its manifestations may vary across groups. Some research has found few meaningful differences across diverse groups, although some associations have been found with socioeconomic status. Overall, the research on the association between ethnic/racial differences and depression has yielded mixed results, and no firm conclusions can be made (Merikangas et al., 2010).

Social factors are important considerations in depression, because social functioning is one of the major impairments in depressed children and youth. Depressed children are more socially isolated, derive less enjoyment from the environment, do not respond as well to positive overtures from others, receive less positive feedback, and may have social skills deficits. Parent and teacher reports indicate that depressed children have social skills deficits and difficulties with interpersonal relationships, are more withdrawn and isolated, and are hostile and aggressive toward peers (Rudolph, Flynn, & Abaied, 2008).

Family dysfunction and parental psychopathology have consistently been shown to be associated with depression in children and adolescents. Maladaptive parenting and abuse are associated with child and adolescent depression, as well as lower levels of parental warmth and communication and higher levels of intrusiveness and maltreatment. Children who have depressed parents are at much higher risk for developing depression due to the factors associated with dysfunctional parenting that exposes them to increased stress (Goodman & Tully, 2008).

Effects of Depression on Academic Performance

Depression has direct effects on academic performance by interfering with task selection and completion, problem-solving skills, reasoning, concentration, memory, and attention. The majority of research evidence indicates that depressed children and youth are likely to perform below their ability and are at risk for dropping out of school (Klein et al., 2013). Stevenson and Hadwin (2012) found an inverse relationship between school achievement and depression and anxiety in typical 12- and 13-year-old students. The authors proposed that worry and executive cognitive processes mediated the link with negative affect and academic performance.

Effects of Depression on Social Development

Depressed children and adolescents often have limited numbers and quality of interpersonal relationships. Because they tend to be withdrawn, less assertive, and self-conscious, they do not develop the skills necessary to participate effectively in social situations. They may be irritable, rejecting, and less social than their peers, leading to more isolation and reduction in relationships. Over time, they may begin to feel helpless and hopeless that their situation will improve and develop a negative attributional style that affects their social relationships (Stark et al., 2008).

BASIC CONSIDERATIONS

To be an effective resource for anxious and depressed children and youth, the school psychologist must have a thorough knowledge of the developmental patterns and trajectories of anxiety and depression, as well as assessment, intervention, and prevention practices and strategies. Because symptoms of anxiety and depression overlap and most of them are variations of typical developmental patterns, the school psychologist must have a broad range of knowledge and skills, including being informed about cultural beliefs and practices regarding anxiety, depression, and mental health.

The school psychologist should have a thorough understanding of how anxiety and depression develop and manifest over the span of childhood and adolescence. In particular, school psychologists should have substantial knowledge of typical behavior, typical age of onset of anxiety and depressive disorders, characteristics of the disorders, factors that contribute to atypical variations, and how to differentiate typical from atypical behavior. There are few behaviors that are unique to either disorder. Rather, symptoms are variations in severity, developmental appropriateness, and degree of effect on functioning. Having this knowledge and implementing it in practice helps to accurately identify problems and to avoid "overpathologizing" typical variations in behavior, leading to more effective assessment, intervention, consultation, and prevention practices that are discussed below.

The school psychologist should also not overlook comorbidity of anxiety and depression with externalizing disorders that may also require simultaneous treatment. For example, there is a strong association between conduct disorder and depression that is shared with oppositional defiant disorder (American Psychiatirc Association, 2013).

BEST PRACTICES IN SCHOOL-BASED INTERVENTIONS FOR ANXIETY AND DEPRESSION

Best practices in school-based interventions for anxiety and depression require that the school psychologist have knowledge and skills in four areas: (a) assessment, including obtaining developmental histories, interviewing, observation, objective measures, and self-report scales; (b) interventions, including social skills training, exposure,

problem-solving training, and cognitive–behavioral therapy; (c) consultation; and (d) prevention. Examples of methods and practices for anxiety and depression in these four areas are presented below, but the school psychologist should note that they often overlap in practice.

Assessment

The school psychologist should be familiar with a wide range of assessment methods for clinical assessment of anxiety and depression using a multimethod approach. For anxiety and depression, the multimethod approach should include (a) a thorough developmental history, including consideration of possible family history of anxiety and depression; (b) interviews with parents, teachers, and, as appropriate, the child; (c) systematic observation of symptomatic behaviors across multiple settings and events; (d) standardized behavior ratings from multiple informants; (e) use of self-report measures of anxiety and depression, as appropriate; and (f) multidimensional personality scales completed by children or parents.

Developmental History

A thorough developmental history should be obtained, which cannot be described in detail here. However, important information to gather should include (a) family history of anxiety and depression, especially maternal history; (b) age of attainment of primary developmental milestones; (c) age when primary and secondary symptoms first appeared; (d) type and severity of symptoms; (e) intervention attempts to address the problem, including medications; and (f) effects of intervention efforts.

Interviews With Children, Parents, and Teachers

Interviews with children about anxiety and depression must be adapted to the child's developmental level, because younger children often have difficulty describing their symptoms, especially beliefs and feelings. Interviews with parents and teachers should include obtaining information on the cognitive, behavioral, and physiological characteristics of anxiety and depression, with questions that address when the symptoms occur, their severity, and their impact on functioning. Questions should also include what interventions have been attempted and the informant's assessment of their effectiveness, including whether the child is receiving prescribed psychotropic medications. Interviews should be semistructured with specific goals to be obtained in a flexible discussion format. What follows are examples of questions for children about cognitive, behavioral, and physiological symptoms: Cognitive: Do you worry about a lot of things? If so, what do you worry about most often? Do you find that you can't concentrate when you want to because you are thinking about other things? Do you get nervous or anxious in new situations? Do you think about bad things happening to you? Behavioral: Do you get wiggly in class a lot? Do you participate in groups as much as other kids? Do you like to talk to others? Physiological: Are you sleeping okay? How is your appetite? Do you have a lot of aches and pains?

These kinds of questions can be adapted for anxious or depressed children, but may have to be modified for developmental level. Questions can be focused on symptoms presented in Table 24.1 and Table 24.2, and can be reworded for interviews with parents and teachers to gather information that can be compared across informants. Cross-informant comparisons are useful to determine whether symptoms are similar and pervasive across settings.

Observations in the School Setting

Systematic school-based observations should occur across multiple settings and activities, with attention given to participation, social relationships, attention, latency of response, task completion, task initiation, and response to instructions and directives. Latency, interval, and event recordings are recommended, as well as peer normative comparisons. Because many symptoms of anxiety and depression tend to be less obvious and frequent, sufficient time must be allotted to obtain adequate information.

Standardized Behavior Rating Scales

Several rating scales exist, but the Child Behavior Checklist (Achenbach & Rescorla, 2001) and the Behavior Assessment System for Children–Second Edition (Reynolds & Kamphaus, 2004) have good psychometric properties. They have parent, teacher, and self-report forms that provide information on internalizing and externalizing behaviors, as well as on adaptive and social skills, that are informative about anxiety and depression and associated comorbidity.

Self-Report Measures of Anxiety and Depression

In addition to behavior rating scales, self-report measures are useful sources of information about the child's subjective and objective reports of trait anxiety and depressive symptomatology. Two useful anxiety measures are the Revised Children's Manifest Anxiety Scale–Second Edition (Reynolds & Richmond, 2008) and the Multidimensional Anxiety Scale for Children–Second Edition (March, 2013). The Revised Children's Manifest Anxiety Scale is normed for children ages 5–18, and the Multidimensional Anxiety Scale for Children is normed for ages 8–19. Both measures have good reliability and validity data.

The Children's Depression Inventory–Second Edition (Kovacs, 2010) is appropriate for ages 7–17 and has self-report, parent-report, and teacher-report forms. The Reynolds Adolescent Depression Scale–Second Edition (Reynolds, 2002) is appropriate for ages 11–20. A companion version for children, the Reynolds Child Depression Scale–Second Edition (Reynolds, 2010), is available for children in Grades 3–6. Both forms are self-report formats and contain critical items for indicators of suicidal ideation and high risk. The Beck Youth Inventories II (Beck, Beck, Jolly, & Steer, 2005) contain five self-report inventories for ages 7–18 that are useful in assessing behavior: anxiety, depression, anger, disruptive behavior, and self-concept. They are valuable because they assess anxiety and depression directly, as well as the other areas that often are involved in internalizing disorders. All of these scales have good psychometric properties and are useful measures to include in comprehensive psychological assessments.

Multidimensional Personality Inventories

These types of measures assess relatively stable personality traits that may be indications of psychopathology. They measure specific symptoms as well as provide indices of mental disorders. Perhaps the most well-known and well-researched measure is the Minnesota Multiphasic Personality Inventory–Adolescent (Butcher et al., 1992), which provides multiple scales and subscales of psychopathology, including anxiety and depression. The Adolescent Psychopathology Scale (Reynolds, 1998) provide similar kinds of information about psychopathology in 20 scales that are linked to the fourth edition of the *Diagnostic and Statistical Manual of Mental Disorders* criteria for adolescents ages 12–19. It includes scales for Academic Problems and Anger/Violence Proneness that are useful in schools.

Interventions

Anxiety and depression are complex conditions that require a multimethod approach toward intervention that includes treatment of the cognitive, behavioral, and physiological symptoms. Many children and youth with anxiety or depression have these symptoms, as well as difficulties with social relationships, coping with stress, and social problem solving. It is important that the school psychologist assess these areas, because these areas often are the basis for implementing interventions. Interventions often involve learning about how to manage symptoms, improve social functioning, and reduce the effects of anxiety and depression. It should be noted that the overall goal of interventions is not to eliminate all symptoms, but to help the child learn to manage them effectively. In particular, because anxiety is a normal characteristic of all people and has adaptive value if not excessive, a goal of eliminating anxiety is neither feasible nor desirable. Although depression is not a developmental phenomenon, it is not feasible to eliminate all periods of sadness or unhappiness, and, thus, management and reduction of symptoms are reasonable goals.

Social Skills Training

Many children with anxiety and depression have social skills deficits that cause difficulties in interpersonal relationships with peers and adults. Social skills training approaches have multiple components that are often used together for specific problems using behavioral strategies, including systematic instruction, modeling, rehearsal, feedback, and reinforcement to address interpersonal problem solving and social perception problems. Although anxious and depressed children may benefit from being taught skills that they lack, they should not be taught solely in isolation. Involvement with other children in groups helps them to recognize others' feelings, improve perspective taking, and practice newly learned skills in various social situations.

Exposure Approaches

Children and youth who experience anxiety and depression may tend to avoid situations that produce discomfort. When using exposure approaches, the child is gradually exposed to an anxiety-producing situation in steps that initially cause little anxiety. As each step is successfully mastered and anxiety subsides to a manageable level, the next steps are introduced until the child achieves the behavioral goal of confronting the feared situation successfully with minimal anxiety. Typically, exposure approaches involve the creation of hierarchies that have specific steps that serve as goals to overcome fear of the situation. The hierarchies have the most anxiety-producing step at the top and the least anxiety-producing step at the bottom. The intermediate steps are graded by the child from least to most anxiety-producing and then the school psychologist gradually helps expose the child to each step. This type of intervention is termed *in vivo* exposure and may be accompanied by relaxation training to help reduce the physiological symptoms of anxiety. An example of a hierarchy is when a child is fearful of going to a new classroom and becomes intensely anxious. The school psychologist can create a hierarchy to gradually expose the child to the new classroom where he or she can be comfortable. The example shown in Figure 24.1 is for a young boy fearful of attending a new school. In situations such as these, collaboration with the principal, teachers, and parents is essential.

Figure 24.1. Example of an Anxiety Hierarchy

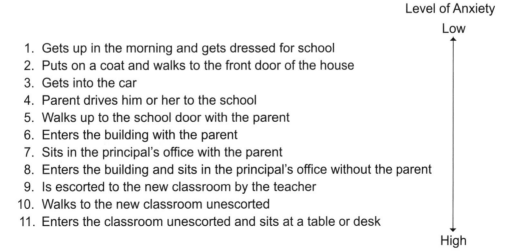

Level of Anxiety
Low

1. Gets up in the morning and gets dressed for school
2. Puts on a coat and walks to the front door of the house
3. Gets into the car
4. Parent drives him or her to the school
5. Walks up to the school door with the parent
6. Enters the building with the parent
7. Sits in the principal's office with the parent
8. Enters the building and sits in the principal's office without the parent
9. Is escorted to the new classroom by the teacher
10. Walks to the new classroom unescorted
11. Enters the classroom unescorted and sits at a table or desk

High

If successful, the child will gradually feel less anxious at each step and will be able to go to the new classroom with little or no anxiety after completing the hierarchy. This approach might require a few days to accomplish and is determined by how the hierarchy is structured, whether it requires changes, and the child's ability to manage anxiety. Some steps may be mastered rather quickly, some steps may need to be repeated, or additional steps may be necessary. The key point is that the child's level of anxiety at each step and how well it is managed determines the progress toward the top level of the hierarchy.

Problem-Solving Training

Children and adolescents with depression have difficulties with social problem solving that are not shown in social anxiety and related conditions. They have difficulties generating solutions to problems, evaluating alternatives, and attempting strategies. Social problem-solving skills training approaches have been applied to address depressive symptoms in several programs, including the Penn Resiliency Program, which has received strong research support (see Gillham, Brunwasser, & Freres, 2008). The program contains a problem-solving component composed of five steps: (a) stop and think, (b) identify goals, (c) brainstorm to generate possible solutions, (d) make a decision on which solution to try based on likely outcomes, and (e) enact the solution.

To implement a similar approach in the school setting, the school psychologist teaches the child how to use this five-step process and then demonstrates how to use it. Then the school psychologist and the child engage in a collaborative intervention process. They create a written list of problems and decide which ones would be focused upon. Those problems are prioritized by those that the child and the school psychologist agree are most problematic. Goals are created that are replacement behaviors, such as participation versus nonparticipation in class. Then, a list of solutions is generated to create these behaviors, followed by selecting those that will be attempted. Finally, the child and the school psychologist develop a plan to implement the solution. This plan should be written in clear terms and could take the form of a behavioral contract or agreement. Although this approach was described for depression, it can be applied to children with anxiety.

Cognitive–Behavioral Therapy

Cognitive–behavioral therapy approaches to treatment of anxiety and depression have been implemented and focus on the child's beliefs, feelings, and behaviors and how all three interact to affect functioning. Numerous studies have been conducted on the effectiveness of these approaches, which have been found to be effective in treating anxiety and depression in children and adolescents (Ollendick, King, & Chorpita, 2006) and can be adapted for use in schools. The majority of these studies have used manualized treatment programs that include a psychoeducatioanal component in which children are taught how to recognize beliefs, feelings, and behaviors, and how each is related to the others, and begin to understand how these three factors affect functioning. This component often comprises about half the sessions and includes learning strategies to cope with the problems. During later sessions, the child applies learned skills with homework, conducts *in vivo* practice, and works with the school psychologist to modify the program as necessary.

Manualized treatment programs can be conducted in individual or group formats and can be adapted to the needs of the child. Many of these programs include learning social skills, coping with stress, problem solving, and enhancing feelings of competence. Methods of muscle relaxation and systematic desensitization that occur in treatments for anxiety and in depression that has anxiety as a co-occurring condition are typically included. Thus, the school psychologist will need to know how to implement these strategies.

Coping Cat (Kendall & Hedtke, 2006) and Taking ACTION (Stark et al., 2008) are examples of well-developed, evidence-based manualized treatment programs for anxiety and depression, respectively. Although complete manualized treatment programs may not be feasible to implement in schools, these programs can be adapted to be compatible with school resources and time constraints. Also, specific cognitive–behavioral strategies that target beliefs, feelings, and behaviors can be developed on an individual or small group basis using homework and practice, which are well suited to a school setting if conducted by trained school psychologists or other mental health professionals. The school psychologist should collaborate with the child to develop a set of specific behaviors and beliefs that will be the targets of the intervention. Homework should be developed that includes learning about beliefs, behaviors, and feelings that affect functioning and strategies to change them. Then, these skills are practiced during the week, which are followed by weekly check-ins on homework, mood monitoring, and informal assessment of the child's efforts. These approaches can be adapted to work with specific interventions that can be implemented and monitored in the school setting.

Depressed children may have similar behaviors, but they are also more likely to have feelings of anger and hostility, which may require anger management strategies. Many depressed children may feel that few people care about them or are interested in their success and may express anger toward parents or others for their difficulties. In particular, depressed children use fewer social and assertive problem-solving strategies than their nondepressed peers, and may take a hostile approach to problem solving (e.g., Rudolph et al., 2008). Therefore, assessment and treatment of anger and hostility shown in depressed children and adolescents often are necessary components to treatment. Many of the approaches toward interventions for anxiety are also applicable to depressed children, including self-monitoring, self-reinforcement, and pleasant activity scheduling. Some anger management techniques that the school psychologist can use or teach to students include relaxation training, problem-solving techniques, thought-stopping, cognitive distraction, positive self-talk, social skills training, role-playing, and assertiveness training.

School-Based Interventions for Academic Anxiety

Interventions can be developed in the school setting and often in collaboration with classroom teachers. These strategies may require training teachers in specific techniques, including how to evaluate their own success, which are skills that the school psychologist will need. Some strategies follow:

- Develop consistent and predictable routines that help to reduce anticipatory worry.
- Give clear and reasonable expectations for performance that the child understands.
- Clearly communicate evaluation criteria and check for the child's understanding.
- Provide opportunities for practice and rehearsal, which may need to be done at home, requiring consultation with parents.
- Use positive approaches and avoid negative attitudes and responses, because anxious children tend to focus on negative rather than positive aspects of their work.
- Pair an anxious child with other children who are calm, confident, and supportive, which may also help with socialization skills.
- Teach the child how to use self-relaxation and positive self-talk strategies.
- Teach the child and teacher how to analyze assignments and break projects into smaller, manageable units that will help to reduce anticipatory worry.

School-Based Interventions for Social Anxiety

In addition to addressing the frequent, academically based difficulties associated with anxiety, some behavioral interventions for social manifestations of anxiety can be considered. These strategies may be done by directly working with the child or in consultation with the teacher. Some of these strategies are discussed above and can be adapted for the school setting.

School-Based Interventions for Depression

Many of the academic strategies listed above can be used with students who experience depression, especially those who have coexisting high levels of anxiety. In general, depressed students have more social difficulties than do anxious students. Some additional strategies for these social difficulties follow:

- Focus on improving social skills and interactions with others.
- Avoid punishment, sarcasm, disparagement, or other negative approaches, because depressed children often have low self-esteem, which is exacerbated when these approaches are used and can contribute to increased difficulties.
- Develop a success-oriented approach toward academic and social functioning using a strengths-based strategy; many depressed children do not view themselves as having strengths, which may affect motivation.
- Emphasize rewarding effort as well as production, because depressed children have difficulty putting forth effort, due to cognitive factors associated with motivation, nonbelief in abilities, and belief that their efforts will not produce positive outcomes.

Consultation

As an indirect service, consultation by school psychologists can be a valuable component of working with students who experience anxiety and depression that affects academic and social performance at school. Direct intervention may not be feasible with some students due to resources, parent consent, or other factors. Nevertheless, indirect consultative services can be valuable in helping to reduce the effects of anxiety and depression in the school setting. The overall goal of consultation is to collaborate with the teacher to identify behaviors that are related to anxiety and depression and develop behavioral interventions to address them. For example, an anxious child may be hesitant to initiate interactions with others in a group activity. The teacher and school psychologist can collaborate to develop a positive behavior plan that could include pairing the child with another child, providing rewards and reinforcement for increased participation, and gradually increasing exposure to others.

Some teachers are hesitant to work with students who are anxious or depressed, due to concerns about working with "emotional problems." Although interested in helping the student, they do not consider themselves able to work with these problems, concerned that they might say or do something incorrectly. In these situations, it is important to emphasize that the goal is not to provide therapy or counseling, but to change behaviors that will help the child to be academically and socially successful. The use of a problem-solving approach that focuses on problem identification, developing an intervention, implementing it, and measuring its effects is recommended (Huberty, 2008).

Prevention

Ideally, prevention of problems is preferred rather than intervening after problems have developed. However, anxiety and depression may have onset at young ages and contributing factors such as genetics and environmental factors are beyond the ability of the school to prevent. Nevertheless, efforts at school-based prevention for anxiety and depression have been attempted with mixed success, including at the universal level of interventions. The FRIENDS program implemented at the universal level for anxiety has been shown to have positive preventive effects that were sustained over several months (Barrett, Farrell, Ollendick, & Dadds, 2006).

Universal prevention programs for depression have not been shown to be as effective, however, showing more mixed results. Horowitz and Garber (2006) conducted a meta-analysis of depression prevention programs in schools and found that these programs were more effective at the selected and indicated levels than at the universal level. Thus, the evidence suggests that universal prevention programs for anxiety may be more effective than depression prevention programs. The school psychologist should nevertheless explore evidence-based programs that have promise for preventing anxiety and depression at the universal level. Because prevention includes preventing the worsening of symptoms or the

development of other disorders, school psychologists can be involved in preventing anxiety and depression-related disorders or complications by working with students who have been identified as being at risk or demonstrate symptoms. Therefore, knowledge and skill in interventions for anxiety and depression at the selected and indicated levels of prevention are essential for school psychologists.

Involvement of Parents

To the extent possible, collaboration with parents should be included when working with anxious and depressed students. Parents can be valuable sources of information about whether the child is improving in social behavior, attitudes toward school, and manifestations of behavior outside of school. In the school setting, parents may not be as directly involved as they might be when participating in community-based treatment, but should be informed about progress on a regular basis with a written plan about the interventions. For both anxiety and depression, the following strategies can be used in the home and may require that the school psychologist help to develop home–school collaboration plans:

- Be consistent in handling problems and administering discipline.
- Avoid being critical, disparaging, or cynical.
- Help the child with school tasks that require preparation and practice.
- Do not expect perfect performance or what is beyond the child's ability.
- Treat feelings as important and not as silly or irrelevant.
- Help the child to learn that mistakes will occur and mistakes can be learning experiences.
- Work on developing organizing skills and setting and complying with routines.
- Maintain flexibility in responsibilities, but nevertheless communicate that the child is expected to meet responsibilities in a timely and proficient manner.

Developmental Considerations

When providing direct interventions, it is important to consider the developmental level of the child. In general, younger children or those with some developmental delays are less able to be active participants in interventions. Differences in language skills and experiences often require that interventions be more specific and concrete for these children than for older children and adolescents. For example, interventions that use cognitive–behavioral techniques must be adapted to be more behavioral and less cognitive in their implementation for these children. For younger children, play activities and use of materials such as puppets or paper and pencil may be needed to put concepts into a format that the child can understand. Although adolescents may be able to participate in typical cognitive–behavioral strategies, younger children often do not have the language skills and experience to be as actively involved in the collaborative process and will need more guidance and direction from the school psychologist.

Multicultural Competencies

Anxiety and depression exist in all cultures, but anxiety and depression are viewed differently in many cultures due to differences in parenting, social expectations of children, attitudes toward emotional expression, mental health as a concept, and attitudes toward participating in psychological services. Therefore, the school psychologist should engage in some self-study to learn more about these cultural perspectives and attitudes and their association with the referral problems. For example, lack of eye contact or not asking questions could be seen as symptoms of anxiety or depression, but the child may be demonstrating culturally related behaviors that are considered respectful to adults. Failure to consider these cultural factors may lead to errors in assessment, diagnosis, and intervention that could have negative outcomes for the student.

Evaluating Effectiveness and Outcomes

The school psychologist should include systematic methods for evaluating change in the child's functioning. Readministration of rating scales or checklists used at the initial problem identification stage will provide information about progress at the conclusion of an intervention. Informal checklists of behaviors that are being targeted should be used at frequent intervals with items that can show progress; that is, "frequent," "occasionally," or "rarely" with definitions for each metric (e.g., "frequent" means daily or almost daily), coupled with observations and interviews with teachers and parents about how the child is progressing. To the extent possible, measures should have acceptable psychometric integrity or be part of a manualized program where the measures are linked to specific interventions. In cases where the child has an

Individualized Education Program (IEP), these methods and their frequency should be described in detail. Examples of behaviors to assess include participation, withdrawal, interactions with others, and other anxiety- and depression-related behaviors that have been identified as intervention targets. These methods can be adapted to assess the effects of direct or indirect interventions. Specific targets for intervention should have the following characteristics: (a) be behaviorally stated, (b) have agreement by all involved, (c) have been shown to be related to problems or impairments in functioning, (d) be able to be modified, and (e) have changes in behavior that can be observed and measured.

Case Example

Erin is a 9-year-old girl in the fourth grade who was referred by her classroom teacher due to concerns about below-average performance, inattention, lack of completion of tasks, off-task behavior, inadequate socialization, and showing little initiative. The teacher suspected that Erin might have attention deficit hyperactivity disorder (ADHD) or a cognitive or learning disability, which would explain her behavior and performance. The teacher had tried various strategies, including giving Erin extra time on assignments, pairing her with capable peers, and positive reinforcement for effort, but with little effect.

Teacher interview: The school psychologist interviewed the teacher and found that when Erin did complete her work, there were indications that it was at grade level or above, but her performance was inconsistent and often the last to be submitted. Inattention was greater on more challenging tasks, especially those that required her to participate in groups or make oral presentations. Her social skills were seen not to be well developed and the teacher described her as "immature." The teacher described Erin as a nice girl who did not cause disruption, but also felt that she was not able to "keep up with the class."

Parent interview: Erin's mother reported that Erin had shown these kinds of patterns since entering school, but they seemed to have increased in the last 2–3 years. Erin's mother reported that Erin was not socially adept and had few close friends, often feeling uncomfortable in social situations. However, Erin has said that she would like to have friends, but did not know how to initiate conversation or play with others. Erin's mother stated that Erin has always been a "worrier" about many things, and that "she is just like me, because I worry a lot, too. I worry about her a lot and watch over her, trying to keep her from getting stressed out and hurt, which helps me not to worry as much. I also have a history of depression." Erin has an older sister age 12 who is socially adept and does well in school. Erin often compares herself to her sister and asks why she cannot be more like her.

Observations: The school psychologist observed Erin in her classroom, at recess, in the cafeteria, and during her physical education classes. In the classroom, Erin's attention varied, depending on the situation. On tasks that she liked and that required individual work, she was attentive and not distracted. On more difficult tasks or group tasks, she was less attentive and doodled on her paper with her pencil. She worked slowly, frequently erasing and correcting her work. Consequently she was often near the last of the students to complete and turn in assignments. Observations of Erin out of the classroom revealed that she had one or two friends, all of whom were not part of the larger group. Erin did not appear to be overtly rejected by others, but she did not attempt to enter into play activities or initiate conversations. In the cafeteria and recess, other students did not approach Erin but did not tease or harass her.

Assessment interview and observations: During the evaluation sessions, Erin was quiet, but cooperative. She reported that some things about school are "hard," but that she wants to do well. She confirmed that she does not have many friends and is "nervous" in groups, but would like to feel more comfortable in social situations. On assessment tasks, she was attentive and tried to do well, although she frequently asked how she was doing. When asked what causes her to feel nervous, she said that speaking to others is "really scary" and "I don't try to talk to my classmates because it makes me too nervous when I do. It's just easier to keep to myself. I have tried but I guess I'm too dumb to do it and I've been dumb a long time."

Assessment results: A cognitive ability test revealed that Erin had average to above average ability, with strengths in verbal comprehension skills. Assessment of her academic achievement placed her in the average to above average range with consistent performance across verbal, mathematics, and language areas. She completed the Multidimensional Anxiety Scale for Children, showing elevations on Social Anxiety, Perfectionism, Anxious Coping, and Total Anxiety. Results on the Children's Depression Inventory–2 showed a clinical level of Low Self-Esteem and borderline scores on Negative Mood and Interpersonal Relations. Behavior ratings by the teacher showed clinical elevations in anxiety and inattention, while the mother's ratings indicated clinically significant levels of anxiety and depression, with anxiety being more elevated. Clinical elevations in hyperactivity and distractibility were not shown on teacher or parent ratings.

Conclusions: The results indicated that Erin did not have a cognitive or learning disability and that her academic performance problems were related to behavioral concerns, specifically generalized anxiety, performance anxiety, and perfectionism. Although Erin showed signs of inattention, they did not correspond with the developmental trajectory of ADHD. Therefore, although the teacher noted that Erin had attention problems and posited that they might be due to ADHD, they were symptoms of general anxiety.

The data supported the conclusion that Erin had generalized anxiety and social anxiety, which were interfering with her participation at school and in social relationships. She demonstrated many of the symptoms in Table 24.1, including worry, inattention, concentration problems, perfectionism, task avoidance, and problems with task completion. She is typical of many children who have high levels of anxiety and desire social relationships but lack the skills and comfort to develop them. Erin is also at risk for the development of depression for several reasons: (a) her mother has a history of anxiety and depression, which are associated with similar patterns in children, especially girls; (b) her mother appears to engage in overprotective behavior that may inhibit the development of Erin's coping skills; (c) anxiety is a risk factor for depression; (d) early onset of anxiety is associated with onset of depression in childhood and early adolescence; and (e) Erin is showing low self-esteem and interpersonal problems that are associated with depression.

Interventions: Upon learning this information, the teacher had a very different perspective of Erin and was apologetic for not having a better understanding of her. The teacher thanked the school psychologist for the work and was more sympathetic to Erin's situation and was very eager to work with the school psychologist to improve Erin's academic and social behavior. The school psychologist worked with Erin on reducing anxiety, developing social skills, and reducing perfectionism. The school psychologist taught Erin how to use systematic relaxation methods, positive self-talk, and distraction techniques. The school psychologist collaborated with the teacher to develop strategies to improve Erin's class participation, task completion, and timely submission of her work, with an emphasis on behavioral techniques. The school psychologist also taught the teacher how to respond to Erin's demonstration of anxiety by providing cues, allowing Erin extra time, and clarifying expectations, which proved to be helpful. Rating scales and systematic observations were used to monitor the effects of the interventions, using changes in teacher ratings and frequency and duration of observational data. After a few weeks, the data and teacher reports indicated that Erin was doing better academically and socially, but she was still showing signs of anxiety that were manageable most of the time.

Anxious and Depressed Students and Special Education

Some children with anxiety and depression may be considered for special services as a student with an emotional disturbance under the Individuals with Disabilities Education Act (IDEA) or Section 504 of the Rehabilitation Act. Eligibility for services under IDEA and Section 504 applies to children who have emotional problems that interfere with school performance, which includes both social and academic performance. When creating behavior intervention programs for anxious and depressed students that comply with these laws, it is important that goals and objectives be behaviorally stated, be measurable, and have a reasonable likelihood of success. Problems associated with behavioral intervention plans in IEPs for anxious and depressed students typically involve nonspecific goals (e.g., "improve social functioning") and nonspecific objectives (e.g., "student will show appropriate behavior 80% of the time"). Although developing specific behavior interventions for anxiety and depression can be challenging, these interventions can be operationalized by focusing on objective data from rating scales, observations, and the results of functional behavioral analyses that include functional interviews with teachers.

Some of these children may be considered to be eligible for services as a student with an emotional disturbance under IDEA. Most often these children will have difficulties with interpersonal relationships and demonstrate achievement problems. To the extent possible, anxious and depressed children should remain in the general education environment, rather than in separate classrooms or settings, because many of their difficulties involve appropriate interactions with typical peers and adults. Keeping them from the opportunity to develop social and problem-solving skills may exacerbate their difficulties. In addition to an IEP or behavior plan under Section 504, these students often need modifications and accommodations in their curriculum

and assignments, such as extended time to complete assignments, practice tests and rehearsals to reduce anxiety, or changes in nonstandardized testing and evaluation procedures. Some of the academic and social intervention strategies can be used as accommodations in Section 504 plans or in IEPs.

SUMMARY

School psychologists can be effective interventionists for children who have anxiety and depression that affect academic and social performance at school. Providing effective services requires knowledge of the causes of anxiety and depression that include genetic, biological, cultural, social, and family factors. School psychologists must have knowledge of typical developmental patterns to determine when anxiety and mood problems become atypical and interfere with functioning. School psychologists also need to know the characteristics of anxiety and depression, typical ages of onset, and their developmental course.

School psychologists must have skills in screening and multimethod psychological and educational assessment in order to gather sufficient information to formulate a clinical picture of the child. Assessment skills include taking developmental histories, observation, interviewing of multiple informants, formal and informal assessment using a variety of measures and procedures, and the ability to differentiate conditions. After this information is obtained, the school psychologist will be better able to use the information to develop direct and indirect interventions. Knowledge of direct interventions should include social skills training, exposure approaches, problem-solving training, and cognitive–behavioral approaches. Consultation skills must include how to work with teachers to promote academic and social success and help the child to manage symptoms in the classroom. Because preventing anxiety and depression is better than treating them, the school psychologist can be highly effective in developing prevention approaches at universal and selected levels, as well as providing direct services. School psychologists can work with parents to implement strategies to address anxiety and depression that affects behavior and meeting responsibilities at home. Finally, services must be provided with a knowledge and sensitivity to cultural factors, and be accompanied by plans to show their effects that are shared with parents.

Some children with anxiety and depression may have problems that interfere with social and academic functioning that may lead to consideration for special education services. A particular challenge in providing these services to these children is developing IEPs that contain goals and objectives that are behaviorally objective and measurable. When developing behavior plans, modifications and accommodations often are necessary to facilitate academic success, such as allowing extra time or making modifications in nonstandardized classroom evaluation. In conclusion, school psychologists should have the skills to serve anxious and depressed children in the classroom and to collaborate with parents.

REFERENCES

Achenbach, T. M., & Rescorla, I. A. (2001). *Manual for the ASEBA school-age forms and profiles.* Burlington, VT: University Associates in Psychiatry.

American Psychiatric Association. (2013). *Diagnostic and statistical manual of mental disorders* (5th ed.). Arlington, VA: Author.

Barrett, P. M., Farrell, L. J., Ollendick, T. H., & Dadds, M. (2006). Long-term outcomes of an Australian universal prevention trial of anxiety and depression symptoms in children and youth: An evaluation of the FRIENDS program. *Journal of Clinical Child & Adolescent Psychology, 35,* 403–411.

Beck, A., Beck, J., Jolly, J., & Steer, R. (2005). *Beck Youth Inventories–Second edition.* Bloomington, MN: Pearson Assessments.

Butcher, J. N., Williams, C. L., Graham, J. R., Archer, R. P., Tellegen, A., Ben-Porath, Y. S., & Kaemer, B. (1992). *Minnesota Multiphasic Personality Inventory–Adolescent.* Minneapolis, MN: University of Minnesota Press.

Costa, N. M., & Weems, C. F. (2005). Maternal and child anxiety: Do attachment beliefs or children's perceptions of maternal control mediate their associations? *Social Development, 14,* 574–590.

Costello, E. J., Egger, H. L., Copeland, W., Erkanli, A., & Angold, A. (2011). The developmental epidemiology of anxiety disorders, phenomenology, prevalence, and comorbidity. In W. K. Silverman & A. Fields (Eds.), *Anxiety disorders in children and adolescents: Research, assessment, and intervention* (2nd ed., pp. 56–75). New York, NY: Cambridge University Press.

Creveling, C. C., Varela, R. E., Weems, C. F., & Corey, D. M. (2010). Maternal control, cognitive style, and childhood anxiety: A test of a theoretical model in a multi-ethnic sample. *Journal of Family Psychology, 24,* 439–448.

Franić, S., Middeldorp, C. M., Dolan, C. V., Ligthart, L., & Boomsma, D. I. (2010). Childhood and adolescent anxiety and depression: Beyond heritability. *Journal of the American Academy of Child and Adolescent Psychiatry, 49,* 820–829.

Gillham, J. E., Brunwasser, S. M., & Freres, D. R. (2008). Preventing depression in early adolescence: The Penn Resiliency Program. In J. R. Z. Abela & B. L. Hankin (Eds.), *Handbook of depression in children and adolescents* (pp. 309–332). New York, NY: Guilford Press.

Goodman, S. H., & Tully, E. (2008). Children of depressed mothers: Implications for the etiology, treatment, and prevention of depression in children and adolescents. In J. R. Z. Abela & B. L. Hankin (Eds.), *Handbook of depression in children and adolescents* (pp. 415–440). New York, NY: Guilford Press.

Gregory, A. M., & Eley, T. C. (2011). The genetic basis of child and adolescent anxiety. In W. K. Silverman & A. Fields (Eds.), *Anxiety disorders in children and adolescents: Research, assessment, and intervention* (2nd ed., pp. 161–178). New York, NY: Cambridge University Press.

Horowitz, J. L., & Garber, J. (2006). The prevention of depressive symptoms in children and adolescents: A meta-analytic review. *Journal of Consulting and Clinical Psychology, 74,* 401–415.

Huberty, T. J. (2008). Best practices in school-based interventions for anxiety and depression. In A. Thomas & J. Grimes (Eds.), *Best practices in school psychology V* (pp. 1473–1486). Bethesda, MD: National Association of School Psychologists.

Kendall, P. C., & Hedtke, K. A. (2006). *Coping Cat workbook* (2nd ed.). Ardmore, PA: Workbook Publishing.

Klein, D. N., Kujawa, A. J., Black, S. R., & Pennock, A. T. (2013). Depressive disorders. In T. P. Beauchaine & S. P. Hinshaw (Eds.), *Child and adolescent psychopathology* (2nd ed., pp. 543–575). Hoboken, NJ: Wiley.

Kovacs, M. (2010). *Children's Depression Inventory–2.* North Tonawanda, NY: Multi-Health Systems.

Lopez-Duran, N. L., Kovacs, M., & George, C. J. (2009). Hypothalamic-pituitary-adrenal axis dysregulation in depressed children and adolescents: A meta-analysis. *Psychoneuroendocrinology, 34,* 1271–1283.

March, J. S. (2013). *Multidimensional Anxiety Inventory for Children–2.* North Tonawanda, NY: Multi-Health Systems.

Merikangas, K. R., He, J., Burstein, M., Swanson, S. A., Avenevoli, S., Cui, L., ... Swendsen, J. (2010). Lifetime prevalence of mental disorders in U.S. adolescents: Results from the National Comorbidity Study–Adolescent Supplement. *Journal of the American Academy of Child and Adolescent Psychiatry, 49,* 980–989.

National Association of School Psychologists. (2010). *Model for comprehensive and integrated school psychological services.* Bethesda, MD: Author. Retrieved from http://www.nasponline.org/standards/2010standards/2_PracticeModel.pdf

Ollendick, T. J., King, N. J., & Chorpita, B. H. (2006). Empirically supported treatments for children and adolescents. In P. C. Kendall (Ed.), *Child and adolescent therapy: Cognitive-behavioral procedures* (3rd ed., pp. 492–520). New York, NY: Guilford Press.

Reynolds, C. R., & Kamphaus, R. W. (2004). *Behavior Assessment System for Children–2.* Bloomington, MN: Pearson Assessments.

Reynolds, C. R., & Richmond, B. O. (2008). *Revised Children's Manifest Anxiety Scale–2.* Los Angeles, CA: Western Psychological Publishing.

Reynolds, W. M. (1998). *Adolescent Psychopathology Scale.* Lutz, FL: Psychological Assessment Resources.

Reynolds, W. M. (2002). *Reynolds Adolescent Depression Scale–2.* Lutz, FL: Psychological Assessment Resources.

Reynolds, W. M. (2010). *Reynolds Child Depression Scale–2.* Lutz, FL: Psychological Assessment Resources.

Rudolph, K. D., Flynn, M., & Abaied, J. L. (2008). A developmental perspective on interpersonal theories of youth depression. In J. R. Z. Abela & B. L. Hankin (Eds.), *Handbook of depression in children and adolescents* (pp. 79–102). New York, NY: Guilford Press.

Stark, K. D., Hargrave, J., Hersh, B., Greenberg, M., Herren, J., & Fisher, M. (2008). Treatment of childhood depression: The ACTION treatment program. In J. R. Z. Abela & B. Hankin (Eds.), *Handbook of depression in children and adolescents* (pp. 224–249). New York, NY: Guilford Press.

Stevenson, J., & Hadwin, J. A. (2012). Anxiety and depression in academic performance: An exploration of the mediating factors of worry and working memory. *School Psychology International, 33,* 443–449.

Varela, R. E., Vernberg, E. M., Sanchez-Sosa, J. J., Riveros, A., Mitchell, M., & Mashunkashey, J. (2004). Anxiety reporting and culturally associated interpersonal biases and cognitive schemas: A comparison of Mexican, Mexican American, and European American families. *Journal of Clinical Child & Adolescent Psychology, 33,* 237–247.

Weems, C. P., & Silverman, W. K. (2013). Anxiety disorders. In T. P. Beauchaine & S. P. Hinshaw (Eds.), *Child and adolescent psychopathology* (2nd ed., pp. 513–541). Hoboken, NJ: Wiley.

25 Best Practices in Interventions for Anxiety-Based School Refusal

Shannon M. Suldo
Julia Ogg
University of South Florida

OVERVIEW

School refusal is a broad term that has been applied to students who miss school for a variety of reasons. Parent-motivated reasons include a student staying home to assist the family. Student-motivated reasons include skipping school to socialize with neighborhood friends. This chapter focuses on a student-motivated reason: anxiety-based school refusal, which refers to youth who avoid regular school attendance or experience challenges remaining at school after arrival owing to overwhelmingly unpleasant emotions, most commonly persistent worries. This chapter distinguishes this form of school avoidance from truancy not associated with anxiety (i.e., skipping school without permission, or without a medical reason; Egger, Costello, & Angold, 2003). This distinction does not preclude students with conduct problems from being considered an anxiety-based case of school refusal, as long as missing school is in part driven by emotional issues that are comorbid with the students' externalizing behaviors. The purposes of this chapter are to define anxiety-based school refusal, summarize primary symptoms and causes, and overview best practices in assessment and intervention strategies. The chapter concludes with a clinical case study to illustrate the topics discussed in text.

References to anxiety-based school refusal are preferable to antiquated or colloquial terms such as *school phobia* or *separation anxiety* because the term *school refusal* reflects the reality that youth can avoid school because of different forms of emotional distress. Although school phobia may correctly characterize students who avoid school because of a specific fear about an aspect of the school environment, it does not pertain to the sizeable number of students who avoid school because of other symptoms associated with social impairments, generalized worry, and/or depression. Owing to the heterogeneity of school refusal, this chapter emphasizes that the first step in intervention often involves a historical, descriptive, and functional assessment to determine the primary causal reason why a particular student is avoiding school. Interventions then follow to treat either the specific underlying internalizing symptomatology or to change a student's reward structure such that the school setting becomes more reinforcing than home.

Early and effective treatment of anxiety-based school refusal is essential in order to prevent strengthening of the problematic behavior via reinforcement patterns in which school absence is followed by anxiety reduction. Additional concurrent challenges associated with reduced time in a classroom include accumulating student skill deficits owing to reduced access to educational and social opportunities. Beyond the student's suffering, families of these students experience significant disturbance, including employment disruptions (i.e., parents stay home or arrive late while balancing the demands of their child who refuses to leave the house), parent–child conflict during efforts to reengage students, and legal ramifications associated with family noncompliance with mandatory attendance laws.

A national survey of school psychologists revealed that school refusal was one of the most common forms of internalizing disorders they encountered in practice, and that prevention and treatment of school refusal were central job roles (Miller & Jome, 2010). Most school psychologists will encounter a student who displays behaviors ranging from a plea to not attend school to absence for extended periods (Kearney, 2008). For a school psychologist, understanding the early warning signs and common correlates of school refusal could assist in the prevention of more significant refusal behaviors and concurrent challenges. For students already exhibiting school refusal, this chapter summarizes evidence-based interventions.

The heterogeneity of the underlying functions or reasons associated with school refusal highlights the importance of operating within a problem-solving, multitiered framework. Collecting data from multiple methods using multiple sources is essential to determine not only why a student is refusing to attend school but also what type of intervention is most likely to be successful and how well the goal of increasing regular student attendance at school is being met. The National Association of School Psychologists (NASP) *Model for Comprehensive and Integrated School Psychological Services* (NASP, 2010) calls for school psychologists to provide services within the domain of Interventions and Mental Health Services to Develop Social and Life Skills. This domain highlights the importance of knowledge and skills to address mental health concerns and to provide a wide range of services across multiple tiers of service delivery.

Working with students who refuse school requires the integration of behavioral assessment with knowledge of evidence-based intervention approaches for youth who meet the diagnostic criteria for several anxiety-based disorders and depression. At a systems level, consideration of the common correlates of school refusal could help a school psychologist determine systematic ways to improve the environmental factors that relate to school refusal.

BASIC CONSIDERATIONS

Anxiety-based school refusal is assumed to be an equal-opportunity problem that strikes students of all demographic backgrounds and geographic locations. However, inconsistencies in how school refusal is defined and reported have limited current understanding of prevalence rates across populations (Kearney, 2008). The body of research on prevalence and treatment of school refusal is also limited by a lack of socioeconomic and ethnic diversity in the samples; that is, most studies include Caucasian youth seeking mental health treatment from outpatient clinics (Lyon & Cotler, 2007). This weakness is particularly unsettling given the higher rates of school nonattendance in schools with more ethnic minority students, in urban and impoverished communities, and among students with disabilities (Kearney, 2008; Lyon & Cotler, 2007).

Prevalence

The frequency of school refusal is difficult to estimate owing to the lack of epidemiological studies and aforementioned inconsistencies in problem definition. Nevertheless, syntheses of research studies generally suggest that 1–2% of students will experience anxiety-based school refusal at some point, with higher rates (5–7%) among clinical samples of youth (Heyne & King, 2004). In a large community sample, approximately 2% of youth (ages 9–16) evidenced anxiety-related school refusal, while the rate of truancy without anxiety features was three times higher (Egger et al., 2003). Such studies that inform the prevalence of school refusal focused on student absences. Information is lacking on the rate of students who exhibit distress when leaving the house or who access the nurse midday in attempts to leave school early.

Some students at all ages demonstrate school refusal, but it is most common during transition periods. These include initial entry to school or changes to a new school (i.e., from elementary to middle school, and middle to high school). Whereas the frequency (Egger et al., 2003) and severity (Hansen, Sanders, Massaro, & Last, 1998) of school refusal is similar in males and females with anxiety-based school refusal, truancy is more common to males and typically begins later (i.e., age 13 versus 10; Egger et al., 2003). Within the subgroup of anxiety-based school refusers, older students are more likely to miss more school (Hansen et al., 1998).

Symptoms

Beyond increasing absences from classes, warning signs of anxiety-based school refusal include a distressed appearance upon separation from parents, requests to call home or leave school, and frequent visits to the school nurse complaining of headaches, stomachaches, nausea, and/or intestinal distress. Symptoms shown at home, especially during the morning routine, include somatic complaints, behavioral outbursts (i.e., tantrums, oppositional behavior, rigidity, and clinginess to parents), and avoidance of leaving the house. School psychologists should be attuned to such symptoms when consulting with teachers, nurses, parents, and other caregivers.

School refusal is not a diagnosis in the fifth edition of the *Diagnostic and Statistical Manual of Mental Disorders*

(DSM-5; American Psychiatric Association, 2013). However, school refusal is included as a symptom of several DSM-5 disorders, including conduct disorder (i.e., "is often truant from school, beginning before age 13 years") and separation anxiety disorder (i.e., "persistent reluctance or refusal to go out, away from home, to school, to work, or elsewhere because of fear of separation"). Our review of the clinical features of samples treated for school refusal at outpatient clinics (e.g., Hansen et al., 1998; Kearney, 2007) or a psychiatric hospital (Bahali, Tahiroglu, Avci, & Seydaoglu, 2011) indicated most of these youth met criteria for one or more of several different internalizing and externalizing psychiatric disorders. The most common primary diagnosis was separation anxiety disorder, reported in 23–75% of samples. Other primary anxiety disorders observed include social anxiety disorder, specific phobia, and generalized anxiety disorder. Depression was the most common psychiatric disorder among a community sample of youth with pure anxiety-based school refusal (Egger et al., 2003) and also a primary diagnosis of some youth in the aforementioned clinical samples. Disruptive behavior disorders such as oppositional defiant disorder were either primary or comorbid disorders in a sizable minority of students with anxiety-based school refusal. Conduct disorder and, to a lesser extent, substance use disorder, were particularly rampant in the community sample of youth with a mixed truancy and anxiety-based school refusal presentation.

In sum, school psychologists working with a student who refuses school should remain on the lookout for anxiety, affective, and disruptive behavior disorders that may require additional (or primary) psychological interventions. Specific interventions for the most common underlying internalizing disorders are recommended later in this chapter. The school psychologist's broad screen for mental health problems, however, should be balanced with an understanding that many students with anxiety-based school refusal do not have a psychiatric disorder. For instance, 24% of the 222 youth who sought treatment for school refusal behavior from Kearney's (2007) specialized outpatient clinic did not meet criteria for any disorder in earlier deitions of the DSM.

School refusal is not recognized as a special education category under the 2004 Individuals with Disabilities Education Act. However, it is important to consider when working with special education populations given that higher levels of absenteeism have been observed among youth with disabilities compared to their peers without disabilities (Kearney, 2008). For this reason, school psychologists should rule out anxiety-based school refusal for youth with disabilities who frequently miss school. Behaviors that may be attributed to a primary disability (e.g., aggression in youth with emotional–behavioral disorders, somatic complaints in youth with other health impairments) could be attempts to escape the school environment or gain access to the home environment. School psychologists may also consider the relevance of Section 504 of the Rehabilitation Act in the case of significant school refusal. Kearney and Albano (2007) suggest that a 504 Plan could facilitate attendance by providing a mechanism to adjust schedules and workload to make it more manageable for a student to return to school.

Etiology

Sudden onset school refusal may occur with a life change, such as a family move, switch to new school, or an emerging stressor in the school environment such as peer victimization or impending discipline. Such transient stress reactions should be treated differently than chronic school refusal associated with unmanaged anxiety, as sudden onset school refusal may resolve itself without excessive resources or necessitate environmental changes that target the stressor.

Functions

When school refusal cannot be associated with an identifiable trigger, the most common reasons entail unmanaged emotional distress associated with the aforementioned psychological disorders. In particular, Kearney and Albano (2007) assert that school refusal is primarily motivated by four reasons: (a) avoid vague symptoms of negative affectivity (e.g., general anxiety, depression) pertinent to school-related fearfulness or general over-anxiety as seen in youth with diagnoses of depression, specific phobia, and/or generalized anxiety disorder; (b) escape anxiety-provoking social interactions (e.g., public speaking, evaluation by others), as evidenced by youth with social anxiety disorder and/or depression; (c) attempts to remain with parents, for attention-seeking purposes or to alleviate separation fears, as evidenced by youth with separation anxiety disorder (generally occurs in younger children); and (d) obtain tangible reinforcement, often in the home environment, which can co-occur with disruptive behavior disorders (generally in older youth). Table 25.1 summarizes these functions, and the indicated interventions for each which are discussed in detail in a later section.

Table 25.1. Function-Based Interventions for Anxiety-Related School Refusal

	Function of School Refusal	Recommended Interventions
Negative reinforcement	Avoid vague symptoms of negative affectivity	• Psychoeducation • Relaxation training for somatic control • Exposure using a fear hierarchy • Self-reinforcement
	Escape anxiety-provoking social interactions	• Psychoeducation • Somatic management • Cognitive restructuring • Practicing coping skills • Exposure • Self-reinforcement
Positive reinforcement	Attempt to remain with parents for attention-seeking purposes or to alleviate separation fears	Parent-based approaches including: • Appropriate and clear commands • Developing effective home routines • Modifying contingencies • Possibly forced attendance
	Obtain tangible reinforcement	Parent-based approaches including: • Developing contracts that modify contingencies • Close monitoring and supervision • Skills training

Note. Based on information from Kearney and Albano (2007).

General Correlates

Factors that co-occur with or predict school refusal include influences within the student, family, and school environment.

Student. In addition to the aforementioned psychological disorders, an anxious temperament puts students at risk. Youth with a general disposition toward worrying and perceiving situations as threatening (termed *trait anxiety*) tend to avoid school-based social situations and prefer proximity to parents to being at school (Richards & Hadwin, 2011). Other student-level factors include somatic symptoms that may have a physical basis but are exaggerated by the student during attempts to avoid school (Kearney, 2008).

Family. On average, parents of children with severe school refusal experience more anxiety and depression compared to parents of children without school refusal issues (Bahali et al., 2011). As such, students' emotionally driven school refusal could be genetically transmitted and/or acquired via modeling of the parent's anxious behavior. In line with the influence of parental mental health on family functioning, school refusal is linked to general family dysfunction (i.e., ineffective parenting) and maladaptive family dynamics, including parent–child relationships that appear enmeshed, high in conflict, or detached, or families that are isolated from others (Kearney, 2008). Regarding isolated and underactive families, greater absenteeism among students with school refusal occurs in families that place a relatively low emphasis on social and recreational activities outside of the home (Hansen et al., 1998).

School. Established school-level correlates of school refusal include on-campus violence and peer victimization, large class and school sizes, unwelcoming school climate, and poor match between coursework and ability level (Kearney, 2008). Whereas overly low academic expectations and demands may contribute to poor attendance because of student boredom, recent research also implicates high academic rigor as a potential correlate of school refusal severity. Specifically, among adolescents with social anxiety disorder, school refusal was harder to treat in students enrolled in more academically rigorous curricula (Heyne, Sauter, Van Widenfelt, Vermeiren, & Westenberg, 2011).

BEST PRACTICES IN INTERVENTIONS FOR ANXIETY-BASED SCHOOL REFUSAL

The next section describes assessment procedures intended to shed light on the form and function of a particular student's school refusal behavior and, when appropriate, the student's underlying psychopathology. The assessment results will guide the intervention team's selection of intervention strategies. The intervention options described in the following sections include a variety of evidence-based cognitive–behavioral strategies and comprehensive treatments. An overview of psycho-pharmacological and systemic interventions is also included. Strategies for monitoring student response to interventions targeting school refusal are discussed.

Assessment

Several resources that outline procedures for assessing school refusal can be used by school psychologists (Kearney & Albano, 2007; King, Heyne, Tonge, Gullone, & Ollendick, 2001; Thambirajah, Grandison, & De-Hayes, 2008). A first step is to collect information from home and school to ensure that school refusal is anxiety based versus the result of truancy, physical illness, or parent-motivated absences (see Thambirajah et al., 2008). Next steps entail a description of the behavioral form and function of the school refusal to inform intervention.

Describe Behavior

School psychologists should use a multiple informant, multimethod approach to develop a behavioral description of the actual school refusal behaviors, which vary widely across students. Regarding the history of the behavior, Kearney and Albano (2007) suggest identifying whether behavioral avoidance, cognitive distortions, and/or physiological reactions are the most problematic presenting symptoms of the school refusal. This stage also includes identification of additional student, parent, school, and medical factors contributing to school refusal (Thambirajah et al., 2008). The tools recommended to collect this information include student, parent, and teacher interviews and rating scales; a review of the student's attendance history and other relevant educational and familial history; behavioral observation conducted when school refusal behaviors are likely to occur; and consultation with medical professionals.

One goal of interviews is to establish the specific behaviors engaged in by the student, as well as symptom frequency and severity. Kearney and Albano (2007) recommend that the student be interviewed first in order to build rapport and to convey that the student's perspective is important. Consider asking parents to keep a log of their child's refusal behaviors, magnitude of distress, how the parent handled the situation, and the outcome (e.g., Did the student attend school? Was the student tardy?; King et al., 2001). Kearney and Albano (2007) provide a reproducible Behavioral Observation for School Refusal Behavior form that can be used to

observe a student's resistance to school preparation activities. The minutes spent in verbal or physical resistance to various activities—arising from bed, dressing, riding to school—are recorded, and the parent and the student rate the student's negative affectivity and noncompliance during these activities. Such data inform the specific manifestation of the refusals.

Rating scales provide an efficient strategy for understanding the student and parent's perceptions of the symptoms and the degree to which the behaviors are atypical. Although not focused specifically on school refusal behaviors, many rating scales help quantify negative affectivity and/or behavioral problems. Relevant rating scales include narrowband instruments of anxiety and depression and broadband scales that assess multiple forms of psychopathology (see McConaughy & Ritter, 2014).

Given the frequency of somatic complaints involved in school refusal, referral to or consultation with the student's physician (and/or collaboration with the school nurse) can establish whether there are legitimate health concerns that have caused the absences. This information is crucial to the school psychologist when developing an intervention plan, as parents may not feel comfortable following through with forced attendance until they are confident that there is not a valid medical concern.

Determine Functions

As described earlier, school refusal is typically motivated by four functions: (a) avoid vague symptoms of negative affectivity, (b) escape anxiety-provoking social interactions, (c) attempts to remain with parents, and (d) obtain tangible reinforcement (Kearney & Albano, 2007). To determine which function best describes a set of school refusal behaviors, a variety of descriptive functional methods can be used (e.g., interviews, observations, rating scales). Observations of the refusal behavior can provide insight by facilitating examination of antecedents and consequences for the behavior. One rating scale specifically designed to assess function is the School Refusal Assessment Scale–Revised (Kearney, 2002; the parent and student versions are available in Kearney & Albano, 2007). This scale provides school psychologists with parent- and student-perceived maintaining functions of the behavior and can help narrow the possible reasons for school refusal. Examinations of the interrater and across-time reliability for clinical judgment using the scale indicated that practitioners should not rely solely on it because of low reliability for individual clinicians. Rather, multiple assessment methods and collaborative decision making should be used to determine school refusal function (Daleiden, Chorpita, Kollins, & Drabman, 1999).

Kearney and Albano (2007) outline an experimental functional approach that can be used to support the hypotheses developed through the School Refusal Assessment Scale–Revised, and describe scenarios that could be compared to determine function. For example, if it is suspected that negative affectivity is maintaining the school refusal, then the school psychologist could compare behavior when the student attends school under normal circumstances versus when some aspects of the typical school environment are removed (e.g., not having to attend full day). In a case where it is believed that a student is attempting to escape an unwanted social or performance situation, school refusal behaviors when that stimuli is present (e.g., basketball game) versus not present (e.g., no basketball game) could be compared. When attention seeking is suspected, the student's response if a parent attends school could be compared to typical circumstances (e.g., no parent present). If the student may be refusing school to obtain tangible rewards, then the school psychologist should observe what occurs when these rewards are provided for school attendance but not unavailable otherwise.

Particularly when dealing with complex cases of school refusal in which the intervention approaches yielded from the assessment methods described here are ineffective, school psychologists should assess for underlying anxiety and depressive disorders (King et al., 2001). A comprehensive self-report measure such as the Adolescent Psychopathology Scale (Reynolds, 1998) is useful in screening for the multitude of psychological disorders commonly associated with school refusal and in suggesting symptoms to be explored further in a clinical assessment.

Forming the Intervention Team

The intervention process starts with forming a team composed of individuals at school and home who can help provide information and support with the implementation of the plan. Clearly communicated intervention goals and steps are essential to ensure consistency across settings and to prevent any stakeholder from inadvertently reinforcing school refusal behaviors. The school psychologist can play a central role in bringing the team together and supporting each member's role once an intervention is implemented, as described in Table 25.2. Key members of the team include the student's teacher to ensure the day-to-day environment is conducive to school attendance, the school nurse to

evaluate medical issues and to serve as a liaison with other medical professionals, school administrators to ensure the school environment supports school attendance, and the student's parent to make sure the student arrives and stays at school each day.

Student-Focused Clinical Interventions Targeting Anxiety-Related School Refusal

While early treatment approaches emphasized immediate full-time attendance, rapid school return is less preferable to a graduated approach that is more in line with ethical clinical interventions for anxiety-based school refusal (King et al., 2001). Behavioral and cognitive–behavioral interventions that emphasize a graduated, progressive return have reduced school refusal in a number of studies of youth with extreme school refusal and comorbid mental health problems (e.g., Heyne et al., 2011). The specific strategies are listed in Table 25.3 and can be used alone or in multicomponent intervention packages. Although the strategies are generally applicable across age levels, school psychologists should consider developmentally appropriate modifications as with any cognitive–behavioral treatment.

Psychoeducation

This common first step in cognitive–behavioral treatment entails using simple terms to teach students that anxious symptoms manifest physically (feelings, such as muscle tension, a racing heart, and rapid breathing), cognitively (thoughts, such as expectations of catastrophe, pessimistic future outcomes, and self-doubt), and behaviorally (actions, typically avoidance, sometimes tears or clinging to parents). Depending on a student's cognitive level, school psychologists can make affective education more concrete by helping students color in body diagrams that indicate their own common symptoms during anxious episodes. Anxiety is also normalized through discussions of its functional nature. A rationale for further assessment and treatment is secured though explaining the importance of acquiring tools to use to cope with anxious symptoms that are essentially false alarms (Chorpita, 2007).

Relaxation Training

To combat the physical component of anxiety, students are taught deep breathing and muscle relaxation strategies to help reduce somatic complaints and tensions. School psychologists can set a peaceful stage by providing a dimly lit room with soft music and

Table 25.2. The Intervention Team: Personnel and Roles

Personnel	Role	How a School Psychologist Can Provide Support
School psychologists	• Assess school refusal • Develop interventions • Provide direct clinical interventions • Support and coordinate the roles of other team members (see specifics below)	n/a
Teachers	• Identify the student who has early warning signs of school refusal • Liaison between home and school • Assist with developing, enacting, and monitoring the intervention	• Provide information about warning signs of school refusal • Facilitate expectations that are consistent with the treatment goals • Encourage matching of academic requirements to the student's current skills to reduce student anxiety • Prepare for roles in exposure tasks (e.g., coach how to respond when the student reacts negatively) • Collaborate to develop feasible progress-monitoring tools
School nurses	• Identify the student at risk for school refusal • Evaluate somatic complaints to rule out medical concerns • Provide a supportive environment for the student	• Provide information about warning signs of school refusal • Collaborate to collect data to determine the function of somatic complaints • Coach the nurse to encourage the student to use coping strategies to return to class
School administrators	• Provide flexibility to students who are refusing school to support their return • Implement universal strategies to improve the school climate	• Provide information on school refusal behaviors and universal strategies to encourage school attendance • Help consider possible escape-oriented behaviors (e.g., is student behavior an attempt to gain access to the parent?) • Assist develop interventions that match escape-oriented functions
Parents	• Provide information about the duration and intensity of refusal behaviors • Implement intervention strategies to keep the student in school • Coach the student to face feared situations and to practice coping skills • Reinforce school attendance appropriately at home • Encourage participation in activities that help the student view school positively • Review and practice coping strategies learned with the therapist	• Provide information about the importance of supporting and reinforcing strategies that help the student remain in school • Help develop skills in coaching the student's school attendance • Help identify appropriate reinforcers for school attendance • Share ideas that can be used at home to reinforce coping strategies learned in therapy

encouraging students to sit in a comfortable position and close their eyes. School psychologists can then use progressive muscle relaxation scripts (see Merrell, 2008) to prompt the students to purposefully tense and relax various muscle groups, with a focus on helping students recognize the contrast and become attuned to when muscles are in a tense state (signaling the need for tension reduction). Recordings of these scripts can facilitate rehearsal outside of the session. Some students need prompts to train their attention to the task of relaxation through repetition of brief self-scripts such as "I feel calm." Ultimately, youth should acquire the self-control to invoke a relaxed state relatively quickly in the natural environment through muscle memory.

Imagined and Assisted Exposure

The active ingredient responsible for most treatment gains in clinical interventions for anxiety reduction is

Table 25.3. Cognitive–Behavioral Interventions for Anxiety-Related School Refusal

Strategy	Description	Purpose
Psychoeducation	Teach students and their families about the tripartite model of anxiety using simple, concrete terms and drawings	Normalize anxious feelings and secure buy-in for further intervention
Relaxation training	Teach students deep breathing and muscle relaxation strategies to be invoked in anxiety-provoking situations	Address the physical component of anxiety by reducing somatic distress and tension
Exposure	Create a hierarchy of feared situations, then help students use coping strategies during gradual exposure (imagined or assisted) to the identified situations	Extinguish the fear response associated with an anxiety-provoking stimulus
Cognitive restructuring	Teach students to replace anxious thoughts with adaptive self-talk that facilitates effective coping	Address the cognitive component of anxiety in order to enable students to attempt exposure tasks
Modify contingencies	Identify students' preferred activities and rewards, then make access to these reinforcers contingent on specified rates of school attendance	Extinguish reinforcement patterns that maintain school refusal behaviors; motivate students to attempt exposure tasks
Skills training	Provide explicit instruction and practice in communication and problem solving	Develop skills needed to navigate social situations successfully

active, repeated exposure to the feared situation (Kendall et al., 2005). School psychologists should avoid tackling the most feared situation first, such as a full day in a classroom in which the student has developed a specific fear of the teacher. Instead, collaborate with the student to create a fear hierarchy, in which the student generates and ranks situations associated with minimal, moderate, and severe emotional distress. Gradual exposure entails brief sessions that slowly move up the fear hierarchy after less emotionally arousing situations are neutralized. School psychologists model nonfearful behavior in the anxiety-provoking situation and then assist the student in facing the same situation.

The behavioral component of anxiety is addressed by prohibiting the avoidance reaction. The student's initial distress about such situations is reduced as he or she learns first hand that these situations were not as fearsome as originally imagined and that he or she could cope with the situations through using anxiety-management tools. While in vivo exposure situations optimize likelihood of generalization outside of school psychologist-assisted sessions, exposure tasks can also be imaginal. This route is preferable when a student's emotional or physical safety cannot be ensured. Particularly in the school environment in which unpredictability is the norm, school psychologists may be most comfortable carrying out imaginal desensitization sessions where students are instructed to switch between states of deep relaxation and vivid imagination of

a particular feared situation for short intervals. Merrell (2008) argued persuasively for following mastery of imaginal situations with in vivo practice when working with students on school-related fears in particular, as "removal from the anxiety-provoking school setting too easily may serve inadvertently to worsen the problem, through the very powerful escape conditioning it might provide" (p. 179). Full cooperation from teachers, administrators, and sometimes peers is essential prior to in vivo situations that involve the presence of others in the feared school environment. Exposure tasks are considered mastered when the formerly feared stimulus is no longer accompanied by debilitating emotional distress or behavioral avoidance.

Cognitive Interventions

Through cognitive restructuring, school psychologists help students replace anxious thoughts (e.g., My mother will get hurt in an accident while I'm at school today.) with coping statements that reflect confidence (e.g., My mother is a careful driver who has not been in a major accident. She'll be fine.). These interventions are useful in ameliorating the cognitive component of anxiety and preparing students for exposure tasks. To be tailored to a student's primary cognitive errors, Chorpita (2007) offers intervention modules/sessions that address probability overestimation, catastrophic thinking, and substituting adaptive thoughts for pessimistic ones. Because many worries have some basis in reality (e.g., car accidents do occur), school psychologists help students focus on the (smaller) likelihood that such fears would actually transpire in order to help students live with the same probabilities for harm faced by high-functioning individuals throughout society. Successful completion of exposure tasks serve to reinforce the realistic statements school psychologists initially help students formulate. Merrell (2008) provides further guidance on self-instructional training, in which students formulate and rehearse adaptive scripts to enact through internal speech when approaching potentially fear-inducing situations or when anxiety is detected.

Modifying Contingencies

Contingency management pertains to both (a) addressing outcomes that often (unintentionally) reinforce school refusal behaviors and (b) providing additional motivation for students to attempt exposure tasks. Regarding the former, school psychologists should help families identify aspects of the home that may be particularly attractive to students and then block access to such reinforcers at times when students should be in class. At the same time, these potential reinforcers should be offered as rewards for predetermined rates of school attendance. In a classic example, a student sent home from school following somatic complaints (without a medical cause) should not be permitted to access videogames or movies during the school day, but such preferred activities may be provided contingent on adequate attendance. Students whose school refusal behavior is motivated by attempts to access parents' attention would be ill-served by being permitted to accompany a parent to work after being sent home from school, but may be motivated to stay in school when special activities with parents are offered for adequate attendance. Particularly when working with students who experience general emotional distress, creation of reward schedules contingent on school attendance and effort in exposure tasks may increase motivation to approach emotionally arousing situations. Merrell (2008) provides further guidance for how school psychologists can conduct reinforcer preference assessments and deliver identified reinforcers to reward and strengthen student behaviors that are incompatible with the avoidant anxious response.

Skills Training

Students who learn to manage physiological symptoms and become sufficiently motivated to approach exposure tasks, but who anticipate or evidence challenges functioning effectively in the situations, may have deficits in the basic competencies needed to navigate the situation. Explicit skills training is appropriate to address such deficits in (a) prior acquisition of knowledge, (b) learning opportunities that may have been thwarted earlier in development owing to absence from the situation, (c) heightened physiological symptoms that precluded action, or (d) vicarious learning of ineffective performances. The most likely skill targets for students with anxiety-based school refusal include family communication, problem solving, and school-based social situations. Given elevated parent–child conflict in adolescence, families of school-refusing older students in particular may benefit from direct instruction in communication skills and decision making (Heyne et al., 2011). Increased competence in family communication can minimize barriers in collaborative parent–child attempts to reengage a student in school. The basic steps in social skills training to be applied across social situations, such as joining a conversation or taking a test, include problem identification and definition, idea generation and modeling of the appropriate behaviors, rehearsal of the behavioral chain, performance feedback, and planning for generalization (Merrell, 2008). Chorpita (2007) offers detailed social skills lessons for anxious students that focus on meeting new people and effective nonverbal communication.

Student-Focused Multicomponent Treatment Package Targeting School Refusal

Kearney and Albano (2007) put forth a manualized cognitive–behavioral intervention that takes a functional approach to ameliorating school refusal that allows school psychologists to meet the heterogeneous needs of students who refuse school. Their individualized treatment plan is organized around the four functions their work has identified and is outlined in Table 25.1.

Two functions involve negative reinforcement, as the student is attempting to avoid or remove himself or herself from an undesirable situation at school. Interventions for such functions are student centered and address maladaptive negative reinforcement patterns. When school refusal is driven by negative affectivity, strategies include psychoeducation, somatic control exercises involving relaxation training, exposure using a fear hierarchy, and self-reinforcement. When the function is to escape social or performance situations, Kearney and Albano (2007) recommend that the intervention package include psychoeducation, somatic management, cognitive restructuring targeting maladaptive thoughts, practicing coping skills, exposure, and self-reinforcement. These student-based strategies can be paired with classroom or school-based efforts to make attendance less aversive (i.e., by reducing requirements for performance).

The remaining two functions entail positive reinforcement from a source outside of the school. Interventions to address both functions are family based, as it is likely that the family plays a role in supporting or maintaining this positive reinforcement. When a student's goal for school refusal is to gain access to a parent, parent-based interventions school psychologists can implement include teaching the parent to give appropriate and clear commands to increase student compliance, working with the family to develop consistent and structured home routines that facilitate timely arrival at school, teaching parents to effectively use contingency management to encourage school attendance (rewards for attending school, combined with reducing reinforcement or punishment for non-attendance), and possibly forced attendance. Finally, when a student is trying to obtain reinforcement outside of school, the school psychologist can work with the family to design a treatment package that focuses on developing contracts that increase reinforcement for school attendance and reducing reinforcement available outside of school, teaching the family skills to solve problems (e.g., setting a time and place to negotiate solutions) and increase effective communication using role plays and feedback to reduce conflict, and teaching students how to refuse peer pressure to miss school. When such proactive strategies are ineffective, the school psychologist should discuss the use of close monitoring and supervision (e.g., a parent escorting his or her child to school).

These methods are described extensively in Kearney and Albano's (2007) therapist manual, which provides session outlines, language for describing treatment components to clients, handouts/worksheets, and example cases. Multiple sessions are outlined for each function. Kearney and Albano's corresponding parent workbook was designed for distribution to participating families.

Outcomes of Kearney and Albano's (2007) prescriptive approach have been promising, albeit limited in number. For instance, three of four students who attended virtually no school at baseline evidenced large improvements in attendance over the course of intervention with an individualized intervention matched to the function of school refusal behavior (Tolin et al., 2009). However, none of these students

continued high attendance over the long-term, and all students eventually selected alternative school placements. Kearney and Silverman (1999) compared four students receiving intervention for school phobia based on a functional approach to four students receiving interventions not matched to function. The functionally based group showed significant improvements (full-time attendance, reductions in anxiety) compared to those without the matched intervention who incurred increases in absences and anxiety. Other studies with small samples have also provided support for the functional model of treatment, as summarized in Tolin et al. (2009).

Student-Focused Clinical Interventions Targeting Underlying Internalizing Disorders

Students who do not respond fully to targeted school refusal interventions, or whose emotional issues have consequences beyond school attendance, may be in need of more intensive clinical interventions. Such time-limited, manualized interventions with empirical support for ameliorating the internalizing disorders most common to school refusal, or that have shown some efficacy for reducing school refusal among students with anxiety disorders, are summarized next.

Social Anxiety Disorder
Among students referred for clinical treatment, school refusal accompanied by a diagnosis of social phobia (i.e., social anxiety disorder) predicted worse outcomes, defined as functioning 3 years after treatment (McShane, Walter, & Rey, 2004). A promising school-based option for adolescents is the Skills for Academic and Social Success, as developed by Masia-Warner, Fisher, Ludwig, Rialon, and Ryan (2011). This intervention is primarily a group counseling modality, with 12–14 small-group sessions that focus on psychoeducation, realistic thinking, social skills training, and exposure tasks. Other components include two brief individual meetings to set goals and problem solve intervention obstacles, four weekend exposure sessions that entail social events with peers without anxiety problems, and meetings with parents and teachers to share intervention goals and strategies. Outcome trials found at least 80% of adolescents who completed Skills for Academic and Social Success demonstrated clinically significant gains, with approximately two thirds no longer meeting diagnostic criteria for social phobia (Masia-Warner et al., 2011).

Coping Cat is a clinic-based intervention option with impressive empirical support for reducing anxiety in students with social phobia, separation anxiety disorder, and/or generalized anxiety disorder (Kendall, Furr, & Podell, 2010). Coping Cat, created for students ages 7–16, entails eight sessions of psychoeducation followed by eight sessions of exposure. Among students who sought outpatient treatment for an anxiety disorder *and* had impairing levels of school refusal, 75% of Coping Cat completers no longer evidenced school refusal afterward (Beidas, Crawley, Mychailyszyn, Comer, & Kendall, 2010). This positive response is remarkable given that Coping Cat does not target school refusal exclusively and instead targets reductions in general anxiety across situations. The finding that 41% of the sample dropped out before the planned end of treatment suggests that not all students are well suited for a lengthy intervention that does not begin exposure tasks until the ninth session. More immediate integration into the school setting may be necessary.

Separation Anxiety Disorder

School psychologists may be interested in a 10-week parent training program, developed by Eisen, Engler, and Sparrow (2006) and Eisen, Raleigh, and Neuhoff (2008) for use with families of young children with separation anxiety disorder. Parents learn several cognitive–behavioral strategies to apply to their children at home, including relaxation training, contingency management, and exposure. Preliminary outcomes with parents of children ages 7–10 indicated positive results, with five of six target children no longer meeting criteria for separation anxiety disorder after intervention (Eisen et al., 2008). Although replication in school (versus clinic) settings is needed, it is notable that the materials for parents are highly accessible and relatable (Eisen et al., 2006).

Specific Phobia

In addition to the behavioral interventions such as systematic desensitization and contingency management that are empirically supported treatments for specific phobia in students, school psychologists should consider One-Session Treatment (see Davis, Ollendick, Reuther, & Munson, 2012), when working with students who have a specific fear of, for example, a teacher, classroom pet, or tests. One-Session Treatment combines graduated exposure to situations identified on a fear hierarchy, clinician modeling and coaching, reinforcement, psychoeducation, cognitive restructuring, and skills training into a single 3-hour cognitive–behavioral intervention (consisting primarily of a functional assessment followed by behavioral experiments) that has not been viewed as particularly aversive by the students. A study of almost 200 students (ages 7–16) diagnosed with specific phobia found that just over 50% were diagnosis free immediately after One-Session Treatment and at 6-month follow up, compared to a remission rate of only 2% among students in a no treatment (wait list) condition (Ollendick et al., 2009).

Depression

A sizable minority of students with emotionally driven school refusal either has primary or comorbid affective disorders, which exacerbate challenges getting to and staying at school. One empirically supported school-based manualized intervention targeting depression is Taking ACTION (Stark, Streusand, Krumholz, & Patel, 2010). This 20-session group-counseling, cognitive–behavioral intervention includes psychoeducation, training in coping skills and the problem-solving process, cognitive restructuring, and facilitating a positive self-image. A school-based trial with depressed girls (Grades 4–7) found that four of five participants no longer met criteria for a depressive disorder after completing Taking ACTION (Stark et al., 2010).

Pharmacological Interventions

Given the co-occurrence between school refusal and anxiety and depressive disorders, and the common use of psychopharmacological interventions for internalizing disorders, students who refuse school may be prescribed psychotropic medications. Medications most often used in the treatment of student anxiety disorders include selective serotonin reuptake inhibitors, tricyclic antidepressants, benzodiazepines, buspirone, beta blockers, and antiepileptics (Kearney, 2008). For a general overview of the classes of medication typically used to treat youth, and the specific FDA-approved medications for anxiety, see Carlson and Shahidullah (2014).

Several studies have specifically examined the use of psychopharmacological treatment targeting school refusal behaviors (versus an anxiety or affective disorder). Those conducted from the 1970s to the early 1990s used tricyclic antidepressants and yielded inconclusive findings. A more recent study was promising: When combined with cognitive–behavioral therapy, school-refusing adolescents with comorbid internalizing disorders who were treated with imipramine had higher rates of attendance and experienced more rapid decreases in depressive symptoms when compared with a cognitive–behavioral therapy-only group (Bernstein et al., 2000).

The dearth of research on psychopharmacology for the treatment of school refusal suggests that close monitoring is warranted.

Systemic Preventive Interventions

School-level strategies for reducing school refusal involve early identification combined with reduction of the ecological risk factors previously referenced, such as bullying and poor school climate. School psychologists can ensure that every school has mechanisms in place to identify students systematically prior to school refusal becoming severe and entrenched. Plans must alert designated educators to abrupt cases of absences or students who are present but evidence the warning signs discussed earlier, such as distress upon arrival and asking to call home. Lyon and Cotler (2007) recommend instituting a cutoff of no more than 10% unexcused nonattendance over a period of up to 3 months in duration. They contend that 10% would reflect a clear pattern of problematic attendance and still remains sufficiently sensitive to identify relatively low-level school refusal cases.

Given increased school refusal during transition periods, it is essential to prepare and support students to manage promotions to the next school level. Strategies include hosting orientations, pairing students with older peers, and facilitating connections with a consistent adult such as a homeroom teacher. To address the resistant school refusal among some students in advanced coursework, Heyne et al. (2011) suggest close monitoring of the academic demands of socially anxious students, with educators reducing demands as needed. Strategies can include being flexible with assignment time lines and/or requirements for group work and giving options for modes of presentation.

Intervention Effectiveness

A progress-monitoring strategy for school refusal should be individually tailored to the function of a student's refusal and the intervention strategies. For many students, in addition to monitoring attendance over class periods and entire days, positive responses to intervention should result in reduced emotional distress and improved attitudes pertinent to attendance. School psychologists may want to use narrowband measures of anxiety and depression, keeping in mind that students' levels of distress may not always correspond directly to their attendance. Parents' reports of cooperation during morning routines, and school nurses' records of

frequency of student visits, may inform evaluations of students' willingness to arrive to and stay at school.

Case Example: Jada

Jada is a seventh-grade student in an urban middle school. She is educated primarily in a small, self-contained classroom for students with emotional and behavioral disabilities. In a weekly student assistance team meeting, Jada's special education teacher expressed concerns with Jada's increasingly aggressive behavior. Most recently, Jada stabbed a classmate in the hand with a pencil, resulting in an immediate out-of-school suspension. The teacher reported Jada expressed little remorse for her actions and had never seemed provoked by the targeted classmate. The teacher also noted that Jada's mother maintains regular communication with teachers and solicits behavior management advice.

A records review indicated Jada was identified with an emotional and behavioral disorder in fourth grade. At that time, problem behaviors were mostly internalizing in nature and included excessive fears and feelings of sadness. The evaluation also noted a history of poor attendance that necessitated the involvement of a school truancy officer. Although attendance subsequently improved to nonalarming levels, the school psychologist's detailed examination revealed a current pattern of partial attendance, where Jada left before lunch time at least twice a week. Despite no prior office referrals for major conduct violations, this year Jada had received five referrals for attempting to harm classmates. The most recent consequences for these referrals included multiday suspensions.

Jada's responses on the Adolescent Psychopathology Scale yielded numerous elevations on clinical disorder scales. The highest were separation anxiety disorder ($T = 76$) and social phobia ($T = 74$). In an interview Jada confirmed she actively avoided contact with all children and adults, with the exception of her immediate family. She shared a room with her mother in her maternal grandparents' home. She spoke of her mother in very warm terms, but became agitated and tearful when relaying extensive concerns about her mother's safety. Jada's most frequent worry was that an airplane would fall from the sky and kill her mother. All Jada's reinforcers entailed either activities with her mother or solitude, such as reading a book in her room.

Jada's mother reported a long history of challenges getting Jada to leave the house. She still escorted Jada to school each morning, and feared legal ramifications associated with repeated giving in to Jada's emotional pleas to accompany her mother to work or return home under the supervision of her grandparents. Current strategies for managing Jada's behavior entailed repeated verbal reassurance that no harm would befall her mother and punishing misbehavior at school with extensive household chores. Jada's mother was flummoxed about Jada's recent aggression, and warily noted that Jada did not seem to mind the additional chores.

The school psychologist reasoned that Jada's school refusal appeared maintained by positive reinforcement in the form of access to her mother and grandparents following suspensions and was also motivated by a chronic desire to escape anxiety-provoking social interactions in the classroom. The school psychologist's interventions to address the first function included collaboration with administrators to devise an alternate school-based consequence for aggression, collaboration with Jada's mother to make activities with, and physical proximity to, her contingent on school attendance whereas consequences for school misbehavior involved social interactions with less-preferred relatives, and collaboration with the special education teacher to create plans for ensuring all students' safety while permitting Jada brief, scheduled text interchanges with her mother following increasingly longer intervals of appropriate classroom behavior. To address the second function, the related services on Jada's Individualized Education Program were revised to include weekly school-based counseling to ameliorate symptoms of anxiety. The school psychologist selected Coping Cat to improve Jada's skills for coping with worries about social interactions and her mother's safety.

To monitor progress toward reducing aggression and increasing full-day attendance, the intervention team accessed school records and reviewed weekly graphs of Jada's office discipline referrals and attendance. To assess progress toward reducing anxiety symptoms, Jada completed a narrowband measure of anxiety every 2 weeks just before regularly scheduled counseling sessions. Classroom violence ceased after the first time that the assistant principal assigned in-school (versus out-of-school) suspension for aggression. Anecdotal reports from the special education teacher suggested Jada's peer interactions increased several weeks after counseling sessions began. Jada's mother, relieved to have concrete prevention and intervention strategies to implement at home, reported diminished verbal protests in the morning and noted that both she and Jada took pleasure in planning and enacting their reward activities.

SUMMARY

School psychologists are likely to encounter students with school refusal and have training in behavioral assessment and prevention/intervention approaches that make them well-suited to support such students. Students with anxiety-based school refusal exhibit a variety of behaviors ranging from emotional distress when leaving parents to problematic absenteeism. Significant levels of school refusal occur in approximately 1–2% of students. Several anxiety, depressive, and disruptive behavior disorders are commonly seen in this population, although not all students who refuse school have a diagnosable disorder. Students exhibiting school refusal are heterogeneous. Student, family, and school-related variables often contribute to the development and maintenance of these behaviors. Assessment of both the form and function is necessary to match interventions to the underlying cause. Primary functions for school refusal include (a) avoidance of vague symptoms of negative affectivity, (b) escape of anxiety-provoking social interactions, (c) attempts to remain with parents, and (d) efforts to obtain tangible reinforcement. Based on the hypothesized function, cognitive–behavioral strategies to address school refusal behaviors include psychoeducation, exposure, skills training, and contingency management, delivered either in isolation or as part of an intervention package. Intensive, manualized interventions or psychopharmacological treatment for internalizing disorders may be warranted for students who are resistant to functional intervention approaches or who have significant internalizing symptomatology. School psychologists should also consider systematic school-based interventions such as screening and transition-support strategies, as they provide an efficient approach to preventing anxiety-based school refusal.

REFERENCES

American Psychiatric Association. (2013). *Diagnostic and statistical manual of mental disorders* (5th ed.). Washington, DC: American Psychiatric Association.

Bahali, K., Tahiroglu, A. Y., Avci, A., & Seydaoglu, G. (2011). Parental psychological symptoms and familial risk factors of children and adolescents who exhibit school refusal. *East Asian Archives of Psychiatry, 21*, 164–169.

Beidas, R. S., Crawley, S. A., Mychailyszyn, M. P., Comer, J. S., & Kendall, P. C. (2010). Cognitive-behavioral treatment of anxious youth with comorbid school refusal: Clinical presentation and treatment response. *Psychological Topics, 2*, 255–271.

Bernstein, G. A., Borchardt, C. M., Perwien, A. R., Crosby, R. D., Kushner, M. G., Thuras, P. D., & Last, C. G. (2000). Imipramine plus cognitive-behavioral therapy in the treatment of school refusal. *Journal of the American Academy of Child and Adolescent Psychiatry, 39*, 276–283.

Carlson, J. S., & Shahidullah, J. D. (2014). Best practices in assessing the effects of psychotropic medication on student performance. In P. Harrison & A. Thomas (Eds.), *Best practices in school psychology: Systems-level services*. Bethesda, MD: National Association of School Psychologists.

Chorpita, B. F. (2007). *Modular cognitive-behavioral therapy for childhood anxiety disorders*. New York, NY: Guilford Press.

Daleiden, E. L., Chorpita, B. F., Kollins, S. H., & Drabman, R. S. (1999). Factors affecting the reliability of clinical judgments about the function of children's school-refusal behavior. *Journal of Clinical Child Psychology, 28*, 396–406. doi:10.1207/S15374424jccp280312

Davis, T. E., Ollendick, T. H., Reuther, E. T., & Munson, M. S. (2012). One-Session Treatment: Principles and procedures with children and adolescents. In T. E. Davis, T. H. Ollendick, & L. Ost (Eds.), *Intensive One-Session Treatment of specific phobias* (pp. 97–125). New York, NY: Springer.

Egger, H. L., Costello, E. J., & Angold, A. (2003). School refusal and psychiatric disorders: A community study. *Journal of American Academic of Child and Adolescent Psychiatry, 42*, 797–807. doi:10.1097/01.CHI.0000046865.56865.79

Eisen, A. R., Engler, L. B., & Sparrow, J. (2006). *Helping your child overcome separation anxiety or school refusal: A step-by-step guide for parents*. Oakland, CA: New Harbinger.

Eisen, A. R., Raleigh, H., & Neuhoff, C. C. (2008). The unique impact of parent training for separation anxiety disorder in children. *Behavior Therapy, 39*, 195–206. doi:10.1016/j.beth.2007.07.004

Hansen, C., Sanders, S. L., Massaro, S., & Last, C. G. (1998). Predictors of severity of absenteeism in children with anxiety based school refusal. *Journal of Clinical Child Psychology, 27*, 246–254. doi:10.1207/s15374424jccp2703

Heyne, D., & King, N. J. (2004). Treatment of school refusal. In P. M. Barrett & T. H. Ollendick (Eds.), *Handbook of interventions that work with children and adolescents: Prevention and treatment* (pp. 243–272). Hoboken, NJ: Wiley.

Heyne, D., Sauter, F. M., Van Widenfelt, B. M., Vermeiren, R., & Westenberg, P. M. (2011). School refusal and anxiety in adolescence: Non-randomized trial of a developmentally sensitive cognitive behavioral therapy. *Journal of Anxiety Disorders, 25*, 870–878. doi:10.1016/j.janxdis.2011.04.006

Kearney, C. A. (2002). Identifying the function of school refusal behavior: A revision of the School Refusal Assessment Scale. *Journal of Psychopathology and Behavioral Assessment, 24*, 235–245.

Kearney, C. A. (2007). Forms and functions of school refusal behavior in youth: An empirical analysis of absenteeism severity. *Journal of Child Psychology and Psychiatry, 48*, 53–61. doi:10.1111/j.1469-7610.2006.01634.x

Kearney, C. A. (2008). School absenteeism and school refusal behavior in youth: A contemporary review. *Clinical Psychology Review, 28*, 451–471. doi:10.1016/j.cpr.2007.07.012

Kearney, C. A., & Albano, A. M. (2007). *When children refuse school: A cognitive-behavioral therapy approach: Therapist guide* (2nd ed.). New York, NY: Oxford University Press.

Kearney, C. A., & Silverman, W. K. (1999). Functionally based prescriptive and nonprescriptive treatment for children and adolescents with school refusal behavior. *Behavior Therapy, 30*, 673–695. doi:005-7894/99/06734369551.0

Kendall, P. C., Furr, J. M., & Podell, J. L. (2010). Child-focused treatment of anxiety. In J. R. Weisz & A. E. Kazdin (Eds.), *Evidence-based psychotherapies for children and adolescents* (2nd ed., pp. 45–60). New York, NY: Guilford Press.

Kendall, P. C., Robin, J. A., Hedtke, K. A., Suveg, C., Flannery-Schroeder, E., & Gosch, E. (2005). Considering CBT with anxious youth? Think exposures. *Cognitive and Behavioral Practice, 12*, 136–150. doi:10.1016/S1077-7229(05)80048-3

King, N. J., Heyne, D., Tonge, B. G., Gullone, E., & Ollendick, T. H. (2001). School refusal: Categorical diagnoses, functional analysis and treatment planning. *Clinical Psychology & Psychotherapy, 8*, 352–360. doi:10.1002/cpp.313

Lyon, A. R., & Cotler, S. (2007). Toward reduced bias and increased utility in the assessment of school refusal behavior: The case for diverse samples and evaluations of context. *Psychology in the Schools, 44*, 551–565. doi:10.1002/pits.20247

Masia-Warner, C., Fisher, P. H., Ludwig, K. A., Rialon, R., & Ryan, J. L. (2011). Adapting treatment of social anxiety disorder for delivery in schools: A school-based intervention for adolescents. In C. A. Alfano & D. C. Beidel (Eds.), *Social anxiety in adolescents and young adults: Translating developmental science into practice* (pp. 281–296). Washington, DC: American Psychological Association.

McConaughy, S. H., & Ritter, D. R. (2014). Best practices in multimethod assessment of emotional and behavioral disorders. In P. Harrison & A. Thomas (Eds.), *Best practices in school psychology: Data-based and collaborative decision making*. Bethesda, MD: National Association of School Psychologists.

McShane, G., Walter, G., & Rey, J. M. (2004). Functional outcome of adolescents with "school refusal." *Clinical Child Psychology and Psychiatry, 9*, 53–60. doi:10.1177/1359104504039172

Merrell, K. W. (2008). *Helping students overcome depression and anxiety: A practical guide* (2nd ed.). New York, NY: Guilford Press.

Miller, D. N., & Jome, L. M. (2010). School psychologists and the secret illness: Perceived knowledge, role preferences, and training needs regarding the prevention and treatment of internalizing disorders. *School Psychology International, 31*, 509–520. doi:10.1177/0143034310382622

National Association of School Psychologists. (2010). *Model for comprehensive and integrated school psychological services*. Bethesda, MD: Author. Retrieved from http://www.nasponline.org/standards/2010standards/2_PracticeModel.pdf

Ollendick, T. H., Ost, L., Reuterskiold, L., Costa, N., Cederlund, R., Sirbu, C., ... Jarrett, M. A. (2009). One-Session Treatment of specific phobias in youth: A randomized clinical trial in the United States and Sweden. *Journal of Consulting and Clinical Psychology, 77*, 504–516. doi:10.1037/a0015158

Reynolds, C. R. (1998). *Adolescent Psychopathology Scale*. (APS). Lutz, Florida: Psychological Assessment Resources.

Richards, H. J., & Hadwin, J. A. (2011). An exploration of the relationship between trait anxiety and school attendance in young people. *School Mental Health*, *3*, 236–244. doi:10.1007/s12310-011-9054-9

Stark, K. D., Streusand, W., Krumholz, L. S., & Patel, P. (2010). Cognitive-behavioral therapy for depression: The ACTION treatment program for girls. In J. R. Weisz & A. E. Kazdin (Eds.), *Evidence-based psychotherapies for children and adolescents* (2nd ed., pp. 93–109). New York, NY: Guilford Press.

Thambirajah, M. S., Grandison, K. J., & De-Hayes, L. (2008). *Understanding school refusal: A handbook for professionals in education, health, and social care.* London, England: Jessica Kingsley.

Tolin, D. F., Whiting, S., Maltby, N., Diefenbach, G. J., Lothstein, M. A., Hardcastle, S., … Gray, K. (2009). Intensive (daily) behavior therapy for school refusal: A multiple baseline case series. *Cognitive and Behavioral Practice*, *16*, 332–344. doi:10.1016/j.cbpra.2009.02.003

Best Practices in Promoting Appropriate Use of Restraint and Seclusion in Schools

Brian M. Yankouski
Thomas Massarelli
Seton Hall University (NJ)

OVERVIEW

Owing to the passage of federal legislation, such as the Individuals with Disabilities Education Improvement Act (IDEIA) and the No Child Left Behind Act, the numbers of students with significant disabilities, emotional or behavioral problems, and mental health disorders have increased in mainstream classrooms (McLeskey, Landers, Hoppey, & Williamson, 2011; McLeskey, Landers, Williamson, & Hoppey, 2010; Yankouski, Massarelli, & Lee, 2012). These students typically require varying levels of academic, behavioral, and psychological supports because they often have a history of serious psychiatric and behavioral problems that have an impact on their daily functioning in school (Koppelman, 2004; Yankouski et al., 2012). Restraint and seclusion procedures that were once restricted to being used in psychiatric institutions have moved with these students into the schools.

Schools have now come under public scrutiny regarding the use of restraint and seclusion because of recent reports nationwide of alleged abuse and death due to school personnel misusing these procedures with students (Ryan & Peterson, 2004; *Seclusions and Restraints: Selected Cases of Death and Abuse at Public and Private Schools and Treatment Centers*, 111th Cong., 2009). The same federal regulations governing the use of restraint and seclusion that protect the rights of psychiatric patients do not apply to schools (Ryan & Peterson, 2004). Therefore, there are no guidelines or systems currently in place to monitor or regulate the use of such procedures in these settings. Both the House (H.R.

1381) and Senate (S. 2020) versions of the proposed federal legislation, Keeping All Students Safe Act (http://thomas.loc.gov/home/gpoxmlc112/h1381_ih.xml), is the first attempt at providing federal guidelines for the use of restraint and seclusion in schools. While many states have enacted state legislation to provide school professionals with guidelines governing the use of these procedures in the schools, the content of these guidelines and policies varies greatly, with no set standards for practice (Ryan, Robbins, Peterson, & Rozalski, 2009; *Seclusions and Restraints: Selected Cases of Death and Abuse at Public and Private Schools and Treatment Centers*, 111th Cong., 2009; U.S. Department of Education, 2010, 2012).

The purpose of this chapter is to examine the school psychologist's role in use of restraint and seclusion procedures in schools. This chapter offers school psychologists best practice recommendations in collaborating with others to implement restraint and seclusion procedures. After reading this chapter, school psychologists will be able to (a) identify preventive techniques to reduce the need for restraint and seclusion procedures in schools, (b) understand best practice procedures in using restraint and seclusion with students in the schools, (c) develop crisis intervention protocols and be able to assist in policy development to ensure the humane and ethical treatment of students when using restraint and seclusion, and (d) utilize postvention strategies for debriefing after the use of restraint and seclusion and implement data-based progress monitoring to monitor the use of restraint and seclusion.

What Is Restraint?

According to the Council for Children with Behavioral Disorders (2009), restraint is defined as a physical method used to restrict the freedom of movement or normal access to the individual's body. Restraint typically falls into three categories: mechanical, chemical, and ambulatory (Council for Children with Behavioral Disorders, 2009). Mechanical restraint involves the use of a device or object in order to restrict a person's body movement (e.g., calming blankets or strapping an individual to a chair; U.S. Department of Education, 2012). Chemical restraint refers to the use of medication (e.g., tranquilizers) to calm or subdue an acting-out person (Council for Children with Behavioral Disorders, 2009). Ambulatory restraint, also referred to as manual restraint or therapeutic holding, entails another person physically using his or her body to restrict the movement of another individual as a means of reestablishing behavior control in order to maintain safety for the acting-out individual and other individuals. Ambulatory restraint is the most common form of restraint currently being used in public schools with students who exhibit aggressive and self-injurious behavior (Council for Children with Behavioral Disorders, 2009; Ryan & Peterson, 2004).

What Is Seclusion?

Seclusion is defined as the involuntary confinement of an individual alone in a room in which the individual is physically prevented from leaving for any period of time (U.S. Department of Education, 2012). Seclusion should not be confused with time-out, which is used as a behavior management procedure in schools. With time-out the student is temporarily removed from the classroom in a monitored, unlocked room or setting for the purpose of helping the student to calm down (U.S. Department of Education, 2012).

Current Issues in Restraint and Seclusion

For years the use of restraint and seclusion had been a common practice with children and adolescents with disabilities and behavior problems within psychiatric facilities. These practices are still used today in psychiatric hospitals and institutions but with much more care and scrutiny than in the past. With the increased number of students with emotional disabilities in the public schools due to the passage of IDEIA, these restraint and seclusion procedures have moved from psychiatric facilities into the public schools. However, the use of these procedures in state hospitals and institutions is monitored by strict policies and legislative oversight on what constitutes proper restraint and seclusion procedures with children and adolescents. Currently, many public schools across the United States do not have such policies in place and lack legislative oversight, yet teachers and staff are being trained to restrain students who are out of control (Ryan & Peterson, 2004). However, without federal guidelines in place, some states are taking a more active role than other states in developing policies and procedures for properly restraining and isolating students who are unmanageable.

Figure 26.1 is a map of states that have statutes and regulations addressing restraint and seclusion in schools. The shaded states represent those states that currently have legislation enacted on restraint and seclusion in these settings. School psychologists are advised to examine this map and to review their state's legislation on restraint and seclusion practices in schools for guidance on how to implement these procedures. If a school psychologist finds that his or her state currently does not have state legislation on restraint and seclusion use in schools, then the school psychologist is encouraged to work with the state school psychology association to advocate for public policy and legislation on restraint and seclusion use.

The domains found within the National Association of School Psychologists (NASP) *Model for Comprehensive and Integrated School Psychological Services* (2010a) are directly connected to the use of restraint and seclusion in schools, specifically the domain Interventions and Mental Health Services to Develop Social and Life Skills. This domain explores the use of evidence-based interventions to promote social–emotional functioning and mental health by providing school psychologists with best practice recommendations in restraint and seclusion. By implementing evidence-based strategies to prevent the use of these procedures in schools, school psychologists can help to ensure the humane and ethical treatment of students.

The practice recommendations for the use of restraint and seclusion in schools found within this chapter are directly linked to the general problem-solving and multitiered themes of this edition of *Best Practices*. School psychologists will find that this chapter provides a conceptual framework for problem solving practical issues related to the use of restraint and seclusion in schools. Furthermore, this chapter examines multitiered prevention and intervention strategies that coincide with

Figure 26.1. Map of States With Statutes and Regulations on Restraint and Seclusion

Note. Based on information from U.S. Department of Education (2012).

other chapters within this edition of *Best Practices* and are connected to other areas within the NASP Practice Model (NASP, 2010a).

BASIC CONSIDERATIONS

Since 2000, school safety has become a paramount issue facing school administrators and superintendents throughout the country (American Association of School Administrators, 2012). The use of restraint and seclusion techniques has received national attention, mostly through the misuse of these procedures. From a school-based perspective, it is the school psychologist who works directly with the mental health needs of the students. The benefits of having school-based interventions available to teachers and staff will help assist them in understanding and reacting appropriately to crisis situations. All too often it is the lack of knowledge and instruction that impedes staff from carrying out a plan of action that can reduce the threat of violence in the school. There have been numerous lawsuits directed at schools for the improper use of restraint and seclusion practices throughout the country (*Seclusions and Restraints: Selected Cases of Death and Abuse at Public and Private Schools and Treatment Centers*, 111th Cong., 2009).

There are many challenges the school psychologist must recognize in helping children to remain safe. All school districts have a limited supply of resources, including hiring additional staff, providing money for inservice training, and purchasing special equipment for working with the most severely disabled students (e.g., use of calming blankets, time-out rooms, and monitoring devices). All of these resources can help promote safe schools and reduce the special education cost of having fewer students attend out-of-district programs that inevitably cost the district more money (McLeskey et al., 2010, 2011).

BEST PRACTICES IN PROMOTING APPROPRIATE USE OF RESTRAINT AND SECLUSION

School psychologists are in a unique position to address and monitor the use of restraint and seclusion in schools and collaborate with others in development and implementation of appropriate procedures. The subsequent sections address best practices in restraint and seclusion use in schools in three main areas: (a) prevention, (b) behavioral crisis intervention, and (c) postvention. Various strategies and recommendations will be discussed in further detail within each of these areas.

Prevention

School psychologists have the capability of collaborating with others in providing prevention programs and curriculum to students that can reduce problematic behaviors (e.g., aggression, self-injury) that could warrant the use of restraint and seclusion. By preventing problem behaviors from occurring and teaching socially acceptable replacement behaviors, school psychologists are in a unique position to help prevent the use of restrictive procedures, such as restraint and seclusion in the schools. This section will provide school psychologists with ideas for approaches, prevention both by reducing problem behaviors and by reducing the need for restraint and seclusion, at the universal, classroom, and individual levels.

Positive Behavioral Interventions and Support
School psychologists and all other school personnel should make use of positive behavioral interventions and supports to prevent the need for using restraint and seclusion with students. Research illustrates that schools utilizing positive behavioral interventions and supports had a reduction in the number of instances in which intensive interventions including restraint and seclusion were perceived as being needed with students, had an increase in the efficacy of comprehensive behavioral interventions, and had an improvement in the maintenance of behavior changes with students (Horner & Sugai, 2009). Therefore, it is recommended that school psychologists implement positive behavioral interventions and supports within their schools to aide in reducing the need for restrictive procedures like restraint and seclusion.

Verbal De-Escalation and Crisis Prevention
School psychologists and all other school personnel should make every attempt to utilize methods of crisis prevention prior to the implementation of more restrictive procedures such as restraint and seclusion. These alternative methods should include training staff in the use of verbal de-escalation techniques to defuse a crisis situation with a student prior to its escalating to a level where restraint or seclusion may become necessary. Acceptable verbal de-escalation techniques include (a) attempting to redirect the student, (b) setting appropriate limits, (c) engaging a student in a discussion of his or her behavior, (d) reflecting the student's feelings, (e) clarifying the student's concerns, and (f) developing a plan to solve the problem together (Dufresne, 2011). Research has shown that training staff in techniques to prevent problem behaviors and defuse crisis situations can reduce the number of situations in which restraint and seclusion may be necessary (Fogt & Piripavel, 2002; Ryan et al., 2009).

Character Education
Character education encourages students to reflect upon the meaning of civic and personal values and the application of those values in their daily lives. Programs such as Project Wisdom (2013) and Character Counts (Josephson Institute, 2013) address the issue of character education in promoting school-wide learning that affect children and staff. These programs and others like them indicate reductions in discipline referrals as well as strong improvements in teacher morale, school climate, and social–emotional competencies (Institute of Education Sciences, 2007). Therefore, the use of character education programs in turn could help reduce disciplinary and behavioral incidents, thus reducing the need for the use of restraint and seclusion.

Social–Emotional Learning
Social–emotional learning is a process for helping students, teachers, and staff achieve the necessary training to foster positive relationships with others, make responsible decisions, and handle challenging situations constructively and ethically (Collaborative for Academic, Social, and Emotional Learning, 2011). Social–emotional learning is a framework for school-wide improvement in teaching skills that help maintain a safe and caring learning environment. Skills that are targeted for students may include making friends, teaching how to calm down and self-regulate, making good choices, and resolving conflicts in an appropriate manner (Taylor & Dymnicki, 2007). Therefore, by promoting the social–emotional learning of students, school psychologists may be able to reduce emotional problems that could result in behavioral episodes potentially requiring the use of restraint and seclusion.

Collaborative Problem Solving
Collaborative problem solving for students is a therapeutic program based in cognitive–behavioral principles that conceptualizes aggressive and maladaptive behaviors as the by-product of lagging cognitive skills in the areas of flexibility, frustration tolerance, and problem solving. Collaborative problem solving provides a framework to understand a student's maladaptive behaviors as impairments in executive functioning, language processing, emotion regulation, cognitive flexibility, and social skills. By identifying deficits in

social and cognitive skills in conjunction with precipitating antecedent events, school personnel and students can examine alternatives to these behaviors. Research has shown that collaborative problem solving as both a prevention and intervention procedure for students can reduce the need for restraint and seclusion (Greene, Ablon, & Martin, 2006; Martin, Krieg, Esposito, Stubbe, & Cardona, 2008).

Designing Behavioral Interventions and Writing Crisis Intervention Plans

To prevent the need for restraint and seclusion in schools, school psychologists must conduct the necessary behavioral assessments and work with school staff to design comprehensive behavior intervention plans to reduce the need for such procedures by identifying the underlying functions and causes of problematic or dangerous behaviors. A functional behavioral assessment can be used to identify and address the causes of disruptive behaviors in the classroom. A school psychologist can conduct and employ various methods and techniques to examine the causes of disruptive behavior. Such methods may include (a) teacher and parent questionnaires and rating forms, (b) direct and indirect methods of classroom observation, (c) various assessment methods such as behavior rating scales, (d) academic and cognitive assessments, and (e) personality inventories. Once the functional behavioral assessment is complete, the school psychologist can meet with the Individualized Education Program (IEP) team (parents, administrators, teachers, and child study team members) to determine the best course of action to help ameliorate the behaviors in question.

A comprehensive behavior intervention plan should then be developed identifying the antecedents of the aberrant behavior and the purposes the behavior serves. The behavior intervention plan should also explore the student's history of behaviors, what previous interventions were tried and were either effective or ineffective, and new interventions to try in the classroom. As part of the behavior intervention plan, follow-up interventions and parental support are crucial. The behavior intervention plan should be a fluid document that can change over time to address what is working in the classroom as well as to identify new behaviors that may result from the interventions used.

Crisis plans are also used in the schools, and most schools today have a crisis plan for dealing with serious and dangerous behaviors. It is recommended that school psychologists become involved in developing a crisis intervention plan for each classroom where there are students who might require the use of restraint or seclusion. This plan should specify the roles of every staff member and his or her responsibility when involved in a crisis situation. Furthermore, the school psychologist may work with others to develop an individualized crisis intervention plan for each student who might require the use of restraint or seclusion. This plan should identify the warning signs the student exhibits before reaching the crisis phase, what behaviors can be seen during the crisis, and ways that the student might act after the crisis. For each of these areas of the individualized crisis intervention plan, the school psychologist and team should outline potential crisis intervention procedures to be employed by school personnel at each phase of the crisis. If the student has an IEP, then this individualized crisis intervention plan may then be amended to his or her IEP. If the student does not have an IEP, then it may be included in the student's file. For a more complete knowledge of a school's crisis prevention and intervention program, the authors suggest referring to the book on the PREPaRE model (i.e., Brock et al., 2009).

Development of School Policies on Restraint and Seclusion

According to NASP's *What Is a School Psychologist?* (NASP, 2011), two of the many roles and duties of school psychologists are to work with school administrators to develop school-wide programs that promote a positive school climate which is conducive to learning and to implement school policies and practices that ensure the safety of all students. School psychologists are in a unique leadership position to provide administrators with input on policies surrounding restraint and seclusion because of their extensive training in mental health, behavioral consultation and management, as well as crisis intervention (Fagan & Wise, 2007).

Owing to the possible risks associated with the use of restraint and seclusion (e.g., trauma), school psychologists can ensure that school policies and procedures on restraint and seclusion will take into account the psychological, behavioral, and social–emotional needs of students. Therefore, given the background and training of school psychologists, it is imperative that they be included in a comprehensive team of school professionals to develop school policies on restraint and seclusion that ensure the humane and ethical treatment of all students. School psychologists should collaborate with other multidisciplinary teams within the school (e.g., behavior teams, disciplinary teams) when developing such policies to ensure continuity of district procedures.

Appendix A provides school psychologists and other school personnel with a checklist of what their school's policy on restraint and seclusion should include in order to provide comprehensive services to students. It is important to remember that when developing a policy on restraint and seclusion that it is not specific to any student population (e.g., students with disabilities). According to the Office for Civil Rights (2012), students with disabilities and ethnic minorities are more likely to be subjected to restraint and seclusion procedures in schools. Therefore, it is imperative that the policy applies to all students in the school and is not written to discriminate against certain student populations. Furthermore, school psychologists should promote including in the school policy a procedure to collect data on the use of restraint and seclusion and to examine trends in which these procedures are being used in student populations. This information should then inform the school administration's creation of a strategic plan designed to reduce the use of these restrictive procedures in the school.

Policies regarding the use of restraint and seclusion should be reviewed regularly and updated as appropriate. School psychologists and other school staff may use data that have been collected throughout the school year on restraint and seclusion practices to inform policy decisions. This information should be shared with school administrators, the superintendent, and the board of education. It is suggested that the school's policy on restraint and seclusion be reviewed and revised on an annual basis.

Also, it is recommended that schools communicate their policies on restraint and seclusion with parents or legal guardians. One way to do this is to include the policy in the student handbook and have parents or legal guardians sign a form stating that they have received and read the student handbook. For those students with an IEP, it is important to talk and preferably meet with parents prior to the actual IEP meeting to address what will be discussed at the IEP meeting. Informing parents or guardians of the school's policies and assuring them of the staff's professionalism may help reduce the risk of an adversarial relationship between school officials and parents or guardians. When approaching the topic of restraint and seclusion, it is important to let the parents or guardians know that these procedures are the last resort measures to be used when all least restrictive alternatives have been tried and have failed. Parents need to know that the individuals performing these procedures are properly trained and have experience in these types of emergency procedures.

It may also be helpful to show parents or guardians images of the restraints that might be used with their child, which can often be found in the training manuals of the crisis intervention training program that the school uses.

Behavioral Crisis Intervention

Owing to the professional training of school psychologists in mental health and counseling services, school psychologists can be effective in providing crisis intervention and counseling to students in need during a behavior incident. Furthermore, school psychologists' skills are valuable in an incident requiring the use of restraint and seclusion in order to assess the student's psychological state and well-being. The subsequent section will provide school psychologists with additional information on best practices in providing behavioral crisis intervention within the context of restraint and seclusion use in schools.

Crisis Intervention Training

School psychologists are encouraged to seek advanced training in crisis intervention, including the use of restraint and seclusion, in order to learn how to manage student behaviors when the student begins to pose a significant danger to self or others. This training is necessary for school psychologists so they can learn how to effectively intervene in a crisis situation in order to minimize the risk of harm to students and staff. School psychologists may refer to the annotated bibliography of this chapter (available at http://www.nasponline.org/publications) for additional reading that will provide a more comprehensive review of training programs and assist them in selecting a crisis intervention training provider (e.g., Couvillon, Peterson, Ryan, Scheuermann, & Stegall, 2010).

Use of a Team Approach to Crisis Intervention

During a crisis incident with a student, school psychologists are strongly encouraged to use a team approach. It is recommended that each school building within the public school district has a designated behavioral crisis response team that can be summoned to provide assistance to classroom teachers and students when there is a potentially volatile situation with a student. This team should have training in crisis prevention and intervention, verbal de-escalation, conflict resolution, use of positive behavioral interventions and supports, collaborative problem solving, and proper use of restraint and seclusion. By using a team approach, the staff will be more likely to maintain professionalism during the crisis because they will know that assistance is nearby and that there are witnesses to the incident in the event of allegations of institutional abuse (Dufresne, 2011). Furthermore, with using a team approach, team members can safely monitor restraint and seclusion use with students to ensure that the student is safe.

Determine When to Use Restraint and Seclusion

School psychologists and other school staff should use restraint and seclusion when a student poses a significant danger to self or others and when all least restrictive alternatives have been tried and have failed (e.g., verbal de-escalation, redirecting the student to a different activity). School psychologists should also consider instances of severe property destruction (e.g., breaking a window) as a situation in which restraint or seclusion may be warranted because it also poses a significant danger to the student. For instance, if a student is running from the school into oncoming traffic, restraint or seclusion could be necessary since it would pose a significant danger to the student if he or she were to run into traffic. School psychologists and school personnel should discontinue the use of restraint or seclusion once the student has regained behavioral control and is no longer posing a danger to self or others (U.S. Department of Education, 2012).

Restraint or seclusion should never be used as a form of punishment or discipline (e.g., placing a student in seclusion for out-of-seat behavior or restraining a student for talking back to a teacher). When selecting behavioral procedures, school psychologists should follow the doctrine of the least restrictive alternative method instead of resorting immediately to more restrictive procedures, such as restraint and seclusion. This doctrine states that less intrusive or aversive interventions must be attempted or considered and found to be inappropriate or ineffective prior to the use of more restrictive or aversive methods. This doctrine provides a general framework for the selection of treatment procedures for students on this least to most restrictive continuum to ensure the ethical, legal, and humane treatment of students (Cooper, Heron, & Heward, 2007; Johnston & Sherman, 1993). Following this doctrine provides school psychologists with four levels of procedures to choose from when designing behavior change procedures: (a) methods that use differential reinforcement strategies, (b) procedures focusing on extinction, (c) techniques such as time-out,

and (d) strategies that are more invasive such as restraint or aversives (Alberto & Troutman, 2008).

The actual implementation of physical restraints in schools should be examined along the same doctrine of least to most restrictive interventions. Figure 26.2 provides school psychologists with a flowchart of strategies that should be considered at each level of the least to most restrictive continuum for intervening in a crisis situation with a student.

Furthermore, the types of restraints being used can also be examined along this spectrum. For example, a standing restraint would be considered less restrictive than a seated or prone restraint. Whenever possible, school psychologists and other school personnel should use the least restrictive restraint first and move to more restrictive restraint procedures if necessary. However, there may be times when a more restrictive restraint procedure may need to be used first due to the severity and intensity of the crisis situation that could have an impact on student and staff safety.

Procedural Safeguards in Using Restraint and Seclusion

When school psychologists and school personnel use restraint or seclusion with students, it is important that someone is monitoring the student at all times. The school psychologist and other school personnel should be monitoring the student to ensure that the student's physical safety and psychological well-being are taken into consideration. Furthermore, no restraint should be performed that prevents a child from being able to breathe. There is a well-developed body of research literature demonstrating that restraint-related positional asphyxia is more likely to occur during a prone or emergency floor restraint (O'Halloran & Frank, 2000; Patterson, Leadbetter, & McComish, 1998; Protection & Advocacy, 2002).

While there has been much controversy over banning the use of prone or emergency floor restraints in schools, it should be noted that not all prone or emergency floor restraints are deadly. It largely depends upon how the restraints are performed and the procedural safeguards that are put in place in the mechanics of the prone or emergency floor restraint (Winston, Fleisig, & Winston, 2009). There are a variety of training companies that teach prone or emergency floor restraints that have procedural safeguards built into the mechanics of these restraints to reduce the likelihood of restraint-related positional asphyxia (see Couvillon et al., 2010, for restraint training programs that teach these prone restraints). It is important that an accredited and

Figure 26.2. Hierarchy of Least to Most Restrictive Strategies for Crisis Intervention

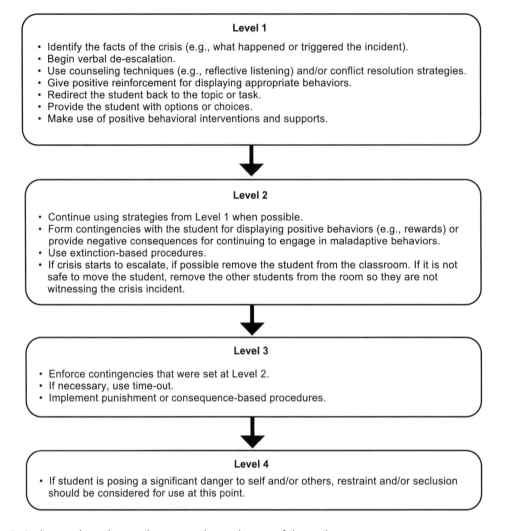

Level 1
- Identify the facts of the crisis (e.g., what happened or triggered the incident).
- Begin verbal de-escalation.
- Use counseling techniques (e.g., reflective listening) and/or conflict resolution strategies.
- Give positive reinforcement for displaying appropriate behaviors.
- Redirect the student back to the topic or task.
- Provide the student with options or choices.
- Make use of positive behavioral interventions and supports.

Level 2
- Continue using strategies from Level 1 when possible.
- Form contingencies with the student for displaying positive behaviors (e.g., rewards) or provide negative consequences for continuing to engage in maladaptive behaviors.
- Use extinction-based procedures.
- If crisis starts to escalate, if possible remove the student from the classroom. If it is not safe to move the student, remove the other students from the room so they are not witnessing the crisis incident.

Level 3
- Enforce contingencies that were set at Level 2.
- If necessary, use time-out.
- Implement punishment or consequence-based procedures.

Level 4
- If student is posing a significant danger to self and/or others, restraint and/or seclusion should be considered for use at this point.

Note. These strategies are based upon the personal experiences of the authors.

reputable training company in restraint and seclusion trains school psychologists and school personnel in these procedures.

Furthermore, it is important to do a brief mental status exam following a crisis. The school nurse can assist with the physical monitoring of the student's respiration, heart rate, and any other areas that may be affected. The school psychologist can look for signs of extreme stress (fight or flight) and determine the level of security needed to bring the student under control. School psychologists can assess the student's orientation to time, place, and people, as well as the student's level of anger and ability to control his or her actions. In some schools, security officers and police are present to oversee the safety of everyone involved and to provide assistance if it is deemed that a student is having a

psychiatric emergency and needs to be transported to the emergency room for psychiatric admittance.

Maintaining the Rights and Dignity of the Student

Policies restricting the use of restraint and seclusion should apply to all children, not just children with disabilities. Any behavioral intervention must be consistent with the child's rights to be treated with dignity and to be free from abuse. NASP's *Principles for Professional Ethics* (2010b) can be applied to the issue of restraint and seclusion use in schools. Specifically, Principle I: The Dignity and Rights of All Persons, states:

School psychologists engage only in professional practices that maintain the dignity of all individuals.

In their words and actions, school psychologists demonstrate respect for the autonomy of persons and their right to self-determination, respect for privacy, and a commitment to just and fair treatment of all persons. (NASP, 2010b, p. 3)

Therefore, school psychologists can take steps to ensure that students are treated with dignity and respect when restraint and seclusion practices are employed in schools.

One way to ensure that students are treated with dignity and respect is to develop a human rights committee in the school. This committee should consist of a cross-disciplinary team of professional staff (e.g., school psychologist, behaviorist, special education teacher, occupational therapist, and school nurse) that reviews all students' behavior intervention plans to ensure the humane and ethical treatment of students and the use of least restrictive behavioral interventions whenever possible to treat behavior problems. Furthermore, the committee should review student incident reports to provide oversight regarding the use of restraint and seclusion environments with students and when necessary consider adjusting behavioral interventions for those students.

Appendix B provides a checklist of questions school psychologists can promote for use in schools to answer in order to guide ethical decision making and to assist school psychologists in ensuring the humane treatment of students. These questions can help guide processing restraint and seclusion use in schools and can serve as a tool for reflection on current practices being used with students in the school. The school's answers to all of the questions in the checklist should be "yes" in order to be certain that the schools have thoroughly processed their plan to use restraint and seclusion and that their plan will ensure the ethical and humane treatment of the student. If a school answers "no" to any of the items on the checklist, then the school should reexamine that item and make a conscious effort in correcting the situation prior to the implementation of restraint and seclusion with the student.

Appendix C offers a self-assessment checklist for school psychologists regarding their professional competencies in the area of restraint and seclusion use in schools through the application of the domains in the NASP Practice Model (NASP, 2010a). School psychologists may use the checklist as a way to explore their own strengths and weaknesses in this topic and as a guide to seek out professional development training in this area. In addition, if school psychologists find that they are responding "no" to the majority of the questions on the checklist, then the school psychologists should examine their own ethical and legal responsibilities to the profession regarding the use of restraint and seclusion in the schools and seek out professional consultation regarding these practices.

Postvention

The following section provides information about what to do after using restraint and seclusion with a student. The recommendations found within this section highlight the roles and responsibilities of school personnel in the areas of ethics and law, documentation, and data-based progress monitoring when using restraint and seclusion with students.

Debriefing With the Team and the Student

After any incident requiring the use of restraint or seclusion, the school psychologist or other school staff member should lead a debriefing session with the school personnel who were involved in the incident. The purpose of the meeting should be to identify what happened before the incident (i.e., antecedents), what occurred during the incident (i.e., behaviors), and what happened after the incident (i.e., consequences). By gathering this information, the school staff can begin to identify some reasons as to why the incident occurred and can formulate ideas to prevent an incident from occurring again in the future. In addition, this debriefing session is a good opportunity for the crisis team and other school personnel who were involved to evaluate their response to the crisis incident and to formulate ideas as to how they can improve their interventions as a team with that particular student again in the future.

Furthermore, the school psychologist or another designated school staff member can also debrief with the student, if appropriate, after the incident to get the student's perspective on what happened during the crisis. This can be an effective process to help identify what the student thinks happened and could provide insight into what the possible triggers are that led to the crisis incident. Also, having this dialogue gives the school psychologist an opportunity to develop and maintain a therapeutic alliance as part of the counseling process and demonstrates to the student that the student's opinion matters.

School personnel may also need to debrief after an incident with all of the students in the class who might have witnessed the crisis incident to ensure the mental health of all students. This is a recommended practice because it could be scary for some students to witness another student in crisis that might have required the use of restraint and seclusion. This is especially crucial if it was an incident that required the student to be hospitalized due to a psychiatric emergency. Also, if schools have students in classrooms who might require the use of restraint or seclusion, schools may want to implement social skills groups in the classroom so that students can discuss feelings and emotions and how some students might display emotions. As part of this dialogue, discussions with students can emphasize that at times if a student is upset and starts to hurt himself or herself or someone else, school staff might have to hold the student in order to keep everyone safe. Students can be reassured that these procedures are done to help protect them and that these procedures are not being performed in a way to hurt them.

Documenting an Incident

After any incident involving the use of restraint or seclusion, school personnel must document the use of these procedures in an incident report form the same day as the incident. It is recommended that school psychologists help their schools develop this incident report form. This form at a minimum should note what had happened, the interventions used, the outcome, and any new interventions that may be employed in the future. These incident reports should be copied and given to the building principal, a district administrator, parents, and others. It is suggested that schools review these incident reports regularly to identify any patterns of behaviors that might be causing an incident to occur and to help school personnel to formulate a plan to reduce the use of restraint and seclusion with those students.

Notifying Parents or Guardians

After any incident involving the use of restraint or seclusion it is suggested that the school psychologist, classroom teacher, or principal notify the student's parents or legal guardians immediately that same day. The parents or legal guardians can be notified in writing either through a letter, by e-mail, in a home–school communication book, or by phone. In addition, if the parents or legal guardians request a copy of the incident report, it should be mailed to the parents or legal guardians within 24–48 hours after the incident has occurred.

Collaboration With Medical Professionals

As part of the IEP team, the school district's consulting medical professional may become involved in performing assessments of children with extreme neurological and social–emotional behavioral problems. These individuals are usually board-approved licensed professionals hired by school districts to lend additional support in terms of addressing severe behavioral problems, helping determine appropriateness of current placement, and recommending outside counseling and/or medication to help manage the more serious explosive disorders affecting some children. Therefore, team collaboration is important in working with students with severe behavior problems. Data regarding behavioral incidents should be shared with these medical professionals in order to determine if problematic behaviors, such as self-injury and severe aggression toward others, have increased or decreased since a change in medication to ensure and maintain staff and student safety. School psychologists and other school personnel should not recommend or use chemical restraint (i.e., medication) or mechanical restraint (i.e., use of straps) unless authorized by a licensed medical professional (U.S. Department of Education, 2012).

Data-Based Progress Monitoring

School psychologists are encouraged to use their professional training in data-based decision making to collaborate with other school staff in monitoring daily progress of students' behaviors. School psychologists may observe students in classrooms daily to determine baseline levels of behavior and then proceed to develop an intervention to help ameliorate the behaviors in question. Behavior monitoring forms such as checklists and observation charts can help identify the problematic behaviors.

In addition, it is recommended that school psychologists work with schools to collect data, such as frequency and duration of restraints and seclusion, in order to monitor the use of such procedures with students. These data will aid them in understanding the trends of the use of these procedures within their school. By analyzing these data, schools can determine whether there are certain students who are being restrained and/or secluded more frequently or if certain classrooms within the school are using these procedures at a higher rate. This information can then be useful to identify staff training needs, and a strategic plan can then be developed to assist in reducing the use of these procedures within the school.

The following case provides an example of how data-based progress monitoring at the school level can be useful to both school psychologists and school administrators.

Each year, a public elementary school collects data on the number of incidents with students who required the use of restraint and seclusion, the number of incidents by classroom, the number of incidents by student demographics, and the types of restraint used in the school. Upon initial examination of the data, the school psychologist determined that two of the six special education classrooms in the school were using restraint and seclusion more than four times as much as the other classrooms. Further analysis revealed that the profile of students in these classrooms was contributing to the increased use of restraint and seclusion. These students had more severe behavioral and psychiatric needs when compared to students in other classrooms. A content analysis of incident reports revealed that some students in each classroom were triggering behavioral incidents of other students. The school psychologist discussed these data with the school principal to identify changing classroom placements for these students next year to help reduce the number of incidents that would require the use of restraint and seclusion. Furthermore, the school psychologist was able to present a case for more professional development training for staff in how to work with students with significant behavioral challenges.

In the scenario above, the school psychologist was able to clearly use his or her knowledge in data-based decision making to help inform professional practice in the schools. The school psychologist was able to identify classrooms that were using restraint and seclusion with students at a significantly higher rate and to further identify the factors contributing to the high usage. Most importantly, the school psychologist was able to become an agent of change by working with administrators to identify appropriate classroom placements for the students next school year, hoping to reduce the need for restraint and seclusion with these students. The school psychologist was also able to identify the professional development needs of school personnel to better enhance their skills in working with students with serious behavior challenges.

Establishment of a Human Rights Committee

School psychologists are strongly encouraged to develop a human rights committee within their school if the school is currently using restraint and seclusion practices with students. The members of this committee should be a cross section of disciplines and should include at a minimum the school psychologist, an administrator, a general education teacher, a special education teacher, and the school nurse. The purpose of this committee should be to review student behavior intervention plans that may contain more restrictive behavioral treatment procedures and to provide oversight regarding the use of restraint and seclusion in the school. The main goal of

this committee is to ensure that all students participating in the school are free from the unnecessary use of restrictive behavioral interventions, including restraint and seclusion, and that they are being treated ethically and humanely throughout this process. For instance, if a student has more than five incidents a month that require the use of restraint and/or seclusion, then a review of the student's behavior intervention plan and incident reports should be conducted. If the student does not have an IEP or behavior intervention plan, then a functional behavioral assessment should be conducted and a behavior intervention plan developed to address the maladaptive behaviors.

The following case is an example of when the human rights committee would have to be involved.

John is an 11-year-old student who is classified as multiply disabled and is currently being served in a self-contained special education classroom within a public school district. He has a one-to-one aide due to his medical concerns (i.e., a feeding tube), self-injurious behavior (i.e., trying to physically remove his feeding tube), and aggressive behaviors (i.e., hitting, spitting, kicking, and head butting staff and other students). In addition, John has a cochlear implant and because he is nonverbal and deaf; his primary means of communication is American Sign Language. Because of his aggressive behaviors staff will have to perform physical restraint with John in order to maintain his safety as well as the safety of others. Instructional staff will typically place him in a one-person standing restraint where his arms will be crossed in front of him up high on top of his chest that will prevent him from being able to sign and communicate with staff. The school psychologist on the human rights committee observes the staff performing this type of restraint and calls a meeting to discuss the rights of this student.

In the case above, John's rights are clearly being violated by placing him in a restraint that prevents him from being able to use his only method of communication. As a result of using this type of restraint, the staff will have no way of de-escalating John because all capabilities of communication have been removed and the staff will be unable to check for John's understanding of whatever directives staff are giving him during the crisis incident. The school psychologist discusses with the staff the clear ethical and human rights issues that are involved with this student. Furthermore, the school psychologist will have to work with the committee to develop a crisis plan and interventions that would allow John to communicate effectively with staff while maintaining the safety of everyone involved in the incident.

Additional Considerations When Using Restraint and Seclusion in Schools

In addition to the aforementioned best practice recommendations, school psychologists need to be mindful of the developmental differences of students of different ages in using restraint and seclusion. For instance, the types of physical restraints that would be conducted with a preschool-age child would be very different from those of a student in high school because of the differences in size and strength. School psychologists and other school personnel should be cautious when performing restraints with younger children because their muscles and body have not fully developed. It is always best to avoid having to restrain a student whenever possible; however, if restraint needs to be performed on a younger child, it should be done only for a brief period of time.

Furthermore, school psychologists and school personnel need to be mindful when intervening with the student to use language that is at the appropriate developmental level of the child. Age-appropriate language is important when intervening with children who are typically developing, but it is even more important when intervening with children with significant developmental disabilities and cognitive impairments. When intervening with students with disabilities, school psychologists and other school staff may find it beneficial to use short, clear, and simple statements to reduce the amount of language the student will have to process. School psychologists may then want to check for the student's understanding of the directive by having the student respond "yes" or "no" through the use of verbal language, sign language, or picture supports.

School psychologists and other school personnel need to be mindful of how culture can have an impact on the way in which staff intervenes with students when using restraint and seclusion (Department of Education and Children's Services, 2011). For example, the concept of physically touching a student of the opposite sex in some cultures could present an area of concern. Therefore, when school psychologists look at developing crisis response teams in schools, it may be best to have professionals on the team who are just as diverse as the student population that they are serving in terms of race, gender, and ethnicity. In addition, it may be helpful to have school personnel on the team who are bilingual to assist in intervening with students in crisis who have limited English proficiency. Also, research has shown that restraint and seclusion have been used more frequently with Hispanic and African American students when compared to other demographic populations (Office for Civil Rights, 2012). Therefore, school psychologists must be mindful of closely monitoring the data on the use of these procedures in schools and offer culturally competent training to staff in order to reduce the use of these restrictive procedures with all students.

SUMMARY

The use of restraint and seclusion in schools is a topic that school psychologists will be faced with for many years to come. With the increase of students with significant behavioral disorders being brought back into mainstream classrooms, school psychologists must be adequately prepared to address the behaviors of these students and have the necessary training in crisis intervention procedures, including the appropriate use of restraint and seclusion, for emergency situations. School psychologists must remember that these restrictive interventions should only be used as a last resort and during emergency situations when students pose a significant danger to themselves or others. School psychologists are encouraged to utilize alternatives to restraint and seclusion (e.g., verbal de-escalation, collaborative problem solving, and positive behavioral interventions and supports) whenever possible. Furthermore, school psychologists are encouraged to use their professional training in assessment to promote the appropriate evaluations of student behavior and design behavioral treatments to reduce the need for restraint and seclusion in schools. Finally, school psychologists must become educated about the use of restraint and seclusion in schools as they have a responsibility to create safe and positive school climates that ensure the ethical and humane treatment of all students.

REFERENCES

Alberto, P. A., & Troutman, A. C. (2008). *Applied behavior analysis for teachers* (8th ed.). Upper Saddle River, NJ: Pearson.

American Association of School Administrators. (2012). *Keeping schools safe: How seclusion and restraint protects students and school personnel.* Alexandria, VA: Author. Retrieved from http://www.aasa.org/uploadedfiles/resources/tool_kits/aasa-keeping-schools-safe.pdf

Brock, S. E., Nickerson, A. B., Reeves, M. A., Jimerson, S. R., Lieberman, R. A., & Feinberg, T. A. (2009). *School crisis prevention and intervention: The PREPaRE model.* Bethesda, MD: National Association of School Psychologists.

Collaborative for Academic, Social, and Emotional Learning. (2011). *Benefits of SEL.* Chicago, IL: Author. Retrieved from http://casel.org/why-it-matters/benefits-of-sel/

Cooper, J. O., Heron, T. E., & Heward, W. L. (2007). *Applied behavior analysis* (2nd ed.). Upper Saddle River, NJ: Pearson.

Council for Children With Behavioral Disorders. (2009). *CCCBD's position summary on the use of physical restraint procedures in school settings.* Arlington, VA: Author. Retrieved from http://higherlogicdownload. s3.amazonaws.com/SPED/820a639f-e64f-4f1f-a998-f94b36273eeb/ UploadedImages/CCBD%20Position%20on%20Use%20of%20 Restraint%207-8-09.pdf

Couvillon, M., Peterson, R. L., Ryan, J. B., Scheuermann, B., & Stegall, J. (2010). A review of crisis intervention training programs for schools. *Teaching Exceptional Children, 42*(5), 6–17.

Department of Education and Children's Services. (2011). *Protective practices for staff in their interactions with children and young people: Guidelines for staff working or volunteering in education and care settings.* Adelaide, Australia: Author. Retrieved from http://www.decd.sa.gov.au/ docs/documents/1/ProtectivePracticesforSta.pdf

Dufresne, J. (2011). *Communication is the key to crisis de-escalation.* Milwaukee, WI: Crisis Prevention Institute. Retrieved from http://www. crisisprevention.com/Resources/Knowledge-Base/De-escalation-Tips

Fagan, T. K., & Wise, P. S. (2007). *School psychology: Past, present, and future* (3rd ed.). Bethesda, MD: National Association of School Psychologists.

Fogt, J. B., & Piripavel, C. M. (2002). Positive school-wide interventions for eliminating physical restraint and exclusion. *Reclaiming Children and Youth, 10,* 227–232.

Greene, R. W., Ablon, J. S., & Martin, A. (2006). Use of collaborative problem solving to reduce seclusion and restraint in child and adolescent inpatient units. *Psychiatric Services, 57,* 610–612. doi:10. 1176/appi.ps.57.5.610

Horner, R., & Sugai, G. (2009). *Considerations for seclusion and restraint use in school-wide positive behavior supports.* Eugene, OR: Positive Behavioral Interventions and Supports. Retrieved from http://www.pbis.org/ common/pbisresources/publications/Seclusion_Restraint_ inBehaviorSupport.pdf

Institute of Education Sciences. (2007). *Character education.* Washington, DC: Author. Retrieved from http://www.eric.ed. gov/PDFS/ED497054.pdf

Johnston, J. M., & Sherman, R. A. (1993). Applying the least restrictive alternative principle to treatment decisions: A legal and behavioral analysis. *The Behavior Analyst, 16,* 103–115.

Josephson Institute. (2013). *Character counts!.* Los Angeles, CA: Author. Retrieved from http://charactercounts.org

Koppelman, J. (2004). Children with mental health disorders: Making sense of their needs and the systems that help them. *National Health Policy Forum Issue Brief, 799,* 1–24.

Martin, A., Kreig, H., Esposito, F., Stubbe, D., & Cardona, L. (2008). Reduction of restraint and seclusion through collaborative problem solving: A five-year prospective inpatient study. *Psychiatric Services, 59,* 1406–1412. doi:10.1176/appi.ps.59.12.1406

McLeskey, J., Landers, E., Hoppey, D., & Williamson, P. (2011). Learning disabilities and the LRE mandate: An examination of national and state trends. *Learning Disabilities Research & Practice, 26,* 60–66. doi:10.1111/j.1540-5826.2011.00326.x

McLeskey, J., Landers, E., Williamson, P., & Hoppey, D. (2010). Are we moving toward educating students with disabilities in less restrictive settings? *Journal of Special Education* (Advance online publication). doi:10.1177/0022466910376670

National Association of School Psychologists. (2010a). *Model for comprehensive and integrated school psychological services.* Bethesda, MD: Author. Retrieved from http://www.nasponline.org/standards/ 2010standards/2_PracticeModel.pdf

National Association of School Psychologists. (2010b). *Principles for professional ethics.* Bethesda, MD: Author. Retrieved from http://www.nasponline.org/standards/2010standards/1_ %20Ethical%20Principles.pdf

National Association of School Psychologists. (2011). *What is a school psychologist?* Bethesda, MD: Author. Retrieved from http://www. nasponline.org/about_sp/whatis.aspx

Office for Civil Rights. (2012). *Seclusion and restraint..* Washington, DC: Author. Retrieved from http://www2.ed.gov/about/offices/list/ ocr/docs/crdc-2012-data-summary.pdf

O'Halloran, R. L., & Frank, J. G. (2000). Asphyxial death during prone restraint. *American Journal of Forensic Medicine and Pathology, 21,* 39–52. doi:10.1097/00000433-200003000-00007

Patterson, B., Leadbetter, D., & McComish, A. (1998). Restraint and sudden death from asphyxia. *Nursing Times, 94*(44), 62–64.

Project Wisdom. (2013). *What is character education?* Carrollton, TX: Author. Retrieved from http://www.projectwisdom.com/ OurApproach/index.asp

Protection & Advocacy. (2002). *The lethal hazard of prone restraint: Positional asphyxiation.* Columbia, SC: Author. Retrieved from http://www.disabilityrightsca.org/pubs/701801.pdf

Ryan, J., & Peterson, R. (2004). Physical restraint in school. *Behavioral Disorders, 29,* 154–168.

Ryan, J., Robbins, K., Peterson, R., & Rozalski, M. (2009). Review of state policies concerning the use of physical restraint procedures in schools. *Education & Treatment of Children, 32,* 487–504.

Seclusions and restraints: Selected cases of death and abuse at public and private schools and treatment centers: Hearings before the Committee on Education and Labor, 111th Cong. 3 (2009) (testimony of Gregory D. Kutz).

Taylor, R. D., & Dymnicki, A. B. (2007). Empirical evidence of social and emotional learning's influence on school success: A commentary on *Building Academic Success on Social and Emotional Learning: What Does the Research Say?,* a book edited by Joseph E. Zins, Roger P. Weissberg, Margaret C. Wang, and Herbert J. Walberg. *Journal of Educational and Psychological Consultation, 17,* 225–231. doi:10.1080/ 10474410701346725

U.S. Department of Education. (2010). *Summary of seclusion and restraint statutes, regulations, policies, and guidance by states and territories.* Washington, DC: Author. Retrieved from http://www2.ed.gov/ policy/seclusion/seclusion-state-summary.html

U.S. Department of Education. (2012). *Restraint and seclusion: Resource document.* Washington, DC: Author. Retrieved from http://www2. ed.gov/policy/seclusion/restraints-and-seclusion-resources.pdf

Winston, M., Fleisig, N., & Winston, L. (2009). *The premature call for a ban on prone restraint: A detailed analysis of the issues and evidence.* Sunrise, FL: Professional Crisis Management Association. Retrieved from http:// www.pcma.com/PDF/PrematureCallBanProneRestraint.pdf

Yankouski, B., Massarelli, T., & Lee, S. (2012). Ethical issues regarding the use of restraint and seclusion in schools. *The School Psychologist, 67,* 47–55.

APPENDIX A. CHECKLIST FOR A COMPREHENSIVE SCHOOL POLICY ON RESTRAINT AND SECLUSION

When developing your policy, ask yourself, "Does the policy…"

1. Have an introduction that illustrates the school's commitment to providing a safe school climate or environment for all students and school personnel? ☐ Yes ☐ No

2. Include a section on positive behavior supports or other preventive strategies to reduce the need for restraint and seclusion? ☐ Yes ☐ No

3. List clear and objective definitions on restraint and seclusion based upon the research literature on these practices? ☐ Yes ☐ No

4. Delineate the differences between mechanical restraint, chemical restraint, physical restraint, and physical escort? ☐ Yes ☐ No

5. Establish that aversives will not be used with students and that restraint and seclusion will not be considered as aversives when used as an emergency procedure? ☐ Yes ☐ No

6. Specifically state when restraint and seclusion will be used with a student? ☐ Yes ☐ No

7. Have a description of the seclusion environment (i.e., physical attributes and characteristics, such as size, ventilation)? ☐ Yes ☐ No

8. Detail a protocol on the use of seclusion environments? ☐ Yes ☐ No

9. Provide regulations on the use of seclusion environments (e.g., not as punishment or as a form of convenience)? ☐ Yes ☐ No

10. Specifically state training requirements for all school personnel on using seclusion environments? ☐ Yes ☐ No

11. Discuss the training and authorization of the school's crisis response team? ☐ Yes ☐ No

12. Provide information on how to access the school's crisis response team? ☐ Yes ☐ No

13. Detail a protocol on restraint for all school personnel and the school's crisis response team? ☐ Yes ☐ No

14. Specifically state what crisis intervention training program(s) school personnel will be trained in? ☐ Yes ☐ No

15. Mention the initial training requirements for school personnel and the crisis response team in restraint and annual refresher trainings to renew/maintain certification? ☐ Yes ☐ No

16. Offer regulations on the use of restraint (e.g., not as a form of punishment)? ☐ Yes ☐ No

17. Specify what restraints will be used by school personnel and the crisis response team? ☐ Yes ☐ No

18. Prohibit any specific restraints? ☐ Yes ☐ No

19. Discuss a time limit on restraints? ☐ Yes ☐ No

20. Incorporate best practices in the use of restraints (e.g., face-to-face monitoring, not using restraints that restrict speaking or breathing)? ☐ Yes ☐ No

21. Include that school personnel are trained in cardiopulmonary resuscitation, first aid, and the use of automated external defibrillator devices? ☐ Yes ☐ No

22. Tell how the use of restraint and seclusion will be documented? ☐ Yes ☐ No

23. Discuss reporting requirements at the local, state, and/or national levels? ☐ Yes ☐ No

24. State how parents/guardians will be notified after the use of restraint and/or seclusion with their child? ☐ Yes ☐ No

25. Mention how parental consent will be obtained if restraint and seclusion will not be used as an emergency procedure but instead as part of a planned behavioral intervention for a student with an IEP? ☐ Yes ☐ No

26. Establish a human rights committee and discuss the committee's responsibilities in monitoring restraint and seclusion within the school? ☐ Yes ☐ No

27. Discuss data-based progress monitoring and data collection on the use of restraint and seclusion? ☐ Yes ☐ No

28. Include a clause on law enforcement or other state agencies? ☐ Yes ☐ No

29. Establish complaint procedures for parents/guardians on restraint and seclusion? ☐ Yes ☐ No

30. Include legal references and references from the research literature? ☐ Yes ☐ No

APPENDIX B. CHECKLIST OF QUESTIONS TO GUIDE ETHICAL DECISION MAKING AND HUMANE TREATMENT OF STUDENTS

Student

1. Does the student's behavior pose a significant danger to self or others? ☐ Yes ☐ No

2. Has a functional behavioral assessment been conducted to determine the functions of the student's behavior(s)? ☐ Yes ☐ No

3. Does the student have a comprehensive behavior intervention plan in place? ☐ Yes ☐ No

4. Has data-based progress monitoring been used to check for student progress toward behavioral goals? ☐ Yes ☐ No

5. Have least restrictive alternatives to restraint and seclusion been used in the behavior intervention plan (e.g., positive behavior supports)? ☐ Yes ☐ No

Parents/Guardians

1. Has a meeting occurred with the parents/guardians, school personnel, student (if applicable), and all other parties involved to discuss the student's behavior(s) that may warrant the use of restraint and seclusion? ☐ Yes ☐ No

2. Have all behavioral intervention strategies, including restraint and seclusion, that will be used with the student been outlined for the parents/guardians from least restrictive to most restrictive? ☐ Yes ☐ No

3. Have the parents/guardians been assured that no restraint will be used that will intentionally prevent their child from speaking or breathing? ☐ Yes ☐ No

4. Have the parents/guardians been informed of the risks and benefits of using restraint and seclusion with their child? ☐ Yes ☐ No

5. Have the parents/guardians provided the school with a signed consent form giving the school permission to use restraint and seclusion with their child? ☐ Yes ☐ No

School Personnel

1. Have school personnel been trained to implement the student's behavior intervention plan, including data collection to monitor the student's progress toward behavioral goals? ☐ Yes ☐ No

2. Have school personnel been trained to use restraint and seclusion through an accredited crisis intervention training program? ☐ Yes ☐ No

3. Have school personnel who will be using restraint and seclusion with the student been trained in cardiopulmonary resuscitation, first aid, and the use of an automated external defibrillator? ☐ Yes ☐ No

4. Will school personnel be documenting the use of restraint and seclusion in an incident report? ☐ Yes ☐ No

5. Will school personnel have a meeting with the parents/guardians to discuss behavioral incidents and revise the behavior intervention plan when necessary? ☐ Yes ☐ No

School

1. Does the school have a written school policy on the use of restraint and seclusion with students? ☐ Yes ☐ No

2. Does the school have a human rights committee that will review the student's behavioral data and incident reports to ensure ethical and humane treatment? ☐ Yes ☐ No

3. Does the school have a protocol in place to notify parents/guardians when their child has been restrained or secluded? ☐ Yes ☐ No

4. Does the school have a grievance procedure in place for parents/guardians to file complaints or express concerns about restraint and seclusion use with their child? ☐ Yes ☐ No

5. Does the school have an established program in positive behavioral intervention supports? ☐ Yes ☐ No

APPENDIX C. SELF-ASSESSMENT CHECKLIST FOR SCHOOL PSYCHOLOGISTS USING THE NASP DOMAINS OF PRACTICE

Data-Based Decision Making and Accountability

1. Do I monitor school-wide data related to the use of restraint and seclusion? ☐ Yes ☐ No

2. Do I monitor school-wide data related to disproportionality in using restraint and seclusion? ☐ Yes ☐ No

3. Do I monitor data on restraint and seclusion use in my school to inform program decisions and professional development needs of my staff? ☐ Yes ☐ No

Consultation and Collaboration

1. Do I consult with school administrators regarding program concerns related to restraint and seclusion use in my school? ☐ Yes ☐ No

2. Do I consult with school administrators to develop school policies on restraint and seclusion use in my school? ☐ Yes ☐ No

3. Do I collaborate with school personnel to develop an action plan to reduce the use of restraint and seclusion in my school? ☐ Yes ☐ No

Interventions and Instructional Support to Develop Academic Skills

1. Do I work with others to develop interventions with students to enhance academic skills that can reduce problematic behaviors with students who could require the use of restraint and seclusion? ☐ Yes ☐ No

2. Do I train instructional staff in effective instructional practices and interventions to reduce the use of restraint and seclusion? ☐ Yes ☐ No

3. Am I knowledgeable of instructional supports and interventions that can enhance academic, behavioral, and social skills while reducing the need of restraint and seclusion with students? ☐ Yes ☐ No

Interventions and Mental Health Services to Develop Social and Life Skills

1. Do I know how to provide mental health services to a student in crisis while using restraint and seclusion? ☐ Yes ☐ No

2. Do I know how to debrief a student after using restraint and seclusion with the student and how to debrief other students who might have witnessed the crisis? ☐ Yes ☐ No

3. Do I collaborate with others to develop interventions that reduce severe behavior problems and teach appropriate social skills in order to reduce the need for restraint and seclusion with students? ☐ Yes ☐ No

School-Wide Practices to Promote Learning

1. Do I work with others to implement school-wide positive behavioral interventions and supports to promote the learning of the students and reduce the need for restraint and seclusion? ☐ Yes ☐ No

2. Am I part of a school-wide team to identify and implement evidence-based practices to reduce the need for restraint and seclusion? ☐ Yes ☐ No

3. Do I have the knowledge of school and systems structure to be an agent of change in my school regarding the use of restraint and seclusion? ☐ Yes ☐ No

Preventive and Responsive Services

1. Have I received training in evidence-based crisis prevention procedures to reduce the need for restraint and seclusion? ☐ Yes ☐ No

2. Have I received crisis intervention training in how to safely implement restraint and seclusion? ☐ Yes ☐ No

3. Am I part of a school-wide human rights committee to make proactive decisions to ensure the ethical and humane treatment of students so the students are not subjected to the inappropriate use of restraint and seclusion? ☐ Yes ☐ No

Family–School Collaboration Services

1. Do I inform parents/guardians when restraint and seclusion are used with their child? □ Yes □ No

2. Do I collaborate with parents/guardians to develop appropriate behavioral interventions to reduce the need for restraint and seclusion use with their child? □ Yes □ No

3. Do I know how to explain clearly to parents/guardians the restraint and seclusion procedures that may be used with their child? □ Yes □ No

Diversity in Development and Learning

1. Am I knowledgeable of developmental factors that can contribute to how to safely intervene with a child when using restraint and seclusion? □ Yes □ No

2. Am I knowledgeable of factors of diversity (e.g., race, class, gender, cultural) that can contribute to crisis intervention with students when using restraint and seclusion? □ Yes □ No

3. Am I aware of issues in language development that can have an impact on intervening with a student in a crisis that requires the use of restraint and seclusion? □ Yes □ No

Research and Program Evaluation

1. Have I stayed abreast of current research on restraint and seclusion in schools? □ Yes □ No

2. Have I conducted a program evaluation of my school district's programs and training regarding the use of restraint and seclusion? □ Yes □ No

3. Do I have the skills to conduct an appropriate evaluation of the efficacy of restraint and seclusion procedures in my school as an effective crisis intervention procedure? □ Yes □ No

Legal, Ethical, and Professional Practice

1. Have I received training in restraint and seclusion laws in my state? □ Yes □ No

2. Have I received training in restraint and seclusion procedures in my district? □ Yes □ No

3. Do I have a communication procedure to prevent and report abuse related to restraint and seclusion? □ Yes □ No

27 Best Practices in Making Manifestation Determinations

Robert J. Kubick Jr.
Akron (OH) Public Schools
Katherine Bobak Lavik
Kent State University (OH)

OVERVIEW

The purpose of this chapter is to provide school psychology practitioners with some best practices in making manifestation determinations. The reader will learn about the federal laws and regulations that introduced the manifestation determination mandate and the evolutionary processes that brought the mandate to its current form. In particular, the significant changes in the manifestation determination mandate brought about by evolving federal guidelines are reviewed. Specific guidelines will be shared for effectively conducting the "relationship test," which lies at the heart of making manifestation determinations. After reviewing specific best practice recommendations, the reader will be cautioned about the many problems associated with the conceptualization of the manifestation determination process and its practical implementation.

The content of this chapter is subsumed within the National Association of School Psychologists (NASP) *Model for Comprehensive and Integrated School Psychological Services* (NASP, 2010a), specifically in the Interventions and Mental Health Services to Develop Social and Life Skills domain. The involvement of school psychologists in the manifestation determination process is provided as a direct service to students, families, and schools. In collaborating with others, school psychologists use their skills in the manifestation determination process to intervene with students who manifest significant behavioral, social, and emotional needs.

BASIC CONSIDERATIONS

A manifestation determination is a review process undertaken by a team whose task is to determine whether an instance of misbehavior by a student with a disability is a manifestation of that student's disability. The manifestation determination process is similar to the legal process of determining if an individual should be held accountable for his or her behavior due to a preexisting mental condition (Lee, 2005). There are three key components to the manifestation determination process: (a) disciplining students with disabilities, (b) determining when a manifestation determination is required, and (c) conducting a manifestation determination.

Disciplining Students With Disabilities

The need to conduct manifestation determinations can be traced back to a U.S. Supreme Court ruling that unilateral expulsions of students with disabilities constituted a "change in placement" under the Individuals with Disabilities Education Act (IDEA) and, as such, were subject to the procedural requirements of that legislation (Katsiyannis & Maag, 2001). IDEA 1997 clarified the conditions under which school personnel could apply existing disciplinary options for the general student population to students with disabilities. When disciplining students, IDEA 1997 required schools to treat special education students and their general education peers differently, particularly when considering removal from school (Lee, 2005). The core of this framework was left intact in the 2004 Individuals with Disabilities Education Improvement Act (IDEA), yet there are notable differences between the two.

Under IDEA 2004, long-term removals of students with disabilities from school for disciplinary reasons (e.g., suspension, expulsion) are permitted only in situations where there is no direct and substantial relationship between the student's disability and the behavior for which he or she is being referred. If a student's misbehavior is found to be the result of his or her disability, then there are restrictions in the typical options for disciplinary removal (Lee, 2005). The removal of a student with a disability from school for disciplinary reasons constitutes a "change in placement" from the student's Individualized Education Program (IEP) if a disciplinary removal from school is greater than 10 consecutive days or it establishes a "pattern of removals" (Lee, 2005). There is no clear legal definition of what constitutes a pattern of removal, but practitioners should investigate and consider the length of time a student is removed, the duration of each removal, and the proximity of removals to each other (Lee, 2005).

Removal can define a wide range of potential disciplinary actions (e.g., suspension, expulsion) that remove a student from the educational placement described on his or her IEP or that might otherwise be considered a "change in placement." For example, "partial removals," such as suspensions for portions of the school day, or "in-school" suspensions might also constitute a change in placement, particularly when they are combined with other types of longer-duration removals and consequently form a pattern of removals and/or exceed 10 days in one school year (Gates & Cheramie, 2004).

Determining When a Manifestation Determination Is Required

IDEA 2004 requires conducting manifestation determinations whenever students with disabilities are (a) suspended out of school for more than 10 consecutive days, (b) suspended out of school for more than 10 cumulative days with a pattern, or (c) removed to an interim alternative educational setting for possession of drugs and/or weapons or for having inflicted serious bodily injury (Katsiyannis, Losinski, & Prince, 2012). The manifestation determination meeting must occur within 10 days of the intended removal. During that time, school officials collect data, which may include a current functional behavioral assessment, a review of school records, any previous psychoeducational evaluation or diagnostic reports, the student's current IEP and placement, and (when possible) an observation of the student (Lee, 2005). State departments of education have provided disciplinary action flowcharts for students with disabilities as guidance documents for the legal requirements behind manifestation determinations (e.g., Massachusetts Department of Education, 2007; Ohio Department of Education, 2012). These flowcharts and the IDEA 2004 were consulted to develop a disciplinary flowchart for students with disabilities and manifestation determinations (see Figure 27.1).

If it is determined that there was no substantial and direct relationship between the "critical behavior event" and the student's disability, then the student may be subjected to the disciplinary procedures of his or her general education peers, including removals beyond 10 days. If it is determined that there is a substantial and direct relationship between the critical behavior event and the student's disability, then the student may not be removed beyond the 10-day limit. The initial assumption is that the behavior is a manifestation of the student's disability (Zilz, 2006). It is important to know that schools appear to shoulder the burden of proof that a given behavior was not a manifestation of a disability (Katsiyannis & Maag, 2001). Parents or guardians may request an expedited evaluation during the manifestation determination process. If such an evaluation is requested, it is expected to take place as soon as possible, though there is no legal deadline for a certain number of days in which the evaluation must take place.

Decisions as to whether a critical behavior event is related to a student's disability are made collectively by the manifestation determination review team. These decisions are to reflect the consensus of the team. There is no voting by the various team members on the question of whether a behavior was a manifestation of a disability. Instead, the law strongly implies that the final decision is to be unanimous among the team members. Manifestation determinations are subject to the appeals process outlined in IDEA 2004. The parents may request an expedited hearing to appeal the results of a manifestation determination. If the parents or guardians of the student disagree with the findings or result of the manifestation determination, then they may invoke their right to a due-process hearing with an impartial hearing officer (Lee, 2005). During this appeal period, "stay put" provisions are in effect and it is impermissible for the school to unilaterally remove the student from his or her current placement. If the current placement is in an alternative educational placement, then the student must remain there during the hearing, unless the time

Figure 27.1. Disciplinary and Manifestation Determination Flowchart

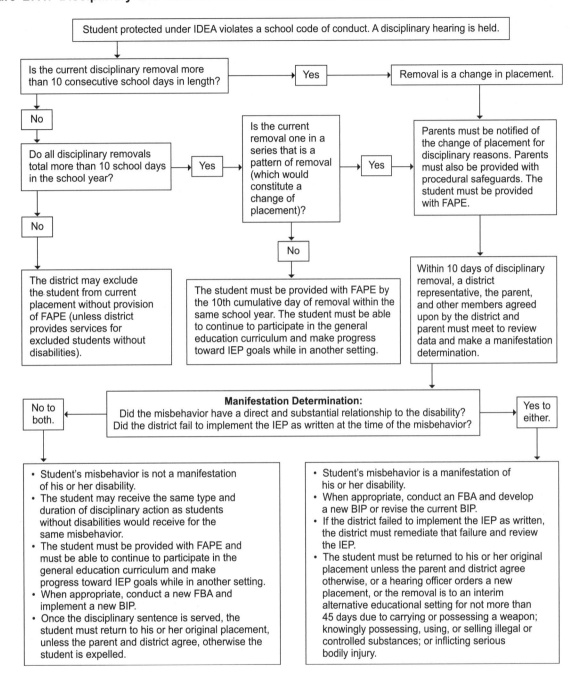

Note. This chart summarizes IDEA 2004 standards. Based on information from Ohio Department of Education (2012) and the Massachusetts Department of Education (2007). BIP = behavior intervention plan; FAPE = Free and Appropriate Public Education; FBA = functional behavior assessment; IEP = Individualized Education Program.

period for the placement expires before the hearing process has concluded (Disability Rights California, 2006). At that point, the student would return to his or her previous educational placement. Similarly, if the student was not in an alternative educational placement when the hearing process began, then the student would remain in his or her current educational placement and may not be removed (Disability Rights California, 2006). The exception to this prohibition is that schools may assign a student to an interim alternative educational setting for no more than 45 days (regardless of whether a behavior is a manifestation of the student's disability) in situations where a student does any of the following at school, on school premises, or at a school function under the jurisdiction of the school: (a) carries or possesses a weapon, (b) knowingly possesses or uses illegal drugs or sells or solicits the sale of a controlled substance, or (c) inflicts serious bodily injury upon another person. The stay put provisions do not apply to appeals of disciplinary decisions, however. If a parent or guardian appeals the disciplinary decision, not the manifestation determination, then the school may continue to provide the discipline to the student as the school had planned. If a student's behavior is found to be related to the disability, a manifestation determination must be implemented.

Conducting a Manifestation Determination

IDEA 2004 simplified the manifestation determination process by requiring a "direct and substantial" relationship between the behavior and a student's disability (Ryan, Katsiyannis, Peterson, & Chmelar, 2007). Part of the rationale for limiting the scope only to instances of a direct and substantial relationship was to ensure that school administrators had the tools that they needed to maintain safe learning environments (Katsiyannis et al., 2012). IDEA 2004 required only that the IEP be implemented but eliminated any considerations as to whether the IEP was appropriate (as was required in IDEA 1997).

There has been concern that IDEA 2004 minimized due process procedures as these procedures relate to manifestation determinations. For example, Meloy (2008) noted that the number of questions for the review team to address has effectively been reduced to only two: (a) Is there a direct relationship between the conduct in question and a student's disability? (b) Has the IEP been appropriately implemented? Meloy (2008) noted that the reauthorization eliminated from consideration factors such as the student's ability to control his or her behavior in order to follow the code of student conduct, the indirect relationship between a student's disability and his or her behavior, and the appropriateness of the student's IEP and placement.

IDEA 2004 requires a district representative, parent, and "other relevant members" (to be determined by agreement of the school and parent) to be participants in a manifestation determination. Members of the IEP team are not required participants. The manifestation determination team must consider relevant information from the parent, teacher observations of the child, and the child's IEP.

Zirkel (2006) stated that IDEA 2004 focused on two causal factors. The first was whether the student's disability caused (or had a direct and substantial relationship to) the conduct subject to discipline. The second was whether the conduct subject to discipline was the direct result of the school's failure to implement the IEP. There has been a shift from focusing on the IEP to focusing on causality. To the extent that the IEP is considered, it is only in its implementation rather than its formulation. Case law has indicated a greater likelihood of manifestation determination teams finding that there is no relationship between disability and behavior (Zirkel, 2006).

IDEA 2004 also included subtle differences in the inclusion of functional behavioral assessments and behavior intervention plans in the manifestation determination process (Zirkel, 2011). When the team determines that the conduct in question was a manifestation of a student's disability, the team is still prompted to develop or modify the functional behavioral assessment and behavior intervention plan during the manifestation review. However, when it is found that the conduct was not a manifestation of a student's disability and/or a student is placed into a 45-day interim alternative educational setting, the language of the reauthorization requires that functional behavioral assessments and behavior intervention plans be designed as appropriate in order to address the behavior violation so that it does not recur.

Conducting the Relationship Test

The study by the manifestation determination team as to whether a specific instance of misbehavior is a manifestation of a student's disability has been termed the *relationship test* (Hartwig & Ruesch, 1995). There is nothing in the IDEA statutes or court decisions that provides much guidance as to how this test is to be conducted or how to obtain definitive findings (Yell, 2006). It is clear that the relationship test must be made on an individualized basis and, as such, reflexive determinations based solely on disability label are proscribed (Kubick, Bard, & Perry, 2000). When conducting the relationship test, there are multiple factors that potentially can be considered to illuminate the extent of any existing relatedness between disability and behavior. Of the original four factors considered in making the relationship test, only two factors appear to be relevant to the IDEA 2004 language: (a) the student's disability did not impair his or her understanding of the consequences of the misbehavior and (b) the student's disability did not impair his or her ability to control the behavior subject to disciplinary action (Katsiyannis & Maag, 2001; Lee, 2005).

Some researchers (e.g., Hartwig & Ruesch, 1995; Kubick et al., 2000) have offered some specific questions for teams to answer when conducting the relationship test. Noteworthy, in particular, were those presented by Gates and Cheramie (2004), in which they focused on the two key standards of relatedness that remain relevant under IDEA 2004: (a) whether the student's disability impaired his or her ability to understand the impact or consequences of the misconduct and (b) whether the student's disability impaired his or her ability to control the misconduct.

Questions for manifestation determination teams to consider under the first standard include (a) Are the student's thought processes logical? (b) Did the student understand the consequences for breaking school rules? (c) Did the student have the capacity to know which behaviors are unacceptable? (d) Has the student received a copy and adequate explanation of the school's code of conduct? (e) Has the student demonstrated the ability to follow school rules? (f) Has the student expressed that this or similar conduct is wrong? (g) Has the student expressed an understanding of the consequences of this or similar behavior?

Questions for manifestation determination teams to consider under the second standard include (a) Has the student followed school rules in the past? (b) What features of the disability has the student exhibited in the past? (c) In what situations can the student control his or her behavior? (d) Are there other factors that explain the misconduct? (e) Is this an isolated or recurrent behavior? (f) Was the behavior premeditated? (g) Would similarly situated students without disabilities react in a similar manner in this circumstance?

Evaluating the Implementation of the IEP

Conducting the relationship test is only one of the two factors that the manifestation determination team must consider. IDEA 2004 also mandates that the team determine if the critical behavior event for which the student was referred was the direct result of the school's failure to implement the student's IEP. In order to make this determination, the team must analyze whether the student's IEP was being implemented as written at the time of the misconduct. The team should verify, in particular, that all special education services, interventions, accommodations, and other related supports were being provided to the student as prescribed in his or her IEP.

As they were in providing resources to conduct the relationship test, Gates and Cheramie (2004) were helpful in compiling the following questions for teams to consider when trying to establish whether the school has implemented the IEP: (a) Was the IEP legally developed? (b) Was the IEP implemented as written? (c) Have the services been provided consistent with the IEP? (d) Is the student making educational progress? (e) Did the IEP address all of the student's needs? (f) Are behavioral goals and objectives included in the IEP? (g) Was there a developing pattern of conduct that should have been detected?

BEST PRACTICES IN MAKING MANIFESTATION DETERMINATIONS

The intent of this chapter is not to provide an exhaustive step-by-step approach to conducting manifestation determinations, as these have been offered elsewhere (e.g., Hartwig & Ruesch, 1995; Kubick et al., 2000). Aside from a comprehensive how-to guide in conducting manifestation determinations, several key best practice guidelines for school psychologists are offered here.

Adopt a Preventive Orientation

Perhaps the best guidance in dealing with the entire issue of manifestation determinations is to take proactive and tangible steps that will reduce (or even eliminate) their necessity. School psychologists, educators, and parents should develop positive behavior management plans for all students with disabilities who need them, provide consistent disciplinary policies for students with special needs, and ensure the use of accurate and comprehensive documentation systems. In addition, systemic and school-wide efforts in developing positive behavior supports can be implemented. These positive behavior supports should include developmentally and culturally responsive practices.

These efforts can be accomplished, in part, by school officials assessing student populations for behavioral and social–emotional concerns within a response-to-intervention framework. In this manner, baseline behavioral concerns of students can be appreciated, and responses to various individual and group interventions can be measured. Students who continue to manifest behavioral concerns, or otherwise demonstrate needs in this area, can be identified and served within the three-tiered model. This framework is best equipped to identify chronic student misbehavior and to activate efforts to meet student needs more effectively than reactive removals that follow misbehavior.

School officials (school psychologists, teachers, principals) can work closely to provide students with disabilities with explicit instructions about their code of student conduct and ensure that all students understand the standards of the educational community (Kubick & Bard, 2004). These professionals can ensure the development of effective and responsive IEPs and positive behavior supports to identify and meet the needs of students (Kubick & Bard, 2004). Teams can conduct comprehensive functional behavior assessments (before a manifestation determination requires it) that further illuminate students' needs and root causes of problematic and seemingly intractable behaviors. Student performance can be measured accurately and frequently to study progress (or lack thereof) over time and intervene as conditions warrant. School officials can team with other stakeholders to develop robust alternative programs for students who struggle in traditional learning environments.

Hartwig and Ruesch (1995) recommended that school psychologists and other team members assess for the presence of social–emotional and behavioral concerns whenever initial evaluations and reevaluations are being conducted with students who demonstrated behavioral concerns. These actions can provide what they termed a *reference system* that can be used as a source of data should the need to conduct a manifestation determination arise in the future. The reference system can be quantified and made more intelligible for others via the use of, for example, charts, tables, and graphs. In addition, the development and implementation of comprehensive behavior intervention plans is a necessity in responding to chronic student misbehavior. Properly conducted, functional behavioral assessments can illuminate the reasons behind various problem behaviors and provide teams with ideas for replacing misbehavior with functional alternative behaviors.

Identify Roles of School Psychologists

It is highly recommended that a school psychologist be a member of the manifestation determination team (Meloy, 2008). In some settings, school psychologists may be the only individuals in the school district who have heard of the term manifestation determination. Though other school-based professionals might have some exposure to the concept and potential outcomes of manifestation determination processes, school psychologists are likely to be the only team members with significant training in this area. Procedural leadership in conducting comprehensive evaluations is often provided by school psychologists, and they should lead other school professionals in identifying

the entire array of academic and behavioral needs for each student evaluated.

School psychologists are often the school-based team members with the requisite training in compliance with special education law, and they can assist manifestation determination teams in gathering all pertinent and necessary information that will be useful in making and supporting informed decisions, all while focusing on student needs. School psychologists can be useful in providing documentation that cites the data that were used to make decisions and in completing a manifestation determination.

Beyond being familiar with the legal requirements of manifestation determinations, school psychologists have several other advantages and attributes that are often unique to their discipline and call for their participation in the review process. As professionals operating at the nexus between education and psychology, school psychologists have singular insights into the ways that an individual student's disability might express itself in misbehavior. Likewise, they have a depth of understanding in terms of the ecological context in which behavior occurs, including appreciating antecedents to behaviors and how different consequences and intervening variables may support continuation of various behaviors (Meloy, 2008). School psychologists frequently benefit from advanced training that informs them about developmental differences among students of different ages, backgrounds, and exceptionalities, and how various practices and programs need to be adapted to meet the needs of all students. Related to this respect and appreciation for individual differences, school psychologists benefit from strong multicultural awareness, training in developmental differences, and competencies needed for effective practice in analyzing a variety of student disabilities and related behaviors.

School psychologists often provide philosophical direction and support to help school-based professionals embrace the concept of special education, including multiple dimensions of teaching and learning that are not limited to academic skills development but extend to the behavioral, social, and emotional needs of students, as well (Meloy, 2008). Toward that end, school psychologists can appreciate how some laws, regulations, and district practices (e.g., zero tolerance policies) might conflict with the federal laws regulating the disciplining of students with disabilities. As research-practitioners, school psychologists are continuously evaluating their own professional effectiveness by analyzing the impact of their services on student outcomes.

Use Culturally and Developmentally Responsive Practices

When disciplining a student with a disability, the school district must take into consideration not only the student's disability but also the student's cultural background and developmental stage. School staff, including school psychologists, should ensure that disciplinary strategies are culturally responsive. Students from ethnic minority backgrounds are disciplined at a disproportionately higher rate than their majority-background peers. Specifically for African American and Hispanic American students, this disparity is often referred to as the discipline gap (e.g., Monroe, 2005). Teachers' and students' cultural norms about appropriate and inappropriate behaviors may vary, which can lead to higher rates of discipline against students from a cultural background different from those of their teachers (Monroe, 2005). These disciplinary actions are sometimes even more severe than those that their majority peers receive for the same misbehaviors (Monroe, 2005). One method to assist in ameliorating this cultural disparity would be to increase the diversity of school staff (Monroe, 2005). School districts should also take steps to educate staff about cultural differences in behavioral and disciplinary norms that are present in the community. Home–school–community collaboration on disciplinary guidelines could lead to disciplinary actions that are more culturally responsive and lead to closing the discipline gap (Monroe, 2005). While teacher training programs may offer coursework intended to raise multicultural awareness, few teacher training programs specifically give teachers the skills necessary to develop classroom-based disciplinary strategies that are culturally responsive (Monroe, 2005). School districts and educator training programs should implement professional development opportunities and coursework that address the specific relationship between school-based discipline and cultural responsiveness.

Likewise, discipline should also be developmentally appropriate, and school psychologists can collaborate with others to assist in identifying practices that are effective for students of different ages and developmental levels. The behavioral expectations for students in early childhood grade levels should not be the same as the behavioral expectations of students in high school. Developmentally, younger students will respond to and think about discipline differently. Many early childhood programs contain developmentally inappropriate disciplinary strategies, however (Longstreth, Brady, & Kay, 2013). For example, two strategies that work well for correcting misbehavior in young students include immediate feedback and an emphasis on positive behavioral support. Many early childhood programs still rely on excluding students from the general education curriculum, however, which is inappropriate for the age level (Longstreth et al., 2013). Removing a younger student from class as a punitive consequence for misbehavior is inappropriate for younger students because the removal does not focus on the more appropriate actions of rewarding students for positive behavior and continuing their education in the classroom.

Other examples of developmentally appropriate policies include (a) taking an instructional, proactive approach to teaching prosocial behavior; (b) implementing a three-tier model of prevention and intervention support; (c) creating clear and consistent definitions for behavioral expectations; (d) focusing on developmentally appropriate variables (e.g., behavioral expectations on an elementary playground versus in a mechanical vocational technology classroom); (e) providing developmentally appropriate adult supervision (e.g., supervised bathroom trips in elementary school versus hallway passes for middle/high school); (f) engaging family in the curriculum (e.g., classroom parent volunteer versus career-day presentation); (g) training staff on developmental stages of cognition and self-awareness; and (h) evaluating disciplinary policies, procedures, actions, and outcomes through the use of behavioral progress monitoring (Longstreth et al., 2013).

One-size-fits-all disciplinary codes that have been developed without regard to cultural or linguistic background or developmental stage should be modified using the research-based suggestions provided above. Culturally and developmentally responsive disciplinary practices could lead to decreased disciplinary referrals. School psychologists have advanced training on cultural and linguistic variables that can affect discipline. They also have advanced training in child and adolescent development of behavior and cognition that can be useful in modifying disciplinary codes to be more developmentally appropriate. School psychologists have the training, knowledge, and experience in ensuring that school districts implement evidence-based practices that are also culturally and developmentally responsive.

Maintain Collaboration Between Home and School

School psychologists can be particularly helpful throughout a manifestation determination process by mediating between the school district, the student and his or her family, and other parties involved in the process. Communicating with parents and involving them in a variety of school procedures is vital in safeguarding positive student outcomes. It is important to recognize that the potential consequences of a manifestation determination can be considerable and, as such, there can be powerful external factors that can influence the process (Kubick & Bard, 2004). The potential consequences can include, on one side, school staff desiring the removal of a student with chronic misbehavior and, on the other, the family members of the student who have full recognition that any protracted disciplinary removals might have life-altering consequences. Seen within this context, the possibility of contentious and adversarial meetings is omnipresent.

School psychologists can lead school-based professionals in establishing a routine and robust communication system with students' families, particularly those who manifest chronic behavioral concerns. By doing so, school professionals can better understand the needs of students who manifest problematic behavior and work together with families to reduce misconduct. In the event that a critical behavior event should arise, the prospects for a successful review can be optimized if there has been a sustained and healthy working relationship between home and school. At the very least, efforts should be made to ensure that a manifestation determination review is not the first time that school officials are meeting with a particular family.

Provide Ongoing Professional Development

Effective professional development is often critical to enacting policies and procedures that benefit all students. Training of teachers and other school professionals will be a necessary component of having an effective response to chronic student misbehavior and providing positive behavior supports to reduce their recurrence. Effective professional development must enable systems to build the capacity to support the comprehensive educational servicing of students with a variety of behavioral concerns. A model for ecological and individual support, curriculum-based assessment, and empirically supported instructional practice was offered by Sawka, McCurdy, and Mannella (2002).

School officials are advised to conduct training on a variety of topics that may ultimately culminate in manifestation determinations, including identification of and intervention with problem behaviors and development and implementation of comprehensive IEPs and behavior intervention plans. Training should

also be provided on (a) conducting informative functional behavioral assessments that can provide data to direct future intervention efforts and (b) creating developmentally and culturally responsive discipline practices. Each of these areas is a training prerequisite; that is, it is best that school professionals have competency in these areas before becoming regularly involved with manifestation determinations. By developing the professional capacity of individual staff members in these areas, manifestation determinations can be made by a team of individuals who have the expertise to understand the many factors surrounding the process. School psychologists, counselors, social–workers, and other mental health professionals, in particular, can benefit from training in manifestation determinations in order that their unique understanding of students' social–emotional and behavioral issues can be brought to bear in addressing the mandates of public policy. In addition, school psychologists are often leaders for designing effective professional training for other educators.

Enact Systems-Level Initiatives

Systems-level initiatives have enjoyed increased recognition as an effective and efficient means to bring comprehensive school psychological service delivery to the greatest number of students. An important part of preventing students from engaging in perpetual rule breaking is providing comprehensive educational services at the systems level. School psychologists can lead the way in building system capacity to successfully intervene with ongoing problem behavior in schools via a multitiered model for delivering services to students, including mental health services, social skills training, modeling, peer mediation, and role modeling. School officials should develop clear expectations and rules for student behavior, as well as consequences for misbehavior (Lee, 2005). As such, school officials should develop comprehensive and understandable discipline policies, including procedures for students with disabilities. Students who manifest behavioral concerns can be identified through screening efforts in Tier 1 and subsequently immersed in positive behavior supports, which would maintain relatively mild aversive consequences but focus on strong, robust, and reinforcing incentives for appropriate behaviors.

In Tier 2, targeted interventions can be employed in the service of students who fail to respond to universal treatments. In this framework, social–emotional domains must be a central consideration in determining the educational needs of students with disabilities who find themselves the subject of repeated disciplinary referrals, regardless of their special education eligibility category. This would include assessments in multiple domains that extend beyond restriction of the narrow domains that are implicated by different eligibility categories. The range of concerns might not rise to a level where eligibility under the serious emotional disturbance criteria is met, but the presence of such problems should be acknowledged, described, and treated (Morrison & D'Incau, 2000). All students who demonstrate ongoing behavioral needs should be provided with comprehensive behavior intervention plans and, as necessary, functional behavioral assessments, before a manifestation determination is needed.

In Tier 3, for those students who have exhausted the aforementioned efforts, substantial individualized intervention becomes necessary. For some students, this might include explicit social skills training in, for example, conflict resolution. Perhaps development of coping and communication strategies is warranted. For other students, placement into highly structured school-based alternative programs might be beneficial. Regardless of the tier of intervention in which a student's concerns might be identified, all students should be provided with an array of prevention programs to reduce or eliminate future occurrences of problem behavior (Lee, 2005). Morrison and D'Incau (2000) maintained that a close examination of school disciplinary practices should be undertaken to determine what impact these practices have on the ability to serve students with disabilities who demonstrate emotional and/or behavioral problems. There should be adequate prevention mechanisms to intervene early with students who show evidence of emotional and/or behavioral problems. In addition, disciplinary measures should be graduated in terms of severity, and consequences should be appropriately matched to behavioral violations.

Progress may be monitored by keeping track of behavior in multiple ways. The school could generate counts of the number of suspensions, detentions, and disciplinary actions for the building as a whole, a specific grade level, an individual classroom, or an individual student. School-wide data could pinpoint specific classrooms, grade levels, locations (e.g., hallway, cafeteria, playground), or times of day (e.g., mornings, lunch, transitions between periods) that are most likely to trigger behavior problems. In the classroom, teachers could monitor specific concerning behaviors using various methods. Countable behaviors, such as disruptions, talking out, or number of times out of seat, could

be monitored using tally marks. Behaviors that are more disruptive due to the amount of time they last, such as tantrums, could be monitored using timers. For any behavior that is monitored, teachers should note what happened before the behavior (i.e., its antecedents) and what happened after the behavior (i.e., its consequences). Intervention programs should be designed around improving the circumstances surrounding antecedent events and the student's and others' reactions to the behavior. These types of data collection procedures could easily provide graphs and charts that could document student improvements or failures in response to interventions. School psychologists' expertise in data collection, analysis, program evaluation, and use of data for effective decision making can be valuable for monitoring progress in systems-level practices.

Another consideration for systems-level initiatives and capacity building is one of treatment for chronic behavioral disorders. Such pathologies can be managed with behavior intervention plans with some success but may often require intervention beyond the school or classroom setting. Important distinctions must be made between misbehavior that is due to emotional disturbance versus social maladjustment, as the prescribed treatments may differ as a consequence.

Appreciate Political Contexts

It has been noted that, more than even specific skills training in conducting manifestation determinations, understanding the political dynamics in which these decisions occur is often vital to a successful conclusion (Kubick et al., 2000). For example, it is important to explore the attitudes of school personnel and address these attitudes in order that they not prove detrimental to the process. Many educators may be reluctant to engage with students who demonstrate chronic behavioral concerns, and their attitudes about disciplining special education students may have undue influence on the manifestation process. Such attitudes might result in an avoidance of the process altogether, so as to not add legitimacy to differential disciplinary outcomes for students with disabilities (as opposed to their peers without disabilities).

At the other extreme, other educators may view the manifestation determination as a useful tool in quickly removing behaviorally problematic students from the school. They may attempt to stack the deck against students by making numerous referrals for manifestation determinations and consistently finding no relationships between various behaviors and disabilities, regardless of any evidence to the contrary. These individuals can potentially abuse power to remove students with disabilities from the school/classroom setting. School psychologists might even overhear other school-based individuals state, in some manner, that they are trying to "win" a manifestation determination (Kubick, 2008).

School psychologists understand that disciplinary removals, particularly those of a long-term nature, often have significant consequences for students, including the possibility of the student's educational trajectory being irrevocably altered. As such, they can often serve as the conscience of a team that might potentially make a highly impactful and disruptive decision based on short-term frustrations, political considerations, and/or simply the desire to send a message.

As detailed previously, establishing good home and school communication can be helpful in conducting manifestation determination. This is particularly true when one considers how vital it is that school psychologists earn the trust and confidence of parents as they navigate through what can be an emotional process. Failure to appreciate the affective aspects of the manifestation determination review process could potentially lead to hostility, embitterment, and distrust. Moreover, poorly controlled emotionality from various team members will increase the likelihood of disagreements, appeals, and legal actions, and none of these outcomes will be consonant with providing a free and appropriate public education to the referred student.

Recognize Problems With Disciplinary Removals for Students With Disabilities

Problems with manifestation determinations often reflect larger concerns with discipline itself. For example, students with disabilities (in spite of differential discipline standards) are more likely to be subject to disciplinary exclusions than their same-age peers (Data Accountability Center, 2011; Katsiyannis et al., 2012). With school systems demonstrating a propensity to exclude students with conduct problems, students who have disabilities and rule-breaking incidents are particularly vulnerable to being excluded (Morrison & D'Incau, 2000). The need for maintaining a balanced approach in removing students for disciplinary reasons is vital, particularly when the significant consequences of the removal are considered. Maag and Katsiyannis (2006) noted that students with disabilities are disproportionately represented in disciplinary exclusions, and moreover, students with emotional and behavioral disorders are excluded even more than other students with disabilities. They observed that these students have

higher rates of absenteeism, dropping out of school, and incarceration, all of which can be presumed to worsen in the face of prolonged and/or multiple disciplinary exclusions.

In contrast to the motives of school officials who seek to quickly remove students with problematic behavior from schools, there is little empirical support for disciplinary removals as helpful in changing challenging student behaviors. The effectiveness of suspensions and expulsions has long been considered a dubious practice in terms of positively changing problem student behavior (Kubick et al., 2000). It has been argued that removals are only effective if the student perceives the environment from which he or she is being removed to be more interesting and more reinforcing than the environment to which he or she is being sent (Rutherford, 1978). Other studies have been critical of disciplinary removals based on their (a) displacing school problems to the larger community, (b) exacerbating the original problem behavior, (c) reinforcing truancy and inappropriate behavior, (d) interfering with educational progress, and (e) failing to address the underlying problems that caused the misbehavior (Hundley, 1994).

Morrison and D'Incau (2000) demonstrated that students subjected to manifestation determinations have a variety of risk conditions in their lives, including family neglect, family disruption, absenteeism, and emotional and/or behavioral problems. All students subjected to manifestation determinations in their study showed documented evidence of emotional, familial, or behavioral risk indicators that paralleled their special education histories. Morrison and D'Incau's (2000) results suggested that students with disabilities, who already have co-occurring environmental and individual complications, may experience and exhibit compounded emotional and behavioral difficulties that place them at risk for school maladjustment and potential exclusion from school. In many cases, it is difficult to adequately fit many of these students into IDEA diagnostic categories or design appropriate interventions within the typical service delivery model of instructional services, and alternatives to manifestation determinations and subsequent removals should be explored.

A particularly interesting finding of Morrison and D'Incau (2000) was that the paramount protective factor in the final decision to expel or not to expel a student with a disability was the presence of an advocate (e.g., parent, attorney, clergy, counselor, or teacher) who pleaded and/or demanded that a student remain in school. In all cases of advocacy, the decision to expel was not sustained. Other findings were that students were more likely to be expelled as they grew older and/or engaged in more severe offenses (e.g., physical assault, brandishing or threatening with a knife, or possession/use of illegal drugs).

Weigh Ethical Considerations

School psychologists should be vigilant in maintaining the highest ethical standards whenever they engage in professional practice. The process of conducting a manifestation determination, even in ideal contexts, can often present challenges to the NASP *Principles for Professional Ethics* (NASP, 2010b). The application of professional ethics to specific school psychological practices is paramount in all aspects of service delivery.

The first principle of the NASP (2010b) ethics code embodies school psychologists respecting the dignity and rights of all persons. Section I.3, in particular, indicates that school psychologists are to promote fairness and justice. They are to use their expertise in cultivating school climates that are safe and welcoming to all persons, including students with chronic behavioral concerns. This section also promotes the maintenance of developmentally and culturally responsive practices. Embedded within this principle is a standard that holds school psychologists to work to correct school practices that are unjustly discriminatory or deny students their legal rights. As such, school psychologists are duty bound to prevent manifestation determination processes from devolving into vehicles to remove troublesome students with disabilities en masse from the public school setting. Another embedded standard is that school psychologists ensure that all students participate in and benefit from school programs, as well as have access to school psychological services. The systemic and total removal of students with disabilities from the public schools is in direct conflict with this tenet.

The fourth principle of the NASP (2010b) ethics code embodies the responsibility that school psychologists have to schools, families, communities, the profession, and society. School psychologists must assume a proactive role in identifying social injustices that affect children and schools. They must strive to reform systems-level patterns of injustice. Embedded within this principle is a standard that holds school psychologists to use their professional expertise to promote changes and advocate for policies in schools that benefit students. As the research demonstrating any benefit of long-term disciplinary removals to students is dubious at best, school psychologists are well advised to advocate for building systems-level capacities and enacting programs that have been empirically demonstrated to bring about these benefits, such as school-wide positive behavior interventions.

Recognize Inherent Limitations of Manifestation Determinations

It has been argued that the viewpoints that underlie the manifestation determination process embrace a medical model orientation, which subscribes to the concept of problem behavior as being within the person and independent from the context of his or her environment (Lee, 2005). Maag and Katsiyannis (2008) posited that there are inherent problems with special education eligibility determination criteria in reflecting the medical model. One of the problems is that social constructions of disability categories often resist objective definition. One example of this limitation is the emotional disturbance eligibility category, which is vague and inconsistent. Another weakness of the medical model is that it might unwittingly exclude some diagnoses (e.g., learning disability) that do not readily incorporate emotional–behavioral aspects into their definition. Consequently, the medical model is not a view embraced by modern psychology as many problematic behaviors are often viewed in a manner that, if not context dependent, clearly appreciates the significant influence of environments on such behavior (Lee, 2005).

Maag and Katsiyannis (2008) maintained that one possible solution to the limitations of the medical model would be using a response-to-intervention approach to eligibility for students with emotional and/or behavioral disorders. They conceptualized that Tier 1 would involve focusing on increasing student engagement and modifying instruction. Tier 2 would involve group and embedded interventions in social skills training and other supportive interventions for targeted students. Tier 3 would include an expanded team of professionals with functional assessments focusing on generalization and maintenance of learned skills. With this grounding, school professionals, including school psychologists, can make more defensible determinations by assessing whether a given student possessed the necessary skills to monitor his or her behavior and engage in appropriate alternative behaviors. Assessments can include information about whether the student can analyze problems factually (free of significant distortion or bias), generate solutions, and evaluate the effectiveness of these solutions. Deficiencies in these skills could result in a determination that there was a relationship between an instance of misbehavior and the student's disability. There has been some early support for practical uses of this model (e.g., Fairbanks, Sugai, Guardino, & Lathrop, 2007).

It has been argued by Katsiyannis and Maag (2001) that the manifestation determination process is conceptually and methodologically flawed and appears to serve more of a political than educational purpose. Because disability categories are socially constructed and not medically validated, it is logically impossible to make a valid manifestation determination unless there is a known physical cause for the behavior problem. Disability categories, as social constructions, are subject to a variety of social and political pressures, which makes the ability to identify causal relationships subjective rather than objective (Lee, 2005).

Case Study Example

The following case study is provided based on similar case studies described or referenced in the literature (e.g., Katsiyannis et al., 2012; Kubick, 2008; Morrison & D'Incau, 2000; Zirkel, 2006) and the authors' own experiences. Instead of being a play-by-play description of one specific case, this case study example takes real conditions and decisions from multiple cases and condenses them into an easily digestible example that demonstrates the best practices procedures to follow during a manifestation determination. At the end of the case study example, best practices for follow-up actions after a manifestation determination are provided based on the information provided earlier in this chapter.

An eighth-grade student, Gabe, identified with a learning disability in reading comprehension and listening comprehension, is suspended from school. Gabe receives 45 minutes a day of specially designed instruction in reading/language arts in a resource room, plus 20 minutes of tutoring daily during a 45-minute study hall period. The reading/language arts instruction also focuses on listening comprehension skills. Gabe has begun to skip classes regularly, along with a small group of other students, but no pattern is established as to which classes he skips, and the students do not engage in any other unlawful behaviors while skipping class. Gabe had only skipped class twice before this year, once in sixth grade and once in seventh grade, with the same small group of other students. Because of the frequency with which Gabe is skipping classes the current school year, he has received 11 total suspensions. Although he was not given 11 days of suspension consecutively, these suspensions all stem from Gabe's skipping behavior and are each thus considered to be one in a pattern of removals. This pattern of removals means that Gabe's

placement is changed, his parents must be notified, and a manifestation determination must take place.

The school team consists of the principal, Gabe's teachers and parents, and the school psychologist. At the manifestation determination meeting, the team follows several steps to determine whether or not Gabe's behavior is a manifestation of the disability. The team follows a question-and-answer process similar to the flowchart provided in Figure 27.1. The team also answers questions outlined in this chapter for determining whether the behavior had a direct and substantial relationship with Gabe's disability and whether the IEP was appropriately implemented.

There is general agreement that the IEP was implemented as written. There is also agreement that Gabe's disability did not impair his ability to control his misconduct. While he has skipped twice in the past, it was only once per year and with the same small group of other students. The team concludes that he is generally able to control his behavior and that skipping with a group of other students requires forethought and planning to skip all together at the same time. There is disagreement about whether or not Gabe's disability impairs his ability to understand the impact or consequences of his misconduct, however.

The parents claim that Gabe's skipping behavior has a direct relationship to his disability, because Gabe has a learning disability in reading comprehension and listening comprehension, thus (a) causing him difficulties in understanding class work in all areas and thus wanting to skip and (b) impairing his ability to understand the consequences of the misconduct. The parents claim that he does not understand the consequences of his misconduct because he was only given the same information as all other students regarding consequences for skipping class; that is, the student handbook and an overview of school rules at the beginning of the school year. Parents claim this information is not substantial enough for Gabe to learn the school rules because, as stated in previous evaluation team reports and IEPs, Gabe needs repetition and breakdown of complicated information into smaller steps. The parents claim that Gabe needs similar repetition and breakdown of the school rules in order for him to completely understand the possible consequences for any misbehavior.

The principal and teachers note that Gabe was provided with additional opportunities to understand the consequences of skipping class. He received the student handbook, he received an overview of school rules at the beginning of the year, there were school rules posted around the building, and he had previous experience skipping, so he would know what the consequences for skipping class are. Gabe always turns in his homework, completes class work on time, raises his hand to talk in class, and has received no other behavioral referrals from classroom teachers. The work that he completes receives low average grades overall, with some work below average. Gabe's teachers suggest that he understands class materials and rules well enough to turn in homework, earn passing grades, and follow class rules (aside from this recent bout of skipping). Gabe has shown an ability to follow all other school-wide rules. The school psychologist notes that the team agreed Gabe's IEP was appropriately implemented as written, suggesting that Gabe had received the necessary repetition and breakdown of complicated procedures into smaller steps.

Objectively, it would seem that Gabe's behavior was not a manifestation of his disability because the evidence provided does not support that his behavior has a direct and substantial relationship to his disability. Following the questions outlined earlier in this chapter, Gabe's thought processes were logical because he had to plan with the other students when to skip class together. Gabe has demonstrated an ability to follow all other school rules this year and all school rules in previous years (with the only exceptions being the two skipping instances in two previous years), suggesting he also has the capacity to know which behaviors are unacceptable. His mainly low average grades and previous academic and cognitive performance may also be used to support his capacity to understand whether a behavior is acceptable or not. Gabe understood the consequences of misbehavior because he received a copy and adequate explanation of the school rules in the form of the student handbook and an explanation provided at the beginning of each school year, in addition to school rules being posted and a lack of other violations. Gabe additionally understood the consequences of misbehavior and the specific consequences of skipping because of his prior experience with being reprimanded for skipping and because of his previous receipt of copies and explanations of school rules.

Although no specific data were presented as to whether or not Gabe has expressed whether he knows the skipping behavior is wrong, the team could easily gather that information by speaking with Gabe. As was mentioned earlier in this chapter, however, not all of the guiding questions have to be answered to prove whether the behavior had a direct and substantial relationship with the disability. These are guiding questions that are useful to investigate in order to provide the evidence

necessary to prove whether or not a behavior had a direct and substantial relationship to the disability. The district is responsible to bear the burden of proof that a behavior was not related to a disability in manifestation determination hearings (Katsiyannis & Maag, 2001). Objectively, then, it would appear that the district was able to provide the necessary data to support that Gabe's behavior was not a manifestation of determination. Subjectively, however, the principal, teachers, parents, school psychologist, and other staff members may have emotional ties to the situation, and this conclusion may not be reached easily and may not be unanimously determined. If the school supports the decision and the parents disagree, the parents would be able to file for due process. If the entire team agrees that a behavior was not a manifestation of the student's disability, the procedures outlined in Figure 27.1 should be followed.

Whether a manifestation determination decision is unanimous or whether the parents move for due process, the school district should examine a few points following any manifestation determination. Best practices would suggest that school districts should prevent manifestation determinations, and the occurrence of a manifestation determination meeting would mean that prevention efforts failed. The district should evaluate its preventive systems for weak spots. The student's specific IEP should also be examined and the IEP team should evaluate whether the behavior in question should be addressed on the student's IEP. The student should be monitored and an FBA and behavior intervention plan implemented to prevent the specific behavior from happening again. In Gabe's case, the FBA could support that the function of his skipping behavior was for peer acceptance, rather than for reasons related to his disability. The behavior intervention plan would then focus on rewarding Gabe for refraining from skipping and making more positive decisions about his peers. Gabe's friends who skipped with him may also benefit from behavioral interventions to prevent skipping behavior, as it would also be best practices for school districts to work with all students on improving undesirable behaviors. Gabe's friends, for example, did not respond to the school-wide Tier 1 behavior intervention, so they may be identified as in need of group-based Tier 2 or even individualized Tier 3 behavior interventions as a result of their excessive skipping behaviors.

SUMMARY

Manifestation determinations are composed of many steps and components, some of which are well defined and outlined and some of which are vaguely defined with conflicting case law guidance. Overall, manifestation determinations deal with disciplining students with disabilities, determining when a manifestation determination is required, and conducting a manifestation determination.

When disciplining students with disabilities, schools need to evaluate whether the student has been removed from their placement as outlined by their IEP for either 10 consecutive days or 10 cumulative days that represent a pattern of removal. The manifestation determination team then needs to decide whether the misbehavior had a direct and substantial relationship to the student's disability, including whether the disability impaired the student's ability to understand the consequences of the misbehavior and whether the disability impaired the student's ability to control the behavior that was disciplined (Meloy, 2008). The manifestation determination team also needs to decide whether the student's IEP was appropriately implemented during the time of the misbehavior (Meloy, 2008).

The best practice for conducting manifestation determinations, however, lies within preventing misbehavior from occurring in the first place. Evidence-based strategies that work toward preventing misbehavior include (a) adopting preventive practices, (b) involving a school psychologist, (c) engaging in culturally and developmentally responsive practices, (d) promoting home–school collaboration, (e) providing ongoing professional development, (f) implementing systems-level three-tiered frameworks of behavior management, (g) maintaining an awareness of in-district politics, (h) considering the problems inherent in removing students with disabilities from instruction, (i) promoting ethical practices, and (j) recognizing the inherent limitations of manifestation determinations.

REFERENCES

Data Accountability Center. (2011). *IDEA Part B Data Reports Table 5: Discipline.* Washington, DC: Author.

Disability Rights California. (2006). *YIKES! My child with a disability is being considered for expulsion!* Sacramento, CA: Author. Retrieved from http://www.disabilityrightsca.org/pubs/546301.htm

Fairbanks, S., Sugai, G., Guardino, D., & Lathrop, M. (2007). Response to intervention: Examining classroom behavior support in second grade. *Exceptional Children, 73,* 288–310.

Gates, G. E., & Cheramie, G. M. (2004, March). *Conducting manifestation determinations for students with disabilities.* Paper presented at the annual meeting of the National Association of School Psychologists, Dallas, TX.

Hartwig, E. P., & Ruesch, G. M. (1995). *How to make a manifestation determination* [Video]. Horsham, PA: LRP Publications.

Hundley, C. A. (1994). The reduction of childhood aggression using the brainpower program. In M. Furlong & D. Smith (Eds.), *Anger, hostility and aggression: Assessment, prevention, and intervention strategies for youth* (pp. 313–344). Brandon, VT: Clinical Psychology.

Katsiyannis, A., Losinski, M., & Prince, A. M. T. (2012). Litigation and students with disabilities: A persistent concern. *NASSP Bulletin, 96,* 23–43. doi:10.1177/0192636511431008

Katsiyannis, A., & Maag, J. W. (2001). Manifestation determination as a golden fleece. *Exceptional Children, 68,* 85–96.

Kubick, R. J. (2008). Best practices in making manifestation determinations. In A. Thomas & J. Grimes (Eds.), *Best practices in school psychology V* (pp. 827–835). Bethesda, MD: National Association of School Psychologists.

Kubick, R. J., & Bard, E. M. (2004). Manifestation determination: Guidelines for parents and educators. In A. S. Canter, L. Z. Paige, M. D. Roth, I. Romero, & S. A. Carroll (Eds.), *Helping children at home and school II: Handouts for families and educators* [CD-ROM version] (S8–213–S8–216). Bethesda, MD: National Association of School Psychologists.

Kubick, R. J., Bard, E. M., & Perry, J. D. (2000). Manifestation determinations: Discipline guidelines for children with disabilities. In C. Telzrow & M. Tankersley (Eds.), *IDEA amendments of 1997: Practice guidelines for school-based teams* (pp. 199–240). Bethesda, MD: National Association of School Psychologists.

Lee, S. W. (2005). Manifestation determination. In S. W. Lee (Ed.), *Encyclopedia of school psychology* (pp. 303–305). Thousand Oaks, CA: SAGE.

Longstreth, S., Brady, S., & Kay, A. (2013). Discipline policies in early childhood care and education programs: Building an infrastructure for social and academic success. *Early Education and Development, 24,* 253–271.

Maag, J. W., & Katsiyannis, A. (2006). Behavioral intervention plans: Legal and practical considerations for students with emotional and behavioral disorders. *Behavioral Disorders, 31,* 348–362.

Maag, J. W., & Katsiyannis, A. (2008). The medical model to block eligibility for students with EBD: A response-to-intervention alternative. *Behavioral Disorders, 33,* 184–194.

Massachusetts Department of Education. (2007). *Discipline of special education students under IDEA 2004.* Boston, MA: Author. Retrieved from http://www.doe.mass.edu/sped/IDEA2004/spr_meetings/disc_chart.pdf

Meloy, L. L. (2008). Minimalist approach to manifestation determination: Possible compromise of due process rights. *Communiqué, 36*(6), 1–6.

Monroe, C. R. (2005). Understanding the discipline gap through a cultural lens: Implications for the education of African American students. *Intercultural Education, 16,* 317–330.

Morrison, G. M., & D'Incau, B. (2000). Developmental and service trajectories of students with disabilities recommended for expulsion from school. *Exceptional Children, 66,* 257–272.

National Association of School Psychologists. (2010a). *Model for comprehensive and integrated school psychological services.* Bethesda, MD: Author. Retrieved from http://www.nasponline.org/standards/2010standards/2_PracticeModel.pdf

National Association of School Psychologists. (2010b). *Principles for professional ethics.* Bethesda, MD: Author. Retrieved from http://www.nasponline.org/standards/2010standards/1_%20Ethical%20Principles.pdf

Ohio Department of Education. (2012). *Discipline of special education students under IDEA*. Columbus, OH: Author. Retrieved from http://www.edresourcesohio.org/videos/discipline/docs/Ohio%20Discipline%20Action%20Flow%20Chart.pdf

Rutherford, R. (1978). Theory and research on the use of aversive procedures in the education of behaviorally disordered and emotionally disturbed children and youth. In F. Wood & K. Lankin (Eds.), *Punishment and aversive stimulation in special education* (pp. 41–64). Reston, VA: Council for Exceptional Children.

Ryan, J. B., Katsiyannis, A., Peterson, R., & Chmelar, B. (2007). IDEA 2004 and disciplining students with disabilities. *NASSP Bulletin, 91*, 130–140.

Sawka, K. D., McCurdy, B. L., & Mannella, M. C. (2002). Strengthening emotional support services: An empirically based model for training teachers of students with behavioral disorders. *Journal of Emotional and Behavioral Disorders, 10*, 223–232.

Yell, M. I. (2006). *The law and special education* (2nd ed.). Upper Saddle River, NJ: Pearson/Merrill.

Zilz, W. A. (2006). Manifestation determination: Rulings of the courts. *Education and the Law, 18*(2–3), 193–206.

Zirkel, P. A. (2006). Manifestation determinations under the Individuals with Disabilities Education Act: What the new causality criteria mean. *Journal of Special Education Leadership, 19*(2), 3–12.

Zirkel, P. A. (2011). State special education laws for functional behavioral assessment and behavior intervention plans. *Behavioral Disorder, 36*, 262–278.

28

Best Practices in Service Learning for School-to-Work Transition and Inclusion for Students With Disabilities

Felicia L. Wilczenski
Paula Sotnik
Laura E. Vanderberg
University of Massachusetts–Boston

OVERVIEW

The domain Interventions and Mental Health Services to Develop Social and Life Skills, of the National Association of School Psychologists (NASP) *Model for Comprehensive and Integrated School Psychological Services* (NASP, 2010), emphasizes the competencies of school psychologists in understanding the biological, cultural, developmental, and social influences on behavior and mental health as well as their impacts on learning and independent functioning. School psychologists are called upon to provide a continuum of developmentally appropriate learning experiences to promote life skills. The passage from youth to adulthood is a particularly critical transition for an individual's personal growth and life adjustment.

Transition from school to work is a challenging time for all young people, especially for young people with disabilities. Currently, the bulk of U.S. social institutions designed to support vulnerable populations cease this support between the ages of 18 and 21. U.S. social policy for the most part still assumes adulthood at 18 or 21, leaving many young people without a safety net (Furstenberg, Rumbaut, & Settersten, 2005). The period of developmental transition immediately following high school presents both opportunities and challenges for individual adaptation (Schulenberg, Sameroff, & Cicchetti, 2004). School psychologists are well aware that not all individuals flourish in this developmental period, and the increasing lack of structure in these years proves particularly challenging for vulnerable populations (Osgood, Foster, Flanagan, & Ruth, 2005).

A large part of a fulfilling and productive future depends upon finding and maintaining employment. Despite legislation aimed at supporting career development, such as the Individuals with Disabilities Education Act, the Vocational Rehabilitation Act, and the Americans with Disabilities Act, youth and adults with disabilities continue to experience high unemployment. Statistics indicate that students with disabilities have a high school dropout rate that is twice that of students without disabilities. Only 21.1% of people with disabilities ages 16 and older were in the labor force in May 2011 in comparison with 69.7% of people without disabilities (Bureau of Labor Statistics, 2011; National Collaborative on Workforce and Disability for Youth, 2012). Although the legislation was intended to create equal access to appropriate education, as well as equity and opportunity within the workplace, many people with disabilities lack access to traditional forms of skill building that lead to employment.

Transition refers to the period during which students end their high school experiences and move into the first phase of adult life. Transitions for students with disabilities represent the intersection of two pedagogical challenges: special education and inclusion. Transition planning is designed to help adolescents with disabilities move into adult roles in independent living, civic engagement, and employment. Transition work focuses on the connections between the classroom and the community.

Service learning, where the community becomes the classroom, provides a vehicle to address goals related to employment in a student's Individual Transition Plan. Service learning has been shown to be a powerful experiential pedagogy for academic, personal, social, and career development (Wilczenski & Coomey, 2007), and growing evidence suggests its effectiveness as a strategy for transition planning (Wilczenski, Timmons, Martell, & Vanderberg, 2012). Service learning can bridge the gap between high school and post-high school environments such as higher education, community life, and the workforce. It differs from other work-based activities in that students gain employment skills while giving back to their community and, consequently, transforming those communities to full inclusion. Service learning also creates the opportunity to demonstrate valuable contributions that can be made by students with disabilities in work settings.

BASIC CONSIDERATIONS

In pedagogy, service learning integrates community work with curriculum goals. A widely accepted definition of service learning is based upon the National and Community Service Act of 1990, and includes the following four core characteristics: (a) students learn through participation in organized experiences that meet actual community needs and are coordinated with school and community; (b) the program is integrated into the academic curriculum with time to reflect upon those experiences; (c) students are given opportunities to use their knowledge and skills in real-life situations in communities; and (d) learning is extended beyond the classroom into the community, which fosters the development of a sense of caring.

In addition to being a pedagogical technique, service learning is a philosophy and a community development strategy that can optimize postsecondary transitions for students with disabilities. Service-learning curricula incorporate individualized goals based on the characteristics of the participants and the community setting. Using this curriculum framework, service learning is an intentional developmental strategy in planning and implementing projects that promote personal growth, community growth, and inclusion. Inclusion is at once a process, a state of being involved, and a method for integrating into the community those who are, or are at risk of, being excluded. Service-learning projects are multifaceted and, through principles of universal design, can be arranged to include all students with different learning variabilities.

For an educational activity to be considered service learning, certain criteria of reflection and reciprocity must be met (Eyler, 2002). Service learning is a dynamic reciprocal relationship between students and the community resulting in mutual benefits. Various service-learning programs assign different weight to the two components of service and learning. Sigmon (1998) offers the following typology, suggesting four variations in the relationship between service and learning: (a) service *learning*, where the emphasis is on learning objectives; (b) *service* learning, which is service oriented; (c) service learning with separate service and learning goals; and (d) *service learning*, where service and learning goals are of equal weight and enhance each other.

Engaging in community service—for volunteers both with and without disabilities—is an effective avenue for personal and professional development. Service participants actively contribute to the strengthening of their communities, while at the same time gaining valuable skills, exploring career paths, and developing social networks that can lead to meaningful employment. Volunteering and serving others can be transformative in two regards: (a) persons with disabilities, who typically have been recipients of services rather than providers, offer a valuable service to the community and therein transform from the servee to the server; and (b) peers without disabilities transform to see persons with disabilities as contributors rather than only recipients of service. Teachers implementing an inclusive service-learning class in Brooke Point High School in Stafford, Virginia, described how the participation of students with and without disabilities in that class facilitated learning on both sides and described how traditional students developed an appreciation of their peers' strengths and weaknesses. Students without disabilities began to regard their peers with disabilities as typical servers and learners, not only as students with disabilities (for more information, see Lacey, 2009).

The Edward M. Kennedy Serve America Act of 2009 reauthorized and expanded national service programs administered by the Corporation for National and Community Service (2011). Although the legislation is not specific to disabilities, it increased eligibility of individuals with disabilities for national service and implicitly charged national service programs to increase access and accommodations in order to actively engage youth and adults in Senior Corps, AmeriCorps, and

Learn and Serve America. In so doing, it supported greater involvement in service for people with disabilities. The following mandates taken directly from the Universal Design for Learning bill language (Corporation for National and Community Service, 2009) require national service entities to

- identify and implement methods of recruitment to increase the number of participants who are individuals with disabilities in the programs receiving assistance under the national service laws,
- effectively accommodate individuals with disabilities to increase the participation of individuals with disabilities in national service programs,
- provide and disseminate information regarding methods to make service-learning programs and programs offered under the national service laws accessible to individuals with disabilities, and
- collaborate with organizations with demonstrated expertise in supporting and accommodating individuals with disabilities.

For people who have had limited vocational experience, national service such as AmeriCorps can be an important transition option and a component of a long-range employment plan. Completing a structured service-learning project allows people with disabilities to develop their vocational and interpersonal skills and to use skills they already possess in new ways while experiencing the sense of contribution that may result from giving back to their communities. Involvement in community service has been found to break down barriers to employment while building confidence, careers, and community for its participants (Timmons & Zalewska, 2012).

The Corporation for National and Community Service Strategic Plan (Corporation for National and Community Service, 2011) provides a blueprint to carry out the spirit and intent of Universal Design for Learning. The plan states that outcomes for both the service participant and the communities in which they serve are improved when the participant has a positive service experience that includes opportunities for professional, educational, and personal growth. National service offers the participant a unique combination of professional, educational, and life benefits. Corporation for National and Community Service–supported participants may receive an education award to pay education training costs at qualified institutions of higher education or to repay qualified student loans. Additionally, Corporation for National

and Community Service–supported participants may develop a wide range of skills during their experience, ranging from hard skills such as construction and weatherizing and disaster response planning and operations to softer skills such as counseling, leadership, teamwork, appropriate workplace behaviors, and cultural competency.

Results from a longitudinal alumni study (Corporation for National and Community Service, 2008) revealed impressive growth across educational, career, and personal domains. Concerning participant satisfaction, AmeriCorps members are not only satisfied with their service experiences but are more likely to be very satisfied with almost every aspect of their lives than a comparison group and are less likely to experience depression. Possibly, the benefits of service go beyond the activity itself as participants may generalize positive service experiences. The study also demonstrated that AmeriCorps service gives members the chance to explore different career paths, gain job-related skills, develop leadership capabilities, and network with community leaders while gaining hands-on experience. High percentages of AmeriCorps members reported that they earned valuable skills that they used in later employment, also suggesting that participants generalize and transfer their hard and soft skills for career development. Members from different levels of service were also surveyed about whether their experience in AmeriCorps helped them see the importance of education. For state and national members, 66% of members reported that serving in AmeriCorps helped them see the importance of education. Fifty-seven percent of National Civilian Community Corps members report that AmeriCorps helped them see the importance of education. Within the state and national subgroups of Hispanics/Latinos, Blacks/African Americans, and members from disadvantaged circumstances, the percentages were 82%, 72%, and 74%, respectively. Overall, these reports indicate that service has a positive impact on considerations for further education and that these effects may be more robust for certain populations.

The conceptual model illustrated in Figure 28.1 frames service learning in terms of intended targets, outcomes, and impact on educational and employment transitions. The base shows service learning integrating three critical transition target variables previously identified in the literature: (a) career development, (b) self-determination, and (c) social skill building. By intentionally integrating these targets, service-learning experiences enable positive outcomes in character, career, and community development (Timmons &

Figure 28.1. Conceptual Model for Service Learning as a Transition Process for Students With Disabilities

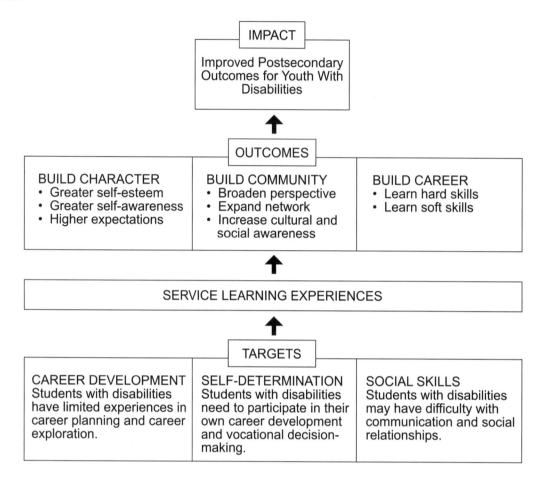

Zalewska, 2012), as well as promote inclusive post-secondary outcomes for students with disabilities. This conceptual model shows the skill and character domains that are affected by the use of service learning as an inclusive school-to-work transition strategy.

BEST PRACTICES IN SERVICE LEARNING

School psychologists have a vested interest in the outcomes of their work; that is, preparing all students, including those with disabilities, for postschool life. This section offers ideas for school psychologists to use to promote and support inclusive service-learning experiences for students and to integrate community engagement as a valuable transition strategy for youth with disabilities. Through the intentional promotion of service learning for transition planning, school psychologists will become more effective in supporting career development, self-determination, and social skills building. These are vital life skills that have been shown to have an impact on

postsecondary education, employment, and independent living outcomes. The following evidence-based and best practices in service learning can assist all youth in achieving positive transition and inclusion outcomes.

Service Learning: Critical Elements

What follows are best practices for service learning outlined by the National Youth Leadership Council (2008):

- Service learning actively engages participants in meaningful and personally relevant service activities.
- Service learning is intentionally used as an instructional strategy to meet learning goals and/or content standards.
- Service learning incorporates multiple challenging reflection activities that are ongoing and that prompt deep thinking about oneself and one's relationship to society.

- Service learning promotes understanding of diversity and mutual respect among all participants.
- Service learning provides youth with a strong voice in planning, implementing, and evaluating service-learning experiences with guidance from adults.
- Service-learning partnerships are collaborative, mutually beneficial, and able to address community needs.
- Service learning engages participants in an ongoing process to assess the quality of implementation and progress toward meeting specified goals, and uses results for improvement and sustainability.
- Service learning has sufficient duration and intensity to address community needs and meet specified outcomes.

Implementation of Universal Design and a PARR Model

A PARR model (see, e.g., Duckenfield & Swanson, 1992; Roehlkepartain, Bright, & Margolis-Rupp, 2000; Schon, 1983) is a cyclical process of planning, action, reflection, and recognition. Following PARR and using principles of Universal Design for Learning ensure best practices in the implementation and assessment of student response to the inclusive service-learning experience.

Universal design, and particularly Universal Design for Learning (Rose & Meyer, 2006), provides an approach for creating instructional goals, methods, materials, and assessments that work for everyone, that is, not a single, one-size-fits-all solution but rather, flexible approaches that can be customized and adjusted for individual needs. Universal Design for Learning offers a set of principles for curriculum development that gives all individuals equal opportunities to learn the instructional goals. Universal Design for Learning principles (Center for Applied Special Technology, 2011) can be directly applied in service-learning projects to support inclusion. Specifically, service learning should provide multiple means of representation to optimize understanding for all students. Additionally, service learning should provide multiple means of expression to allow students to demonstrate what they know. Finally, service learning should provide multiple means of engagement to appeal to different engagement and motivational preferences of students.

Table 28.1 outlines the strategies of Universal Design for Learning that can be employed at each step of a PARR model.

Transition Planning

Guideposts for Success (National Collaborative on Workforce and Disability for Youth, 2006) includes a compilation of research-based educational and career development interventions that can make a positive difference in the lives of all youth, including those with disabilities. The guideposts integrate research findings on what all youth need to successfully transition to adulthood and outline basic practices in transition planning. For instance, interventions should hold the highest expectations for all youth, those with and without disabilities. Programs should provide equality of opportunity for everyone and promote integration and inclusion. Furthermore, interventions should foster full participation through self-determination, informed choice, and participation in decision making and transition planning that are culturally and linguistically appropriate. For transition goals, all programs should aim for independent living, including skill development and long-term supports and services. Program staff should encourage competitive employment and economic self-sufficiency, with supports if necessary, as everyone's life goal (see http://www.ncwd-youth.info/guideposts/key-principles).

Additionally, Table 28.2 indicates how the Guideposts for Success provide a systematic structure for service learning as a transition experience that will ensure youth move successfully from school to work (Timmons & Zalewska, 2012).

School and Service Partnerships

Successful collaborations develop knowledge, trust, and relationships that enable schools and community organizations to achieve more in partnership than they could independently (Corporation for National and Community Service, 2004; Timmons & Zalewska, 2012). Collaborations can be mutually beneficial. While schools create community service opportunities for youth that allow them to gain valuable experience, the service programs also gain access to qualified, committed participants (Timmons & Zalewska, 2012). The local service community may be unfamiliar with the school and disability community, and vice versa. Therefore, a critical first step in successful partnerships involves learning more about each other. The Corporation for National and Community Service (2004) identifies ways to identify potential partners and shared information to build collaborations:

- Every state has a service commission with a disability coordinator on staff. Contact the state's coordinator to

Table 28.1. Universal Design for Service Learning Using a PARR Model

PARR Model	Universal Design Examples
Preparation: Introduce students to the issues or topics that will be addressed in the program, select appropriate projects, and provide background information and training. This stage involves everything from selecting a project to preparing students with the knowledge and skills to be effective. Prepare students to serve by giving them a basic overview of what they will be doing and why. Specific tasks may include building enthusiasm, selecting a project, and introducing social issues.	• Students conduct an accessibility assessment of all sites when selecting a project. • The importance of community needs is expressed in multiple formats (e.g., text, photographs, and auditory means). • All students can identify, understand, and value each other's diverse learning styles and perspectives. • A variety of technologies and methods are used to enable all students to express choices and make decisions.
Action: Engage in either direct or indirect service to help others in the community. This action moves social issues from students' heads to their hearts and hands. The action step of the model includes not just the act of serving, but also the necessary supports for successfully engaging in that service. Specific tasks may include providing a supportive environment, coping with change, ensuring safety, building relationships with the people being served, and documenting the experience.	• Multiple means (e.g., voice recorders, photovoice, photographs) are used to capture students' work. • Digital storytelling enables students to have a voice in documenting their service experiences. • Supports guide students in working with community partners to address accessibility issues and provide appropriate accommodations within the service setting.
Reflection: Look back on the experience, raise and address questions, explore opportunities, and assess the project or program. Reflection is an intentional process of guiding students to discover and interpret the meaning of learning from serving. Have students keep a journal of experiences and insights. Specific reflection tasks may include remembering the experience, identifying issues that surfaced and skills used to address those issues, exploring possibilities within and beyond the service for continuing to make a difference, and assessing what worked and what did not work.	• Video recorders are used to record students' considerations of "what, so what, now what." • Creative art projects, photo collages, and drawings are used to express what students learned.
Recognition: Evaluate and honor the service experience. Recognize the major findings from the reflections and assessments, celebrate accomplishments, recognize and value learning variabilities, and make plans and commitments for the future. This step should provide a sense of accomplishment of the work done and set the stage for ongoing involvement and commitment. Specific recognition tasks may include celebrating the experiences, sharing learning, and making commitments with others.	• All students describe how inclusive approaches led to accomplishments and benefits for all participants. • Each student contributes to a variety of outcome evidence, including written text, photographs, visual graphs, and audio recordings.

Note. Based on information from Duckenfield and Swanson (1992) and Roehlkepartain, Bright, and Margolis-Rupp (2000).

learn more about the range of service options and how youth with disabilities can be included. A full list of state coordinators can be seen at http://serviceandinclusion. org/index.php?page=coordinatorslist. The coordinator, or other members of the service commission, can help identify inclusive service programs in the community. They also may be able to share promising practices and examples of partnerships between the disability community and national service programs that facilitated successful engagement of individuals with disabilities.

• Once a local service program is identified, set up short, informal meetings with its leadership. Be prepared to explain the program and the goals.
• Invite service staff to meet school staff and students. Ask them to present an overview of the community service options other youth have engaged in recently.
• Coordinate a service day for students to serve at an organization or within the school community.
• Service programs have state- or county-level conferences and meetings. Present a workshop or attend sessions to stay abreast of local initiatives.

Table 28.2. Addressing the Guideposts to Success Through Service Learning

Five Guideposts to Success	Service-Learning Transition Strategies
School-based preparatory experiences: In the school setting, preparatory experiences should be grounded in standards, clear performance expectations, and graduation exit options.	• Provide a hands-on career and interest assessment by trying out different roles and experiences. • Provide learning experiences in a community setting, creating opportunities to define what future workplaces and careers might look like. • Provide a concrete activity relevant to expectations of the Individualized Education Program.
Career preparation and work-based learning experiences: These precareer and prework experiences should expose youth to a range of opportunities for learning and development.	• Increase employability by developing soft skills, such as interpersonal, communication, and time-management and teamwork skills. • Expose youth to new career ideas and people of diverse ages, backgrounds, and cultures, including people with and without disabilities. • Provide an opportunity to gain real-world experience. • Allow youth to gain perspective on abilities and limitations in a work environment.
Youth development and leadership: Experiences should focus on development and leadership through coordinated activities that encourage competency and self-esteem.	• Encourage and empower youth as they discover their abilities and talents. • Create opportunities to develop, practice, and master problem-solving skills. • Help students develop personal goals and objectives through exploration and reflection activities. • Foster self-advocacy skills through guided disclosure and advocacy for appropriate accommodations in the service setting. • Enhance self-esteem through the pride and satisfaction of addressing a community need.
Connecting activities: Community-based experiences should be in partnership with programs and services that help students gain access to chosen postschool options.	• Help students develop a commitment to service as another postschool option. • Increase access and connection to employment, education, and community resources through newly formed networks composed of peers, mentors, and professionals. • Increase exposure to businesses in the community through intentional consideration of how future employment connects to the service project.
Family involvement and supports: Service-family connections should promote social, emotional, and occupational growth.	• Connect youth with mentors and other caring adults. • Expand peer and professional networks that can be used for occupational growth.

Case Study: Project Impact

Project Impact (Martell, 2012) is a 5-month intensive community service experience for youth with disabilities in Florida that includes a student-led community mapping exercise. In community mapping, students identify a community problem and the resources needed to address it. The students develop a plan for a service activity that will address the problem, and then implement the service activity. Students follow this model with guidance from trained AmeriCorps facilitators and mentors (Martell, 2012).

Implementation

The case study of Project Impact shows the four steps of a PARR (preparation, action, reflection, and recognition) process in action. Each month students meet with peers and their facilitator, and together they engage in various aspects of preparation. They decide on a service activity to address an identified community problem.

Once the plan is developed, the students identify supplies for the activity and determine expenses. They discuss areas of collaboration with other entities in the community and a plan for marketing the service project. Together the students outline exactly how the service project will unfold, their roles, and their responsibilities. Then students enter the action step as they engage in the service activity to address the community problem. Throughout the service, they participate in regular reflection activities that allow them to consider the skills they are developing and the impact they are having in their community. After completion of the service project, they reflect further on and celebrate their accomplishment in the recognition step. Through Project Impact, Florida AmeriCorps programs, in conjunction with a range of community partners, have implemented 30 community-service projects (e.g., work in soup kitchens, homeless shelters, beach cleaning), with 300 students with disabilities in 12 Florida counties (Martell, 2012).

Outcomes

Findings indicate that Project Impact leads to increased employability skills for youth with disabilities (Wilczenski, Timmons, Martell, & Vanderberg, 2012). Interviews conducted with 24 Project Impact participants reveal how the experience contributed to employment skill building and career exploration. A few representative statements by the study participants are included below to illustrate how their participation in Project Impact influenced them in terms of personal, vocational, and community development, all of which together can influence employability (see NextSTEP, 2012, pp. 3–5).

Personal development: Students experienced an expanded understanding of their own abilities and challenges, and increased self-confidence. Specifically, students reported the following gains:

- Expanded self-concept: Participants viewed themselves in a new light, discovering abilities and talents of which they were not previously aware.
- Greater self-awareness: These new discoveries made the participants more cognizant of their strengths and thus more confident. Many participants recognized abilities such as creativity, leadership, and courage. Students who previously struggled with low self-esteem or felt confined to their disability-specific labels reported seeing themselves as more successful after the service experience. Though they still understood their disability and its challenges, they no longer saw themselves as different and disabled.

- Sense of pride and accomplishment: New confidence encouraged many participants to engage in new activities and to feel proud of what they had accomplished. Many of these activities were previously unfamiliar, so completing them gave the participants great satisfaction and confidence in their own abilities.
- Adequacy and belonging: Participation in Project Impact provided an opportunity to practice personal and professional interactions. Through these new friendships, networks, and connections, participants perceived they were meaningful, contributing members of a group. Participants reported opening up to others and often feeling—sometimes for the first time—that they belonged and were just as worthy and adequate as anybody else.

One Project Impact participant spoke of his personal development in this way:

> … [Project Impact] was a turning point for me. It helped me be more open, and being more accepting and trying to make me break out of that fear, like I'm not labeled, I'm just like everyone else. But I just have one difference than some other people.

Vocational development: Students practiced workplace skills and explored different career choices, interests, and options in Project Impact. In particular, students had the following opportunities that positively influenced their vocational development.

- The occasion to practice workplace behavior: The service included practicing and mastering the soft skills necessary for work, such as interpersonal, communication, time management, and teamwork skills. Participants also had an opportunity to develop their work ethic (personal responsibility, collaboration with others, dependability, and accountability). As a result, participants increased their employability and developed identities as employees.
- The opportunity to try different roles and experiences: The experience helped participants narrow their career choices and workplace preferences. By engaging in a variety of tasks (woodworking, helping children to read, caring for animals, creating flyers), participants discovered strengths and talents that contributed to feeling more capable and confident as a future worker. Although the tasks were unfamiliar, and at times overwhelming and challenging, after

completing them participants expressed pride and increased confidence. In the end, participants became more aware of what their future career might look like. Will they work in an office, work outside, have direct contact with people, or be independent? Will they want to do something creative? Project Impact helped many to get closer to a clear vision of their future career.

As another participant said of her vocational development, "[My community service experience] taught me how to be more responsible, to stay on task and work harder, keep working at a steady pace and not overdo it." In this participant's words, "[Project Impact] basically can help you experience a career choice or give you a taste of a career that you really never thought you could do or skills that you never thought you had."

Community development: Students enhanced their connection to and integration into their communities in their new roles as problem solvers. They experienced these aspects of community development:

- Increased connection and integration: Participants changed the way they viewed their surroundings and their role in society. Through community service, the participants were able to interact with a variety of people of different ages, backgrounds, cultures, and disabilities. For many, this was an opportunity to, for the first time, experience communities different from their own immediate surroundings. They learned how to accept others and how to feel accepted in a large group. They reported that participation made them feel more included in their communities.
- Ability to view themselves as providers: Many of the participants came to view themselves not as recipients of services, but rather as providers of solutions. Participants mentioned wanting to "help other people" as a result of their Project Impact experience.
- Sense of ownership and meaningful contribution: Hands-on participation and completion of the project made the participants feel that they were important and capable contributors. Seeing positive outcomes of their work gave them an empowering sense that they are capable of doing something very important for their communities.

A Project Impact facilitator made this comment about students:

They're able to go out and have that joy, receive that joy of giving back to their community, too.

And that makes people feel good. It makes them feel good. It shows them that … there are a lot of things they can do.

Service and transition: Interviews with Project Impact participants indicate that the service experience positively influenced them personally, vocationally, and within their communities. Through increasing their self-confidence, learning and practicing workplace skills, trying out different vocational choices, and providing meaningful solutions to problems in their community, they have become more employable. Employability, or the ability to gain and maintain employment, can be achieved only when an individual has acquired assets that can be presented to and valued by employers. As a result, service-learning experiences such as Project Impact can be a great option for youth with disabilities transitioning between secondary school and adult life.

Replication of Project Impact

Project Impact can be revised and replicated by school psychologists needing to provide school-to-work transition services for students with disabilities. Consider the tasks that can be incorporated in a PARR process (see Table 28.3).

National Service as a Transition Option

Students may be interested in participating in a more formal service opportunity, such as the AmeriCorps programs, where members serve full time or part time. AmeriCorps provides a structured opportunity for members to gain experience, work skills, and connections they can use later in a job search. Members can also receive a modest living allowance and an education award to be used for postsecondary educational assistance. To participate in AmeriCorps programs, students need to have completed high school, or have earned an equivalency certificate, or need an independent assessment conducted by the grantee showing the student to be incapable of obtaining a high school diploma or its equivalent. To obtain further information about AmeriCorps:

- Look at the service programs listed on the AmeriCorps website (http://www.americorps.gov/about/programs/index.asp). See how they relate to each youth's interests, abilities, and location. Use the interactive program selector to help choose the right program (http://www.nationalservice.gov/for_individuals/ready/selector.asp). If the student plans

Table 28.3. Tasks for Implementing Service-Learning Transitions Using a PARR Model

Preparation:
- Create structure by establishing a timeline for identification and implementation of the service project and stick to it
- Identify one community problem to address
- Choose a service project to address the identified problem
- Choose a location where the service project will take place
- Identify necessary resources (supplies) needed and determine project cost
- Identify additional partners
- Outline exactly how the service project will unfold
- Create a formal agenda for each planning meeting that ensures full participation
- Allow time for discussion about how each activity is building a skill needed for employment
- Consider assessing the physical space and attitudes/sensitivity of staff at the service location
- Identify needed accommodations for accessing the service project, such as transportation

Action:
- Use team-building exercises to increase peer connections, promote group problem solving, and build decision-making skills
- Use committees to plan and implement different aspects of the project
- At the service site, provide accommodations, training on disability etiquette, and incorporate Universal Design
- Complete the service project

Reflection:
- Incorporate regular reflection activities that create an intentional platform for connecting each phase of the experience to skills gained and future career options
- Discuss the link between service and employment
- Discuss the kinds of careers/occupations associated with the service project
- Think creatively about using Universal Design for Learning and adaptations to ensure all students can demonstrate their learning

Recognition:
- Celebrate and reflect on the completion of the service project
- Participate in a meta reflection activity, discussing accomplishments and how they relate to employment
- Complete a reflection activity, discussing what was learned, the types of skills built, how these skills might prepare them for employment, and what type of careers they might consider as a result of participating

Note. Based on information from NextSTEP (2012, p. 8).

to stay local, contact the state service commission and disability coordinator to learn more about in-state service options.

- Identify skills and behaviors that the student can practice in preparing for a potential service experience.

- Help the student apply for a service program. Most service programs have an online application process. Remember, this is a competitive process, so all students will not automatically be selected to serve. It may also take some time for applications to be reviewed. Many service positions require a formal interview, an excellent opportunity for building job-search skills.

- Discuss any accommodations necessary for working at a service program. Create a plan for support and monitoring progress toward personal and vocational goals. Engage the state's department of vocational rehabilitation in the process.

The National Service Inclusion Project (NSIP) can assist to broker relationships between national service programs and schools and can help students and their families learn about national service options. NSIP is a cooperative agreement between the Corporation for National and Community Service and the Institute for Community Inclusion at the University of Massachusetts–Boston. NSIP provides training and technical assistance to ensure meaningful service experiences for all Americans, regardless of their abilities. NSIP also builds partnerships between disability organizations and national service organizations to increase the participation of people with disabilities in national service. Refer to the NSIP website for contact information (http://www.serviceandinclusion.org).

In situations where it may not be feasible for a student with disabilities to be physically present at a service site, virtual volunteering or an e-service partnership in cyberspace may be an alternative. For example, NSIP was consulted when an AmeriCorps participant with a disability was not able to continue, because of a medical concern, as a volunteer tutor face to face in a GED class. Instead, online tutoring was arranged so the volunteer could continue her work.

SUMMARY

Service-learning experiences, such as Project Impact, offer students with disabilities the opportunity to build the personal and professional skills necessary to be employed. Service during the transition from school to work enables students to obtain real-world work experience, explore careers, and practice and master the soft skills essential for employment (NextSTEP, 2012). Through the examples and recommendations in this chapter, school psychologists working with youth can promote involvement in inclusive service learning as a means for developing life skills, facilitate personal growth and community connections, and create a transition pathway to meaningful employment, particularly for students with disabilities. School psychologists working at the intersection of special and general education are uniquely positioned to provide professional development for addressing transition issues and to advocate that service-learning opportunities be incorporated as part of the life skills goals and objectives of Individual Transition Plans.

AUTHOR NOTE

The authors acknowledge the significant contribution to this chapter by Paul Martell, Jaimie Timmons, and Agnieszka Zalewska, whose work with Project Impact using service learning as a vehicle to smooth the passage from school to work is an important addition to transition research and practice.

Disclosure. Felicia L. Wilczenski has a financial interest in books she authored or coauthored that are referenced in this chapter.

REFERENCES

Bureau of Labor Statistics. (2011). *Employment situation report: May 2011: Table A-6. Employment status of the civilian population by sex, age, and disability status, not seasonally adjusted.* Washington, DC: Author. Retrieved from http://www.bls.gov/news.release/empsit.t06.htm

Center for Applied Special Technology. (2011). *Universal Design for Learning guidelines version 2.0.* Wakefield, MA: Author. Retrieved from http://www.udlcenter.org/aboutudl/udlguidelines

Corporation for National and Community Service. (2004). *Creating an inclusive environment: A handbook for the inclusion of people with disabilities in national and community service programs.* Washington, DC: Author. Retrieved from http://www.serviceandinclusion.org/handbook/index.php?page=sectionix

Corporation for National and Community Service. (2008). *Still serving: Measuring the eight-year impact of AmeriCorps on alumni.* Washington, DC: Author.

Corporation for National and Community Service. (2009). *The Edward M. Kennedy Serve America Act.* Washington, DC: Author. Retrieved from http://www.nationalservice.gov/help/serve_america_act/Serve_America_Act.htm

Corporation for National and Community Service. (2011). *Strategic plan 2011–2015.* Washington, DC: Author. Retrieved from http://www.nationalservice.gov/about/focus_areas/index.asp

Duckenfield, M., & Swanson, L. (1992). *Service-learning: Meeting the needs of youth at risk.* Clemson, SC: Clemson University, National Dropout Prevention Center.

Eyler, J. (2002). Reflection: Linking service and learning: Linking students and communities. *Journal of Social Issues, 58,* 517–534.

Furstenberg, F. F., Rumbaut, R. G., & Settersten, R. A. (2005). On the frontier of adulthood: Emerging themes and new directions. In R. A. Settersten, F. F. Furstenberg, & R. G. Rumbaut (Eds.), *On the frontier of adulthood: Theory, research, and public policy* (pp. 3–28). Chicago, IL: University of Chicago Press.

Lacey, L. (2009). *Case study from the Brooke Point Learn and Serve peer program.* Washington, DC: Corporation for National and Community Service. Retrieved from http://www.servicelearning.org/lsa/lsa_page/2009mtg.php

Martell, P. (2012). *Creating a generation of change through awareness and action: Project Impact activity guide.* Tallahassee, FL: The Governor's Commission on Volunteerism and Community Service.

National Association of School Psychologists. (2010). *Model for comprehensive and integrated school psychological services.* Bethesda, MD: Author. Retrieved from http://www.nasponline.org/standards/2010standards/2_PracticeModel.pdf

National Collaborative on Workforce and Disability for Youth. (2006). *Guideposts for success.* Washington, DC: Institute for Educational Leadership. Retrieved from http://www.ncwd-youth.info/guideposts

National Collaborative on Workforce and Disability for Youth. (2012). *Improving high school outcomes for all youth: Recommendations for policy and practice.* Washington, DC: Institute for Educational Leadership. Retrieved from http://www.ncwd-youth.info/policy-brief-04

National Youth Leadership Council. (2008). *K–12 service-learning standards for quality practice.* St. Paul, MN: Author. Retrieved from http://www.nylc.org/sites/nylc.org/files/files/Standards_Oct2009-web.pdf

NextSTEP. (2012). *Lessons learned from Project Impact: Community service during the transition to employment for youth with disabilities.* Boston, MA: University of Massachusetts, Institute for Community Inclusion.

Osgood, D. W., Foster, E. M., Flanagan, C. A., & Ruth, G. R. (2005). Why focus on the transition to adulthood for vulnerable populations? In D. W. Osgood, E. M. Foster, C. A. Flanagan, & G. R. Ruth (Eds.), *On your own without a net: The transition to adulthood for vulnerable populations* (pp. 1–26). Chicago, IL: University of Chicago Press.

Roehlkepartain, E. C., Bright, T., & Margolis-Rupp, B. (2000). *An asset builder's guide to service-learning.* Minneapolis, MN: Search Institute.

Rose, D. H., & Meyer, A. (2006). *A practical reader in Universal Design for Learning.* Cambridge, MA: Harvard Education Press.

Schon, D. A. (1983). *The reflective practitioner: How professionals think in action.* London, England: Temple Smith.

Schulenberg, J. E., Sameroff, A. J., & Cicchetti, D. (2004). The transition to adulthood as a critical juncture in the course of psychopathology and mental health. *Development and Psychopathology, 16,* 799–806. doi:10/1017/S0954579404040015

Sigmon, R. L. (1998). *Linking service with learning.* Washington, DC: Council of Independent Colleges.

Timmons, J., & Zalewska, A. (2012). *Considering national service as a pathway to employment for youth with disabilities: Lessons learned from Project Impact.* Boston, MA: University of Massachusetts, Institute for Community Inclusion.

Wilczenski, F. L., & Coomey, S. M. (2007). *A practical guide to service learning: Strategies for positive development in schools.* New York, NY: Springer.

Wilczenski, F. L., Timmons, J., Martell, P., & Vanderberg, L. (2012, June). *Service-learning initiatives for youth in transition: Building character, career, and community.* Poster presented at the annual meeting of the American Association on Intellectual and Developmental Disabilities, Charlotte, NC.

Index

A

absenteeism, 41
academic engaged time
    available time, 21
    components, 21–23, 32
    defined, 22
    engaged time, 21–22
    increasing, 19–35
    instructional strategies, 28–30
    instructional time, 21
    managerial strategies, 26–28
    practices for maximizing, 25
    scheduled time, 21
    student self-regulated strategies, 30–32
    transition time, 21
    wait time, 21
academic engagement, 38, 39–40, 41
    formal interventions, 39–40
academic performance
    ADHD, individualized supports, 345
    anxiety and depression and, 352, 357
    competence, 67
    enablers, 67, 213
    failure, 121, 143–155
    focus, 28–29
    improvement rate, 54, 60, 61, 62, 63
    interventions, effective, 129–141
    learning time, 20
    profile, updated, 192
    students with learning disabilities, preparation, 188–189
    study skills, 68
    universal interventions, 340–341
    website, 56
academic press, social support and, 47–48

accountability, 84
activities, 46
ADHD. *See* attention deficit hyperactivity disorder
adults, interacting with students, 276–277
advocacy
    gifted students, 168–169
    students with disabilities, 183, 188, 408–409
affect
    positive psychology, 202–203
    study skills, 74
affective engagement, 38, 44, 47–48
    formal interventions, 48
    strategies to promote, 41
after-school interventions, 92–93
alliteration, 98
alphabetic principle, 98–99
Americans with Disabilities Act (ADA), 174, 190
AmeriCorps, 416–417, 423
anxiety
    academic performance and, 350–351, 352
    assessment, 353–354
    behavioral component, 372
    case example, 359–361
    causes, 350, 352
    characteristics, 349–350
    consultation, 357–358
    development and, 350, 353, 358–359
    hierarchy, 355
    intervention, 354–357
      effectiveness and outcomes, 359
    multicultural competencies, 359
    parents and, 358
    prevalence, 350
    prevention, 358
    school-based interventions, 349–363
    social development and, 351, 352–353

special education and, 361
tests and, 74
Appropriate Academic Supports to Meet the Needs of All Students, NASP and, 144
assessment
    academic engaged time, 25
    ADHD, 334, 346
    anxiety and depression, 353–354
    gifted students, 165
    group counseling, ongoing, 316
    ongoing, 340
    school refusal, 369–370
    social skills, 215
    students with disabilities, 178–179, 180
    timed, 134
Association on Higher Education and Disability (AHEAD), 191
attendance, behavior engagement and, 40–41
attention deficit hyperactivity disorder (ADHD), 335–336
    assessment, 334, 346
    collaboration and consultation, 336–337
    cultural factors, 337
    executive skills, 283
    interventions, 279, 334, 338
attention problems
    conceptual underpinnings, 337–338
    interventions, 335–347
    primary prevention, 339–341
    secondary prevention, 341–343
    teacher-mediated strategies, 338–339
    tertiary intervention, 343–346
attitudes, intergroup, 219
authoritative discipline, 254–255, 262–263
authoritative teaching style, engaged time and, 27–28
automaticity, 116
autonomy, student, 79

B

Baumrind, Diana, 254
Beck Youth Inventories II, 354
Beginning Teacher Evaluation Study, 20
behavior
    challenging, special education and, 321–322
    effect on others, 264
    indicators, collecting and disaggregating data, 324
    reductive techniques, 259
    social skills and, 216
Behavior Education Program, 45
behavioral engagement, 38, 40–45

formal interventions, 44–45
    strategies, 42
behavior problems
    crisis intervention, 386–389
    mild, 260
    moderate, 261–262
    restraint and seclusion, 385, 386–389
    retention and, 145
    serious or chronic, 263
behavior rating scales
    anxiety and depression, 354
    executive skills, 273–274
behavior supports
    culturally responsive, 321–334
    individualized, 344
    tiered-level supports, 321–334
    token reinforcement and response cost, 344
belonging and bonding with school, 47
benchmarks, minimal expected performance, 54, 57
Bilingual Verbal Ability Test-Normative Update, 162
blending, 98
Building Hope for the Future, 209

C

Caring School Community, 245
Carl D. Perkins Career and Technical Education Act, 174
Carl D. Perkins Vocational and Applied Technology Education Act, 174
Carroll's model of school learning, 20
CBM. *See* curriculum-based measurement
challenge, level of, 130–132
CHAMPS (conversation, help, activity, movement, participation, and success), 245
changes
    facilitating, 288–289
    small, 290
character, 204–205
    positive psychology, 204–205
character education
    restraint and seclusion, 384
    self-discipline, 256
Check & Connect, 45, 246–247
child-rearing patterns, executive skills and, 279
Children's Manifest Anxiety Scale–Second Edition, 354
classroom
    academic engaged time, 26–28
    arrangement, 26
    climate, 256
    discipline problems, prevention of, 257–258

engaged time, 26
evidence-based techniques, 257
executive skills, 274
flipped, 90
management, 257
pedagogy, core components, 10
routines and procedures, 339
see also discipline
client factors, interviewing, 288–289
clinical interventions, school refusal, 374–375
coaching, executive skills, 275, 283
cognition
    inflexibility, 274
    learning strategies, 30–31
    oral reading fluency, 116
cognitive assessment, gifted students, 161
cognitive–behavioral interventions
    anxiety and depression, 356–357
    school refusal, 372–373
cognitive engagement, 38, 45–47
    formal interventions, 47
    strategies to promote, 43
collaboration
    discipline, 265
    executive skills, 284
    interviewing, 291
    multicultural considerations, 79
    medical professionals, 390
    restraint and seclusion, 384, 390
    teachers, 10
Collaborative for Academic, Social, and Emotional
    Learning (CASEL), 256
college, students with learning disabilities, 188, 190,
    193
community
    development, 423
    service, 416
computer-assisted instruction, ADHD, 345–346
Concept-Oriented Reading Instruction, 47
confidentiality, group counseling, 314
consultation
    administrators, 168
    anxiety and depression, 357–358
    executive skill, 275
    gifted students, 168
    teachers, 168
    transitioning students, 194
contingency management
    homework, 94
    school refusal, 373
cooperation, change and, 289–290

cooperative learning, social skills, 220
Corporation for National and Community Service
    Strategic Plan, 417
counseling, individual, 247–248
    college-supported, students with learning disabil-
      ities, 193
    see also group counseling
creativity tests, gifted students, 162
credits, monitoring, 40
crisis intervention and prevention, restraint and
    seclusion, 384, 385
    hierarchy of least to most restrictive strategies, 388
    team approach, 386–387
    training, 386
critical behavior event, 400
cross-ethnic interactions, social skills, 220
cross-gender interactions, social skills, 220
cultural factors
    attention, 337
    background, 324–327
    case example, 326–327
    resilience, 233–234
    restraint and seclusion, 392
    social skills, 217, 219
    social support, 244
culturally responsive practices, manifestation determi-
    nations, 405
curriculum-based measurement (CBM)
    oral reading fluency, 116–117
    progress monitoring, 52, 139

D

data-based decision making and accountability, 51
debriefing, restraint and seclusion, 389–390
decision-making model, students with disabilities, 174
defiance and disruptive behavior, 257
demandingness, 254, 262
depression
    academic performance and, 352
    assessment, 353–354
    case example, 359–361
    causes, 352
    characteristics, 351
    consultation, 357–358
    development, 351–352, 353, 358–359
    effectiveness and outcomes, 359
    intervention, 354–357
    multicultural competencies, 359
    parents and, 358
    prevalence, 351–352

prevention, 358
school-based interventions, 349–363
school refusal, 375
social development and, 352–353
special education and, 361
development
academic interventions, 138–139
anxiety and depression, 351–352, 353, 358–359
discipline, 253
executive skills, 270–271, 283
gifted students, 164–165
interviewing, 302–303
manifestation determinations, 405
positive psychology, 201
social support, 243
differentiated instruction, 14–15
dignity, student's, restraint and seclusion, 388–389
directions, comprehension, 70–71
disabilities coordinator, students with learning disabilities, 193
disability, legitimate, 321
discipline
authoritative, 254–255, 262–263
classroom, 251–267
components, 255
educational opportunities, 263
evidence-based strategies and techniques, 253
flowchart, 401
gap, 254
manifestation determinations, 408–409
multitiered system, 254
preventive strategies, 254, 257–258
purposes, 265
referrals, 254, 257
removals, 408–409
disparity, discipline referrals, 254
disproportionality, responding to, 322–323
disruptive behaviors, 407
diversity
gifted students, 161–162
positive psychology, 201
resilience, 233–234
social skills, 217
documenting, restraint and seclusion, 390
dropping out, 154
retention and, 146, 147–148, 154
students at risk, 48–49
student engagement and, 38–39
Dynamic Indicators of Basic Early Literacy Skills (DIBELS), 54, 56, 57, 62, 63

E

early intervention, 324–327
case example, 326–327
early warning systems, engagement, 48–49
Education for All Handicapped Children Act of 1975, 158
Edward M. Kennedy Serve America Act of 2009, 416–417
elementary level, retention, 145–146
Elkonin boxes, 104–105
emotion coach, 263
emotional intelligence, 256
employment skills, students with disabilities, 178
engagement, 37, 67
engagement-based interventions, 49
environmental factors, 297
culturally responsive, 325
executive skills, 276–277
errors, 133–134
ethics
group counseling, 307
manifestation determinations, 409
restraint and seclusion, checklist, 395
ethnic minorities
retention, 143
social skills, 219
evaluation
anxiety and depression intervention, 359
gifted students, 169
group counseling, 317
evidence-based practices
discipline, 259
reading, 15–16, 102–110
Tier 1, 102–104
Tier 2 and 3, 104–110
excellence gaps, 169
executive skills, 269–285
assessment, 273–275
case examples, 280–281
cultural considerations, 279–280
defined, 269–270, 271, 272
development, 283
interventions, 275–280, 283–284
multitiered model, 281
observation, direct, 274
role, 270, 275
school performance, 271
systems-level models, 281–283
teaching, 277
expectations

discipline, 253
engaged time, 26–27
exposure
anxiety and depression, 355–356
imagined and assisted, 371–372
expulsion, 251, 408
extracurricular participation, 42–43

F

facilitators, group counseling, 308–310
coleaders, 309–310
qualifications, 309
failures, monitoring, 40
family
gifted students, 168
school refusal, 368
family–school collaboration, positive psychology and,
199
feedback, 132, 135–136
interviewing, 292–296
performance, 29, 123–124
firmness and fairness, 263–264
flashcards, 134
flow, positive psychology, 206–207
formative assessment, reading, 12–13
functional assessment
attention problems, 344–345
students with disabilities, 179
functional discrepancy, 194
functional process, transition, students with learning
disabilities, 186
future-oriented thinking, facilitating, 46–47

G

gender, social skills and, 217, 219
generalization
facilitators, 222–223
social skills, 222–223
gifted students
achievement tests, 162
advocacy and research, 168–169
case study, 166–167
characteristics, 162–163
conceptualizations, 158
consulting with administrators and teachers, 168
educational services, 164–166
evaluating services, 169
identification and assessment, 161, 164
methods to support, 160

national initiatives and legislation, 158–159
nonverbal assessment, 161–162
portfolios, 163
professional knowledge, 168
psychosocial development, 167–168
services for, 157–171
goal setting, 63, 64, 298–299
academic areas, 63
competency-based models, 55–56
conceptual frameworks, 55
decision rules, group level, 56–58
future goals linked with past goals, 209
group level, 53, 56–58
individual levels, 53–54, 58–61
local vs national data, 55
normative approach, 55
progress monitoring, 53–55
student, 31–32
at grade level, 61–63
below grade level, 58–59
Good Behavior Game, 44–45
grade level, executive skills, 282
grade point averages, 204
Grade Retention and Social Promotion, NASP and,
144
gratitude, positive psychology, 205–206
group counseling, 305–319
ethics, 307
evaluation, 317
evidence-based programs, 312
group development, 307–308
group logistics and implementation, 308–314
multicultural and diversity considerations, 307
multitiered model of intervention, 306–307
needs assessment, 308
participant selection, 310–311
precounseling assessment, 314
progress monitoring, 316
scheduling, 311, 313
school setting, 306
strategies, 314–315, 315–316
structure, 314
supplies and space, 313–314
theoretical orientation, 316
Tier 1, 306
Tier 2, 306–307
Tier 3, 307
troubleshooting, 316–317
see also counseling
groups
flexible, 14

nature of, 306
size, 310
small learning groups, engaged time, 27

H

happiness, 202
helping process, interviewing, 291
helping relationship
    factors of change, 288
    interviewing, 291–292
high school
    reform, student engagement, 39
    students with learning disabilities, 188
        transcripts, 193
higher education trend, students with learning
    disabilities, 186–187
home–school collaboration
    executive skills, 282–283
    individualized supports, 346
    manifestation determinations, 405–406
home support, 79
homework
    academic engaged time, 32
    accommodations, 93
    amount, 85, 86
    anti-homework movement, 84
    completion, 40
    developmental differences, 85–86
    group contingencies, 94
    history, 84
    incentives, 93–94
    lower grades, 95
    management, 83–96
    negative effects, 88
    noncompliance, 89, 94–95
    noninstructional implications, 85, 87
    parents and, 87, 91–92
    parent–teacher communication, 93
    positive effects, 87, 88
    practice, 85, 87
    purpose, 85, 86
    special education and, 86, 88–89
    value of, 95
hope
    interviewing, 289
    positive psychology, 209–210
Human Rights Committee, establishment, example, 391
Hunter, Phyllis C., 9

I

"I do, We do, You do" format, 15
IDEA. *See* Individuals with Disabilities Education Act
IDEIA. *See* Individuals with Disabilities Education Improvement Act
IEP. *See* Individualized Education Program
incentives, 126
incremental rehearsal, 134
Individual Transition Plans, 425
Individualized Education Program (IEP)
    anxiety and depression, 362
    discipline, 253
    gifted students, 166
    implementation, 403
    retention and, 144
    stages, 178
    students with disabilities, 178, 181
individualized intervention, 407
Individuals with Disabilities Education Act (IDEA)
    anxiety and depression, 361
    discipline, 253, 192
    manifestation determinations, 399–400, 402, 403
    reading and, 10
    transition from school to work, 174
Individuals with Disabilities Education Improvement Act (IDEIA)
    restraint and seclusion, 381
    students with disabilities, 180, 181
induction, 264–265
informed consent, group counseling, 311
inservice training
    executive skills, 275
    retention, 153
institutional expectations, students with learning disabilities, 193–194
instruction
    attention problems, 341–342
    content, 125
    design, 29–30
    differentiated, 29
    dosage, 13–14
    explicit, 130, 132, 133
    gifted students, 166
    guided, 75
    hierarchy, 132
    level, 130–132, 133–134
    pace, 30
    retention, 153
    time analysis, 35
    time checklist, 35

intensive interventions and expanded services,
329–332
case study, 332
culturally responsive, 330
interest surveys
gifted students, 163
students with disabilities, 179
intergroup interactions, 219
social skills, 220
internalization, 255
interspersal procedures, 107
interventions, 324
ADHD, assessment data and, 346
after-school, 92–93
anxiety and depression, 354–357
attention problems, 339, 343–346
behavioral concerns, serious, 327–329
case study, 329
components, 139
design, 275–276
checklist, 278
early, 324–327
evaluation, 79–80, 140, 376
exceptions to the problem, 300–301
executive skills, 275
school psychologists' role, 275
formal, 40
group counseling, 308
individualized, case example, 79
mathematics, 137–138
multicultural competencies, 139
preventive interventions, systemic, 376
reading, 136–137
research support for, 277–279
school refusal, 370, 371, 375–376
skill-by-treatment interaction, 129–141
examples, 136–138
students' natural resources, 301–302
targeted, 135
manifestation determinations, 406–407
study skills, 69
team, 370, 371
Interventions and Mental Health Services to Develop
Social and Life Skills, 252
interviews
anxiety and depression, 353–354
assumptions, 289–290
change, facilitating, 288–289
collaboration, 291–296
developmental factors, 302–303
executive skills, 273

goals, 298–300
interventions, 300–302
model/technique factors, 289
setting, 291
solution-focused, 296–297
student-driven, 287–304
student interview questions, 77
students with disabilities, 180
tasks and strategies, 290, 303
IQ, gifted students, 161

K

Keeping All Students Safe Act, 381
kindergarten
delayed entry, 154
retention, 145–146

L

language, 290
restraint and seclusion, 392
students', 299–300
law-related approach, 264–265
Learn and Serve America, 417
learning
inventories, 78
structure and support for, 28–29
time, 32–33
learning disability. *See* students with learning
disabilities
lecture, 264–265
legislation
gifted education, 158–159
students with disabilities, 173–174
see also particular Act
letter–sound associations, 98
literacy components, oral reading fluency, 118
lonely student, positive affect and, positive psychology,
210

M

manifestation determinations, 399–413
case study, 410–411
conducting, 402–403
culturally and developmentally responsive practices, 405
defined, 399
disciplinary removals, 408–409
ethics, 409

flowchart, 401
home–school collaboration, 405–406
IDEA requirement, 400–402
limitations, 409–410
political contexts, 407–408
preventive orientation, 403–404
professional development, 406
students with disabilities, 408–409
systems-level initiatives, 406–407
manipulation, 98
manualized treatment
anxiety and depression, 356–357
group counseling, 310
mastery goal orientation, 46
mathematics
developmental differences, 138–139
effective intervention, example, 137–138
meta-analyses, 131
medical model, limitations, 409–410
medical professionals, restraint and seclusion, 390
medications, school refusal, 375
memory, 73, 130
mental health, 287
needs, 317–318
problems, incidence, 305
meta-analyses, 130, 131
minimal sufficiency, 264
misbehavior, 41–42
consequences, 265
contributing factors, 264
correcting, 258–265
preventing, 410
miscommunications, 219
Model for Comprehensive and Integrated School Psychological Services
academic skill improvement, 51
discipline, 251
executive skills, 270
manifestation determinations, 399
mental health, 305
positive psychology, 199
restraint and seclusion, 382
retention, 144
social skills, 213
study skills, 67
monitoring
behavioral challenges, 324, 328
social skills, 222
student-based, 75
mood disorders, causes of, 352
motivation, study skills, 74

multicultural competencies/considerations
anxiety and depression, 359
gifted students, 166
group counseling, 307
skill-by-treatment interaction, 139
study skills, 79
Multidimensional Anxiety Scale for Children-Second Edition, 354
multidimensional personality inventories, 354
multiple intervention packages, social skills, 217
multitiered systems
attention problems, 346
case example, 75, 78
executive skills, 281, 282
group counseling, 306–307
social support, 243
study skills, 75, 78–79

N

Naglieri Nonverbal Ability Test 2, 162
NASP Advocacy Roadmap, 153
A Nation at Risk, 269
Nation's Report Card, 9
National Association for Gifted Children, 158–159
National Center on Response to Intervention (NCRTI), 52
National Civilian Community Corps, 417
National Education Commission on Time and Learning, 19
national service
entities, 417
transition option, 423–424
National Service Inclusion Project (NSIP), 424
negative reinforcement
classroom discipline, 258, 259
school refusal, 373–374
No Child Left Behind (NCLB)
executive skills, 269
gifted children, 158
reading and, 10, 15
restraint and seclusion, 381
retention and, 143
school to work for students with disabilities, 174
nonverbal cues, 27
note taking, 71

O

optimism
consultation with teachers, 208–209

formal school-based curriculum, 207–208
positive psychology, 207–209
oral reading fluency. *See* reading
organizational skills
ADHD, 279
development, 92
study skills, 69–70
organizers, graphic, 109
out-of-school time, 43–44
outcomes
anxiety and depression, 359
behavioral challenges, 325–326
engagement and, 49
positive psychology, 201–202
student engagement, 39

P

paired peer practice, 134
paragraph shrinking, 108–109
parents
anxiety and depression, 358
attention problems, 341
educating, 343
gifted students, 162–163
homework, 87
restraint and seclusion, notifying, 390
students with disabilities, 183
parent–teacher communication, homework, 93
PARR (preparation, action, reflection, and recognition) model, 419, 420, 421, 424
participation in learning, engaged time, 28
passage previewing, 125
Patient Protection and Affordable Care Act (ACA), 177–178
peer relationships, difficulties in, 213
peer-tutoring, oral reading fluency, 118
Penn Resiliency Program, 207–208
perceptions, students', 299–300
PERMA model, 202
personal development, 422
phobia, school refusal, 375
phoneme awareness, 97–98, 118–119
phonics, 118–119
phrase drill error correction, 124
political contexts, manifestation determinations, 407–408
positive behavioral interventions and supports (PBIS), 45
restraint and seclusion, 384
positive psychology, 290

age and developmental levels, 201, 209, 211
applying in schools, 199–212
character strengths, 204–205
criticism, 200
diverse populations, 201
examples, 203–204
flow, 206–207
gratitude, 205–206
history, 200
hope, 209–210
implications for schools, 201
lonely student, positive affect and, 210
optimism, 207–209
orientation, 200
outcomes, 201–202
positive affect and resiliency, 202–203
self-discipline, 256
strengths, 203–204
student engagement, 206–207
troubled youth, 210
positive reinforcement
discipline, 258, 259
school refusal, 374
possibilities, focus, 290
praise, 257–258
prevention, 324
anxiety and depression, 358
attention problems
primary, 339–341
secondary, 341–343
discipline, 254, 257–258
barriers, 253
manifestation determinations, 403–404
prevention, universal level, 339–341
restraint and seclusion, 384–386
school refusal, 376
universal, 358
previewing, 71
problems
changeable, 296–297
discussion, 296
influence, 297
problem solving
anxiety and depression, 356
culturally responsive, 326, 328–329, 331
discipline, 260
restraint and seclusion, 384–385
process–outcome research, 20
professionals
gifted students, 168
learning disabilities, 194

manifestation determinations, 406
professors, students with learning disabilities, 193
programming for behavior, culturally responsive,
    327–328
progress monitoring
    academic skill improvement, goal-setting processes,
        51–66
        CBM, 52
        group level, 56–58
        individual student level, 58–61
        other academic areas, 63
        student enrolled at grade level, 61–62
        tool charts, 52
        types and applications, 52–53
    attention problems, 340
    group counseling, 316
    manifestation determinations, 407
    restraint and seclusion, 390–391
    social skills, 222
    subskill mastery measurement, 52–53
    system-wide approaches, 51
Project Impact, 425
    case study, 421–423
    replication, 423
prompting function, 279
prosocial behavior, interventions to increase, 339–340
    strategies, 342–343
prosody, 115–116
protective assets
    discipline, 253
    resilience, 227, 228–229
psychoeducation, school refusal, 370
psychosocial development, gifted students, 167–168
punishment, 258, 259, 264
    corporal, 251
    limitations, 259
    spanking, 251, 254
    see also discipline

Q

questioning
    generation, 109
    techniques, 28

R

rating scale
    child outcome, 293
    gifted behavior, 163
    interviews, 292–294
    children, 295
    social skills, 215
reading
    acquisition phase, 103
    comprehension, 71–72, 100
    critical skills, 100–102
    demonstration, 103
    difficulty, incidence, 9, 16
    general education
        differentiated instruction, 14–15
        early reading, 11
        instructional dosage, 13–14
        EBI strategies, 15–16
        instructional strategies, 9–17
        secondary reading, 11–12
        formative assessment, multitiered model, 12–13
    generalization, 104
    guided practice, 103
    independent practice with feedback, 103
    instruction, Tier 1, 102–103
    meta-analyses, 131
    oral fluency, 99, 103–104, 115–128
        educators' view, 116
        instructional target, 126
        interventions, 121–126
        it is too hard, 126
        prerequisite skills, 118–119
        target for instruction, 116–117
        texts for, 119–120
        they don't want to do it, 123–124
        they have not had enough help to do it, 124–125
        they have not had to do it that way before,
         125–126
        they have not spent enough time doing it, 124
        treatment ingredients, 120–121
    patterns, 126
    problems
        critical reading skills, 97–100
        developmental differences, 138–139
        example, 136–137
        incidence, 97
        interventions, 97–113
        multitiered service delivery, 100–102
        Tier 1 strategies, 102–104
        Tier 2 and 3, 104–110
    repeated readings, 107–108
Reading Mastery, 120
referrals
    discipline, 254, 257
    reading problems, 110
    study skills, 67

Rehabilitation Act of 1973, 190
relationships
    interviewing, 289
    social skills, 220–221
    supportive, 247
    testing, 402–403
relaxation training, school refusal, 370–371
removal, 400
repeated readings, 125
replacement techniques, 259
research-based instructional strategies, 15
resilience, 225–237
    defined, 226
    evaluation of services, 234–235
    positive psychology, 202–203
    protective factors, 227, 228–229
    risk factors, 226–228
    student engagement and, 39
    Tier 1–3, 230–233
responding
    active, 28
    opportunities, 132, 134
response to intervention (RTI)
    components, 51–52
    decision-making frameworks, 129
    gifted students, 163–164
    homework, 89, 90, 91–95
    learning disability, 191
    progress monitoring, 51, 139
    Tier 1, 89, 90–92
    Tier 2, 92–94
    Tier 3, 94–95
responsibility
    acceptance, 265
    challenging avoidance, 265
responsiveness, 254, 257, 262
restraint
    additional considerations, 392
    appropriate use, 381–397
    behavioral crisis intervention, 386–389, 395, 396–397
    current issues, 382–383
    defined, 382
    determining when to use, 387
    ethical decision making and humane treatment, checklist, 395
    postvention, 389–391
    prevention, 384–386
    procedural safeguards, 387–388
    school policy checklist, 394
    self-assessment checklist, NASP domains, 396–397

retention, 143–155
    benefits, 148, 154
    case studies, 149–152
    cost, 153
    defined, 143, 145
    effects, 146
    efficacy, 144, 145
    incidence, 143
    individual decisions, 149–152
    kindergarten and elementary level, 145–146
    policies, 144–145
    programmatic interventions, 152–153
    school district/system level, 152, 154
    secondary level, 147–148
    special education and, 148–149
    state education agencies, 153
    studies, 146–147
    systemic solutions, 149
rewards, 257–258
Rey Osterrieth Complex Figure, 274
Reynolds Adolescent Depression Scale–Second Edition, 354
Reynolds Child Depression Scale–Second Edition, 354
rights, students'
    learning disabilities, 193
    restraint and seclusion, 388–389
risk factors
    discipline, 253
    resilience, 226–228
routines, engaged time and, 26–27
RTI. *See* response to intervention

S

Sanford Harmony Program, 221–222
school climate, discipline, 253, 256
school district/system
    executive skills, 281–282
    retention, 152
school policy
    restraint and seclusion, 385–386
        checklist, 394
school psychologists' role
    group counseling, 305
    manifestation determination, 404
    outsiders and insiders, 10
    skill-by-treatment interaction, 129
    students with learning disabilities, 195, 287
school refusal, 210, 368
    anxiety-based, 365–379
    assessment, 369–370

case example, 376–377
clinical interventions
    anxiety-related school refusal, 370–373
    internalizing disorders, 374–375
cognitive–behavioral strategies, 377
etiology, 367
family, 368
functions, 367–368
incidence, 377
interventions
    effectiveness, 376
    manualized, 377
    multicomponent, 373–374
    pharmacological, 375–376
    preventive, 376
    psychopharmacological, 377
    systemic preventive, 376
    team, 370
prevalence, 366
primary functions, 377
school setting, 368
student, 368
symptoms, 366–367
school setting
    attention problems, 338
    school refusal, 368
school–service partnerships, 419–420
    state coordinators, 420
school site mentor, 176
School-to-Work Opportunity Act, 174
school-to-work transition, students with disabilities,
        415–426
school-wide positive behavior interventions and sup-
        ports approach (SWPBIS), 252, 254, 258
screening, 328
    behavior, 325–326
seclusion
    additional considerations, 392
    appropriate use, 381–397
    behavioral crisis intervention, 386–389, 395,
        396–397
    current issues, 382–383
    defined, 382
    determining when to use, 387
    ethical decision making and humane treatment,
        checklist, 395
    postvention, 389–391
    prevention, 384–386
    procedural safeguards, 387–388
    school policy checklist, 394
    self-assessment checklist, NASP domains, 396–397

secondary level
    retention, 147–148
    students with learning disabilities, 190
    teachers, reading and, 11–12
segmenting, 98
segregation, social skills, 220
SEL. *See* social and emotional learning
self-advocacy
    students with disabilities, 183
    students with learning disabilities, 193, 194–195
self-assessment, NASP domains, restraint and seclusion,
        checklist, 396–397
self-awareness, 256
self-checking behaviors, 31
self-correcting techniques, 31
self-determination
    students with disabilities, 179
    students with learning disabilities, 194–195
self-discipline, 252, 253, 257, 258, 265
self-disclose, students with learning disabilities, 193
self-efficacy, 46, 68
self-evaluation system, ADHD, 345
self-instruction, 74
self-management
    academic engaged time, 31
    attention problems, 345
    study skills, 73
self-monitoring
    academic engaged time, 31, 32
    reading, 109–110
    study skills, 73–74
self-questioning, 31, 74
self-reflection, 74
self-regulation
    engaged time and, 30–32
    inventories, 78
    learning strategies, 45–46, 47
    multicultural considerations, 79
    parents, 204
    reading, 72
    study skills, 75
Self-Regulation Empowerment Program, 47
self-report, anxiety and depression, 354
Semantic Mapping and Semantic Feature Analysis,
        73
seminars, executive skill, 275
Senior Corps, 416–417
separation anxiety disorder, school refusal, 375
service
    delivery level, attention problems, 338
    transition, 423

service learning
    conceptual model, 417–418
    critical elements, 418–419
    defined, 416
    guideposts to success, 421
    PARR model, 419, 420
    school and service partnerships, 419–420
    school-to-work transition, students with
        disabilities, 415–426
    state coordinators, 420
    transition planning, 419
    universal design, 419, 420
setting
    group counseling, 308
    students with learning disabilities, 187–188
skill-by-treatment interaction, 129–141
skills
    school refusal, 373
    targeted, 132, 134–135
social and academic functioning, anxiety and depression, 361–362
social and emotional learning (SEL)
    applying, 256
    discipline, 252, 254
    self-discipline, 256
    skills, 256
social anxiety disorder, school refusal, 375
social development and, anxiety and depression, 352–353
social–emotional functioning
    competencies, 256
    discipline and, 252–253
    restraint and seclusion, 384
social promotion, 143
social skills
    anxiety and depression, 355
    assessment, 215–216
    challenges, 222–223
    cultural and gender considerations, 217, 218–221
    evidence-based program, 218
    features, 213–214
    learning, 214, 217
    program components, 216
    self-segregation, 220
    teaching and supporting, 216–217
    training, 213–224
    top 10, 214
social support
    academic press and, 47–48
    assessing and promoting, 239–249
    assessment, 241–244
    models and theories, 239–240

    outcomes, 240–241
    promotion, 244–248
    rating scales, 242
social validity, 216
solution attempts, 297
sound and letter boxes, 104–105
spanking, 251, 254
special education
    anxiety and depression and, 361
    executive skills, 283
    homework and, 86, 88–89
    referring to, 331
    retention and, 148–149
state education agencies, retention, 153
state law
    gifted domains, 159
    restraint and seclusion in schools, 382
stimulus-preference assessment, 123
Strong Start/Strong Kids/Strong Teens, 245–246
student engagement, 37–50
    defined, 37
    positive psychology, 206–207
    subtypes, 38–39
student/parent involvement, students with disabilities, 181–182
student-regulated approach, 31–32
students
    achievement, 9, 67
    at risk, 48
    concerns, 296
    engaged time, 30–32
    executive skill, 275, 276
    learning disabilities, 187
    motivation, 29–30, 67
    perceptions, 48
    population, monitoring, 48
    school refusal, 368
    strengths and resources, 290
students with disabilities
    behavior, 321
    discipline, 399–400, 410
    expulsions, 399–400
    manifestation determinations, 408–409
    restraint and seclusion, 392
    school-linked services, 177–178
    school-to-work transition, 173–184, 415–426
        assessment, 178–179, 180
        barriers to services, 182
        case study, 182–183
        decision-making model, 174
        functional assessment, 179

IEP, 178
  interest surveys, 179
  interviews, 180
  legislation, 173–174
  planning, 187, 188, 192, 195
  school-linked services, 177–178
  self-determination, 179
  student/parent involvement, 181–182
  three-tier model, 174–175
  transition coordinator, 176–177
  transition IEP meeting, 180
  vocational evaluations, 179
  vocational personality types, 179
 strengths, 203
students with learning disabilities, transition to college,
    195–196
  academic preparation, 188–189
  adult status, 193
  disclosing, 191–192
  documentation, 190–191
  effective, 192–194
  example, 185–186
  planning, 187, 188
  qualifying for services in college, 190
  secondary preparation, 190
  setting focus, 187–188
  student advocacy, 188
  student focus, 187
  Tier 1, 189
  Tier 2, 189
  Tier 3, 189–190
  transition responsibilities, 194–195
study
  guides, 72–73
  skills, 67–81
    academic goals and, 68
    assessment, 74–75, 76, 77, 78
    autonomous, 68
    checklist, 76
    instruction in, 80
    modeling, 75
    multicultural considerations, 79
    multitiered systems, application to, 75, 78–79
    school psychologists' effectiveness, 79–80
    strategies, 69–74
    tiered supports, 78–79
  strategies, 30–31, 68–69, 78–79, 340–341
summer courses, students with learning disabilities, 193
supportive systems and services, 256–257
suspension, 251, 408

SWPBIS. *See* school-wide positive behavior interven-
    tions and supports approach
systemic solutions, retention, 149, 154
systems level
  executive skills, 276, 281–283
  manifestation determinations, 406–407
  positive psychology, 199

T

targets, 53
  behavior, time and space, 337
tasks
  modifying, 276
  directions, explicit, 29
  interest/value, 68
teachers/teaching
  attention, 29
  attention problems, 338, 339–340
  gifted students, 168
    nomination, 163
  intervention agent, 338
  methods, 30
teacher–student relationships, 257
teams, students with learning disabilities, 192
temperament, 279
tests, executive skills, 274–275
test taking, 72–73, 75
text, summarizing, 108–109
three-tier model, students with disabilities, 174–175
Tier 1
  academic and behavior support, 25
  behavioral challenges, 324–327
  questions and interventions, 326
  resilience, 230–231
  social support, 244–245
  students with learning disabilities, 189
Tier 2
  behavioral challenges, 327–329
  guiding questions, 329
  resilience, 231–232
  students with learning disabilities, 189
Tier 2 and 3
  academic engaged time and, 25
  social support, 246–248
Tier 3
  behavioral challenges, 329–332
  guiding questions, 331
  resilience, 232–233
  students with learning disabilities, 189–190
tiered-level supports, 321–334

time use
    analysis, 22–23
    confrontation and social problem solving, 264
    delay procedures, 105–106
    group analysis, 22–23
    individual classroom analysis, 23
    learning, 32
    limit, 27
    making the most of available time, 39–40
    see also academic engaged time; instructional time
To Aid Gifted and High-Ability Learners by
        Empowering the Nation's Teachers (TALENT
        Act), 159
transition coordinator, 175–176, 177
    students with disabilities, 176–177
transition, school-to-college, students with learning
        disabilities, 195–196
    academic preparation, 188–189
    effective, 192–194
    example, 185–186
    planning, 187
    qualifying for services in college, 190
    responsibilities, 194–195
    secondary preparation, 190
    setting focus, 187–188
    student advocacy, 188
    Tier 1, 189
    Tier 2, 189
    Tier 3, 189–190
transition, school to work, students with disabilities,
        173–184
    barriers, 182
        case study, 182–183
    IEP meeting, 180–181
        notification for, 180
        students with disabilities, 180
    students with learning disabilities 173, 175, 176,
            182, 194–195, 415–416, 419
        case study, 182–183
    planning 173, 175, 176, 415–416, 419
    services, 175
    team program, 177

transitions
    attention problems, 340
    engaged time and, 27
    support, 48
treatment barriers, counseling, 318
troubled youth, positive psychology, 210
troubleshooting, group counseling, 316–317
tutoring
    homework management, 92
    students with learning disabilities, 192

U

universal design, 419, 420
Universal Design for Learning, 417
universal programming, culturally responsive, 325

V

value of school, student beliefs, 47
verbal cues, 27
verbal de-escalation, restraint and seclusion, 384
vocabulary, 99–100
    development, 422–423
vocational evaluations, students with disabilities, 179
vocational personality types, students with disabilities,
        179

W

warm demander approach, 27
well-being, 202, 211
What Works Transition Research Synthesis Project,
        175
words, recorded, 106–107
writing
    developmental differences, 138–139
    meta-analyses, 131

Z

zero tolerance approach, 251

Best Practices in School Psychology: Series List

Best Practices in School Psychology: Data-Based and Collaborative Decision Making

INTRODUCTION AND FRAMEWORK

1. The National Association of School Psychologists Model for Comprehensive and Integrated School Psychological Services
   Rhonda J. Armistead and Diane L. Smallwood
2. Problem-Solving Foundations for School Psychological Services
   Kathy Pluymert
3. A Comprehensive Framework for Multitiered Systems of Support in School Psychology
   Karen Callan Stoiber
4. The Evolution of School Psychology: Origins, Contemporary Status, and Future Directions
   James E. Ysseldyke and Daniel J. Reschly

DATA-BASED DECISION MAKING AND ACCOUNTABILITY

5. Best Practices in Problem Analysis
   Theodore J. Christ and Yvette Anne Arañas
6. Best Practices in Data-Analysis Teaming
   Joseph F. Kovaleski and Jason A. Pedersen
7. Best Practices in Universal Screening
   Craig A. Albers and Ryan J. Kettler
8. Best Practices in Facilitating and Evaluating the Integrity of School-Based Interventions
   Andrew T. Roach, Kerry Lawton, and Stephen N. Elliott
9. Best Practices in Diagnosis of Mental Health and Academic Difficulties in a Multitier Problem-Solving Approach
   Frank M. Gresham
10. Best Practices in Curriculum-Based Evaluation
    Kenneth W. Howell and John L. Hosp

11. Best Practices in Curriculum-Based Evaluation in Early Reading
    Michelle K. Hosp and Kristen L. MacConnell
12. Best Practices in Written Language Assessment and Intervention
    Christine Kerres Malecki
13. Best Practices in Instructional Assessment of Writing
    Todd A. Gravois and Deborah Nelson
14. Best Practices in Mathematics Assessment and Intervention With Elementary Students
    Ben Clarke, Christian T. Doabler, and Nancy J. Nelson
15. Best Practices in Mathematics Instruction and Assessment in Secondary Settings
    Yetunde Zannou, Leanne R. Ketterlin-Geller, and Pooja Shivraj
16. Best Practices in Neuropsychological Assessment and Intervention
    Daniel C. Miller and Denise E. Maricle
17. Best Practices in Play Assessment and Intervention
    Lisa Kelly-Vance and Brigette Oliver Ryalls
18. Best Practices in Conducting Functional Behavioral Assessments
    Mark W. Steege and Michael A. Scheib
19. Best Practices in Rating Scale Assessment of Children's Behavior
    Jonathan M. Campbell and Rachel K. Hammond
20. Best Practices in Can't Do/Won't Do Academic Assessment
    Amanda M. VanDerHeyden
21. Best Practices in Clinical Interviewing Parents, Teachers, and Students
    James J. Mazza
22. Best Practices in Identification of Learning Disabilities
    Robert Lichtenstein
23. Best Practices in the Assessment and Remediation of Communication Disorders
    Melissa A. Bray, Thomas J. Kehle, and Lea A. Theodore
24. Best Practices in Multimethod Assessment of Emotional and Behavioral Disorders
    Stephanie H. McConaughy and David R. Ritter
25. Best Practices in the Assessment of Youth With Attention Deficit Hyperactivity Disorder Within a Multitiered Services Framework
    Renée M. Tobin, W. Joel Schneider, and Steven Landau
26. Best Practices in Early Identification and Services for Children With Autism Spectrum Disorders
    Ilene S. Schwartz and Carol A. Davis
27. Best Practices in Assessment and Intervention of Children With High-Functioning Autism Spectrum Disorders
    Elaine Clark, Keith C. Radley, and Linda Phosaly
28. Best Practices in Writing Assessment Reports
    Robert Walrath, John O. Willis, and Ron Dumont

CONSULTATION AND COLLABORATION

29. Best Practices in School Consultation
    William P. Erchul and Hannah L. Young
30. Best Practices in School-Based Problem-Solving Consultation: Applications in Prevention and Intervention Systems
    Thomas R. Kratochwill, Margaret R. Altschaefl, and Brittany Bice-Urbach
31. Best Practices in Behavioral/Ecological Consultation
    Tammy L. Hughes, Jered B. Kolbert, and Laura M. Crothers
32. Best Practices in School-Based Mental Health/Consultee-Centered Consultation by School Psychologists
    Jonathan Sandoval
33. Best Practices in Instructional Consultation and Instructional Consultation Teams
    Sylvia Rosenfield

34. Best Practices in Facilitating Consultation and Collaboration With Teachers and Administrators
    Robin S. Codding, Lisa M. Hagermoser Sanetti, and Florence D. DiGennaro Reed
35. Best Practices in School Psychologists' Promotion of Effective Collaboration and Communication Among School Professionals
    Tanya L. Eckert, Natalie Russo, and Bridget O. Hier
36. Best Practices as an Internal Consultant in a Multitiered Support System
    Kathy McNamara
37. Best Practices in Implementing School-Based Teams Within a Multitiered System of Support
    Matthew K. Burns, Rebecca Kanive, and Abbey C. Karich
38. Best Practices in Providing Inservices for Teachers and Principals
    Laura M. Crothers, Jered B. Kolbert, and Tammy L. Hughes
39. Best Practices in Establishing Effective Helping Relationships
    Julia E. McGivern, Corey E. Ray-Subramanian, and Elana R. Bernstein

Best Practices in School Psychology: Student-Level Services

INTERVENTIONS AND INSTRUCTIONAL SUPPORT TO DEVELOP ACADEMIC SKILLS

1. Best Practices in Instructional Strategies for Reading in General Education
   Rebecca S. Martinez
2. Best Practices in Increasing Academic Engaged Time
   Maribeth Gettinger and Katherine Miller
3. Best Practices in Fostering Student Engagement
   Amy L. Reschly, James J. Appleton, and Angie Pohl
4. Best Practices in Setting Progress Monitoring Goals for Academic Skill Improvement
   Edward S. Shapiro and Kirra B. Guard
5. Best Practices in Promoting Study Skills
   Robin Codding, Virginia Harvey, and John Hite
6. Best Practices in Homework Management
   Lea A. Theodore, Melissa A. Bray, and Thomas J. Kehle
7. Best Practices on Interventions for Students With Reading Problems
   Laurice M. Joseph
8. Best Practices in Oral Reading Fluency Interventions
   Edward J. Daly III, Maureen A. O'Connor, and Nicholas D. Young
9. Best Practices in Delivering Intensive Academic Interventions With a Skill-by-Treatment Interaction
   Matthew K. Burns, Amanda M. VanDerHeyden, and Anne F. Zaslofsky
10. Preventing Academic Failure and Promoting Alternatives to Retention
    Mary Ann Rafoth and Susan W. Parker
11. Best Practices in Services for Gifted Students
    Rosina M. Gallagher, Linda C. Caterino, and Tiombe Bisa-Kendrick
12. Best Practices in Planning for Effective Transition From School to Work for Students With Disabilities
    Fred Jay Krieg, Sandra S. Stroebel, and Holly Bond Farrell
13. Best Practices in Facilitating Transition to College for Students With Learning Disabilities
    Raymond Witte

INTERVENTIONS AND MENTAL HEALTH SERVICES TO DEVELOP SOCIAL AND LIFE SKILLS

14. Best Practices in Applying Positive Psychology in Schools
    Terry M. Molony, Maureen Hildbold, and Nakeia D. Smith
15. Best Practices in Social Skills Training
    Jennifer R. Frey, Stephen N. Elliott, and Cindy Faith Miller
16. Best Practices in Fostering Student Resilience
    Amity L. Noltemeyer
17. Best Practices in Assessing and Promoting Social Support
    Michelle K. Demaray and Christine K. Malecki
18. Best Practices in Classroom Discipline
    George G. Bear and Maureen A. Manning
19. Best Practices in Assessing and Improving Executive Skills
    Peg Dawson
20. Best Practices in Solution-Focused, Student-Driven Interviews
    John J. Murphy
21. Best Practices in Group Counseling
    Julie C. Herbstrith and Renée M. Tobin
22. Best Practices in Delivering Culturally Responsive, Tiered-Level Supports for Youth With Behavioral Challenges
    Robyn S. Hess, Vanja Pejic, and Katherine Sanchez Castejon
23. Best Practices in Classroom Interventions for Attention Problems
    George J. DuPaul, Gary Stoner, and Mary Jean O'Reilly
24. Best Practices in School-Based Interventions for Anxiety and Depression
    Thomas J. Huberty
25. Best Practices in Interventions for Anxiety-Based School Refusal
    Shannon M. Suldo and Julia Ogg
26. Best Practices in Promoting Appropriate Use of Restraint and Seclusion in Schools
    Brian M. Yankouski and Thomas Massarelli
27. Best Practices in Making Manifestation Determinations
    Robert J. Kubick Jr. and Katherine Bobak Lavik
28. Best Practices in Service Learning for School-to-Work Transition and Inclusion for Students With Disabilities
    Felicia L. Wilczenski, Paula Sotnik, and Laura E. Vanderberg

Best Practices in School Psychology: Systems-Level Services

SCHOOL-WIDE PRACTICES TO PROMOTE LEARNING

1. Best Practices in Systems-Level Change
   Jose M. Castillo and Michael J. Curtis
2. Best Practices in Strategic Planning, Organizational Development, and School Effectiveness
   Howard M. Knoff
3. Best Practices in Implementing Evidence-Based School Interventions
   Susan G. Forman, Audrey R. Lubin, and Alison L. Tripptree

4. Best Practices in Curriculum Alignment
   Bradley C. Niebling and Alexander Kurz
5. Best Practices in Facilitating Professional Development of School Personnel in Delivering Multitiered Services
   Melissa Nantais, Kimberly A. St. Martin, and Aaron C. Barnes
6. Best Practices in Decreasing Dropout and Increasing High School Completion
   Shane R. Jimerson, Amy L. Reschly, and Robyn S. Hess
7. Best Practices in Focused Monitoring of Special Education Results
   W. Alan Coulter
8. Best Practices in Supporting the Education of Students With Severe and Low Incidence Disabilities
   Franci Crepeau-Hobson
9. Best Practices for Working in and for Charter Schools
   Caven S. Mcloughlin

PREVENTIVE AND RESPONSIVE SERVICES

10. Best Practices in Developing Prevention Strategies for School Psychology Practice
    William Strein, Megan Kuhn-McKearin, and Meghan Finney
11. Best Practices in Population-Based School Mental Health Services
    Beth Doll, Jack A. Cummings, and Brooke A. Chapla
12. Best Practices in Developing a Positive Behavior Support System at the School Level
    Brian C. McKevitt and Angelisa Braaksma Fynaardt
13. Best Practices in the Use of Learning Supports Leadership Teams to Enhance Learning Supports
    Howard S. Adelman and Linda Taylor
14. Best Practices in School–Community Partnerships
    John W. Eagle and Shannon E. Dowd-Eagle
15. Best Practices in School Crisis Intervention
    Stephen E. Brock, Melissa A. Louvar Reeves, and Amanda B. Nickerson
16. Best Practices in School Violence Prevention
    Jim Larson and Sarah Mark
17. Best Practices in Bullying Prevention
    Erika D. Felix, Jennifer Greif Green, and Jill D. Sharkey
18. Best Practices in Threat Assessment in Schools
    Dewey Cornell
19. Best Practices in Suicide Prevention and Intervention
    Richard Lieberman, Scott Poland, and Cheryl Kornfeld
20. Best Practices in Crisis Intervention Following a Natural Disaster
    Melissa Allen Heath
21. Best Practices for Responding to Death in the School Community
    Scott Poland, Catherine Samuel-Barrett, and Angela Waguespack
22. Best Practices in Using the DSM-5 and ICD-10 by School Psychologists
    Susan M. Swearer, Kisha Radliff, and Paige Lembeck
23. Best Practices in Pediatric School Psychology
    Thomas J. Power and Kathy L. Bradley-Klug
24. Best Practices in Medication Treatment for Children With Emotional and Behavioral Disorders: A Primer for School Psychologists
    James B. Hale, Margaret Semrud-Clikeman, and Hanna A. Kubas
25. Best Practices in Assessing the Effects of Psychotropic Medication on Student Performance
    John S. Carlson and Jeffrey D. Shahidullah
26. Best Practices in Collaborating With Medical Personnel
    Sarah E. Glaser and Steven R. Shaw

27. Best Practices in Meeting the Needs of Children With Chronic Illness
    Cynthia A. Riccio, Jessica Beathard, and William A. Rae
28. Best Practices in Working With Children With Traumatic Brain Injuries
    Susan C. Davies
29. Best Practices in Responding to HIV in the School Setting
    Tiffany Chenneville

FAMILY–SCHOOL COLLABORATION SERVICES

30. Best Practices in Promoting Family Engagement in Education
    Susan M. Sheridan, Brandy L. Clarke, and Sandra L. Christenson
31. Best Practices in Systems-Level Organization and Support for Effective Family–School Partnerships
    Laura Lee McIntyre and S. Andrew Garbacz
32. Best Practices in Reducing Barriers to Parent Involvement
    Patricia H. Manz and Julie C. Manzo
33. Best Practices in Partnering With Parents in School-Based Services
    Dawn D. Miller and Nancy P. Kraft
34. Best Practices in Family–School Collaboration for Multitiered Service Delivery
    Gloria Miller, Cathy Lines, and Megan Fleming
35. Best Practices in Facilitating Family–School Meetings
    Kathleen M. Minke and Krista L. Jensen
36. Best Practices in Linking Families and Schools to Educate Children With Attention Problems
    Jennifer A. Mautone, Kristen Carson, and Thomas J. Power

Best Practices in School Psychology: Foundations

DIVERSITY IN DEVELOPMENT AND LEARNING

1. Best Practices in Increasing Cross-Cultural Competency
   Antoinette Halsell Miranda
2. Best Practices School Psychologists Acting as Agents of Social Justice
   David Shriberg and Gregory Moy
3. Best Practices in Primary Prevention in Diverse Schools and Communities
   Sherrie L. Proctor and Joel Meyers
4. Best Practices in Providing Culturally Responsive Interventions
   Janine Jones
5. Best Practices in Nondiscriminatory Assessment
   Samuel O. Ortiz
6. Best Practices in the Assessment of English Language Learners
   Catharina Carvalho, Andrea Dennison, and Ivonne Estrella
7. Best Practices in Assessing and Improving English Language Learners' Literacy Performance
   Michael L. Vanderwood and Diana Socie
8. Best Practices in School-Based Services for Immigrant Children and Families
   Graciela Elizalde-Utnick and Carlos Guerrero

9. Best Practices in Conducting Assessments via School Interpreters
   Emilia C. Lopez
10. Best Practices in Working With Children From Economically Disadvantaged Backgrounds
    Christina Mulé, Alissa Briggs, and Samuel Song
11. Best Practices in Providing School Psychological Services in Rural Settings
    Margaret Beebe-Frankenberger and Anisa N. Goforth
12. Best Practices in Working With Homeless Students in Schools
    Brenda Kabler, Elana Weinstein, and Ruth T. Joffe
13. Best Practices in Working With Children Living in Foster Care
    Tracey G. Scherr
14. Best Practices in Service to Children in Military Families
    Mark C. Pisano
15. Best Practices in Supporting Students Who Are Lesbian, Gay, Bisexual, Transgender, and Questioning
    Emily S. Fisher
16. Best Practices in Working With LGBT Parents and Their Families
    Julie C. Herbstrith
17. Best Practices in School Psychologists' Services for Juvenile Offenders
    Janay B. Sander and Alexandra L. Fisher
18. Best Practices in Planning Effective Instruction for Children Who Are Deaf or Hard of Hearing
    Jennifer Lukomski
19. Best Practices in School-Based Services for Students With Visual Impairments
    Sharon Bradley-Johnson and Andrew Cook

RESEARCH AND PROGRAM EVALUATION

20. Best Practices in Conducting School-Based Action Research
    Samuel Song, Jeffrey Anderson, and Annie Kuvinka
21. Best Practices Identifying, Evaluating, and Communicating Research Evidence
    Randy G. Floyd and Philip A. Norfolk
22. A Psychometric Primer for School Psychologists
    Cecil R. Reynolds and Ronald B. Livingston
23. Best Practices in Developing Academic Local Norms
    Lisa Habedank Stewart
24. Best Practices in Designing and Conducting Needs Assessment
    Richard J. Nagle and Sandra Glover Gagnon
25. Best Practices in Program Evaluation in a Model of Response to Intervention/Multitiered System of Supports
    Jose M. Castillo
26. Best Practices in the Analysis of Progress Monitoring Data and Decision Making
    Michael D. Hixson, Theodore J. Christ, and Teryn Bruni
27. Best Practices in Evaluating Psychoeducational Services Based on Student Outcome Data
    Kim Gibbons and Sarah Brown
28. Best Practices in Evaluating the Effectiveness of Interventions Using Single-Case Methods
    Rachel Brown, Mark W. Steege, and Rebekah Bickford

LEGAL, ETHICAL, AND PROFESSIONAL PRACTICE

29. Trends in the History of School Psychology in the United States
    Thomas K. Fagan
30. History and Current Status of International School Psychology
    Thomas Oakland and Shane Jimerson

31. Best Practices in Applying Legal Standards for Students With Disabilities
    Guy M. McBride, John O. Willis, and Ron Dumont
32. Best Practices in Ethical School Psychological Practice
    Susan Jacob
33. Best Practices in the Application of Professional Ethics
    Laurie McGarry Klose and Jon Lasser
34. Ethical and Professional Best Practices in the Digital Age
    Leigh D. Armistead
35. Best Practices in Using Technology
    William Pfohl and Susan Jarmuz-Smith
36. Best Practices in Using Technology for Data-Driven Decision Making
    Benjamin Silberglitt and Daniel Hyson
37. The Status of School Psychology Graduate Education in the United States
    Eric Rossen and Nathaniel von der Embse
38. Best Practices in Assessing Performance in School Psychology Graduate Programs
    Joseph S. Prus and Enedina Garcia-Vazquez
39. Best Practices in the Supervision of Interns
    Jeremy R. Sullivan, Nicole Svenkerud, and Jane Close Conoley
40. Best Practices in National Certification and Credentialing in School Psychology
    Eric Rossen
41. Best Practices in Early Career School Psychology Transitions
    Arlene E. Silva, Daniel S. Newman, and Meaghan C. Guiney
42. Best Practices in Supervision and Mentoring of School Psychologists
    Virginia Smith Harvey, Joan A. Struzziero, and Sheila Desai
43. Best Practices in School Psychologists' Self-Evaluation and Documenting Effectiveness
    Barbara Bole Williams and Laura Williams Monahon
44. Best Practices in the Professional Evaluation of School Psychologists Utilizing the NASP Practice Model
    Anastasia Kalamaros Skalski and Mary Alice Myers
45. Best Practices in Continuing Professional Development for School Psychologists
    Leigh D. Armistead
46. Best Practices in Using Technology for Continuous Professional Development and Distance Education
    Jack A. Cummings and Susan Jarmuz-Smith
47. Best Practices in Maintaining Professional Effectiveness, Enthusiasm, and Confidence
    Brian P. Leung and Jay Jackson

National Association of School Psychologists